THE DRAMATIC WORKS IN
THE BEAUMONT AND
FLETCHER CANON

This is the tenth and final volume in the definitive series of critical, old-spelling texts of the plays in the Beaumont and Fletcher canon, in which the texts are established on modern bibliographical principles. This volume contains the texts of six plays written by Fletcher and his collaborators, Nathan Field, Philip Massinger, Ben Jonson, George Chapman, John Ford and John Webster. Each play is introduced by a discussion of the text and its authorship, and is accompanied by detailed textual notes, a list of press variants, emendations of accidentals and a historical collation.

The plays are *The Honest Man's Fortune, Rollo, Duke of Normandy, The Spanish Curate, The Lovers' Progress, The Fair Maid of the Inn* and *The Laws of Candy*.

At the back of this concluding volume, there is a useful index showing how the plays are distributed between the volumes, and a table giving the authorship of the plays.

VOLUME I

The Knight of the Burning Pestle
The Masque of the Inner Temple and Gray's Inn
The Woman Hater   The Coxcomb
Philaster   The Captain

VOLUME II

The Maid's Tragedy   A King and No King
Cupid's Revenge   The Scornful Lady
Love's Pilgrimage

VOLUME III

Love's Cure   The Noble Gentleman
Beggars' Bush
The Tragedy of Thierry and Theodoret
The Faithful Shepherdess

VOLUME IV

The Woman's Prize   Bonduca
The Tragedy of Valentinian
Monsieur Thomas   The Chances

VOLUME V

The Mad Lover   The Loyal Subject
The Humorous Lieutenant   Women Pleased
The Island Princess

VOLUME VI

Wit Without Money   The Pilgrim
The Wild-Goose Chase   A Wife for a Month
Rule a Wife and Have a Wife

VOLUME VII

Henry VIII   The Two Noble Kinsmen
Wit at Several Weapons   The Nice Valour
The Night Walker   A Very Woman

VOLUME VIII

The Queen of Corinth   The False One
Four Plays, or Moral Representations, in One
The Knight of Malta
The Tragedy of Sir John van Olden Barnavelt
The Custom of the Country

VOLUME IX

The Sea Voyage   The Double Marriage
The Prophetess   The Little French Lawyer
The Elder Brother   The Maid in the Mill

THE
DRAMATIC WORKS IN
THE BEAUMONT AND
FLETCHER CANON

GENERAL EDITOR
FREDSON BOWERS

VOLUME X

THE HONEST MAN'S FORTUNE

ROLLO, DUKE OF NORMANDY

THE SPANISH CURATE   THE LOVERS' PROGRESS

THE FAIR MAID OF THE INN   THE LAWS OF CANDY

CAMBRIDGE
UNIVERSITY PRESS

Published by the Press Syndicate of the University of Cambridge
The Pitt Building, Trumpington Street, Cambridge CB2 1RP
40 West 20th Street, New York, NY 10011-4211, USA
10 Stamford Road, Oakleigh, Melbourne 3166, Australia

First published 1996

Printed in Great Britain by Woolnough Bookbinding Ltd.
Irthlingborough, Northants.

A catalogue record for this book is available at the British Library

Library of Congress cataloguing in publication data

Beaumont, Francis, 1584–1616.
The dramatic works in the Beaumont and Fletcher
canon.
Includes index (v. 10)
v.1:B66–13195
I. Fletcher, John, 1579–1625, joint author.
II. Bowers, Fredson Thayer, ed.
PR2420   1966   822.3   66–74421

ISBN 0 521 36189 3 hardback

SE

CONTENTS

Foreword   *page* vi

THE HONEST MAN'S FORTUNE   I

    Edited by CYRUS HOY, *John B. Trevor Professor of*
    English, University of Rochester

ROLLO, DUKE OF NORMANDY   145

    Edited by GEORGE WALTON WILLIAMS, *Professor of*
    English, Duke University

THE SPANISH CURATE   293

    Edited by ROBERT KEAN TURNER, *Professor of*
    English, University of Wisconsin–Milwaukee

THE LOVERS' PROGRESS   425

    Edited by GEORGE WALTON WILLIAMS

THE FAIR MAID OF THE INN   553

    Edited by FREDSON BOWERS, *formerly Linden Kent*
    Professor of English Literature, University of Virginia

THE LAWS OF CANDY   659

    Edited by CYRUS HOY

INDEX

    Titles of the Dramatic Works in the Beaumont and   749
       Fletcher Canon
    Authors of the Dramatic Works in the Beaumont and   751
       Fletcher Canon

FOREWORD

These volumes contain the text and apparatus for the plays conventionally assigned to the Beaumont and Fletcher canon, although in fact Fletcher collaborated with dramatists other than Beaumont in numerous plays of the canon and some of the preserved texts also represent revision at a later date by various hands. The plays have been grouped chiefly by authors; this arrangement makes for an order that conveniently approximates the probable date of composition for most of the works.

The texts of the several plays have been edited by a group of scholars according to editorial procedures set by the general editor, who closely supervised in matters of substance as well as of detail the initially contrived form of the texts. Otherwise the individual editors have been left free to develop their concepts of the plays according to their own views. We hope that the intimate connection of one individual, in this manner, with all the different editorial processes will lend to the results some uniformity not ordinarily found when diverse editors approach texts of such complexity. At the same time, the peculiar abilities of the several editors have had sufficient free play to ensure individuality of point of view in its proper role; and thus, we hope, the deadness of compromise that may fasten on collaborative effort has been avoided, even at the risk of occasional internal disagreement.

The principles on which each text has been edited have been set forth in detail in 'The Text of this Edition' prefixed to volume 1, pp. ix–xxv, followed by an account on pp. xxvii–xxxv of the Folio of 1647. Necessary acknowledgements will be found in the present volume in each Textual Introduction.

Charlottesville, Virginia   F.B.

THE HONEST MAN'S FORTUNE

edited by

CYRUS HOY

TEXTUAL INTRODUCTION

The Honest Man's Fortune (Greg, *Bibliography*, no. 662) exists in two versions: a manuscript text of the play (MS Dyce 9), now preserved in the Victoria and Albert Museum, London, and the text printed in the 1647 Beaumont and Fletcher Folio. The manuscript is in the hand of the scribe Edward Knight, book-keeper of the King's Company. Its titlepage states that *The Honest Man's Fortune* was 'Plaide In the yeare 1613'. At the end of the manuscript text, in the hand of Sir Henry Herbert, Master of the Revels, is the statement that 'This Play, being an olde one, and the Originall lost was reallowd by mee this 8. Febru. 1624 Att the Intreaty of Mr   .' The last word has been torn away, but in the margin a different hand has added the word 'Taylor' (i.e. Joseph Taylor, one of the leading actor–managers of the King's Company). The entry in Herbert's office-book re-states this:

For the king's company. An olde play called *The Honest Man's Fortune*, the originall being lost, was re-allowed by mee at Mr Taylor's intreaty, and on condition to give mee a booke, this 8 Februa. 1624.[1]

The cast-list printed with the text of the play in the 1679 Beaumont and Fletcher Folio suggests that the original performers were members of Lady Elizabeth's Company.[2] The six actors named there (Nathan Field, Rob. Benfield, Emanuel Read, Joseph Taylor, Will. Eglestone, Thomas Basse) are all known to have been members of Lady Elizabeth's in 1613, and this confirms the manuscript's statement that the play was 'plaide' (presumably for the first time) in that year. Field, who had been a child actor with the Queen's Revels, had by now become leading man with Lady Elizabeth's and had begun to write plays. Two comedies of his single authorship had appeared (*A Woman is a Weathercock*, c. 1609–10, and *Amends for Ladies*, c. 1610–11). Sometime during the years c. 1612–15 he had written the *Four Plays, or Moral Representations, in One* with Fletcher, and *The Honest Man's Fortune* seems to be a product of the same period. In this case Field turned for aid not only to the more experienced Fletcher, but to a beginning dramatist, Philip Massinger. The three would continue to

3

work together after all of them had moved on from Lady Elizabeth's to the King's Company. Their collaboration would produce two more extant plays (*The Knight of Malta* and *The Queen of Corinth*) and a third now lost (*The Jeweller of Amsterdam*) before it ended with Field's death *c.* 1619–20. The authorial division of *The Honest Man's Fortune* seems to be as follows:[3]

FIELD: I; II; III.i.144–206, ii; IV
FIELD AND MASSINGER: III.iii
FIELD AND FLETCHER: V.i, iv
MASSINGER: III.i.1–143
FLETCHER: V.ii, iii.

The Honest Man's Fortune, like a number of other plays in the Beaumont and Fletcher canon written originally for Lady Elizabeth's Men, passed eventually into the possession of the King's Men, and it is there that we first hear of it when the company plans to revive it in the early months of 1625. Thereafter, it is rarely heard of again. It is included in the Lord Chamberlain's list (dated 7 August 1641) of plays to be protected for the King's Company against unauthorized publication.[4] On or around 4 September 1646, it was entered in the Stationers' Register by Humphrey Robinson and Humphrey Moseley in their list of some thirty plays that were to comprise the first Beaumont and Fletcher Folio, published in the following year.

After the Restoration, *The Honest Man's Fortune* is encountered merely as a title. It appears in a list of plays allowed to the Duke's Company under the date of 20 August 1668,[5] but it seems to have been rarely, if ever, performed in the last four decades of the seventeenth century. It was included for publication in the second Beaumont and Fletcher Folio (1679). Gerard Langbaine, citing Heywood's *History of Women* as its source, includes it among the plays of Beaumont and Fletcher in *Momus Triumphans* (1688, p. 58), and provides a somewhat fuller note on it in *An Account of the English Dramatick Poets* (1691, p. 209; the importance of this text for establishing the name of the play's principal character will be discussed later in this introduction). Apart from its inclusion in the collected editions of Beaumont and Fletcher published in 1711, 1750 and 1778, *The Honest Man's Fortune* is not otherwise heard of in the eighteenth century until 1790 when Malone reports his possession of the manuscript in his

Historical Account of the English Stage. In 1836, Alexander Dyce acquired the manuscript at the Heber sales, and his edition of the play (printed in vol. III of his *Works of Beaumont and Fletcher*, 1843) was the first to take into account its important textual variants.

The relation of what has come to be known as the Dyce Manuscript to the text of the 1647 Folio, and the choice of a copy-text, pose the principal issues that face the editor of *The Honest Man's Fortune*. The relation of the two texts is very close. It would appear that both derive from the same manuscript: the foul papers of the three authors who wrote the play. What Herbert refers to as 'the Originall' (meaning, presumably, the original licensed prompt-book) was said to be missing in 1625, and the authorial foul papers appear to have served as the copy from which Knight prepared the new one (now the Dyce Manuscript). They also appear to have served, twenty-two years later, as copy for the printed text in the 1647 Folio. The two most immediately apparent differences between the two texts — MS's omission of one scene (V.iii), and its altered version of the final scene (V.iv.246ff.) — do not call into question the basic identity of the sources from which each derives. F1 gives us the earlier, pre-1625 version of the play; MS gives us a somewhat altered version prepared (presumably) for the 1625 revival, with the unnecessary V.iii cut in the interest of shortening a long play, and the rewritten V.iv.246ff. serving to replace the indelicacy of the original ending.

In preparing a new prompt-book that would be coming under the severe gaze of Sir Henry Herbert, who would need to license it anew if the play were to be revived, Knight and the stage-adapter (whose hand also appears from time to time in the Dyce MS) seem to have been consciously on guard against the inclusion of material that the censor might find offensive. Thus Herbert's sensitivity on the score of oaths seems to be acknowledged in MS, which regularly uses the word 'Heaven' where F1, twenty-two years later, more boldy uses the name of 'God' (and is probably following the authorial foul papers in doing so). Elsewhere in the F1 text, however, oaths are typically omitted, their omission indicated by a long dash. Since a prompt-book would need to supply words of some sort to be spoken on the stage at these points in the text, MS generally supplies an oath to fill these blanks, but MS oaths are notably mild, and are unlikely to represent the original ones; here the F1 compositors may have acted as their own censors.

Ironic allusions to established social institutions and references to morally questionable contemporary behaviour are vigorously deleted in the Dyce MS with strokes of the pen intended to render them illegible (but modern scholars have managed to read them). Whether the pen was wielded by Herbert himself (or one of his aids), or by scribe or stage-adapter anticipating trouble from the censor, is not always clear. In addition to these alterations in the text of the play, MS also exhibits the scribal signs (vertical bars) marking theatrical cuts made to tighten and quicken the pace of the stage action. Most of these probably originated in 1625 when the new prompt-book was being prepared. We cannot know how many of MS's vertical bars enclosing material to be omitted had a precedent in the copy from which it was derived. Whatever the source or the motive, the passages marked in one way or another for omission in the Dyce MS are as follows.

The proposed cuts in Act I are two in number: I.i.222–41 (Longavile's fanciful account of the difficulties and dangers attendant on making one's way into a crowded court-room), and I.iii.2–4 (a play on words that may have been deemed too obscure). At II.i.15–27, Longavile and Duboys' plans for setting up a male brothel is not only marked for omission with the usual vertical line, but deleted by means of a series of loops that cross out each of the twelve lines that comprise the passage (it remains, however, decipherable). Also heavily crossed out (but also still readable) is the slighting reference to a courtier at II.ii.44–6. Both these Act II cuts were evidently made out of deference to the censor.

A number of passages are marked for omission in Act III: part of Lamira and Lady Orleans' discussion of marriage at III.i.34–50; Veramour's laboured speech at III.i.80–87; Veramour's offer to sing, Lady Orleans' acceptance of the offer, and the stage-direction for a song at III.i.137–43.1 (there was apparently no provision for music in the 1625 revival). What was evidently deemed an offensive reference to a lord's arrest at III.ii.54–5 is heavily crossed out (but has proved to be decipherable). Laverdure, La-poope and Mallicorne's discussion of the prevalence and the inevitability of bribery and corruption in the Court and the City at III.iii.9–37 is curtailed. Laverdure's indelicate reference at III.iii.156–8 to ladies who mistake their horse-keepers for their husbands is to be omitted.

Act IV is the most heavily cut: nine moralizing lines of the twenty-two that comprise Montaigne's opening soliloquy are marked for omission at IV.i.8–16; soon some twenty-one lines of the sentimental exchange between Montaigne and Veramour that follows are marked to go, at IV.i.27–48, and more cuts are marked at IV.i.72–80, 103–7 (a rude remark about women). Charlotte's elaborate sixteen-and-a-half line speech to Montaigne in praise of patience under adversity at IV.i.168–84 loses all but its last crucial line and a half ('Will you ... marry me ...?'). Another rude remark about women is to be cut at IV.i.270–2. At V.ii.84–5, two lines of a speech of Mallicorne's are cut for no apparent reason. The scene of the four servants gossiping about the events of the play as they prepare to serve a banquet (V.iii) is omitted altogether from MS (as has already been noted). At V.iv.67, La-poope's reference to 'a Psalme of mercy' was evidently considered irreverent and deleted (but remains legible). A bit later, the same character's 'Pray God' has been crossed out and replaced with 'I wish' in MS at V.iv.98, and it is presumably Herbert's sensitivity on the subject of oaths that causes Laverdure's 'Troth tis wondrous hot, God blesse us from him' to be cut at V.iv.153–4. MS's more restrained ending (V.iv.246ff.) replaces F1's boisterous finale.

Many years ago, W. W. Greg drew attention to the manner in which cuts are sometimes signalled in this play by the use of repeated words that serve for cues to bridge an omitted passage.[6] Three passages displaying repetitions of this sort have been noted in the F1 text: at I.i.222–41 (marked for omission in MS); I.i.298–316 (no indication of a cut in MS); IV.ii.84–8 (MS version of this passage, unlike MS versions of the other two, contains the repeated phrase that marks the cut, but one occurrence of it has been deleted). That there are signs for cuts in both the F1 and MS texts of the first and third of these passages contributes to the evidence that both texts were printed from the same manuscript. All three passages are discussed in the Textual Notes for this edition.

The Dyce MS provides what, on balance, is a text that is verbally superior to that of F1, but it is sophisticated, and it would be a mistake to select it as the copy-text for an old-spelling edition of the play. Though it is the earlier of the two texts, and so closer to the date of the play's original composition and performance, it is doubtful that it is the more trustworthy witness to the accidentals – the spelling and the punctuation – of the authorial foul papers that presumably served as copy for both it and F1. Sometimes what seem unusual spellings of particular words are found in both texts (*e.g.*, 'Sawsiges' at II.iv.136), and a distinctive manner of pointing a given passage will appear in each; these things occur frequently enough to suggest a common manuscript source for both the Dyce MS and F1; but these occurrences do not obscure the fact that the spelling and punctuation of each text is *sui generis*. The spelling and punctuation of the text of the Dyce MS is essentially that of the scribe Edward Knight, a professional who knew how to prepare a theatrical prompt-book; and the Dyce MS shows us the text of *The Honest Man's Fortune* in the process of being prepared for the stage. At II.ii.90, Knight has corrected the authorial slip that, in F1, gives the name 'Annabella' to the character elsewhere known as Lamira. MS shows plans for casting the 1625 revival: stage-directions at I.i.316, I.ii.0.1, and I.ii.96.1 contain the names of three actors (George Vernon, John Rhodes and George Rickner) who would be playing minor roles (see Historical Collation).[7]

The F1 text of the play, on the contrary, often seems maddeningly unprofessional. It is a wretched job of printing. Yet the compositors who set the 1647 Folio text of the play were probably truer to its accidentals in their blundering fashion than Knight, who was generally inclined to impose his own personal preferences in these matters. In justice to the F1 compositors, it must be said that the presumptive foul papers serving as their copy posed serious difficulties. Even the capable Knight had problems with them in 1625; by 1647 they seem to have been in an even more ruinous condition. Not only did the various authorial hands pose problems of legibility that resulted in the omission of words and phrases due to eye-skip, and the often egregious verbal blunders that reduce much of the F1 text to imbecility; the hands often seem to have been altogether illegible, at which points the compositors resort to the long dashes that occur throughout the text. These are not dashes put to any conventional use, such as punctuating an interrupted sentence (though that is sometimes the case, as at I.i.115); often the dashes indicate a suppressed oath (as has been noted); most often they are used simply as a sign of defeat: either the copy was defective at that point, or it was illegible.

Fortunately, MS can usually be depended on to supply the missing F1 readings at such points. At other times, when it is evident from the nature of MS/F1 variants that something more than manuscript illegibility or compositorial misreading is involved, the evidence of MS will frequently show that either the scribe or the stage-adapter has altered it for some reason: to straighten out the grammar or the syntax of the authors, to adjust the dialogue in order to accommodate a projected cut, to modify a word or phrase that might seem to give offence. MS variants that do not correct an F1 misreading must be treated with caution. They might indeed be authorial revisions; usually they are alterations, sophistications introduced by scribe or stage-adapter. Thus the best policy for the editor of the play is to follow Greg's classic instructions regarding the choice of copy-text for old-spelling editions: to base his edition on that one of the early texts that best preserves the spelling and punctuation of the authors, and to introduce into this, from such other contemporary texts as are available, such substantive emendations as are necessary.[8] The copy-text for the present edition is, then, the 1647 Folio, emended at practically every line with substantive readings from MS.

The Honest Man's Fortune was printed in Section 5 of the 1647 Folio, the section assigned to Edward Griffin. It occupies sigs. 5T1 to 5X4v (the latter half of sig. 5X4v contains Fletcher's verses 'Upon an Honest Mans Fortune'). The evidence of running-titles suggests three-skeleton work for the three quires, with three verso and three recto titles appearing in an orderly sequence:

Verso: I   5T1v, 5V1v, 5V2v, 5X3v
       III 5T2v, 5T4v, 5V4v, 5X2v, 5X4v
       V   5T3v, 5V3v, 5X1v
Recto: II   5T2, 5V2, 5X4
       IV 5T3, 5V1, 5X1, 5X3
       VI 5T4, 5V3, 5V4, 5X2

Editors of the six plays printed by Griffin that have previously appeared in these volumes have discovered all of them to have been set by three compositors (designated *A*, *B* and *C*) whose preferences in spellings and contractions have differed sufficiently to make it possible to identify the work of each.[9] Of the three, Compositor *B* has regularly exhibited the most clearly defined spelling practices (he tends, for example, to set *Ile* or *ile* rather than *I'le* or *i'le*; *do* and *go* rather than *doe* and *goe*; *tis*, *twas*, *twill* rather than *'tis*; *'twas*, *'twill*; *Countrey* rather than *Country*). Compositors *A* and *C* share a number of spelling habits, however, and neither has ever displayed such a readily identifiable set of spelling characteristics as are available in the case of Compositor *B*, but in all six of the Griffin plays previously edited in these volumes, spelling tendencies augmented by other evidence (variant contracted forms for speech-prefixes, for example) have made it possible to differentiate the work of Compositors *A* and *C*, and to recognize the ways in which it relates to the more readily recognizable work of Compositor *B*.

In the case of *The Honest Man's Fortune*, the share of Compositor *B* is, as usual, readily apparent. He set exactly half of the F1 text (one page of each two-page forme) as follows:

Compositor *B*: 5T1–5T2v (I.i.0.1–I.ii.20); 5V1–5V2v (II.ii.231–III.ii.7); 5X1–5X2v (IV.i.145–V.ii.33).

The other half of the text presents a *mélange* of spellings and contracted forms common to both Compositors *A* and *C* with no discernible pattern of occurrences that would serve to separate the work of one from that of the other. It could be the work of a single compositor (and if so, Compositor *C* seems the more likely), but the possibility that Compositor *A* shared in the work ought not to be ruled out. What is clear is that work on the text of *The Honest Man's Fortune* was evenly divided between Compositor *B* on the one hand, and Compositor *A* and/or Compositor *C* on the other. The section of the text not set by Compositor *B* corresponds exactly in length to Compositor *B*'s own share.

Compositor *A* and/or *C*: T3–T4v (I.ii.21–II.ii.231); V3–V4v (III.ii.8–IV.i.145); X3–X4v (V.ii.34–V.iv.272).

There are at least two sufficient reasons why evidence from spellings and contractions of the sort that has previously served to differentiate the work of Compositors *A* and *C* might break down in the case of a text like *The Honest Man's Fortune*. One is bibliographic: copy was cast off for the two compositorial shares, and the exigencies of space often required a good deal of compression to fit a given stretch of text into a given folio signature. Verse is often set as prose, and the spelling of words is often clipped whenever possible. Thus spellings such as *do*, *go*, *bin*, *yong*, *wil*, *believe*, *Mistris*, which previous editors of the Griffin plays have found to be characteristic of Compositor *C*, appear in *The Honest Man's Fortune* on the same folio signature, often in the same folio column, with spellings that have hitherto been thought of as representative of Compositor *A* (*doe, goe, been, young, will, beleeve, Mistresse*).

The other reason why certain features of the evidence for compositor identification is obscured in this case is the nature of the copy from which the 1647 Folio text was printed. This consisted of the foul papers of at least three different authors. By the time they were used for F1 printers' copy they were some thirty-five years old. That they posed difficulties for the compositors is evident from the many confusions and misreadings in the F1 text; that they were often illegible or otherwise defective is evident from the many occasions in the F1 text when the compositors resort to the use (already noted) of long dashes to indicate gaps in the manuscript copy, or readings that they cannot decipher. But precisely because their copy was proving so difficult, they seem to have done their best to follow it, even to the suppression of their own usual habits of spelling and contraction; thus, some of the eccentric spellings and abbreviations that they produce would seem to result not only from repeated attempts to read an all but illegible hand, but also from an effort to reproduce the sundry forms that names and their abbreviations seem to have taken in what were, presumably, the manuscript papers of the various authors.

Here, as in the F1 text of *The Sea Voyage*, the efforts on the part of Griffin's compositors to read an all but illegible hand often result in a blizzard of variant spellings for the names of the play's characters. All the occurrences of the spelling *Duboys* (sigs. T1, T1v, T2, T2v, V1, V1v, V2, X1v) are the work of Compositor *B*. In the non-*B* sections of the text, the character's name is spelled more variously: *Duboyes* (sigs. T3v, T4v), *Duboies* (sig. T4v), *Dubois* (sigs. T3v, T4v, V3, X3). Speech-prefixes for this character are always given as *Dub.* except on sig. T4v, where six occurrences of *Du.* appear. Compositor *B* normally sets the name *Longueville* (sigs. T1, T2, X1, X1v, X2), but he sometimes sets *Longeville* (sigs. T2v, V2v); and the spellings *Longaville* (sigs. T3v, V1, X1, X2) and *Longavile* (sigs. T4v, X3, X3v) appear in both the text's compositorial divisions. The name of the page-boy is correctly given as *Veramour* at various points throughout the text (sigs. V2, V3v, V4v, X1, X4), but along the way we also have *Voramer* (sig. T1), *Vercamor* (sig. T3), *Viramour* (sig. V2v) and *Viramor* (sig. V4). His speech-prefixes are normally printed as *Ver.* in both compositorial divisions, but occasionally they appear as *Vir.* (sigs. V2v, X4), *Vera.* (sig. T3v) and *Veram.* (sigs. V3v, V4). The name *Mallicorne* (sigs. T4, T4v, V1v) also appears as *Malicorne* (sigs. V3, X1v), *Malycorne* (sigs. X1, X2v), *Mallycorne* (sig. V1v), and *Mallycorn* (sig. X3). The name that first appears as *La-poope* (sig. T3v; later sigs. V2, X2v) is the occasion of much typographical indecision: *La Poope* (sig. X1), *La-poop* (sigs. V3, X1, X1v), *La-Poop* (sig. V4), *La-Poope* (sig. X3). The contractions for his speech-prefixes are almost equally various. They appear normally throughout the text as *La-p.*, but we also find *La p.* (sig. T3v), *La.p.* (sigs. T4, T4v), and *Lap-p* (sig. T4, V3).

Variants such as these seem to be the result either of compositorial misreading or inconsistency. There is, however, another class of variant abbreviations for speech-prefixes that might be said to reflect variant forms in the manuscript copy. Throughout the play, from her first appearance on sig. V2 until her last on sig. X4, Lamira's speech-prefixes appear as *Lam.* However, near the end of the play, on sigs. X3v–X4, there appear fifteen occurrences of the abbreviation *Lami.* This may reflect Fletcher's revision of Field's fifth act. Speech-prefixes for Charlotte also display a variety of abbreviated forms in these latter pages of the play: the prevailing form has previously been *Charl.* (sigs. V2v, V4v, X1), but to this is now added *Cha.* (sigs. V3v, X4), and *Char.* (sigs. X2, X2v). The character's full name is also variously spelled: *Charlo* in a stage-direction on sig. V3v; *Charlote* in another on sig. V4v (and again on sigs. X2 and X3); *Charlot* in still another on sig. X1.

The various terms used for referring to Lady Orleans in F1's speech-prefixes and stage-directions seem to shed a particularly revealing light on the nature of the F1 copy. On the character's first appearance (Act I), Compositor *B* set her speeches with the heading *Lady* (sig. T2v), and Compositor *A/C* who set sigs. T3–T3v tended to head them *La.* (interspersed with an occasional *Lady*). When Compositor *B* sets her speeches in Act IV (sigs. X1, X1v, X2) he again heads them *Lady*, and Compositor *A/C* sets *La.* to head her single speech (her last in the play) on sig. X3. But between these two sections of the text, the simple references to *Lady* change both in speech-prefixes and in references to the character in stage-directions. Act III opens with the stage-direction: '*Enter Madam Lamira, Madam le Orleans ...*' (sig. V2), and throughout III.i speech prefixes for the *Lady* are headed *L.Orl.* (sigs. V2–V2v). It is unlikely that the opening stage-direction was devised by a compositor; its use of the word 'Madam' for the two characters so designated is unique in the F1 text, and this is what relates it to the play's manuscript tradition. The F1 stage-direction seems, indeed, to be the compositor's somewhat muddled version of the stage-direction that stands in the Dyce MS at this point: '*Ent: Maddam Lamira: Ladye Orleance …*'. Manuscript copy for the F1 text of III.i was apparently different from that for the first two acts of the play. Since these were the work of Field, and Massinger's share of the play begins with III.i, it seems likely that the F1 text of this scene was set from a manuscript in Massinger's hand.

It is ironic that the two names in the play's *dramatis personae* that receive the most consistent treatment, both in their spelled-out and their abbreviated forms, are wrong. Throughout the F1 text, the titular character is named *Montague* (abbreviatd *Mont.* in speech-prefixes). There is nothing wrong with *Mont.*, but *Montague* is certainly a mistake for *Montaigne*. This is the name that occurs in the Dyce MS, where the spelling *Montagne* also appears. Both spellings of the name seem to have stood in the F1 copy. Once in F1 (sig. T3) the spelling *Montaigue* appears, the only time F1 ever reproduces the letter -*i* in the -*aig* of MS. But here, as throughout F1, both or all the compositors persist in misreading the minim strokes representing the letter -*n* and printing instead the letter -*u*.

That MS's name for the play's protagonist is correct is established by the reference in Langbaine's account of the play's source: 'As to the plot of *Montaign*'s being prefer'd by *Lamira* to be her Husband, when he was in Adversity, and least expected: the like Story is related by *Heywood* in his *History of Women*, Book 9. pag. 641.' That *Montaigne* was the name the character was known by in the theatre is conclusively shown by Langbaine's use of it. The corresponding figure in the Heywood source is unnamed. The manuscript text of the play was unpublished at the time, and the only printed editions of *The Honest Man's Fortune* (the Folios of 1647 and 1679) that were available in 1691 when Langbaine's *Account of the English Dramatic Poets* appeared give the name as Montague. In the present edition of the play, all occurrences of *Montague* are changed without further notation to *Montagne* (the form of the name the F1 compositors seem to have been aiming at). Speech-prefixes are given as *Montaigne*.

The other character whose name F1 has got wrong is there

consistently spelled *Laverdine*. The name in MS is spelled *Laverdure* or *Laverduer*, though the scribe (Knight) began by nearly making the same mistake the F1 compositors persisted in making. When in MS the name occurred for the first time, it was there spelled *Lauerdine* (Dyce MS, fol. 10), but Knight caught the error and the last three letters were changed to *uer*. Gerritsen has noted (p. lxiv) that 'as *La Verdure* the name acquires a meaning' (from the French *verdeur*, the vigour of old age) that it cannot have as *Laverdine*, and he cites the reference to 'your old Merchant, *Leverdure*' in *The Wild-Goose Chase*, V.ii.77. In the present edition of *The Honest Man's Fortune*, all occurrences of *Laverdine* are changed without further notation to *Laverdure*.

Since, as has been shown above, the spelling *Longueville* is the product of Compositor *B*, and since the spelling *Longavile* (or *Longaville*) appears in both F1's compositorial divisions as well as throughout MS, *Longavile* is the spelling used for the character's speech-prefixes in the present edition. F1 variants in the spelling of the name are preserved in the text for whatever evidence they may have for differentiating authorial or compositorial shares in the composition. It may be noted that *Longavile* is the spelling found for two like-named characters in two other plays in the Beaumont and Fletcher canon, *The Noble Gentleman* and *Four Plays in One* (in 'The Triumph of Death').

Anyone who works on the difficult text of *The Honest Man's Fortune* will be deeply indebted to the critical edition of the Dyce Manuscript published in 1952 by Dr J. Gerritsen. It has been of immense help to me in the preparation of this edition, and I wish to express my appreciation and respect for Dr Gerritsen's meticulous scholarship.

NOTES

1 *The Dramatic Records of Sir Henry Herbert, Master of the Revels, 1623–1673*, ed. Joseph Quincy Adams (New Haven, 1917), p. 30.
2 E. K. Chambers, *The Elizabethan Stage* (Oxford, 1923), III, 227.
3 I have discussed the evidence on which the following attribution is based in 'The shares of Fletcher and his collaborators in the Beaumont and Fletcher canon (IV)', *Studies in Bibliography*, XII (1959), 100–8.

4 Gerald Eades Bentley, *The Jacobean and Caroline Stage* (Oxford, 1941), I, 65–6.

5 *The London Stage: 1660–1800*, Part I: '1660–1700', ed. William Van Lennep (Carbondale, Ill., 1965), p. 140.

6 W. W. Greg, 'A question of plus or minus', *Review of English Studies*, VI (1930), 300–4.

7 For these three actors, see Bentley, *Jacobean and Caroline Stage*, II, 544–6, 547, 611–12.

8 W. W. Greg, 'The rationale of copy-text', *Studies in Bibliography*, III (1950–1), 19–36 (especially statements on pp. 21, 29).

9 I have edited two of these (*The Pilgrim*, vol. VI in this series, and *The Double Marriage*, vol. IX, and have had a hand in editing a third, Professor Bowers' unfinished edition of *The Sea Voyage*, vol. IX). The other three Griffin plays have been edited by Professor Williams (*Love's Cure*, vol. III and *The Knight of Malta*, vol. VIII), and Professor Bowers (*The Woman's Prize*, vol. IV).

THE PERSONS REPRESENTED IN
THE PLAY.

Duke of *Orleans, a spleenful detracting Lord.*
Earl of *Amiens, Brother-in-law* to Orleans, *a noble accomplish'd Gentleman, servant to* Lamira.
Montaigne, *an honest Lord.*
Duboys, ⎫
Longavile, ⎬ *Two faithful followers of* Montaigne.
Veramour, *the loving and loyal Page of* Montaigne.
Laverdure, *a knavish Courtier.*
La-poope, *a foisting Captain.* 10
Mallicorne, *a sharking Citizen.*
Two Lawyers.
Three Creditors.
Officers.
Servants.
[Drawers, Lacqueys, Page.]

WOMEN.

Duchess of *Orleans, a virtuous Lady, and chaste, (but suspected) wife to the Duke.*
Lamira, *a modest Virgin, and a Lady, rich and noble.* 20
Charlotte, Lamira's *Woman.*

The Scene France

The principal Actors were

Nathan Field,	*Joseph Taylor,*
Rob. Benfield,	*Will. Eglestone,*
Emanuel Read,	*Thomas Basse.*

The Persons ... *Basse.*] *adapted from* F2; *omit* F1
*13 Three Creditors] *stet* F2

THE HONEST MAN'S FORTUNE

Enter the Duke of Orleans, *and the* Earle of Amiens *at severall*   I.i
doores.

Amiens.   Morrow my Lord of *Orleance.*
Orleans.   You salute me
   Like a stranger; brother *Orleance*
   Were to me a Title more belonging,
   Whom you call the husband of your sister.
Amiens.   Would the circumstances of
   Our brotherhood had never offer'd cause
   To make our conversation lesse familiar:
   But I meet you like a hinderance in your way:
   Your great law suit is now upon the tongue,
   And ready for a judgement.
Orleans.   Came you from   10
   The Hall now?
Amiens.   Without stay; the Court is full,
   And such a presse of people does attend
   The issue, as if some great man were brought
   To his araignment.
Orleans.   Every mothers sonne
   Of all that multitude of hearers went
   To be a witnesse of the misery
   Your sisters fortunes must have come to, if
   My adversary who did love her first,
   Had been her husband.
Amiens.   The successe may draw
   A testimony from them to confirme   20
   The same opinion, but they went prepar'd
   With no such hope or purpose.
Orleans.   And did you
   Encrease the number of them that are gone

6 Our] MS (o'); your F1   8 But] MS; *omit* F1
23 Encrease] Dyce (Heath, Mason *conj.*); intreat F1; Entreate MS   23 gone] MS; come F1

17

With no such hope or purpose?

Amiens.   Tush, your own
Experience of my heart can answer ye.

Orleans.   This doubtfull answer makes me clearly understand
Your disposition.

Amiens.   If your cause be just,
I wish you a conclusion like your cause.

Orleans.   I can have any common charity
To such a prayer, from a friend I would   30
Expect a love to what I prosper in,
Without exceptions; such a love as might
Make all my undertakings thankfull to't;
Precisely just is seldome faithfull in
Our wishes to another mans desires:
Farewell.

Exit Orleans.

Enter Montagne *having a Purse,* Duboys, Longueville, *and*
Voramer *the Page with two Caskets.*

Duboys.   Here comes your adversaries brother in law.

Longavile.   The Lord of *Amiens.*

Duboys.   From the Hall I thinke.

Amiens.   I did so:——save your Lordship.

Montaigne.   That's a wish
My Lord, as courteous to my present state,   40
As ever honest mind was thankfull for;
For now my safety must expose it selfe
To question: yet to look for any free
Or hearty salutation (sir from you)
Would be unreasonable in me.

Amiens.   Why?

Montaigne.   Your sister is my adversaries wife;
That neernesse needs must consequently draw
Your inclination to him.

Amiens.   I will grant

---

26 answer] MS *corrected*; question MS *originally*; *omit* F1
31 what I] MS; *omit* F1

18

Him all the neernesse his alliance claimes,   50
And yet be nothing lesse impartiall
My Lord of *Montagne.*
Montaigne.   Lord of *Montagne* yet:
But (sir) how long the dignity or state
Belonging to it will continue, stands
Upon the dangerous passage of this houre,
Either for ever more to be confirm'd,
Or like the time wherein twas pleaded, gone:
Gone with it, never to be call'd again.
Amiens.   Justice direct your processe to the end;   60
To both your persons my respect shall stil
Be equall; but the righteous cause is that
Which bears my wishes to the side it holds,
Where, ever may it prosper.
Montaigne.   Then my thanks
Are proper to you, if a man may raise
A confidence upon a lawfull ground
I have no reason to be once perplexed
With any doubtfull motion,——   *Exit* Amiens.
                    Longueville,
That Lord of *Amiens,* (didst observe him?) has
A worthy nature in him.
Longavile.   Either tis   70
His nature or his cunning.
Montaigne.   That's the vizard
Of most mens actions, whose dissembled lives
Do carry onely the similitude
Of goodnesse on 'em, but for him (*Duboys*)
Honest behaviour makes a true report,
What disposition does inhabit him,
Essentiall vertue.
Longavile.   Then tis pitty that
Injurious *Orleance* is his brother.
Duboys.   He
Is but his brother in law.
Longavile.   Law? that's as bad.

74 (*Duboys*)] MS; *omit* F1

19

Duboys.   How is your Law as bad? I rather wish   80
    The hangman thy executor: then that

        Enter two Lawyers, *and two* Creditors.

    Equivocation should be ominous.
Longavile.   Some of your Lawyers.———
1. Lawyer.   What is ominous?
2. Lawyer.   Let no distrust trouble your Lordships thought.
1. Lawyer. The evidences of your question'd land
    Ha' not so much as any literall
    Advantage in 'em to be made against
    Your title.
2. Lawyer.   And your Councell understands
    The businesse fully.
1. Lawyer.   Th'are industrious, just.
2. Lawyer.   And very confident.
1. Lawyer.   Your state endures   90
    A voluntary tryall; like a man
    Whose honours are maliciously accus'd.
2. Lawyer.   The Accusation serves to cleare his cause.
1. Lawyer.   And to approve his truth more.
2. Lawyer.   So shall all
    Your adversaries pleadings strengthen your
    Possession.
1. Lawyer.   And be set upon record
    To witnesse the hereditary right
    Of you and yours.
2. Lawyer.   Courage, you have the law.
Longavile.   And you the profits.
Montaigne.   If discouragement
    Could worke upon me, your assurances   100
    Would put me strongly into heart again;
    But I was never fearfull: and let fate
    Deceive my expectation, yet I am
    Prepared against dejection.
1. Creditor.   So are we.
2. Creditor.   We have received a comfortable hope

86 so] MS; *omit* F1

That all will speed well.

Longavile.   What is he *Duboys?*

Duboys.   A Creditor.

Longavile.   I thought so, for he speaks
As if he were a partner in his state.

Montaigne.   Sir, I am largely indebted to your loves——

Longavile.   More to their purses.

Montaigne.   Which you shall not lose.   110

1. Creditor.   Your Lordship——

Duboys.   That's another creditor.

1. Creditor.   Has interest in me——

Longavile.   You have more of him.

1. Creditor.   And I have had so many promises
From these and all your learned Councellors,
How certainly your cause wil prosper, that——

Longavile.   You brought no Serjeants with you?

Duboys.   To attend his ill successe.

Montaigne.   Good sir, I will not be
Unthankfull either to their industries
Or your affections.

1. Lawyer.   All your land (my Lord)   120
Is at the bar now, give me but ten Crowns
Ile save you harmlesse.

Longavile.   Take him at his word;
If he does lose, you're sav'd by miracle,
For I never knew a lawyer yet undone.

1. Lawyer.   Then now you shall sir, if this prospers not.

Longavile.   Sir, I beseech you doe not force your voyce
To such a loudnesse, but be thrifty now;
Preserve it till you come to plead at bar,
It wil be much more profitable in
The satisfaction then the promise.

1. Lawyer.   Is   130
Not this a satisfaction, to engage
My selfe for his assurance?

Duboys.   If he dare trust ye.

---

132 for his assurance? | *Duboys.* If he dare trust ye.] MS; for this assurance, if he——F1

Montaigne.   No sir, my ruine never shall import
Anothers losse, if not by accident,
And that my purpose is not guilty of:
You are engaged in nothing but your care.

Exeunt Lawyers.

Attend the Procurator to the Court,
Observe how things incline, and bring me word.
Longavile.   I dare not sir; if I be taken there,
Mine eares will be in danger.
Montaigne.   Why? hast thou   140
Committed something that deserves thine eares?
Longavile.   No, but I feare the noyse; my hearing will
Be perished by the noise; and tis as good
To want a member, as to loose the use.
Montaigne.   The ornament excepted.
Longavile.   Well my Lord,
Ile put 'em to the hazzard.   *Exit* Longueville.
1. Creditor.   Your desires
Be prosperous to you.
2. Creditor.   Our best prayers waite
Upon your fortune.   *Exeunt* Creditors.
Duboys.   For your selves, not him.
Montaigne.   Thou canst not blame 'em: I am in their debts.
Veramour.   But had your large expence (a part whereof   150
You owe 'em) for unprofitable Silkes
And Laces, been bestowed among the poore,
They would have prayd the right way for you:
Not upon you.
Montaigne.   For unprofitable Silkes
And Laces? now believe me honest boy
Th'ast hit upon a reprehension that
Belongs unto me.
Veramour.   By my troth my Lord,
I had not so unmannerly a thought,
To reprehend you.

143 and] MS (&); *omit* F1   143–144 good | To want] MS; good't want F1
145 ornament excepted] MS; ornament is excepted F1   153 They] MS; That F1
157 By my troth my] MS; By——my F1

22

Montaigne.   Why I love thee for't.
   Mine own acknowledgement confirmes thy words: 160
   For once I do remember, comming from
   The Mercers, where my Purse had spent it selfe
   On those unprofitable toyes thou speakst of,
   A man halfe naked with his poverty
   Did meet me, and requested my reliefe:
   I wanted whence to give it, yet his eyes
   Spoke for him, those I could have satisfied
   With some unfruitfull sorrow, (if my teares
   Would not have added rather to his griefe,
   Then eas'd it) but the true compassion that   170
   I should have given I had not: this began
   To make me think how many such mens wants
   The vaine superfluous cost I wore upon
   My outside would have clothed, and left my selfe
   A habit as becomming: to encrease
   This new consideration there came one
   Clad in a garment plaine and thrifty, yet
   As decent as these faire deare follies; made
   As if it were of purpose to despise
   The vanity of show: his purse had still   180
   The power to doe a charitable deed,
   And did it.
Duboys.   Yet your inclination, sir,
   Deservd no lesse to be commended, then
   His action.
Montaigne.   Prethee do not flatter me;
   He that intends well, yet deprives himselfe
   Of means to put his good thoughts into deeds,
   Deceives his purpose of the due reward
   That goodnesse merits: O antiquity
   Thy great examples of Nobility
   Are out of imitation, or at least   190
   So lamely follow'd, that thou art as much
   Before this age in vertue, as in time.

   186 thoughts into deeds] thought into deeds MS; thoughts into deed F1

23

Duboys. Sir, it must needs be lamely followed, when
    The chiefest men that love to follow it
    Are for the most part cripples.
Montaigne.   Who are they?
Duboys. Souldiers, my Lord, souldiers.
Montaigne.   Tis true *Duboys*:
    But if the Law disables me no more
    For Noble actions, then good purposes,
    Ile practice how to exercise the worth
    Commended to us by our ancestors;   200
    The poore neglected souldier shall command
    Me from a Ladies Courtship, and the forme
    Ile study shall no more be taught me by
    The Taylor, but the Scholler; that expence
    Which hitherto has been to entertaine
    Th' intemperate pride and pleasure of the taste
    Shall fill my Table more to satisfie,
    And lesse to surfeit.
    What an honest worke it would be, when we finde
    A Virgin in her poverty, and youth   210
    Inclining to be tempted, to imploy
    As much perswasion, and as much expence
    To keep her upright as men use to do
    Upon her falling.
Duboys.   Tis a charity
    That many mayds wil be unthankful for,
    And some will rather take it for a wrong,
    To buy 'em out of their inheritance,
    The thing that they were born to.
                      Enter Longueville.
Montaigne.   Longueville
    Thou bringst a cheerfull promise in thy face.
    There stands no pale report upon thy cheeke,   220
    To give me feare or knowledge of my losse,
    Tis red and lively.

---

194 that] MS; *omit* F1   214 a] MS; *omit* F1
*222 lively. *Longavile.* That's] MS; lively. How proceeds my suit? *Longueville.* That's F1 (*cf.*
   below, line 241)

Longavile.   That's with labour sir,
A labour that to those of *Hercules*
May adde another; or (at least) be cald
An imitation of his burning shirt:
For twas a paine of that unmercifull
Perplexity, to shoulder through the throng
Of people that attended your successe:
My sweaty linnen fixt upon my skin,
Still as they puld me, tooke that with it; 'twas   230
A feare I should have left my flesh among 'em:
Yet I was patient, for (me thought) the toyle
Might be an emblem of the difficult
And weary passage to get out of Law.
And to make up the deare similitude,
When I was forth seeking my handkircher
To wipe my sweat off, I did finde a cause
To make me sweat more, for my Purse was lost
Among their fingers.
Duboys.   There twas rather found.
Longavile.   By them.
Duboys.   I mean so.
Montaigne.   Well, I will restore   240
Thy dammage to thee: how proceeds my suit?
Longavile.   Like one at Brokers; I thinke forfeited.
Your promising councellor at the first
Put strongly forward with a labour'd speed,
And such a violence of pleading, that
His fee in Sugar-candie scarce will make
His throat a satisfaction for the hurt
He did it, and he carried the whole cause
Before him with so cleare a passage, that
The people in the favour of your side   250
Cried *Montagne, Montagne:* in the spight of him
That cryed out silence, and began to laugh
Your adversaries Advocate to scorn:
Who like a cunning foot-man, set me forth

225 An] MS; A F1   225 his] MS; this F1   239 fingers] MS finger F1
243 councellor] MS; councell F1

With such a temperate easie kind of course
To put him into exercise of strength,
And follow'd his advantages so close,
That when your hot mouthed pleader thought 'had wonne,
Before he reacht it, he was out of breath,
And then the other stript him.
Montaigne.   So all is lost.   260
Longavile.   But how I know not; for (me thought) I stood
Confounded with the clamour of the Court,
Like one embarqued upon a storm at Sea,
Where the tempestuous noise of Thunder mixt
With roaring of the billows, and the thick
Imperfect language of the Sea-men, takes
His understanding and his safety both
Together from him.
Montaigne.   Thou dost bring ill news.
Longavile. Of what I was unwilling to have been
The first reporter.
Montaigne.   Didst observe no more?   270
Longavile.   At least no better.
Montaigne.   Then th'art not inform'd
So well as I am; I can tell thee that
Will please thee, for when all else left my cause,
My very adversary tooke my part.
Longavile.   Pox on him, whosoever told you that
Abused you.
Montaigne.   Credit me, he took my part
When all forsook me.
Longavile.   Took it from you.
Montaigne.   Yes
I meane so, and I think he had just cause
To take it when the verdict gave it him.
Duboys.   His Spirit would ha' sunke him, ere he could   280
Have carried an ill fortune of this waight
So lightly.
Montaigne.   Nothing is a misery

274 adversary] MS; adversaries F1
275 Pox on him, whosoever] MS;——whosoever F1

26

Unlesse our weaknesse apprehend it so;
We cannot be more faithfull to our selves
In any thing that's manly, then to make
Ill fortune as contemptible to us
As it makes us to others.

Enter [the two] Lawyers.

Longavile.   Here come they
Whose very countenances will tell you how
Contemptible it is to others.

Montaigne.   Sir?

Longavile.   The sir of Knighthood may be given em,   290
Ere they heare you now.

Montaigne.   Good sir but a word.

Duboys.   How soon the losse of wealth makes any man
Grow out of knowledge.

Longavile.   Let me see I pray sir,
Never stood you upon the pillory?

1. Lawyer.   The Pillory?

Longavile.   O now I know you did not.
Y'ave eares, I thought ye had lost 'em; pray observe,
Here's one that once was gracious in your eyes.

1. Lawyer.   O my Lord.

Longavile.   But ha' you nere a Counsell to redeeme
His Land yet from the judgement?

2. Lawyer.   None but this,   300
A writ of errour to remove the cause.

Longavile.   No more of errour, we have been in that
Too much already.

2. Lawyer.   If you will reverse
The judgement, you must trust to that delay.

Longavile.   Delay? Indeed he's like to trust to that,
With you has any dealing.

2. Lawyer.   Ere the Law
Proceeds to an *habere facias*
Possessionem.

Duboys.   That's a language sir,

290 em] MS; him F1   297 your] MS; our F1
*298 Lord.] MS; Lord, have an eye upon him. F1 (*cf. below, line* 316)

I understand not.

Longavile.   Th'art a very strange
Unthankfull fellow to have taken Fees   310
Of such a liberall measure, and then give
A man hard words for's money.

Montaigne.   So, tis gone.

1. Lawyer.   If men will hazzard their salvations,
What should I say? I've other businesse.

Exeunt Lawyers.

Montaigne.   Y'are ith' right; that's it you should say now
Prosperity has left me.

Enter two Creditors.

1. Creditor.   Have an eye upon him; if
We lose him now, he's gone for ever; stay
And dog him: Ile goe fetch the officers.

Longavile.   Dog him you blood-hound: by this point thou
Shalt more safely dog an angry Lion   320
Then attempt him.   [*Draws his sword.*]

Montaigne.   What's the matter?

Longavile.   Doe but stir
To fetch a Serjeant, and (besides your losse
Of labour) Ile have you beaten, till
Those casements in your faces be false lights.

Duboys.   Falser then those you sell by.

Montaigne.   Who gave you
Commission to abuse my friends thus?

Longavile.   Sir,
Are those your friends that would betray you?

Montaigne.   Tis
To save themselves rather then betray me.

1. Creditor.   Your Lordship makes a just construction of it.

2. Creditor.   All our desire is but to get our own.   330

Longavile.   Your wives desires and yours do differ then.

Montaigne.   So far as my ability will goe
You shall have satisfaction.——*Longeville,*——

Longavile.   And leave your selfe neglected; every man

312 *Montaigne.* So, tis gone.] MS; *omit* F1
314.1 *Exeunt* Lawyers.] *Exit Law.* MS; *omit* F1   321 stir] MS; steere F1

28

Is first a debtor to his own demands,
Being honest.
Montaigne.   As I take it sir, I did
Not entertaine you for my counsellor.
Longavile.   Counsel's the office of a servant, when
The master fals upon a danger, as
Defence is. Never threaten with your eyes,   340
They are no cockatrices; do you heare?
Talke with a Girdler, or a Milner,
They can informe you of a kind of men
That first undid the profit of those trades
By bringing up the forme of carrying
Theire *Morglayes* in their hands: with some of those
A man may make himselfe a priviledge
To aske a question at the prison gates,
Without your good permission.
Both Creditors.   By your leave——
Montaigne.   Stay sir, what one example since the time   350
That first you put your hat off to me, have
You noted in me to encourage you
To this presumption? by the justice now
Of thine own rule, I should begin with thee,
I should turn thee away ungratified
For all thy former service, and forget
Thou ever didst me any; (sirs) tis not feare
Of being arrested makes me thus incline
To satisfie you; for you see by him,
I lost not all defences with my state;   360
The curses of a man to whom I am
Beholding terrifie me more, then all
The violence he can pursue me with.
Duboys, I did prepare me for the worst;
These two small Cabinets doe comprehend
The sum of all the wealth that it hath pleased

343 They] MS; He F1   *346 Theire *Morglayes*] MS; There morglachs F1
349 *Both Creditors.*] MS (*Both Cred:*); 2. *Cred.* F1
356 service, and forget] MS; kindnesse, forget F1
357 any; (sirs) tis] MS; any service: tis F1

29

Adversity to leave me, one as rich
As th' other, both in Jewels; take thou this,
And as the Order put within it shall
Direct thee, distribute it half between   370
Those Creditors, and th' other halfe among
My servants: for (sir) they are my creditors
As well as you are, they have trusted me
With their advancements: if the value faile,
To please you all, my first increase of meanes
Shall offer you a fuller payment; be content
To leave me something, and imagine that
You put a new beginner into credit.

Creditors.   So prosper our own blessings, as we wish
     You to your merit.

Montaigne.   Are your silences   380
     Of discontentment, or of sorrow?

Duboys.   Sir,
     We would not leave you.

Longavile.   Do but suffer us
     To follow you, and what our present means,
     Or industries hereafter can provide,
     Shall serve you.

Montaigne.   O desire me not to live
     To such a basenesse, as to be maintained
     By those that serve me; pray be gone, I wil
     Defend your honesties to any man
     That shal report you have forsaken me;
     I pray be gone.

          Exeunt Servants [Duboys, Longavile] *and Creditors.*
               Why dost thou weep my boy,   390
     Because I doe not bid thee goe too?

Veramour.   No,
     I weep (my Lord) because I would not goe;
     I feare you will command me.

Montaigne.   No my child,
     I wil not; that would discommend th' intent

Of all my other actions: thou art yet
Unable to advise thy selfe a course,
Should I put thee to seeke it; after that
I must excuse or at the least forgive
Any uncharitable deed that can
Be done against my selfe.

Veramour.   Every day   400
(My Lord) I tarry with you, Ile account
A day of blessing to me; for I shall
Have so much lesse time left me of my life
When I am from you: and if misery
Befall you (which I hope so good a man
Was never born to) I wil take my part,
And make my willingnesse increase my strength
To beare it. In the Winter I will spare
Mine own clothes from my selfe to cover you;
And in the Summer, carry some of yours   410
To ease you: Ile doe any thing I can.

Montaigne.   Why, thou art able to make misery
Ashamed of hurting, when thy weaknesse can
Both beare it, and despise it: Come my boy
I will provide some better way for thee
Then this thou speakst of; tis the comfort that
Ill fortune has undone me into the fashion:
For now in this age most men do begin,
To keep but one boy, that kept many men.

                                                    Exeunt.

          Enter Orleans, *a Servant, his* Ladie *following.*   [I.ii]

Orleans.   Where is she? call her.
Lady Orleans.   I attend you sir.
                                             [*Exit Servant.*]
Orleans.   Your friend sweet Madam——
Lady Orleans.   What friend, good my Lord?
Orleans. Your *Montagne*, Madam, he will shortly want

                    *0.1 a Servant] stet F1

                            31

Those Courtly graces that you love him for;
The means wherewith he purchased this, and this,
And all his own provisions to the least
Proportion of his feeding or his clothes,
Came out of that inheritance of land
Which he unjustly lived on: but the law
Has given me right in't, and possession; now   10
Thou shalt perceive his bravery vanish, as
This Jewell does from thee now, and these Pearles
To him that owes 'em.   [*Taking them from her.*]

Lady Orleans.   Ye are the owner sir
Of every thing that does belong to me.

Orleans.   No, not of him, sweet Lady.

Lady Orleans.   O good God!

Orleans.   But in a while your mind will change, and be
As ready to disclaime him; when his wants
And miseries have perish'd his good face,
And taken off the sweetnesse that has made
Him pleasing in a womans understanding.   20

Lady Orleans.   O Heaven, how gratious had Creation been
To women, who are borne without defence,
If to our hearts there had been doores through which
Our husbands might have lookt into our thoughts,
And made themselves undoubtfull.

Orleans.   Made 'em madde.

Lady Orleans.   With honest women?

Orleans.   Thou dost still pretend
A title to that vertue: prethee let
Thy honesty speak freelie to me now.
Thou knowest that *Montaigne*, of whose Land
I am the master, did affect thee first,   30
And should have had thee, if the strength of friends
Had not prevail'd above thine own consent.
I have undone him; tell me how thou doest
Consider his ill fortune and my good.

Lady Orleans.   Ile tell you justly his undoing is

An argument for pitty, and for teares
In all their dispositions that have known
The honour and the goodnesse of his life:
Yet that addition of prosperity,
Which you have got by't, no indifferent man   40
Will malice or repine at, if the Law
Be not abused in't; howsoever since
You have the upper fortune of him, 'twill
Be some dishonour to you to beare your selfe
With any pride or glory over him.
Orleans.   This may be truly spoken, but in thee
  It is not honest.
Lady Orleans.   Yes, so honest, that
  I care not if the chast *Penelope*
  Were now alive to hear me.
Orleans.   Who comes there?

                    Enter Amiens.

Lady Orleans.   My brother.
Amiens.   Save yee.
Orleans.   Now sir, you have heard   50
  Of prosperous *Montagne*.
Amiens.   No sir, I have heard
  Of *Montagne*, but of your prosperity.
Orleans.   Is he distracted?
Amiens.   He does beare his losse
  With such a noble strength of patience that,
  Had fortune eyes to see him, she would weepe
  For having hurt him, and pretending that
  Shee did it but for triall of his worth,
  Hereafter ever love him.
Orleans.   I perceive
  You love him, and because (I must confesse)
  He does deserve it, though for some respects   60
  I have not given him that acknowledgement,
  Yet in mine honour I did still conclude
  To use him nobly.
Amiens.   Sir, it will become

60 it,] MS; that ∧ F1   63 it] MS; that F1

33

Your reputation, and make me grow proud
Of your alliance.
Orleans.   I did reserve
The doing of this friendship till I had
His fortunes at my mercy, that the world
May tell him 'tis a willing courtesie.
Lady Orleans.   This change wil make me happy.
Orleans.   Tis a change;
Thou shalt behold it, then observe me. When   70
That *Montagne* had possession of my Land,
I was his rivall, and at last obtain'd
This Lady who by promise of her own
Affection to him, should ha bin his wife;
I had her, and withheld her like a pawne,
Till now my Land is rendred to me againe,
And since it is so, you shall see I have
The conscience not to keep her. Give him her,

                                        Draws [his sword].

For by the faithfull temper of my sword,
Shee shall not tarry with me.
Amiens [to Lady Orleans]*.*   Give me way——   *Draws.* 80
Thou most unworthy man——give me way
Or by the wrong he does thy Innocence,
Ile end thy misery and his wickednesse,
Together.
Lady Orleans.   Stay and let me justifie
My husband in it, I have wrong'd his bed——

                                        Exit Amiens *in amazement.*

Never——all shames that can afflict me fall
Upon me if I ever wrong'd you.
Orleans.   Didst
Thou not confesse it?
Lady Orleans.   Twas to save your blood
From shedding, it has turn'd my brothers edge;
He that beholdes our thoughts as plainely as   90

---

82 thy Innocence] MS; the Innocent F1   85 it] MS; that F1
85.1 *Exit ... amazement.*] *Enter ... amazement, the servants following him.* F1 (*see Textual Note
    on* I.ii.0.1)   89 it] MS; that F1

Our faces, knowes that I did never hurt
My honesty but by accusing it.

Orleans.   Womens consents are sooner credited
Then their denials: and Ile never trust
Her body that prefers any defence
Before the safety of her honour.——Here,

                    Enter two Servants.

Show forth that stranger.——Give me not a word,
Thou seest a danger readie to be tempted.

Lady Orleans.   Cast that upon me rather then my shame,
And as I am a-dying I wil vowe   100
That I am honest.

Orleans.   Put her out of dores;
But that I feare my land may go againe
To *Montagne*, I would kill thee, I am loth
To make a beggar of him that way; or else——
Go, now you have the liberty of flesh,
And you may put it to a double use,
One for your pleasure, th' other to maintaine
Your wel beloved, he wil be in want.

                    Exit Lady [*and Servants*].

In such a charitable exercise
The vertue wil excuse you for the vice.   110

                    Exit Orleans.

Enter Amiens [*with his sword*] *drawne, meeting* Montagne *and*   [I.iii]
                    Veramour.

Montaigne.   What meanes your Lordship?
Veramour.   For the love of God——
Amiens.   Thou hast advantage of mee, cast away
This buckler.
Montaigne.   So he is Sir, for he lives
With one that is undone.——Avoid us boy.

---

91 that I] MS; it, I F1   96.1 *two* Servants] MS; *servant* F1
100 a-dying] MS; now dying F1   100–101 vowe | That] MS now—— | That F1
108 be in] MS; *omit* F1

0.1–2 *Enter* Amiens . . . *drawne, meeting* Montagne *and* Veramour.] *Ent: Amiens: At one doore:*
    Montaigne: and Veramour. At Another: MS; *Enter Amiens drawne, Montagne, Vercamor*
    meeting. F1   *2–4 cast away . . . undone.] *stet* F1

Veramour. Ile first avoid my safety,
Your Rapier shall be button'd with my heade,
Before it touch my Master.
Amiens.   *Montagne?*
Montaigne.   Sir.
Amiens.   You know my sister?
Montaigne.   Yes sir.
Amiens.   For a whore?
Montaigne.   You lye, and shall lie lower if you dare
Abuse her honor.

Enter Lady Orleans.

Lady Orleans.   I am honest.
Amiens.   Honest!   10
Lady Orleans.   Upon my faith I am.
Amiens.   What
Did then perswade thee to condemn thy self?
Lady Orleans.   Your safety.
Amiens.   I had rather be expos'd
To danger, then dishonor; th'ast betray'd
The reputation of my familie
More basely by the falsenesse of that word,
Then if thou hadst delivered me asleepe
Into the hands of a base enemie.
Reliefe will never make thee sensible
Of thy disgraces; let thy wants compell thee to it.   20

Exit.

Lady Orleans.   O I am a miserable woman.
Montaigne.   Why Madam? are you utterly without
Means to relieve you?
Lady Orleans.   I have nothing sir,
Unlesse by changing of these cloaths for worse,
And then at last the worst for nakednesse.
Montaigne.   Stand off boy.——Nakednesse would be a change
To please us Madam, to delight us both.
Lady Orleans.   What nakednesse sir?

10 *Enter* Lady Orleans.] *Ent: the Ladye Orleans:* MS; *Enter Lady.* F1
17 if thou hadst] MS; *that thou hast* F1   18 a] MS; *omit* F1

36

Montaigne.   Why the nakednesse
   Of body Madam, we were Lovers once.
Lady Orleans.   Never dishonest Lovers.
Montaigne.   Honestie   30
   Has no allowance now to give our selves.
Lady Orleans.   Nor you allowance against honestie.
Montaigne.   Ile send my Boy hence, opportunitie
   Shall be our servant, come and meet me first
   With kisses like a stranger at the doore,
   And then invite me neerer to receive
   A more familiar inward welcome, where
   Instead of tapers made of virgine wax
   Th' increasing flames of our desires shall light
   Us to a banquet: and before the taste   40
   Be dull with satisfaction, Ile prepare
   A nourishment compos'd of every thing
   That beares a naturall friendship to the bloud,
   And that shall set another edge upon't,
   Or else between the courses of the feast
   Wee'l dallie out an exercise of time,
   That ever as one appetite expires
   Another may succeede it.
Lady Orleans.   O my Lord,
   How has your nature lost her worthinesse?
   When our affections had their liberty,   50
   Our kisses met as temperatelie as
   The hands of sisters, or of brothers, yet
   Our blouds were then as moving; then you were
   So noble, that I durst have trusted your
   Embraces in an opportunity
   Silent enough to serve a ravisher,
   And yet come from you undishonor'd. How
   You think me altered, that you promise your
   Attempt successe I know not; but were all
   The sweet temptations that deceive us set   60

---

31 give] *i.e.* gyve (= fetter, restrain; Heath MS Notes)
38 virgine] MS; Virgins F1   51 Our] MS (o'); Or F1
52 yet] MS; that F1

On this side, and on that side all the wantes,
These neither should perswade me nor they force.
Montaigne.   Then misery may waste your body.
Lady Orleans.   Yes,
But lust shall never.
Montaigne.   I have found you still
As uncorrupted as I left you first.
Continue so; and I wil serve you with
As much devotion as my word, my hand
Or purse can show you; and to justifie
That promise, here is half the wealth I have,
Take it, you owe me nothing, till you fall   70
From vertue, which the better to protect
I have bethought me of a present meanes.
[*To* Veramour] Give me the Letter;———this commends my Boy
Into the service of a Lady, whose
Free goodnesse you have bin acquainted with,
Lamira.
Lady Orleans.   Sir I know her.
Montaigne.   Then believe
Her entertainment wil be noble to you;
My boy shall bring you thither: and relate
Your manner of misfortune if your own
Report needs any witnesse: so I kisse   80
Your hand good Lady.
Lady Orleans.   Sir, I know not how
To promise, but I cannot be unthankfull.
Montaigne.   All that you can imploye in thankfulnesse
Be yours, to make you the more prosperous.
Farwell my boy,———

Exeunt Lady *and* Veramour.
I am not yet oppress'd,
Having the power to helpe one that's distress'd.

Exit.

61 on that] MS; one that F1   61 wantes] MS; waiters F1   62 they] MS; the F1
83 imploye] MS; implore F1
85 Exeunt ... Veramour.] Exit Lady | Vera. F1 (printed in right-hand margin of lines 85–86);
     omit MS   86.1 Exit.] Exeunt. F1

Enter Longaville *and* Dubois.   II.i

Longavile.   What shall we do now: swords are out of use,
And words are out of credit.
Duboys.   We must serve.
Longavile.   The meanes to get a service will first spend
Our purses; and except we can allow
Our selves an entertainment, service will
Neglect us; now tis grown into a doubt
Whether the Master or the servant gives
The countenance.
Duboys.   Then fall in with Mistresses.
Longavile.   They keep more servants now (indeed) then men,
But yet the age is grown so populous   10
Of those attendants, that the women are
Grown full to.
Duboys.   What shall we propound our selves?
Longavile.   I'le think on't.
Duboys.   Do; old occupations have
Too many setters up to prosper, some
Uncommon trade would thrive now.
Longavile.   Wee'l ee'n
Make up some half a dozen proper men,
And set up a male stewes, we should get more
Then all your female sinners.
Duboys.   If the house
Be seated as it should be privately.
Longavile.   I, but that would make a multitude   20
Of witches.
Duboys.   Witches? how I prethee?
Longavile.   Thus,
The bauds would all turn witches to revenge
Themselves upon us; and the women that
Come to us, for disguises must wear beards,
And that's they say, a token of a witch.

12 to] *i.e.* too (*also at* II.ii.168, 277; III.iii.18; V.iii.45; V.iv.24, 135)
17 And set up a male stewes, we should get] MS; And should not we get F1
21 I] MS; *omit* F1

Duboys.   What shall we then do?

Longavile.   We must study on't,
With more consideration, stay *Duboyes*;
Are not the Lord of *Orleans* and the Lord
Of *Amiens* enemies?

Duboys.   Yes, what of that?

Longavile.   Methinks the factions of two such great men   30
Should give a promise of advancement now
To us that want it.

Duboyus.   Let the plot be thine,
And in the enterprize Ile second thee.

Longavile.   I have it, wee will first set down our selves
The Method of a quarrell; and make choyce
Of some frequented Taverne; or such a place
Of common notice to perform it in
By way of undertaking to maintaine
The severall honours of those enemies,
Thou for the Lord of *Orleanes*; I for *Amiens*.   40

Duboys.   I like the project, and I think 'twill take
The better, since their difference first did rise
From his occasion whom we followed once.

Longavile.   We cannot hope lesse after the report,
Then entertainment or gratuity,
Yet those are ends, I do not aime at most;
Great spirits that are needy, and will thrive,
Must labour whiles such troubles are alive.

                                        Exeunt.

            Enter Laverdure, *and* La-poope.   [II.ii]

La-poope.   Hunger is sharper then the sword. I have fed this three
days upon leafe *Tobacco*, for want of other Victuals.

Laverdure.   You have liv'd the honester Captaine; but be not so
dejected, but hold up thy head, and meate wil sooner fall i'thy
mouth.

La-poope.   I care not so much for meat, so I had but good liquor, for
which my guts croak like so many Frogs for raine.

Laverdure.   It seemes, you are troubled with the wind-Collick,

        47 Great] MS; Greater F1   *1 Hunger] MS; Slander F1

                            40

Captaine. If you be Captaine, swallow a bullet: tis present remedy
i'le assure you.   10

La-poope.   A bullet! why man my panch is nothing but a pile of
bullets; when I was in any service I stood between my Generall and
the shot, like a mud-wall; I am all lead, from the crown of the head
to the soale of the foot, not a sound bone about me.

Laverdure.   It seems you have bin in terrible hot service Captaine.

La-poope.   It has ever bin the fault of the low Country wars to spoile
many a man, I ha' not bin the first nor shall not be the last: but ile tell
you sir, (hunger has brought it in to minde) I served once at the
Siege of *Brest*, 'tis memorable to this day, where we were in great
distresse for victuals, whole troops fainted more for want of food   20
then for blood, and died, yet we were resolved to stand it out; I my
self was but then Gentleman of a Company, and had as much need
as any man, and indeed I had perished had not a miraculous
providence preserved me.

Laverdure.   As how good Captaine?

La-poope.   Marry sir ee'n as I was fainting and falling down for want
of sustenance, the enemy made a shot at me, and struck me full ith'
paunch with a penny loaf.

Laverdure.   Instead of a bullet!

La-poope.   Instead of a bullet.   30

Laverdure.   That was miraculous in deed; and that loaf sustained
you.

La-poope.   Nourished me or I had famished with the rest.

Laverdure.   You have done worthy acts being a souldier, and now
you shall give me leave to requite your tale, and to acquaint you
with the most notorious deeds that I have done being a Courtier. I
protest Captain I wil lie no more then you have done.

La-poope.   I can indure no lies.

Laverdure.   I know you cannot Captaine, therefore ile only tell you
of strange things. I did once a deed of charity for it self; I assisted a   40
poor widdow in a sute, and obtained it, yet I protest I took not a
penny for my labour.

---

*8–9 wind-Collick, Captaine. If you be Captaine, swallow] winde collick. | yf you be Captaine
      swallow MS; wind-Collick Captaine, swallow F1
11 bullet! why man my panch] MS; bullet; if you be Captain, my panch F1
16 fault] MS; fate F1

La-poope.   Tis no such strange thing.

Laverdure.   By *Mars* Captaine, but it is, and a very strange thing too
in a Courtier, it may take the upper hand of your penny loaf for a
miracle. I could ha' told you how many Ladies have languished for
my love, and how I was once sollicited by the mother, the daughter,
and grand-mother out of the least of which I might have digg'd my
selfe a fortune; they were all great Ladies, for two of them were so
big I could hardly embrace them: but I was sluggish in my rising 50
courses, and therefore let them passe; what meanes I had is spent
upon such as had the wit to cheat me; that wealth being gon, I have
only bought experience with it, with a strong hope to cheat
others;———but see here comes the much declined *Montagne*, who
had all his Manor houses, which were the body of his estate
overthrowen by a great winde.

Enter Montagne, Mallicorne.

La-poope.   How by a great winde? was he not overthrown by law?

Laverdure.   Yes, marry was he: but there was terrible puffing and
blowing before he was overthrown, if you observ'd, and believe it
Captain, ther's no wind so dangerous to ruine a building as a 60
lawyers breath.

La-poope.   What's he with him?

Laverdure.   An eminent Citizen, Mounsier *Mallicorne*, lets stand a
side and listen their designs.

Mallicorne.   Sir, profit is the Crown of labour, it is the life, the soule
of the industrious Merchant, in it he makes his paradise, and for it
neglects Wife, Children, Friends, Parents, nay all the world, and
delivers up himselfe to the violence of stormes, and to be toss'd into
unknown ayres; as there is no faculty so perillous, so ther's none so
worthy profitable.   70

Montaigne.   Sir, I am very well possest of it, and what of my poore
fortunes remaines, I would gladly hazzard upon the Sea; it cannot
deale worse with me then the Land, though it sinck or throw it into
the hands of Pirats. I have yet five hundred pounds left, and your
honest and worthy acquaintance may make me a young Merchant;
th'one moity of what I have I would gladly adventure.

55 his Manor] MS; the Manor F1   60 ruine] MS; *omit* F1
64 designs] MS; design F1   73 into] MS; in F1

42

Mallicorne. How adventure? you shall hazzard nothing: you shall
only joyne with me in certaine commodities that are safe arrived
unto the Key; you shall neither be in doubt of danger nor dammage;
but so much mony disburst, so much received; sir I would have you   80
conceive I pursue it not for any good your money wil do me, but
meerly out of mine own freenesse and courtesie to pleasure you.

Montaigne. I can believe no lesse, and you expresse a noble nature,
seeking to build up a man so ruin'd as my selfe.

Laverdure. Captaine here is subject for us to worke upon if we have
wit; you hear that there is money yet left, and it is going to be layd
out in Rattels, Bels, Hobby-Horses, brown paper, or some such
like sale commodities; now it would do better in our purses, or
upon our backs in good Gold-lace, and Scarlet, and then we might
pursue our projects, and our devices towards my Lady *Lamira*; go   90
to, ther's a conceit newly landed; harck I stand in good reputation
with him, and therefore may the better cheat him: Captaine, take a
few instructions from me.

Montaigne. What monies I have is at your disposing, and upon
twelve I will meete you at the Pallace with it.

Mallicorne. I wil there expect you, and so I take my leave.

Exit.

Laverdure. You apprehend me?

La-poope. Why do ye think I am a dunce?

Laverdure. Not a dunce Captaine, but you might give me leave to
misdoubt that pregnancy in a Souldier, which is proper and   100
hereditary to a Courtier; but prosequte it, I wil both second, and
give credit to it.——Good Mounsier *Montagne*, I would your
whole revenues lay within the circuit of mine armes, that I might as
easily bestow it or restore it unto you as my curtesie.

La-poope. My zealous wishes sir, do accompany his for your good
fortune.

Laverdure. Believe it sir, our affection towards you is a strong band
of friendship.

Montaigne. To which I shall most willingly seale. But believe me
Gentlemen, in a broken estate the bond of friendship oft is   110

---

80 received] MS; receive F1   88 or] MS; *omit* F1   90 *Lamira*] MS; *Annabella* F1
104 bestow it or] MS; bestow, or F1   106 fortune] MS; fortunes F1

forfeited, but that it is your free and ingenuous natures to renew it.

Laverdure. Sir, I wil amply extend my self to your use, and am very zealously afflicted as not one of your least friends for your croocked fate; but let it not seise you with any dejection, you have as I hear a sufficient competency left, which wel disposed may erect you as high in the worlds account as ever.

Montaigne. I cannot live to hope it, much lesse injoy it, nor is it any part of my endeavour; my study is to render every man his own, and to containe my self within the limits of a Gentleman.

Laverdure. I have the grant of an Office given me by some noble 120 favorites of mine in Court, there stands but a small matter between me and it, if your ability be such to lay down the present sum, out of the love I bear you, before any other man, it shall be confirmed yours.

Montaigne. I have heard you often speak of such a thing; if it be assur'd to you I wil gladly deale in it; that portion I have, I would not hazard upon an unknowne course, for I see the most certainest is incertain.

La-poope. Having money sir, you could not light upon men that could give better direction; there is at this time a friend of mine 130 upon the Seas; to be plain with you, he is a Pyrate, that hath wrote to me to work his freedom, and by this Gentlemans meanes, whose acquaintance is not small at Court, we have the word of a worthy man for it, only there is some money to be suddainly disburst, and if your happinesse be such to make it up you shall receive treble gaine by it, and good asssurance for it.

Montaigne. Gentlemen out of the weaknesse of my estate you seem to have some knowledge of my brest that wood if it were possible advance my declined fortunes, to satisfie all men of whom I have had credit, and I know no way better then these which you propose; 140 I have some money ready under my command, some part of it is already promis'd, but the remainder is yours to such uses as are propounded.

Laverdure. Appoint some certain place of meeting, for these affaires require expedition.

Montaigne. I wil make it my present businesse: at twelve, I am to

111 natures] MS; nature F1   114 not] MS; *omit* F1
127 an unknowne] MS; one F1   145 require] MS; requires F1

meet *Monsir Mallicorne* the Marchant at the Pallace, you know him
sir, about some negotiation of the same nature, there I wil be ready
to tender you that money, upon such conditions as wee shall
conclude of.   150

Laverdure.   The care of it be yours, so much as the affaire concernes
you.

Montaigne.   Your caution is effectuall, and till then I take my leave.

Laverdure.   Good Master *Montagne.*

Exit [Montaigne].

[*Voices within.*]   Down with their weapons.

Enter Longavile *and* Dubois, *their swords drawn,* Servants *and
others between them.*

1. Servant.   Nay Gentlemen what meane you, pray be quiet, have
some respect unto the house.

Longavile.   A treacherous slave.

Duboys.   Thou dost revile thy self base *Longavile.*

Longavile.   I say thou art a villaine and a corrupt one, that hast some   160
seaven years fed on thy masters trencher, yet never bredst good
bloud towards him: for if thou hadst, thou'dst have a sounder heart.

Duboys.   So sir, you can use your tongue something nimbler then
your sword.

Longavile.   Wood you cood use your tongue well of your Masters
friend, you might have better imployment for your sword.

Duboys.   I say againe and I wil speak it loud and often, that *Orleans* is
a noble Gentleman with whom *Amiens* is to light to poyse the scale.

Longavile.   He is the weaker for taking of a prayse out of thy mouth.

Duboys.   This hand shall seale his merit at thy heart.   170

Laverdure.   Part them my masters, part them.

1. Servant.   Part them sir, why do not you part them, you stand by
with your sword in your hand, and cry part 'em.

---

147   *Monsir*] MS; *omit* F1   150 of] MS; off F1
151   the affaire] MS; they affaire F1
155   *Voices ... weapons.*] *Within a clamor, down with their weapons.* F1; *Wthin: Clashing of
weapons: some crying downe wth theire weapons:* MS
*155.1–2 Servants *and others*] stet F1   156, 172 *1. Servant.*] *Ser.* F1, MS
162   thou'dst] MS; *omit* F1   165–166 Masters friend] MS; Master, friend F1
172   not you] MS; you not F1

Laverdure.   Why you must know my friend my cloaths are better
then yours, and in a good suit, I do never use to part any body.
La-poope.   And it is discretion.
Laverdure.   I marry is it Captaine.
Longavile.   Duboies,

Though this place priviledge thee, know where next we meet,
The bloud which at thy heart flowes drops at thy feet.   180

[*Exit.*]

Duboys.   I would not spend it better then in this quarrell,
And on such a hazard.

Enter Amience *in hast, his sword drawne.*

Amiens.   What uprores this, must my name here be question'd
In Tavern brawels, and by affected Ruffins?
Laverdure.   Not we indeed sir.
Duboys.   Fear cannot make me shrink out of your fury,
Though you were greater then your name doth make you,
I am one, and the opposer; if your swolne rage
Have ought in mallice to inforce, expresse it.
Amiens.   I seek thee not nor shalt thou ever gaine   190
That credit, which a blow from me wood give thee.
By my blood, I more detest that fellow
Which took my part then thee, that he durst offer
To take my honour in his feeble armes,
And spend it in a drinking room; which way went he?
Laverdure.   That way sir,——[*aside*] I wood you wood after for I
do fear we shall have some more scuffling.
Amiens.   Ile follow him, and if my speed o're take him, I shall ill
thank him for his forwardnesse.

Exit.

Laverdure.   I am glad he's gon, for I do not love to see a sword drawn   200
in the hand of a man that lookes so furious, ther's no jesting with
edge tooles, how say you Captaine?
La-poope.   I say tis better jesting then to be in earnest with them.

Enter Orleance.

182.1 *hast*] *i.e., haste; omit* MS   192 my blood, I] MS; my——I F1
203   *La-poope.*] MS; *Cap.* F1

Orleans.   How now?
What's the difference? they say there have bin swords drawn,
And in my quarrell, let me know that man,
Whose love is so sincere to spend his bloud
For my sake, I will bounteously requite him.

Laverdure.   We were all of your side, but there he stands begun it.

Orleans.   What's thy name?   210

Duboys.   *Duboyes.*

Orleans.   Give me thy hand, thou hast receaved no hurt?

Duboys.   Not any, nor were this body
Stuck full of wounds, I should not count them hurts,
Being taken in so honorable a cause
As the defence of my most worthy Lord.

Orleans.   The dedication of thy love to me
Requires my ample bounty, thou art mine,
For I do finde thee made unto my purposes.
Mounsieur *Laverdure*, pardon my neglect   220
I not observed you, and how runs rumour?

Laverdure.   Why, it runs my Lord like a foot man without a cloak, to
show that what's once rumour'd it cannot be hidde.

Orleans.   And what say the rable, am not I the subject of their talk?

Laverdure.   Troth my Lord the common mouth speakes foule
words.

Orleans.   Of me, for turning away my wife do they not?

Laverdure.   Faith the men do a little murmer at it and say, 'tis an ill
president in so great a man, marry the women they rayle, out right.

Orleans.   Out upon them rampallions, Ile keepe my selfe safe enough   230
out of their fingers, but what say my prity Idlye composed gallants
that censure every thing more desperatly then it is dangerous; what
say they?

Laverdure.   Marry they are laying wagers, what death you shall die;
one offerd to lay five hundred pounds; and yet he had but a groat
about him, and that was in two two-pences too to any man that
wo'd make it up a shilling; that you were kil'd with a Pistoll charg'd

213 were] MS; wear F1
231 Idlye] MS; jolly F1 (catchword, sig. 5T4v); Jelly F1 (sig. 5V1)
231 gallants] MS; gallant F1   232 desperatly] MS (desperatlye); desperate F1
235 offerd] MS; offers F1

with white Powder; another offerd to pawne his soule for five
shillings, and yet no body wo'd take him, that you were stab'd to
death and sho'd die with more wounds then *Cesar*.   240

Orleans.   And who sho'd be the *Brutus* that sho'd do it? *Montagne*
and his associates?

Laverdure.   So tis conjectured.

La-poope.   And believe it, sweet Prince, it is to be feared, and
therefore prevented.

Orleans.   By turning his purpose on himself, were not that the way?

Laverdure.   The most direct path for your safety. For where doth
danger sit more furious then in a desperate man?

La-poope.   And being you have declined his meanes, you have
increast his malice.   250

Laverdure.   Besides the generall report that steems in every mans
breath, and staines you all over with infamy, that Time the
devourer of all things cannot eat out.

La-poope.   I, for that former familiarity, which he had with your
Lady.

Laverdure.   Men speak it as boldly as words of complement; good
morrow, good even, or God save you sir, are not more usuall; if the
very word cuckold had been written upon your forehead in great
Capitall Letters, it could not have been dilated with more
confidence.   260

Orleans.   He shall not sleepe another night, I will have his blood,
though it be required at my hands again.

Laverdure.   Your Lordship may, and without hazzarding your own
person; here's a Gentleman in whose looks I see a resolution to
perform it.

Duboys.   Let his Lordship give me but his honourable word for my
safetye, Ile kill him as he walks.

Laverdure.   Or pistoll him as he sits at meat.

La-poope.   Or at game.

Laverdure.   Or as he is drinking.   270

Duboys.   Any way.

Orleans.   Wot thou? call what is mine thine own, thy reputation shall

241 *Brutus*] MS; Butchers F1   258 very] MS (verie); *omit* F1
264 here's] MS; he's F1   267 safetye] MS; life F1

48

not be brought in question for it, much lesse thy life; it shall be
namd a deed of valour in thee, not murder: Farewell.   *Exit.*

Duboys.   I need no more encouragement, it is a worke I will
perswade my selfe that I was borne to.

Laverdure.   And you may perswade your selfe to that you shall be
sav'd by it, being that it is for his honourable Lordship.

Duboys.   But you must yield me means, how, when and where.

Laverdure.   That shall be our taskes; nay more, we will be agents   280
with thee: this houre we are to meet him, on the receipt of certain
moneys, which indeed we purpose honestly to cheat him of,

> And that's the main cause I wo'd have him slain,
> Who works with safety makes a double gain.

Exeunt.

Enter Longaville, Amiens *following him.*   [II.iii]

Amiens.   Stay sir, I have took some pains to overtake you.
Your name is *Longaville?*

Longavile.   I have the word of many honest men for't.——
I crave your Lordships pardon,
Your sudden apprehension of my steps
Made me to frame an answer unwitting and
Unworthy your respect.

Amiens.   Doe you know me?

Longavile.   Yes, my Lord.

Amiens.   I know not you; nor am I well pleased to make
This time, as the affaire now stands, the induction   10
Of your acquaintance; you are a fighting fellow?

Longavile.   How my Lord?

Amiens.   I think I too much grace you;
Rather you are a fellow dares not fight,
But spet and puffe and make a noyse whilst
Your trembling hand drawes out your Sword, to try it
Upon Andirons, stooles or tables, rather
Then on a man.

Longavile.   Your honour may best speake this;

---

283 main cause] MS; many causes F1   5 of] MS; on F1   15 try] MS; lay F1

Yet by my life with little safety, if
I thought it serious.

Amiens.   Come, you are a mere braggart,
And you have given me cause to tell you so: 20
What weaknesse have you ever seen in me
To prompt your selfe, that I could need your helpe,
Or what other reasons could induce you to it?
You never yet had a meales meat from my Table,
Nor as I remember from my Wardrop
Any cast Suite.

Longavile.   Tis true,
I never durst yet have such a servile spirit,
To be the minion of a full swolne Lord;
But alwaies did detest such slavery: 30
A meales meat, or a cast sute?
I wo'd first eate the stones, and from such rags
The dunghill does afford pick me a garment.

Amiens [*aside*].   I have mistook the man, his resolute spirit
Proclaimes him generous, he has a noble heart
As free to utter good deeds as to act them;
For had he not been right, and of one piece,
He would have crumpled, curled, and shrunck himselfe
Out of the shape of man into a shaddow.——
But prethee tell me, if no such fawning hope   40
Did lead thee on to hazzard life for my sake;
What was it that incited thee? Tell me; speak it
Without the imputation of a Sicophant.

Longavile.   Your own desert, and with it was joyn'd
The unfained friendship that I judged you ever
Held unto my former Lord.

Amiens.   The noble *Montagne*?

Longavile.   Yes, the noble and much injured *Montagne*.

Amiens.   To such a man as thou art, my heart shall be
A Casket: I will lock thee up there,   50
And esteem thee as a faithfull friend,
The richest Jewell that a man enjoyes;

18 Yet by my life with] MS; yet——| with F1   19 mere] MS; merry F1
33 dunghill] W; dunghills MS, F1 (dunghils)   38 shrunck] MS; struck F1

50

And being thou didst follow once my friend,
And in thy heart still dost, not with his fortunes
Casting him off,
Thou shalt goe hand in hand with me, and share
As well in my ability as love;
Tis not my end
To gaine men for my use, but a true friend.

Exeunt.

Enter Duboys.   [II.iv]

Duboys.   There's no such thriving way to live in grace,
As to have no sence of it; his backe nor belly
Shall not want warming that can practise mischiefe;
I walke now with a full purse, grow high and wanton,
Prune and briske my selfe in the bright shine
Of his good Lordships favours; and for what vertue?
For fashioning my selfe a murderer.
O noble *Montagne*, to whom I owe my heart,
With all my best thoughts, tho my tongue have promisd
To exceed the malice of thy destiny,   10
Never in time of all my service knew I
Such a sinne tempt thy bounty; those that did feed
Upon thy charge had merit or else need.

Enter Laverdure *and* Lapoope, *with disguises.*

Laverdure.   *Duboys*, most prosperously met.
Duboys.   How now? will he come this way?
Laverdure.   This way, immediately; therefore thy assistance, deere
    Duboys.
Duboys.   What, have you cheated him of the money you spoke of?
Laverdure.   Fough, as easily as a silly Countrey wench of her
    maydenhead; we had it in a twinkling.   20
Duboys.   Tis well——Captaine, let me helpe you [*aids* La-poope *in
    putting on his disguise*], you must be our leader in this action.
La-poope.   Tut, feare not, Ile warrant you if my Sword hold, we'l
    make no sweating busines of it.

3 practise mischiefe] MS; practise me mischiefe F1   24 busines] MS; sicknesse F1

Duboys.   Why that's well said, but let's retire a little, that we may come on the more bravely; this way, this way.   *Exeunt.*

Enter Montagne *in the hands of three* Officers, *and three* Creditors.

1. Creditor.   Officers look to him, and be sure you take good security before he part from you.

Montaigne.   Why but my friends,
You take a strange course with me; the sums I owe you   30
Are rather forgetfulnesse they are so slight,
Then want of will or honesty to pay you.

1. Creditor.   I sir, it may be so; but we must be paid, and we will be paid before you scape: we have wife and children, and a charge, and you are going down the wind, as a man may say; and therefore it behooves us to looke to't in time.

2. Creditor.   Your cloak here wo'd satisfie me, mine's not above a three pound matter, besides the arrest.

3. Creditor.   Faith and mine is much about that matter too; your Girdle and Hangers, and your Beaver, shall be sufficient baile for't.   40

1. Creditor.   If you have ever a plain black sute at home, this with your Silke-stockings, Garters, and Roses shall pacifie me too; for I take no delight, if I have a sufficient pawne, to cast any Gentleman in prison; therefore tis but an untrussing matter, and you are free, we are no unreasonable creatures you see; for mine own part, I protest I am loth to put you to any trouble but for security.

Montaigne.   Is there no more of you? he wo'd next demand my skinne.

1. Creditor.   No sir, here's no more of us, nor do any of us demand your skin, we know not what to doe with it: but it may be if you   50
ow'd your Glover any money, he knew what use to make of it.

Montaigne.   Ye dregs of basenesse, vultures amongst men,
That tyer upon the hearts of generous spirits.

1. Creditor.   You doe us wrong sir, we tyre no generous spirits, we tyre nothing but our hackneys.

Enter Mallicorne.

Montaigne.   But here comes one made of another piece;

41 this with] MS; this Silken one, with F1   46 but] MS; *omit* F1

52

A man well meriting that free born name
Of Citizen; welcome my deliverer, I am falne
Into the hands of blood-hounds, that for a sum
Lesser then their honesties, which is nothing,   60
Wo'd teare me out of my skin.

Mallicorne. Why sir, what's the matter?

1. Creditor. Why sir, the matter is, that we must have our money,
which if we cannot have, we'l satisfie our selves with his carcasse,
and be payd that waies:——you had as good sir not have been so
peremptory.——Officers, hold fast.

1. Officer. The strenuous fist of vengeance now is clutcht; therefore
feare nothing.

Mallicorne. What may be the debt in grosse?

Montaigne. Some forty Crowns, nay rather not so much,   70
Tis quickly cast.

Mallicorne. Tis strange to me, that your estate sho'd have
So low an ebbe, to sticke at such sleight sums:
Why my friends, you are too strict in your accounts,
And call too sudden on this Gentleman,
He has hopes left yet to pay you all.

1. Creditor. Hopes? I marry pray bid him pay his friends with his
hopes, and pay us with currant Coyne: I knew a gallant once that
fed his creditors still with hopes, and bid 'em they sho'd feare
nothing, for he had 'em tyed in a string; and trust me so he had 80
indeed, for at last he and all his hopes hopt in a haltar.

Montaigne. Good sir, with what speed you may free me out of the
company of these slaves, that have nothing but their names to show
'em men.

Mallicorne. What wo'd you wish me do sir? I protest I ha' not the
present summe (small as it is) to lay down for you; and for giving
my word, my friends no later then yesternight made me take bread
and eate it, that I sho'd not do it for any man breathing ith' world;
therefore I pray hold me excused.

Montaigne. You doe not speake this seriously?   90

Mallicorne. As ever I said my prayers, I protest to you.

66 Officers] MS; Officer F1   77 pray] MS; *omit* F1
77–78 with his hopes] MS; with hopes F1   82 free me out of the] MS; free out the F1
87 later] MS; latter F1

Montaigne. What may I think of this?

Mallicorne. Troth sir thought is free for any man; we abuse our
betters in it, I have done it my selfe.

Montaigne. Trust me, this speech of yours doth much amaze me,
Pray leave this language, and out of that same sum
You lately did receive of me, lay down
As much as may discharge me.

Mallicorne. You are a merry man sir, and I am glad you take your
crosses so temperately; fare you well sir, and yet I have something 100
more to say to ye, a word in your eare I pray; to be plaine with you I
did lay this plot to arrest ye to enjoy this money I have of yours,
with the more safety. I am a foole to tell you this now; but in good
faith I could not keepe it in. And the money wo'd a done me little
good else. An honest Citizen cannot wholly enjoy his own wife for
you, they grow old before they have the true use of them, which is a
lamentable thing, and truely much hardens the hearts of us Citizens
against you: I can say no more, but am heartily sorry for your
heavinesse, and so I take my leave.   *Exit* Mallycorne.

1. Creditor. Officers laye hold on him againe, for Mounsier 110
Mallycorne will doe nothing for him I perceive.

Enter Duboys, Lapoope, *and* Laverdure.

Duboys. Nay come on my masters, leave dauncing of the old
measures, and let's assault him bravely.

Laverdure. By no means; for it goes against my stomacke to kill a
man in an unjust quarrell.

La-poope. It must needs be a clog to a mans conscience all his life
time.

Laverdure. It must indeed Captaine: besides doe ye not see he has
gotten a guard of friends about him, as if he had some knowledge of
our purpose?   120

Duboys. Had he a guard of Devils as I think them little better, my
Sword should doe the message that it came for.

Laverdure. If you will be so desperate, the blood lie upon your own
neck, for we'l not meddle in't.

Duboys [*aside to* Montaigne]. I am your friend and servant,

102 ye] MS; you F1   106 the] MS; *omit* F1   110 laye] MS; take F1
112 on] MS; *omit* F1

Struggle with me and take my Sword.

> Duboys *runs upon* Montagne, *and strugling yeelds him his*
> *Sword; the* Officers *draw,* Laverdure *and* La-poope *in the*
> *scuffling retire,* Montagne *chaseth* [*the* Officers] *about the*
> *Stage, himselfe wounded.* [The Third Officer *falls.*]

Noble sir make your way, you have slaine an Officer.

> [*Exit* Duboys.]

Montaigne.   Some one of them has certainly
Requited me; for I do lose much blood.   *Exit.*

1. Officer.   Udsprecious, we have lost a brother, pursue the   130
Gentleman.

2. Officer.   Ile not meddle with him: you see what comes on't; besides
I know he will be hang'd ere he be taken.

1. Officer.   I tell thee yeoman he must be taken ere he be hanged; he is
hurt in the guts, run afore therefore and know how his wife will rate
his Sawsiges a pound.

3. Officer.   Stay brother, I may live, for surely I finde i'm but hurt in
the leg, a dangerous kick on the shin-bone.

> *Exeunt.*

Enter Madam Lamira, Lady Orleans, Veramour.   III.i

Lamira.   You see Lady
What harmlesse sports our Countrey life affords;
And though you meet not here with City dainties,
Or Courtly entertainment, what you have
Is free and hearty.

Lady Orleans.   Madam, I finde here
What is a stranger to the Court, content,
And receive curtesies done for themselves,
Without an expectation of returne,
Which binds me to your service.

Lamira.   Oh your love;
My homely house built more for use then shew   10
Observes the Golden mean equally distant
From glittering pompe, and sordid avarice;

126.1–4 Duboys ... *wounded.*] *printed between lines* 124 *and* 125 *in* MS, F1
126.3 *the* Officers] *them* F1, *em* MS   126.3 *about*] MS; *off* F1
129 *Exit.*] MS; *omit* F1   0.1 Lady Orleans] MS (*Ladye Orleance*); *Madam le Orleans* F1

For Maskes we will observe the workes of nature
And in the place of visitation read.
Our Physick shall be wholsome walkes, our viandes,
Nourishing not provoking: for I finde
Pleasures are tortures, that leave stings behind.

Lady Orleans.   You have a great estate.

Lamira.   A competency
Sufficient to maintaine me and my ranke,
Nor am I, I thank Heaven, so Courtly bred   20
As to imploy the utmost of my Rents
In paying Tailors for phantastick Roabes;
Or rather then be second in a fashion,
Eate out my Officers and my Revenues
With grating usury; my back shall not
Be the base on which your soothing Citizen
Erects his Summer-house; nor on the other side
Will I be so penuriously wise,
As to make money (thats my slave) my Idoll,
Which yet to wrong, merits as much reproof,   30
As to abuse our servant.

Lady Orleans.   Yet with your pardon
I thinke you want the Crown of all contentment.

Lamira.   In what good Madam?

Lady Orleans.   In a worthy husband.

Lamira.   Humh! It is strange the galley-slave should praise
His Oare, or stroakes; or you, that have made shipwracke
Of all delight upon this Rock cal'd marriage,
Should sing Encomions of't.

Lady Orleans.   Madam, though one fall
From his horse and breake his neck, will you
Conclude from that it is unfit to ride?
Or must it follow, because *Orleance*   40
My Lord is pleased to make his passionate triall
Of my suspected patience, that my brother,
(Were he not so, I might say, worthy *Amiens*)
Will imitate his ills, that cannot fancy

23 a] MS; the F1   27 Summer-house] MS; Summer-houses F1
34 Humh! It] MS;——It F1   37 of't] MS; o't F1   41 Lord is] MS; Lord's F1

56

What's truely Noble in him?
Lamira.   I must grant
There's as much worth in him as can be lookt for
From a young Lord, but not enough to make
Me change my golden liberty and consent
To be a servant to it, as wives are
To the Imperious humors of their Lords: 50
Me thinks I'm well, I rise and goe to bed
When I thinke fit, eate what my appetite
Desires without controle, my servants study
Is my contentment, and to make me merry
Their farthest ayme; my sleeps are enquired after,
My rising up saluted with respect:
Command and liberty now waite upon
My Virgin state; what would I more? change all,
And for a husband? no; these freedomes die,
In which they live with my Virginity;   60
Tis in her choice that's rich to be a wife,
But not being yoakt to chuse the single life.———
Boy!
Veramour. Madam.
Lamira.   How like you the Countrey?
Veramour. I like the ayre of it well Madam, and the rather because as
   on Irish Timber your Spider will not make his web, so for ought I
   see yet your Cheater, Pander, and Informer being in their
   dispositions too foggy for this piercing climate, shun it, and choose
   rather to walk in mists in the City.
Lamira. Who did you serve first boy?
Veramour. A rich Merchants widdow, and was by her preferred to a   70
   young Court-lady.
Lady Orleans. And what difference found you in their service?
Veramour. Very much: for looke how much my old City Madam
   gave to her young visitants, so much my Lady received from her
   hoary Court-servants.
Lamira. And what made you to leave her?
Veramour. My father (Madam) had a desire to have me a tall man,

55 ayme] MS; ayms F1   61 her] MS (hir); their F1   63 Boy] MS; *omit* F1
65 Spider] MS; Spiders F1   74 from] MS; for F1   77 tall] MS; tale F1

57

took me from thence.

Lamira.   Well, I perceive you inherit the wag, from your father.

Veramour.   Doves beget Doves; and Eagles, Eagles, Madam: A 80
Citizens heire, tho left never so rich, seldome at the best proves but
a griffin Gentleman: the sonne of an Advocate, tho dub'd like his
father, will shew a relish of his discent, and the fathers thriving
practice: as I have heard, she that of a Chambermayd is
metamorphosed into a Madam, will yet remember how oft her
father's daughter by her mother ventured to lie upon the rushes
before she could get in that which makes many Ladies.

Lady Orleans.   But what think you of your late Master?

Veramour.   Oh Madam——   *Sighes.*

Lamira.   Why doe you sigh? you are sorry that you left him,   90
He made a wanton of you.

Veramour.   Not for that:
Or if he did, for that my youth must love him.
Oh pardon me, if I say liberty
Is bondage, if compared with his kind service;
And but to have power now to speake his worth
To its desert, I should be well content
To be an old man when his praise were ended:
And yet, if at this instant you were pleased
I should begin, the livery of age
Would take his lodging up upon this head   100
Ere I should bring it to a period.
In briefe he is a man (for God forbid
That I should ever live to say he was)
Of such a shape as would make one beloved,
That never had good thought; and to his body
He hath a mind of such a constant temper
In which all vertues throng to have a room:
Yet 'gainst this noble Gentleman, this *Montagne*,
For in that name I comprehend all goodnesse,
Wrong, and the wrested law, false witnesses,   110
And envy sent from hell, have rose in Armes,

---

81 Citizens heire] MS; Citizen here F1   81 but] MS; *omit* F1
*82 griffin] MS; *omit* F1   *86 father's] Mason; *omit* MS, F1
89 *Sighes*] MS; *Sigh* F1   100 up] MS; *omit* F1   107 all] MS; *omit* F1

And tho not pierced, battered his honourd shield.
What shall I say? I hope you will forgive me,
That but your selfe, if you were pleas'd to love,
I know no *Juno* worthy such a *Jove*.

Enter Charlot *with a letter.*

Lamira.   Tis well yet that I have the second place
    In your affection:——From whence?
Charlotte.   From the Lord *Amiens*, Madam.
Lamira.   Tis welcome, though it beare his usual language:

                                              [*Reads.*]

    I thought so much, his love-suit speakes his health.   120
    'Twolld showe well in a night cap.
Lady Orleans.   But in him
    I hope as he meanes, appeares honorable.
Lamira.   On those termes I receave it. What's he that brought it?
Charlotte.   A Gentleman of good ranke, it seems.
Lamira.   Where is he?
Charlotte.   Receiving entertainment in your house
    Sorting with his degree.
Lamira.   Tis well.
Charlotte.   He waites
    Your Ladiships pleasure.
Lamira.   He shall not waite long:
    Ile leave you for a while; nay stay you boy,
    Attend the Lady.

                                Exeunt Lamira, Charlotte.

Veramour.   Would I might live once
    To waite on my poore Master.
Lady Orleans.   That's a good boy: 130
    This thankfulnesse looks lovely on thy forehead,
    And in it, as a book, me thinks I read
    Instructions for my selfe, that am his debtor,
    And wo'd do much that I might be so happy
    To repaire that which to our griefe is ruin'd.
Veramour.   It were a worke a King might glory in,

114 That but your selfe, if you were pleas'd] MS; That if you were but pleas'd F1
120 speakes] MS; speake F1   *121–123 'Twolld ... receave it.] MS; *omit* F1

If he saw with my eyes: If you please Madam,
For sure to me you seem unapt to walke,
To sit, although the churlish Birds deny
To give us musicke in this grove, where they   140
Are prodigall to others: Ile strain my voyce
For a sad Song, the place is safe and private.
Lady Orleans.   Twas my desire; begin good *Viramour*.

Musick a Song, at the end of it enter Montagne *fainting, his Sword
drawn.*

Lady Orleans.   What's he *Viramour?*
Veramour.   A goodly personage.
Montaigne.   Am I yet safe? or is my flight a dream?
My wounds and hunger tell me that I wake:
Whither have my feares borne me? no matter where,
Who hath no place to goe to, cannot erre:
What shall I doe? cunning calamity
That others grosse wits uses to refine,   150
When I most need it duls the edge of mine.
Lady Orleans.   Is not this *Montagnes* voyce?
Veramour.   My Masters? fie.
Montaigne.   What sound was that, pish,
Feare makes the wretch think every leafe oth' Jury:
What course to live, beg? better men have done it,
But in another kind: steale? *Alexander*
Though stiled a Conquerour, was a proud thiefe
Though he robd with an Army; fie how idle
These meditations are: though thou art worse
Then sorrows tongue can speak thee, thou art still   160
Or shouldst be, honest *Montagne.*
Lady Orleans.   Tis too true.
Veramour.   Tis he:
What villaines hande did this? oh that my flesh
Were Balme; in faith sir, I would plucke it off
As readily as this; pray you accept
My will to doe you service: I have heard

138 seem unapt] MS; seem to me unapt F1   163 hande] MS; hands F1

The Mouse once sav'd the Lyon in his need,
As the poore Scarab spild the Eagles seed.

Lady Orleans.   How do you?

Montaigne.   As a forsaken man.   170

Lady Orleans.   Do not say so, take comfort,
  For your misfortunes have been kind in this,
  To cast you on a hospitable shoare,
  Where dwels a Lady——

Veramour.   She to whom, good Master,
  You prefer'd me.

Lady Orleans.   In whose house, whatsoere
  Your dangers are, Ile undertake your safety.

Montaigne.   I feare I am pursued, and doubt that I
  In my defence have kild an Officer.

Veramour.   Is that all? there's no law under the Sunne
  But will I hope confesse, one drop of blood   180
  Shed from this arme is recompence enough
  Though you had cut the throats of all the Catchpoles
  In France, nay in the world.

Montaigne.   I would be loth
  To be a burthen, or feed like a drone
  On the industrious labour of the Bee,
  And baser far I hold it to owe for
  The bread I eate, what's not in me to pay,
  Then that since my full fortunes are declined,
  To their low ebb I fashion my high mind.
  It was no shame to *Hecuba* to serve   190
  When Troy was fired: if't be in your power
  To be a means to make her entertain me,
  And far from that I was, but to supply
  My want with habit fit for him that serves,
  I shall owe much to you.

Lady Orleans.   Leave that care to me.

Veramour.   Good sir, leane on my shoulder; helpe good Madam:
  Oh that I were a horse for halfe an houre,

---

177 feare I] MS; feare that I F1   185 the Bee] MS; a Bee F1
188 that] MS; *omit* F1   189 I] MS; Ile F1
192 entertain me] MS; entertainment F1

61

That I might carry you home on my backe:
I hope you wil love me still?
Montaigne.   Thou dost deserve it boy.   200
That I should live to be thus troublesome!
Lady Orleans.   Good sir, tis none.
Veramour.   Trouble most willingly; I would be changd
Like *Apuleius*, weare his Asses eares,
Provided I might still this burthen beare.
Lady Orleans.   Tis a kind boy.
Montaigne.   I finde true proofe of it.

                                              Exeunt.

              Enter Amiens *and* Longeville *with a Paper.*   [III.ii

Amiens.   You'l carry it?
Longavile.   As I live although my packet
Were like *Bellerophons.* What have you seen
In me or my behaviour since your favours
So plentifully showerd upon my wants,
That may beget distrust of my performance?
Amiens.   Nay, be not angry, if I entertained
But the least scruple of your love, or courage,
I would make purchase of one with my state
Should do me right in this, nor can you blame me
If in a matter of such consequence   10
I am so importunate.
Longavile.   Good my Lord,
Let me prevent your further conjurations
To rayse my spirit, I know this is a challenge
To be delivered unto *Orleance* hand,
And that my undertaking ends not there,
But I must be your second, and in that
Not alone search your enemy, measure weapons,
But stand in all your hazzards, as our blouds
Ran in the self same veines, in which if I
Better not your opinion, as a limbe   20
That's putrifyed and uselesse, cut me off,

---

4 showerd] MS; showed F1   8 purchase] MS *corrected;* choice MS *originally;* omit F1
8 with] MS (wth); which F1   12 Let] MS (let); tell F1

And underneath the Gallowes bury it.

Amiens.   At full you understand me, and in this
Binde me and what's mine to you and yours.
I wil not so much wrong you as to adde
One sylable more, let it suffice I leave
My honor to your guard: and in that prove
You hold the first place in my heart and love.

Exit Amiens.

Longavile.   The first place in a Lords affection? very good; and how
long doth that last? perhaps the changing of some three shirts in the   30
Tennis Court; wel it were very necessary that an order were taken
(if it were possible,) that younger brothers might have more wit, or
more money: for now how ever the foole hath long bin put upon
him that inherits, his revenew hath brought him a spunge, and wip't
off the imputation, and for the understanding of the younger, let
him get as much rhetorick as he can to grace his language, they wil
see he shall have glosse little enough to set out his barck.——

Enter Dubois.

Stand *Dubois.* Look about. All safe?

Duboys.   Approach not neer me but with reverence,
Lawrell and adoration, I have done   40
More then deserves ten thousand ducketts.

Longavile.   How now what's the matter?

Duboys.   With this hand only aided by this brain,
Without an *Orpheus* Harp, redeem'd from hels
Three headed Porter, our *Euridice.*

Longavile.   Nay prithee speak sence, this is like the stale braggart in a
Play.

Duboys.   Then in plaine Prose thus, and with as little action as thou
canst desire, the three headed Porter were three unexorable Catchpoles out of whose jawes with out the help of *Orpheus* Harp, bayle   50
or bribe, (for those too stringes makes the Musique that mollifies

32 brothers] MS; brother F1   *37 barck] *stet* F1
37.1 *Enter* Dubois.] *after* 'language' (*line* 36) *in* F1   40 adoration] MS; adorations F1
41 deserves ten thousand ducketts] MS; deserve a 100 thanks F1
50 bayle] MS; baite F1

those flinty furies,) I rescued our *Euridice*, I meane my old Master
Montagne.

Longavile.   And is this all, a poor rescue? Pretious, tis allmost as
common as to have a lord arrested, and lye by it. I thought thou
hadst reverst the judgement for his overthrow, in his sute, or
wrought upon his adversary *Orleance*, taken the shape of a Ghost,
frighted his mind into distraction, and for the appeasing of his
conscience forc'd him to make restitution of *Montagnes* Lands, or
such like. Rescued? Slight, I would have hired a Crohieture for two   60
Cardekues to have done so much with his whip.

Duboys.   You wood sir, and yet tis more then three on their foot-
cloathes durst do for a sworne Brother, in a Coach.

Longavile.   Besides what proofe of it? for ought I know, this may be
a trick. I had rather have him in prison where I might visit him, and
do him service, then not at all, or I know not where.

Duboys.   Well sir, the end wil shew it. What's that, a challenge?

Longavile.   Yes, wher's *Orleance*? though we fight in jest he must
meet with *Amiens* in earnest,——

Enter Orleans [behind].

Fall off, we are discovered.   70

Orleans.   My horse, garcon, ha!

Duboys.   Were it not in a house, and in his house
To whom I owe all duty——

Longavile.   What would it do?
Prate as it do's? but be as far from stricking
As he that owes it, *Orleans*.

Duboys.   How?

Longavile.   I think thou art his Porter,
Set here to answer creditors, that his Lordship
Is not within or takes the diet. I am sent,
And wil grow here untill I have an answer,   80
Not to demand a debt of money, but

---

*54–55 Pretious ... lye by it.] MS (*heavily crossed out*); *omit* F1   60 a] MS; *omit* F1
*60 a Crohieture] *stet* F1   64 proofe] MS; proofs F1
65 in prison] MS; a Prisoner F1   69.1 *Enter* Orleans] MS; *omit* F1
71 *Orleans*] MS (Orle:); *omit* F1 (*where Orleans' words are printed following* 'discovered' *at the
end of Longavile's preceding speech*)   72 his house] MS; his presence F1
*73 What would it do?] *stet* F1

To call him to a strict account for wrong
Done to the honor of a Gentleman,
Which nothing but his hearts-bloud shall wash off.
Duboys.   Shall I hear this?
Longavile.   And more, that if I may not
Have accesse to him, I will fix this here
To his disgrace and thine.
Duboys.   And thy life with it.
Longavile.   Then have the coppies of it pasted on posts,
Like Pamphlet titles that sue to be sold;
Have his disgrace talk for Tobacco shops,   90
His picture bafful'd.
Duboys.   All respect away,
Wer't in a Church——   *Draw both.*
Longavile.   This is the book I pray with.
Orleans [*coming forward*].   Forbear upon your lives.
Longavile.   What are you rous'd? I hope your Lordship can read
(though he staine not his birth with scholler-ship). [*Gives paper.*]
Doth it not please you? Now if you are a right Mounsier, muster up
the rest of your attendance, which is a page, a cook, a pander,
coach-man, and a foot man, in these dayes a great Lords traine;
pretending I am unworthy to bring you a challenge, in stead of
answering it, have me kik't.   100
Duboys.   If he does thou deserv'st it.
Longavile.   I dare you all to touch me, I'le not stand still,
What answer you?
Orleans.   That thou hast done to *Amience*
The office of a faithfull friend which I
Would cherish in thee were he not my foe.
How ever since on honorable tearmes
He cals me forth, say I will meet with him,
And by *Dubois* ere Sun-set make him know
The time and place, my swords length, and what ever
Scruple of circumstance he can expect.   110
Longavile.   This answer comes unlookt for, fare you well,

83 honor] MS; honors F1   84 hearts-bloud] MS (hearts bloud); heart-bloud F1
111 fare] MS; far F1

Finding your temper thus, wood I had sayd lesse.

Exit.

Orleans.   Now comes thy love to the test.
Duboys.   My Lord 'twill hold,
And in all dangers prove it selfe true gold.

Exeunt.

Enter Laverdure, La-poop, Malicorne, Servant.   [III

Servant.   I wil acquaint my Lady with your comming.
Please you repose your selves here.
Mallicorne.   Ther's a tester, nay now I am a woer I
must be bountifull.
Servant.   If you would have two three-pences for it sir,
To give some of your kindred as you ride,
I'le see if I can get them; we use not
(Tho Servants) to take Bribes.   *Exit.*
Laverdure.   Then thou art unfit, to be in office either in Court or
City.   10
La-poope.   Indeed corruption is a Tree whose branches are of an
unmeasurable length, they spread every where, and the dew that
drops from thence have infected some chayres and stooles of
authority.
Mallicorne.   Ah Captaine, lay not all the fault upon Officers. You
know you can shark though you be out of action, witnesse
Montagne.
Laverdure.   Hang him, hee's safe enough; you had a hand in it to and
have gained by him; but I wonder you Citizens that keep so many
bookes, and take such strict accounts for every farthing due to you 20
from others, reserve not so much as a memorandum for the
curtesies you receive.
Mallicorne.   Would you have a Citizen book those? thankfulnes is a
thing we are not sworn to in our indentures: you may as well urge
conscience.
Laverdure.   Talke no more of such vanities. *Montagne* is irrecover-
ably sunk, I would we had twenty more to send after him; the Snake
that would be a Dragon and have wings must eate a spider; and

3 woer] *i.e.,* wooer (*the* MS *reading*). *Cf. below, lines* 47, 193, *and* IV.i.147, 282.
*27–28 the Snake that would be a Dragon] *stet* F1   28 a spider] MS; *omit* F1

66

what implyes that but this, that in this Canniball age he that would
have the sute of wealth must not care whom he feeds on? and as I   30
have heard no flesh battens better, then that of a profest friend; and
he that would mount to honour must not make dainty to use the
head of his mother, back of his father, or neck of his brother, for
ladders to his preferment; for but observe, and you shall finde for
the most part cunning villany sit at a feast as principall guest, and
Innocent honesty waite as a contemn'd servant with a trencher.
La-poope.   The Ladies.

Enter Mountagne *bare-headed* [*and dressed as a servant*], Lamira,
    Lady Orleance, Charlot, Veramour, *salute.*

Montaigne.   Do yee smell nothing?
Charlotte.   Not I sir.
Montaigne.   The carrion of three knaves is very strong in my   40
    nostrels.
Laverdure.   We came to admire, and finde fame was a niggard
    Which we thought prodigall in your report
    Before we saw you.
Lamira.   Tush sir, this Courtship's old.
La-poope.   Ile fight for thee sweet wench,
    This is my tongue and woes for me! [*Touching his sword.*]
Lamira.   Good man of War,
    Hands of; if you take me it must be by siege,
    Not by an onset; and for your valour, I   50
    Think that I have deserved few enemies,
    And therefore need it not.
Mallicorne.   Thou needst nothing sweet Lady, but an obsequious
    husband, and where wilt thou finde him, if not in the City? we are
    true Moscovits to our Wives, and are never better pleased, then
    when they use us as slaves, bridle and saddle us; have me, thou shalt
    command all my wealth as thine own, thou shalt sit like a Queen in
    my ware house; And my factors at their returne with my ships shall
    pay thee tribute of all the rarities of the earth; thou shalt wear gold,
    feed on delicates, the first peascods, strauberies, grapes, cherries   60
    shall——

29 implyes] MS *corrected*; imployes MS *originally*, F1   40 three] MS; *omit* F1
43 your] MS (yoʳ); our F1   58 their] MS; the F1

Lamira.   Be mine; I apprehend what you would say.
   Those dainties which the City payes so dear for,
   The Country yeilds for nothing, and as early;
   And credit me your far fet viandes please not
   My appetite better then those that are neer hand.
   Then for your promis'd service and subjection
   To all my humors, when I am your wife,
   Which as it seemes is frequent in the City,
   I cannot finde what pleasure they receive   70
   In using theire fond husbands like their Maydes;
   But of this more hereafter; I accept
   Your proffer kindly, and yours; my house stands open
   To entertain you; take your pleasure in it,
   And ease after your journey.
Lady Orleans.   Do you note
   The boldnesse of these fellowes?
Lamira.   Alas Madam,
   A virgin must in this be like a lawyer,
   And as he takes all fees, shee must hear all suitors;
   The one for gaine, the other for her mirth;——
   [*To* Montaigne] Stay with the Gentlemen, wee'l to the Orchard. 80
         Exeunt Lamira, Lady Orleans, Veramour, Charlotte.
La-poope.   Hum, what art thou?
Montaigne.   An honest man, though poor;
   And look such like to monsters, are they so rare?
Laverdure.   Rose from the dead?
Mallicorne.   Do you heare Mounsier Serviture, didst thou never
   heare of one *Montagne* a prodigall gull, that lives about Paris?
Montaigne.   So sir.
Laverdure.   One that after the losse of his maine estate in a Law sute,
   bought an Office in the Court.
La-poope.   And should have letters of Mart, to have the Spanish
   treasure as it came from the Indies; were not thou and he twins? put 90
   of thy hat, let me see thy forehead.
Montaigne.   Though you take priviledge to use your tongues,

*69 frequent] *stet* F1   71 theire] MS; there F1   76 these] MS; the F1
80 Orchard] MS; Orchards F1   81 Hum, what] MS;——what F1
*82 such] MS *corrected*; they MS *originally*, F1

68

I pray you hold your fingers,
'Twas your base cozenage made me as I am,
And were you some where else I would take off
This proud filme from your eyes, that will not let
You know I am *Montagne*.

     Enter Lamira [*and conceals herself*] *behinde the Arras.*

Lamira [*aside*].   I will observe this better.
Laverdure.   And art thou he? I wil do thee grace; give me thy hand; I
  am glad thou hast taken so good a course; serve God and please thy 100
  Mistris; if I prove to be thy Master as I am very likely, I will do for
  thee.
Mallicorne.   Faith the fellow's well made for a servingman, and will
  no doubt carry a chyne of Beefe with a good grace.
La-poope.   Prithee be carefull of me in my chamber, I will remember
  thee at my departure.
Montaigne.   All this I can indure under this roof,
And so much owe I her, whose now I am,
That no wrong shall incense me to molest
Her quiet house; while you continue here,   110
I will not be ashamed to do you service
More then to her, because such is her pleasure.
But you that have broke thrice, and fourteen times
Compounded for two shillings in the pound,
Know I dare kick you in your shop; do ye hear?
If ever I see *Paris*, though an army
Of musty Murrions, rusty brown bils and clubs,
Stand for your guard——I have heard of your tricks,
And you that smell of Amber at my charge,
And triumph in your cheat; well I may live   120
To meet thee, be it among a troop of such
That are upon the faire face of the Court
Like running ulcers, and before thy whore
Trampell upon thee.
La-poope.   Is this a language for a livery? take heed, I am a Captaine.
Montaigne.   A Cox-comb are you not? that thou and I

96 let] MS; tell F1   104 with a good] MS; with good F1   125 Is] MS; *omit* F1

To give proof, which of us dares most, were now
In mid'st of a rough Sea, upon a piece
Of a split ship, where only one might ride,
I would——but foolish anger makes me talke   130
Like a Player.

                   Lamira [comes forward] from the Arras.

Lamira.   Indeed you act a part
Doth ill become my servant; is this your duty?
Montaigne.   I crave your pardon,
And wil hereafter be more circumspect.
Laverdure.   Oh the power of a Womans tongue! it hath done more
then we three with our swords durst undertake: put a madde man to
silence.
Lamira.   Why Sirra these are none of your comrades
To drink with in the celler; one of them   140
For ought you know may live to be your Master.
La-poope [aside].   Ther's some comfort yet.
Lamira.   Here's choyce of three, a wealthy Merchant——
Mallicorne [aside].   Hem, shee's taken, she hath spy'd my good Calf,
And many Ladies chuse their husbands by that.
Lamira.   A Courtier that's in grace, a valiant Captaine,
And are these mates for you? away be gon.
Montaigne.   I humbly pray you will be pleased to pardon,
And to give satisfaction to you Madam,
(Although I break my heart) I will confesse   150
That I have wrong'd them too, and make submission.
Lamira.   No I'le spare that; goe bid the Cook haste Supper.

                             Exit Montaigne.

La-poope.   Did she talke of supper? Oh brave Lady thou art worthy
to have servants, to be commandresse of a Family, that knowst how
to use and govern it.
Laverdure.   You shall have many Mistresses that will so mistake as to
take their horse keepers, and footemen insteed of their Husbands,
thou art none of those.

131.1 Lamira...*Arras.*] *Ent: Lamyra:* | *from the Aras* MS (*in the margin to the left of lines* 132–
    133); *Exit Lamira* | *from the* | *Arras.* F1 (*in the margin to the right of lines* 129–131).
133 become my] MS; become you my F1   136 hath] MS; had F1
153 Did she talke of supper?] MS; *omit* F1

Mallicorne.   But she that can make distinction of men, and knowes
   when she hath gallants, and fellowes of rank and quality in her   160
   house——
Lamira.   Gallants indeed, if it be the Gallants fashion
   To triumph in the miseries of a man,
   Of which they are the cause: one that transcends
   (In spight of all that fortune hath, or can)
   A million of such things as you; my doores
   Stand open to receive all such as wear
   The shape of Gentlemen, and my gentlier nature
   (I might say weaker) weighes not the expence
   Of entertainment; think you i'le forget yet   170
   What's due unto my selfe? do not I know,
   That you have dealt with poor *Montagne*, but like
   Needy Commanders, cheating Citizens,
   And perjured Courtiers? I am much mov'd, else use not
   To say so much, if you will bear your selves
   As fits such you would make me think you are,
   You may stay; if not the way lies before you.   *Exit.*
Mallicorne.   What think you of this Captaine?
La-poope.   That this is a baudy house, with Pinacles and Turrets, in
   which this disguised *Montagne* goes to rut gratis, and that this is a 180
   landed pandresse, and makes her house a brothell for charity.
Mallicorne.   Come, that's no miracle; but from whence derive you
   the supposition?
Laverdure.   Observe but the circumstance; you all know that in the
   height of *Montagnes* prosperity, hee did affect and had his love
   return'd by this Lady *Orleans*; since her divorcement, and his decay
   of estate, it is knowne, they have met; not so much as his boy is
   wanting; and that this can be any thing else then a meer plot for
   their night work, is above my imagination to conceive.
Mallicorne.   Nay it carries probability, let us observe it better, but   190
   yet with such caution as our prying be not discovered: here's all
   things to be had without cost, and therefore good staying here.
La-poope.   Nay that's true, I would we might woe her twenty years
   like *Penelopes* sutors; come *Laverdure.*
                                   Exeunt Mallicorne, La-Poop.

   165 can)] MS; can be done) F1

Laverdure.   I follow instantly,——yonder he is.

Enter Viramor.

The thought of this Boy hath much coold my affection to his Lady,
and by all conjectures, this is a disguised whore; I will try if I can
search this Mine. Page——

Veramour.   Your pleasure sir?

Laverdure.   Thou art a pritty Boy.   200

Veramour.   And you a brave man: now I am out of your debt.

Laverdure.   Nay prithy stay.

Veramour.   I am in haste sir.

Laverdure.   By the faith of a Courtyer——

Veramour.   Take heed what you say, you have taken a strange oath.

Laverdure.   I have not seene a youth that hath pleased me better, I
would thou could'st like me, so far as to leave thy Lady and waite
on me, I would maintaine thee in the bravest Cloaths——

Veramour.   Though you took them up on trust, or bought 'em at the
brokers.   210

Laverdure.   Or any way: then thy imployments should bee so neate
and cleanly, thou shouldst not touch a payre of Pantables in a
Moneth, and thy lodging——

Veramour.   Should be in a brothell.

Laverdure.   No, but in mine armes.

Veramour.   That may be the circle of a Baudy house, or worse.

Laverdure.   I meane thou shouldest lie with me.

Veramour.   Lie with you? I had rather lie with my Ladies Monkey;
'twas never a good World since our French Lords learned of the
Neopolitans to make their Pages their Bed-fellowes; it doth more   220
hurt to the Suburbe Ladies then twenty dead Vacations; Tis Supper
time sir.   *Exit* Veramour.

Laverdure.   I thought so, I know by that 'tis a Woman, for because
peradventure she hath made tryall of the Monkey, she preferrs him
before me, as one unknown; well,
These women are strange Creatures, and have strange desires;
And men must use strange meanes to quench strange fires. *Exit.*

---

216 may] MS; my F1   220 it] MS; *omit* F1
226 These women are strange Creatures] MS; these are standing Creatures F1

Enter Montagne, *alone, in meane habit.*

Montaigne.   Now *Montagne*, who discerns thy spirit now?
    Thy breeding or thy bloud? here's a poor cloud
    Ecclipseth all thy splendor; who can reade
    In thy pale face, dead eye, or lenten sute,
    The liberty thy ever giving hand
    Hath bought for others, manacling it selfe
    In gives of parchment indissoluble?
    The greatest hearted man supplyed with meanes,
    Nobility of birth and gentlest parts,
    I, though the right hand of his Soveraigne,   10
    If vertue quit her seat in his high soule,
    Glitters but like a Pallace set on fire,
    Whose glory whilst it shines, but ruins him,
    And his bright show each houre to ashes tending
    Shall at the last be rak't up like a sparkle,
    Unlesse mens lives and fortunes feede the flame.
    Not for my own wants though blame I my Stars,
    But suffering others to cast love on me,
    When I can neither take nor thankfull be.
    My Ladies woman, faire and vertuous,   20
    Young as the present moneth, sollicits me
    For love and marriage, now being nothing worth.

Enter Veramour *with Counters.*

Veramour.   Oh Master, I have sought you a long hour,
    Good faith, I never joye out of your sight;
    For Gods sake sir be merry, or else beare
    The Buffets of your fortune with more scorn;
    Do but begin to raile, teach me the way,
    And Ile sit down and help your anger forth:
    I have known you weare a suit full worth a Lordship,
    Give to a man whose need nere frighted you   30
    From calling of him friend, five hundred Crowns

---

4 sute] MS; shute F1   7 gives] *i.e.* gyves (*the* MS *reading*). *Cf. above,* I.iii.31.
10 I] *i.e.* Ay   *22.1 *with Counters*] *stet* F1   24 joye] MS; joyd F1
26 fortune] MS; fortunes F1

Ere sleep had left your sences to consider
Your own important present uses; yet
Since I have seen you with a trencher waite,
Voide of all scorne, therefore Ile waite on you.

Montaigne.   Would God thou wert lesse honest.

Veramour.   Would to God
You were lesse worthy: I am even w'ee sir.

Montaigne.   Is not thy Master strangely fallen, when thou
Servest for no wages, but for charity?
Thou dost surcharge me with thy plenteous love: 40
The goodnesse of thy vertue shown to me,
More opens still my disability
To quit thy pains: Credit me loving boy,
A free and honest nature may be opprest,
Tir'd with curtesies from a liberall spirit,
When they exceed his means of gratitude.

Veramour.   But tis a vice in him that to that end
Extends his love or duty.

Montaigne.   Little world
Of vertue, why dost love and follow me?

Veramour.   I will follow you through all Countries,   50
Ile run (fast as I can) by your horse side,
Ile hold your stirrop when you doe alight,
And without grudging waite till you returne:
Ile quit assurd meanes, and expose my selfe
To cold and hunger still to be with you;
Fearlesse Ile travell through a wildernesse,
And when you are weary, I will lay me down
That in my bosome you may rest your head,
Where whilst you sleep, Ile watch that no wild beast
Shall hurt or trouble you: and thus we'l breed   60
A story to make every hearer weep,
When they discourse our fortunes and our loves.

Montaigne.   Oh what a scoffe might men of Women make,
If they did know this boy? but my desire
Is that thou wouldest not (as thou usest still

47 vice] MS; due F1   54 assurd] MS; offerd F1
63 Women] MS (woemen); Wormes F1

74

When like a servant I 'mong servants sit)
Waite on my Trencher, fill my cups with wine:
Why shouldst thou doe this boy? prethee consider,
I am not what I was.

Veramour.   Curst be the day
When I forget that *Montagne* was my Lord,   70
Or not remember him my Master still.

Montaigne.   Rather curse me, with whom thy youth hath spent
So many houres, and yet untaught to live
By any worldly qualitie.

Veramour.   Indeed
You never taught me how to handle Cards
To cheat and cozen men with oathes and lies;
Those are the worldly qualities to live
Some of our Scarlet Gallants teach their boyes.
Since stumbling fortune then leaves vertue thus
Let me leave fortune, ere be vicious.   80

Montaigne.   Oh lad, thy love will kill me.

Veramour.   By my troth
I think in conscience I shall die for you:
Good Master weep not, doe you want aught sir?
Will you have any money? here's some Silver;
And here's a little Gold, 'twill serve to play,
And put more troublesome thoughts out of your mind:
I pray sir take it, Ile get more with singing,
And then Ile bring it you; my Lady ga't me,
And by my troth it was not covetousnesse,
But I forgot to tell you sooner on't.   90

Montaigne.   Alasse boy, thou art not bound to tell it me,
And lesse to give it, buy thee Scarfes and Garters,
And when I have money, I will give thee a Sword:
Nature made thee a beauteous caskanet
To lock up all the goodnesse of the Earth.

Enter Charlote.

---

77 worldly] MS; wordly F1
*78–79 boyes. | Since] MS; boyes ∧ | These worldly qualities. | Since F1
81 By my troth] MS; In truth F1   89 And by my troth it] MS; And——it F1
94 caskanet] MS; Cabinet F1   95 goodnesse] MS; godnesse F1

Veramour [*aside*].   I have lost my voyce with the very sight of this
   Gentlewoman:———good sir steale away, you were wont to be a
   curious avoyder of womens company.

Montaigne.   Why boy, thou darst trust me any where, darst thou
   not?   100

Veramour.   I had rather trust you by a roaring Lyon, then a ravening
   woman.

Montaigne.   Why boy?

Veramour.   Why truly she devoures more mans flesh.

Montaigne.   I, but she roares not boy.

Veramour.   No sir? why she is never silent but when her mouth is
   full.

Charlotte.   Mounsier *Montagne.*

Montaigne.   My sweet fellow, since you please to call me so.

Veramour.   On my conscience she would be pleased well enough to   110
   call you bedfellow: oh Master, do not hold her by the hand so: a
   woman is a lyme-bush, that catcheth all she toucheth.

Charlotte.   I do most dangerously suspect this boy to be a wench; art
   thou not one? come hither, let me feele thee.

Veramour.   With all my heart.

Charlotte.   Why dost thou pull off thy glove?

Veramour.   Why, to feele whether you be a boy, or no.

Charlotte.   Fie boy, goe too, Ile not looke your head, nor combe your
   locks any more, if you talke thus.

Veramour.   Why, ile sing to you no more then.   120

Charlotte.   Fie upon't, how sad you are! a young Gentleman that was
   the very Sunne of *France*———

Montaigne.   But I am in the eclipse now.

Charlotte.   Suffer himselfe to be over-run with a Lethargy of
   melancholy and discontent! rouze up thy spirit, man, and shake it
   off:

> A Noble soule is like a ship at Sea,
> That sleepes at Anchor when the Ocean's calme;
> But when she rages, and the wind blows high,
> He cuts his way with pride and Majesty.   130

110 On] MS; Ah F1   130 pride] MS; skill F1

I would turn foole, or Poet, or any thing, or marry, to make you
merry; prethee let's walke: good *Veramour* leave thy Master and
me, I have earnest businesse with him.

Veramour.   Pray doe you leave my Master, and me; we were very
merry before you came, he does not covet womens companie.
What have you to do with him?——come sir will you goe? And ile
sing to you again:——I'faith his mind is stronger then to credit
womens vows, and too pure to be capable of their loves.

Charlotte.   The boy is jealous; sweet lad leave us; my Lady call'd for
you I sweare: that's a good child, there's a piece of Gold for thee, go   140
buy thee a Feather.

Veramour.   There's two pieces for you, do you goe and buy one, or
what you will, or nothing so you goe.—— Nay then I see you
would have me go sir; why, 'faith I will, now I perceive you love
her better then you doe me; but God blesse you whatever you do,
or intend; I know you are a very honest man.   *Exit.*

Charlotte.   Still shall I woe thee, whilst thy teares reply
I cannot, or I will not marry thee?
Why hast thou drawn the blood out of my cheekes,
And given a quicker motion to my heart?   150
Oh thou hast bred a fever in my veines
Call'd love, which no Physitian can cure;
Have mercy on a maid whose simple youth——

                                                        [*Kneels.*]

Montaigne.   How your example fairest teacheth me
A ceremonious Idolatry!   *Kneels.*
By all the joy of love I love thee better
Then I or any man can tell another;
And will expresse the mercy which thou crav'st,
I will forbeare to marry thee: consider
Thou art natures heire in feature, and thy parents   160
In faire inheritance; rise with these thoughts,
And look on me but with a womans eye,
A decayd fellow, voyd of means and spirit.

Charlotte.   Of spirit?

131 turn foole] MS; turn a foole F1   141 buy thee a] MS; buy a F1
147 teares] Dyce (Heath, Mason *conj.*); yeares MS; eares F1
161 inheritance] MS; inheritances F1

Montaigne.   Yes, could I else tamely live,
  Forget my fathers blood, waite and make legs,
  Staine my best breeches, with the servile drops
  That fall from others draughts?
Charlotte.   This vizard wherewith thou wouldst hide thy spirit
  Is perspective, to shew it plainlier.
  This under-value of thy selfe is but   170
  Because I should not buy thee; what more speaks
  Greatnesse of man, then valiant patience,
  That shrinks not under his fates strongest strokes?
  These Roman deaths, as falling on a Sword,
  Opening of veines, with poyson quenching thirst,
  (Which we erroneously doe stile the deeds
  Of the heroicke and magnanimous man)
  Was dead-eyd cowardise, and white cheek'd feare,
  Who doubting tyranny, and fainting under
  Fortunes false Lottery, desperately runne   180
  To death for dread of death; that soules most stout,
  That bearing all mischance, dares last it out;
  Will you performe your word, and marry me,
  When I shall call you to't?
Montaigne.   I'faith I will.
Charlotte.   Who's this alights here?

Enter Longueville *with a riding-rod.*

Longavile.   With leave faire creature,
  Are you the Lady Mistris of the house?
Charlotte.   Her servant sir.
Longavile.   I pray then favour me,
  To inform your Lady, and Duke *Orleans* wife,
  A businesse of emport awaites 'em here,   190
  And craves for speedy answer.
Charlotte.   Are you in post sir?
Longavile.   No, I am in Satin Lady;
  I would you would be in post.
Charlotte.   I will returne Sweet.   *Exit.*

---

164 else] MS; *omit* F1   170 selfe] MS; life F1   178 cheek'd] F2; cheeke F1, MS

78

Longavile.   Honest friend, doe you belong to the house?
    I pray be covered.
Montaigne.   Yes Sir, I doe.
Longavile [*aside*].   Ha, dreamst thou *Longaville?* sure tis not he:——
    Sir I should know you.
Montaigne.   So should I you, but that I am asham'd.
    But though thou knowst me, prethee *Longaville*,   200
    Mock not my poverty, pray remember your selfe;
    Showes it not strangely for thy cloathes to stand
    Without a hat to mine? mocke me no more.
Longavile.   The pox embroyder me all over sir,
    If ever I began to mocke you yet.
    The devill on me, why should I weare Velvet
    And Silver Lace, hart I will teare it off.
Montaigne.   Why mad-man?
Longavile.   Put on my Hat? yes, when I am hangd I will:
    Death, I could break my head   210
    For holding eyes that knew not you at first:
    But time and fortune run your courses with him,
    He'l laugh and scorne you, when you shew most hate.

    Enter Lamira, Orleans Lady, Laverdure, La Poope, Malycorne,
        Veramour, Charlot.

Lamira.   Your affaire Mounsier?
Longavile.   Doe you mocke me Lady?
Lamira.   Your businesse sir, I mean.
Lady Orleans.   Regard your selfe good Mounsier *Longueville.*
Lamira.   You are too negligent of your selfe and place,
    Cover your head sweet Mounsier.
Longavile.   Mistake me not faire Ladies, by my blood,
    Tis not to you, nor you, that I stand bare.   220
Laverdure.   Nay sweet deere Mounsier, let it not be to us then.
La-poope.   A pox a complement.

---

204 The pox embroyder] MS; The——embroyder F1
206 The devill on] MS; The——on F1   207 Lace, hart I] MS; Lace,——I F1
210 Death, I could] Dyce; I could MS;——I could F1   213 scorne] MS; storm F1
*214 Your affaire] MS; You're a fair F1   219 by my blood] MS; *omit* F1
222 A pox a] MS;——a F1

Mallicorne.   And a plague of manners.
  Pray hide your head, you gallants use to do't.
Longavile.   And you your foreheads.
  Why you needfull accessary rascals,
  That cannot live without your mutuall knaveries,
  More then a Bawd, a Pandor, or a Whore
  From one another; how dare you suspect
  That I stand bare to you? what make you here?
  Shift your house Lady of 'em, for I know 'em,   230
  They come to steale your Napkins, and your Spoons;
  Look to your Silver-bodkin, (Gentlewoman)
  Tis a dead utensil, and Page 'ware your pockets;
  My reverence is unto this man, my master,
  Whom you with protestations, and oaths
  As high as Heaven, as deep as hell, which would
  Deceive the wisest man of honest nature,
  Have cozned and abus'd; but I may meet you,
  And beate you one with t'other.
Montaigne.   Peace, no more.   240
Longavile.   Not a word sir.
Laverdure.   I am something thicke of hearing; what said he?
La-poope.   I heare him, but regard him not.
Mallicorne.   Nor I, I am never angry fasting.
Longavile.   My love keeps back my duty, noblest Lady;
  If husband or brother merit love in you,
  Prevent their dangers, this houre brings to triall
  Their hereto sleeping hates; by this time each
  Within a yerd is of the others heart,
  And met to prove their causes and their spirits   250
  With their impartiall Swords points; haste and save,
  Or never meet them more but at the grave.   *Exit.*
Lady Orleans.   Oh my distracted heart, that my wrackt honour
  Should for a brothers, or a husbands life,
  Throwe the undoing die.

222 And a plague of] MS; And——of F1   223 you gallants] MS; your gallants F1
231 steale your Napkins] MS; steale Napkins F1   246 in] MS; from F1
249 yerd] *i.e.* yard (*the* MS *reading*)   252 *Exit*] MS; *omit* F1
255 Throwe the] MS; through thy F1

Lamira.   *Amiens* engagd;
  If he miscarry all my hopes and joys,
  I now confesse it loudly, are undone:
  Caroch, and haste, one minute may betray
  A life more worth then all time can repay.
                    Exeunt Ladies [Lamira, Lady Orleans, Charlotte],
                              and Montaigne.

Mallicorne [*aside*].   Hump: Mounsier *Laverdure* pursues this boy   260
  extreamly.——Captaine what will you doe?

La-poope.   Any thing but follow to this land service; I am a Sea-
  captaine you know, and to offer to part 'em, without we could do't
  like water-men with long staves, a quarter of a mile off, might be
  dangerous.

Mallicorne.   Why then let's retire and pray for 'em. I am resolv'd to
  staie the event; abus'd more then we have been we cannot be,
  without they fall to flat beating on's, and that were unkindly done
  i'faith.

                              Exeunt Malycorne, La-poop.

Veramour.   Never stirre, but you are the troublesomest Asse that ere   270
  I met with; retire, you smel like a womans chamber, she newly up,
  before she have pinsht her vapours in with her cloathes.

Laverdure.   I will haunt thee like thy Grandames ghost, thou shalt
  never rest for me.

Veramour.   Well, a pox of your muske tongue for me, I perceive tis
  vaine to conceale a secret from you: believe it sir, indeed I am a
  woman.

Laverdure.   Why la; I knew't, this Propheticall tongue of mine never
  faild me; my mother was halfe a witch, never any thing that she
  forespake, but came to passe: a woman? how happy am I? now we   280
  may lawfully come together without feare of hanging; Sweet
  wench, be gracious, in honourable sort I woe, no otherwise.

Veramour.   Faith the truth is I have loved you long——

Laverdure.   See, see.

Veramour.   But durst not open it.

262 land service] MS; Sea-service F1   267 staie the event] MS; stop your intent F1
268 on's] MS; o'us F1   268–269 and that ... i'faith] MS; *assigned to Laverdure in* F1
270 Never stirre, but] MS;——but F1   271 she newly] MS; that's newly F1
275 a pox ... for me,] MS; *omit* F1

Laverdure.   By gad I think so.

Veramour.   But briefly, when you bring it to the test, if there be not
    one Gentleman in this house, wil challenge more interest in me,
    then you can, I am at your disposure.

Laverdure.   Oh *Fortunatus*, I envie thee not   290
    For cap, or pouch, this day Ile prove my Fortune,
    In which your Lady doth elect her husband,
    Who will be *Amiens*, 'twill save my wedding dinner,
    Povera La-poop and *Malicorne*: if all faile,
    I will turne Citizen, a beauteous wife
    Is the horn-booke to the richest Tradesmans life.

                                              Exeunt.

Enter Duboys, Orleans, Longueville, Amiens, *two Lacqueys*, a   [IV.
                Page *with two Pistols.*

Duboys.   Here's a good even piece of ground my Lord:
    Will you fix here?

Orleans.   Yes anywhere;——Lacquey, take off my spurs;——
    Upon a bridge, a raile but my Swords bredth,
    Upon a battlement, Ile fight this quarrell.

Duboys.   O' the ropes, my Lord?

Orleans.   Upon a line.

Duboys.   So all our Countrie Duels
    Are carried, like a fire-worke on a thred.

Orleans.   Go now stay with the horses, and doe you heare
    Upon your lives, till some of us come to you,   10
    Dare not to looke this way.

Duboys.   Except you see
    Strangers or others that by chance or purpose
    Are like to interrupt us.

Orleans.   Then give warning.

                        [*Exeunt Lacqueys and Page.*]

Longavile.   Who takes a Sword? the advantage is so small,
    As he that doubts hath the free leave to choose.

Orleans.   Come give me any, and search me; tis not

    The ground, weapon, or seconds that can make
    Oddes in these fatall trials: but the cause.
Amiens.   Most true, and but it is no time to wish
    When men are come to do, I would desire   20
    The cause 'twixt us were other then it is;
    But where the right is, there prevaile our Swords,
    And if my sister have outliv'd her honour,
    I doe not pray I may outlive her shame.
Orleans.   Your sister *Amiens*, is a whore, at once.
Amiens.   You oft have spoke that sence to me before,
    But never in this language *Orleance*;
    And when you spoke it faire, and first, I told you
    That it was possible you might be abus'd:
    But now,   30
    Since you forget your manners, you shall free me
    If I transgresse my custome. You doe lie,
    And are a villaine, which I had rather yet
    My Sword had prov'd, then I been forc'd to speake:
    Nay give us leave, and since you stand so haughtily
    And highly on your cause, let you and I,
    Without engaging these two Gentlemen,
    Singly determine it.
Longavile.   My Lord, you'l pardon us.
Duboys.   I trust your Lordships
    Meane not to doe us that affront.
Amiens.   As how?   40
Duboys.   We kisse your Lordships hand, and come to serve you
    Here with our Swords.
Longavile.   My Lord, we understand
    Our selves.
Duboys.   We have had the honour to be call'd
    Unto the businesse, and we must not now
    Quit it on terms.
Amiens.   Not terms of reason?
Longavile.   No,

---

   18 these] MS; those F1   31 free me] MS; finde F1
   40 Meane not to doe] MS; may not doe F1
   42 Here with our Swords] Dyce; here with swords F1; with our swords MS

No reason for the quitting of our calling.

Duboys.   True,
If I be call'd to't I must aske no reason.

Longavile.   Nor heare none neither, which is lesse, nor looke for't.
It is a favour if my throat be cut,   50
Your Lordship does me, which I never can
Nor must have hope how to requite:——what noise,
    A noise within, crying down with their Swords.
What cry is that?——My Lord upon your guard,
Some treachery is a foot.

    Enter Lady Orleans, Lamira, Montagne [*followed by the*] *two*
        Lacqueys, [*and*] Page.

Lady Orleans.   O here they are:——
My Lord (deare Lady helpe me) help me all;
I have so woefull interest in both,
I know not which to feare for most: and yet
I must prefer my Lord. Deare brother,
You are too understanding, and too Noble
To be offended, when I know my duty,   60
Though scarce my teares will let me see to do it.

Orleans.   Out loathed strumpet.

Lady Orleans.   O my dearest Lord,
If words could on me cast the name of whore,
I then were worthy to be loath'd; but know,
Your unkindnesse cannot make me wicked;
And therefore should lesse use that power upon me.

Orleans.   Was this your art to have these actors come,
To make this interlude? withdraw, cold man,
And if thy spirit be not frozen up,
Give me one stroke yet at thee for my vengeance.   70

Amiens.   Thou shalt have stroakes, and stroakes, thou glorious man,
Till thou breathst thinner ayre then that thou talkest.

Lamira.   My Lord Count *Amiens.*

Lady Orleans.   Princely husband.

Orleans.   Whore.

49 nor looke for't] MS; *omit* F1   54 *two* Lacqueys ... Page] MS; *omit* F1
61 see] MS (se); so F1

Lamira.   You wrong her impudent Lord; O that I had
   The bulke of those dull men; look how they stand,
   And no man will revenge an innocent Lady.
Amiens.   You hinder it Madam.
Lamira.   I would hinder you;
   Is there none else to kill him?
Lady Orleans.   Kill him Madam?
   Have you learn'd that bad Language? O repent,
   And be the motive rather both kill me.   80
Orleans.   Then die my infamy.
Montaigne.   Hold bloody man.
Orleans.   Art thou there Basiliske?
Montaigne.   To strike thee dead,
   But that thy fate deserves some weightier hand.
Orleans.   O here's a plot; you bring your champion with you;
   Madame Adultresse your Adulterer:
   Out howling bitch wolfe.
Duboys.   Good my Lord.
Orleans.   Are you
   Her Graces countenance Lady, the receiver
   To the poore vertuous couple?
Duboys.   Sweet my Lord.
Orleans.   Sweet rascall, didst not thou tell me, false fellow,
   This *Montagne*, here was murdered?
Duboys.   I did so;   90
   But he was falser, and a worthlesse Lord,
   Like thy foule selfe, that would have had it so.
Longavile.   *Orleance* tis true, and shall be prov'd upon thee.
Montaigne.   Thy malice Duke, and this thy wicked nature,
   Are all as visible as thou; but I
   Borne to contemne thy injuries, doe know,
   That though thy greatnesse may corrupt a Jury,

---

*80 And be the motive rather both kill me.] *stet* F1   *82 there] MS; their F1
*83–84 hand. | *Orleans.* O here's] hand. | *Dub.* Sweet my Lord. | *Orl.* O here's F1, MS (*where*
   '*Dub.* Sweet my lord' *is marked for omission*). Cf. Duboys' speech at line 88, below.
84 champion] MS; champions F1
85 Madame Adultresse your Adulterer] MS; the adultresse with the adulterer F1
86 howling bitch wolfe] MS; howling——F1   88 vertuous] MS; vicious F1

And make a Judge afraid, and carry out
A world of evils with thy title: yet
Thou art not quit at home, thou bearest about thee   100
That, that doth charge thee, and condemne thee too.
The thing that grieves me more, and doth indeed
Displease me, is, to thinke that so much basenesse
Stands here to have encountered so much honour:——
[*To* Amiens] Pardon me my Lord what late my passion spake,
When you provok'd my innocence.

Orleans.   Yes doe,
  O flattery, courser then the sute he weares;
  Give him a new one *Amiens.*

Amiens.   *Orleance,*
  Tis here nor time nor place, to jest or raile
  Poorely with you, but I will finde a time to   110
  Whisper you forth to this or some fit place,
  As shall not hold a second interruption.

Montaigne.   I hope your Lordships honour, and your life
  Are destined unto higher hazzards; this
  Is of a meaner arme.

Duboys.   Yes faith, or none.

Longavile.   He is not fit to fall by an honest Sword,
  A Prince and lie!

Duboys.   And slander, and hire men
  To publish the false rumours he hath made.

Longavile.   And sticke 'em on his friends, and innocents.

Duboys.   And practice gainst their lives after their fames.   120

Longavile.   In men that are the matter of all leudnesse,
  Bauds, thieves, and cheaters, it were monstrous.

Duboys.   But in a man of blood, how more conspicuous?

Amiens.   Can this be? Heaven!

Lady Orleans.   They doe slander him.

Orleans.   Hang them, a paire of railing hangbies.

Longavile.   How?

---

99 evils] MS; devils F1   100 quit] MS; quiet F1
107 courser] MS; becomes him better F1   109 nor time] MS; no time F1
*115 a meaner arme] *stet* F1   120 gainst] MS; against F1
124 Heaven] MS; *omit* F1

86

Stand *Orleance;*———stay, give me my Pistols boy,———
                              [*Takes pistol from* Page.]
Hinder me not,———by that foule life of which
Thou art no longer master, I will kill thee.
Lady Orleans.   O stay his fury.
Amiens.   *Longueville,* my friend.
Longavile.   Not for my selfe, my Lord, but for mankind,   130
And all that have an interest to vertue,
Or title unto innocence———
Amiens.   Why heare me.
Longavile.   For justice sake———
Amiens.   That cannot be.
Longavile.   To punish
His wives, your honours, and my Lords wrongs here,
Whom I must ever call so; for your loves
I sweare, Ile scrifice———
Amiens.   *Longaville,*
I did not thinke you a murtherer before.
Longavile.   I care not what you thought me.
Amiens.   By my soule,
And what it hopes for, if thou attempt his life,   140
Thy own is forfeit.
Montaigne.   Foolish frantick man,
The murder will be of us, not him.
Lady Orleans.   O God.
Montaigne.   We could have kild him, but we would not take
The justice out of fates,———before my God
Singe but a haire of him, thou diest.
Longavile.   No matter.
                                        Shoots.
Amiens.   Villaine.   [*Lady Orleans falls.*]
Duboys.   My Lord, your sister is slaine.
Amiens.   *Biancha?*

127–128 by that ... I will kill thee] MS; by———| I will kill him F1
134 honours] MS; honour F1   136 I sweare] MS; Ile sweare F1
*139–140 By my soule, | And what it hopes for, if] MS; By———If F1
144 fates,———before my God] MS; fates.———F1
145–145.1 matter. | *Shoots.*] MS; matter, shoot F1 (*where the s.d. 'Shoots' is printed as* 'shoot' *at
the end of Longavile's speech*)

Montaigne.   O haplesse and most wretched chance.
Lamira [*to* Orleans].   Standst thou
    Looking upon the mischief thou hast made?
    Thou Godlesse man, feeding thy blood-shot eyes
    With the red spectacle, and art not turn'd   150
    To stone with horrour? hence and take the wings
    Of thy blacke infamy, to carry thee
    Beyond the shoot of looks, or sound of curses,
    Which will pursue thee till thou hast out-fled
    All but thy guilt. That still be present with thee.
Orleans.   O wish it off again, for I am crack'd
    Under the burden, and my heart will breake.
    How heavy guilt is, when men come to feele.
    If you could know the mountaine I sustaine
    Of horror, you would each take off your part,   160
    And more, to ease me: I cannot stand, forgive
    Where I have wrong'd I pray.
Amiens.   Looke to him *Montagne.*
Longavile.   My Lords and Gentlemen, the Lady's well,
    But for her feare, unlesse that have shot her;
    I have the worst on't, that needs would venture
    Upon a tricke had like to ha' cost my guts:
    Look to her, she'l be well, it was but Powder
    I chargd with, thinking that a guilty man
    Would have been frighted sooner; but I am glad
    He's come at last.
Lamira.   How, is *Byancha* well?   170
Montaigne.   Not hurt.
Amiens.   Lives she? see sister, doth she breath?
Lady Orleans.   O Gentlemen, think you I can breath,
    That am restored to the hatefull sense
    Of feeling in me my deare husbands death?
    O no, I live not; life was that I left;
    And what you have cal'd me to, is death indeed;
    I cannot weep so fast as he doth bleed.

---

154 till ᴧ thou] MS; still: | Thou F1   155 That ... thee] MS; *omit* F1
160 Of] MS; With F1   163 Lady's] MS (ladyes); Lady is F1
164 for her feare] MS; for feare F1   171 *Montaigne.* Not hurt.] MS; *omit* F1

Duboys.   Pardon me Madam, he is well.

Lady Orleans.   Ha? my husband.

Orleans.   I cannot speake whether my joy or shame
Be greater, but I thank thee Heaven for both.   180
O look not black upon me, all my friends,
To whom I will be reconciled, or grow unto
This earth, till I have weept a trench
That shall be great enough to be my grave,
And I will think them too most manly teares,
If they do move your pities: it is true,
Man should do nothing that he should repent;
But if he have, and say that he is sorry,
It is a worse fault if he be not truly.

Lamira.   My Lord, such sorrow cannot be suspected: 190
Here take your honoured wife, and joyn your hands.
I will be she hath married you again:
And Gentlemen, I do invite you all,
This night to take my house, where on the morrow,
To heighten more the reconciling feast,
Ile make my selfe a husband and a guest.

                                        Exeunt.

                    Enter Montagne *and* Charlote.   V.i

Charlotte.   Well now I am sure you are mine.

Montaigne.   I am sure I am glad
I have one to own me then; you'l finde me honest
As these daies go, enough; poore without question,
Which beggars hold a vertue; give me meat,
And I shall do my worke, else knock my shooes off,
And turn me out again.

Charlotte.   You are merry, fellow.

Montaigne.   I have no great cause.

Charlotte.   Yes thy love to me.

Montaigne.   That's as we make our game.

Charlotte.   Why you repent then?

Montaigne.   Faith no. Worse then I am I cannot be;

---

180 thee Heaven] MS; the Heavens F1   192 I will be she] MS;——she F1
2 own me then] MS; own then F1   *6 are merry] MS; are a merry F1

89

Much better I expect not: I shall love you,   10
And when you bid me goe to bed, obey,
Lie still or move, as you shall minister,
Keep a foure-nobles Nag, and a Jack Merlin,
Learn to love Ale, and play at two-hand Irish,
And there's the all I aime at.

Charlotte.   Nay sweet fellow,
Ile make it something better.

Montaigne.   If you doe, you'l make me worse:
Now I am poore, and willing to doe wel,
Hold me in that course: of all the Kings creatures,
I hate his coyne; keep me from that, and save me;   20
For if you chance out of your housewifery
To gleane a hundred pound or two, bestow it
In Plum-broth ere I know on't, else I take it,
Seeke out a hundred men that want this money,
Showre it among 'em, they cry noble *Montagne*,
And so I stand again at livery.

Charlotte.   You have pretty fancies sir, but married once,
This charity will fall home to your selfe.

Montaigne.   I would it would, I am afraid my loosenesse
Is yet scarce stopt, though it have nought to worke on   30
But the meere aire of what I have had.

Charlotte.   Pretty.

Montaigne.   I wonder sweet heart why you'l marry me.
I can see nothing in my selfe deserves it,
Unlesse the handsome wearing of a band,
For that's my stocke now, or a paire of garters,
Necessity will not let me loose.

Charlotte.   I see sir
A great deale more, a hansome man, a husband
To make a right good woman truely happy.

Montaigne.   Lord, where are my eyes? either you are foolish
As wenches once a yeere are, or far worse,   40
Extreamly vertuous; can you love a poore man

---

*13 Jack Merlin] MS; black Merling F1   15 the] MS; then F1
22 gleane] MS; leave F1   23 on't] MS; it F1   25 Showre] MS; Share F1
25 they] MS; they'l F1

That relies on cold meat and cast stockings,
One onely suit to his backe, which now is mewing?
But what will be the next coate will pose *Tristram*.
If I should leavy from my friends a fortune
I could not raise ten groats to pay the Priest now.

Charlotte.   Ile do that duty; tis not means nor money
Makes me pursue your love; were your mind bankrupt,
I would never love you.

Enter Lamira.

Montaigne.   Peace wench, here's my Lady.
Lamira.   Nay never shrinke i'th wetting, for my presence;   50
D'ee finde her willing *Montagne?*
Montaigne.   Willing Madam?
Lamira.   How dainty you make of it, doe not I know
You two love one another?
Montaigne.   Certaine Madam,
I thinke ye'ave revelations of these matters:
Your Ladyship cannot tell me when I kist her.
Lamira.   But she can, sir.
Montaigne.   But she will not Madam;
For when they talke once, tis like fairy-money,
They get no more close kisses.
Lamira.   Thou art wanton.
Montaigne.   God knows I need not, yet I would be lusty:
But by my troth my provender scarce pricks me.   60
Lamira.   It shall be mended *Montagne*, I am glad
You are grown so merry.
Montaigne.   So am I too Madam.
Lamira.   You two will make a pretty hansome consort.
Montaigne.   Yes Madam, if my fiddle faile me not.
Lamira.   Your Fiddle? why your Fiddle?
I warrant thou meanest madly.
Montaigne.   Can you blame me?
Alasse I am in love.
Charlotte.   Tis very well sir.

*43–44 mewing ... Tristram] stet F1   60 But by my troth my] MS; But——my F1
*60 provender ... pricks me] stet F1

91

Lamira.   How long have you been thus?

Montaigne.   How thus in love?

Lamira.   You are very quick sir: no, I mean thus pleasant.

Montaigne.   By my troth madam, ever since I was poore.   70

Lamira.   A little wealth would change you then.

Montaigne.   Yes Lady,
   Into another suit, but never more
   Into another man: Ile bar that mainly.
   The wealth I get henceforward shal be charm'd
   For ever hurting me, Ile spend it fasting:
   As I live noble Lady there is nothing
   I have found directly cures the melancholy,
   But want and wedlocke; when I had store of money
   I simper'd sometime, and spoke wondrous wise,
   But never laught out-right; now I am empty   80
   My heart sounds like a bell, and strikes a' both sides.

Lamira.   You are finely temper'd *Montagne.*

Montaigne.   Pardon Lady,
   If any way my free mirth have offended,
   Twas meant to please you: if it prove too sawcie,
   Give it a frown, and I am ever silenc'd.

Lamira.   I like it passing well; pray follow it:
   This is my day of choice, and shall be yours too,
   Twere pity to delay ye: call to the Steward,
   And tell him tis my pleasure he should give you
   Five hundred Crowns: make your selfe hansome *Montagne,*   90
   Let none weare better cloathes, tis for my credit;
   But pray be merry still.

Montaigne.   If I be not,
   And make a foole of twice as many hundreds,
   Clap me in Canvas Lady.

                                        Exeunt.

          Enter La-poope, Laverdure, *and* Malycorne.   [V.ii]

Laverdure [aside].   I am strangely glad, I have found the mystery
   Of this disguised boy out: I ever trusted

---

70 By my troth madam, ever] MS;——Ever F1   81 a'] MS (a); at F1

92

It was a woman, and how happily
I have found it so; and for my selfe, I am sure
One that would offer me a thousand pound now
(And that's a pretty sum to make one stagger)
In ready Gold for this concealment, could not
Buy my hope of her, she's a dainty wench,
And such a one I finde I want extreamly
To bring me into credit: beauty does it.   10

Mallicorne.   Say we should all meach here, and stay the feast now,
What can the worst be? we have plai'd the knaves,
That's without question.

La-poope.   True, and as I take it this is the first truth
We told this seven yeers, and for any thing
I know may be the last: but grant we are knaves,
Both base and beastly knaves——

Mallicorne.   Say so then.

Laverdure.   Well.

La-poope.   And likewise let it be considered, we have wrongd
And most maliciously, this Gentlewoman,
We cast to stay with, what must we expect now?   20

Mallicorne.   I there's the point, we would expect good eating.

La-poope.   I know we would, but we may find good beating.

Laverdure.   You say true Gentlemen, and by my faith
Though I love meat as well as any man,
I care not what he be, if a eate a Gods name;
Such crab-sauce to my meat wil turn my pallate.

Mallicorne.   There's all the hazzard, for the frozen *Montagne*
Has now got spring againe, and warmth in him,
And without doubt dares beat us terribly.
For not to mince the matter, we are cowards,   30
And have and shall be beaten when men please
To call us into cudgelling.

La-poope.   I feele
We are very prone that way.

Laverdure.   The sonnes of *Adam*.

---

*7 this concealment] *stet* F1   *11 meach] *stet* F1
*15 this seven] MS (this 7.); these ten F1   23 by my faith] MS; by——F1
30 mince] MS (*corrected*); mynt MS (*originally*); mint F1

La-poope.   Now here then rests the state o'th· question,
Whether we yeild our bodies for a dinner
To a sound dog-whip, for I promise ye
If men be given to correction,
We can expect no lesse, or quietly
Take a hard Egge or two, and ten mile hence
Baite in a ditch, this we may do securely;   40
For to stay here about will be all one,
If once our morall mischiefes come in memory.
Mallicorne.   But pray ye hear me, is not this the day
The Virgin Lady doth elect her husband?
Laverdure.   The dinner is to that end.
Mallicorne.   Very well then,
Say we all stay, and say we scape this whipping,
And be well entertained, and one of us
Carry the Lady.
La-poope.   'Tis a seemly saying,
I must confesse, but if we stay, how fitly
We may apply it to our selves (i'th end)   50
Will aske a Christian feare; I cannot see
If I say true, what speciall ornaments
Of art or nature, lay aside our lying,
Whoring and drinking, which are no great vertues,
We are endued withall to win this Lady.
Mallicorne.   Yet women go not by the best parts ever;
That I have found directly.
Laverdure.   Why should we fear then?
They choose men as they feed; some times they settle
Upon a white broth face, a sweet smooth gallant,
And him they make an end of in a night;   60
Sometimes a Goose, sometimes, a grosser meat,
A rump of beef will serve 'em at some season,
And fill their bellies too: though without doubt
They are great devourers: stock fish is a dish,
If it be well drest, for the tufnesse sake
Wil make the proud'st of 'em long and leap for't.

46 we scape] MS; we all scape F1   59 broth] MS; broth'd F1

   They'l run mad for a pudding ere thy'l starve.
La-poope.   For my own part I care not, come what can come,
   If I be whipt, why so be it; if cudgel'd,
   I hope I shall out live it, I am sure   70
   'Tis not the hundreth time I have bin serv'd so,
   And yet I thank God I am here.
Mallicorne.   Here's resolution.
La-poope.   A little patience, and a rotten Apple
   Cures twenty worse diseases; what say you sir?
Laverdure.   Marry I say sir, if I had bin acquainted
   With lamming in my youth, as you have bin
   With whipping, and such benefits of nature,
   I should do better: as I am, i'le venture,
   And if it be my luck to have the Lady,
   I'le use my fortune modestly; if beaten   80
   You shall not hear a word, one I am sure of,
   And if the worst fall she shall be my physick.
La-poope.   Lets go then, and a merry winde be with us.
Mallicorne.   Captaine your shooes are old, pray put 'em off,
   And let one fling 'em after us; be bold sirs,
   And howsoever our fortune fals, lets beare
   An equall burden; if there be an odde lash,
   Wee'l part it afterwards.
La-poope.   I am arm'd at all points.

                                                    Exeunt.

            Enter foure [Servants] *serving in a Banquet.*   [V.iii]

1. Servant.   Then my Lady will have a bedfellow to night.
2. Servant.   So she sayes, heaven what a dainty armefull shall he
   enjoy that has the launching of her, what a fight shee'l make.
3. Servant.   I mary boyes, there will be sport indeed, there will be
   grapling, she has a murderer lies in her prow, I am affraid will fright
   his maine mast *Robin.*

---

83   *La-poope.*] MS; *omit* F1
*0.1–50.1   *Enter . . . serving in a Banquet . . . Exeunt.*] F1; *omit* MS. *Throughout the F1 text of this*
        scene, speech-prefixes for the Servants consist only of numerals ('1', '2', '3', '4').
2, 37 dainty] F2; danty F1

THE HONEST MAN'S FORTUNE [V.iii

4. Servant.   Who dost thou think shall have her of thy conscience? thou art a wise man.

3. Servant.   If she go the old way, the way of lot, the longest cut sweeps all without question.   10

1. Servant.   She has lost a friend of me else; what think yee of the Courtier?

2. Servant.   Hang him hedgehogge, h'as nothing in him but a piece of Euphues, and twenty dozen of twelve penny riband all about him, he is but one Pedlers shop of gloves and garters, pickteeth and pomander.

3. Servant.   The Courtier! marry God blesse her *Steven*, she is not mad yet, she knowes that trindle tayle too well, he's crest falne, and pinbuttock't with leaping Landresses.

4. Servant.   The Merchant sure shee will not be so base to have him.   20

1. Servant.   I hope so *Robin*, hee'l sell us all to the Moors to make mummy; nor the Captaine.

4. Servant.   Who Potgun, that's a sweet youth indeed, will he stay thinke ye?

3. Servant.   Yes, without question, and have half din'd too ere the grace be done; he's good for nothing in the world but eating, lying and sleeping; what other men devour in drink, he takes in Pottage, they say has bin at Sea, a Herring fishing, for without doubt he dares not hayle an Ele-boate, ith way of War.

2. Servant.   I think so, they would beate him off with Butter.   30

3. Servant.   When he brings in a prize, unlesse it be Cockles, or Callis sand to scoure with, I'le renounce my five mark a year, and all the hidden art I have in carving, to teach young Birds to whistle Walsingham; leave him to the lime boates; now, what think you of the brave *Amiens*?

1. Servant.   That's a thought indeed.

2. Servant.   I marry ther's a person fit to feed upon a dish so dainty, and hee'l do't I warrant him ith nick boyes, has a body world without end.

4. Servant.   And such a one my Lady will make no little off; but is not   40
Montagne married to day?

3. Servant.   Yes faith, honest *Montagne* must have his bout too.

2. Servant.   Hee's as good a lad as ever turnd a trencher; must we leave him?

3. Servant.   Hee's to good for us *Steven*, I'le give him health to his
good luck to night ith old Beaker, and it shall be sack too.

4. Servant.   I must have a Garter; and boyes I have bespoke a Posset,
some body shall give me thanks for't, 'tas a few toyes in't will rase
commotions in a bed lad.

1. Servant.   Away; my Lady.   50

                                                            Exeunt.

      Enter Orleance, *and his* Lady *arme in arme*, Amiens, Lamira,   [V.iv
      Charlote, *like a Bride*, Montagne *brave*, Laverdure, Longavile,
           Dubois, Mallycorn, La-Poope.

Lamira.   Seate your selves noble Lords and Gentlemen,
You know your places; many royall welcomes
I give your grace; how lovely shewes this change!
My house is honor'd in this reconcilement.

Orleans.   Thus Madam must you do:
My Lady now shall see you made a Woman;
And give you some short lessons for your voyage.
Take her instructions Lady, she knowes much.

Lamira.   This becomes you sir.

Lady Orleans.   My Lord must have his will.   10

Orleans.   Tis all I can do now sweet heart.——Faire Lady,
This to your happy choyce;——brother *Amiens*,
You are the man I meane it to.

Amiens.   I'le pledge you.

Orleans.   And with my heart.

Amiens.   With all my love I take it.

Lamira.   Noble Lords,
I am proud ye have done this day, so much content,
And me such estimation yet this hour
(In this poor house) to knit a league for ever,
For so I know ye mean it.

Amiens.   I do Lady.

Orleans.   And I my Lord.

Omnes.   Y'ave done a work of honor.   20

Amiens.   Give me the Cup, where this health stops, let that man

---

1 Seate] MS; Stur F1   17 yet] Gerritsen; that F1, MS   18 to knit] MS; shall be F1

Be either very sick, or very simple,
Or I am very angry;——sir, to you;——
Madam me thinks this Gentleman might sit to;
He would become the best on's.

Orleans.   Pray sit down sir,
I know the Lady of the feast expects not
This day so much old custom.

Lamira.   Sit down *Montagne*;
Nay never blush for the matter.

Montaigne.   Noble Madam,
I have too tyes against it, and I dare not;
Duty to you first, as you are my Lady,   30
And I your poorest servant; next the custome
Of this dayes ceremony.

Lamira.   As you are my servant,
I may command you then.

Montaigne.   To my life Lady.

Lamira.   Sit down, and here, i'le have it so.

Amiens.   Sit down man,
Never refuse so faire a Ladies offer.

Montaigne.   It is your pleasure Madam, not my pride,
And I obey;——ile pledge yee now my Lord,——
Mounsier *Longavile.*

Longavile.   I thank you sir.

Montaigne.   This to my Lady,
And her faire choyce to day, and happinesse.   40

Longavile.   Tis a faire health, i'le pledge you though I sinke for't.

Lamira.   *Montagne* you are too modest; come i'lde adde
A little more wine t'ee, 'twill make you merry,
This to the good I wish you.

Montaigne.   Honord Lady,
I shall forget my selfe with this great bounty.

Lamira.   You shall not sir; give him some Wine.

Amiens.   By heaven
You are a worthy woman, and that Man is blest
Can come neer such a Lady.

29 too] *i.e.* two   29 tyes] MS; reasons F1   44 wish you.] MS; wish.——F1
46 Wine] MS; Vine F1

98

Lamira.　　　　　　　　Such a blessing
　Wet weather washes off, my Lord.
Montaigne.　　　　　　　At all!
　I will not go a lip lesse.
Orleans.　　　　　　Tis well cast sir.　　　　　　50
Mallicorne.　If *Montagne* get more Wine, we are like to heare on't.
Laverdure.　I do not like that sitting there.
Mallicorne.　　　　　　　Nor I,
　Me thinks he looks like Justice.
La-poope.　　　　　　Now have I
　A kinde a grudging of a beating on me,
　I fear my hot fit.
Mallicorne.　　　　Drink apace, ther's nothing
　Allays a cudgell like it.
Lamira.　　　　　*Montagne,* now
　I'le put my choyce to you; who do you hold
　In all this honor'd company a husband
　Fit to enjoy thy Lady? speak directly.
Montaigne.　Shall I speak Madam?
Lamira.　　　　　　*Montagne,* you shall.　　60
Montaigne.　Then as I have a soule i'le speak my conscience,
　Give me more wine, *in vino veritas,*
　Here's to my self, and *Montagne* have a care.
Lamira.　Speak to th' cause.
Montaigne.　Yes, Madam;
　First i'le begin at the lower ende.
Laverdure.　　　　　　Have at us.
La-poope.　Now for a Psalme of mercy.
Montaigne [*to* Laverdure].　　　You good Mounsier,
　You that bely the noble Name of Courtier,
　And think your claime good here, hold up your hand;
　Your Worship is endited here, for a　　　　70
　Vaine glorious foole——
Laverdure.　　　　Oh sir.
Montaigne.　　　　　　For one whose wit

49 washes off, my Lord.] washes of ∧ my lord. MS; washes. F1
50 lesse.] lesse,——MS; lesse my Lord. F1　53 Justice] MS; a Judge F1
66 at the lower ende.] MS; to thee. F1　71 Oh sir] MS; Good, oh sir F1

Lies in a ten pound wastcoat, yet not warme;
Ye have travel'd like a Fidler to make faces,
And brought home nothing but a case of tooth-picks.
You would be married, and no lesse then Ladye,
And of the best sort can serve you; thou silke worm
What hast thou in thee to deserve this woman?
Name but the poorest piece of man, good manners,
Ther's nothing sound about thee, faith thou'ast none,
It lies pawn'd at thy silke mans, for so much lace   80
Thy credit with his wife cannot redeem it,
Thy cloaths are all the soule thou hast, for so
Thou sav'st them hansome for the next great tilting
Let who wil take the t'other, thou wert never christen'd
Upon my conscience but in barbers water,
Thou art never out o'th basen, thou art rotten,
And if thou darst tell truth, thou wilt confesse it;
To kill the noysomnesse of itch, thy skin
Looks of a Chestnut colour, greas'd with Amber.
All women that on earth do dwell thou lov'st,   90
Yet none that understand love thee again,
But those that love the Spittle. Get thee home
Poor painted butter fly, thy summers past;
Go sweat and eat dry Mutton, thou mayst live
To do so well yet, a bruis'd Chamber Maide
May fall upon thee, and advance thy follies.
You have your sentence; now it followes Captaine,
I treat of you.
La-poope.   Pray God I may deserve it.
Orleans. Beshrow my heart, he speaks plaine.
Amiens.   That's plain dealing.
Montaigne. You are a rascall Captaine.
La-poope.   A fine calling.   100
Montaigne. A water coward.
Amiens.   He would make a pretty stuffe.
Montaigne. May I speak freely Madam?
Lamira.   Here's none ties you.

75 Ladye] MS; Ladies F1   81 with his wife] MS; which is worse F1
88 To kill the noysomnesse of itch, thy] MS;————thy F1   102 May] MS; Nay F1

100

Montaigne.   Why should'st thou dare come hither with a thought
  To finde a wife here fit for thee? are all
  Thy single money whores that fed on Carrots,
  And fild the high grasse with familiars
  Falne of to footmen? prethee tell me truly,
  For now I know thou dar'st not lie, couldst thou not
  Wish thy selfe beaten well with all thy heart now,
  And out of paine? say that I broke a rib,   110
  Or cut thy nose off, wert not mercifull
  For this ambition?
La-poope.   Do your pleasure sir,
  Beggars mut not be choosers.
Orleans.   He longs for beating.
Montaigne.   But that I have nobler thoughts possesse my soule,
  Then such brown bisket, such a peice of dog-fish,
  Such a most mangy Mackrell eater as thou art
  That dares do nothing that belongs to th' Sea,
  But spue, and catch rats, and fear men of war,
  Though thou hast nothing in the world to loose
  Abord thee, but one piece of beefe, one Musket   120
  Without a cock for peace sake, and a pitch barrell,
  I'le tell thee if my time were not more pretious
  Then thus to loose it, I would so rattle thee,
  It may be beat thee, and thy puefellow,
  The Merchant there of Eele skins, till my words,
  Or blowes, or both, made ye two branded wretches
  To all the world hereafter;———
                  [*To* Mallicorne.] you would faine to
  Venture your bils of lading for this Lady.
  What would you give now for her? some five frayle
  Of rotten Figs, good Godson, would you not sir?   130
  And halfe a pinte of olives, and a Parrat
  That speaks high Dutch? can all thou ever saw'st
  Of thine own fraughts from Sea, or cosonage
  (At which thou art as expert as the devill),
  Nay sell thy soul for wealth to, as thou wilt do,

123 so] MS; *omit* F1   124 puefellow] MS; pure fellow F1
*125 Eele skins] MS; Catskins F1   131 And halfe a pinte of olives,] MS; *omit* F1
131 and a] MS (& a); Or a F1

Forfeit thy friends, and raise a mint of Money,
Make thee dream all these double could procure
One kisse from this good Lady? can'st thou hope
She would lie with such a nook of hell as thou art,
And hatch young Merchant-furies? oh ye dog-bolts   140
That fear no God but Dunkirks, I shall see you
Serve in a lowsy Limeboat, ere I die,
For mouldy cheese and butter Billingsgate
Would not endure, or bring in rotten Pippins
To cure blew eyes, and swear they came from *China*.

Lamira.   Vex 'em no more, alas they shake.

Montaigne.   Down quickly
  On your marrow bones, and thank this Lady.
  I would not leave you thus else, there are blankets,
  And such delights for such knaves; but fear still;
  'Twill be revenge enough, to keep you waking.   150
  Ye have no minde to marrie, ha' ye?

La-poope.   Surely
  No great mind now.

Montaigne.   Nor you?

Mallicorne.   Nor I, I take it.

Montaigne.   Two eager sutors.

Laverdure.   Troth tis wonderous hot,
  God blesse us from him.

Lamira.   You have told me *Montagne*
  Who are not fit to have me, let me know
  The man you would point for me.

Montaigne.   There he sits;
  My Lord of *Amiens*, Madam, is my choyce,
  Hee's noble every way, and worth a wife
  With all the dowers of vertue.

Amiens.   Do you speak sir
  Out of your friendship to me?

Montaigne.   Yes, my Lord,   160
  And out of truth, for I could never flatter.

138 One] MS; A F1
151 to marrie] MS; of Marriage F1   156 point for] MS; point out for F1
158 worth] MS; worthy F1   159 dowers of vertue.] MS; dowries of——F1

102

Amiens.   I will not say how much I owe you for it,
    For that were but a promise, but Ile think ye,
    As now I find you, in despite of fortune,
    A faire and noble Gentleman.
Lamira.   My Lords,
    I must confesse the choyce this man hath made
    Is every way a great one, if not too great,
    And no way to be slighted: yet because
    We love to have our own eyes, sometimes in't,
    Give me a little liberty to see   170
    How I could fit my selfe, if I were put to't.
Amiens.   Madam we must.
Lamira.   Are yee all agreed?
Omnes.   We be!
Lamira.   Then as I am a maid, I shall choose here.
    Montagne, I must have thee.
Montaigne.   Oh Madam I have learnt to suffer more
    Then you can (out of pitty) mock me with,
    This way especially.
Lamira.   Thou think'st I jest now;
    But by the love I bear thee, I will have thee.
Montaigne.   If you could be so weak, to love a falne man,
    He must deserve more then I ever can,   180
    Or ever shall (deer Lady); look but this way
    Upon that Lord and you will tell me then
    Your eyes are no true choosers of good men.
Amiens.   Do you love him truely lady?
Lamira.   Yes my Lord,
    And will obey him truly, for i'le marry him,
    And justly thinke he that has so well serv'd mee
    With his obedience, being borne to greatnesse,
    Must use me nobly of necessity
    When I shall serve him.
Amiens.   'Twere a deepe sin to crosse ye.——Noble *Montagne*,   190
    I wish ye all content, and am as happy
    In my friends good as it were meerly mine.

162 will] MS; would F1   163 think] MS; thank F1   169 in't] MS; now F1
175 Oh] MS; Why F1   184 lady] MS; *omit* F1   185 And] MS (&); I F1

Montaigne.   Your Lordship does ill to give up your right;
I am not capable of this great goodnesse,
There sits my wife that holds my troth.
Charlotte.   I'le end all.
I wooed ye for my Lady, for her wonne ye,
And now give up my title, alas poor wench,
My aimes are lower far.
Montaigne.   How's this sweet heart?
Lamira.   Sweet heart tis so, the drift was mine, to hide
My purpose till it struck home.
Omnes.   God give ye joy.   200
Lamira.   Prethee leave wondring, by this kisse i'le have thee.
Montaigne.   Then by this kisse, and this i'le ever serve ye.
Longavile.   This Gentleman and I sir must needs hope
Once more to follow yee.
Montaigne.   As friends and fellows,
Never as servants more.
Longavile. Duboys.   You make us happy.
Orleans.   Friend *Montagne,* ye have taught mee so much honor,
I have found a fault in my self, but thus
I'le purge my conscience of it, the late land
I took by false play from you, with as much
Contrition, and entirenesse of affection   210
To this most happy day, again I render;
Be master of your own, forget my malice,
And make mee worthy of your love, Lord *Montagne.*
Montaigne.   You have won me and honor to your name.
Mallicorne.   Since your Lordship has begun good deeds, wee'l
follow;
Good sir forgive us, we are now those men
Fear you for goodness sake; those sums of money
Unjustly we detaine from you, on your pardon
Shall bee restord again, and we your servants.
La-poope.   You are very forward sir, it seems you have money,   220
I pray you lay out, i'le pay you or pray for you,
As the Sea works.

196 wooed ye] MS; wooed you F1   196 for her wonne ye,] MS; *omit* F1
200 ye] MS; you F1   203 hope] MS; hop F1   *208 land] *stet* F1

104

Laverdure.   Their pennance sir i'le undertake, so please ye
   To grant me one concealement.
Longavile.   Right courtier, still a begging.
Montaigne.   What is it sir?
Laverdure.   A Gentlewoman.
Montaigne.   In my gift?
Laverdure.   Yes sir, in yours.
Montaigne.   Why bring her forth and take her.
                                   Exit Laverdure.

Lamira.   What wench would he have?
Montaigne.   Any wench I think.

      Enter Laverdure *and* Veramour, *like a Woman.*

Laverdure.   This is the Gentlewoman.
Montaigne.   This, 'tis my Page sir.
Veramour.   No sir, I am a poor disguis'd Lady   230
   That like a Page have followed you full long
   For love god-wot.
Omnes.   A Lady!
Laverdine.   Yes, yes, tis a Lady.
Montaigne.   It may be so, and yet we have laine together,
   But by my troth I never found her Lady.
Lady Orleans.   Why wore you boyes cloathes?
Veramour.   I'le tell you Madam,
   I took example by two or three playes, that methought
   Concernd me.
Montaigne.   Why made you not me acquainted with it?   240
Veramour.   Indeed sir I knew it not my selfe,
   Untill this Gentleman opend my dull eyes,
   And by perswasion made me see it.
Amiens.   Could his power in words make such a change?
Veramour.   Yes, as truly woman as your selfe my Lord.
Laverdure.   Why but hark you, are not you a woman then?
Veramour.   If hands and face make it not evident,

224 one] MS; on F1   227.1 *Exit* Laverdure.] MS; *omit* F1
*228 he] *stet* F1   229 This, 'tis] MS; 'Tis F1
233–234 *Omnes.* A Lady! | *Laverdine.* Yes, ... Lady.] MS (*subs.*); *Omnes.* A Lady——
    Laverdine——yes, yes, tis a Lady. F1   246 then] MS; *omit* F1

105

You shall see more.

Mallicorne.   Breeches, breeches, *Laverdure.*

La-poope.   Tis not enough, women may wear those cases.   250
Search further Courtier.

Omnes.   Ha, ha, ha.

La-poope.   Oh thou freshwater Gudgeon, wouldst thou come
To point of Marriage with an Ignoramus?
Thou shouldst have had her urin to the doctors,
The foolishest Phisitian could have made plaine
The liquid Epicæne; a blind man by the hand
Could have discoverd the ring from the stone.
Boy, come, to Sea with me, ile teach thee to climb,
And come down by the rope, nay to eate Rats.   260

Veramour.   I shall devour my Master before the prison then,
Sir, I have began my Trade.

Mallicorne.   Trade? to the Citie, child,
A flatcap will become thee.

Montaigne.   Gentlemen
I beseech you molest your selves no further,
For his preferment it is determin'd.

Laverdure.   I am much ashamed, and if my cheek
Gives not satisfaction, break my head.

Montaigne.   Your shame's enough sir.

Amiens.   *Montagne*, much joy attend thy marriage Bed;
By thy example of true goodnesse, envie is exil'd,   270
And to all honest men that truth intend,
I wish good luck, faire fate be still thy friend.

                                        Exeunt.

            FINIS.

Upon an Honest Mans Fortune
By Mr. *John Fletcher*.
[Printed in italic at the end of the play's text (F1647, sig. 5X4v)]

You that can look through Heaven, and tell the Stars,
Observe their kind conjunctions, and their wars;
Find out new lights, and give them where you please,
To those men honors, pleasures, to those ease;
You that are Gods surveyers, and can show
How far, and when, and why the wind doth blow;
Know all the charges of the dreadfull thunder,
And when it will shoot over, or fall under:
Tell me, by all your art I conjure ye,
Yes, and by truth, what shall become of me?   10
Find out my star, if each one, as you say,
Have his peculiar Angel, and his way;
Observe my fate, next fall into your dreames,
Sweep clean your houses, and new line your sceames,
Then say your worst: or have I none at all?
Or is it burnt out lately? or did fall?
Or am I poor, not able, no full flame?
My star, like me, unworthy of a name?
Is it, your art can only work on those
That deale with dangers, dignities, and cloaths?   20
With love, or new opinions? you all lye,
A fishwife hath a fate, and so have I,
But far above your finding; he that gives,
Out of his providence, to all that lives,
And no man knowes his treasure, no not you:
He that made Egypt blind, from whence you grew
Scaby and lowsy, that the world might see
Your calculations are as blind as ye,
He that made all the stars, you dayly read,
And from thence filtch a knowledge how to feed;   30
Hath hid this from you, your conjectures all
Are drunken things, not how, but when they fall;
Man is his own star, and the soule that can
Render an honest, and a perfect man

107

Command all light, all influence, all fate,
Nothing to him fals early or too late.
Our acts our Angels are, or good or ill,
Our fatall shadowes that walke by us still,
And when the stars are labouring, we believe
It is not that they govern, but they grive   40
For stubborn ignorance; all things that are
Made for our generall uses are at war,
Even we among our selves, and from the strife
Your first unlike opinions got a life.
O man, thou image of thy makers good,
What canst thou fear, when breath'd into thy blood
His spirit is, that built thee? what dull sence
Makes thee suspect, in need, that providence?
Who made the morning, and who plact the light
Guid to thy labours? who cal'd up the night,   50
And bid her fall upon thee, like sweet flowers
In hollow murmurs, to lock up thy powers?
Who gave thee knowledge, who so trusted thee,
To let thee grow so neer himselfe, the Tree?
Must he then be distrusted? shall his frame
Discourse with him, why thus, and thus I am?
He made the Angels thine, thy fellowes all,
Nay even thy servants, when devotions call.
Oh canst thou be so stupid then, so dim,
To seek a saving influence, and loose him?   60
Can Stars protect thee? or can poverty,
Which is the light to Heaven, put out his eye?
He is my star, in him all truth I find,
All influence, all fate, and when my mind
Is furnished with his fullnesse, my poor story
Shall outlive all their Age, and all their glory.
The hand of danger canot fall amisse,
When I know what, and in whose power it is.
Nor Want, the curse of man, shall make me groan,
A holy hermit is a mind alone.   70

69 curse] Seward; cause F1–2

Doth not experience teach us all we can
To work our selves into a glorious man?
Love's but an exhalation to best eyes
The matter spent, and then the fooles fire dyes?
Were I in love, and could that bright star bring
Increase to wealth, honour, and every thing:
Were she as perfect good as wee can aime,
The first was so, and yet she lost the Game.
My mistris then be knowledge and faire truth;
So I enjoy all beauty and all youth,   80
And though to time her lights and lawes she lends,
She knowes no Age that to corruption bends.
Friends promises may lead me to believe,
But he that is his own friend knowes to live.
Affliction when I know it is but this,
A deep allay whereby man tougher is
To bear the hammer, and the deeper still,
We still arise more image of his will.
Sicknesse an humorous cloud twixt us and light,
And Death, at longest but another night.   90
Man is his own Star, and that soule that can
Be honest is the only perfect man.

FINIS.

THE END OF THE PLAY (V.iv.246 ff.) IN MS DYCE 9

[The following text is based on J. Gerritsen's edition of the Dyce MS, and accepts his emendations at lines 247 (where damage to MS has resulted in the loss of the speech-prefix) and 249 (where the phrase 'truth is, I' is only partially preserved in MS in its present damaged state), and at line 260 (where MS omits 'him'). The lineation is that of Gerritsen's edition. The abbreviations of MS speech-prefixes have been expanded to accord with those of the present edition of the play.]

*

Laverdure.   why but harke you; are not you a woeman then.
Veramour.   yes, as much as you are, but since I am heere,
   amidst so faire a presence, Ile open all.
   truth is, I am no other then that I seem'd
   at first to bee, a boy, only as poore suspected   250
   Innocents sometimes, to quit their vexed bodies
   from the plague of tortors, by force'd paines
   confesse those things they never did, so forced
   was I to this exchange
Laverdure.   I am gulld, I am gulld
Veramour.   for trust me gent, never did the ghost
   of a deceased churle haunt the place where hee
   had hid his gold wth more Insatiate greedines,
   then this blinde conceited youth did me, no place
   could free me from him, tell at last I agreed   260
   to say as he would haue me, & by that meanes got
   some rest, & now I dare be my selfe againe.
Montaigne.   I'st ene so, how doe you like yor masculine ladye.
Laverdure.   so well, that yf it please you to change,
   I shall be much thankefull.
Lamira.   O keepe yor first choice.
Laverdure.   ha! crost in my first loue, I'me ene ashame'd
   of my selfe.
Montaigne.   come, chere vp, wee are all frends, I haue not
   receiud more wrongs then I am willing to forgiue,
   but you shall not hence vntell the marriage feast be past.   270

Amiens.   *Montaigne*, much Ioye attend thy marriage bed.
  by thy example of true goodnes, *Envy* is exild,
  & to all honest men, that truth Intend,
  I wish good luck, faire *Fate* be still thy frend.
                    ——*ffinis*   ——*Exeunt*

TEXTUAL NOTES

The Persons represented in the Play.

13 Three Creditors] The F2 cast-list specifies 'Two', but 'three Creditors' are brought on in the stage-direction at II.iv.26.1, and the third creditor speaks at II. iv. 39. Only two creditors enter, together with the two lawyers, in the play's opening scene (I.i.81.1).

I.i

222 lively.] Following this word F1 prints the words 'How proceeds my suit?' which also occur at line 241. The repetition is the result of an intended cut marked in MS involving lines 222–41 ('That's with labour sir, ... Thy dammage to thee:'). If the cut were observed, Montaigne's final words in line 241 ('how proceeds my suit?') would provide the necessary cue for Longavile's speech at line 242. Though the cut has not been made in F1, it was evidently marked in the F1 printers' copy, and the cue words have been brought forward to the place where they would have served to bridge it. This explanation for the textual problem that the passage poses was first presented by W. W. Greg, 'A question of plus or minus', *Review of English Studies*, VI (1930), 300–4. For its acceptance by later scholars, see R. C. Bald, *Bibliographical Studies in the Beaumont and Fletcher Folio of 1647*, Supplement to the Bibliographical Society's Transactions, No. 13 (Oxford University Press, 1938 (for 1937)), pp. 79–80, where examples of this practice for indicating cuts are noted in the texts of *The Woman's Prize* and *Beggars' Bush*), and J. Gerritsen, *The Honest Mans Fortune: A Critical Edition of MS Dyce 9 (1625)* (Groningen, 1952), pp. xlix, liii, who suggests that such repeated phrases as those found in the present passage and in those at I.i.298–316 and IV.ii.84–8 were intended to aid the scribe in the preparation of actors' parts.

298 Lord.] The first Lawyer's full speech in F1 reads 'O my Lord, have an eye upon him.' The repetition of the words 'Have an eye upon him' at line 316 (where they are spoken by the first Creditor) suggests (as Greg, *op. cit.* noted) another intended cut in the F1 copy, this one involving lines 298–316. The repeated words would again represent a cue for bridging the cut, as in the case of the passage at lines 222–41, noted above. Unlike lines 222–41, however, lines 298–316 are not marked for cutting in MS.

346 *Morglayes*] 'Morglay' was the sword of Bevis of Southampton. Field refers to it again in *A Woman is a Weather-cock*, IV.iii.34: '*Beauis* on *Arundell* with Morglay in hand'.

I.ii

0.1 *a Servant*] Before these words in MS the name '*G: Rick:*' (for 'George Rickner') has been interlined above a caret in Knight's hand. No exit is provided for the servant in either MS or F1, but he must leave the stage at some point because MS calls upon him to enter again at line 96.1, where Knight inserts the name '*G: Rick:*' again below MS stage-direction *Ent: 2: Seruants*. F1 calls for only a single servant to enter at this point, in response to Orleans' call for one to escort his Lady off-stage (line 96). This is of a piece with the uncertainty evident throughout this scene regarding the number of servants on hand and the entourage (Orleans' or Amiens') to which they belong. F1's confused version of the stage-direction at 85.1 reads '*Enter Amiens in amazement, the servants following him.*' But no servants have accompanied him in his entrance at 49.1, and he is now, at 85.1, exiting, not entering. The simplest means of resolving the problem of the servants is to let 'G: Rick:' exit as soon as he has entered (I.ii.1.1); to have him return as one of the two servants MS calls for at 96.1; and to omit the reference to the servants who follow Amiens in his amazement. For George Rickner, see G. E. Bentley, *The Jacobean and Caroline Stage* (Oxford, 1941), II, 384, 547.

I.iii

2–4 cast away . . . undone] The 'buckler', as Dyce explained, is Veramour, who has thrown himself in front of Montaigne, his master. What follows turns on a pun on 'cast away'. Amiens challenges Montaigne to come out from behind (to cast away) the protection of the page, his buckler. Montaigne replies that Veramour is indeed cast away (undone) since he continues to serve a financially ruined master. The passage 'So he is Sir, for he lives | With one that is undone' (lines 3–4) is marked for omission in MS. Bald (p. 55) thought it 'was probably omitted in performance because it was liable to provoke an unintended laugh'. Gerritsen (p. 138), commenting that 'a writer who inserts a pun usually intends a laugh', thought it more likely that the words were cut 'because the pun was too obscure'.

II.ii

1 Hunger] This, the MS reading, is certainly correct, not F1's 'Slander', it being 'of hunger, not slander, that La Poop complains, who was indeed a wretch that could not be slandered' (J. Monck Mason, *Comments on the Plays of Beaumont and Fletcher* (London, 1798), p. 385). But the phrase 'slander is sharper than a sword' seems to have been current (cf. Shakespeare, *Cymbeline*, III.iv.33–4, and *The Winter's Tale*, II.iii.86–7), and the F1 compositor apparently found it more familiar. The proverb is not included in Tilley's *Dictionary*, though Tilley's S522 ('Slander leaves a score (scar) behind it') is close. The present passage is cited (with a query) by R. W. Dent in *Shakespeare's Proverbial Language: An Index* (Berkeley and Los Angeles, 1981), p. 211.

8–9 wind-Collick ... swallow]   The phrase 'If you be' has been omitted from line 9 in F1 (which here reads 'troubled with the wind- | Collick,Captaine, swallow'), but appears in F1's version of line 11 ('A bullet; if you be Captain, my panch'). The MS version of line 11 replaces F1's 'if you be' with the words 'why man' and omits 'Captain'. Gerritsen (p. li) suggests that in the copy for F1, 'the words "yf you be Captaine" would have been inserted either below the line or in the margin, and the compositor then mistook the place where they should go'. Though Gerritsen considered that 'the word "Captaine" could hardly have been repeated here', the repetition is typical of Laverdure's garrulous speech.

155.1–2 Servants *and others*]   In MS the word '*Seruants*' is crossed out and replaced with '*Drawers*': perhaps they are the '*others*' to whom the F1 stage direction refers. In line 157 'the house' is a tavern. Cf. the references to 'Tavern brawels' (line 184) and 'a drinking room' (line 195).

III.i

82 griffin]   Here used as an emblem of incongruity; the fabulous animal had the head and wings of an eagle, and the body and hind quarters of a lion.

86 father's]   Both MS and F1 read 'how oft her daughter by her mother ventured to lie'. Mason (p. 387) called this nonsense, adding: 'Veramour is describing the woman herself: we must therefore read – "how oft her *father's* daughter, by her mother, ventured to lie".' Subsequent editors (Weber, Dyce) have accepted the word 'father's' into their texts. Gerritsen, however (p. 150), declares that 'the meaning is perfectly clear if we read "how oft the daughter by the mother ventured to lie".' This yields a possible meaning, but Gerritsen's reading seems to impart a rather more innocent sense to the passage than its context implies. In the drama of this period, the phrase 'to lie upon the rushes' is seldom entirely innocent (cf. 'the wanton rushes' of Shakespeare's *1 Henry IV*, III.i.211). And the phrase 'get in' certainly carries a bawdy innuendo. Mason's emendation is necessary.

121–123 'Twolld ... receave it.]   Gerritsen, who seems not to have understood this passage, thought it might be an uncomplimentary hit at the legal profession, and that this might account for its omission from F1 (he suggested that 'night cap' here is probably intended to mean a lawyer). The sense of the passage is quite simple: Lamira responds with sarcasm to a letter from her suitor, Amiens, in which presumably he complains of how he languishes in health for her: his love-lorn language, she says, would better become an invalid in a night-cap. Lady Orleans, Amiens' sister, tries to defend her brother's sincerity. Bald (p. 55) is surely right in suggesting that, to judge from the evidence of fol. 17v of the MS, the lines were 'an afterthought of the author's or were added on revision, either in the margin or on an inserted slip, and that they were omitted from the folio for the same reason that they were nearly omitted from the manuscript'. Gerritsen (p. lii) notes that 'with these lines the passage is metrically regular, without them it is irregular', and thinks it 'more likely that the author revised them in composing the scene'.

III.ii

37 barck] Gerritsen (p. 153), failing to see any meaning in this passage as it stands, and acting on an annotation of Dyce's in his copy of the Folio, emended 'barck' (the reading of both MS and F1) to 'boock', thereby establishing a parallel between 'rhetoric' and 'gloss', 'language' and 'book'. But 'barck' is correct. Here as elsewhere Field uses the word in a sense that combines two meanings of 'bark': (1) 'rind', 'husk', 'outer covering', and (2) a small sailing vessel. Cf. *The Knight of Malta*, V.i.102–3 (a Field scene): 'I would not for *Aleppo*, this fraile Bark, | This barke of flesh, no better steeres-man had'. In the present passage, Longavile is saying: younger brothers, no matter how elegant their discourse, will find it to be of little avail, in the absence of money, to launch them in society.

54–55 Pretious . . . lye by it.] The passage, heavily crossed out in MS and omitted from F1, was presumably deemed offensive either by the stage-reviser or the censor. W. W. Greg (*Dramatic Documents from the Elizabethan Playhouses* (Oxford, 1931), p. 290) found the passage to be undecipherable but recognized that it 'does not seem to be a scribal error'. The crossed-out words were first read by R. C. Bald (p. 55).

60 Crohieture] a porter (*O.E.D.*, s.v., 'Crocheteur'). MS spells the word 'Croiheture'.

73–74 What would it do? | Prate as it do's?] Longavile insults Duboys by addressing him here in a form of baby-talk.

III.iii

27–8 the Snake that would be a Dragon] Apparently a variant of the proverb 'A Serpent must eat another serpent before he can become a dragon' (Tilley, S228). Dyce cited parallels in Jonson's *Catiline* (III, 523–4: 'A serpent, ere he comes to be a dragon, | Do's eate a bat'), and Dryden and Lee's *Oedipus* (III.i.24–5: 'A Serpent ne're becomes a flying Dragon, | Till he has eat a Serpent'). In the following line (28) the words 'a Spider' are omitted from F1, and Gerritsen (p. xlvii) notes that in MS 'Knight left a blank for the word "spider", probably because he could not read it, and did not insert it until after he had mended his pen . . . eight lines farther down.' Thus it is not altogether 'certain that "spider" was the original word of [the] text' (Gerritsen, p. 155).

69 frequent] The word used in the sense 'widely current' is familiar in Massinger. Cf. *The Roman Actor*, I.i.43, and *The Elder Brother*, I.ii.153 (a Massinger scene).

82 look such] F1 reads 'look they'; in the MS, Knight first wrote 'look they', then changed it to 'look such'. In his edition of MS, Gerritsen rejects its altered reading on the grounds that 'it would be too remarkable if scribe and compositor had both misread "such" as "they"'. But misreading is not necessarily in question here. There are other places where F1 follows a MS reading that has subsequently been changed (e.g., III.i.77, III.iii.29, IV.i.289, V.ii.30, V.iv.172).

IV.i

22.1 *with Counters*.]   The reference presumably is to the imitation coins, or tokens, used in counting money: what the Clown in *The Winter's Tale* (IV.iii.36) and Troilus in *Troilus and Cressida* (II.ii.28) refer to as 'compters'. The reference is omitted from the MS version of this stage-direction, as it is from all printed editions of the play from F2 through Dyce. The inclusion of the Counters in the F1 stage-direction is evidently a relic of the author's original conception of the scene, where the weighing out – and exchange – of money may have been imagined to figure more prominently than it does in the scene as we have it. Veramour offers Montaigne 'some Silver' and 'a little Gold' at lines 84–5, and at line 142 he offers Charlotte 'two pieces' of gold if she will leave Montaigne and him alone together. The 'Counters' may have been intended for use in the stage business attendant on occasions such as these.

78–79 boyes. | Since]   F1's insertion of the words 'These wordly qualities' followed by a period between lines 78–9 seems (as Gerritsen, p. xxxviii, has noted) to be an effort 'to make sense of a passage that could have been corrected by removing a colon two lines above' (after 'live', line 77).

214 Your affaire]   This, the MS reading, conveys the sense of Lamira's remark, while the F1 reading ('You're a fair') reflects the sense in which Longavile understands it.

289 disposure.]   Following this word, both F1 and MS in its original state had an *Exit* marked for Veramour, but MS *Exit* has been deleted, and only the *Exeunt* at 296.1 remains to clear the stage at the end of the scene. F1 retains both the *Exit* at line 289, and the *Exeunt* at 296.1. Gerritsen (p. lxi) suggests that Veramour 'is meant to go off slowly but not actually leave the stage until the end'. He presumably is still on stage at line 292 when Laverdure makes reference to 'your Lady'.

IV.ii

80 And be the motive rather both kill me.]   I.e. 'and rather persuade them both to kill me' (Seward's explanation of this difficult passage is generally accepted).

82 there]   Again, as at IV.i.214 above, MS and F1 spellings differentiate the homophones (an adverb in MS, a possessive pronoun in F1). Field uses the phrase again in *Four Plays in One* ('The Triumph of Honour', scene ii, lines 167–8: 'Art thou there, Basilisk? remove thine eyes, | For I am sick to death with thy infection.').

83–4 hand. | Orleans. O here's]   Both MS and F1 follow Montaigne's 'But that thy fate deserves some weightier hand' with a three-word speech by Duboys: 'Sweet my Lord.' It is marked for omission in MS, and anticipates Duboys' words at line 88. It obviously signals a cut involving lines 84–8 ('O here's a plot ... vertuous couple?'), in the manner of the cuts noted above at I.i.222, 298. See Gerritsen, p. lii.

115 a meaner arme]   This, the F1 reading, is not altogether satisfactory, but the MS reading ('to [i.e., too] meane an arme') is even less so. The general import of the F1 text is clear however: Montaigne's hope for Amiens is that he is destined to put his honour and his life at risk in conflict with a worthier adversary than Orleans;

chastising Orleans is work for 'a meaner arm' than Amiens'. As Gerritsen notes, the manuscript's 'to meane an arme' makes nonsense of Duboys' following remark ('Yes faith, or none') which MS marks for omission.

139–140 By my soule . . . if]   One of many occasions when the F1 compositor found his copy illegible; between the words 'By' and 'If' he merely inserted a long dash. MS fills the gap, but the scribe too had his difficulties with the copy at this point; the word 'soule' is crossed out, a caret is inserted before it and the word 'blood' interlined above, and then erased. See Gerritsen, pp. 166–7.

V.i

6 are merry]   Dyce noted that by 'fellow', Charlotte means 'fellow-servant' and compared her speech at line 15, below, and Montaigne's speech at IV.i.109. F1's 'You are a merry fellow' loses this meaning.

13 Jack Merlin]   Dyce, noting that 'the merlin is a small species of hawk', quotes Robert Holme's *Academy of Armory* (1688; ii, 236): 'A Jack is the Male of a Merlin, some call him a *Jack-Merlin*.'

43–44 mewing . . . *Tristram*]   'Mewing' (moulting, shedding, as the feathers of a hawk) suggests Tristram de Lyones, Arthurian hero and reputed authority on matters relating to hawking and hunting. *The Booke of Hawking, Hunting and Blasing of Arms* (1486) was attributed to him.

60 provender . . . pricks me]   Proverbial; Tilley, P615.

V.ii

7 this concealment]   The allusion is to the contemporary practice of bringing to light, and reporting to specially appointed government commissions, lands that had formerly been part of monastic properties but which had been quietly taken over by private individuals and not surrendered to the Crown. These were referred to as 'concealed' lands, and the commissions charged with the discovery of 'conceal-ments' were widely held to be susceptible to bribes. It was commonly assumed that a person with influence at Court could manage to have land that he wished to possess shown to be concealed land and then acquire it, either as a gift or for a nominal sum. Laverdure refers to the practice again at V.iv.224.

11 meach]   Though Mason (p. 390) announced that 'there is no such word as meache' (and lamely proposed emending to 'mess'), 'meach' (meaning 'skulk' or 'lurk') is common in the drama of the period. Cf. Dekker, *Satiromastix*, IV.iii.73: 'I did but mych heere'. For the MS spelling of the word in the present passage ('meich'), cf. (in the Beaumont and Fletcher canon) *The Noble Gentleman*, I.ii.78–9: 'my meiching varlet'. Beaumont and Fletcher's *The Scornful Lady* contains references to 'some Meeching raskall' (V.i.12) and to 'Michers' (II.ii.16).

15 this seven]   For 'this seven' F1 reads 'these ten'. Gerritsen (p. 169) accounts for the variant by suggesting that F1 copy read 'this seven' but the compositor mistook *v* for *t*.

V.iii

0.1 *serving in a Banquet*]   In the absence of this scene from the MS text, the Banquet is provided for by the stage-direction that opens the MS version of V.iv: '*A Banquet: Set out: then Enter: Orleance: & his Ladye* ...'

V.iv

125 Eele skins]   The MS reading; F1's 'Catskins' is a mistake. The phrase 'a merchant of eelskins' (meaning a merchant without money or wares) is proverbial. See Tilley, M882.

208 land]   The MS is defective at this point, and the reading 'landes' of Gerritsen's edition is conjectural, but F1 'land' is preferable. Montaigne's disputed property is almost always referred to in the singular (e.g., I.i.85, 120, 300; I.ii.8, 29, 71, 76, 102); only once in the plural (III.ii.59).

228 he]   MS reads 'ye' and Gerritsen (p. 178) considered this to be correct on the assumption that the question Lamira addresses to Montaigne as given there ('what wench wolld ye haue') shows her to 'be more interested in the female appanages of her future husband than in those of a disreputable scoundrel'. If so, one is left wondering what she makes of his answer in both MS and F1 ('Any wench I think'). Lamira and Montaigne's remarks to each other clearly have reference to Laverdure, who has just left the stage. 'What wench would he have?' asks Lamira in F1, which is certainly right.

PRESS VARIANTS IN F1 (1647)

SHEET 5Ti (*outer forme*)

Uncorrected: MB, MnU, ViU[1], WMU[2], WU
First-stage corrected: Hoy, NIC, NjP, ViU[2], WaU, WMU[1,3]

Sig. 5T4v
  Head-line 156] 56

Second-stage corrected: IU, NcD, RoU

Sig. 5T1
  I.i.6 cause] rause

119

EMENDATIONS OF ACCIDENTALS

I.i

I.i] *Actus: I: Scæna: I:* MS; *Actus primus*——*Scena prima:* Fı
1–27 You ... disposition.] *prose in* Fı
6 cause] MS, Fı (c); rause Fı (u)
24 purpose?] ~ . Fı; ~ ∧ MS
29–31 I can ... prosper in,] Fı *lines:* I can ... prayer │ From ... prosper in;
30 prayer,] MS; ~ ∧ Fı
31 in,] ~ : MS; ~ ; Fı
32 exceptions;] ~ , MS; ~ ∧ Fı
34–36 Precisely ... Farewell.] Fı *lines:* Precisely ... wishes │ To ... Farewell.
39 so:——] ~ , ∧ MS; ~ : ∧ Fı
39–40 That's ... state,] *one line in* Fı
68 motion,——] ~ : ∧ MS; ~ , ∧ Fı
68 *Exit* Amiens.] *after* 'prosper.' (*line* 64) *in* MS, Fı
70–72 Either ... lives] Fı *lines:* Either ... cunning. │ *Mont.* That's ... actions │ Whose ... lives
78–79 He ... law.] *one line in* Fı
81 executor:] MS; ~ ∧ Fı
81.1 *Enter ... Creditors.] after line* 82 *in* Fı
109 loves——] ~ , MS; ~ . Fı
111 Lordship——] MS; ~ . Fı
112 me——] ~ ∧ MS; ~ . Fı
114 Councellors] MS; Conncellors Fı
115 prosper,] MS; ~ : Fı
128 bar,] MS; ~ ∧ Fı
130–131 Is ... engage] *one line in* Fı
131 satisfaction,] MS; ~ ∧ Fı
132 assurance?] ~ . MS; ~ , Fı
136.1 *Exeunt* Lawyers.] *Exit Law.* Fı; *Exit (after line* 138) MS

142–144 No, but ... the use.] Fı *lines:* No, but ... will be │ Perished ... want │ A member ... the use——
144 use.] MS; ~ ——Fı
145 Lord,] MS; ~ ∧ Fı
146–147 Your ... you.] *one line in* Fı
148 Creditors] MS; *Cred.* Fı
156–157 Th'ast ... me.] Fı *lines:* Th'ast ... belongs │ Unto me.
183–184 Deservd ... action.] *one line in* Fı
196–197 Tis ... more] *one line in* Fı
205 hitherto] MS (hetherto); hitherro Fı
209 be,] MS; ~ ; Fı
213–214 To keep ... falling.] *one line in* Fı
214–215 Tis ... for] *one line in* Fı
218–219 *Longueville* ... face.] *one line in* Fı
221–222 To give ... lively.] *one line in* Fı
222–223 That's ... *Hercules*] *one line in* Fı
254 foot-man,] ~ ? MS, Fı
275–276 Pox ... │ Abused you.] *one line in* Fı
277–278 Yes ... cause] *one line in* Fı
281–282 Have ... lightly.] *one line in* Fı
282–283 Nothing ... so;] *one line in* Fı
290–291 The sir ... │ Ere] *one line in* Fı
300–301 None ... cause.] *prose in* Fı
302–303 No more ... already.] *prose in* Fı
303–304 If ... delay.] *prose in* Fı
306–308 Ere ... *Possessionem.*] *one line in* Fı
308–309 That's ... not.] *one line in* Fı

309–312 Th'art ... money.] *prose in* F1
315–316 Y'are ... me.] F1 *lines:* Y'are
    ... right; | That's ... me.
319–321 Dog him ... attempt him.]
    prose in F1
321–322 Doe ... losse] *one line in* F1
322 Serjeant,] MS; ~ ; F1
325–326 Who ... thus?] *prose in* F1
326–327 Sir, ... you?] *one line in* F1
327–328 Tis ... me.] *one line in* F1
333 satisfaction.——] ~ . ‸ MS; ~
    ‸ ‸ F1
333 *Longeville,*——] ~ , ‸ MS, F1
335–336 Is ... honest.] *one line in* F1

338–339 Counsel's ... as] F1 *lines:*
    Counsel's ... servant, | When ... as
339 danger,] MS; ~ : F1
340 is. Never] MS; ~ ‸ never F1
349 leave——] ~ ‸ MS; ~ . F1
379–380 So ... merit.] *prose in* F1
380–381 Are ... sorrow?] *one line in* F1
381–382 Sir, ... you.] *one line in* F1
382–385 Do ... serve you.] *prose in* F1
391–392 No, ... goe;] *one line in* F1
399–400 Any ... selfe.] *one line in* F1
400–401 Every ... account] *one line in*
    F1

I.ii

2 Madam——] ~ . MS, F1
13–14 Ye ... me.] *prose in* F1
26 women?] ~ ‸ MS; ~ . F1
36 pitty,] ~ ? MS, F1
47–48 Yes ... *Penelope*] *one line in* F1
50–51 Now ... *Montagne.*] *one line in*
    F1
51–52 No ... prosperity.] F1 *lines:* No
    ... *Montag/n/e,* | But ...
    prosperity.
53 distracted?] ~ ‸ MS; ~ . F1
53–54 He ... that] F1 *lines:* He ...
    strength | Of ... that
57 worth,] ~ ‸ MS; ~ : F1
58–59 I perceive ... confesse)] *one line*
    in F1
60 respects‸] MS; ~ , F1
62–63 Yet ... nobly.] *prose in* F1
63–65 Sir ... alliance.] *prose in* F1
65–66 I did ... had] *one line in* F1
69–70 Tis ... When] *one line in* F1

70 me. When] ~ ‸ when F1; ~ , ‸
    MS
78 her. Give ... her,] ~ , ~ ... ~ ,
    MS; ~ —— ~ ... ~ ——F1
78.1, 80 *Draws*] drawes MS; draws F1
79–80 For ... me.] *prose in* F1
83–84 Ile ... Together] MS; *one line in*
    F1
85 bed——] ~ , MS; ~ ‸ F1
87–88 Didst ... it?] *one line in* F1
88–89 Twas ... edge] F1 *lines:* Twas
    ... has | Turn'd ... edge
93 sooner] MS; sonner F1
96 honour.——Here,] ~ .——
    here‸ MS; ~ ‸ ——here——F1
97 stranger.——Give] ~ .——giue
    MS; ~ ‸ ——give F1
97 word,] MS; ~ ‸ F1
101–103 Put ... loth] *prose in* F1
103 loth‸] MS; ~ , F1
105 Go,] MS; ~ ‸ F1

I.iii

0.2 Veramour] MS; *Vercamor* F1
2–3 Thou ... buckler.] *one line in* F1
4 undone.——Avoid] ~ . ‸ avoide
    MS; ~ ‸ ——a voyd F1
6–7 Your ... Master.] *prose in* F1

6 button'd‸] MS; ~ , F1
6 heade,] MS; ~ ‸ F1
9–10 You ... honor.] MS; *one line in*
    F1
11–12 What ... self?] *one line in* F1

22–23 Why ... you?] *prose in* F1
23–25 I have ... nakednesse.] *prose in*
F1
26 boy.——Nakednesse] ~ . ∧ nak-
ednes MS; ~ , ∧ nakednesse F1
28–29 Why ... once.] *prose in* F1
30–31 Honestie ... selves.] *one line in*
F1
37 welcome,] MS; ~——F1
37 where∧] MS; ~ , F1
47–48 That ... it.] *one line in* F1
48–49 O my ... worthinesse?] *one line*
in F1

57 you∧ undishonor'd. How] MS;
~——~——how F1
63–64 Yes ... never.] *one line in* F1
64–65 I have ... first.] *one line in* F1
65 first.] MS; ~ ∧ F1
72 meanes.] MS; ~ ∧ F1
73 Letter;——] ~ ,——MS; ~ ; ∧
F1
75–76 Free ... *Lamira.*] *one line in* F1
75 with,] MS; ~ ∧ F1
76–77 Then ... you;] *one line in* F1
80–81 Report ... Lady.] *one line in* F1
81–82 Sir ... unthankfull.] *prose in* F1
85 oppress'd,] MS; ~ . F1

II.i

II.i] *Actus: Secundj: Scæna: Pri:* MS;
Actus Secundi Scæna Prima. F1
7–8 Whether ... countenance.] *one*
line in F1
7 Master] Mr. MS, F1
12 propound] MS (propounde); pro-
pund F1
13–15 Do ... now.] *prose in* F1
13 old] MS (olde); Old F1
15–16 Wee'l ... men,] *one line in* F1
18 sinners.] ~ ∧ MS; ~ ? F1
18–19 If ... privately.] *one line in* F1
20 I,] MS; ~ ∧ F1

20–21 I, ... witches.] *one line in* F1
21 Thus,] MS; ~ ∧ F1
21–22 Thus, ... revenge] *one line in* F1
23 upon us;] ~ ∧ ~ , MS; ~ ; ~ ∧
F1
26 do?] ~ . MS, F1
27 consideration,] MS; ~ ; F1
27 *Duboyes;*] MS; ~ ∧ F1
29 that?] ~ . MS, F1
30 men∧] MS; ~ . F1
32–33 Let ... thee.] *one line in* F1
39 enemies,] MS; ~ . F1

II.ii

8 Collick,] ~ . MS; ~ ∧ F1
19 *Brest,*] MS; Braste∧ F1
40 things.] MS; ~ , F1
52 that] MS; That F1
54 others;——] ~ ,——MS; ~ ; ∧
F1
63 Citizen,] MS; ~ . F1
68 toss'd] tossd MS; tos'd F1
80 but] MS; But F1
101 prosequte] prosecute MS; prose-
quute F1
102 it.——] ~ ,——MS; ~ . ∧ F1

110 Gentlemen,] gent, MS; ~ ∧ F1
110 estate∧] ~ , MS, F1
114 but] MS; But F1
126 in it;] MS; ~ ~ ∧ F1
132 freedom] freedome MS; fre- | dom
F1
133 Court,] MS; ~ ; F1
138 ∧to ... brest∧] MS; (to ... brest)
F1
156 you,] MS; ~ ∧ F1
162 if∧ ... hadst,] MS; ~ , ... ~ ∧ F1
171 masters,] MS; ~ ∧ F1

178 *Duboies,*] MS; ~ ∧ F1
178–180 *Duboies ... feet.*] *prose in* F1
183–184 What ... Ruffins?] *prose in* F1
186–189 Fear ... expresse it.] *prose in*
    F1
189 inforce,] MS; ~ ∧ F1
191 thee.] MS; ~ , F1
196 sir,——] ~ , ∧ MS, F1
203 say] MS; Say F1
204–208 How ... him.] *prose in* F1

211 *Duboyes.*] MS; ~ ? F1
213–221 Not ... rumour?] *prose in* F1
221 rumour?] ~ . MS, F1
235 and yet] & yet MS; And yet F1
236 and that] & that MS, F1
236 too,] MS; ~ ∧ F1
273 much ∧ lesse] MS; much- | lesse F1
280–282 That ... of,] F1 *lines:* That ...
    taskes; | Nay ... thee: | This ...
    moneys, | Which ... of,

II.iii

2 ∧ Your] MS;——Your F1
3–7 I have ... respect.] *prose in* F1
3 for't.——] ~ . ∧ MS; ~ , ∧ F1
9–11 I know not ... fellow?] *prose in*
    F1
12–33 I think ... garment.] *prose in* F1
39 shaddow.——] ~ . ∧ MS, F1

42–43 What ... Sicophant.] F1 *lines:*
    What ... thee? | Tell ... Sicophant.
44–46 Your own ... Lord.] *prose in* F1
55 Casting ... off,] casting ... off, F1
    (*where the line is indented four spaces
    from the left-hand margin*)
57–58 As well ... end] *one line in* F1

II.iv

15 way?] ~ ∧ MS, F1
18 What,] MS; ~ ∧ F1
21 well——] ~ , MS; ~ ∧ F1
29–32 Why ... pay you.] *prose in* F1
65 waies:——] ~ ; ∧ MS; ~ : ∧ F1
66 peremptory.——] ~ . ∧ MS, F1

72–76 Tis ... all.] *prose in* F1
95–98 Trust ... discharge me.] *prose in*
    F1
126 Sword.] MS; ~ ; F1
138 leg,] ~ . MS; ~ ∧ F1

III.i

III.i] *Actus: 3: Scæna: I:* MS, *Actus
    Tertius. Scæna prima.* F1
2 our] MS (or); ous F1
62 life.——] ~ . ∧ MS, F1
63 Boy!] ~ , MS; *omit* F1
84 practice:] ~ ; MS; ~ , F1
84 heard,] ~ ∧ MS; ~ : F1
96 desert,] MS; ~ ; F1
98 pleased ∧] MS; ~ , F1
103 was)] ~ ∧ MS, F1
105 thought; ∧] ~ , ∧ MS; ~ ;) F1
117 affection:——] MS; ~ : ∧ F1

126–127 He ... pleasure.] *one line in* F1
162–163 Tis ... flesh] *one line in* F1
176 undertake] MS; undetake F1
187 pay,] ~ ∧ MS; ~ ; F1
191 if't] yf't MS; ift F1
193 was,] MS; ~ ; F1
196–199 Good ... still?] *prose in* F1
200–201 Thou ... troublesome!] F1
    lines: Thou ... live | To ...
    troublesome.
200 boy.] MS; ~ , F1
201 troublesome!] ~ , MS; ~ . F1

III.ii

1 it?] ~ ∧ MS; ~ . F1
1–5 As ... performance?] *prose in* F1
2 *Bellerophons*.] ~ ∧ MS; ~ , F1
2 What] what MS, F1
11–12 Good ... conjurations] *one line in* F1
11 Lord,] MS; ~ ∧ F1
12 me∧] MS; ~ , F1
22 Gallowes] MS (gallowes); Gallous F1
24 yours.] MS; ~ , F1
32 brothers∧] MS; brother, F1
34 inherits,] ~ ∧ MS, F1
36–38 language, they ... | *Enter Dubois*. | Stand] language. | *Enter Dubois*. | They ... stand F1
37 barck.——] MS; ~ ; ∧ F1
38 Stand *Dubois*. Look about. All safe?] MS; stand *Dubois* ∧ look about ∧ all safe. F1
39 reverence,] MS; ~ ∧ F1
40–41 Lawrell ... ten thousand ducketts.] *one line in* F1 (*which reads* 'deserve a 100 thanks' *for* 'deserves ten thousand ducketts')
44 Harp,] MS; ~ ∧ F1
49 Porter∧] ~ , MS, F1
51–52 (for ... furies,)] ∧ ~ ... ~ , ∧ MS, F1
51 stringes∧] MS; ~ , F1
54 rescue? Pretious,] ~ . pretious, MS;

~ , I thought F1
60 like. Rescued?] ~ ! rescued? MS; ~ ∧ rescued; F1
60 Slight,] light∧ MS; slight∧ F1
64 it?] ~ . MS; ~ , F1
65 trick.] MS; ~ , F1
65 prison∧] MS; a Prisoner, F1
67 it. What's] ~ . whats MS; ~ , what's F1
67 that,] ~ ∧ MS, F1
70 Fall] fall MS, F1
70 discovered.] MS; ~ ; F1
71 horse, garcon, ha!] MS; ~ ∧ ~ ∧ ~ . F1
72 a house,] MS; ~ ~ ∧ F1
72 his house∧] MS; his presence, F1
73–75 What ... *Orleans*.] *prose in* F1
75 it,] MS; ~ ∧ F1
89 Pamphlet] MS (pamphlet); Phamplet F1
91–92 All ... Church——] *one line in* F1
92 *Draw*] draw MS, F1
95 scholler-ship).] scholership.) MS; scholler-ship)∧ F1
96 Doth] doth MS, F1
96 you? Now∧] ~ . now∧ MS; ~ ∧ now? F1
98 traine;] MS; ~ , F1
105 foe.] MS; ~ , F1
113 comes] MS; Comes F1

III.iii

0.1 Laverdure, La-poop, ... Servant.] ~ ∧ ~ ∧ ... servant. F1
6–8 To give ... Bribes.] *prose in* F1
12 length,] MS; ~ ∧ F1
15 Officers.] MS; ~ ∧ F1
15 You] you MS, F1
30 care∧ whom] MS; care——whom F1
37.2 Charlot] MS; *Charlo* F1

47 me!] ~ . MS; ~ ? F1
60 peascods,] MS; ~ ——F1
62 say.] MS; ~ , F1
75–76 Do ... fellowes?] *one line in* F1
76–80 Alas ... Orchard.] F1 *lines*: Alas ... lawyer, | And ... the | One ... with the | Gentlemen, ... Orchard. (F1 'Orchards.')
79 mirth;——] ~ . ∧ MS; ~ ; ∧ F1

80.1 Lady Orleans, Veramour, Char-
lotte.] *La.Orle.Veram.* | *Charl.* F1
83 dead?] ~ . MS, F1
96–97 This ... *Montagne.*] F1 *lines:*
This ... you, | Know ... *Mon-*
tagne. (F1 '*Montague.*')
134–135 I ... circumspect.] *prose in* F1
143 Merchant——] ~ , MS; ~ . F1
149 Madam,] MS; ~ . F1
153 supper?] ~ . MS; *omit* F1
166 you;] ~ , MS, F1
187 met;] MS; ~ ∧ F1

195 instantly,——] ~ . ∧ MS; ~ , ∧
F1
204 Courtyer——] ~ ∧ MS; ~ . F1
208 Cloaths——] ~ . MS, F1
220 Neopolitans∧] MS; ~ ; F1
220 Bed-fellowes;] ~ , MS, F1
221 twenty] MS; tweenty F1
222 Veramor.] *Vir.* MS; *Veram.* F1
225 well,] MS; ~ ∧ F1
226 These] these MS, F1
226–227 These ... fires.] MS; *prose in*
F1

IV.i

IV.i] *Actus Quartij: Scæna: Prj* MS;
Actus Quartus, Scæna Prima. F1
(*where 'Actus' may be 'Actas'*)
10 I,] MS; ~ ∧ F1
20 vertuous,] MS; ~ ∧ F1
22 marriage,] MS; ~ ∧ F1
22 worth.] ~ ∧ MS; ~——F1
36–37 Would to God ... sir.] *prose in*
F1
60–61 Shall ... weep,] F1 *lines:* Shall
... story | To ... weep,
69–71 Curst ... still.] *prose in* F1
74–75 Indeed ... Cards] *one line in* F1
77 live∧] MS; ~ : F1
78 boyes.] MS; ~ ∧ F1
81–82 By my troth ... you] *one line in*
F1 (*which reads* 'In truth' *for* 'By my
troth)
87 singing,] MS; ~ . F1
97 Gentlewoman:——] ~ . ∧ MS;
~ : ∧ F1
103 boy?] ~ . MS, F1
104 flesh.] MS; ~——F1
105 but] MS; But F1
106 sir?] ~ , MS, F1
121 are!] ~ , MS; ~ ? F1
122 *France*——] ~ . MS, F1
136–138 What ... loves.] F1 *lines:*
What ... goe? | And ... again: |
I'faith ... vows, | and ... loves.

136 him?——] ~ . ∧ MS; ~ ? ∧ F1
137 again:——] *omit* MS; ~ : ∧ F1
143 goe.——] ~ . ∧ MS
144 will,] MS; ~ ; F1
155 *Kneels*] kneels MS, F1
162 me∧] MS; ~ ; F1
167 draughts?] ~ . MS, F1
185.1 *Enter ... riding-rod.*] *printed below*
'call you to't?' (*line* 184) *in* F1
186–187 With ... house?] *prose in* F1
188–189 I pray ... wife.] *prose in* F1
192–193 No ... post.] *prose in* F1
197–198 Ha, ... know you.] *prose in* F1
197 he:——] ~ . ∧ MS; ~ : ∧ F1
214 Mounsier?] ~ ∧ MS; ~ . F1
224–225 And you ... rascals] *prose in* F1
224 foreheads.] ~ , MS, F1
254–255 Should ... die.] *prose in* F1
255–256 *Amiens* engagd; ... joys,] *one*
line in F1
259.2 Montaigne.] *Mont.* MS, F1
261 extreamly.——] ~ . ∧ MS, F1
266 'em.] MS; ~ , F1
268–269 on's, and that ... i'faith.] MS;
o'us. | *Lav.* And that ... i'faith. F1
269.1 *Exeunt ... La-poop.*] MS; *printed*
below 'beating o'us.' (*line* 268) *in* F1
283 long——] ~ ∧ MS; ~ . F1
294 *Povera* ∧] MS; ~ , F1
294 and] & MS; *and* F1

IV.ii

0.1 *Lacqueys*] *Lacqueyes* MS; *Lacques*
    F1
0.2 *with*] MS (wth); *wish* F1
3 anywhere;——] ~ . ‸ MS; ~ ; ‸
    F1
3 spurs;——] ~ . ‸ MS; ~ ; ‸ F1
4–5 Upon a bridge ... quarrell.] F1
    lines: Upon a bridge ... battlement,
    | Ile ... quarrell.
6 Lord?] ~ . MS, F1
7–8 So ... thred.] *prose in* F1
11–13 Except ... us.] *prose in* F1
22 Swords,] MS; ~ . F1
28 you spoke] MS; yov spoke F1
30–31 But ... free me] *one line in* F1
    (*which reads* 'finde,' *for* 'free me ‸')
32 custome. You] ~ , you MS, F1
37–38 Without ... it.] *one line in* F1
39–40 I trust ... affront.] *prose in* F1
41–42 We ... Swords.] *prose in* F1
42–43 My ... selves.] *one line in* F1
43–45 We ... terms.] *prose in* F1
45–46 No, ... calling.] *one line in* F1
47–48 True, ... reason.] *one line in* F1
47 True,] true, MS; True ‸ F1
49 lesse,] MS; ~ : F1
51 me,] MS; ~ ; F1
51 can ‸] MS; ~ , F1
52 requite:——] ~ ‸ ——MS; ~ :
    ‸ F1
53 that?——My Lord] ~ . ‸ my lord
    MS; ~ ‸ ‸ my Lord F1
53 guard,] MS; ~ ? F1
54 are:——] ~ . ‸ MS; ~ : ‸ F1
74–76 You wrong ... Lady.] F1 *lines*:
    You wrong ... the bulke | Of those
    ... no man| Will ... Lady.
77–78 I would ... him?] *prose in* F1
78–79 Kill ... repent,] F1 *lines*: Kill ...
    bad | Language? O repent,
80 motive ‸] ~ , MS, F1
82–83 To strike ... hand.] *prose in* F1
85 Adultresse ... Adulterer] *Adul-*

tresse ... *Adulterer* MS; adultresse
    ... adulterer F1
86–88 Are ... couple?] *prose in* F1
88 couple?] ~ . MS, F1
90–91 I did ... Lord,] *one line in* F1
94–109 Thy malice ... jest or raile]
    prose in F1
104 honour:——] ~ . ‸ MS; ~ : ‸
    F1
114–115 Are ... arme.] F1 *lines*: Are ...
    is of | A ... arme.
124 Heaven!] ~ . MS; *omit* F1
125–126 How? ... boy,——] *one line in*
    F1
126 *Orleance;*——] ~ . ‸ MS; ~ ; ‸
    F1
126 boy,——] ~ , , MS, F1
127 not,——] ~ , ‸ MS, F1
132 innocence——] ~ . MS, F1
133 sake——] ~ ‸ MS; ~ . F1
133–136 To punish ... sacrifice——]
    prose in F1
137–138 *Longaville* ... before.] *prose in*
    F1
139–141 By ... forfeit.] F1 *lines*: By—
    —If thou attempt | His life, thy
    own is forfeit.
141–142 Foolish ... him.] *prose in* F1
147–148 Standst ... made?] *one line in*
    F1
148 made?] F1 (*where the question mark
    has become displaced near the side
    rule at the end of line* 146); ~ ‸ MS
150–155 With the red ... present with
    thee.] F1 *lines*: With the ... stone |
    With horrour ... blacke | Infamy,
    ... looks, | Or ... still: | Thou ...
    guilt. (*For* 'till' F1 *reads* 'still:' (*line*
    154), *and omits* 'That still be present
    with thee' (*line* 155))
158 feele.] MS; ~ ‸ F1
161–162 And more ... pray.] F1 *lines*:
    And more ... stand, | Forgive ...
    pray.

163–164 My Lords ... shot her;] F1
    lines: My Lords ... feare, | Unlesse
    ... shot her;

170 How,] MS; ~ ∧ F1
170 *Byancha*∧] MS; ~ ? F1
178 Ha?] MS; ~ ∧ F1

V.i

V.i] *Actus Quintj: Scæna Prj* MS; *Actus
    Quintus. Scæna prima.* F1
4–5 Which ... off] F1 *lines:* Which
    ... and I | Shall ... off,
6 merry,] MS; ~ ∧ F1
8 then?] ~ . MS, F1
9 no. Worse] MS (~ . worse); ~ ∧
    wors F1
13–14 Keep ... Irish] F1 *lines:* Keep
    ... black | Merling, ... Irish (*where
    for* 'Jack Merlin' F1 *reads* 'black
    Merling')
15–16 Nay ... better.] *one line in* F1
19 course:] ~ , MS, F1
20 coyne;] ~ , MS, F1
23 it,] ~ ∧ MS; ~ ; F1

32 me.] MS; ~ , F1
36–37 I see ... husband] *one line in* F1
41 vertuous;] MS; ~ , F1
45 fortune∧] MS; ~ : F1
53–54 Certaine ... matters:] *one line in*
    F1
61–62 It shall ... merry.] *prose in* F1
65–66 Your ... madly.] *prose in* F1
66–67 Can ... love.] *one line in* F1
71–72 Yes ... more] *one line in* F1
73 mainly.] MS; ~ , F1
82–83 Pardon ... offended,] *one line in*
    F1
90 Five hundred] 500 MS, F1
92–93 If ... hundreds] *one line in* F1

V.ii

11–13 Say ... question.] *prose in* F1
11 feast∧ now,] MS; ~ , ~ ∧ F1
32–33 I ... way.] *one line in* F1
34 question,] MS; ~ ? F1
45–48 Very ... Lady.] *prose in* F1
48–49 'Tis ... fitly] *one line in* F1

52 speciall] MS; spetiall F1
53 lying,] ~ ∧ MS, F1
56–57 Yet ... directly.] *prose in* F1
57–58 Why ... settle] F1 *lines:* Why
    ... men | As ... settle
86 howsoever] MS; howosever F1

V.iii
(*Omitted from* MS)

2, 37 dainty] danty F1
7 conscience?] ~ , F1
10 question.] ~ ? F1
12 Courtier?] ~ . F1

15 Pedlers] *Pedlers* F1
23 Potgun] *Potgun* F1
47 bespoke∧] ~ , F1

V.iv

0.2 Longavile,] ~ ∧ F1
3 change!] ~ . MS; ~ ? F1
5–6 Thus ... Woman] F1 *lines:* Thus
    ... see | You ... Woman

5 do:] ~ . MS; ~ , F1
11 heart.——] ~ . ∧ MS; ~ , ∧ F1
11 Faire] faire MS, F1
11 Lady,] MS; ~ ; F1

12 choyce;——] ~ ; ∧ MS; ~ ∧ ∧
   F1
15–17 Noble ... hour] *prose in* F1
15 Lords,] MS; ~ ∧ F1
21–22 Give ... simple] F1 *lines:* Give
   ... let | That ... simple
22 simple,] MS; ~ ; F1
23 angry;——] ~ . ∧ MS; ~ ; ∧ F1
23 you;——] ~ ,——MS; ~ ; ∧ F1
25–33 Pray ... then.] *prose in* F1
34–35 Sit down man, ... offer.] *prose in*
   F1
37–38 And I ... *Longavile.*] *prose in* F1
37 obey;——] ~ . ∧ MS; ~ ; ∧ F1
37 Lord,——] ~ . ∧ MS; ~ , ∧ F1
39–45 This ... bounty.] *prose in* F1
46–48 By ... Lady.] F1 *lines:* By ...
   and that | Man ... Lady.
48–49 Such ... Lord.] *one line in* F1
   (*which omits* 'off, my Lord')
49–50 At ... lesse.] *one line in* F1
   (*which adds the words* 'my Lord')
49 all!] ~ , MS, F1
52–53 Nor ... Justice.] *one line in* F1
   (*which reads* 'a Judge' *for* 'Justice')
53–59 Now ... directly.] *prose in* F1
65–66 Yes ... ende.] *one line in* F1
   (*which reads* 'to thee' *for* 'at the
   lower ende')
67–71 You ... foole——] *prose in* F1
71 foole——] ~ . MS, F1
80 lace ∧] MS; lace; F1
85 ∧but ... water∧,] (but ...
   water) ∧ F1; *paren. in* MS *encloses
   words* 'Let ... conscience' (*lines*
   84–85)
88 itch] ich MS; *omit* F1
89 Amber.] MS; ~ ∧ F1
92 Spittle. Get] ~ , get MS, F1
93 past] MS; pa'st F1
95 yet,] MS; ~ ; F1
99 heart,] ~ ∧ MS, F1
99 speaks∧] ~ , MS, F1
102 Madam?] ~ . MS, F1
102 Here's] MS (heres); Her's F1

111–112 Or ... ambition?] *one line in* F1
112–113 Do ... choosers.] *one line in* F1
127 hereafter;——] ~ . ∧ MS; ~ ; ∧
   F1
128 Lady.] MS; ~ ; F1
130 Figs, good∧] ~ ∧ ~ ∧ MS; ~
   ∧ ~ , F1
134 devill),] MS; ~) ∧ F1
146–147 Down ... Lady.] *prose in* F1
151–152 Surely ... now.] *one line in* F1
152 you?] ~ ∧ MS; ~ . F1
153–154 Troth ... him.] *one line in* F1
156–159 There ... vertue.] *prose in* F1
159–160 Do ... me?] *one line in* F1
160–161 Yes ... flatter.] *one line in* F1
165–166 My ... made] *one line in* F1
165 Lords,] MS; ~ ∧ F1
169 in't,] MS; now ∧ F1
170 see∧] MS; ~ , F1
172 be!] ~ . MS; ~ ? F1
176–177 Then ... especially.] *prose in*
   F1
176 with,] MS; ~ ∧ F1
181 Lady);] ~) ∧ MS; ~ ;) F1
184–189 Yes ... him.] *prose in* F1
187 obedience,] ~ ∧ MS, F1
190 ye.——] ~ . ∧ MS; ~ , ∧ F1
190 Noble] noble MS, F1
195–198 I'le ... far.] *prose in* F1
195 all.] MS; ~ , F1
199 mine,] MS; ~ ∧ F1
203–204 This ... yee.] *prose in* F1
204–205 As ... more.] *one line in* F1
206–213 Friend ... *Montagne.*] *prose in*
   F1
207 self,] MS; ~ ∧ F1
209 play∧] MS; ~ , F1
209 you,] ~ ∧ MS, F1
211 day, again∧] MS; ~ ∧ ~ , F1
213 Lord] MS; L. F1
215–222 Since ... works.] *prose in* F1
229 'tis] MS (tis); 'Tis F1
230 Lady∧] MS; ~ ? F1
231–232 That ... god-wot] *one line in*
   F1

232 god-wot] F1; god ∧ wot MS
236 her ∧] MS; ~ , F1
238 two or three] MS; 2 or 3. F1
240 it?] ~ ∧ MS, F1

247–248 If ... more.] *one line in* F1
262–263 Trade? ... thee.] *one line in* F1
263–264 Gentlemen ... further] *one line
    in* F1

HISTORICAL COLLATION

[NOTE: The F1 (Folio 1647) copy-text has been collated with MS Dyce 9 (1625) and with the following editions: F2 (Folio 1679), L (*Works*, 1711, intro. Gerard Langbaine), S (*Works*, 1750, ed. Theobald, Seward and Sympson; *The Honest Man's Fortune*, ed. Seward); C (*Works*, 1778, ed. George Colman the Younger), W (*Works*, 1812, ed. Henry Weber), D (*Works*, 1843–6, ed. Alexander Dyce), G (*The Honest Mans Fortune: A Critical Edition of MS Dyce 9*, ed. J. Gerritsen (for the editor's emendations to MS)). Omission of a siglum indicates that the text concerned agrees with the reading of the lemma. Variants concerning the use of *ye/ you* and contracted or uncontracted forms of speech are noted only when they occur between F1 and MS. In the following entries, reference is made to 'original' and 'corrected' readings in MS. When the altered readings appear to be the result of intervention from the scribe or the stage-adapter they are not, in fact, corrections, and so in a number of cases have not been received into the text of this edition.]

I.i

6 Our] your F1–2, L–W
8 But] *omit* F1–2, L–W
23 Encrease] Entreate MS; intreat F1–2, L–W
23 gone] come F1–2, L–W
24 hope or] *omit* MS
25 ye] you MS
26 answer] *omit* F1–2, L–W
31 what I] *omit* F1–2, L–W
36 Farewell] fare you well MS
74 (*Duboys*)] *omit* F1–2, L–W
78 *Duboys.*] *Mont.* MS
84 *2. Lawyer.*] *1 Law.* L
86 Ha'] Have MS
86 so] *omit* F1
99 profits] profitt MS, D
106 That] *omit* MS
110, 123 lose] loose MS
132 his assurance? | *Duboys.* If he dare trust ye.] this assurance, if he—— F1–2, L–W
136 You are] You're F2, L, S
143 and] *omit* F1–2, L–W

143–144 tis as good | To want] tis as good't want F1–2; 'tis as good 'twant L, S; it is as good to want C, W
144 a member, as to loose the use] *the line appears twice in* F2 (*bottom of sig. 3S3v, top of sig. 3S4*)
145 ornament excepted] ornament is excepted F1–2, L–W
148 For] *omit* W
152 among] upon MS
153 They] That F1–2, L–W
157 By my troth my] By——my F1–2, L, S; By my soul, my C, W
179 were] weare MS
186 thoughts into deeds] thoughts into deed F1–2, L–D; thought into deeds MS
194 that] *omit* F1–2, L; who S, C, W
214 Tis a charity] Tis charity F1–2, L–C; It is charity W
222 lively.] lively. | How proceeds my suit? F1–2, L–W

130

222–241 *Longavile. That's with labour
. . . Thy dammage to thee:*] *marked
for omission in* MS
222 labour] leave F2–W
225 An] A F1
225 his] this F1
226 unmercifull] merciful F2, L
232 Yet] It MS
236 seeking my] seeking of my L, S
239 fingers] finger F1
243 councellor] councell F1–2, L–W
258 'had] h'had F2–C; he had W
259 he reacht] he had reach'd W
274 My] for my MS
274 adversary] adversaries F1–2, L–W
275 Pox on him, whosoever]——whosoever F1–2; Whosoever L–W
290 em] him F1–2, L–W
296 Y'ave] ye aue MS; You've L, S, C,
D; You have W
297 your] our F1
298 Lord.] Lord, have an eye upon him.
F1–2; Oh, oh! my Lord,——I
have an Eye upon him. S, C; Oh!
my lord! I have an eye upon him.
W, D
299 ha'] have MS
303 reverse] reserve S
308 *Duboys.*] *Mont.* S, C, W
309 very] *omit* L, S
311 then give] then to give S, C, W
312 *Montaigne. So, tis gone.*] *omit* F1–
2, L–W
315 Y'are] you are MS; You're L, D;
You are S, C, W
316 *Enter two* Creditors.] *Ent: ye credi-*

tors MS (*where just below are added
the names* 'G:Ver:I:Rho:' *(George
Vernon and John Rhodes). See Textual Introduction, p. 8*).
319 him you] you him MS
321 stir] steere F1
323 Ile] I will S, C, W, D
324 casements] casement F2
342 a . . . a] the . . . the F2, L–D
343 They] He F1–2, L–W
346 Theire *Morglayes*] There morglachs F1
346 hands] Heads S
349 *Both Creditors.*] *Both Cred:* MS
(*original reading*); *1. Cred:* MS (*altered by Knight*); *2 Cred.* F1–2; L–D
354 should] shall L, S
356 service, and forget] kindnesse, forget F1–2, L, W; kindnesses, forget
S, C
357 any; (sirs) tis] any service: tis F1–2,
L–W; any. 'Tis D
374 advancements] advancement F1–2,
L–W
379 *Creditors.*] *Cred.* F1
380 your silences] you silences F2
381 discontentment] discontent F1–2,
L–W
381 or of sorrow] or Sorrow S
399 uncharitable] charitable F2, L
402 for I shall] for at least I shall S
416 the comfort that] the comfort it MS;
thy comfort that S; the comfort yet
D (*conj.*)
417 Ill] I'll F2

I.ii

*0.1 *a Servant*] *G: Rick:* MS (*for
'George Rickner'; inserted above a
caret before 'A'. See Textual Introduction, p. 8*).
9 on] one MS
15 God] heaven MS, F2, L–D

19 off] of MS
24 Our] Or F1
26 still] stile F1
29 of whose] he of whose S
30 I am] I'm F2, L
30 thee] three F1

44 dishonour to you] dishonour t' you
S
60 it] that F1–2, L, C, W
63 it] that F1–2, L–D
70 When] omit MS
74 ha] have MS, C, W
81 man——give] man!——God!—
——give C, W; man——death give
MS, D
82 thy Innocence] the Innocent F1–2,
L–D
85 it] that F1–2, L–W
85.1 Exit Amiens in amazement.] Exit
Amiens MS, C, D; Enter Amiens in

amazement, the servants following
him. F1; Exeunt Am: Orl: | Enter
Orleans in amazement, the servants
following him. F2, L, S; Exeunt
Amiens and Servant. W
89 it] that F1–2, L–W
91 that I] it, I F1–2, L–W
96.1 Enter two Servants] 'G: Rick:'
added below s.d. 'Ent: 2: Seruants' in
MS; Enter Servant F1–2, L–W
100 a-dying] now dying F1–2, L–W
100–101 vowe | That] now—— | That
F1; vow—— | That F2, L, S
108 be in] omit F1–2, L–W

I.iii

0.1–2 Enter Amiens ... drawne, meeting Montagne and Veramour.]
Enter Amiens drawne, Montague, |
Vercamor meeting. F1–2; Ent:
Amiens: At one doore: Montaigne:
and | Veramour. At Another: MS
1 Lordship?] Lordship? (they drawe:)
MS
1 God] heaven MS, F2–C, D
3 This] MS (originally), F1–2, L–W;
That MS (corrected), D
3–4 So ... undone.] marked for omission in MS
17 if thou hadst] that thou hast F1
18 hands] and C, W

18 of a base enemie] of base enemie F1;
of base enemies F2, L; of basest
enemies S
38 virgine] Virgins F1–2, L, W
44 edge] hedge MS
51 Our] Or F1
52 yet] that F1–2, L, C; tho' S
61 on that] one that F1–2, L
61 wantes] waiters F1–2, L; tortures S,
C, W
62 they] the F1; these F2, W; those L,
S, C
79–80 if ... witnesse:] omit MS
83 imploye] implore F1–2, L–D
86 that's] omit S

II.i

7 Master] Mr F1–2; mr MS
7 servant] servants F2, L, S
7 gives] give S
14 setters up] fetters-up C
15–27 Wee'l ... consideration,]
marked for omission and crossed out
in MS
17 And set up a male stewes, we should
get] And should not we get F1–2,
L–W

21 I] omit F1–2, L–D
22 all turn] turn all S
24 Come] came MS
25 a token] the token MS
28 Are] is MS
47 Great] Greater F1
48 whiles] whilest MS; while C; whilst
W

II.ii

0.1 La-poope] Captaine Lapoop] MS
1 Hunger] Slander F1–2, L, S, C
1 this] these S, C, W
4 dejected, but hold] dejected, hold S
4 i'thy] into thy S; in thy C
6 so I] yf I MS
8–9 wind-Collick, Captaine] wind collick. MS, D
9 If you be] omit F1–2, L–W
9 tis present] tis a present S; it is present S
11 why man] if you be Captain F1; I'll tell you Sir F2, L–W
16 fault] fate F1–2, L–W
17 nor shall not be the last] nor shall be last S
21 then for blood] than Blood S
23 a miraculous] a most miraculous S
27 sustenance] substenance L
41 yet] & yet MS
43 Tis] this is MS, D; It is C
44–45 and a very ... in a Courtier,] crossed out in MS
46 ha'] have MS, C, W
47 mother, the daughter] mother, daughter S
48 of which] omit MS
49 of them] of em MS
52 upon] on S
53 hope to cheat] hope too to cheat S
55 his Manor] the Manor F1–2, L–W
60 ruine] omit F1–2. L–D
64 designs] design F1–2, L–W
67–68 world, and delivers up himselfe to the] world, delivers himself to th' S
69 ther's] there is MS, S, C, D
70 worthy profitable] worthy as the Profitable S; worthy-profitable D
72 fortunes remaines] Fortune yet remains S
72 hazzard upon] hazard it upon S
73 into] in F1–2, L–W

75 honest] honesty L, S
76 th' one] the one MS, C, W, D
77 How] omit S
79 Key] quay C
79 nor dammage] nor of damage S
80 received] receive F1–2, L–W
85 here is subject for us] here's subject f'r us S; here's subject for us C
87 brown paper, or some] or browne paper, some MS
88 or] omit F1–2, L–W
90 Lamira] Annabella F1–2, L–W
94 monies] money S, C
94 upon] at S
96 so I take] so take S
98 ye] you MS
104 bestow it or] bestow. or F1–2, L–D
106 fortune] fortunes F1–2, L–D
107 band] bond S–D
109 me] it MS
111 ingenuous natures] ingenuous nature F1–2, L, C, W; Ingenious natures MS; most ingenuous nature S
114 not] omit F1
118 endeavour] endeavours L, S
127 an unknowne] one F1–2, L–W
127 certainest] certain F2, L–W
128 incertain] Incertaintye MS; uncertain S, C, W
130 give better] give you better MS
131 wrote] writ MS
138 it were] omit S
140 no way better] no better way S
141 under] at S
142–143 are propounded] you have propounded S
144 meeting, for] meeting then, for S
145 require] requires F1
147 Monsir] omit F1
150 of] off F1
151 the affaire] they affaire F1
153 and] omit MS

133

154 Master] *Monsir* MS
155 *Voices ... weapons.*] *Within a clamor, down with their weapons.* F1–2; *Within: Clashing of weapons: some crying downe | wth theire weapons:* MS
155.1–2 *Enter ... them.*] *then Enter Longauile: | Dubois: their Swords drawne: 3: or: 4: Drawers | betwene em:* MS
157 some] *omit* L, S
162 thou'dst] *omit* F1
165–166 Masters friend] Master, friend F1
172 them ... them] em ... em MS
172 not you] you not F1–2, L–W
174 know my friend] know, friend S
182.1 Amience *in hast, his sword*] *Amiens: | wth Sword* MS
192 my blood, I] my——I F1–2, L, S; my soul C, W
196 after] after him MS
197 some] *omit* MS
201 hand] hands MS
203 *La-poope.*] *Cap.* F1–2, L
209 begun] began MS, D
212 thou] *omit* F2, L, S
213 were] wear F1
223 what's once rumour'd it cannot] what once is rumour'd cannot MS,

D; what's once rumour'd can't S; what's once rumour'd it can't C
224 say] saies MS
229 they] *omit* S
231 Idlye] jolly F1 (catchword, sig. 5T4v), F2, L–D; Jelly F1 (sig. 5V1)
231 gallants] gallant F1
232 desperatly] desperate F1
235 offerd] offers F1–2, L–D
241 *Brutus*] Butchers F1–2, L–D
245 therefore prevented] therefore to be prevented S
251 every] each S
252 and] *omit* S
252–253 the devourer] the great devourer S
254 that] the L, S
257 morrow, good] morrow, or good S
257 God] *omit* F2, L, S
258 very] *omit* F1–2, L–W
258 upon] on S
262 at] of W
263 own] *omit* S
264 here's] he's F1
267 safetye] life F1–2, L–D
272 Wot] Willt MS; Wou't F2, L–D
277–278 be sav'd] merit MS
278 being that it is] seeing't is S
283 main cause] many causes F1

II.iii

5 of] on F1–2, L–D
7 Unworthy] worthy MS
10 now] *omit* MS
13 dares] dare MS
14 noyse whilst] noise, the whilst S
15 try] lay F1–2, L–D
16 Upon] on S
18 Yet by my life with] yet——|with F1–2, L, S; yet, with C, W
19 mere] merry F1; verie F2, L–W
22 could] should MS
23 reasons] reason MS, F2, L

24 yet] *omit* MS
25 Nor] *omit* S
25 remember from] remember, nor from S
33 dunghill] dunghils F1–2, MS, L, S, C, D
33 does] doe F2, L, S, C, D
38 shrunck] struck F1–2, L–W
44 desert, and] desert, sir, and S
46 unto] to S
49 art] *omit* S

II.iv

3 practise mischiefe] practise me mischiefe F1–2, L, C

5 briske] baske MS, D; brisk up S

16 therefore] and therefore S

19 Fough] phue MS

24 busines] sicknesse F1–2, L–D

33 and we will] and will S

34 scape] escape W

34 have wife] have a wife S

37 a] omit MS

39 Faith and mine] 'Faith mine S

40 Hangers] Hanger S, C

40 and your Beaver, shall] and beaver,
shall MS; and your Beaver here,
shall S

41 this with] this Silken one, with F1–
2, L–D

42 and Roses] and your Roses S

43 I have a sufficient] I have sufficient
L; I've sufficient S

46 but] omit F1–2, L–W

49 here's] here are S, C

50 with it] wth't MS

60 then their] than ev'n their S

65 not have been] you had not beene
MS

66 Officers] Officer F1–2, L–W

74 my] omit S

76 left yet] yet left MS

77 pray] omit F1–2, L–D

77–78 with his hopes] with hopes F1–

2, L–D

81 all] omit S

82 free me out of the] free out the F1

87 later] latter F1

101 ye] you MS

102 ye] you F1–2, L–D

102 this] MS originally; the MS (corrected), D

104 wo'd a] wolld have MS; would ha'
C, W, D

106 the] omit F1

106 them] em MS

110 laye] take F1–2, L–W

112 on] omit F1–2, L–W

112 of] omit MS

114 for] omit S

116 a mans] his MS

119 gotten] got S

123 upon] on S

126.2–3 in the scuffling] omit MS

126.3 retire] retires MS

126.3 the Officers] them F1–2, L–W; em
MS

126.3 about] off F1–2, L–W

126.4 The Third Officer falls.] omit F1–
2, MS, L–W

130 Udsprecious] spretious MS

133 he be] he will be S

137 i'm but] I am not MS

138 a dangerous ... shin-bone] omit MS

III.i

0.1 Enter ... Veramour.] Enter
Madam Lamira, Madam le Or-
leans, Veramour. F1–2; Ent: Mad-
dam Lamira: Ladye Orleance: |
And Viramour the Page: MS

23 a] the F1–2, L–D

27 Summer-house] Summer-houses
F1–2, L–W

30 yet] put G

34 Humh! It]——It F1–2, L, S; God!
It C, W

34–50 Humh! It is ... their Lords:]
marked for omission in MS

37 of't] o't F1; on't F2, L–D

37 though] although S

41 Lord is] Lord's F1–2, L

44 that cannot] that you can't S

51 I'm] I am MS

55 ayme] ayms F1–2, L–W
57 waite] waites MS
61 her] their F1–2, L–W
63 Boy] *omit* F1–2, L; Veramor S, C, W
65 on] In MS
65 Spider] Spiders F1
66 yet] that MS
74 from] for F1
77 had] MS *originally*, F1–2, L, C, W, G; having MS *corrected*, S, D
77 tall man] tale- | man F1
78 from] *omit* S
80–87 Doves beget ... Ladies] *marked for omission in* MS
81 Citizens heire, tho left never] Citizen here, tho left never F1–2, L, C; Citizen left ne'er S
81 at the best] at best S
81–82 proves but a griffin Gentleman] MS; proves a Gentleman F1–2, L–D
86 father's] *omit* MS, F1–2, L, S, C
89 Sighes] *Sigh* F1
100 lodging up upon] lodging upon F1–2, L, C, W; lodging on S
102 God] heaven MS, F2, L, S, C, D
103 I should ever] ever I shold MS
107 all] *omit* F1–2, L
112 his] this MS

114 That but your selfe, if you were pleas'd] That if you were but pleas'd F1–2, L, C, W; That unless you yourself were pleas'd S
116 that] *omit* S
118 Lord *Amiens*] lord of *Amience* MS
120 speakes] speake F1
121–123 'Twolld ... receave it.] *omit* F1–2, L–D
126 with] *omit* MS
132 a] I MS
137–143 If you please ... begin good *Viramour*] *marked for omission in* MS (*where 'Ent: Montaigne' has been added in the margin to the left of lines* 135–136 *to fit the cut*)
138 seem unapt] seem to me unapt F1
152 Masters] mr MS
154 oth'] a MS
163 hande] hands F1–2, L–W
168 spild] spoil'd S, C, W
177 feare I] feare that I F1–2, L–W
185 the Bee] a Bee F1–2, L–W
188 that] *omit* F1–2, L–W
188 my full] my once full S, W
189 I] Ile F1–2, L–W
192 entertain me] entertainment F1–2, L
204 eares] ear S, C, W

III.ii

0.1 *Enter ... Paper.*] *Ent: Amience: Longauile: hauing A paper in's hand.* MS
1 live although] liue I will, although MS
4 showerd] showed F1
8 purchase] MS *corrected*, D, G; choice MS *originally*, F2, L–W; *omit* F1
8 with] which F1–2, L, C
12 Let] tell F1

24 what's] what is S, C, W, D, G
30–31 in the Tennis Court] at tennis MS
31 very] *omit* S
32 brothers] brother F1
32 might have] might either have S
34 brought] bought F2, L–D
37 have] *omit* MS
37 barck] boock G
38 All] 's all F2; is all L–W
40 adoration] adorations F1–2, L–W

41 deserves] deserve F1

41 ten thousand ducketts] MS ('10000
    duckets'); a 100 thanks F1; a
    hundred thanks F2, L–D

49 were] was MS, D

49 unexorable] inexorable S, C, W

50 bayle] baite F1–2, L–W

51 too] two F2, L–D

51 makes] make F2, L–D

54 all, a poor] all? Poor S

54–55 Pretious ... lye by it.] omit F1–
    2, L–D

60 Rescued] rescue F2, L

60 Slight] light MS

60 a Crohieture] Crohieture F1; a
    Croiheture MS; Acrocheture F2, L; a
    Crocheteur S–D; a Crocheture G

61 Cardekues] crownes MS

62 tis] it is MS

62 on] one MS

64 proofe] proofs F1, L–W; proof's F2

65 in prison] a Prisoner F1–2, L–W

66 or I] or be I S

69 with] omit S

69.1 Enter Orleans] omit F1–2, L–W

71 Orleans] omit F1–2, L–W

72 his house] his presence F1–2, L–W

83 honor] honors F1–2, L–W

84 hearts-bloud] heart-blood F1–2;
    L–D

90 for] of MS

92.1 after 'pray with.' (line 92) F2, L–
    W print s.d. 'Enter Orleans.' on
    following line. Cf. above, 69.1.

95 he ... his] you ... yor MS, D

100 have me kik't] thrust me downe the
    staires MS

102 all] both MS

103 you] omit F2, L, S

110 circumstance) circumstances L, S

111 fare] far F1

III.iii

0.1 Enter ... Servant.] Enter: Lauer-
    dure: Lapoope: Malycorne: & A
    Seruant: MS

3 woer] wooer MS F2, L—D

7 them] em MS

9–37 Laverdure. Then thou ... La
    poope. The Ladies.] marked for
    omission in MS (where the cut is
    bridged by adding to the end of the
    Servant's speech at line 8 the words
    'but I may spare my labour heeres
    my lady' and by bringing forward the
    s.d. at lines 37.1–2, below, to the
    margin to the right of lines 6–10 thus:
    'Ent: Montaigne: | Lamira: Lady
    Orleance | Charlot: Page:'

13 thence have] them have MS; thence,
    hath F2, L–W; them hath D; them
    has] G

15 Ah] oh MS

20 bookes] shop = bookes MS

20 take] keep L, S

20 accounts] accounte MS

24 we are] wee're MS

28 a spider] omit F1–2, L—W

29 implyes] MS corrected; imployes MS
    originally, F1–2, L; implieth S, C

31 heard no] heard, there's no S

37.1–2 Enter Mountagne ... salute.]
    Ent: Montagne: | bare: Lamyra: |
    Lady Orleance: | Charlot: Viram:
    MS

40 three] omit F1–2, L–W

41 nostrels] nosthrill MS

43 your] our F1–2, L

47 woes] wooes MS, S–D

57 as] is MS

58 their] the F1–2, L–W

59–60 gold, feed] gold, shalt feed S

65 your] you MS; yon G

65 fet] fecht MS; fetcht S

67 promis'd] promise MS

71 theire] there F1
76 these] the F1–2, L–W
78 shee] so she MS
80 Orchard] Orchards F1–2, L—W
80.1 *Exeunt ... Charlotte.*] *Exe: Vir:
     & woemen.* MS
81 Hum, what]——what F1–2, L, S;
     Zounds! C; Pox! W
82 such] MS *corrected*; they MS *orig-
     inally*, F1–2, L–W, G
83 Rose] rise MS
85 lives] liveth S, C
89 have letters ... have the] have had
     letters ... have taken the MS, D
91 of] off F2, L–D
92 tongues] tongue F2, L, S
94 cozenage] cozenages F2, L, S, C
96 This] the MS
96 let] tell F1
97.1 *Enter ... Arras.*] *Lamyra showes |
     hir Selfe at the | Arras:* MS (*in the
     margin to the left of lines* 97–99)
104 with a good] with good F1
115 ye] you MS, F2, L–D
125 Is] *omit* F1–2, L–W
131 Like a Player] I knowe not what MS
131.1 *Lamira comes forward from*] *Ent:
     Lamyra: | from* MS; *Exit Lamira |
     from* F1; *Lamira from* F2, L–W
133 become my] become you my F1–2,
     L, C, W
136 hath] had F1
140 them] those W
153 Did she talke of supper] *omit* F1–2,
     L–D
153 Oh] *omit* S
156–158 *Laverdure.* You shall ... none
     of those.] *marked for omission in* MS
159 But she] *deleted and the words* 'I loue
     a lady' *interlined by the stage reviser*

in MS
159 make distinction] make a distinction
     MS
159 knowes] know D
160 and Fellowes S
165 can] can be done F1–2, C, W, D;
     can do L, S
168 gentlier] gentler F2, L, S
177 if not] *omit* MS
182 miracle] wonder MS
182 from] *omit* S
183 the] this MS
184 circumstance] circumstances S
187 met; not] met and here they are
     together, not S
187 boy is] boy but is F2, L, C
189 their] *omit* S
192 and] *omit* S
193 woe] woo MS; wooe F2, L–D
196 hath much] much hath S
197–198 try if I can search] try to search
     S
207 like] lie F2
209 on] one MS
209 'em] them MS
213 lodging——] lodging
     should——S
214 Should] *omit* S
216 may] my F1
217 meane thou] mean that thou S
219 French Lords] *deleted, and the word*
     'gallants' *interlined above a preceding
     caret in* MS
220 it] *omit* F1
223 for] *omit* MS
226 These women are strange Crea-
     tures] these are standing Creatures
     F1–2, L; these are strange creatures
     S, C, W

IV.i

0.1 *Enter ... habit.*] *Enter Montaigne:
     in meane habit:* MS

4 sute] shute F1
7 gives] gyves MS

8–16 The greatest ... the flame.]
   marked for omission in MS
10 I] Yea S; Ay C, W, D
10 though] thought F2, L
17 my own] myne owne MS
22.1 *with Counters.] omit* MS, F2–D
24 joye] joyd F1–2, L–W
25 Gods] heavens MS, F2, L, S, C
26 fortune] fortunes F1–2, L–W
27–48 Do but begin ... love or duty.]
   marked for omission in MS
30 Give] given MS
36 God ... God] heaven ... heaven
   MS, F2, L, S, C, D
37 w'ee] with you MS
47 vice] due F1–2, L–W
50 I] Sir, I S
53 till] tell MS
54 quit assurd] quit offerd F1–2, L, C,
   W; quit all offer'd S
63 Women] Wormes F1
72–80 Rather curse me ... ere be
   vicious.] *marked for omission in* MS
77 worldly] wordly F1
78–79 boyes. | Since] boyes ∧ | These
   worldly qualities. | Since F1–2,
   L–D
81 By my troth] In truth F1–2, L–D
88 ga't] gave't MS
89 And by my troth it] And——it
   F1–2, L, S; And, by my soul, it C,
   W
94 caskanet] Cabinet F1–2, L–D
95 goodnesse] godnesse F1
96–97 I have lost ... this Gentle-
   woman] O mr. heres a gentlewoman MS
99–107 *Montaigne.* Why boy? ...
   mouth is full.] *marked for omission
   in* MS
106 mouth is] mouthes MS
110 On my] Ah my F1–2, L, C, W; Oh
   my S; O' my D
119 locks] locke MS
129 she] it S

130 pride] skill F1–2, L–D
131 turn foole] turn a foole F1–2, L, C,
   W
133 have earnest] have verie Earnest MS
135 companie] companies MS
136–137 And ile sing to you again] *omit*
   MS
141 buy thee a] buy a F1–2, L–D
144 'faith] i'faith F2, L–W
145 God] heaven MS, F2, L, S, C
147 shall] will F2, L, S
147 woe] wooe MS, F2, L, S, C; woo W,
   D
147 teares] eares F1–2, L–W; yeares MS
158 will] to S
161 In] *omit* MS
161 inheritance] inheritances F1–2, C,
   W
164 could I else tamely] could I tamely
   F1–2, L; else could I tamely W
167 fall] falls MS
168–182 *Charlotte.* This vizard ... last it
   out] *marked for omission in* MS
170 selfe] life F1–2, L–W
178 cheek'd] cheeke, F1, MS
180 runne] ran MS
184 I'faith] By faith MS
185.1 *with a riding-rod] omit* MS
193 Sweet] sweet instantly MS
204 The pox embroyder] The——
   embroyder F1–2, F, L, S
206 The devill on] The——on F1–2,
   L, S; The plague upon C, W
207 Lace, hart I] Lace,——I F1–2, L,
   S; Lace? 'Sdeath, I C, W
210 Death, I could]——I could F1–2,
   L, S, G; I could MS, C; Pox! I could
   W
213 scorne] storm F1–2, L, W
213.1–2 *Enter ... Charlot.] Enter:
   Lamira: Ladye Orleance: Lauer-
   dure: | Lapoop: Malycorne: Charlot:
   Viramour:* MS
214 Your affaire] You're a fair F1–2, L,
   S, C; You are a fair W

219 by my blood] *omit* F1–2, L–W
221 let it not be to] let not be to MS; let it
be not to W
222 A pox a]——a F1–2, L, S
222 *Mallicorne.*] *Mont.* W
222 And a plague of] And——of F1–2,
L, S; and pox of C, W
223 you gallants] your gallants F1–2,
L–W
231 steale your Napkins] steale Napkins
F1–2, L
233 'ware] beware C, W
246 in] from F1–2, L–D
255 Throwe the] through thy F1–2,
L–W
255 die] dice MS
260 Hump] Hum MS
262 land service] Sea-service F1
267 staie the event] stop your intent F1–
2, L; Stop here; your Intent? S, C;
Stop; your intent? W

268 on's] o'us MS
268–269 and that ... i'faith] *assigned to
Laverdine in* F1–2, L–W
270 Never stirre, but you are]——but
you are F1; But you are F2, L;——
You are S; Curse me, but you're C;
Curse me, but you are W
271–272 retire ... cloathes] *marked for
omission in* MS
271 smel like] smell just like S
271 she newly] that's newly F1–2, L–D
275 a pox ... for me] *omit* F1–2, L–D
281 Sweet] my sweet S
282 woe] wooe MS, C; woo L, S, W, D
284 See, see.] So, so! D
286 By gad I think]——I think F1–2,
L;——I thought S; By Heaven, I
think C, W
289 disposure.] MS *corrected*; disposure.
| *Exit.* MS *originally*, F1–2, L–W
291 For] *omit* S

IV.ii

0.1–2 *Enter ... Pistols.*] *Ent: Dubois:
Orleance: Longauile: Amience: .2.
Lacqueyes: A Page wth .2. Pistolls:*
MS
1 Lord] Lords F1–2, L–W
5 Ile] I'de MS
6 O' the] a' the MS
17 The] *omit* MS
18 these] those F1–2, L–W
31 free me] finde F1–2, L–W
40 Meane not to doe] may not doe F1–
2, L, W; may n't do S, C
42 Here with our Swords] here with
swords F1–2, L—W; with our
swords MS
44 Unto] into MS
45 on terms] on any terms S
49 nor looke for't] *omit* F1–2, L—W
52.1 *A noise ... Swords.*] *Wthin: cry; oh
| stay their swords: | stay their
Swords:* MS (*in margin to the left of
lines* 51–53)

54 Some] So S
54 *Enter ... Page.*] *Enter Lady
Orleans, Lamira, Montague.* F1
61 see] se MS; so F1
64 loath'd] both MS
65 Your] That your S
67 have] make F2, L, S
68 this] the MS
71 man] voice MS
72 breathst] bee'st MS
73 Lord] lords MS
74 *Lamira.*] *omit* F2
80 And be] or by MS
80 rather] they will MS
82 there] their F1
83–84 hand. | *Orleans.* O here's] hand.
| *Dub.* Sweet my Lord. | *Orl.* O
here's F1–2, MS (*where* 'Dub.
Sweet my lord' *is marked for omis-
sion*), L–W; hand. | *Dubois.* My
lord! | *Orl.* Oh, here's D
84 champion] champions F1–2, L–W

85 Madame Adultresse your Adul-
     terer] the adultresse with the adul-
     terer F1–2, L–W
86 howling bitch wolfe] howling——
     F1–2, L–W
87 countenance] countenancer F2,
     L–D
88 vertuous] vicious F1–2, L–W
89 didst not thou tell] didst thou not
     tell MS, W, D; didst not tell L, S
89 me, false] me, thou false S
99 evils] devils F1
100 quit] quiet F1–2, L–W
105 me] omit S
105 spake] spoke MS
107 courser] becomes him better F1–2,
     L–W
109 nor time nor] no time nor F1–2, C,
     W; no time or L, S
115 a meaner arme] to meane an arme
     MS
115 Duboys. Yes . . . none.] marked for
     omission in MS
120 gainst] against F1–2, L
124 Heaven] omit F1–2, L–W
125 them] em MS
127–128 by that . . . I will kill thee]
     by—— | I will kill him F1–2, L, S;
     by Heavens, I will kill him C; by
     Heaven, I will kill him W
134 honours] honour F1–2, W
136 I sweare] Ile sweare F1–2, L, S
139–140 By my soule, | And what it
     hopes for, if] By——If F1–2, L, S;

by Heaven, if C, W
142 God] heaven MS, F2, L, S, C, D
144 fates,——before my God] fates.—
     —F1–2, L–W
145–145.1 matter. | Shoots.] matter,
     shoot. F1–2 (where the s.d. 'Shoots'
     is printed as 'shoot' at the end of
     Longueville's speech)
146 Amiens. Biancha?] Lamy: Biancha:
     MS
154 till] still F1–2, L; tell MS
155 That still be present with thee] omit
     F1–2, L–W
158 come] comes MS
159 If . . . sustaine] the line in MS begins
     with the words 'the burden of his'
     which have been deleted
160 Of] With F1–2, L, C, W
163 Lady's] ladyes MS; Lady is F1–2, L,
     S, W
164 for her feare] for feare F1–2, L–W
165 on't] on it G; of it S, C, W
169 I am] I'm F2, L, S, C
170–171 Lamira. How . . . breath?]
     Lam. How is Biancha? well? Lives
     she? See. | Ami. Sister——she
     doth breathe. S
171 Montaigne. Not hurt.] omit F1–2,
     L–W
172 O Gentlemen] omit MS
180 thee Heaven] the Heavens F1–2,
     L–W
192 I will be she]——she F1–2, L, S;
     She hath C, W

<h2 style="text-align:center">V.i</h2>

0.1 Enter . . . Charlote.] Enter: Mon-
     taigne: and Charlote MS
2 own me then] own then F1–2, L–W
5 knock my shooes off] knock off my
     shoes S
6 are merry] are a merry F1–2, L–W
7 thy love to me] my love to ye MS
13 Jack Merlin] black Merling F1; Jack
     Merling F2, L, S

15 the] then F1–2, L–W
22 gleane] leave F1–2, L, S; save C, W
23 on't] it F1–2, L–W
24 Seeke] I seeke MS
25 Showre] Share F1–2, L–D
25 they] they'l F1–2, L–W
29 my] the MS
30 though] thought MS
42 That relies] That but relies S

47 nor] or MS
51 D'ee] doe you MS; D'ye F2, L, S,
   C, D; Do ye W
59 God] heaven MS, F2, L, S, C
60 But by my troth my] But——my
   F1–2, L, S; But, by my soul, my C,
   W
63 pretty] omit MS

70 By my troth madam, ever]——
   Ever F1–2; Ever L, S; E'er C; By
   Heaven, ever W
81 a'] a MS; at F1–2, L–W; o' D
90 Five hundred] 500 F1
93 many hundreds] many a hundreds
   MS

V.ii

0.1 Enter ... Malycorne.] Ent:
    Lauerdure: Lapoope: and Maly-
    =corne MS
11 should] omit MS
15 We told] We have told S
15 this seven] these ten F1–2, L–D
19 Gentlewoman] gent MS
23 Gentlemen] gent MS
23 by my faith] by——F1–2, L, S; by
   my soul C, W
25 if a eate] yf hee eate MS; if he beat C
26 Such crab-sauce] Such a crab-sauce
   F2, L
30 mince] MS corrected; mint F1; mynt
   MS originally
34 rests] rest S

34 o'th] a'th MS
46 we scape] we all scape F1–2, L, C,
   W
57 Why] Who L
58 some times] sometime MS
59 broth] broth'd F1–2, L–W
72 God] the Fates MS; Heaven F2, L,
   S, C, D
72 am here.] am here, too. MS
76 lamming] lamings MS
77 whipping] whippings MS
83 La-poope.] omit F1–2, L–W
84–85 Mallicorne. Captaine ... sirs]
   marked for omission in MS
86 And howsoever] Lauer: and how so
   ever MS, D

V.iii

0.1–50.1 Enter ... Exeunt.] omit MS
2, 37 dainty] danty F1
10 without question] without all

question S
46 Beaker] Baker L
47 a Posset] a | a Posset F1

V.iv

0.1–3 Enter ... La-Poope.] A Ban-
   quet: Set out: then Enter: Orleance: |
   & his Ladye: Arme in Arme:
   Amience: Lamira: | Charlott drest as
   A Bride: Montaigne: Ve[r]ie braue.
   | Longauile: Dubois: Lauerdure:
   Malycorne: | Lapoop: & Atten-
   dants; MS
1 Seate] Stur F1

1 Gentlemen] gent MS
17 yet] that MS, F1–2, L–D
18 to knit] shall be F1–2, L—D
20 Y'ave] ye haue MS
24 Gentleman] gent MS
24 to] too MS
29 too] two L–D
29 tyes] reasons F1–2, L–D
34 Amiens.] Lami: MS

44 wish you.] wish.——F1–2, L
46 him] me W
46 Wine] Vine F1
46 By heaven] I sweare MS
49 washes off, my Lord.] washes of my lord. MS; washes. F1–2, L, W; wishes S, C
50 lesse.] lesse,——MS; lesse my Lord F1–2, L–W
51 are like] are all like F2, L, S
51 on't] of it S, C, W
53 Justice] a Judge F1–2, L–D
54 kinde a] kinde of MS, F2, L–W; kind o' D
59 Fit] fiting MS
63 Here's to] heere, to MS
63 and *Montagne* have a care.] and——| *Lam.* Montague, have a care. S, C
66 at the lower ende] to thee F1–2, L–W
67 *La-poope.* Now for a Psalme of mercy.] *deleted in* MS
71 Oh sir] Good, oh sir F1–2, L–D
75 Ladye] Ladies F1–2, L–W
81 with his wife] which is worse F1
84 the t'other] the other C, W
86 o'th] ath MS; o'the S, D
88 To kill the noysomnesse of itch, thy]————thy F1–2, L–W
93 thy] the F2, L, S
98 Pray God] *deleted and replaced with the words* 'I wish' *in* MS; Pray Heaven F2, L, S, C, D
99 *Orleans.* Beshrow … dealing.] *omit* MS
102 May] Nay F1
102 Here's] Her's F1
105 fed] feede MS
113 not be] be no MS
123 so] *omit* F1–2, L–D
124 puefellow] pure fellow F1–2, L–W
125 Eele skins] Catskins F1–2, L–D
131 And halfe a pinte of olives,] *omit* F1–2, L–W

131 and a] Or a F1–2, L–D
138 One] A F1–2, L–W
141 God] Hell F2, L–D
141 Dunkirks] Dunkirk F2, L–D
143 mouldy] walkinge MS
147 On] a Ms; Upon S, C, W
151 to marrie] of Marriage F1–2, L–D
151 ha'] haue MS
153–154 *Laverdur.* Troth … from him.] *marked for omission in* MS
154 God] Heaven F2, L–D
156 point for] point out for F1–2, L–W
158 worth] worthy F1–2, L–W
159 dowers of vertue.] dowries of—— F1–2, L–W
162 will] would F1–2, L–W
163 think] thank F1–2, L–W
169 in't] now F1, S, C, W, D; new F2, L
172 We be] MS *originally*, F1–2, L–W; all laydy MS *altered by stage reviser*, D
173 shall] should MS
175 Oh] Why F1–2, L–W
180 I ever can] ever I can S
182 then] them S
184 you love] you then love S
184 lady] *omit* F1–2, L–W
185 And] I F1–2, L–W
194 this great] this this great MS
196 wooed ye] wooed you F1–2, L–D
196 for her wonne ye] *omit* F1–2, L–W
200 God] *omit* MS, F2, L–D
200 ye] you F1–2, L–D
203, 242 Gentleman] gent MS
203 hope] hop F1
206 ye have] you have MS, W, D; you've C
208 land] landes MS (*conj.*)
210 and entirenesse] As with entireness S, C
213 Lord] L. F1–2
218 detaine] MS *corrected*, F1–2, L–D; detainde MS *originally*
224 one] on F1
225 Right courtier] *omit* MS; A right

Courtier F2, L–D
225 still a begging] still begging S
227.1 *Exit* Laverdure] *omit* F1–2
228 he] ye MS
228.1 *Enter . . . a Woman.*] *Ent: Lauer-
    dure: & Viram:* | *as A woeman:* MS
229 This, 'tis] 'Tis F1–2; L–W
231 have] hath MS
231 you] *omit* MS
232 wot] MS *originally*, F1–2, L–D;
    sooth MS *corrected*

234 Yes, yes, tis] yes, tis MS
239 Concernd me.] concearnd me
    madame I tooke that habit, MS
243 perswasion] perswasions MS
246 then] *omit* F1–2, L–W
256 foolishest] foolish L, S
266 I am] Sirs, I am S
267 Gives] Giveth S, D
270 By thy example of true] by th'
    Example of thy true S
272 thy] their S

ROLLO, DUKE OF NORMANDY

edited by

GEORGE WALTON WILLIAMS

TEXTUAL INTRODUCTION

The first record of *The Tragedy of Rollo, Duke of Normandy, or The Bloody Brother* (Greg, *Bibliography*, no. 565) occurs in lists of plays given before the royal household; *Rollo* was presented at Court on 7 November 1630, on 21 February 1631 and again on 17 January 1637.[1] The play was entered for publication in the Stationers' Register on 4 October 1639 for John Crooke and Richard Sergier; it appeared in two substantive and independent quartos in 1639 and 1640, the first in consequence of this entry.

The first edition of the play was printed in London by 'R. Bishop, for Thomas Allott and John Crook ... to be sold in Pauls Churchyard'. The printer's copy was a scribal transcript, with 'literary improvements'. The second edition was printed in Oxford by Leonard Lichfield, '*Printer to the University*'. Lichfield would seem to have secured his copy from the King's Men themselves while they were playing for the King at Oxford.[2] The third edition, printed in the Second Folio (1679), was set up from the first quarto; from the Folio was printed a third quarto in 1686. A fourth quarto, printed for Tonson in 1718, reprints his edition of 1711.[3]

Critical understanding of the transmission of the 'received text' of *Rollo* has had a curious history. A direct line of derivation in fact extends from Q1 to F2 and to the eighteenth-century editors. These editors, however, were unaware of the existence of Q1, and they believed that Q2 had been the first edition. Seward wrote: 'the old quarto of 1640 [is] the first edition of this Play' (p. 83); Colman, similarly, termed Q2 'the first copy we meet with' (p. 83). Their editions, therefore, were based on the assumption that the text had been transmitted from Q2 to F2. By 1812, the first quarto had been discovered, and Weber's and Dyce's editions were edited with a clear understanding of the presence of two substantive quartos. Jump's edition (1948), however, was the first to have been 'based upon [the text] of the second quarto';[4] the present edition is the second.

Weber explains the variation between the two texts: 'both copies were printed from manuscripts copied by ... [different] transcribers,

and we have reason to be glad [?] that ... [the two printed copies] did
not use both one manuscript, and that the second [quarto] did not copy
from the first'. Weber's analysis of the transmission would seem in the
main to have been correct. The manuscript behind Q1 was 'of a ...
"literary" type ... the work of a scribe who took it upon himself to
edit the text', modernizing certain Massingerian idioms and spellings,
and 'almost invariably [altering] the Fletcherian *ye* to *you*'; his work is
marked by 'strict logicality and his rather elementary notion of regular
metre'.[5] The manuscript behind Q2 would appear, on the basis of
three theatrical directions, to have been either 'a prompt-book or a
manuscript in the direct line of descent from a prompt-book'.[6]

That the two substantive quartos derive from a single common
ancestor not far removed is supported by the presence of what most
editors consider as shared and common errors, such as these:

	Qq	Editors
III.i.18	provok'd	provoke
29	[*half-line omit*]	herself too deere
IV.ii.177	*Almuter*	Almuten
195	partly	partile
204	*Algell*	Algoll
207	*Hyley*	Hyleg
IV.iii.75	affaire	affaires
V.i.21	talke	taske

The present edition would offer these additions to this list:

II.ii.66	shoote	shooe	(*this edition*)
IV.i.97	those	these	(*this edition*)
V.ii.12	roving	roring	(Dyce *conj.*)

There are other cruxes (in both quartos) involving repetition of words
that might seem to be common errors but about which there is no
critical agreement:

II.i.91 + 1, 98 + 1	A crowne ... | A crowne ...
II.ii.40	drawne ... draw ...
III.i.66–7	justice ... | ... justice
V.ii.194–5	place ... | ... place

In thirty-one of some thirty-two entry- and exit-directions, comparable in Q2 and Q1, the sequence of characters entering or leaving is

identical in both quartos, regardless of the order in which the characters speak. The single exception tests the rule:

III.i.306.1   Q2 *Exit Baldwin with the Guard.* (E4)
               Q1 *Exit Guard, Count Bald.* (F3)

The identity in sequence is most remarkable in directions where a comparatively large number of characters enters. For example: at I.i.147, Q2 lists seven characters followed by those three already on stage – Q1 lists the seven in the same order;[7] at II.ii.0.1–2, Q2 lists four characters with two stage-properties – Q1 lists the four and the props and prints them with the same line-division as in Q2; at II.iii.7.1–2, Q2 lists eleven characters (counting '*attendants*' as two) – Q1 lists the eleven in the same sequence. (Q1 includes at the end of the list '*Edith*', a character not needed in the scene.) This parity suggests strongly that the printed quartos are close to the common manuscript ancestor.

The nature of the manuscript behind Q1 may be guessed in part by the differences between Q1 and Q2. The substantive variants sampled below are evidently introduced by the scribe of that manuscript. Though it is not always absolutely demonstrable that either quarto is right or wrong, the assumption is that the Q1 readings are sophistications, intrusions by a non-authorial agent, and that the Q2 readings are closer to the authors' holograph. Some variants seem to be attempts to improve grammatical forms perceived as inelegancies or crudities:

	Q2	Q1
I.i.149	who	whome [!]
259, 261	Are	Be
II.ii.3	a	of
141	drawd	drawne
IV.i.19, 138	gin	begin

('Whome' is a super-sophisticated 'correction'; 'who' is grammatically correct.) One such change is of a religious nature, avoiding presumed blasphemy:

II.ii.115   good god   gods

Some of the variants are literary changes which seem to have been made because the scribe thought to improve the play:

I.i.42	eldest	Elder
I.i.103	roots	weeds
II.ii.22	*Arion* on	*Arion* like
67	Dad	Lad
77	daies	nights
iii.115	*Ilion*	*Illium*
IV.i.213	stooles	tooles
V.ii.208	twenty	ten

The scribe of the manuscript behind Q1, with the prompt-book before him and charged with preparing a 'literary' copy, saw it as his duty to remove extraneous or theatrical items. So he imposed a correct English scene division on his text (deleting all the classical divisions of Act I and adjusting the style of entry-directions to the English form, the standard of Acts II–V, twice adding '*to them*' to his directions), and he changed two theatrical directions '*Exit Lator.*' and '*Exeunt Juglers.*' (V.ii.210.1, 225) to phrases indicating his interest in the sense of the dramatic moment as a reader would like to visualize it: '*He is led out.*', '*They are lead* [sic] *out.*' (V.ii.198, 212). He omitted one descriptive direction found in Q2: '*He disarms him.*' (III.i.181),[8] and he included three directions not in Q2 ('*To Norbret.*' IV.ii.72; '*Exit.*' IV.ii.81; '*Exeunt.*' V.ii.107) (these four may reasonably be regarded as oversights). The scribe treated three directions that might seem to be specifically characteristic of the prompt-book in three different ways:

III.i.0.1	Q2	*A Stoole set out.* (D3)
	Q1	[*omitted*]
V.ii.0.1	Q2	*Enter Edith and a boy.* | *A banquet set out.* (I2)
	Q1	*Enter Edith, a Boy, and a Banquet set out.* (H4)
V.ii.135	Q2	*Sophia, Matilda, Aubrey,* | *and Lords at the doore.* (I4)
	Q1	*within.* (I2v)

These variants suggest the 'literary' attitude of Q1, which regarded the theatrical necessity of a stool as of no concern to a reader, and the presence of half-a-dozen actors '*at the doore*', fully satisfied by '*within*'.

As has been suggested, the second quarto derives from 'a prompt-book or a manuscript in the direct line of descent from a prompt-book'. The book-keeper's directions, noted just above, strongly indicate a prompt origin. By virtue of the presence of these directions and of the prominence of the Fletcherian *ye*, it is assumed that the manuscript behind Q2, if not the prompt-book itself, was a close transcript that preserved aspects of the prompt-book more authentic in substantives and in accidentals than did the manuscript behind Q1, which was prepared, as the evidence reveals, to satisfy certain perceived literary requirements. Though printing directly from the prompt-book is certainly unusual in the conditions of the London trade, it is conceivable that in Oxford the players might have been willing to send their unique copy to the printer, who was, after all, 'Printer to the University', and in this particular venture may have thought of himself as enjoying royal patronage. Still, the presence of the 'classical' scene divisions in Act I of the printed quarto (Q2) remains puzzling. If such divisions stood in the author's foul papers, there is no reason – beyond simple scribal fidelity to copy (not automatically to be expected here) – why they should have been copied into the prompt-book. But Act I is the only act which observes the *liaison de scènes* and in which such division might have seemed appropriate, since that division might represent a specific author's deliberate attempt to create a particular effect – possibly copying a French custom for a play set in France. If they were added in a transcript intervening between the prompt-book and the quarto (Q2), one must wonder why the transcriber abandoned his plan after Act I, since he could scarcely have expected Acts II to V to exhibit a form of scene division different from that of Act I.

At all events, there is evidence that a non-authorial agent has intervened between the prompt-book and Q1 and there is no unequivocal or compelling evidence that any such agent has intervened between the prompt-book and Q2. In consequence, the second quarto is chosen as the copy-text of this edition.

The composition of the second quarto was shared by Compositor *P* and Compositor *Q*, their work being most readily distinguished by the habits of spacing after medial punctuation. An analysis of this single characteristic divides the stints;[9] in addition, normally Compositor *P* prefers the speech-prefixes '*Roll.*' and '*Lator.*', and Compositor *Q* '*Rollo.*' and '*Lat.*'. On pages E2v and E3 both forms appear in alternation, as both compositors are at work at this point of change-over.

P: A4–4vB1–2v   C3–4vD1–2v   E(2v)3–4v
Q: A2–3v   B3–4vC1–2v   D3–4vE1–2v(3)
P: F3–4v   G3–4v   H3–4vI1–2v   K1–2
Q: F1–2v   G1–2v   H1–2v   I3–4v

The scheme reveals that – normally – one compositor set four consecutive pages of a sheet while his fellow set the other four.[10] In sheets B and C, C and D, D and E, H and I, each compositor's stint consisted of eight consecutive pages – i.e., B3–4vC1–2v. For the twenty-four pages from E3 to H1v, the alternation proceeded by four-page units.[11] Shortages of italic sorts of 'R' suggest *seriatim* setting and reveal that for pages E2v and E3 the two compositors were working alternately from the same cases.

The quarto is printed with two-skeletons, alternating regularly. The running-titles are '*The Tragœdy of* Rollo' (verso) and '*Duke of Normandy*.' (recto). The skeletons are interchanged between sheets D and E, between sheets F and G, and again between sheets G and H:

Skeleton A works the outer formes of sheets B, C, D, G and the inner formes of sheets
    E, F, H, I;
Skeleton B works the inner formes of sheets B, C, D, G and the outer formes of sheets
    E, F, H. I.

In shifting from sheet D to sheet E, skeleton A is turned. The heading for A2v spells the word '*Tragœdy*'; it is reset for B2v to the uniform standard spelling of the title and of the other running-titles. The headings for A3v and A4v reappear in equivalent positions in B, a new heading being devised for B1v. The heading for A4 reappears in B4; the heading for A3 may have been realigned for B3. From the disposition of heads in sheet K, it would appear that that sheet was set by half-sheet imposition.

The act and scene divisions of the second quarto are strange. In Act I the scenes are numbered after the classical manner (1 to 6), a new scene beginning with each important entry (the stage is never clear); in Acts II–V, the scenes are numbered after the English manner, though the system is defective in each act: there are no headings for the act or first scene in Act II, no headings for the second scenes in Acts III and V, no heading for the third scene in Act IV. In this edition, to conform to the style of this series, the English style has been imposed on Act I, and the directions omitted from the other acts have been supplied after the same system. The spelling for the scenes is 'Scena' except at I.vi.0.1 where it is 'Scæna' and II.ii.0.1 where it is 'Scœna'.[12] As these aberrant settings are the work of, respectively, Compositors *P* and *Q* – who also regularly set the normal form – the two headings would seem to have derived from the manuscript. The act headings are printed from two settings of type left standing, the 'short' form (4.4 cm.) appearing at the head of Acts I, III, IV, the 'long' form (4.8 cm.) at Act V (Act II lacks a heading). The same headings were used in the printing of the companion piece, *Rule a Wife and Have a Wife*.[13] The word 'Scene' in headings for I.iii, II.iii, and IV.ii (A3v, D1, G3: all the work of Compositor *P*) may also have been standing.

An unusual feature of the second quarto is the form of exit-direction stipulating exceptions, *Exeunt omnes præter* ... Such forms of the Latin preposition appear at I.i.100.1, 396; III.i.385.1–2; IV.i.148 (A3v, B4, F1, G1v).[14] As these directions occur in the presumed shares of three different authors, they may derive from a non-authorial source or, more likely, from the work of a single author retouching the whole piece – from any one of the authors who might here be exhibiting a classical predilection.

The names of the characters present a few minor difficulties – Gisbert is 'Gilbert' once (I.i.104.1); Hamond is 'Hamon' once (II.iii.7.31); Grandpree and Russee appear both once each with a single final '-e' (I.i.390.2, IV.ii.0.1). In 'The Names of the Actors', Baldwin is 'Balwin', Trevile is 'Trevite', Duprete is 'Du Prette'; Pipeau is 'Pipeane', and La Fiske is 'La-Fiske'. (The error for Pipeau – the French word for 'bird call' (IV.ii.42) – is clearly caused by a '*n/v*' misreading, with a final '-e' for elegance). The only problematic name is De Bube, 'De Bubie' in the 'Names'. Of the four uses of this name in the text (IV.ii.0.1, 59, 85, 97.1) three spell the name as two words (line 59 is the exception), three spell the first syllable 'De' (line 85 is the exception, 'La Bube' – contaminated from 'La Fiske' in the line above), two do and two do not capitalize the second syllable. The name is here standardized to 'De Bube'. Though its listing in the 'Names' would require a trisyllable, the pronunciation of the name would appear to be disyllabic (IV.ii.59, 85) and 'Bube' must therefore be the preferred form, a form that would suggest the parallel with the name of Captain Bubb, the supposed original of this figure. Russee would also appear to be disyllabic (IV.i.199, ii.84), though it is spelled once in a direction 'Russe' (IV.ii.0.1), the spelling of the name of one of the supposed originals of this figure.[15] (See below.)

For the 'Names of the Actors', Q1 in 'Drammatis personæ' gives these notes: Rollo, Otto – 'Brothers, Dukes of *Normandy*; Aubrey – 'their kinsman'; Gisbert – 'the Chancellour'; Baldwin – 'the Princes Tutour'; Grandpree, Verdun – 'Captaines, of *Rollo's* faction'; Trevile, Duprete – Captaines, of *Otto's* faction'; Latorch – '*Rollo's* Earewig'; the Astrologers – 'Five cheating Rogues'. In the copy of Q2 in the Perkins Library at Duke University, an early italic hand describes Latorch as 'an infamous wretch'. The cast-list of 1686 in Q3 assigns Rollo to 'Mr Kynnaston' and Pipeau to 'Miss Cockye, the little Girl'.

The second quarto would seem to exhibit an unusual number of errors, presumably compositorial, resulting from anticipation or recollection. A sample of these instances (an asterisk indicates that the crux is discussed in the Textual Notes):

Anticipations (?)

	Q2	Q1 and Editors
III.i.74	By ... by	Be ... by
115–16	or ... | Or *	and ... | Or
IV.i.218–9	that ... that	of ... that
V.ii.174–5	presently ... presently	[*omit*] ... presently
(?) III.i.143–4	both ... breath	too ... breath

Recollections (?)

I.i.163–4	then when ... | Wer't then	... | Wert thou
III.i.111–12	bloud | To bloudy	... | To colour
149	left ... heaven 'sleft halfe	... heaven's halfe (*this edn*)
ii.17–18	sheep ... sheep	... chip
IV.i.147	so ... so	so ... [*omit*]
IV.iii.80	endlesse ... worthlesse	... worthy

Reversal (?)

III.ii.86	*chipt ... clipt**	*clipt ... chipt*

Single letter transfers (?)

I.i.302	turnes treasons *	turne ...
III.i.254	perswasions ... brothers treasons *	persuasion ...
373	oblivions ... sences	oblivion ...
IV.i.108	sleight clauses	... causes
ii.222	Persons brings *	Person brings (*this edn.*)
		Persons bring (Q1)

The edition emends four readings on the basis of the supposed desire of the compositor (Compositor Q in each instance) to avoid turning over the end of his line, or to keep his matter within his short stick:

	Q2	Q1 and Editors
II.i.54	him*	his peace
III.i.10	affection *	affections
329	high	highest
IV.i.193	Highnes	Highnesse

Another instance, less compelling (Compositor P):

	Q2	Q1 and Editors
I.i.180	lawe	laws (lawes [this edn])

Here, it may be argued, the compositor, misunderstanding the sentence structure and having space for only four letters, chose to change MS 'lawes' (cf. line 190) to 'lawe' rather than to 'laws'; but the plural is clearly necessary as the pronoun in the next line demonstrates.

The treatment of possessive pronouns 'my/mine', 'thy/thine' before vowels or aspirants is curious. Massinger writes 'my owne' in I.i.202, 310, and perhaps 'my innocence' in V.i.106 (all of these pronouns are 'mine' in Q1); the other authors seem to prefer 'mine' and 'thine' in comparable phrases (many of which are represented in Q1 by 'my' and 'thy'). No significant pattern in the varying practices appears.[16]

Jump has argued that the play was written about 1625, possibly completed after Fletcher's death, Fletcher's contributions being in his 'latest style'. On the other hand, Bertha Hensman has proposed for the date of composition the summer of 1617 or not long thereafter, drawing parallels between the comic sections and events of the day of topical interest. Particularly, in I.i, the threats of the braggart knights might suggest the speech of James I against duelling and his creation of many new knights in 1617; in II.ii, the Cook's recipes for exotic and poisonous foods would seem to allude to the Great Powder Poison Trial of 1615–16 that determined the guilt of some of those implicated in the death of Sir Thomas Overbury; in IV.ii, the names of the astrologers are weak disguises for the names of Fisk, Bretnor and Bubb, notorious necromancers and fortune-tellers much in the public eye in 1616–18. She argues also for a major revision by Massinger about 1630, basing her argument for that date on the age of the actor John Lowin (Aubrey). Finally, Drs John Jowett and Gary Taylor, finding no evidence for such a late revision, have adopted as important dating evidence the chronicle of André Du Chesne published in 1619, which Hensman had already advanced as a source for the play, thus placing the final writing of the piece in 1619 or in 1620. They support a date of composition of 1617–20, admitting 'some degree of revision or adaptation', probably before the performances in 1630 and 1631.[17]

The main plot of the play, based, strangely enough, on Roman history, derives from the accounts of the brothers Antoninus Bassianus (Rollo), better known as 'Caracalla' (the older son), and Geta (Otto) (the younger son), available to the author(s) in Innocent Gentillet, *Discours sur les moyens de bien gouverner ... Contre Machiavel*, translated into English by Simon Patericke as *A Discours upon the Meanes of Wel Governing a Kingdome ... Against N. Machiavell*, and published in London in 1602. The germ of the play must lie in the immediate relationships of these brothers and their parents, explicitly recorded from classical history. The father, L. Septimius Severus Augustus, on his death (in York in 211 AD), fearing the ferocity of his older son, appointed his younger son joint heir. That politic device merely exacerbated the fury of Caracalla who, after several attempts, all frustrated by the vigilance of Geta, succeeded in murdering his brother, just one year after their father's death. Feigning a desire for reconciliation, Caracalla contrived a meeting in his mother's rooms where he and Geta should exchange forgiveness; the meeting was, however, an ambush where Caracalla and his flatterers (his 'Marmosets') murdered Geta even 'betwixt his mothers armes, who was all bloody with the blood of her sonne'; she was then forced to approve the deed in order to avoid the like fate herself.[18] This episode, exactly represented in III.i, must constitute the earliest conception of the play and provide its sanguinary title, 'The Bloody Brother'. To this stage of composition must then be added the writing of a subplot of topical references, of interest in 1615–16, II.ii and III.ii (the suborning of the kitchen staff and their execution) and II.iii (the conciliatory banquet). It might seem appropriate to include at this stage also IV.ii (the fortune-tellers) and I.i. (the reference to the profusion of knights). Perhaps some uneasiness was sensed in the imposing of these 'renaissance' concepts on a classical tale, and the authors transferred the events of that classical account to a 'pseudo-historical' setting in medieval Normandy, the background for which, as Hensman has noted, they took from Sebastian Munster's *Cosmographie Universelle* (1575). The figure for Caracalla would be Rollo, the first Duke of Normandy (an ancestor of William the Conqueror). But Rollo, the record of whose life 'n'est connue que par des sources tardives, normandes, puis scandinaves', had traditionally been regarded as an admirable hero; J. P. Collier calls attention to a ballad, printed in 1617–18, which speaks of 'brave Rollo'.[19] The figure of a bloodthirsty Rollo, however, probably derives from the compilation by André Du Chesne, *Historiae Normannorum Scriptores antiqui* (Paris: R. Fouet, 1619), specifically the section 'Gesta Normannorum in Francia Ante Rollorem Ducem', where Rollo is depicted as 'tyrannus', 'perfidus', '*Christi ... crudelissimus persecutor*'.[20] Since Hensman and Jowett and Taylor report that no earlier (and, indeed, no other) accounts of a tyrannous Rollo have been found,[21] the play in its present form must postdate the publication of the Du Chesne chronicle; but as such a date – post-1619 – would seem to be too late to capitalize fully on the topical events of 1615–17, we must suppose that the play was several years in preparation. Unusual, but perhaps not unlikely for a play that seems to have enjoyed many collaborators.

The determination of the authorship which, not surprisingly, is closely linked to the problem of dating, is one of the most vexed of all such questions in the canon. The entry in the Stationers' Register reports that the play is 'By I: B.'; the first quarto claims that the play is 'By *B. J. F.*'; the second quarto assures us that it is 'Written by John Fletcher *Gent.*'.[22] Modern critics have not accepted Lichfield's ascription of sole authorship and have sought diligently over the years to pluck out the secrets of the mysterious initials of the Stationers' Register and of Q1. No recent critic has found the work of Beaumont ('*B.*') in the play; some have detected the work of Jonson ('I: B' or '*J.*' or '*B. J.*'); and all have seen the hand of Fletcher ('*F.*'). All have found also the work of Massinger. The editors of the standard edition of Massinger's *Plays and Poems* decline to comment on the authorship of *Rollo*, 'the impossible problem', though they believe that 'Massinger himself probably revised [the play] in the late 1620's'.[23]

The most careful and extended accounts of the problem among the recent critics have been those of Jump (1948), Hoy (1961) and Jowett and Taylor (1993).[24] These three critics agree that

Act I is the work of Massinger,
Act II is the work of Fletcher and
Act III, scene ii is the work of Fletcher.

The remainder of the play is contested.

	Jump	Hoy	Jowett and Taylor
III.i. 11–263	Chapman	Fletcher	Field/Chapman
264–330	Chapman	Fletcher	Fletcher
331–6	Chapman	Fletcher	Field/Chapman
337–87	Chapman	Chapman	Field/Chapman
388–420	Chapman	Chapman	Field
IV.i,ii	Jonson	Jonson	Field/Chapman
iii	Chapman	Chapman	Field
V.i. 1–89	Massinger	Massinger	Massinger
90–119	Fletcher	Fletcher/Massinger	Fletcher
ii. 1–104	Fletcher	Fletcher/Massinger	Fletcher
105–47	Fletcher	Fletcher/Massinger	Fletcher
148–244	Fletcher	Fletcher	Fletcher

No matter which allocation is right – if any is – such an intricate system of collaboration strains the principle of neatness that critics desire; nevertheless, it is neither impossible nor implausible.

Dr Hoy asserts that the unassisted shares of Fletcher and Massinger 'present no difficulty' (p. 57). He is less certain about the shared sections, proposing that Fletcher and Massinger are both at work in the last section of V.i.90–119 (Aubrey's long speech) and that Massinger has revised Fletcher's work in the early section of V.ii.1–147 (Edith and Rollo and the latter's death). It is generally agreed that in the other sections of the play a third or possibly a fourth author has been involved. Of the sections remaining, scenes IV.i, ii have been assigned to Ben Jonson by Crawford, Garnett, Wells and Jump. Dr Hoy accepts these assignments, although he observes, 'the linguistic evidence of Jonson's share ... is pitifully slight'. He supports also the argument by Wells for Chapman's authorship of the remaining sections of III and of IV.iii, observing likewise that 'the linguistic evidence for [Chapman's] share in *Rollo* is painfully slight'. Hoy's linguistic evidence demonstrates that Act IV and Act III.1–263, 337–

420 'cannot have been written by either Massinger or Fletcher'. Jowett and Taylor reject Jonson on the basis of chronology – there is no indication that Jonson was in a collaborative mood at the time *Rollo* was written – and there is insufficient evidence in terms of linguistics or content to require his presence. On the other hand, Richard Field was collaborating with both Fletcher and Massinger in 1613–19, and Jowett and Taylor assign to him, perhaps by default, the sections of Act IV previously assigned to Jonson.[25]

As for the fourth collaborator, since his name was first suggested in 1928, Chapman has been most often advanced. Jowett and Taylor, however, can find little to support that candidacy. But Chapman and Field were close associates, and it is not unlikely that while Field was working on this play he enlisted the services of his mentor, Chapman, who was at this time returning to dramatic writing after completing his translations of Homer and Hesiod.

The assignments of authorship cannot be said to have been concluded, but it is clear that this play is the work of Fletcher and Massinger, assisted by one, two or three collaborators, most likely Field for one, possibly Field or Chapman or Field and Chapman for another, and improbably Jonson for a third. Such diversity of authorship and of critical opinion requires an hypothesis of revision or of revisions at several different dates. Perhaps speculation may be admitted that Fletcher undertook the writing of the play in 1615–16, seeking to develop the theme of the bloody brother from classical history supporting it with a subplot of topical interest (II, III.ii; IV.ii); he was aided by Massinger (I.i). The central scene of the death of Geta (III.i) would have been Fletcher's also, but when the decision was made to 'modernize' the story, Field or Chapman was invited to contribute. Jowett and Taylor point out that all of Chapman's tragedies are set in France;[26] it may be that Chapman, knowing French history and knowing also of the 1619 publication of the Du Chesne chronicle, converted the death of Geta into the death of Otto and became responsible for the change of scene from Rome to France, and for the new title of 'Rollo, Duke of Normandy'.

The title of the play has also been subject to fluctuation. The records of the royal household call it 'Rollo'; the entry in the Stationers' Register names it '*A Tragedy called The Bloody Brother*' and the titlepage of the first quarto (1639) names it 'The Bloody Brother. A Tragedy.'. Reprinting this quarto, the Second Folio (1679) names the play in the 'Catalogue' 'Rollo, Duke of Normandy' (sig. A4v) and in the text 'The Bloody Brother; or, Rollo. A tragedy'. Since they evidently knew the popular name was Rollo, the Folio printers may have been responding to publishing interests or to popular sentiment.

The second quarto printed in 1640 calls the play 'The Tragœdy of Rollo Duke of Normandy', adding the toponymic 'Duke of Normandy', and dropping the fratricide. The compositor of Q3 in 1686 solved the problem by combining what had now become the three elements (and the generic term) into 'Rollo, Duke of Normandy: or, The Bloody Brother. A tragedy.'[27]

The Folio title, 'The Bloody Brother; or Rollo. A tragedy', with two elements, reappeared in the editions of Langbaine and Seward. Apparently unaware of Q3 (as well as of Q1), Colman took his title from the second quarto. Weber explained Colman's omission of 'the Bloody Brother' by suggesting that Colman 'conceived [that fratricidal phrase] to have been a mere unauthorized addition to the title, for which the editors of the folio printed in 1679 were responsible',[28] and he named his edition 'The Bloody Brother, or Rollo, Duke of Normandy'; Dyce followed; Jump adopted the Q3 title, no doubt as a convenient way of combining the two traditions while giving preference to the more elevated form.

Rollo contains three songs: 'Drinke today and drown all sorrowe' at II.ii.47–58; 'Come fortunes a whore' at III.ii.46–90; 'Take oh take those lipps away' at V.ii.21–32. The first song is a 'three-man song', scored in the single surviving manuscript for one tenor and two basses. Though (as we discover later) the Cook can sing, here only the Yeoman, the Pantler and the Butler sing, the Cook serving as director and as audience (II.ii.45–7, 59) as the three others sing in 'close' (line 44) harmony. The music is probably the work of John Wilson.[29] (In Q1, 'The drinking Song, to the second Act.' appears on A3v, having been omitted from its proper place in the print on D3.) The second song, an offering of these comic characters, is a jolly piece sung on the way to the gallows. Though the refrain suggests that this too might have been a three-man song, it is evidently sung by four men, each having a solo verse (assigned first by Weber), supported perhaps by the other three joining to sing 'Three merry men' as the refrain. No music or manuscript sources are known for this text, and hence there are no aids to suggest what the author's original conception of the lineation and rhyme scheme may have been. That conception is reflected in differing systems in Q2 and Q1, and editors have devised their own schemes of representing the lines and rhymes of the varying stanza forms. The present edition sees the song as one increasing in prosodic complexity as it progresses. (See further in Textual Note.) The third song, sung by 'a Boy', survives in several prints and manuscripts, thus indicating a popularity that derives, no doubt, from the appealing setting composed for it by John Wilson.[30] The metre of the six lines is trochaic tetrameter (final syllable omitted), the rhyme scheme *a b a b c c*. Such formal simplicity serves well the tone of the scene in which Edith seeks to disarm Rollo and lure him to his death. The first stanza of the song appears also in Shakespeare's *Measure for Measure* (IV.i.1–6), first printed in the 1623 First Folio. (See further in Textual Note.)

The present edition owes much to the edition prepared by J. D. Jump for the Master of Arts degree in 1936 at the University of Liverpool and published by the Press of that University in 1948. Unable to include all of his specific data on press variation in quarto 1 and in quarto 2, on parallel passages linking *Rollo* with other contemporary plays, and on metrical statistics, Professor Jump deposited his 'Materials Supplementary' to his edition in the Library of the University of Liverpool. Through the kindness of Mr J. Clegg, Assistant Librarian (Special Collections), I have been able to utilize the materials, drawing on them heavily for the collations of Q2 and entirely for the collations of Q1. I am obliged to Mr Clegg and to Professors Philip Edwards and Ann Thompson (both late) of the University of Liverpool for their assistance in making them available.

I express my appreciation also for assistance in editing the scene of the 'Juglers' (IV.ii) to Dr J. C. Eade of the Australian National University. The technical language of the scene – regardless of the problems associated with its authorship – has frightened off many critics, who have been, understandably, ready to regard it all as meaningless jargon. That it is entirely coherent and well informed, though complex, has been clearly demonstrated by Dr Eade whose work on this scene has been published in *Studies in Bibliography* and in his volume, *The Forgotten Sky*.[31]

Professor Gary Taylor of the University of Alabama most generously sent me in advance of publication a typescript of his and John Jowett's study, *Shakespeare Reshaped 1606–1623* (Oxford, 1993). I am particularly grateful to him for this courtesy. I am much obliged also to two specialists for their assistance in the discussion of the song in Act V, Professor Donald Foster of Vassar College and Professor Thomas A. Pendleton of Iona College. I very much regret that Dr Bertha Hensman's edition of the play (New York: Vantage Press, 1991) reached me too late in the preparation of this edition for me to profit from its observations.

The present text is based on the copy of the second quarto in the William R. Perkins Library at Duke University collated with other examplars as indicated in the note at the head of the Press Variants. Eleven formes are press variant. Because of the unusual progress of the transmission of the text of this play, two special sigla have been used in the apparatus: the siglum 'Qq' represents the concurrence of Q2 and Q1 only; the siglum 'Q1–Q3' represents the concurrence of Q1–F2–Q3 only (not of Q2). The Historical Collation includes the three seventeenth-century quartos, the Second Folio, the eighteenth- and nineteenth-century collected editions and the twentieth-century edition of J. D. Jump. I have consulted also the textual studies of J. Monck Mason (1798), John Mitford (1856), Kenneth Deighton (1896).

NOTES

1 Gerald Eades Bentley, *The Jacobean and Caroline Stage* (Oxford, 1956), III, 401–2.
2 At the same time he secured also the manuscript of Fletcher's *Rule a Wife and Have a Wife* and published the first edition of that work concurrently or, at least, conjointly with *Rollo*. One copy of this edition of *Rollo* was in the collection of Charles II. For a discussion of the printing of these two quartos and of Lichfield's publishing ventures see the Textual Introduction to *Rule a Wife* in this series, vol. VI, pp. 487, 489–92.
3 It is therefore not included in the Historical Collation. The derivation of Q4 from Langbaine's edition is demonstrated by several errors common to those editions only: e.g., 'kissing' (I.i.83) for 'killing' F2, Q3; 'softer' (III.i.298) for 'foster' F2, Q3; etc. Q3, set from F2, agrees nevertheless with Q2 in 'presidents' (for F2 'precedents' (I.i.369), 'doubts and' (for 'doubts or' II.iii.75), 'future' (for 'further' II.iii.101).

4 J. D. Jump (ed.), *Rollo Duke of Normandy or The Bloody Brother A Tragedy* (London, 1948; reissued 1969), p. xv; and see also for an early printing of the Textual Section of the Introduction, *The Library*, XVIII (1937), 279–86.

5 Weber, p. 118; Jump, pp. xiii, xiv.

6 Cyrus Hoy, 'The shares of Fletcher and his collaborators in the Beaumont and Fletcher canon (VI)', *Studies in Bibliography*, XIV (1961), 56, quoting Jump, pp. xiii, xii. See below. John Jowett and Gary Taylor, *Shakespeare Reshaped 1606–1623* (Oxford, 1993), offer several different stemmata for the transmission of the texts of this play (pp. 290–5).

7 The sequence of those seven listed fails to indicate the dramatic division of the forces; Dyce was the first to correct the error. This edition supposes that the two factions enter at different doors.

8 Another such stage-direction, omitted in uncorrected Q1, appears in the corrected state: '*Latorch gives each a paper.*' (II.ii.104).

9 I am indebted to my former student, Mrs (now Dr) Barbara Fitzpatrick for the details of this analysis. The line numbers of these stints are as follows: Compositor Q: I.i.0.1–104, 297–II.ii.39, II.iii.109–III.i.230, 359–ii.72, IV.i.108–236.1, IV.ii.121–243, V.ii.63–177; Compositor P: I.i.104.1–296, II.ii.40–iii.108, III.i.231–358, III.ii.73–IV.i.107, IV.ii.0.1–120, 244–V.ii. 62, 178–245.1.

10 Both compositors set B2v and C2v, the compositor who was to set the next page (B3, C3) assisting his fellow by finishing the lower part of the page (the changes occurring at I.i.273b(?) and II.ii.15). Both compositors set E2v–3 in four stints: Q set from the head of E2v, III.i.198, to line 219 (the middle of E2v); then P to line 246 (the middle of E3); then Q to line 259, the bottom of E3. (A tenuous case can be made that Q assisted P for 228–9 and that P assisted Q for 256b–57.)

11 The same change in the method of setting occurs in *Rule a Wife* at the same place, E3, though in that quarto the second system extends for only sixteen pages, to G2v.

12 This spelling occurs also in *The Prophetesse* at III.ii.0.1 (4E1v unc.) but is proof corrected.

13 For further comment on the interlocking of these headings, see this series, vol. VI, pp. 490–1.

14 At the equivalent positions in the first quarto *praeter* is 'translated' as '...*manent* ...' (B2v, C3, Compositor X), as '...Praeter...' (F4 – conceived as a character, Compositor Z?), and as '...*all but...*' (G4v, Compositor Y). As these three different interpretations may be explained as the efforts of the several Q1 compositors, we may assume that the scribe of the manuscript behind Q1 retained the Latin. I am indebted to Professor Alan C. Dessen, of the University of North Carolina–Chapel Hill, for assistance in the matter of stage directions; he writes: 'Massinger, more than any other dramatist I have found (including Chapman, who uses more Latinisms than any other) is especially fond of this usage [of *praeter*] ... (although he is anything but consistent)' (correspondence, 31 March 1995). On the basis of this observation, we may say with some confidence that Massinger is the 'single author retouching the whole piece'.

15 Jump (following E. F. Bosanquet (1917) records the name of Walter Russe, who published a prognostication in 1559–60 (p. 76); Bertha Hensman suggests that 'Russe' is 'clearly a stage representation of the medieval necromancer, Friar Rush'

(*The Shares of Fletcher, Field and Massinger in Twelve Plays of the Beaumont and Fletcher Canon* (Salzburg, 1974), p. 267). See also Dyce, p. 438.

16 At V.ii.85, in a Fletcher passage, where Q1 supplies a line containing the phrase 'thy eyes', omitted from Q2, this edition, adopting the entire line, emends to read 'thine eyes' to accord with Fletcher's style.

17 Jump, pp. xxx–xxxi; Hensman, *The Shares of Fletcher, Field and Massinger*, pp. 267; Jowett and Taylor, *Shakespeare Reshaped*, Appendix III, 'The date and authorship of *Rollo, Duke of Normandy*', pp. 260–71, esp. pp. 264, 270.

18 Gentillet, *A Discours upon the Meanes of wel governing a Kingdom*, pp. 47–8. As an indication of the closeness with which the author(s) followed Gentillet, cf. the Chancellor's answer: 'That it was not so easy to excuse a parricide as it was to commit it', the source for the passage at III.i.218–19. The figure of Latorch is 'Laetus', who persuaded Bassianus 'to slay his brother *Geta*' Smith, *Biographical Dictionary*. Hensman gives a detailed and circumstantial account of the influence of several sources, notably Nicholas Symth's translation of *The History of Herodian* (1550), relating the various sources to the various authors, but her analysis has not proved persuasive to later critics (*The Shares of Fletcher, Field and Massinger*, pp. 242–76).

19 Michel de Bouard, *Histoire de la Normandie* (Toulouse, 1970), p. 97; Dyce notes the Collier ballad (p. 373). The *Biographie universelle* (Paris, 1824), provides the traditional view of Rollo: 'un prince humain, équitable, ami de la paix et protecteur zélé de la réligion. ... Il a mérité de ses sujets, dont il était adoré, le surnom de *Juste*' XXXVIII, 489) – as in III.i.367, IV.i.34 (this title, interestingly enough, the Rollo of this play claims for himself, just after his murder of three victims – III.i.345).

20 See I, 34; Rollo wished to be a Christian, we are told, 'Et postquam permissu divino multa Franciae bona diripuit, vastavit, incendit, atque consumpsit: factus est fidelissimus Christi cultor, cuius ante fuerat crudelissimus persecutor' (*ibid.*). He was baptized in the year 912 (p. 84). The atrocities listed here by Du Chesne, it should be noted, are all military; those committed in the play are all political or personal and derive from the classical account.

21 The career of Antoninus 'is so different from' that of the historical Rollo that it is difficult to see why or how 'the Roman story might be reclothed in the trappings of Rollo and his friends', but Du Chesne's *Scriptores antiqui* would seem to have provided the means for the transfer. The names of almost all of the characters of the play are found in Du Chesne's chronicle 'in juxtaposition with records of the life of Rollo which depict him as a murderer and a tyrant who also had a brother equal with him in honour and power. It is likely that the author of *The Bloody Brother* [drew either] upon Du Chesne's volumes, or upon early Norman chronicles similar to them [which have not been identified]' (Bertha Hensman, 'John Fletcher's "The Bloody Brother or Rollo Duke of Normandy"', Unpublished dissertation, University of Chicago, 1947, pp. 135–6). Taylor and Jowett, *Shakespeare Reshaped*, p. 270. Hensman's claims are perhaps a little extreme. Rollo's younger brother, Gurim, was killed in a battle which the brothers were waging against the King of Dacia (Du Chesne, pp. 70–1). (I am obliged to my colleague Professor Francis L. Newton for assistance here.) The name of

Odo(?) appears in Du Chesne (p. 34); the names of Alain, Aubert (?) Bauldouyn, Haymon, Mathilde appear in Belleforest's *Cosmographie* (pp. 85, 86 [second system, sig. Zii], 304, 459–60).

22 Since Lichfield printed *Rule a Wife and Have a Wife* concurrently with *Rollo* in 1640, using the same setting of type for the authorial ascription, it is very probable that he thought both plays the unaided work of Fletcher or, at least, primarily Fletcher's.

23 Philip Edwards and Colin Gibson, *The Plays and Poems of Philip Massinger* (Oxford, 1976), I, xx; IV, 5.

24 In addition to the arguments in his edition, Jump has included in his 'Materials Supplementary' (see below) a list of many passages parallel to others in the undoubted works of the various proposed authors.

25 Charles Crawford, 'Ben Jonson and "The Bloody Brother"', *Jahrbuch der Deutschen Shakespeare-Gesellschaft*, XLI (1905), 163–76; R. Garnett, 'Ben Jonson's probable authorship of Scene 2, Act IV, of Fletcher's "Bloody Brother"', *Modern Philology*, II (1904–10), 489–95; William Wells, '"The Bloody Brother"', *Notes and Queries*, CLIV (1928), 6–9; Hoy, 'The shares of Fletcher and his collaborators', pp. 61, 63; Jowett and Taylor, *Shakespeare Reshaped*, pp. 265–6. The jargon of the astrologers in IV.ii might because of its esoteric learning represent Jonson's work, but as such satire was not uncommon in the period that argument is not conclusive. The error in the handling of the classical background at IV.i.213 suggests that the section of satire there is also not Jonson's (not Chapman's either, probably). Had Jonson wished to demonstrate the pretentiousness of his characters he would have used an allusion less arcane that would more clearly have exposed to the audience that pretentiousness. Dr Hoy has reviewed these paragraphs on attributions of authorship; he writes: 'while I am much impressed with Taylor and Jowett's argument concerning Field's share in *Rollo*, I am not entirely persuaded by it . . . I simply do not think Field is clever enough [to have written the scenes they attribute to him] . . . if Field wrote any of [these scenes,] . . . they are better than just about anything else he ever did . . . [The] evidence for Field's presence in *Rollo* is purely circumstantial' (29 January 1994).

26 *Shakespeare Reshaped*, p. 271.

27 The head-title of Q3 (sig. A1) reverses the order: 'The Bloody Brother; or Rollo. A Tragedy.' A slippery title, indeed.

28 Weber, p. 118; Greg: 'the obviously unauthoritative character of the first edition discredits its title' (II, 703).

29 John P. Cutts, *Musique de scène de la troupe de Shakespeare* (Paris, 1959), p. 171.

30 Cutts argues that Wilson adapted a setting originally composed in 1604(?) by an unknown musician, perhaps Robert Johnson, and that it was because of this adaptation that the song 'connut un grand succès' (*ibid.*, p. 172).

31 'Astrological analysis as an editorial tool: the case of Fletcher's *The Bloody Brother*', *Studies in Bibliography*, XXXIV (1981), 198–204; *The Forgotten Sky* (Oxford, 1984), pp. 189–97.

THE NAMES OF THE ACTORS.

Rollo, *⎱ Sonnes to the deceased Duke of* Normandy.
Otto, *⎰*

Aubrey, *Kinsman to* Rollo.

Gisbert, *⎱ Two Counsellors of State.*
Baldwin, *⎰*

Latorch, *Favorite to* Rollo.

Hamond, *Captaine of the Guard.*

Allan, *His brother.*

Granpree, *⎱ Servants to* Rollo.
Verdon, *⎰*

Trevile, *⎱ Servants to* Otto.
Duprete, *⎰*

Russee,
De Bube,
La Fiske, *⎬ Cheaters.*
Norbret,
Pipeau,

Cooke.

Butler.

Pantler.

Yeoman of the Cellar.

Cittizens.

Guard.

Servants.

Boyes.

Sophia, *The old Dutchesse.*

Matilda, *Her daughter.*

Edith, *Daughter to* Baldwin.

[*Scene*: Caen, Rhoane.]

166

THE TRAGŒDY OF ROLLO
Duke of Normandy.

Baldwin.   The brothers then are met?
Gisbert.   They are.
Baldwin.   Tis thought
  They may be reconcil'd.
Gisbert.   Tis rather wish'd.
  For such whose reason does direct their thoughts
  Without self flattery, dare not hope it *Baldwin*:
  The fires of love which the dead Duke believ'd
  His equall care of both would have united,
  Ambition hath divided; and there are
  Too many on both parts that know they cannot
  Or rise to wealth or honour, their maine ends,
  Unlesse the tempest of the Princes fury   10
  Make troubled Seas, and those Seas yeeld fit Billowes
  To heave them up; and these are too well practis'd
  In their bad arts to give way to a calme,
  Which yeelding rest to good men proves their ruine.
Baldwin.   And in the shipwrack of their hopes and fortunes
  The Dukedome might be sav'd, had it but ten
  That stood affected to the generall good,
  With that confirm'd zeale which brave *Aubrey* does.
Gisbert.   He is indeed the perfect character
  Of a good man, and so his actions speak him.   20
Baldwin.   And did you observe the many doubts and cautions
  The brothers stood upon before they met?
Gisbert.   I did, and yet that ever brothers should
  Stand on more nice termes then sworne enemies
  After a war proclaimed, would with a stranger,

Wrong the reporters credit; they saluted
At distance, and so strong was the suspicion
Each had of other, that before they durst
Embrace, they were by severall servants searcht,
As doubting conceal'd weapons; antidotes   30
Tane openly by both, fearing the roome
Appointed for the enterview was poysoned;
The chaires and cushions with like care survai'd.
And in a word, in every circumstance
So jealous on both parts, that it is more
Then to be fear'd, concord can never joyne
Mindes so divided.

Baldwin.   Yet our best endeavours
Should not be wanting *Gisbert.*

Gisbert.   Neither shall they,

Enter Granpree *and* Verdon.

[*Apart*] But what are these?

Baldwin [*apart*].   They are without my knowledge,
But by their manners and behaviours   40
They should expresse themselves.

Granpree.   Since we serve *Rollo*
The eldest Brother, weel be *Rollians,*
Who will maintaine us lads as brave as Romans;
You stand for him?

Verdon.   I doe.

Granpree.   Why then observe,
How much the businesse, the so long'd for businesse,
By men that are nam'd from their swords concernes you:
Lechery, our common friend, so long kept under
With whips and beating fatall hemp shall rise;
And baudry in a French-hood plead before her
Where it shall be concluded, after twelve   50
Virginity shall be carted.

Verdon.   Excellent!

Granpree.   And Hell but grant the quarrell thats betweene

43 us lads,] us Q2; us, lads, Q1   49 plead] Q1; shall plead Q2

The Princes may continue, and the businesse
That's of the sword, t'outlast three sutes in law,
And we will make Atturneys lans-prizadoes,
And our brave Gown-men practisers of back-sword;
The pewter of all Serjeants Maces shall
Be melted and turn'd into common Flaggons,
In which it shall be lawfull to carrouse
To their most lowsey fortunes.

Baldwin [*aside*].   Here's a statesman!   60

Granpree.   A Creditor shall not dare but by petition
To make demand of any debt, and that
Only once every leap yeare, in which if
The debtor may be won for a French Crown
To pay a souse, he shall be registred
His benefactor.

Verdon [*aside*].   The Chancellour heares you.

Granpree.   Feare not, I now dare speak as lowd as he,
And will be heard, and have all that I speak law.
Have you no eyes? there is a reverence due
From children of the gowne to men of action.   70

Gisbert.   How's this?

Granpree.   Ev'n so, the times, the times are chang'd,
All businesse is not now prefer'd in parchment,
Nor shall a grant passe which wants this broad seale,
                                        [*Shows his sword.*]
This seale, doe you see? your gravity once laid
My head and heeles together in the dungeon
For cracking a scald officers crowne, for which
A time is come for vengeance and expect it;
For know you have not full three houres to live.

Gisbert.   Yes somewhat longer.

Granpree.   To what end?

Gisbert.   To hang you,
Think on that Ruffion.

Granpree.   For you Schoolemaster,   80
You have a pretty daughter; let me see,
Neere three a clock, by which time I much feare
I shall be tir'd with killing some five hundred,

Provide a bath, and her to entertaine me.
And that shall be your ransome.
Baldwin.   Impudent raskall!

Enter Trevile, *and* Duprete.

Gisbert.   More of the crue.
Granpree.   What, are you *Rollians?*
Trevile.   No: this for *Rollo* and all such as serve him:
    We stand for *Otto.*
Granpree.   You seeme men of fashion,
    And therefore ile deale fairely, you shall have
    The honour this day to be chronicled   90
    The first men kill'd by *Granpree;* you see this sword,
    A prettie foolish toy, my valours servant,
    And I may boldly say a Gentleman,
    It having made when it was *Charlemaines*
    Three thousand Knights; this Sir shall cut your throat,
    And doe you all faire service else.
Trevile.   I kisse
    Your hands for the good offer: here's another
    The servant of your servant, which shall be
    Proud to be scowr'd in your sweet guts, till when,
    Pray you command me.
Granpree.   Your Idolater Sir.   100
                    Exeunt omnes præter Gisbert *and* Baldwin.
Gisbert.   That ever such should hold the names of men!
    Or justice be held cruelty, when it labours
    To pluck such roots up.
Baldwin.   Yet they are protected,
    And by the great ones.
Gisbert.   Not the good ones *Baldwin.*

Enter Aubrey.

Aubrey.   Is this a time to be spent thus by such
    That are the principall minsters of the State?
    When they that are the heads have fill'd the Court
    With factions, a weake woman only left

To stay their bloudy hands? can her weake arme
Alone divert the dangers ready now   110
To fall upon the Common-wealth, and bury
The honours of it, leaving not the name
Of what it was? O *Gisbert* the faire tryalls
And frequent proofes which our late Maister made
Both of your love and faith, gave him assurance
To choose you at his death a Guardian, nay
A Father of his Sonnes, and that great trust
How ill doe you discharge? I must be plaine
That at the best y'are a sad looker on
Of those bad practises you should prevent.   120
And where's the use of your Philosophy
In this so needfull time? be not secure,
For *Baldwin* be assur'd since that the Princes
When they were young and apt for any forme,
Were given to your instruction and grave ordering,
'Twill be expected that they should be good,
Or their bad manners will be imputed yours.
Bladwin. 'Twas not in me my Lord to alter nature.
Gisbert. Nor can my Counsells work on them that will not
Vouchsafe me hearing.
Aubrey.   Doe these answers sort   130
Or with your place or persons? or your years?
Can *Gisbert* being the piller of the Lawes
See them trod under foot, or forc't to serve
The Princes unjust ends, and with a frowne
Be silenc'd from exclaiming on the abuse,
Or *Baldwin* only weepe the desperate madnesse
Of his seduced Pupills? See those minds
Which with good arts he labour'd to build up,
Examples of succeeding times oreturn'd
By undermineing Parasites; no one precept   140
Leading to any act, or great or good
But is forc'd from their memory, in whose roome
Black Counsailes are receiv'd; and their retirements
And secret conference, produceing only

Divelish designes, a man would shame to father.
But I talke when I should doe, and chide others
For that I now offend in.

Enter Rollo, Latorch, Verdon, Granpree, [*and at another doore*]
Otto, Trevile, Duprete.

                    [*aside*] See't confirm'd:
Now doe or never speak more.
Gisbert [*aside*].   We are yours.
Rollo.   You shall know who I am.
Otto.   I doe, my equall.
Rollo.   Thy Prince, give way, were we alone ide force thee   150
    In thy best bloud to write thy selfe my subject,
    And glad I would receive it.
Aubrey.   Sir——
Gisbert.   Deare Lord——
Otto.   Thy subject?
Rollo.   Yes, nor shall tame patience hold mee
    A minute longer, only halfe my selfe,
    My birth gave me this Dukedome, and my sword
    Shall change it to the common grave of all
    That tread upon her bosome, ere I part with
    A peece of Earth, or title that is mine.
Otto.   I need it not, and would scorne to receive
    Though offer'd what I want not, therefore know   160
    From me though not deliver'd in great words,
    Eies red with rage, poore pride, and threatning action;
    Our father at his death, then when no accent
    (Wert thou a sonne) could fall from him in vaine,
    Made us co-heires, our part of land and honours
    Of equall waight, and to see this confirm'd
    The oath of these is yet upon record,
    Who though they should forsake me, and call downe
    The plagues of perjury on their sinfull heads,
    I would not leave my selfe.

116 a] Q1; to be a Q2
147–148 See't ... | *Gisbert.* We] Q1; *Gisb.* See't ... | We Q2   *158 title] *stet* Q2
164 Wert] Colman; Wer't Q2, Q1–Q3   164 thou] Q1; then Q2

172

Trevile.   Nor will we see   170
  The will of the dead Duke infring'd.
Latorch.   Nor I
  The elder rob'd of what's his right.
Granpree.   Nor you?
  Let me take place: I say I will not see it,
  My sword is sharpest.
Aubrey.   Peace you tinder-boxes,
  That only carry matter to make a flame,
  Which will consume you.
Rollo (*to* Baldwin).   You are troublesome,
  This is no time for Arguments, my title
  Needs not your schoole defences, but my sword
  With which the Gordian of your Sophistry
  Being cut, shall shew the Imposture.
      (*To* Gisbert)   For your lawes,   180
  It is in me to change them as I please,
  I being above them: would you have me protect them?
  Let them then now stretch their extreamest rigour,
  And seize upon that Traitor, and your tongue
  Make him appeare first dangerous and then odious,
  And after under the pretence of safety
  For the sick State, the Lands and Peoples quiet,
  Cut off his head, and Ile give up my sword,
  And fight with them at a more certaine weapon
  To kill, and with authority.
Gisbert.   Sir I graunt,   190
  The Lawes are usefull weapons, but found out
  To assure innocence not to oppresse.
Rollo.   Then you conclude him innocent?
Gisbert.   The power
  Your father gave him, must not prove a crime.
Aubrey.   Nor should you so receive it.
Baldwin.   To which purpose,
  All that dare challenge any part in goodnesse
  Will become Suppliants to you.

---

180 Imposture. For] Q1; Imposture for Q2   180 lawes] Q1; lawe Q2
*182 them:] (Dyce *conj.*); them (*Gisbert*) Q2, Q1–Q3   *189 at] *stet* Q2

Rollo.   Such have none,
That dare move mee in this, hence, I defy you:
Be of his party, bring to it your lawes,
And thou thy double heart, thou popular foole: 200
Your morrall rules of justice, and her ballance.
I stand on my owne Guard.

Otto.   Which thy injustice
Will make thy enimies; by the memory
Of him whose better part now suffers for thee,
Whose reverend ashes with an impious hand,
Thou throwst out to contempt, in thy repineing
At his so just decree; thou art unworthy
Of what his last will, not thy merit gave thee,
That art so swolne within, with all those mischiefes
That ere made up a Tyrant, that thy brest   210
The prison of thy purposes, cannot hold them
But that they break fourth, and in thy owne words
Discover, what a monster they must serve,
That shall acknowledge thee.

Rollo.   Thou shalt not live
To be so happy.

>   *Offers his sword at* Otto: *the factions joyneing,*
>   Aubrey, *between, severs the Brothers.*

Aubrey.   Nor your misery
Begin in murder; duty, allegeance,
And all respect of what you are forsake mee.
Doe you stare ons? is this a theater?
Or shall these kill themselves, like to mad fencers,
To make you sport? keepe them assunder, or   220
By Heaven ile charge on all.

Granpree.   Keepe the peace,
[*To* Rollo] I am for you my Lord, and if you'l have me
Ile act the Constables part.

Aubrey.   Live I to see this!
Will you doe that your Enimies dare not wish,
And cherish in your selves those furies which

---

199 to it] Weber; it to Q2, Q1–Q3   *215 *factions*] *faction* Q2, Q1–Q3
218 ons?] Q2(c); ons, Q2(u); on? Q1   219 mad fencers] Q1; manfencers Q2

Hell would cast out? doe, I am ready, kill me,
And these that would fall willing sacrifices
To any power that would restore your reason
And make you men againe, which now you are not.
Rollo.   These are your bucklers boy.
Otto.   My hinderances,   230
And were I not confirm'd, my justice in
The taking of thy life, could not waigh downe
The wrong, in shedding the least drop of blood
Of these, whose goodnesse only now protects thee.
Thou should'st feele, I in act would prove my selfe
What thou in words dost labour to appeare.
Rollo.   Heare this and talke againe? Ile break through all
But I will reach thy heart.
Otto.   Tis better guarded.

Enter Sophia.

Sophia.   Make way or I will force it, who are these
My sonnes, my shames; turne all your swords on mee,   240
And make this wretched body but one wound,
So this unnaturall quarrell finde a grave
In the unhappy wombe that brought you forth.
Dare you remember that you had a Mother,
Or looke on these gray haires, made so with teares
For both your goods, and not with age, and yet
Stand doubtfull to obay her? from me you had
Life, nerves and faculties to use those weapons,
And dare you raise them against her, to whome
You owe the meanes of being what you are?   250
Otto.   All peace is meant to you.
Sophia.   Why is this warre then?
As if your armes could be advanc'd, and I
Not set upon the wracke, your blood is mine
Your danger's mine, your goodnesse I should share in,
And must be branded with those impious markes
You stamp on your owne foreheads, and on mine

247 her?] Q1; hers? Q2   253 wracke] Q1 (rack); wracks Q2

If you goe on thus: for my good name therefore
Though all respects of honour in your selves
Are in your fury choakt, throw downe your swords.
Your duty should be swifter then my tongue,   260
And joyne your hands while they are innocent,
You have heat of blood and youth apt to ambition
To plead an easy pardon for what's past;
But all the ills beyond this houre committed,
From Gods or men must hope for no excuse.

Gisbert. Can you heare this unmov'd?

Aubrey.   No Syllable
Of this so pious charme, but should have power
To frustrate all the juggling deceipts
With which the Divell blindes you.

Otto.   I begin
To melt, I know not how.

Rollo.   Mother, Ile leave you,   270
And Sir, be thankfull for the time you live
Till wee meet next, (which shall be soone and suddaine)
To her perswasion for you.

Sophia.   O yet stay,
And rather then part thus, vouchsafe me hearing
As enimies; how is my soule divided!
My love to both is equall as my wishes,
But are return'd by neither, my griev'd heart
Hold yet a litle longer, and then break;
I kneele to both, and will speak so, but this
Takes the authority of a Mothers power,   280
And therefore like my selfe, *Otto* to thee,
And yet observe sonne, how thy Mothers teares
Outstrip her forward words to make way for 'em,
Thou art the younger *Otto*, yet be now
The first example of obedience to me,
And grow the elder in my love.

Otto.   The meanes
To be so happy?

*280 of] i.e., off

176

Sophia.   This, yeeld up thy sword,
    And let thy pietie give thy mother strength
    To take that from thee, which no enimies force
    Could ere dispoile thee of: [*Gives her his sword.*]
                    why dost thou tremble?   290
    And with a fearefull eye fixt on thy brother,
    Observ'st his ready sword as bent against thee?
    I am thy armour and will be pierc't through
    Ten thousand times before I will give way
    To any perill may arrive at thee,
    And therefore feare not.
Otto.   Tis not for my selfe
    But for you Mother; you are now engag'd
    In more then lies in your unquestion'd vertue.
    For since you have disarm'd me of defence,
    Should I fall now, though by his hand, the world   300
    May say it was your practise.
Sophia.   All worlds perish
    Before my pietie turne treasons parent.
    Take it againe, and stand upon your guard,
    And while your brother is, continue arm'd.
    And yet this feare is needlesse, for I knowe
    My *Rollo*, though he dares as much as man,
    So tender of his yet untainted valour,
    So noble, that he dares doe nothing basely.
    You doubt him, he fears you, I doubt and feare
    Both, for the others safety not my owne.   310
    Know yet my sonnes when of necessity
    You must deceive or be deceiv'd, 'tis better
    To suffer treason then to act the traytor;
    And in a war like this, in which the glory
    Is his that's overcome: consider then
    What 'tis for which you strive: is it the Dukedome,
    Or the command of these so ready subjects?
    Desire of wealth, or whatsoever else
    Fires your ambition? 'tis still desperate madnesse,

*302 turne] Q₁; turnes Q₂   *310 the] Weber; *omit* Q₂, Q₁–Q₃

To kill the people which you would be Lords of, 320
With fire and sword to lay that countrey wast,
Whose rule you seek for, to consume the treasures
Which are the sinewes of your government,
In cherishing the factions that destroy it.
Far, far be this from you, make it not question'd,
Whither you can have interest in that Dukedome,
Whose ruine both contend for.

Otto.   I desire
But to enjoy my owne which I will keep.

Rollo.   And rather then posteritie shall have cause
To say I ruin'd all, divide the Dukedome, 330
I will accept the moietie.

Otto.   I embrace it.

Sophia.   Divide me first or teare me limb by limb,
And let them find as many severall graves
As there are Villages in *Normandy*,
And 'tis lesse sinne, then so to weaken it.
To heare it mention'd doth already make me
Envy my dead Lord, and almost blaspheame
Those powers which heard my prayers for fruitfulnesse,
And did not with my first birth close my wombe.
To me alone, my second blessing proves 340
My first, my first of misery, for if heaven
That gave me *Rollo*, there had staid his bounty,
And *Otto* my deere *Otto* nere had been,
Or being, had not been so worth my love,
The streame of my affection had run constant
In one faire current, all my hopes had been
Laid up in one, and fruitfull *Normandy*
In this division had not lost her glories.
For as 'tis now 'tis a faire dyamond
Which being preserv'd intire exceeds all value, 350
But cut in peeces, (though these peeces are
Set in fine gold by the best workmans cunning)
Parts with all estimation: so this Dukedome

*341 My first, my first] *stet* Q2

178

As tis yet whole, the neighbouring Kings may covet
But cannot compasse, which divided will
Become the spoile of every barbarous foe
That will invade it.
Gisbert.   How this workes in both!
Baldwin.   Prince *Rolloes* eyes have lost their fire.
Gisbert.   And anger,
That but ev'n now wholly possessed good *Otto*,
Hath given place to pitty.
Aubrey.   End not thus   360
Madam, but perfect whats so well begun.
Sophia.   I see in both faire signes of reconcilement
Make them sure proofes they are so: the fates offer
To your free choice, either to live examples
Of piety or wickednesse, if the latter
Blindes so your understanding that you cannot
Pierce through her painted outside, and discover
That she is all deformitie within,
Boldly transcend all presidents of mischiefe,
And let the last and the worst act of tryannies,   370
The murther of a Mother but begin
The Scene of bloud, you after are to heighten;
But if that vertue and her sure rewards
Can win you to accept her for your guide,
To lead you up to heaven and there fix you
The fairest starres in the bright sphere of honour,
Make me the parent of a hundred sonnes
All brought into the world with joy not sorrow,
And every one a Father to his countrey
In being now made mother of your concord.   380
Rollo.   Such and so good: loud fame for ever speak you.
                 The brothers throw down their swords and embrace.
Baldwin.   I, now they meet like brothers.
Gisbert.   My hearts joy
Flowes through my eyes.
Aubrey.   May never womans tongue

---

376 starres] Q1; starre Q2

179

Hereafter be accus'd, for this ones goodnesse.
Otto.   If we contend, from this houre it shall be
How to overcome in brotherly affection,
Rollo.   *Otto* is *Rollo* now, and *Rollo Otto*,
Or as they have one minde, rather one name,
From this attonement let our lives begin,
Be all the rest forgotten.
Aubrey.   Spoke like *Rollo*.   390
Sophia.   And to the honour of this reconcilement
We all this night will at a publique feast
With choice wines drowne our late feares, and with Musick
Welcome our comforts.
Baldwin.   Sure and certaine ones.
Sophia.   Supported thus I am secure o sonnes,
This is your Mothers triumph.
Rollo.   You deserve it.
          Exeunt omnes præter Granpree, Verdon, Trevile, Duprete.
Granpree.   Did ever such a hop'd for businesse end thus?
Verdon.   Tis fatall to us all, and yet you *Granpree*
Have the least cause to feare.
Granpree.   Why, what's my hope?
Verdon.   The certainty that you have to be hang'd;   400
You know the Chancellours promise.
Granpree.   Plague upon you.
Verdon.   What think you of a bath, and a Lords daughter
To entertaine you?
Granpree.   Those desires are of.
Fraile thoughts: all friends, no *Rollions* now, nor *Ottoes*,
The severall curtesies of our swords and servants
Deferr till apter consequence: let's make use
Of this nights freedome, a short Parliament to us,
In which it will be lawfull to walk freely;
Nay to our drink we shall have meat too, and thats
No usuall businesse to the men oth' sword.   410
Drink deep with me to night, we shall to morrow
Or whip or hang the merrier.

Trevile.   Lead the way then.

                                                            Exeunt.

                    Enter Latorch *and* Rollo.   [II.i]

Latorch.   Why should this trouble you?
Rollo.   It does and must doe,
    Till I finde ease.
Latorch.   Consider then and quickly,
    And like a wise man take the current with you
    Which once turn'd head will sink you. Blest occasion
    Offers it selfe in thousand safeties to you,
    Time standing still to point you out your purpose,
    And resolution (the true child of vertue)
    Ready to execute: what dull cold weaknesse
    Has crept into your bosome, whose meere thoughts
    Like tempests ploughing up the sayling Forrests   10
    Ev'n with their swing were wont to shake down hazards.
    What, ist your mothers teares?
Rollo.   Prethee be patient.
Latorch.   Her hands held up, her prayers, or her curses?
    O Power of prayer: dropt through by a woman.
    Take heed the Souldiers see it not, 'tis miserable,
    In *Rollo*, below miserable; take heed your friends
    The sinewes of your cause, the strength you stir by,
    Take heed I say, they finde it not; take heed
    Your own repentance (like a passing bell)
    Too late and too lowd tell the world you are perish'd.   20
    What noble spirit eager of advancement,
    Whose imployment is his plough, what sword whose sharpnesse
    Waits but the arme to weild it, or what hope
    After the world has blowne abroad this weaknesse
    Will move againe, or make a wish for *Rollo?*
Rollo.   Are we not friends againe, by each oath ratified,
    Our tongues the Heralds of our hearts?
Latorch.   Poore hearts then.
Rollo.   Our worthier friends.

                *10 sayling] Q1; soyling Q2   *14 prayer] *stet* Q2

                                   181

Latorch.   No friends Sir to your honour,
    Friends to your fall: where is your understanding,
    The noble vessell that your full soule sail'd in,   30
    Rib'd round with honours, where is that? tis ruin'd,
    The tempest of a womans sighes hath sunk it.
    Friendship, take heed Sir, is a smiling harlot
    That when she kisses, killes a soder'd friendship
    Peec'd out with promises; o painted ruine!
Rollo.   *Latorch*, he is my brother.
Latorch.   The more doubted,
    For hatred hatch'd at home is a tame Tiger
    May fawne and sport, but never leave his nature.
    The jarres of brothers, two such mighty ones,
    Are like a small stone throwne into a river,   40
    The breach scarce heard, but view the beaten current
    And you shall see a thousand angry rings
    Rise in his face, still swelling and still growing;
    So jarres circling in distrusts, pull down dangers,
    And dangers death, the greatest extreame shadow,
    Till nothing bound them but the Shoars, their graves.
    There is no manly wisdome nor no safety
    In leaning to this league, this peece patcht friendship,
    This rear'd up reconcilement on a billow
    Which as he tumbles, totters down your fortune.   50
    Ist not your own you reach at? law and nature
    Ushring the way before you, is not he
    Borne and bequeath'd your subject?
Rollo.   Ha?
Latorch.   What fool
    Would give a storme leave to disturb his peace
    When he may shut the casement? can that man
    Has woon so much upon you by your pitty,
    And drawne so high, that like an ominous Comet
    He darkens all your light, can this couch'd Lyon

---

34 killes] Q1; kisses Q2   41 breach] Q1; breath Q2
*44 circling ... pull down] circling in distrusts, distrusts pull down Q2; circling distrusts,
    distrusts breed Q1–3   46 Shoars] Showers Q2; shoare Q1–3
*54 his peace] Q1; him Q2

(Though now he licks and locks up his fell pawes
Craftily humming like a Cat to cozen you)   60
But when ambition whets him and time fits him,
Leap to his prey, and seiz'd once, suck your heart out?
Doe you make it conscience?

Rollo.   Conscience *Latorch?* what's that?

Latorch.   A feare they tye up fooles in: natures coward,
  Pauling the bloud and chilling the full spirits
  With apprehension of meere cloudes and shadowes.

Rollo.   I know no conscience, nor I feare no shadowes.

Latorch.   Or if you did, if there were conscience,
  If the free soule could suffer such a curbe
  Toth' fiery minde, such puddle to put it out,   70
  Must it needs like a rank vine run up rudely,
  And twine about the top of all our happinesse,
  Honour and rule, and there sit shaking of us?

Rollo.   It shall not nor it must not: I am satisfied,
  And once more am my selfe againe.
  My mothers teares and womanish cold prayers
  Farewell, I have forgot yee. If there be conscience,
  Let it not come betwixt a Crowne and me,
  Which is my hope of blisse, and I believe it:
  A crowne, a crowne, o sacred rule now fire me: 80
  Otto, our friendship thus I blowe to ayre
  A bubble for a boy to play withall,
  And all the vowes my weaknesse made like this,
  Like this poore heartlesse rush, I rend a peeces.

Latorch.   Now you goe right Sir, now your eyes are open.

Rollo.   My Fathers last petition's dead, as he is,
  And all the promises I clos'd his eyes with,
  In the same grave I bury.

Latorch.   Now you are a man Sir.

Rollo.   *Otto* thou shewst my winding sheet before me,
  Which ere I put it on, like heavens blest fire   90
  In my descent ile make it blush in bloud.

---

  61 when] Q1; *omit* Q2   64 feare] Q1; teare Q2
  *65 Pauling] Q1; Palling F2; Tasting Q2   69 such a curbe] Q1; *omit* Q2
  *70 Toth'] To the Q1; The Q2   *80 A crowne ... me:] *omit* Q2, Q1–Q3

Nor shall the pitty of thy youth false brother,
Although a thousand Virgins kneele before me,
And every dropping eye a Court of mercy,
The same bloud with me, nor the reverence
Due to my Mothers blessed wombe, that bred us
Redeem thee from my doubts: thou art a woolfe here
Fed with my feares, and I must cut thee from me,
No safety else.

Latorch.   But be not too much stirr'd Sir,
Nor too high in your execution; swallowing waters   100
Run deep and silent till they are satisfied,
And smile in thousand curles, to guild their craft;
Let your sword sleep, and let my two-edg'd wit work,
This happy feast, the full joy of your friendship
Shall be his last.

Rollo.   How my *Latorch?*

Latorch.   Why thus Sir,
Ile presently goe dive into the Officers
That minister at Table, gold and goodnesse
With promise upon promise, and time necessary
Ile poure into 'em.

Rollo.   Canst thou doe it neatly?

Latorch. Let me alone and such a bait it shall be   110
Shall take off all suspition.

Rollo.   Goe and prosper.

Latorch. Walk in then and your smoothest face put on Sir.

              Exeunt.

Enter the Master Cook, Butler, Pantler, Yeoman *of the Seller,* [II.
with a Jack of beere and a dish.

Cook. A hot day, a hot day, vengeance hot boyes,
Give me some drink; this fire's a plaguy fretter.
Body a me I am dry still, give me the Jack boy,
This wooden skiffe holds nothing.

Pantler.   And faith master,

91–92 bloud. | Nor] bloud. | A crowne, a crowne, o sacred rule now fire me, | Nor Q2, Q1–Q3
98–99 me, | No] me, | A crowne, a crowne. o sacred rule now fire me, | No Q2, Q1–Q3
4 skiffe] *i.e.,* bowl (*Latin,* scyphus)

What brave new meats? for here will be old eating.
Cook.   Old and young boy, let em all eat, I have it,
    I have ballasse for their bellies, if they eat, a Gods name
    Let em have ten tire of teeth a peece, I care not.
Butler.   But what new rare munition?
Cook.   Peuh a thousand,
    Ile make yee Pigs speak French at table, and a fat Swan   10
    Come sailing out of *England* with a challenge.
    Ile make yee a dish of Calves feet dance the Canaries,
    And a consort of cram'd Capons fiddle to em.
    A Calves head speak an Oracle, and a dozen of Larkes
    Rise from the dish, and sing all supper time;
    Tis nothing boyes, I have fram'd a fortification,
    Out of Rye past, which is impregnable,
    And against that for two long houres together,
    Two dozen of maribones shall play continually.
    For Fish ile make ye a standing lake of White-broth,   20
    And Pikes come ploughing up the plumbes before 'em.
    Arion on a Dolphin playing Lachrimae,
    And brave King *Herring* with his oyle and onyon
    Crownd with a leomon pill, his way prepar'd
    With his strong guard of pilchers.
Pantler.   I marry maister.
Cook.   All these are nothing, ile make ye a stubble goose
    Turne oth toe thrice, doe a crosse point presently
    And then sit downe againe, and cry, come eate mee.
    These are for mirth, now Sir, for matter of mourning
    Ile bring ye in the lady loyne of Veale   30
    With the long love she bore the Prince of Orenge.
Officers.   Thou boy, thou!
Cook.   I have a trick for thee too,
    And a rare trick, and I have done it for thee.
Yeoman.   What's that good master?
Cook.   Tis a sacrifice,
    A full vine bending like an Arch, and under
    The blowne god *Bacchus* sitting on a hogs-head

*11 sailing] Q1 (sayling); sculing Q2   24 pill] *i.e.*, peel

185

His altar heere, before that a plump Vintner,
Kneeling and offering incense to his Deity,
Which shall be only this, red spratts and pilchers.
Butler.   This when the Tables drawne, to draw the wine in.   40
Cook.   Thou hast it right, and then comes thy Song Butler.
Pantler.   This will be admirable.
Yeoman.   O Sir, most admirable.
Cook.   If you'l have the pastie speak, 'tis in my power,
   I have fire enough to worke it:——come stand close,
   And now rehearse the Song it may be perfect,
   The drinking song, and say I were the Brothers.

The Song.

Drinke to day and drowne all sorrow,
You shall perhaps not doe it to morrow.
Best while you have it use your breath,
There is no drinking after death.

Wine works the heart up, wakes the wit,
There is no cure gainst age but it.
It helps the head-ach, cough and tissick,
And is for all diseases Physick.

Then let us swill boyes for our health,
Who drinkes well loves the common wealth.
And he that will to bed goe sober,
Falls with the leafe still in October.

Cook.   Well have you borne your selves, a red-deere pye boies,
   And that no leane one, I bequeath your vertues.   60
   What friends hast thou to day, no Cittizens?
Pantler.   Yes father the old Crew.
Cook.   By the Masse, true wenches:
   Sirrha, set by a chaine of beefe and a hot pastie,
   And let the jole of Sturgion be corrected,
   And doe you marke sir, stalke me to a Pheasant

*40 drawne] *stet* Q2   *43 pastie] Q1; paste Q2
*47–58 *Drinke ... October.] *stet* Q2   63 chaine] *i.e.,* chine

186

And see and yee can shooe her into the Seller.
Pantler.   Godamercy dad, send me thy roaring bottles
And with such Nectar I will see 'em fill'd,
That all thou speak'st shall be pure Helicon.

Enter Latorch.

[*Aside*] Mounsieur *Latorch*, what newes with him?——Save ye.   70
Latorch.   Save ye maister, save ye Gentlemen,
You are casting for this preparation,
This joyfull supper for the royall brothers?
I'me glad I have met yee fitly, for to your charge
My bountifull brave Butler, I must deliver
A beavy of young lasses, that must looke on
This daies solemnity, and see the two Dukes
Or I shall loose my credit; you have stowage?
Butler.   For such freight ile finde roome, and be your servant.
Cook.   Bring 'em, they shall not starve here, ile send 'em victualls   80
Shall worke you a good turne, though it be ten daies hence sir.
Latorch.   Godamercy noble maister.
Cook.   Nay ile doe't.
Yeoman.   And Wine they shall not want, let 'em drink like ducks.
Latorch.   What misery it is that mindes so royall,
And such most honest bounties as yours are,
Should be confin'd thus to uncertainties?
Butler.   I, were the State once setled, then we had places.
Yeoman.   Then we could shew our selves and helpe our friends sir.
Cook.   I, then there were some savour in't, where now
We live betweene two stooles, every hower ready   90
To tumble on our Noses, and for ought we know yet
For all this supper, ready to fast the next day.
Latorch.   I would faine speake to you out of pitty,
Out of the love I beare you, out of honesty,
For your own goods, nay for the generall blessing.
Cook.   And we would as fain hear you, pray goe forward.
Latorch.   Dare yee but think to make your selves up certainties,

*66 shooe] shoote Q2, Q1–Q3   *67 *Pantler.*] *stet* Q2
*70 with him?] Q1; within? Q2
70–71 Save ye. *Latorch.* Save ye] Q1; *Lat.* Save ye, | Save ye Q2

Your places and your credits ten times doubled,
The Princes favour, *Rolloes*?
Butler.   A sweet gentleman.
Yeoman.   I, and as bounteous if he had his right too.   100
Cook.   By th'masse a royall gentleman indeed boies,
   Hee'd make the Chimnies smoake.
Latorch.   He would doe friends,
   And you too, if he had his right, true Courtiers,
   What could ye want then? dare yee?———
Cook.   Pray be short sir.
Latorch.   And this my soule upon't, I dare assure you,
   If you but dare your parts.
Cook.   Dare not me Monsieur,
   For I that feare neither fire nor water sir,
   Dare doe enough a man would think.
Yeoman.   Beleeve't sir,
   But make this good upon us you have promis'd,
   You shall not finde us flinchers.
Latorch.   Then ile be suddaine.   110
Pantler [*aside*].   What may this meane, and whether would he drive
      us?
Latorch.   And first for what you must doe, because all danger
   Shall be apparently ti'de up and mussel'd,
   The matter seeming mighty, there's your pardons.
                                        [*Gives papers.*]
Pantler [*aside*].   Pardons? is't come to that? good god defend us.
Latorch.   And here's five hundred crownes in bounteous earnest.
                                        [*Gives money.*]
   And now behold the matter.   *Latorch gives each a paper.*
Butler.   What are these Sir?
Yeoman.   And of what nature? to what use?
Latorch.   Imagine.
Cook.   Will they kill rats? they eat my pies abhominably,
   Or worke upon a woman, cold as Christmasse?   120
   I have an old jade sticks upon my fingers.
   May I tast 'em?

Latorch.   Is your will made?
  And have you said your prayers? for they'l pay ye;
  And now to come up to you for your knowledge,
  And for the good you never shall repent yee,
  If ye be wisemen now.
Cook.   Wise as you will sir.
Latorch.   These must be put then into the severall meats
  Young *Otto* loves, by you into his wine sir,
  Into his bread by you, by you into his linnen.
  Now if you desire, ye have found the meanes   130
  To make yee, and if ye dare not ye have
  Found your ruine, resolve me ere you goe.
Butler.   You'l keep faith with us?
Latorch.   May I no more see light else.
Cook.   Why 'tis done then.
Butler.   Tis done.
Pantler.   Tis done——[*aside*] which shall be
  Undone.
Latorch.   About it then, farewell, ye are all
  Of one mind?
Cook.   All.
Butler, Pantler, Yeoman.   All, all.
Latorch.   Why then, all happy   *Exit.*
Butler.   What did we promise him?
Yeoman.   Doe you aske that now?
Butler.   I would be glad to know what 'tis.
Pantler.   Ile tell yee,
  It is to be all villaines knaves and traitors.
Cook.   Fine wholsome titles.
Butler.   But if we dare goe forward?   140
Cook.   We may be hang'd drawd and quartred.
Pantler.   Very true Sir.
Cook.   What a goodly swinge shall I give the gallowes,
  Yet I thinke too,
  This may be done, and we may be rewarded
  Not with a rope, but with a Royall master,

124 up] Q1; *omit* Q2   136 *Butler, Pantler, Yeoman.*] Dyce; *Omn.* Q2; *All.* Q1–3
*140 *Butler.*] *stet* Q2   *142 swinge] *stet* Q2

And yet we may be hang'd too.
Yeoman.   Say 'twere done,
Who is it done for? is it not for *Rollo*
And for his right?
Cook.   And yet we may be hang'd too.
Butler.   Or say he take it, say we be discover'd.
Yeoman.   Is not the same man bound still to protect us?   150
Are we not his?
Butler.   Sure he will never faile us.
Cook.   If he doe friends, we shall finde that will hold us,
And yet me thinks this prologue to our purpose,
These Crownes should promise more. Tis easly done,
As easy as a man would rost an egge,
If that be all; for look ye gentlemen,
Here stands my broths: my finger slipps a litle,
Downe drops a dose, I stirre him with my ladle,
And there's a dish for a Duke: *Olla podrida*:
Here stands a bak't meate, he wants a litle seasning,   160
A foolish mistake, my spice-boxe gentlemen,
And put in some of this, the matters ended:
Dredge ye a dish of Plovers, there's the art on't,
Or in a galingale a little does it.
Yeoman.   Or as I fill my wine.
Cook.   Tis very true Sir
Blessing it with your hand, thus, quick and neatly
First, tis past.
Yeoman.   And done once tis as easy
For him to thank us for it, and reward us.
Pantler.   But 'tis a damned sinne.
Cook.   I never feare that,
The fire's my playfellow, and now I am resolv'd boyes.   170
Butler.   Why then have with yee.
Yeoman.   The same for mee.
Pantler.   For me too.
Cook.   And now no more our worships, but our Lordships.
[*Exeunt.*]

159 podrida] F2; podrilla Q2, Q1

190

Pantler.   Not this yeare o' my knowledge, ile un-lord ye.

Exit.

Enter Servant *and* Shewer [*and Officers, Guard, and Ushers*].   [II.] iii

Servant.   Perfume the roome round: and prepare the table:
Gentlemen officers waite in your places.
Shewer.   Make roome there,   *Banquet* [*brought in*].
Roome for the Dukes meate, Gentlemen be bare there,
Cleere all the entrance, Guard put by those gapers,
And Gentlemen Ushers see the Gallery cleere
The Dukes are coming on.   *Hoboyes* [*sound*].

Enter Sophia *between* Rollo *and* Otto, Aubrey, Latorch, Gisbert,
Baldwin, *attendants*; Hamond, Matilda.

Servant [*apart*].   Tis certainly inform'd.
Otto [*apart*].   Reward the fellow,
And looke you mainely to it.
Servant [*apart*].   My life for yours Sir.
Sophia.   Now am I straight my Lords, and young againe,   10
My long since blasted hopes shoote out in blossomes,
The fruits of everlasting love appearing.
O my blest boyes, the honour of my yeares,
Of all my cares the bounteous faire rewarders!
O let me thus embrace you, thus for ever
Within a mothers love lock up your friendships,
And my sweet sonnes, once more with mutuall twineings,
As one chast bed begot you, make one body:
Blessings from heaven in thousand showers fall on yee.
Aubrey.   O womans goodnesse never to be equall'd,   20
May the most sinfull creatures of thy Sex,
But kneeling at thy Monument, rise Saints.
Sophia.   Sit downe my worthy sonnes, my Lords your places.
I, now me thinks the Table's nobly furnish't,
Now the meat nourishes, the wine gives Spirit,
And all the roome stuck with a generall pleasure,

173 o' my] Q2(c); o my Q2(u); on my Q1   *5 gapers] Q1; papers Q2
*7 coming on.] *stet* Q2   9 yours] Q1; you Q2

Shewes like the peacefull bower of happinesse.

Aubrey.   Long may it last, and from a heart fill'd with it
Full as my cup, I give it round my Lords.

Baldwin.   And may that stubborne heart be drunk with sorrow   30
Refuses it, men dying now should take it,
And by the vertue of this Ceremony
Shake off their miseries and sleepe in peace.

Rollo.   You are sad my noble brother.

Otto.   No indeed Sir.

Sophia.   No sadnesse my sweet sonne this day.

Rollo.   Pray ye eate,
Something is here you have lov'd, tast of this dish,
It will prepare your Stomack.

Otto.   Thank you brother,
I am not now dispos'd to eate.

Rollo.   Or that,
You put us out of heart man, come these bak'd meats
Were ever your best dyet.

Otto.   None I thanke you.   ⟍ 40

Sophia.   Are you well noble Child?

Otto.   Yes gratious mother.

Rollo.   Give him a cup of wine then, pledge the health,
Drinke it to me, ile give it to my mother.

Sophia.   Doe my best child.

Otto.   I must not my best mother,
Indeed I dare not, for of late my body
Has been much weakned, by excesse of dyet.
The promise of a feaver hanging on mee,
And even now ready, if not by abstinence——

Rollo.   And will you keep it in this generall freedome;
A little health preferrd before our friendship.   50

Otto.   I pray you excuse mee, sir.

Rollo.   Excuse your selfe sir,
Come tis your feare, and not your feaver brother,
And you have done me a most worthy kindnesse.
My Royall mother, and my noble Lords,

50–52 *Rollo.* And . . . mee, sir.] Q1; *omit* Q2

192

Heare, for it now concernes me to speak boldly,
What faith can be expected from such vowes,
From his dissembling smiles, what fruit of friendship,
From all his full embraces, what blest issue,
When he shall brand me here with base suspition?
He takes me for a poysoner.

Sophia.　　　　　　　　Gods defend it sonne.　　　60

Rollo.　For a foule knave, a villaine, and so feares mee.

Otto.　I could say something too.

Sophia.　　　　　　　　You must not so sir,
Without your great forgetfulnesse of virtue.
This is your brother and your honour'd brother,
Indeed your loving brother.

Rollo.　　　　　　　If he please so.

Sophia.　One noble Father with as noble thoughts,
Begot your minds and bodies, one care rockt you,
And one truth to you both was ever sacred;
Now fye my *Otto*, whether flyes your goodnesse?
Because the right hand has the power of cutting,　　70
Shall the left presently cry out, hee's maymde?
They are one my childe, one power and one performance,
And joyn'd together thus one love, one body.

Aubrey.　I doe beseech your Grace, take to your thoughts,
More certaine Counsailors then doubts and feares,
They strangle nature, and disperse themselves
If once beleev'd, into such foggs and errors,
That the bright truth her selfe can never sever.
Your brother is a Royall gentleman,
Full him selfe of honour and honesty,　　80
And take heed Sir, how nature bent to goodnesse,
(So straight a Cedar to himselfe) uprightnesse
Being wrested from his true use, prove not dangerous.

Rollo.　Nay my good brother knowes I am to patient.

Latorch.　Why should your grace think him a poysoner?
Has he no more respect to piety,
And but he has by oath tyde up his fury,

80 him selfe of] of him selfe Q2, Q1–Q3　　　83 Being] Seward; Be Q2, Q1–Q3

193

Who durst but think that thought?
Aubrey.   Away, thou firebrand.
Latorch.   If men of his sort, of his power and place,
The eldest sonne in honour to this Dukedome.——   90
Baldwin.   For shame contain thy tongue, thy poysonous tongue,
That with her burning Venome will infect all,
And once more blow a wildfire through the Dukedome.
Gisbert.   *Latorch*, if thou bee'st honest or a man,
Containe thy selfe.
Aubrey.   Goe to, no more, by heaven
You'l finde you have plaid the foole else, not a word more.
Sophia.   Prethee, sweet sonne.
Rollo.   Let him alone sweet mother, and my Lords
To make you understand how much I honour
This sacred peace, and next my innocence,   100
And to avoid all future difference
Discourse may draw on, to a way of danger,
I quit my place, and take my leave for this night,
Wishing a generall joy may dwell among yee.
Aubrey.   Shall we waite upon your Grace?
Rollo.   I dare not break yee:——
  Latorch.   *Exeunt* Rollo *and* Latorch.
Sophia.   Doe you now perceive your brothers sweetnesse?
Otto.   O mother that your tendernesse had eyes,
Discerning eyes, what would this man appeare then?
The tale of *Synon* when he took upon him
To ruine *Troy*, with what a cloud of cunning   110
He hid his heart? nothing appearing outwards
But came like innocence and dropping pitty,
Sighes that would sinke a Navy, and had tales
Able to take the eares of Saints beliefe too,
And what did all these? blew the fire to *Ilion*.
His crafty art (but more refin'd by study)
My brother has put on, oh I could tell yee
But for the reverence I beare to nature,
Things that would make your honest bloud move backward.

116 His ... study)] Q1; *omit* Q2

194

Sophia.   Yee dare tell me.
Otto.   Yes in your private closet,   120
  Where I will presently attend you, rise,
  I am a litle troubled but twill off.
Sophia.   Is this the joy I lookt for?
Otto.   All will mend.
  Be not disturb'd deere mother: Ile not faile you.

> *Exeunt* Sophia, *and* Otto [*severally,*
> *Guests and Attendants*; *manent* Baldwin, Aubrey].

Baldwin.   I doe not like this.
Aubrey.   That's still in our powers,
  But how to make it so that we may like it——
Baldwin.   Beyond us ever. *Latorch* me thought was busie,
  That fellow, if not lookt to narrowly,
  Will doe a suddaine mischiefe.
Aubrey.   Hell look to him,
  For if there may be a divell above all yet,   130
  That rogue will make him. Keep your selfe up this night.
  And so will I, for much I feare a danger.
Baldwin.   I will, and in my watches use my praiers.

> *Exeunt.*

A Stoole set out.   III.i
Enter Sophia, Otto, Matilda, Edith.

Otto.   You wonder (Madam) that for all the shewes
  My brother *Rollo* makes of hearty love,
  And free possession of the Dukedome twixt us,
  I notwithstanding should stand still suspicious;
  As if beneath those vailes, he did convey
  Intents and practises of hate and treason.
Sophia.   It breeds indeed my wonder.
Otto.   Which makes mine.
  Since tis so safe and broad a beaten way
  Beneath the name of friendship to betray.
Sophia.   Though in remote and further off affections   10
  These falshoods are so common, yet in him

---

*10 affections] Q1; affection Q2

They cannot so force nature.

Otto.   The more neere
The bonds of truth binde, the more oft they sever,
Being better cloakes to cover falshood ever.

Sophia.   It cannot be that fruits (the tree so blasting)
Can grow in nature; take heed (gentle sonne)
Lest some suborn'd suggester of these treasons
Beleev'd in him by you, provoke, the rather
His tender envies to such fowle attempts.
Or that your too much love to rule alone   20
Bred not of him this jealous passion;
There is not any ill we might not beare
Were not our good held at a price too deere.

Otto.   So apt is treachery to be excus'd
That innocence is still aloud abus'd,
The fate of vertue ev'n her friends perverts
To plead for vice oftimes against their hearts;
Heavens blessing is her curse, which she must beare,
That she may never love herself too deere.

Sophia.   Alas (my sonne) nor fate nor heaven it selfe   30
Can or would wrest my whole care of your good
To any least securenesse in your ill.
What I urge issues from my curious feare,
Lest you should make your meanes to scape your snare,
Doubt of sincerenesse is the only meane,
Not to incense it but corrupt it cleane.

Otto.   I rest as far from wrong of all syncerenesse,
As he flies from the practise, trust me (Madam)
I know by their confessions he suborn'd,
What I should eat, drink, touch, or only have sented   40
This evening feast was poyson'd; but I feare,
His open violence more, that trecherous odds
Which he in his insatiate thirst of rule
Is like to execute.

Sophia.   Beleeve it sonne,

---

14 to cover falshood ever] to falshood ever Q2; to cover falshood over Q1–Q3
*18 provoke] Seward; provok'd Q2, Q1–Q3   *21 Bred ... of] *stet* Q2
29 herself too deere] Seward; *omit* Q2, Q1–Q3   43 Which he] Q1; *omit* Q2

If still his stomack be so foule, to feed
On such grosse objects, and that thirst to rule
The state alone, be yet unquencht in him,
Poysons and such close treasons ask more time
Then can suffice his fiery spirits hast,
And were there in him such desire to hide   50
So false a practise, there would likewise rest
Conscience and feare in him of open force,
And therefore close nor open you need feare.

Matilda.   Good Madame stand not so inclin'd to trust,
What proves his tendrest thoughts to doubt it just;
Who knowes not the unbounded flood and sea,
In which my brother *Rollo's* appetites
Alter and rage with every puffe of breath
His swelling bloud exhales? and therefore heare
What gives my temperate brother cause to use   60
His readiest circumspection, and consult,
For remedy gainst all his wicked purposes;
If he arme, arme, if he strow mines of treason
Meet him with countermines, 'tis justice still
(For goodnesse sake) to encounter ill with ill.

Sophia.   Avert from us such justice (equall heaven)
And all such cause of justice.

Otto.   Past all doubt,
(For all the sacred priviledge of night)
This is no time for us to sleep or rest in,
Who knowes not all things holy are prevented   70
With ends of all impiety? all but
Lust, gaine, ambition.

Enter Rollo *arm'd and* Latorch.

Rollo.   Perish all the world
Ere I but loose one foot of possible Empire:
Be sleights and colour us'd by slaves and wretches,
I am exempt by birth from both those curbes,
And sit above them in all justice, since

49 hast] *i.e.,* haste   61 readiest] Q1; *omit* Q2   65 with] Q1; for Q2
74 Be] Q1; By Q2

197

I sit above in power; where power is given,
Is all the right suppos'd of earth and heaven.
Latorch.   Prove both Sir, see the Traitour.
Otto.   He comes arm'd.
See mother now your confidence.
Sophia.   What rage   80
Affects this monster!
Rollo.   Give me way or perish.
Sophia.   Make thy way Viper if thou thus affect it.
Otto.   This is a Treason like thee.
Rollo.   Let her goe.
Sophia.   Embrace me, weare me as thy sheild my sonne,
And through my brest let his rude weapon run
To thy lives innocence.
Otto.   Play not two parts,
Treacher and coward both, but yeeld a sword,
And let thy arming thee be odds enough
Against my naked bosome.
Rollo.   Loose his hold.
Matilda.   Forbeare base murtherer.
Rollo.   Forsake our Mother.   90
Sophia.   Mother, do'st thou name me,
And put off nature thus?
Rollo.   Forsake her, traitour,
Or by the spoile of nature thorough hers
This leads unto thy heart.
Otto.   Hold.
Sophia.   Hold me still.
Otto.   For twenty hearts and lives I will not hazard
One drop of bloud in yours.
Sophia.   O thou art lost then.
Otto.   Protect my innocence heaven.
Sophia.   Call out murder.
Matilda.   Be murdred all, but save him.
Edith.   Murder, murder.
Rollo.   Cannot I reach you yet?
Otto.   No, fiend. [*They grapple.*]

Rollo.   *Latorch*
  Rescue, I am downe.
Latorch.   Up then, your sword cooles Sir,   100
  Ply it i'th flame and work your ends out.
Rollo.   Ha,
  Have at you there Sir.   [*Stabs* Otto.]

                    Enter Aubrey.

Aubrey.   Author of prodigies,
  What sights are these!
Otto.   O give me a weapon *Aubrey.*
Sophia.   O part em, part 'em.
Aubrey.   For heavens sake no more.
Otto.   No more resist his fury, no rage can
  Adde to his mischiefe done.   *Dies.*
Sophia.   Take spirit my *Otto,*
  Heaven will not see thee dye thus.
Matilda.   He is dead,
  And nothing lives but death of every goodnesse.
Sophia.   O he hath slain his brother, curse him heaven.
Rollo.   Curse and be curst, it is the fruit of cursing.   110
  Latorch, take off here; bring too of that bloud
  To colour ore my shirt, then raise the Court,
  And give it out how he attempted us
  In our bed naked; shall the name of brother
  Forbid us to enlarge our state and powers?
  Or place affects of bloud above our reason,
  That tells us all things good against another,
  Are good i'th same line against a brother.   *Exit* [*with* Latorch].

                    Enter Gisbert, Baldwin.

Gisbert.   What affaires informe these outcries?
Aubrey.   See and grieve.
Gisbert.   Prince *Otto* slaine!
Baldwin.   O execrable slaughter!   120
  What hand hath author'd it?

        112 colour] Q1; bloudy Q2   *115 and] Q1; or Q2

                          199

Aubrey.   Your Schollers, *Baldwin.*
Baldwin.   Unjustly urg'd Lord *Aubrey*, as if I
   For being his schoolemaster must teach this doctrine.
   You are his Counsellour did you advise him
   To this foule parricide?
Gisbert.   If rule affect this license, who would live
   To worse then dye, in force of his obedience?
Baldwin.   Heavens cold and lingring spirit to punish sinne,
   And humane bloud so fiery to commit it?
   One so outgoes the other it will never   130
   Be turn'd to fit obedience.
Aubrey.   Burst it then
   With his full swing given, where it brooks no ground,
   Complaints of it are vaine, and all that rests
   To be our refuge (since our powers are strengthlesse)
   Is to conforme our wills to suffer freely
   What with our murmures we can never master.
   Ladies be pleas'd with what heavens pleasure suffers,
   Erect your Princely countenances and spirits,
   And to redresse the mischiefe now resistlesse,
   Sooth it in shew, rather then curse or crosse it,   140
   Wish all amends and vow to it your best,
   But till you may performe it let it rest.
Gisbert.   Those temporizings are too dull and servile
   To breath the free ayre of a manly soule
   Which shall in me expire in execrations
   Before for any life I sooth a murderer.
Baldwin.   Powr lives before him till his own be drye
   Of all lives services and humane comforts,
   None left that looks at heaven's halfe so base
   To doe these black and hellish actions grace.   150

              Enter Rollo, Latorch, Hamond, *and Guard.*

Rollo.   Hast *Latorch,*
   And raise the City as the Court is rais'd,

143 too] Q1; both Q2   *147 Powr] (*i.e.,* Pour) *stet* Q2 (Power)
149 heaven's halfe] Q1 (heaven is halfe); heaven 'sleft halfe Q2

200

Proclaiming the abhorr'd conspiracy
In plot against my life.
Latorch.   I shall my Lord.   *Exit.*
Rollo.   You there that mourne upon the justly slayne,
   Arise and leave it if you love your lives,
   And heare from me, what (kept by you) may save you.
Matilda.   What will the Butcher doe? I will not stir.
Rollo.   Stir, and unforc't stir, or stir never more.
   Command her you (grave Beldam) that know better   160
   My deadly resolutions, since I drew them
   From the infective fountaine of your own,
   Or if you have forgot, this fiery prompter
   Shall fix the fresh impression in your heart.
Sophia.   Rise daughter serve his will in what we may,
   Lest what we may not he enforce the rather,
   Is this all you command us?
Rollo.   This addition
   Only admitted, that when I endeavour
   To quit me of this slaughter, you presume not
   To crosse me with a syllable, nor your soules   170
   Murmur, nor think against it, but weigh well,
   It will not help your ill, but help to more;
   And that my hand wrought thus far to my will
   Will check at nothing till his circle fill.
Matilda.   Fill it so, I consent not, but who soothes it
   Consents, and who consents to tyranny does it.
Rollo.   False Traiteresse dye then with him.
Aubrey.   Are you mad
   To offer at more bloud, and make your selfe
   More horrid to your people? Ile proclaime
   It is not as your instrument will publish.   180
Rollo.   Doe, and take that along with you——
                    [Rollo *strikes at him;*] Aubrey *disarms him.*
                                        so nimble:
   Resigne my sword, and dare not for thy soule

To offer what thou insolently threatnest,
One word proclaiming crosse to what *Latorch*
Hath in commission, and intends to publish.
Aubrey.   Well Sir, not for your threats, but for your good,
Since more hurt to you would more hurt your countrey,
And that you must make vertue of the need
That now compells you, ile consent as far
As silence argues to your will proclaim'd.   190
And since no more sonnes of your princely Father
Survive to rule but you, and that I wish
You should rule like your Father, with the love,
And zeale of all your subjects, this foule slaughter
That now you have committed made asham'd
With that faire blessing that in place of plagues
Heaven tries our mending disposition with,
Take here your sword, which now use like a Prince,
And no more like a Tyrant.
Rollo.   This sounds well.
Live and be gratious with us.
Gisbert and *Baldwin.*   O Lord *Aubrey.*   200
Matilda [*apart*].   He flatter thus?
Sophia [*apart*].   He temporizes fitly.
Matilda [*apart*].   Wonder invades me.
Rollo.   Doe you two think much
That he thus wisely and with need consents
To what I author for your countries good,
You being my Tutor, you my Chancellour?
Gisbert.   Your Chancellour is not your flatterer Sir.
Baldwin.   Nor ist your Tutors part to shield such doctrine.
Rollo.   Sir first know you,
In praise of your pure Oratory that rais'd you,
That when the people who I know by this   210
Are rais'd out of their rests and hastning hither,
To witnesse what is done here are arriv'd
With our *Latorch*, that you (extempore)
Shall fashion an Oration to acquit

*202 *Matilda.* Wonder ... *Rollo.* Doe] *Rollo.* Wonder ... doe Q2, Q1–Q3
209 rais'd you] raise you Q1; rais'd me Q2   213 that] Q1; *omit* Q2

And justifie this forced fact of mine,
Or for the proud refusall loose your head.
Gisbert.   I fashion an oration to acquit you?
Sir know you then that 'tis a thing lesse easy
T'excuse a parricide then to commit it.
Rollo.   I doe not wish you Sir to excuse me,   220
But to accuse my brother as the cause
Of his owne slaughter, by attempting mine.
Gisbert.   Not for the world, I shold powre bloud on bloud,
It were another murder to accuse
Him that fell innocent.
Rollo.   Away with him,
Hence, haile him straight to execution.
Aubrey.   Far fly such rigor your amendfull hand.
Rollo.   He perishes with him that speaks for him.
Guard doe your office on him, on your lives paine.
Gisbert.   Tyrant 'twill hast thine own death.
Rollo.   Let it wing it,   230
He threatens mee, villaines teare him peece-meale hence.
Guard.   Avant Sir,
Hamond.   Force him hence.
Rollo.   Dispatch him Captaine,
And bring me instant word he is dispatch't,
And how his Rhetorique takes it.
Hamond.   Ile not faile sir.
Rollo.   Captaine besides, remember this in chiefe,
That being executed you deny
To all his friends the Rites of funerall,
And cast his carcase out to doggs and fowles.
Hamond.   Tis done my Lord.
Rollo.   Upon your life not faile.
                    Exit [Hamond *with* Gisbert *and Guard*].
Baldwin.   What impious dareing is there here of heaven!   240
Rollo.   Sir now prepare your selfe, against the people
Make here their entry, to discharge the Oration
He hath denyde my will.

232 *Hamond. . . . hence.*] Q1; *omit* Q2

Baldwin.   For feare of death?
  Ha, ha, ha.
Rollo.   Is death ridiculous with you?
  Workes misery of age this, or thy Judgement?
Baldwin.   Judgement false Tyrant.
Rollo.   You'l make no Oration then?
Baldwin.   Not to excuse
  But agravate thy murther if thou wilt,
  Which I will so inforce, ile make thee wreack it
  (With hate of what thou win'st by't) on thy self   250
  With such another justly merited murther.

                    Enter Latorch.

Rollo.   Ile answer you anon.
Latorch.   The Citizens
  Are hasting Sir in heapes, all full resolv'd
  By my perswasion of your brothers treasons.
Rollo.   Honest *Latorch.*

        Enter Hamond [*with the head, and the Guard*].

Hamond.   See Sir here's *Gisberts* head.
Rollo.   Good speed, wast with a sword?
Hamond.   An axe my Lord.
Rollo.   An axe, twas vilely done: I would have had
  Mine own fine headsman done it with a sword,
  Goe, take this dotard hence, and take his head
  Off with a sword.
Hamond.   Your Schoolemaster?
Rollo.   Even he.   260
Baldwin.   For teaching thee no better, 'tis the best
  Of all thy damned Justices, away
  Captaine, ile follow.
Edith.   O stay there Duke,
  And in the midst of all thy bloud and fury
  Heare a Poore maids petitions, heare a daughter
  The only daughter of a wretched father,

O stay your hast, as you shall need this mercy.

Rollo.   Away with this fond woman.

Edith.   You must heare mee:
  If there be any sparke of pitty in you,
  If sweet humanity and mercy rule you.   270
  I doe confesse you are a Prince, your anger
  As great as you, your execution greater.

Rollo.   Away with him.

Edith.   O Captaine by thy man-hood,
  By her soft soule that bare thee:——I doe confesse sir,
  Your doome of justice on your foes most righteous;
  Good noble Prince looke on me.

Rollo.   Take her from me.

Edith.   A curse upon his life that hinders me,
  May fathers blessing never fall upon him,
  May heaven never heare his prayers. I beseech you,   [*Kneeles.*]
  O Sir, these teares beseech you, these chast hands woe you,   280
  That never yet were heav'd but to things holy,
  Things like your selfe, you are a God above us,
  Be as a God then, full of saving mercy,
  Mercy, O mercy sir, for his sake mercy,
  That when your stout heart weepes, shall give you pitty.
  Here I must growe.

Rollo.   By heaven Ile strike thee woman.

Edith.   Most willingly, let all thy anger seize mee,
  All the most studyed torments, so this good man,
  This old man, and this innocent escape thee.

Rollo.   Carry him away I say.   290

Edith.   Now blessing on thee: o sweet pitty
  I see it in thy eyes. I charge ye souldiers,
  Even by the Princes power release my Father,
  The Prince is mercifull, why doe ye hold him?
  The Prince forgets his fury, why doe ye tug him?
  He is old, why doe ye hurt him? speak O speak sir,
  Speak, as you are a man, a mans life hangs sir,
  A friends life and a foster life, upon you.
  'Tis but a word, but mercy, quickly spoke sir,
  O speake Prince speake.

Rollo.   Will no man here obay mee?   300
  Have I no rule yet? as I live he dies
  That does not execute my will and suddenly.
Baldwin.   All thou canst doe takes but one short houre from me.
Rollo.   Hew off her hands.
Hamond.   Lady hold off.
Edith.   No, hew 'em,
  Hew off my innocent hands as he commands you,
  Theyle hang the faster on for deaths convulsion.
                Exit Baldwin *with* [Hamond *and*] *the Guard.*
  Thou seed of rocks, will nothing move thee then,
  Are all my teares lost, all my righteous prayers
  Drown'd in thy drunken wrath? I stand up then,   [*She rises.*]
  Thus boldly bloudy Tyrant,   310
  And to thy face in heavens high name defy thee,
  And may sweet mercy when thy soule sighs for it,
  When under thy black mischiefes thy flesh trembles,
  When neither strength nor youth, nor friends nor gold,
  Can stay one hower, when thy most wretched conscience
  Wak'd from her dreame of death, like fire shall melt thee,
  When all thy mothers teares, thy brothers wounds,
  Thy peoples feares and curses, and my losse,
  My aged fathers losse shall stand before thee——
Rollo.   Save him I say, run save him, save her Father,   320
  Fly and redeeme his head.   *Exit* Latorch.
Edith.   May then that pitty,
  That comfort thou expect'st from heaven, that mercy
  Be lockt up from thee, fly thee, howlings finde thee,
  Dispaire, O my sweet father! stormes of terrors,
  Bloud, till thou burst againe.
Rollo.   O faire sweet anger!

    Enter Latorch *and* Hamond *with a head* [*and Guard*].

Latorch.   I came too late Sir, 'twas dispatch't before,
  His head is heere.
Rollo.   And my heart there; goe bury him,

Give him faire rites of funerall, decent honours.
                    [*Exit* Hamond *with the head.*]
Edith.   Wilt thou not take mee monster? highest heaven,
Give him a punishment fit for his mischiefe.   330
Latorch.   I feare thy prayer is heard, and he rewarded:
Lady have patience, 'twas unhappy speed,
Blame not the Duke, 'twas not his fault but fates,
He sent you know to stay it, and commanded
In care of you, the heavy object hence
Soone as it came, have better thoughts of him.

                    Enter the Citizens.

Citizen 1.   Where's this young Traitor?
Latorch.   Noble Citizens, heere,
And heere the wounds he gave your Soveraigne Lord.
Citizen 1.   This Prince of force must be
Belov'd of Heaven, that heaven hath thus preserv'd.   340
Citizen 2.   And if he be belov'd of heaven you know,
He must be just and all his actions so.
Rollo.   Concluded like an Oracle, O how great
A grace of heaven is a wise Citizen!
For heaven 'tis makes them wise, as't made mee just,
As it preserv'd mee, as I now survive,
By his strong hand to keep you all alive,
Your wives, your children, goods and lands kept yours,
That had been else prey to his Tyrannous power.
That would have prey'd on mee, in bed assaulted mee   350
In sacred time of peace, my mother heere,
My sister, this just Lord, and all had fill'd
The Curtian Gulfe of this conspiracy,
Of which my Tutor and my Chancellor,
(Two of the gravest and most counted honest
In all my Dukedome) were the monstrous heads.
O trust no honest men for their sakes ever
My politique Citizens, but those that beare,
The names of Cutthroats, Userers, and Tyrants.

329 highest] Q1; high Q2   *340 preserv'd.] *stet* Q2   341 belov'd] Q1; lov'd Q2
348 children,] Q1; childrens Q2   352 fill'd] Seward (Sympson *conj.*); felt Q2, Q1–Q3

O those beleeve in; for the foule mouth'd world   360
Can give no better tearmes to simple goodnesse,
Even me it dares blaspheme, and thinks me tyrannous
For saving mine own life, sought by my brother;
Yet those that sought his life before by poison,
(Though mine own servants hoping to please me)
Ile lead to death for't which your eyes shall see.

Citizen 1.   Why what a Prince is here!

Citizen 2.   How just?

Citizen 3.   How gentle?

Rollo.   Well now my deerest subjects, or much rather
My nerves, my spirits, or my vitall bloud,
Turne to your needfull rest, and setled peace,   370
Fixt in this root of steele, from whence it sprung
In heavens great help and blessing, but ere sleep
Binde in his sweet oblivion your dull sences,
The name and vertue of heavens King advance
For yours (in chiefe) for my deliverance.

Citizens.   Heaven and his King save our most pious Soveraign.

Rollo.   Thanks my good people: *Exeunt* Citizens.
                              mother, and kind sister,
And you my noble kinsman, things borne thus,
Shall make yee all command what ever I
Enjoy in this my absolute Empery.   380
Take in the body of my Princely brother,
For whose death since his fate no other way
Would give my eldest birth his supreme right,
Wee'l mourne the cruell influence it beares,
And wash his Sepulcher with kindly teares.

                    Exeunt [bearing off Ottos *body]* omnes
                    præter [Aubrey,] Latorch *and* Edith.

Aubrey.   If this game end thus, heavens will rule the seat:
What we have yeelded to, we could not let.   [*Exit* Aubrey.]

Latorch.   Good Lady rise and raise your spirits withall
More high then they are humbled, you have cause

As much as ever honour'd happiest Lady,   390
And when your eares are freer to take in
Your most amendfull and unmatched fortunes,
Ile make yee drowne a hundred helplesse deaths
In sea of one life pour'd into your bosome
With which shall flowe into your armes the riches,
The pleasures, honours, and the rules of Princes.
Which though death stop your eares me thinks should ope them:
Assay to forget death.
Edith.   O slaughtered Father!
Latorch.   Cast off what cannot be redrest, and blesse
The fate that yet you curse so, since for that   400
You spake so movingly, and your sweet eyes
With so much grace fill'd, that you set on fire
The Dukes affection, whom you now may rule
As he rules all his Dukedome, ist not sweet?
Does it not shine away your sorrowes cloudes?
Sweet Lady take wise heart, and heare and tell me.
Edith.   I heare no word you speak.
Latorch.   Prepare to heare then,
And be not barr'd up from your selfe, nor adde
To your ill fortune with your far worse judgement,
Make me your servant to attend with all joyes   410
Your sad estate, till they both blesse and speake it:
See how theil bow t'ye, make me wait, command me
To watch out every minute, for the stay
Your modest sorrow fancies, raise your graces,
And doe my hopes the honour of your motion
To all the offer'd heights that now attend you.
O how your touches ravish! how the Duke
Is slaine already with your flames imbrac't!
I will both serve and visit you and often.
Edith.   I am not fit Sir.
Latorch.   Time will make you Lady.   420
                                        Exeunt.

Enter Guard, three or four boyes, then the Sheriffe, [*leading the*   [III.
Master] Cook, Yeoman *of the Seller*, Butler, *and* Pantler *to*
execution.

Guard 1.   Come bring these fellowes on, away with em.
Guard 2.   Make roome afore there, roome there for the prisoners.
Boy 1.   Lets run afore boyes, we shall get no place else.
Boy 2.   Are these the youths?
Cook.   These are the youths you look for.
   And pray my honest friends be not so hasty.
   Ther'le be nothing done till we come I assure you.
Boy 3.   Heres a wise hanging, are there no more?
Butler.   Doe you heare Sir,
   You may come in for your share ift please you.
Cook.   My friend if you be unprovided of a hanging
   You look like a good fellow, I can afford you   10
   A reasonable penniworth.
Boy 2.   Afore, afore boyes,
   Heres e'en enough to make us sport.
Yeoman.   Pox take you,
   Doe you call this sport? Are these your recreations?
   Must we be hang'd to make you mirth?
Cook.   Doe you heare Sir,
   You Custard-pate, we goe too't for high treason,
   An honourable fault, thy foolish father
   Was hang'd for stealing sheep.
Boyes.   Away, away boyes.
                        [*Exeunt boyes.*]
Cook.   Doe you see how that sneaking rogue lookes now? you chip
   Pantler,
   You peaching rogue that provided us these necklaces,
   You poore rogue, you costive rogue you.
Pantler.   Pray, pray fellowes.   20
Cook.   Pray for thy crusty soul, where's your reward now
   Good goodman manchet, for your fine discovery?
   I doe beseech you Sir, where are your dollers?

        18 chip] Q1; sheep Q2   *19 peaching] *stet* Q2
        22 manchet] (a small loaf of fine bread)

Draw with your fellows and be hang'd.

Yeoman.   He must now,
For now he shall be hang'd first, that's his comfort,
A place too good for thee, thou meale-mouthd rascall.

Cook.   Hang handsomely for shame, come leave your praying
You peaking knave, and die like a good Courtier,
Die honestly and like a man, no preaching
With——I beseech you take example by me,   30
I liv'd a lewd man, good people——pox on't,
Die me as thou had'st din'd, say grace and God be with you.

Guard.   Come will yee forward?

Cook.   Good Master Sheriffe your leave too.
This hasty work was never done well, give us so much time
As but to sing our own Ballad, for weel trust no man
Nor no tune but our own, 'twas done in Ale too,
And therefore cannot be refus'd in justice,
Your penny-pot-Poets are such pelting theeves,
They hang men ever twice, we have it here Sir,
And so must every marchant of our voyage,   40
Heele make a sweet returne else of his credit.

Yeoman.   One fit of our own mirth, and then we are for yee.

Guard 1.   Make hast then and dispatch.

Yeoman.   Theres day enough Sir,

Cook.   Come boyes sing cheerefully, we shall never sing younger,
We have chose a loud tune too because it should like well.

                    They sing.

> Come fortune's a whore I care not who tell her,
> Would offer to strangle a page of the Celler.
> That should by his oath to any mans thinking
> And place, have had a defence for his drinking.
>   But this she does still when she pleases to palter,   50
>   Instead of his wages she gives him a halter.
>   Three merry boyes, and three merry boyes,
>   And three merry boyes are we,

45–90+3 They sing.] stet Q2   50 *still]* Q1; *omit* Q2

As e're did sing three parts in a string,
All under the triple tree.

But I that was so lusty,
And ever kept my bottles,
That neither they were musty,
And seldome lesse then pottles,
For me to be thus stopt now   60
With hemp insteed of Corke Sir,
And from the Gallows lopt now
Shewes that there is a forke Sir
In death, and this the Token.
Man may be two waies killed,
Or like the bottle broken,
Or like the wine be spilled.
Three merry boyes, etc.

O yet but looke on the master Cook
The glory of the kitchin,   70
In sowing whose fate at so lofty a rate
No Tayler had a stitch in,
For though he make the man,
The Cook yet makes the dishes:
The which no Tailor can,
Wherein I have my wishes.
That I who at so many a feast
Have pleas'd so many Tasters,
Should come my selfe for to be drest,
A dish for you my masters.   80
Three merry boyes, etc.

O Man or Beast or you at least,
That wears or Brow or Antler,
Prick up your eares unto the teares,
Of me poore Paul *the Pantler.*
That am thus clipt, because I chipt.
The cursed crust of Treason
With loyall knife, O dolefull strife,

*86 *clipt ... chipt*] Q1; *chipt ... clipt* Q2

212

> *To hang thus without Reason.*
> Three merry boyes, etc.   90

There's a few copies for ye; now Farewell
Friends, and good Master Sheriffe let me not
Be printed with a brasse pot on my head.
Butler.   March faire, march faire, afore good Captaine Pantler.

Exeunt.

Enter Aubrey *and* Latorch [*at two doores*].   IV.i

Aubrey.   *Latorch* I have waited here to speake to you
And you must hearken: set not forth your leggs
Of hast, nor put your face of businesse on,
An honester affaire then this I urge too,
You will not easily thinke on, and twill be
Reward to entertaine it. 'Tis your fortune
To have our maisters Eare above the rest
Of us that follow him, but that no man envies,
For I have well considered, truth sometimes
May be convay'd in by the same conduits   10
That falshood is. These courses that he takes
Cannot but end in ruine, Empire got
By bloud and violence must so be held,
And how unsafe that is, he first will prove,
That toyling still to remove Enemies
Makes himselfe more: it is not now a Brother,
A faithfull Counsailor of state or two,
That are his danger, they are faire dispatcht,
It is a multitude that gin to feare
And think, what began there must end in them,   20
For all the fine Oration that was made 'em;
And they are not an easy monster quell'd.
Princes may pick their suffering nobles out,
And one by one employ them to the block:
But when they once grow formidable to
Their Clownes and Coblers, ware then guard themelves;

2 leggs] Q2, Q1(u); leg Q1(c)   14 that] Q1; it Q2   23 out] Q1; on't Q2

213

If thou durst tell him this *Latorch*, the service
Would not discredit the good name you hold
With men: besides the profit to your maister,
And to the publique.

Latorch.   I conceive not so Sir,   30
They'r ayery feares, and why should I object 'em
Unto his fancy, wound what is yet sound?
Your Counsells colour not with reason of state,
Where all that's necessary still is just.
The actions of the Prince, while they succeed,
Should be made good and glorifide, not question'd:
Men doe but shew their ill affections
That——

Aubrey.   What? speake out.

Latorch.   Doe murmure gainst their maisters.

Aubrey.   Is this to mee?

Latorch.   It is to whosoever,
Mislikes o'the Dukes courses.

Aubrey.   I? is't so?   40
At your state ward sir.

Latorch.   I am sworne to heare,
Nothing may prejudice the Prince.

Aubrey.   Why? doe you?
Or have you? ha?

Latorch.   I cannot tell: mens hearts
Shew in their words sometimes.

Aubrey.   I ever thought thee
Knave o'th chamber: art thou the spy too?

Latorch.   A watchman for the State, and one that's known
Sir, to be rightly affected.

Aubrey.   Baude of the State,
No lesse then of thy maisters lusts; I now
See nothing can redeeme thee, dar'st thou mention,
Affection or a heart that ne're hadst any?   50
Know'st not to love or hate, but by the scale
As thy Prince does't before thee, that dost never

---

27 thou] Q1; you Q2   30 so] Q1; *omit* Q2   31 They'r] Q1 (They are); Their Q2

Weare thine own face, but putst on his, and gatherst
Baites for his eares, liv'st wholy at his beck,
And ere thou darst utter a thought thine owne,
Must expect his, creep'st forth and wad'st into him,
As if thou wert to passe a ford, there proving
Yet, if thy tongue may step on safely or no,
Then bringst his virtue a sleepe, and staist the wheele
Both of his reason and Judgement that they move not,   60
Whit'st over all his vices, and at last
Dost draw a cloud of words before his eyes,
Till neither he can see thee nor himselfe.
Wretch I dare give him honest Counsells, I,
And love him whil'st I tell him truth: old *Aubrey*
Dares goe the straightest way, which still's the shortest.
Walke on the thornes thou scaterst, Parasite,
And tread 'em unto nothing: and if thou
Then letst a looke fall of the least dislike,
Ile rip thy Crowne up with my sword at height,   70
And pluck thy skinne over thy face in sight
Of him thou flattrest: unto thee I speake it
Slave, against whom all lawes should now conspire,
And e'ry creature that hath sence be arm'd,
As 'gainst the common enimy of mankind,
That slip'st within thy maisters eare, and whisper'st,
'Tis better for him to be fear'd then lov'd,
Bid'st him trust no mans friendship; spare no bloud
That may secure him; Tis no cruelty
That hath a spetious end: for soveraignety,   80
Break all the lawes of kind, if it succeed,
An honest noble and praiseworthy deed,
While he that takes thy poysons in, shall feele,
Their virulent workings in a point of time,
When no repentance can bring aide, but all
His spirits shall melt, which what his conscience burn'd,
And dying in a flatterers armes shall fall unmourn'd.
There's matter for you now.

55 darst] Q1; durst Q2   *76 slip'st] (Dyce *conj.*); sleep'st Q2, Q1–Q3
80 spetious] F2; spatious Q2, Q1

Latorch.   My Lord this makes not,
For loving of my maister.
Aubrey.   Loving? no,
They hate ill Princes most that make 'em so.   90

Enter Rollo, Hamond, Allan, *Guard.*

Rollo.   Ile heare no more.
Hamond.   Alas tis for my brother,
I beseech your highnesse.
Rollo.   How? a brother?
Had not I one my selfe? did title move mee,
When it was fit that he should dye? away.
Allan.   Brother loose no word more, leave my good cause
To upbraid the Tyrant. Ime glad I am falne
Now in these times that will'd some great example
T'assure men we can dye for honesty.
Rollo.   Sir you are brave, pray that you hold your neck
As bravely forth anon unto the headsman.   100
Allan.   Would he would strike as bravely, and thou by,
Rollo, 'twould make thee quake to see me dye.
Aubrey.   What's his offence?
Hamond.   For giving *Gisbert* buriall
Who was sometimes his Maister.
Allan.   Yes Lord *Aubrey,*
My gratitude and humanity are my Crimes.
Rollo.   Why beare you him not hence?
Aubrey.   My Lord, (stay souldiers)
I doe beseech your highnesse doe not loose,
Such men for so sleight causes, this is one
Hath still been faithfull to you, a try'd soule
In all your fathers battailes. I have seen him   110
Bestride a friend against a score of foes;
And look, he looks as he would kill his hundred
For you Sir, were you in danger.
Allan.   Till he killd
His Brother, his Chancellour, then his master,

*97 these] those Q2, Q1–Q3   108 causes] Q1; clauses Q2
113 killd] Q1; kills Q2

To which he can adde nought to equall *Nero*
But killing of his mother.
Aubrey.   Peace, brave foole,
Thou valiant Asse:——here's his brother too Sir,
A Captaine of your Guard hath serv'd you long
With the most noble witnesse of his truth
Mark'd in his face, and ev'ry part about him   120
That turnes not from an enemie: but view him,
And doe not grieve him, Sir, if you doe meane
That he shall hold his place: it is not safe
To tempt such spirits, and let 'em weare their swords,
You make your Guards your terrours by these Acts,
And throw more hearts off from you then you hold,
And I must tell you Sir (with my old freedome,
And my old faith to boot) you have not liv'd so,
But that your state will need such men, such hands,
Of which here's one shall in an houre of triall   130
Doe you more certaine service with a stroke,
Then the whole bundle of your Flatterers,
With all th' unsavorie unction of their tongues.
Rollo.   Peace, talker.
Aubrey.   One that loves you yet my Lord,
And would not see you pull on your own ruines,
Mercy becomes a Prince, and guards him best,
Awe and affrights they are no ties of love,
And when men 'gin to feare the Prince, they hate him.
Rollo.   Am I the Prince or you?
Aubrey.   My Lord, I hope
I have not utter'd ought should urge that question.   140
Rollo.   Then practise your obedience:——see him dead.
Aubrey.   My Lord.
Rollo.   Ile heare no word more.
Aubrey.   I am sorry then:
There is no small dispaire Sir of their safety,
Whose eares are blocked up against the truth.
Come Captaine.
Hamond.   I doe thank you Sir.
Aubrey.   For what?

For seeing thy brother dye a man and honest?
Live thou so Captaine, I will, I assure thee,
Although I die for't too. Come.

Exeunt omnes præter Rollo, *and* Latorch.

Rollo.   Now *Latorch*,
What doe you think?
Latorch.   That *Aubries* speech and manners
Sound somewhat of the boldest.
Rollo.   Tis his custome.   150
Latorch. It may be so, and yet be worth a feare.
Rollo. If we thought so it should be worth his life,
And quickly too.
Latorch.   I dare not Sir be author
Of what I would, he is so dangerous,
But with your highnesse favour and your license——
Rollo. He talkes 'tis true, and he is licens'd: leave him,
We now are Duke alone, *Latorch* secur'd,
Nothing left standing to obscure our prospect,
We look right forth, beside, and round about us,
And see it ours with pleasure: only one   160
Wisht joy there wants to make us so possesse it,
And that is *Edith*, *Edith*, she that got me
In bloud and teares in such an opposite minute,
As had I not at once felt all the flames,
And shafts of love shot in me (his whole armory)
I should have thought him as far off as death.
Latorch. My Lord expect a while, your happinesse
Is ne'rer then you think it, yet her griefes
Are greene and fresh, your vigilant *Latorch*
Hath not been idle, I have leave already   170
To visit her and send to her.
Rollo.   My life.
Latorch. And if I find not out as speedy waies,
And proper instruments to work and bring her
To your fruition, that she be not watch'd
Tame to your highnesse wish, say you have no servant

147 will] Q1; will so Q2   159 beside,] Q1; besides Q2   175 wish] Q1; *omit* Q2

218

Is capable of such a trust about you,
Or worthy to be slave of your delight.
Rollo.   O my *Latorch*, what shall I render thee
For all thy travells, care, and love?
Latorch.   Sir, one sute,
Which I will ever importune till you grant me.   180
Rollo.   About your Mathematitians.
Latorch.   Yes, to have
The scheme of your nativity judg'd by them.
I hav't already erected; O my Lord,
You doe not know the labour of my feares.
My doubts for you are such as cannot hope
Any security but from the starres,
Who being rightly ask'd can tell man more,
Then all power else, there being no power beyond them.
Rollo.   All thy petitions still are care of us.
Aske for thy selfe.
Latorch.   What more can concerne me   190
Then this?
Rollo.   Well rise true honest man and goe then,
We'le study our selves a meanes how to reward thee.
Latorch.   Your Grace is now inspir'd, now, now your Highnesse
Begins to live, from this houre count your joyes,
But Sir, I must have warrants with blanck figures
To put in names such as I like.
Rollo.   You shall.
Latorch.   They dare not else Sir offer at your figure,
O I shall bring you wonders, there's a Fryer,
Russee an admirable man, *De Bube*
Another Gentleman, and then *La Fiske*,   200
The mirrour of his time, 'twas he that set it,
But theres one *Norbret*, (him I never saw)
Has made a mirrour, a meere looking-glasse
In show you'd think't no other, the forme ovall,
As I am given to understand by letter,

---

*177 be slave] be——Q2; be secretary Q1–Q3
*199–200 *De Bube* | Another Gentleman] | Another Gentleman Q2; another | A gentleman
          Q1–Q3

Which renders you such shapes, and those soe differing
And some that will be question'd, and give answers,
Then has he set it in a frame that wrought
Unto the revolutions of the starres,
And so compact by due proportions   210
Unto their harmony doth move alone
A true *Automaton*: Thus *Dedalus* Statues
Or *Vulcans* stooles——

Rollo.   Do'st thou beleeve this?

Latorch.   Sir,
Why what should stay my faith or turn my sence,
He has been about it above twenty yeares,
Three seavens, the powerfull and the perfect numbers,
And art and time Sir can produce such things:
What doe we read there, of *Hiarbaes* banquet
The great Gymnosophist that had his Butlers
And Carvers of pure gold wait at the table: 220
The images of *Mercury* too, that spoke,
The wooden Dove that flew, a Snake of Brasse
That hist: and Birds of silver that did sing.
All these were done Sir by the Mathematiques:
Without which there's no science nor no truth.

Rollo.   You are in your own sphere (*Latorch*) and rather
Then Ile contend with you for it, ile beleeve you.
Yo' have woon upon me that I wish to see
My fate before me now, what ere it be.

Latorch.   And Ile endeavour you shall know't with speed,   230
For which I should have one of trust goe with me,
If you please, *Hamond*, that I may by him
Send you my first dispatches: after I
Shall bring you more, and as they come still more,
And accurate forth from them.

Rollo.   Take your way,
Choose your own meanes, and be it prosperous to us.

                                        Exeunt.

---

210 compact] Q1; compacted Q2   *213 stooles] *stet* Q2   218 of] Q1; that Q2
234 and] Q1; *omit* Q2   234 still] Q1; *omit* Q2

Enter Russee, De Bube, La Fiske, Norbret, Pipeau.   [IV.] ii

Russee.   Come beare up Sirs, we shall have better daies,
  Mine Almanack tells mee.
De Bube.   Whats that, your rumpe?
Russee.   It never itch't in vaine yet; 'slid *La Fiske*,
  Throw off thy sluggish face, I cannot abide
  To see thee look like a poore Jade i'th pound,
  That saw no meat these three daies.
La Fiske.   'Slight, to me,
  It seemes thirteen daies since I saw any.
Russee.   How?
La Fiske.   I cannot remember that I ever saw
  Or meat or mony, you may talke of both,
  To open a mans Stomack or his purse,   10
  But feed 'em still with aire.
De Bube.   Fryer, I feare
  You doe not say your office well adaies,
  I cannot heare your beads knack.
Norbret.   Pox, he feeds
  With lechery, and lives upon th'exchange
  Of his two eggs and puddings, with the market-women.
Russee.   And what doe you sir with the Advocates wife,
  That you perswade upon your Doctorall bed,
  To take the Mathematicall trance so often?
La Fiske.   Come we are starke nought all; bad's the best on's,
  Foure of the Seaven deadly spots we are: 20
  Besides our lechery we are envious
  And most, most gluttinous when we have it thus,
  Most covetous now we want it: then our boy,
  He is a fift spot, sloth, and he undoes us.
De Bube.   Tis true the child was wont to be industrious,
  And now and then send in a Merchants wife
  Sick o'th husband, or a swearing Butler
  That mist one of his Boles; a crying maid
  Had lost a silver spoone; the Curry-combe

---

3 'slid] Seward; slid Q2; slide Q1–Q3   6 'Slight,] F2; Slight, Q1; S'light Q2
*15 puddings] *stet* Q2

221

Sometimes was wanting: there was something gotten   30
But now——

Pipeau.   What now, did I not yester-morning
Bring you in a Cardicue there from the Peasant,
Whose Asse I had driven aside and hid that you
Might conjure for him? and then last night
Six souse from the Cookes wife, yee shar'd among yee
To set a figure for the pestle I stole,
It is not at home yet. These things my maisters,
In a hard time they would be thought on, you
Talke o'your Lands, and Castles in the aire
O'your twelve houses there, but it is I   40
That bring you in your rents for 'em, tis *Pipeau*
That is your bird call.

Norbret.   Faith he does well,
And cuts through the Element for us, I must needs say
In a fine dextrous line.

La Fiske.   But not as he did
At first, then he would saile with any winde
Int' ev'ry creek and corner.

Pipeau.   I was light then,
New built and rigg'd, when I came to you Gentlemen,
But now with often and farre ventring for you,
Here be leakes sprung, and whole plancks wanting, see you,
If you'l new sheath me againe, yet I am for you   50
To any bay or streights, wh'ere you'l send mee,
For as I am, where can this ragged barke
Put in for any service, lesse it be
I'th ile of Rogues, and there turne Pyrate for you.

Norbret.   Faith he saies reason, Fryer you must leave
Your neat crispe Clarret, and fall to your Sider
A while; and you *La Fiske* your larded Capons
And Turkies for a time, and take a good
Cleane tripe in your way; *De Bube* too must content him
With wholsome two sous'd pettitoes, no more crowne Ordinaries,   60

42 call] Q1; cal'd Q2   *51 bay] Weber (Mason *conj.*); bog Q2, Q1–Q3
*51 streights] Seward; sleights Q2, Q1–Q3   51 wh'ere] where Q2; where ere Q1–Q3
*56 crispe] Q1; crispt Q2   60 two sous'd] *i.e.*, worth two sous each

Till we have clothd our Infant.

De Bube.   So you'l keepe
Your owne good motions Doctor, your deere selfe.

La Fiske.   Yes for we all doe know the latitude
O'your concupiscence.

Russee.   Heere, about your belly.

De Bube.   You'l pick a bottle open, or a whimsey
As soone as the best on us.

La Fiske.   And dip your wrist-bands,
(For cuffes you ha'none) as comely in the sawce,
As any Courtier——   *Bells Ring within.*
                    heark, the Bell, who's there?

Russee.   Good luck I doe conjure thee, boy look out.
                            Exit Pipeau *and enter againe.*

Pipeau.   They are Gallants, Courtiers, one of 'em   70
Is of the Dukes Bedchamber.

Russee.   *Latorch!*——downe,
(*To* Norbret) On with your Gowne, there's a new sute arriv'd:
Did I not tell you Sonnes of honger? Crownes,
Crownes are comming towards you: wine and wenches
You shall have once againe, and Fidlers:
Into your studies close, each lay his eare
T'his doore, and as you heare mee to prepare you,
So come, and put me on that visour only.
                    [*Exeunt* De Bube, La Fiske, Norbret.]

                Enter Latorch *and* Hamond.

Latorch.   Youl not be farre hence Captain, when the businesse
Is done, you shall receive present dispatch.   80

Hamond.   Ile walke sir i'th cloister.   *Exit.*

Russee.   Mounsieur *Latorch*, my sonne,
The starres are happy still that guide you hither.

Latorch.   I am glad to heare their Secretary say so,
My learned Father *Russee*, where's *La Fiske*,
Mounsieur *De Bube*, how doe they?

Russee.   At their studies,
They are the Secretaries of the Starres sir,
Still at their books, they will not be pull'd off,

                        223

They stick like cupping glasses; if ever men
Spoke with the tongue of destiny, 'tis they.
Latorch.   For loves sake lets salute 'em.
Russee.   Boy goe see,   90
Tell 'em who's heere, say that their friends doe challenge
Some portion of their time, this is our minute,
Pray them they will spare it: [*Exit* Pipeau.]
                         they are the Sunne and Moone
Of knowledge, pitty two such noble lights
Should live obscur'd, heere in a University,
Whose beams were fit t'illumine any Court
Of Christendome——
Latorch.   The Duke will shortly know 'em.

Enter La Fiske, De Bube, *and* Pipeau.

La Fiske.   Well look upon the Astrolobe, you'l finde it
Four Almucanturies at least.
De Bube.   It is so.
Russee.   Still of their learned stuffe, they care for nothing,   100
But how to know; as negligent of their bodies
In Dyet or else, especially in their clothes
As if they had no change.
Pipeau [*aside*].   They have so little,
As may well free 'em from the name of shifters.
La Fiske.   Mounsieur *Latorch.*
Latorch.   How is it learned Gentlemen,
With both your vertues?
De Bube.   A most happy houre
When we see you sir.
Latorch.   When you heare me then,
It will be happier; The Duke greets you both
Thus, and though you may touch no mony father,
Yet you may take it.   [*Gives gold to* Pipeau.]
Russee.   Tis his highnesse bounty,   110
But yet to me and these that have put off

95 heere] Q1; heere, heere Q2   96 illumine] Q1; illuminate Q2
97 *Latorch.* The ... 'em.] Q1; *omit* Q2   99 Four] Q1; For Q2
*110 you may] *stet* Q2   111 these] Q1; those Q2

224

The world superfluous.

La Fiske.   We have heard of late
His highnesse good successe.

De Bube.   And gratulate it.

Latorch.   Indeed he hath scap't a strange conspiracy,
Thanks to his starres, which starrs he prayes by mee,
You would againe consult and make a judgement
On what you lately erected for my love.

Russee.   O sir, we dare not.

La Fiske.   For our lives.

De Bube.   It is
The Princes Scheme.

Latorch.   T'incounter with that feare
Here's to assure you, his signet, write your names,   120
And be secur'd all three.   [*Gives papers.*]

De Bube.   We must intreat some time Sir.

Latorch.   I must then
Intreat, it be as present as you can.

La Fiske.   Ha'you the Scheme here?

Latorch.   Yes.

Russee.   I would you had Sir
Another warrant.

Latorch.   What would that doe?

Russee.   Marry,
We have a Doctour Sir that in this businesse
Would not performe the second part.

Latorch.   Not him
That you writ to me of?

Russee.   The very same.

Latorch.   I should have made it Sir my sute to see him,
Here is a warrant (Father), I conceiv'd   [*Gives paper.*] 130
That he had soly apply'd himselfe to Magick.

Russee.   And to these studies too Sir, in this field
He was initiated: but we shall hardly
Draw him from his chaire.

Latorch.   Tell him he shall have gold.

133 initiated] Q1; imitated Q2

La Fiske.   O such a syllable would make him forsweare
   Ever to breath in your sight.
Latorch.   How then?
La Fiske.   Sir, he
   (If you doe please to give him any thing)
   Must hav't convai'd under a paper.
Russee.   Or left behinde some book in his study.
De Bube.   Or in some old wall.
La Fiske.   Where his Familiars   140
   May tell him of it, and that pleases him sir.
De Bube.   Or else Ile goe and assay him.
Latorch.   Take gold with you.
Russee.   That will not be amisse, give it the boy sir,
                                 [*Latorch gives gold.*]
   He knowes his holes, and how to bait his spirits.
Pipeau.   We must lay in severall places sir.
Russee.   That's true,
   That if one come not, the other may hit.   [*Latorch gives gold.*]
Latorch.   Well goe then;   [*Exeunt* Russee *and* Pipeau.]
                    is he so learn'd Gentlemen?
La Fiske.   The very top of our profession, mouth of the Fates,
   Pray Heaven his spirts be in good humour to take,
   They'le fling the gold about the house else.
De Bube.   I,   150
   And beat the Fryer, if he goe not well
   Furnisht with holy water.
La Fiske.   Sir you must observe him.
De Bube.   Not crosse him in a word: for then he's gone.
La Fiske.   If he doe come, which is a hazard yet——
   Mas he's here, this is speed.

                    Enter Norbret, Russee, Pipeau.

Norbret.   Where is your scheme?
   Let's see't; dispatch: nay fumbling now? who's this?
                                 [*Latorch gives scheme.*]
Russee.   Chiefe Gentleman of the Dukes chamber, Doctour.

---

136 *Latorch.* How then? | *La Fiske.*] Q1; *omit* Q2   137 him] Q1; *omit* Q2
155 here] Q1 there Q2   *155 scheme] *stet* Q2

Norbret.   O let him be, good even to him, he's a Courtier,
   Ile spare his complement tell him: whats here?
   The geniture nocturnall: longitude   160
   At twenty one degrees, the latitude
   At forty nine and ten minutes; how are the *Cardines?*
La Fiske.   *Libra* in twenty foure, forty foure minutes,
   And *Capricorne*——
Norbret.   I see't, see the Planets
   Where, how they are dispos'd; the Sunne and *Mercury,*
   Mars with the Dragons taile, in the third house,
   And *pars fortunæ* in the *Imo cœli.*
   Then *Jupiter* in the twelfth, the *Cacodæmon.*
De Bube.   And *Venus* in the second, *inferna porta.*
Norbret.   I see it, peace; then *Saturne* i'th fift,   170
   Luna ith' seaventh. And much of *Scorpio*
   (Thats *Mars* his *gaudium*) rising in the ascendant,
   That joint with *Libra* too, the house of *Venus;*
   And *In imo Coeli, Mars* his exaltation;
   Ith' seaventh house, *Aries,* being his naturall house,
   And where he is now seated: and all these shew him
   To be the *Almuten.*
Russee.   Yes he's Lord of the geniture,
   Whether you examine it by *Ptolomies* way,
   Or *Masahales, Zaell,* or *Alkindus.*
La Fiske.   No other Planet hath so many dignities   180
   Either by himselfe, or in regard o'th' *Cuspes.*
Norbret.   Why hold your tongue then, if you know it; *Venus*
   The Lady of the *Horoscope,* being *Libra,*
   The other part *Mars* rules: so that the geniture
   Being nocturnall, *Luna* is the highest,
   None else being in sufficient dignitie,
   She being in *Aries* in the seaventh house
   Where *Sol* exalted is the *Alchocoden.*

---

*166 in] Q1; *omit* Q2   *167 *fortunæ*] F2; *fortuna* Q2; Fortune Q1
168 twelft] F2 (twelfth); twelve Q1; twelfe Q2
*172 Thats] (Eade *conj.*); That Q2; Then Q1–Q3
*174 *In imo*] (Eade *conj.*); *Imum* Q2; *Juniu* Q1–Q3   *174 exaltation] Q1; exultation Q2
*177 geniture] Q1; genitures Q2   *179 *Zaell*] (Garnett *conj.*); *Laell* Q2, Q1–Q3

De Bube.   Yes for you see he hath his termine
   In the degrees where she is and enjoyes   190
   By that six dignities.
La Fiske.   Which are cleerely more
   Then any else that view her i'the scheme.
Norbret.   Why I saw this, and could ha told you too
   That he beholds her with a trine aspect
   Here out of *Sagitary*, almost partile,
   And how that *Mars* out of the selfe same house,
   (But another signe) here by a platique aspect
   Looks at the hilage with a quartile, ruling
   The house where the sunne is; all this could I
   Have told you, but that you will out-run me, and more,   200
   That this same quartile aspect to the Lady of life,
   Here in the seaventh promises some danger,
   Cauda Draconis being so neere *Mars*,
   And *Caput Algoll* in the house of death.
Latorch.   How Sir? I pray you cleere that.
Norbret.   What is the question first?
Russee.   Of the Dukes life, what dangers threaten him?
Norbret.   Apparent and those suddaine: when the *Hyleg*,
   Or *Alchocoden* by direction come
   To a quartile opposition of the place
   Where *Mars* is in the geniture (which is now   210
   At hand) or else oppose to *Mars* himselfe, expect it.
Latorch.   But they may be prevented.
Norbret.   Wisdome only,
   That rules the starres may doe it, for *Mars* being
   Lord of the geniture in *Capricorne*,
   Is (if you mark it) now a Sextile here
   With *Venus* Lady of the Horoscope,
   So she being in her *exilium*, which is *Scorpio*
   And *Mars* his *gaudium*, is o're rul'd by him,
   And cleere debillitated, five degrees
   Beneath her ordinary power, so   220
   That at the most she can but mittigate.

195 partile] F2; partly Q2, Q1   *202 in] Q1; *omit* Q2

Latorch.   You cannot name the Person brings this danger?

Norbret.   No, that the starres tells not us, they name no man;
   That is a work Sir of another place.

Russee.   Tell him whom you suspect, and hee'l guesse shrewdly.

Latorch.   Sir, we doe feare one *Aubrey*, ift were he
   I should be glad, for we should soone prevent him.

La Fiske [*aside to* Norbret].   I know him, the Dukes kinsman, a tall
      man.

   Lay hold on't *Norbret.*

Norbret.   Let me pause a litle,
   Is he not neere of bloud unto the Duke?   230

Latorch.   Yes reverend sir.

Norbret [*aside*].   Fart for your reverence,
   Keep it till then,——and somewhat high of stature?

Latorch.   He is so.

Norbret [*aside*].   How old is he?

La Fiske [*aside*].   About seaven and fifty.

Norbret.   His head and beard inclining to be gray?

Latorch.   Right Sir.

La Fiske [*aside*].   And fat.

Norbret.   He's somewhat corpulent, is he not?

Latorch.   You speak the man Sir?

Norbret.   Well look to him, farewell.

                                        Exit Norbret.

Latorch.   O it is *Aubrey*: Gentlemen I pray you
   Let me receive this under all your hands.

Russee.   Why he will shew you him in his Magick glasse
   If you intreat him; and but gratifie   240
   A spirit or two more.

Latorch.   He shall eat gold
   If he will have it, so you shall all, there's that   [*Gives gold.*]
   Amongst you first: let me have this to send
   The Duke inth' meane time, and then what sights
   You please to shew Ile have you so rewarded
   As never Artists were: you shall to Court
   Along with mee; and there not waite your fortunes.

*222 Person] Persons Q2, Q1–Q3   226 ift were] ift twere Q2; if 'twere Q1–Q3

De Bube.   We have a pretty part on't in our pockets:

                                                    [*Exit* Latorch.]

    Boy we will all be new, you shall along too.

                                                    Exeunt.

                    Enter Sophia, Matilda, Edith.   [IV.

Matilda.   Good Madam heare the sute that *Edith* urges
    With such submisse beseeches, nor remaine
    So strictly bound to sorrow for your sonne,
    That nothing else, though never so befitting,
    Obtaines your eares or observation.
Sophia.   What would she say? I heare.
Edith.   My sute is Madam,
    That you would please to think as well of justice,
    Due to your sonnes revenge, as of more wrong added
    To both your selves for it, in only grieving.
    Th'undaunted power of Princes should not be,   10
    Confin'd in deedlesse cold calamity.
    Anger (the twin of sorrow) in your wrongs,
    Should not be smother'd when his right of birth
    Claimes th'ayre as well, and force of comming forth.
Sophia.   Sorrow is due already, anger never
    Should be conceiv'd but where it may be borne
    In some fact fit t'employ his active flame,
    That else consumes who bears it, and abides
    Like a false starre that quenches as it glides.
Edith.   I have such means t'employ it as your wish   20
    Can think no better, easier or securer
    And such, as but for th'honours I intend
    To your partakings, I alone could end,
    But your parts in all dues to crying bloud
    For Vengeance in the shedder, are much greater,
    And therefore should worke your hands to his slaughter,
    For your consent to which, 'twere infinite wrong,
    To your severe and most impartiall justice,
    To move you to forget so false a sonne,

                    17 flame] Q1; fame Q2

As with a mothers duty made you curse him.   30

Matilda.   *Edith* he is forgot for any sonne
   Borne of my mother, or to mee a brother,
   For should we still performe our rights to him,
   We should pertake his wrongs, and as foule be
   In bloud and damned Parracide as he:
   And therefore tell the happy means that heaven
   Puts in thine hand, for all our long'd for freedome,
   From so abhorr'd and impious a Monster.

Sophia.   Tell what she will ile lend nor hand nor eare,
   To whatsoever heaven puts in her power.   *Exit.* 40

Matilda.   How strange she is to what she chiefly wishes,
   Sweet *Edith*, be not any thought the more
   Discourag'd in thy purpose, but assur'd
   Her heart and prayers are thine: and that we two
   Shall be enough to all we wish to doe.

Edith.   Madam my selfe alone I make no doubt,
   Will be afforded power enough from heaven
   To end the Murderer: all I wish of you,
   Is but some richer ornaments and jewels,
   Then I am able to provide my selfe,   50
   To help out the defects of my poore beauty,
   That yet have beene enough as now they are,
   To make his fancy mad with my desire;
   But you know Maddam, women never can,
   Be too faire to torment an Amorous man;
   And this mans torments I would heighten still,
   Till at their highest he were fit to kill.

Matilda.   Thou shalt have all my jewells and my mothers,
   And thou shalt paint too, that his blouds desire,
   May make him perish in a painted fire.   60
   Hast thou been with him yet?

Edith.   Been with him? no;
   I set that hower back t'hast more his longing,
   But I have promis'd to his Instruments,
   Th'admittance of a Visit at our house,

<hr>

*52 have ... they are] *stet* Q2

231

Where yet I would receive him with all luster
My sorrow would give leave too, to remove
Suspition of my purpose.
Matilda.   Thou shalt have,
   All I can adde, sweet wench, in jewels, tires,
   Ile be my selfe thy dresser: nor may I
   Serve mine owne love with a contracted husband,   70
   More sweetly nor more amptly then maist thou,
   Thy forward will with his bewich'd affections:
   Affects thou any personall aide of mine,
   Mine noblest *Edith?*
Edith.   Nought but your kind prayers,
   For full effect and speed of my affaires.
Matilda.   They're thine (my *Edith*) as for me mine owne,
   For thou well know'st if bloud shed of the best,
   Should coole and be forgotten, who would feare
   To shed bloud still, or where (alas) were then,
   The endlesse love we owe to worthy men.   80
Edith.   Love of the worthiest ever blesse your highnesse.

                                        Exeunt.

          Enter Rollo *with a glasse,* Aubrey *and Servants.*   V.i

Rollo.   I never studied my glasse till now,
   'Tis exceeding well, now leave me;   [*Exeunt Servants.*]
                              cosen,
   How takes your eye the object?
Aubrey.   I have learnt
   So much Sir of the Courtier, as to say
   Your person does become your habit, but
   Being call'd unto it by a noble warre,
   Would grace an Armour better.
Rollo.   You are still
   For that great Art, of which you are the maister,
   Yet I must tell you, that to th'encounters
   We oft attempt, arm'd only thus we bring   10
   As troubled bloud, fears mixt with flattering hopes,

    The danger in the service too as great,
    As when we are to charge quite through and through
    The body of an Army.
Aubrey.   Ile not argue
    How you may ranke the dangers, but will dye in't,
    The ends which they arrive at, are as distant
    In e'ry circumstance, as farre as honour
    Is from shame and repentance.
Rollo.   You are soure.
Aubrey.   I would speak my free thoughts yet not appeare so,
    Nor am I so ambitious of the title   20
    Of one, that dares taske any thing that runnes
    Against the Torrent of his owne opinion,
    That I affect to speake ought may offend you.
    And therefore gratious Sir, be pleas'd to think,
    My manners or discretion have inform'd mee,
    That I was borne in all good ends to serve you,
    And not to check at what concernes me not;
    I look not with sore eyes on your rich outside,
    Nor wrack my thoughts to finde out to what purpose
    'Tis now employ'd; I wish it may be good,   30
    And that I hope offends not. For a Subject
    Towards his Prince in things indifferent,
    To use the austerenesse of a censuring *Cato*,
    Is arrogance not freedome.
Rollo.   I commend
    This temper in you, and will cherish it.

           Enter Hamond *with letters.*

Rollo.   They come from *Rhoane*, *Latorch* imploy'd you?
Hamond.   True sir.
Rollo.   I must not now be troubled with a thought,
    Of any new designe, good *Aubrey* read them,
    And as they shall direct you, use my power
    Or to reply or execute.
Aubrey.   I will Sir.   40

      21 taske] Weber (Mason *conj.*); talke Q2, Q1–Q3
      36–37 *Hamond.* True sir. | *Rollo.*] Q1; *omit* Q2

Rollo.   And Captaine bring a squadron of our guard,
    To the house that late was *Baldwins*, and there waite mee.
Hamond.   I shall.
Rollo.   Some two houres hence.
Hamond.   With my best care.
Rollo.   Inspire mee love, and be thy diety
    Or scorn'd or fear'd, as now thou favour'st mee.

                                 Exit Rollo.

Hamond.   My stay to doe my duty, may be wrongs
    Your Lordships privacy.
Aubrey.   Captaine your love
    Is ever welcome. I intreat your patience
    While I peruse these.
Hamond.   I attend your pleasure.
Aubrey [*apart*].   How's this? a plot on mee!
Hamond.   What is contain'd   50
    In the letters that I brought that thus transports him?
Aubrey [*apart*].   To be wrought on by rogues, and have my head
    Brought to the Axe by knaves that cheat for bread,
    The creatures of a Parasite, a slave,
    I finde you here *Latorch*, nor wonder at it;
    But that this honest Captaine should be made
    His instrument, afflicts mee; Ile make tryall,
    Whether his will or weaknesse made him do it.——
    Captaine you saw the Duke when he commanded
    I should doe what these letters did direct mee,   60
    And I presume you think I'le not neglect
    For feare or favour, to remove all dangers,
    How neere soever that man can be to mee,
    From whom they should have birth.
Hamond.   It is confirm'd.
Aubrey.   Nor would you Captaine I beleeve refuse,
    Or for respect of thankfullnesse or hopes,
    To use your sword with fullest confidence,
    Where he shall bid you strike.
Hamond.   I never have don.

    44 diety] *i.e.*, deity   48 *Hamond.* I ... pleasure. | *Aubrey.*] Q1; *omit* Q2
    58 do] Q1; to Q2

Aubrey.   Nor will, I think.

Hamond.   I hope it is not question'd.

Aubrey.   The meanes to have it so is now propos'd you,   70
  Draw, so, 'tis well, and next;——cut off my head.

Hamond.   What means your Lordship?

Aubrey.   Tis sir the Dukes pleasure,
  My innocence hath made me dangerous
  And I must be remov'd, and you the man
  Must act his will.

Hamond.   Ile be a traitor first,
  Before I serve it thus.

Aubrey.   It must be done,
  And that you may not doubt it, there's your warrant,
  But as you read, remember *Hamond* that
  I never wrong'd one of your brave profession,
  And though it be not manly, I must grieve   80
  That man of whose love I was most ambitious,
  Could finde no object for his hate but mee.

Hamond.   It is no time to talke now honour'd Sir,
  Be pleas'd to heare thy servant, I am wrong'd
  And cannot, being now to serve the Duke,
  Stay to expresse the manner how, but if
  I doe not suddenly give you strong proofes,
  Your life is deerer to me then my owne,
  May I live base and dye so: sir your pardon.   *Exit* Hamond.

Aubrey.   I am both waies ruin'd, both waies mark'd for slaughter, 90
  On every side about, behind, before mee,
  My certain fate is fixt, were I a knave now
  I could avoid this: had my actions,
  But meere relations to their own ends, I could scape now:
  O honesty, thou elder child of vertue,
  Thou seed of heaven, why to acquire thy goodnesse,
  Should mallice and distrust stick thornes before us,
  And make us swimme unto thee hung with hazards?
  But heaven is got by suffering, not disputeing:
  Say he know this before hand, where am I then?   100

Or say he doe not know it, where's my loyalty?
I know his nature troubled as the Sea,
And as the Sea devouring, where he is vex'd,
And I know Princes are their own expounders,
Am I afraid of death? of dying nobly?
Of dying in my innocence uprightly?
Have I met death in all his formes and fears,
Now on the points of swords, now pitcht on lances,
In fires, in stormes of arrowes, battles, breaches,
And shall I now shrink from him when he courts mee?   110
Smileing and full of Sanctity? ile meet him,
My loyall hand and heart shall give this to him,
And though it beare, beyond what Poets feigne,
A punishment; duty shall meet that paine,
And my most constant heart to doe him good,
Shall check at neither pale affright nor bloud.

Enter Messenger.

Messenger.   The Duchesse presently would crave your presence.
Aubrey.   I come;   [*Exit Messenger.*]
                    and *Aubrey* now resolve to keepe,
Thy honour living though thy body sleepe.

                                                              Exit.

Enter Edith *and a* Boy.   [V.
A banquet set out.

Edith.   Now for a Fathers murther and the ruine
All chastity shall suffer if he raigne;
Thou blessed soule look downe and steel thy daughter,
Looke on the Sacrifice she comes to send thee,
And through that bloudy cloud behold my piety.
Take from my cold heart feare, from my sexe pitty,
And as I wipe these teares off, shed for thee,
So all remembrance may I loose of mercy,
Give mee a womans anger, bent to bloud,
The wildnesse of the winds to drowne his prayers,   10
Stormelike may my destruction fall upon him,

My rage like roring Billowes as they rise,
Poure on his soule to sinke it; give me flattery,
(For yet my constant soule nere knew dissembling)
Flattery the food of fooles, that I may rock him,
And lull him in the downe of his desires,
That in the height of all his hopes and wishes,
His Heaven forgot, and all his lusts upon him,
My hand like thunder from a cloud may ceize him,

Enter Rollo.

I heare him come, goe boy and entertaine him.   20

The Song.

> *Take ô take those lipps away,*
> *That so sweetly were forsworne,*
> *And those eyes like break of day,*
> *Lights that doe mislead the morne,*
> *But my kisses bring againe,*
> *Seales of love though seal'd in vaine.*
>
> *Hide ô hide those hills of Snow,*
> *That thy frozen bosome beares,*
> *On whose tops the pincks that grow,*
> *Are yet of those that Aprill wears,*   30
> *But first set my poore heart free,*
> *Bound in those Icy chaines by thee.*

[*Exit* Boy.]

Rollo.   What bright starre taking beauties forme upon her,
In all the happy lustre of heavens glory,
Has dropt downe from the skye to comfort mee?
Wonder of nature, let it not prophane thee,
My rude hand touch thy beauty, nor this kisse,
The gentle sacrifice of love and service,

*12 roring] (Dyce *conj.*); roving Q2, Q1–Q3
*13 Poure] Pour'd Q2, F2, Q3; Powr'd Q1
*21–32 *Take ... by thee.*] See Textual Note.

Be offer'd to the honour of thy sweetnesse.

Edith.   My gratious Lord, no diety dwells here,   40
Nor nothing of that vertue but obedience,
The servant to your will affects no flattery.

Rollo.   Can it be flattery to sweare those eyes
Are loves eternall lamps he fires all hearts with,
That tongue the smart string to his bow, those sighes,
The deadly shafts he sends into our soules?
O look upon me with thy spring of beauty.

Edith.   Your Grace is full of game.

Rollo.   By heaven my *Edith*,
Thy mother fed on roses when she got thee.

Edith [*aside*].   And thine on brambles, that hath prickt her heart out.   50

Rollo.   The sweetnesse of th'Arabian winde still blowing,
Upon the treasures of perfumes and spices,
In all their pride and pleasures call thee Mistris.

Edith.   Wilt please you sit Sir?

Rollo.   So you please sit by mee.
Faire gentle maid, there is no speaking to thee,
The Excellency that appears upon thee
Tyes up my tongue, pray speak to mee.

Edith.   Of what sir?

Rollo.   Of any thing, and any thing is excellent,
Will you take my direction? speak of love then,
Speak of thy faire selfe *Edith*, and whilst thou speakst,   60
Let me thus languishing give up my selfe wench.

Edith [*aside*].   Has a strange cunning tongue,——why doe you sigh
sir?——
How masterly he turnes himselfe to catch me.

Rollo.   The way to Paradise (my gentle maid)
Is hard and crooked, scarce repentance finding
With all her holy helps the doore to enter,
Give me thy hand, what dost thou feele?

Edith.   Your teares sir,
You weep extreamly:——strengthen me now Justice,——
Why are these sorrowes Sir?

Rollo.   Thou'lt never love me
If I should tell thee, and yet there is no way left   70

Ever to purchase this blest Paradise,
But swimming thither in these teares.
Edith [*aside*].   I stagger.
Rollo.   Are they not drops of bloud?
Edith.   No.
Rollo.   They are for bloud then,
    For guiltlesse bloud, and they must drop my *Edith*,
    They must thus drop till I have drown'd my mischiefes.
Edith [*aside*].   If this be true I have no strength to touch him.
Rollo.   Pree thee look upon me, turne not from me,
    Alas I doe confesse I'me made of mischiefe,
    Begot with all mens miseries upon me,
    But see my sorrowes minde, and doe not thou,   80
    Whose only sweetest sacrifice is softnesse,
    Whose true condition tendernesse of nature——
Edith [*aside*].   My anger melts, o I shall loose my justice.
Rollo.   Doe not thou learne to kill with cruelty,
    As I have done, to murther with thine eyes,
    (Those blessed eyes) as I have done with mallice;
    When thou hast wounded me to death with scorne,
    (As I deserve it Lady) for my true love,
    When thou hadst loden me with earth for ever,
    Take heed my sorrowes, and the stings I suffer,   90
    Take heed my nightly dreames of death and horrour
    Pursue thee not: no time shall tell thy griefes then,
    Nor shall an houre of joy adde to thy beauties;
    Look not upon me as I kill'd thy father,
    As I was smear'd in bloud doe thou not hate me,
    But thus in whitenesse of my wash'd repentance
    In my hearts teares and truth of love to *Edith*,
    In my faire life hereafter.
Edith [*aside*].   He will foole me.
Rollo.   O with thine Angell eyes behold and blesse me:
    Of heaven we call for mercy, and obtaine it,   100
    To justice for our right on earth, and have it,
    Of thee I beg for love, save me, and give it.

---

*77 Pree thee] *stet* Q2   *80 minde] *stet* Q2   *80 thou,] Q1; thou learne, Q2
85 As ... eyes,] Q1; *omit* Q2   *85 thine] thy Q1–Q3; *omit* Q2

Edith [*aside*].   Now heaven thy help, or I am gone for ever,
His tongue has turn'd me into melting pitty.

Enter Hamond *and Guard.*

Hamond [*apart*].   Keep the doore safe, and upon paine of death
Let no man enter till I give the word.
Guard [*apart*].   We shall Sir.   *Exeunt.*
Hamond [*apart*].   Here he is in all his pleasure.
I have my wish.
Rollo.   How now, why dost thou stare so?
Edith.   A help I hope.
Rollo.   What dost thou here? who sent thee?
Hamond.   My brother, and the base malitious office   110
Thou mad'st me doe to *Aubrey*: pray.
Rollo.   Pray?
Hamond.   Pray,
Pray, if thou canst pray, I shall kill thy soule else,
Pray suddenly.
Rollo.   Thou canst not be so traiterous.
Hamond.   It is a justice:——stay Lady,

[Edith *takes out her knife.*]

For I perceive your end; a womans hand
Must not rob me of vengeance.
Edith.   Tis my glory.
Hamond.   Tis mine, stay and share with me:——By the Gods *Rollo*
There is no way to save thy life.
Rollo.   No?
Hamond.   No,
It is so monstrous no repentance cures it.

[Rollo *seizes* Edith.]

Rollo.   Why then thou shalt kill her first, and what this bloud   120
Will cast upon thy cursed head——
Hamond.   Poore guard Sir.
Edith.   Spare not brave Captaine.
Rollo.   Feare or the divell ha thee.
Hamond.   Such feare Sir as you gave your honour'd mother,

---

108 I ... wish. *Rollo.* How] Q1; *Rollo.* I ... wish. | How Q2

240

When your most vertuous brother sheild-like held her,
Such Ile give you; put her away.
Rollo.   I will not,
I will not dye so tamely.
Hamond.   Murdrous villaine,
Wilt thou draw seas of bloud upon thee?
Edith.   Feare not,
Kill him good Captaine any way dispatch him,
My bodyes honour'd with that sword that through me
Sends his black soule to hell, o but for one hand.   130
Hamond.   Shake him off bravely.
Edith.   He's too strong, strike him.
Hamond.   O I am with you Sir,   [*He frees* Edith *from* Rollo,
                                        who snatches Ediths *knife.*]
                         now keep you from him,
What has he got a knife?
Edith.   Look to him Captaine
For now he will be mischievous.   [Hamond *stabs him.*]
Hamond.   Doe you smile Sir?
Does it so tickle you, have at you once more.   [*Stabs againe.*]
Edith.   O bravely thrust, take heed he comes not in Sir,
To him againe, you give him too much respit.   [Rollo *falles.*]
Rollo.   Yet wilt thou save my life, and ile forgive thee,
And give thee all, all honours, all advancements,
Call thee my friend.
Edith.   Strike, strike and heare him not,   140
His tongue will tempt a Saint.
Rollo.   O for my soules sake.
Edith.   Save nothing of him.
Hamond.   Now for your farewell,
Are you so wary, take you that.   [*Stabs him.*]
Rollo.   Thou that too.   [*Stabs him.*]
O thou hast kil'd me basely, basely, basely.   *Dyes.*
Edith.   The just reward of murder falls upon thee,——
How doe you Sir, has he not hurt you?
Hamond.   No,
I feele not any thing.
Aubrey (*within*).   I charge yee let us passe.

Guard (within).   Yee cannot yet sir.

Aubrey (within).   Ile make my way then.

Guard (within).   We are sworne to our Captaine,
     And till he give the word——

Hamond.   Now let 'em in there.   150

Enter Sophia, Matilda, Aubrey, *Lords and attendants [and Guards].*

Sophia.   O there he lies, sorrow on sorrow seeks me,
     O in his bloud he lies.

Aubrey.   Had you spoke sooner
     This might have beene prevented. Take the Dutches,
     And lead her off, this is no sight for her eyes.
                                        [*Exit* Sophia *attended.*]

Matilda.   O bravely done wench.

Edith.   There stands the noble doer.

Matilda.   May honour ever seek thee for thy justice,
     O 'twas a deed of high and brave adventure,
     A justice even for heaven to envy at.
     Farewell my sorrowes, and my teares take truce,
     My wishes are come round: o bloudy brother,   160
     Till this houre never beautious; till thy life
     Like a full sacrifice for all thy mischiefes
     Flow'd from thee in these rivers, never righteous:
     O how mine eyes are quarri'd with their joyes now,
     My longing heart ev'n leaping out for lightnesse,
     But, dye thy black sinnes with thee, I forgive thee.

Aubrey.   Who did this deed?

Hamond.   I, and I will answer it.   *Dyes.*

Edith.   He faints, o that same cursed knife has kil'd him.

Aubrey.   How?

Edith.   He snatcht it from my hand for whom I bore it,
     And as they grappell'd——

Aubrey.   Justice is ever equall.   170
     Had it not been on him th'had'st dy'de too honest.
     Did you know of his death?

Edith.   Yes, and rejoyce in't.

---

*150.1 *Enter ... Guards*].] *stet* Q2
*164 quarri'd] *i.e.*, provided with quarry or prey (falconry)

Aubrey.   I am sorry for your youth then, for though the strictnesse
    Of law shall not fall on you, that of life
    Must presently; goe, to a Cloyster carry her,
    And there for ever lead your life in penitence.
Edith.   Best father to my soule, I give you thanks Sir
    And now my faire revenges have their ends,
    My vowes shall be my kin, my prayers my friends.

                                              Exit [*attended*].

Enter Latorch *and Juglers* [Norbret, La Fiske, De Bube, Russee
                    and stand apart].

Latorch.   Stay there, ile step in and prepare the Duke.   180
Norbret.   We shall have brave rewards.
La Fiske.   That's without question.
Latorch.   By this time where's my huffing friend Lord *Aubrey*,
    Where's that good gentleman——O I could laugh now,
    And burst my selfe with meere imagination,
    A wise man and a valiant man, a just man
    Should suffer himselfe to be juggl'd out of the world,
    By a number of poore Gipsies: farewell swash-buckler,
    For I know thy mouth's cold enough by this time,
    A hundred on yee I can shave as neatly,
    And nere draw bloud in show: now shall my honour   190
    My power and vertue walke alone; my pleasure
    Observ'd by all, all knees bent to my worship,
    All sutes to mee, as saint of all their fortunes
    Preferr'd and crowded too: what full place of credit
    And what stile now? your Lordship? no 'tis common,
    But that ile think to morrow on, now for my businesse.
Aubrey.   Who's there.
Latorch.   Ha dead? my maister dead? *Aubrey* a live too?
Guard.   *Latorch* sir.
Aubrey.   Ceize his body.   [*Guards ceize him.*]
Latorch.   O my fortune,
    My maister dead?
Aubrey.   And you within this halfe houre;   200

175 carry] Q1; presently carry Q2   178 faire] Q1; faint Q2
193 sutes] Q1; sute's Q2   *195 stile] Seward, place Q2, Q1–Q3

243

Prepare your selfe good Divell, you must to it,
Millions of gold shall not redeeme thy mischiefes,
Behold the justice of thy practise villaine,
The masse of murders thou hast drawne upon us,
Behold thy Doctrine; you look now for reward sir,
To be advanc'd Ime sure for all your labours,
And you shall have it: make his Gallowes higher
By twenty foot at the least, and then advance him.

Latorch.   Mercy, mercy.

Aubrey.   'Tis too late foole.
Such as you meant for mee, away with him.   21

                              Exit Latorch [*with Guard.*]
What peeping knaves are those, bring 'em in fellowes;
Now, what are you?

Norbret.   Mathematicians,
And it like your Lordship.

Aubrey.   And ye drew a figure.

La Fiske.   We have drawn many.

Aubrey.   For the Duke I mean sir.
  Latorches knaves you are.

Norbret.   We know the gentleman.

Aubrey.   What did he promise yee?

Norbret.   We are paid already.

Aubrey.   But I will see you better paid, goe whip 'em.

Norbret.   We doe beseech your Lordship, we were hired.

Aubrey.   I know you were and you shall have your hire,
Whip 'em extreamely, whip that Doctour there,   22
Till he record himselfe a rogue.

Norbret.   I am one Sir.

Aubrey.   Whip him for being one, and when they'r whipt,
Lead 'em to the gallowes to see their Patron hang'd;
Away with 'em.

Norbret.   Ah good my Lord.   *Exeunt Juglers* [*with Guard*].

Aubrey.   Now to mine owne right Gentlemen.

Lord 1.   You have the next indeed, we all confesse it,
And here stand ready to invest you with it.

209–10 *Aubrey.* Tis ... | Such] Q1; 'tis ... | *Aubrey.* Such Q2

Lord 2.   Which to make stronger to you and the surer,
   Then bloud or mischiefe dare infringe againe,
   Behold this Lady sir, this noble Lady,   230
   Full of that bloud as you are, of that neerenesse,
   How blessed would it be?
Aubrey.   I apprehend yee,
   And so the faire *Matilda* dare accept mee,
   Her ever constant servant.
Matilda.   In all purenesse,
   In all humillity of heart and service,
   To the most noble *Aubrey* I submit mee.
Aubrey.   Then this is our first tye, now to our businesse.
Lord 1.   W'are ready all to put that honour on you.
Aubrey.   These sad rights must be done first. Take up the bodies,
   This as he was a Prince so princely funerall   240
   Shall waite upon him: On this honest Captaine
   The decency of Armes, a teare for him too.
   Goe sadly on, and as we view his bloud,
   May his example in our rule raise good.
                         Exeunt. Florish.

FINIS

237 is] Q1; *omit* Q2

245

TEXTUAL NOTES

I.i

3 does] The Q2 'doe' is presumably a compositorial error for 'does', a form that appears quite normally at line 18, though 'doe' is a standard spelling (line 44) of this compositor's.

158 title] Qy: 'tittle'? Though the quartos read 'title', 'peece of Earth' might suggest something small, justifying the emendation 'tittle': for at line 278 Q2 reads 'litle' for 'little' (as in Q1) and at line 365 occurs (the reverse) 'latter' for 'later' (as in Q1). But 'peece of Earth' and 'title' can be seen to refer back to 'Dukedome', in which the two are combined, as they look forward to 'land and honours' (165).

182 them: would] The quartos' '(Gisbert)' Dyce considered 'an interpolation' between the two words presented in the lemma, and Jump suggested that as 'half lines are rare in Massinger', this passage might be corrupt (though he did not suggest how to correct it). It seems likely that the term of address here deleted is an unnecessary repetition of the marginal direction 'to Gis.', a direction which in Q2 parallels the earlier one 'to Baldwin' (which has no repetition in the dialogue). It is reasonable to argue that the irregular scansion of two Q2 lines is due to the intrusion of this additional direction.

189 at] Mason conjectured and Dyce adopted 'as', explaining the choice as a way of describing the law as a weapon 'more certain' than the sword, but Jump cites a passage (in Fletcher, *Humourous Lieutenant*, I.ii.8) in which the phrase 'fight at a weapon' (i.e., with a weapon), is used as a normal idiom. Cf. the title, *Wit at Several Weapons*. The quartos are probably correct.

215 *factions*] It seems that neither quarto has this direction quite right:

Q2 '*the faction joyneing Aubrey between*';
Q1 '*the faction joining, Aubrey between*'.

Q2 is probably meaningless, but Q1 understands the construction is an absolute. Still, it is scarcely good theatre to present two angry brothers, only one of whom has rallied his faction beside him. The members of the other faction, equally contentious, have obviously also rallied behind their candidate. The 'factions' are mentioned at lines 108 and 324.

280 of] Theobald and Seward both recognized that 'of' indicates modern 'off', but Seward, conceiving that there were 'a pleonasm and impropriety in *taking authority from power*', provided his own extreme emendation. Colman disagreed, using the modern 'off'. Presumably the line signifies that Sophia understands that her kneeling nullifies the authority that should reside in a mother's position: 'Mark how this becomes the house'——to borrow a phrase from another distraught parent. The same problem occurs at line 403.

302 turne]   The Q2 'turnes' is probably the result of compositorial anticipation of
the final '-s' on 'treasons'.

310 the]   The 1640 quarto line is not a full pentameter, and Jump explains: 'nine-
syllable pentameters have been common since Chaucer'; but the other texts and
editions have felt the need of regularizing the line. Q1 supplied 'and not mine
owne'; Theobald proposed 'You both, for others safety ...'; Sympson proposed
'For both, for others safety ...'; Seward read 'Both for each others Safety'. Weber
'Both, for the other's safety', 'because "the" appears more likely [than "each"] to
have been dropt at the press'. That thesis seems reasonable, and we may support it
by noting that the scribe had already written 'th' in 'Both' and was about to write it
in 'others'.

341 My first, my first]   The Q2 lineation may provide the solution here. In that text,
the words 'my first' appear at the end of line 340 and reappear at the beginning of
line 341. If the setting reproduces the MS, then it is easy to see why the Q1
compositor, counting line 340 too long, dropped the words in that line, assuming
that the words were fully provided in 341. Then, discovering that 341 was short, he
supplied an extra 'that'. This Massingerian repetition appears also in Fletcher's 'like
this, | Like this' (II.i.82–3). The extended line in the present crux (340) may have a
fellow later in the play, where 'learn' appears at the end of a line, anticipating its use
in a subsequent line (V.ii.80, 84).

403 of]   The MS must have been misleading. Q2 reads: 'These desires are of frail
thoughts:', but the Q1 scribe or compositor grasped the situation and read: 'are off.
| Frail thoughts'. Only Colman has followed Q2.

406 till apter]   Seward objected to the Q1 reading 'to after consequence' as being a
'poor tautology'; Mason (p. 179) and Dyce approved. The *O.E.D.* does mention
the term, 'after-consequence', from a sermon of 1842 ('*after-*' in combinations, no.
7), but in no other of the combined forms listed does the 'suffix' noun automatically
carry the connotation of postponement. I find no entries to support Weber's
assertion that the term is used 'in old plays more than once'. The *f/p* misreading is
plausible (though Kellner gives no instances), but the variation between 'till' and
'to' cannot be disregarded; and in the assumption that 'till' is more likely than 'to' to
have been the author's word, the present edition follows Q2. In fact, the noun
'consequence' itself appears here in what seems a non-standard sense, meaning little
more than 'a later time' or 'a later action' without any sense of causality – or
consequentiality – deriving from the prior or present situation.

II.i

10 sayling]   Q2 'soyling' results from a standard *a/o* misreading of 'sayling' (as in
Q1). At lines 29–32 Latorch repeats the nautical metaphor of a tempest destructive
to a sailing vessel. (See also Textual Note at II.ii.11.)

14 prayer]   Though the Q2 reading is not easy, it is to be preferred to the Q1
'paper'. Presumably Heath was correct in thinking that there should be a break
between 'prayer' and 'dropt'. He suggested an exclamation point (but the colon
seems more appropriate to this text), and the next phrase he understood to signify:

that 'you have been *dropt through*, penetrated, melted ... by a [woman's tears]'.
Mitford conjectured 'tears, dropt though by a woman', as if a woman's tears were
considered the weakest tears of all. Edith's tears in defence of her father (in III.ii)
seem powerful enough to reverse a prince's doom.

44 circling ... pull down]   Every editor has devised a new reading or a gloss to this
crux. Jump followed Q1: 'So jarres circling distrusts, distrusts breed dangers'
which he explained by seeing 'breed' as a verb controlling the first phrase: 'jars
breed circling distrusts, distrusts breed dangers'. Dyce followed the Q2
construction but emended 'pull down' to 'breed': 'So jars circling in distrusts,
distrusts breed dangers', which he justified by saying that 'the sense positively
requires us to read "... in ..." [with Q2], i.e., swelling out into circles of distrusts'.
Neither reading satisfies: the first is too contorted to be readily grasped, the second
emends the Q2 'pull down' to achieve metrical smoothness. The present edition
argues that the scribe of the prompt-book erroneously duplicated 'distrusts';
deleting the second 'distrusts' perfects the metre, allows us to keep the homely 'pull
down' (which the Q1 compositor was (also) obliged to emend to a more elevated
term for metrical smoothness), and suports Dyce's interpretation. So the 'jarres of
brothers', 'swelling out into circles of distrusts' (Qy: distrust?), pull down dangers,
and dangers pull down death. The cumulative effect desired does not require the
repetition of 'distrusts'.

54 his peace]   The Q2 compositor, with more concern for justification than for
accuracy, substituted 'him' to fill his stick and his line without the trouble of a
turn-over.

65 Pauling]   The Q1 'Pauling', modernized to a variant spelling by F2 and later
editors to 'Palling', seems a strange word for this line. The Q2 'Tasting' cannot be
correct, but Seward (unaware of Q1) based his emendation on it, 'Tainting', and
conjectured 'Taking'. The latter term Colman adopted because, of the two, 'it is
nearer the trace of the letters'. That argument is open to dispute, but Seward and
Colman both cite 'taking' in *The False One* (IV.iii.27), with the sense 'infectious'.

   Though I can accept neither of their emendations, I am satisfied that an attempt
must be made to find the correct MS form in the Q2 error. All critics agree that II.i is
a Fletcher scene, yet it is a scene that contains two of the most serious cruces of the
play, those discussed in these Textual Notes at line 44 above and at line 80 below.
Midway between these documented problems occurs this word 'Tasting'. Jump,
reading 'Pauling' with Q1, gives the definition 'paling, making pale', only
minimally satisfactory since, when applied to blood, the word has an acutely
technical meaning: 'to become pale (?) by separation of clot and serum' (pall, v^1 3,
O.E.D.). That haematological exactness, I venture to say, is a transferred or
extended meaning for the word which principally refers in the *O.E.D.* to beverages
– ale, wine, drink, beer, canary, cider (pall, v1 3; palled, *ppl. a.*[1] 2). From 1430 to the
mid-seventeenth century the term is so used, with one exception: Palsgrave (1530)
– 'I palle, as drinke or blood dothe, by longe standyng in a thynge ... This drinke
wyll pall ... if it stande uncovered all nyght.' The basic application is to 'fermented
or aerated liquors; to lose briskness or sharpness by exposure to the air' (pall, v^3 [a]).
I do not believe that this is the sense intended here; and I do believe that in a difficult

stretch of the original MS the word was unclear and that the Q2 compositor did
what he could with it ('Tasting'), though it must have seemed an odd cannibalistic
idea, and that the scribe of the MS behind Q1 or the compositor did the same,
producing a semi-technical term showing a good deal of medical sophistication
('Pauling').

The first emendation to come to mind is, of course, 'Casting' as in the variant Q2
'Cast', Q1 'Taste' (III.i.399; see also II.i.64), but I find no appropriate meaning of
this word with blood. I suggest, therefore, though with a conviction insufficient to
admit the conjecture to the text, 'Frosting'. Manuscript 'F' might have been
misread as 'P' by the scribe of the manuscript behind Q1 or by the compositor
(Kellner, pp. 196, 205) and might have been misread as 'T' by the compositor of Q2
– as it was in line 64, immediately preceding. (In fact, the collection of 'f' and 't'
initials in the two lines is notable: 'a teare [feare Q1] they tye up fooles in: natures
coward / Tasting [Frosting] the blud') (Kellner, §157; some forms of the initial
letters are indistinguishable (pp. 196–7, 210–11).) The minim of the 'r' might have
been lost in the strokes of the succeeding vowel. The sense of this verbal is glossed
in the *O.E.D.*, covering 'with or as with rime' (frost, *v* 2) with a date of 1635.
Though the expected connotation is that of frosting of the surface (as of the earth or
of a cake), the idea offers a serviceable parallel to the context: 'and chilling the full
spirits'.

70 Toth']   This emendation for Q2 'The' and Q1 'To the' is based on the frequent
appearance of the collapsed form in Fletcher's work: *Knight of Malta*, IV.ii.80,
Barnavelt, II.iii.11, IV.i.66 ('intoth' '), IV.iii.133, etc.

80 A crowne ... me.]   This line presents a vexatious problem. In the passage from
line 77 to line 99, it appears after line 91 and again after line 98 in Q2 (*literatim et
punctuatim*) and in Q1. The Q2 reads:

> If there be conscience,   1 [= 77b]
> Let it not come betwixt a Crowne and me,
> Which is my hope of blisse, and I believe it
> *Otto*, our friendship thus I blowe to ayre
> A bubble for a boy to play withall,   5
> And all the vowes my weaknesse made like this,
> Like this poore heartlesse rush, I rend a peeces.
>   *Lat.*   Now you goe right Sir, now your eyes are open.
>   *Rollo.*   My Fathers last petition's dead, as he is,
> And all the promises I clos'd his eyes with,   10
> In the same grave I bury.
>   *Lat.*   Now you are a man Sir.
>   *Rollo*, *Otto* thou shewst my winding sheet before me,
> Which ere I put it on, like heavens blest fire
> In my descent ile make it blush in bloud.   15 [= 91]
> A crowne, a crowne, o sacred rule now fire me,
> Nor shall the pitty of thy youth false brother,
> Although a thousand Virgins kneele before me,
> And every dropping eye a Court of mercy,

The same bloud with me, nor the reverence   20
Due to my Mothers blessed wombe, that bred us
Redeem thee from my doubts: thou art a woolfe here
Fed with my feares, and I must cut thee from me,   [= 98]
A crowne, a crowne, o sacred rule now fire me,
No safety else.   25

Though Rollo's speech often affects the device of repetition (as in lines 6–7 above), it does not seem that the repetition of this high-flown apostrophe is appropriate in this context; in fact, editors since Colman have agreed that only one statement is wanted.

Colman suggested that the line was 'improperly repeated' through 'some accidental interpolation', and he deleted the line in its second appearance at line 24. Weber and Dyce followed, the latter suggesting: 'The printer, most probably, found the repetition in the prompter's copy, but did not understand what was intended by it, viz., that the actor was to shorten this speech by omitting all except the four first lines and the concluding hemistich' (i.e., retaining only lines 13–16, 25). Jump, on the other hand, omitted the line at its first appearance, line 16:

> we are here concerned with what Dover Wilson has termed a 'repetition-bracket', the occurrence of which Greg has proved may indicate either a marginal insertion or a passage marked for omission in the manuscript. [As either of these situations may produce a compositorial misunderstanding,] [on] bibliographical grounds, therefore, it is [line 16] rather than [line 24] that should be omitted. Literary considerations confirm this decision.

No other indications of such a theatrical nature as is posited by Dyce's hypothesis appear in either quarto, and Jump's explanation, though not implausible on bibliographical grounds, is not specific; both seem finally inadequate.

Both of these modern editors agree, however, that only one statement is appropriate, as they disagree on which of the two printings should be deleted. The present editor finds the line intrusive in both of its appearances. In its first appearance (as Jump recognizes) it interrupts the progress of Rollo's thought, as he paints the bloody future and then refuses to consider pity. Similarly, in its second appearance (as Dyce recognizes) it interrupts the linking of lines 23 and 25: 'I must cut thee from me,|No safety else.'

The entire passage here quoted, in fact, though this has not been noted, involves two statements of the same thing; to neither of these is the line appropriate. The first is lines 4–15; the second is lines 17–23. Both of these passages begin with an address to the brother, reject considerations of mercy, refer to the obligations to a parent, and conclude with threats of violence. The pair seems almost to constitute what we may call 'first and second shots' at the same topic. There are variants, of course – 'friendship'/'pitty', 'weaknesse'/'mercy', 'My Fathers'/'my Mothers', 'thou shewst'/'thou art', 'blush in bloud'/'cut thee from me'. We presume in matters of this kind that the statement second on the page replaces the statement first, as being what the author approved secondly, but the variants here seem to suggest that the

second supplements – does not supplant – the first. As no other instances of such
duplication *currente calamo* come to mind in this play, we are best advised to reject
neither version in favour of the other. Both of the statements end – as it were – with
the duplicated line; neither of them leads into it in any way. One can say, of course,
that the line is an impassioned utterance suitably interjected anywhere, and that is
an argument not easy to refute. One can also say, however, that the line can be fitted
into a coherent pattern where it loses none of its fire and responds immediately to its
context. The present editor believes that the apostrophe to the crown belongs with
the earlier references to the crown in lines 1–3. Here the language, which is
theological ('my hope of blisse') and credal ('I believe it'), progresses directly into
the idolatry of 'o sacred rule'. The inspiration that the crown offers will 'fire' Rollo
to the destruction of his brotherhood with Otto, soon to be no more than a bubble
in the air. (This 'fire', we must suppose, is very different from 'heavens blest fire'
with which in Dyce's location the metaphor must be associated – lines 14, 16).

As earlier editors have demonstrated, it is not easy to find 'bibliographical
grounds' to support an argument for any specific location beyond those printed in
the two quartos. Perhaps in dealing with the two passages – lines 4–15, 17–23/25,
one of which he may have intended to cancel – Fletcher failed to indicate clearly
where one of them, an addendum, was to have been inserted (immediately after line
3) and how the other was to have been deleted, with the result that both were
included and the line appeared twice. It is noteworthy that in Q2 the duplicated line
is identical in both printings – as though the scribe copied it from the same text
twice (and the compositor followed as carefully) – and that in Q1 the differences are
negligible. It is now impossible to reconstruct beyond any doubt the process by
which the error occurred.

II.ii

11 sailing]   Though it is tempting to emend the Q2 'sculing' to modern 'sculling'
and so preserve a more interesting reading, a rare word known as a noun by 1611
and as a verbal by 1624, it is unlikely that a MS -ll- would have been misread.
O.E.D. gives no instance of this word with one -l-. See Textual Note above at
II.i.10.

40 drawne]   See Textual Note at V.ii.195.

43 pastie]   Though *O.E.D.* gives one spelling of 'paste' for the pastie, and so might
be thought to justify the Q2 spelling ('paste'), that unique instance occurs in the
plural and so does not provide sufficient argument to retain Q2.

47–58 *Drinke ... October.*]   The song survives in a single manuscript, British
Library 29396, edited in John P. Cutts, *La Musique de scène de la troupe de
Shakespeare* (Paris, 1959), pp. 83–4, 170–1.

Substantive variants with the MS:

48 *shall perhaps*] may perhaps
48 *you ... perhaps*] (*repeated twice*)

49 *while*] whilst

51 *heart*] heart (*cited as* 'heat' *in Cutts*)

58 *Falls with the leafe still*] (*repeated four times*)

58.1 ——] M. Chilmead/.

'The music being probably written for the revival of the play in 1636–7. "[E.] Chilmead."' (*Catalogue of Printed Music* (British Museum, 1908), II, 278).

In spite of the ascription to Chilmead, Cutts assigns the music to Wilson because of his authorship of the third song in this play (p. 171). Though Cutts describes it as a three-part song, set for one tenor and two basses, Professor Andrew J. Sabol questions 'this categorization solely on the basis of the three surviving music parts, only two of which are vocal parts. . . . The third part is a basso continuo . . . of an instrumental accompaniment, and it has no underlay. . . . [Of the two vocal parts,] the first section could be sung by two tenors and two basses, and the second section by solo tenor or by two tenors' (personal correspondence, 10 May 1994). However the vocal parts may have been assigned in the play, the dialogue makes clear that the Cook is not one of the singers (*pace* Cutts); he listens and directs.

66 shooe] This must certainly be the word intended by the 'shoote' in both quartos. It appears in Fletcher and Rowley's *Maid in the Mill* with intransitive directional force: 'Shough, shough, up to your coop, Pea-Hen' (V.i.28). The scribe behind Q1, recognizing the error of 'shoote her into the Seller' changed 'into' to 'in', correct in grammar but unsafe in execution.

67 *Pantler*.] Though the reference to 'roaring bottles' certainly suggests that the speaker should be the man charged with handling bottles – i.e., the Butler (see Textual Note at III.ii.45) – since both quartos agree, the error is likely to have been the author's; it is difficult then to alter the prefix, following Seward. Dyce believed that the speaker might have been the Yeoman of the Cellar, and Dr Turner agrees, pointing out, correctly, that at line 105 it is the Yeoman who describes his task as to 'fill my wine'. At this distance either '*Butler*' or '*Yeoman*' would seem preferable to what Fletcher seems to have written. (See also Textual Note below at line 140.)

70 with him?] The Q2 'within?' evidently results from a hasty reading by the Q2 compositor. The Q1 reading offers a more powerful and dramatic line: 'M. Latorch! what can he possibly be doing below stairs?' That reading perhaps encourages us to follow Q1 also in dividing the speech, allowing the Pantler to greet Latorch as he enters, to whom then Latorch responds specifically – 'Save ye maister' – before turning generally to the other 'Gentlemen'.

102 doe] This form, the pro-predicate 'do', formerly standard in polite speech and, after a lapse, now becoming standard again, is found occasionally in Fletcher's work (so *The Prophetesse*, I.ii.7) and in Massinger's (*ibid.*, III.iii.184, and below, V.i.68: 'Nor would you Captaine I beleeve refuse, . . . To use your sword. . . . *Captain.* I never have don.'). (See Ronald R. Butters, 'Syntactic change in British English propredicates', *Journal of English Linguistics*, XVI (1983), 1–7.) See also II.i.1, V.ii.85–6.

140 *Butler*.] Here Q1 reads '*Pan.*' and Q2 reads '*But.*' The following line of dialogue can be read as indicating either (as in Q1) the Pantler's glum

determination or (as here) the Butler's uncertainty and fearful questioning. In Q1 the Pantler says: 'But if you dare, goe forward.'; the punctuation and the pronoun reflect the attitude of that text. In Q2 the Butler asks: 'But if we dare goe forward [?]'. There is no justification for rejecting Q2.

142 swinge]   Arguably, 'swing' from Q1, appropriate to the gallows, is to be preferred to Q2 'swinge', another noun, meaning with the verb 'give', 'freedom of action, free scope, licence, liberty to follow one's inclination' (*O.E.D.*).

II.iii

5 gapers]   The Q2 'papers' anticipates the reverse error at V.ii.211, where Q2 reads 'peeping' and Q1 erroneously reads 'gaping'. In Fletcher's hand, the initial character could, evidently, be read as either *g* or *p*.

7 coming on.]   The quartos include in one direction instructions for two actions, the music (to accompany the entry) and the banquet: '*Ho boyes and banquet*' (Q2). Perceiving the direction as presenting the sequence in reverse order, editors since Weber have divided it, bringing in the banquet at lines 3–4 (to follow the command of the Shewer) and sounding the oboes at line 7 (to accompany the entrance of the dukes – not of the banquet). Dr Turner argues that the Q2 direction is not of necessity incorrect: the oboes sound, the banquet is brought in, the royal party enters. The sequence preferred here seems more theatrical than that suggested by the quartos and perhaps more suitable in terms of the protocol of dining: only after the banquet has been prepared do the diners enter. (Cf. *Macbeth*, III.iv.0.1: '*Banquet prepared. Enter Macbeth . . .*'.) Delaying the Shewer's entrance until line 3 will provide an effective staging.

III.i

10 affections]   The Q2 'affection' may be explained as the compositor's solution to fit the line into his short stick (as at lines 15, 28, 30, 40 on this page).

18 provoke]   A scribal error, the recollection of the past participial 'beleev'd' imposes itself on MS 'provoke', an error the more likely because of the easy confusion of terminal *e* and *d*. '*Provok'd* . . . implies *Sophia*'s Belief of *Rollo*'s Attempt, which it is evident she did not give Credit to' (Seward).

21 Bred . . . of]   This line is the conclusion of a passage (lines 15–21), substantively equivalent to the text in Q1 with the exception of this variant: 'Breed not in him', and difficult to interpret. The problem begins with the meaning of 'fruits' and 'tree' (line 15). Seward understood the first phrases to signify: 'It cannot be that fruits so blasting the tree from whence they sprung should grow in nature. Here *Rollo* is the fruit, she herself the tree.' Colman offered: '*Falshood* is the supposed fruit, and *Truth* the tree; Rollo being here accused of engrafting treachery on friendship.' Weber is 'inclined to prefer Seward's comment'; Dyce declines to specify, and Jump suggests that 'Rollo is the tree and evil deeds the fruit.' As it seems difficult to believe that a tree of Truth could under any circumstances produce a fruit of

Falsehood, Colman's reading can hardly be correct; and it is unlikely that Sophia should consider herself being blasted by a falsehood that she does not credit. Jump's reading seems nearer the mark, but perhaps closer yet is a reading that supposes Otto is the tree and his imputations ('fruits') (which Sophia thinks are false), so blast the tree himself that they will never grow in nature. We may then gloss: It cannot be that these untrue charges which you, Otto, have lodged against Rollo can have any effect other than that of destroying you yourself – themselves dying in the process, of course, because they had no truth in them; you should therefore take heed, Otto, and mistrust the rumours and scandals which you hear, lest your own believing them will in fact provoke (see preceding Note) in Rollo the foul attempts at your life which are at present merely the fruit of your own imaginings. Or, to continue, that your own lust for power will not, just as in the previous metaphor, have bred in him that jealousy which you impute to him.

Jump's notion that Rollo is the tree is finally untenable as coming from a mother so much devoted to her first son that she can see little good in her second; but his explanation of the Q2 'Bred ... of' allows us to preserve that text: 'lest it was an excessive desire in you to rule alone which gave rise to the suspicion of him which you now display', bred not in you this your passionate jealousy of him. The parallel present tense of 'provoke' and 'Breed' (as in Q1) is attractive, and surely a 'Breed/Bred' misreading can be interpreted in either way. But in judging the Q1 'Breed not in him' as against the Q2 'Bred not of him', we have also to judge the difference in the prepositions: it is not wise to disregard the *in/of* variant. Presumably, the charge of derived sophistication is more likely placed against 'Breed not in' than against 'Bred not of'. So long as we understand that Sophia's use of the phrase 'this jealous passion' does not imply that she believes that Rollo has already been passionate, there is no difficulty in retaining the Q2 reading at line 21. Seward long ago observed: 'The jealous passion therefore is *Otto*'s, not *Rollo*'s'.

At lines 24–5, Otto expresses his understanding of his mother's curious predilection. Before this, again using a tree metaphor, Aubrey (II.iii.81–3) had offered the same sort of caution.

115 and]   The 'or' in line 115 is probably the fusion of the Q2 compositor's recollection of 'our', two words earlier, and his anticipation of 'Or' two words later. See also III.i.66–7, 74.

147 Powr]   The confusing spelling, 'Power' (for modern 'pour'), unique to Q2, should perhaps be emended to 'Powre', as at line 223 (also Chapman), but though both forms are standard variants in the seventeenth century (*O.E.D.*), in the present context confusion is easy ('Power lives' = power is living). See also at V.ii.13 (Fletcher and Massinger): Q2 'Pour'd'; Q1 'Powr'd'; and *The Prophetess*, I.iii.210 (Fletcher): 'Powr'.

153 Proclaiming]   The Q2 'Complaining' results from the compositor's metathesis of *c* and *p*, assisted by the presence of initial *C* in 'Court' and 'conspiracy'; the Q1 word is echoed at lines 179, 184, 190.

202 *Matilda*]   All the seventeenth-century editions print the phrase, 'Wonder invades me.' as the first words of Rollo's speech, and Weber supported that assignment: 'Rollo may either hypercritically pretend astonishment at the surprise

expressed by Gisbert and Baldwin ...; or he may speak the words aside, being himself surprised at Aubrey's speech. I prefer the former supposition.' Dyce replied: 'the words cannot possibly belong to Rollo'. With similar conviction Seward gave them to Sophia, producing thereby a disjointed speech for her; Colman gave them to '*Gis. and Bald.*', for 'Rollo's reply [at 202] authorizes it' (Weber later pointed out that the phrase cannot properly be spoken as a group speech, as can that at line 200); Dyce, accepting Weber's observation, gave them to Gisbert, though, as he says, he might as well have chosen Baldwin. Though the agreement of Q1 and Q2 is striking, the reluctance of most editors to accept their reading suggests some kind of error. Since the phrase does not seem appropriate to Rollo (as Seward noted) – though the present editor lacks Dyce's conviction on the point – and its assignment to two speakers seems odd and to only one of those specific two, the old courtiers, even odder, the present edition assigns it to Matilda, as the conclusion of her private conversation with Sophia: 'He flatter thus? ... Wonder invades me.' Weber and Dyce thought that this exchange should be 'aside', and Dr Turner points out that if it is not 'aside', Rollo's 'you two' must refer to the women. Seward and Sympson concurred in thinking that the phrase could be spoken by any one of the three speakers who have been chosen by later editors.

254 perswasion]   The Q2 plural is probably another instance of compositorial anticipation. See Textual Introduction.

259 hence]   The quartos 'here' probably results from a misreading of MS 'hēce'. The emendation makes this adverb uniform with those at lines 226 and 231 (and 335).

309 up then]   The second quarto reads 'up thus then', producing an awkward line, hypermetrical with an extra stressed syllable in final position (cf. line 307). It can be argued that we have here a double error. It may be that the author wrote in line 309 'stand up thus', decided to reserve the 'thus' for line 310, wrote 'then' in place of it and neglected to delete 'thus'. The scribe of the prompt-book copied both adverbs. The Q1 compositor, attempting to smooth away the awkwardness, omitted the 'up'; but Edith's posture before this line must be kneeling – she adopts the posture of prayer and the metaphor of a plant fixed in the earth (lines 279–86), and she clings to Rollo (lines 304–6). So at line 309 she must be standing to adopt the posture of defiance (lines 311–19). The word 'up' is essential to the text in order to suggest that movement.

There might be some advantage in placing the direction for Edith's rising on the short line (line 310), but her action must precede (or accompany) not follow her statement; we might better, however, think of 'I stand up then' as constituting the beginning of line 310, leaving line 309 'Drown'd ... wrath?' as the short line here.

325 Bloud]   Qy: Floud?

340 preserv'd]   Qy: should the text be relined and supplemented – 'This Prince ... belov'd of Heaven, | That heaven hath thus preserv'd [from envy's hand].'?

386 seat]   I.e., modern 'set': metaphor from tennis (Jump).

418 imbrac't]   Q1 offers the familiar spelling 'embrac'd', but the Q2 form is acceptable as a past tense. Seward misread as 'embrace it'.

III.ii

19 peaching]   This word, 'informing against someone' (*O.E.D.*, citing this line), is presumably to be distinguished from 'peaking' (line 28, 'mean-spirited'), and no doubt Fletcher was using the two words deliberately and distinctively (by 'peaching' the rogue provided the halters); Q1 agrees with Q2. F2, however, changed 'peaching' (line 19) to 'peaking', and Seward, Colman and Weber changed 'peaking' (line 28) to 'peaching'. The two spellings indicate two separable words, and the distinction should be preserved (as in Dyce and Jump).

45 — 90 + 3 *They sing.*]   Because it is misplaced (after line 94) in Q1, the fourth stanza bears the prefix 'Pant.' in that edition, indicating the singer. Weber first supplied prefixes for the other stanzas, and all editors have followed his sequence: Yeoman (line 47), Butler (line 57), Cook (line 69), Pantler (line 85). These assignments are self-evident, but it is worth a note that a Butler is etymologically a bottler (II.ii.67), one who keeps his bottles (in IV.ii.27–8 the Butler is concerned for his 'Boles'), and a Pantler is etymologically one who deals with bread (*panis*) and chips the crust from the loaf (see also the Textual Note to line 86).

Come fortunes a whore . . . triple tree.]   It is not possible to make the four stanzas of this song – unlike the stanzas of the Servitors' song in II.ii – conform to a single metrical pattern. The stanzas are alike only in that each is followed by the same refrain (but even that constant is lacking for stanza four in Q1 (and so F2)), where the faulty positioning of that stanza (after line 94) may have caused the compositor to overlook the single line of the refrain. In Q2 the Cook refers to the vocal as 'our Ballad' (line 35), and Q1 terms it 'our . . . Ballads', though in the next line both texts speak of it in the singular. (Perhaps the Q1 scribe, noting the variety in metre, made the word plural.)

Stanza 1 is formally unique, consisting of six hypermetrical lines of mixed iambic and anapestic feet, having each eleven or twelve syllables and rhyming *aa bb cc*. Q2 (and so this edition) indents the last two lines, though the text hardly exhibits a change justifying the indention.

Stanzas 2, 3 and 4 have in common a system of alternation between an iambic trimeter line (hypermetrical with weak ending) (even-numbered lines, counting the first line as 1) and iambic trimeters or iambic tetrameters (odd-numbered lines). The present edition breaks with earlier editors by regarding the iambic trimeter (even-numbered) line as the constant and in printing, indented, the lines with that constant in the several stanzas, as the norm of all three stanzas. Stanza 2 (three quatrains) exhibits the form with an uncomplicated metrical pattern: lines 2–4–6–8–10–12, hypermetrical iambic trimeter (with disyllabic rhymes) – i.e., the norm – alternate with 1–3–5–7–9–11, hypermetrical iambic trimeter (with disyllabic rhymes). Stanza 4 (two quatrains): in each quatrain, lines 2 and 4 (hypermetrical iambic trimeter), rhyme terminally; lines 1 and 3 (iambic tetrameter) rhyme internally. Stanza 3 offers a mix of the two systems: lines 1–4, 9–12 with the form of stanza 4; lines 5–8 with the form of stanza 2. Fletcher's form is intricate and accomplished, more sophisticated than the simple schemes used in II.ii and in V.ii.

No explanation comes readily to hand for the variant in the refrain. Q2 offers:

'As e're did sing three parts in a string, / All under the triple tree'; Q1 offers: 'As ever did sing in a hempen string, under the gallow-tree.' Since both 'the triple tree' and 'the gallow-tree' are standard expressions in the seventeenth century for the gallows, neither is clearly to be preferred.

There are no manuscript sources for this song, but Professor Andrew Sabol has called to my attention the record in W. Chapell, *Popular Music of the Olden Time* (London, (n.d.)), I, 162, 216, of the refrain: 'Three merry men and three merry men, And three merry men be we a, I'm in the wood, and thou on the ground, And Jack sleeps in the tree.' Reference to this refrain or to a song named by this refrain occur in half a dozen plays of the period (including *Twelfth Night*, II.iii.70). Professor Sabol proposes also that the individual verses utilize the famous tune, 'Fortune, my foe', and he has skilfully demonstrated by the addition and subtraction of musical notes how the varying metrical patterns can be adapted to the single tune. He explains that the Cook's phrase, 'weel trust no man / Nor no tune but our own' (lines 44–5), means that 'he'll trust no other man's arrangement of those extensively varied verses of that quartet but his own, and certainly the tune is not his own' (personal correspondence, 10 May 1994). The Cook could have with entire confidence trusted Professor Sabol, whose ingenious and elegant setting of the song and the refrain would serve a performance admirably.

86 *clipt ... chipt*] Q2 reverses these participles, presumably through compositorial metathesis; the Q1 version (followed by all editors) is surely correct: 'I chipt [the] ... crust'. Chipping crust is what pantlers do; see *2 Henry IV*, II.iv.220–1.

IV.i

76 slip'st] Objecting to the quartos' 'sleepst' (which he retained nevertheless), Seward was correct in thinking that sycophants cannot be said to sleep, 'since they are generally vigilant and eager'; and in a postscript (p. 529), he conjectured 'creep'st' (as in line 56; adopted by Weber). Seward erred in preserving the vowels and not the consonants; Dyce rightly suggested 'slip'st', though he thought 'the old reading to be right'. Dyce's conjecture is surely correct: a verb of intrusive motion is required. 'Step'st' (as in line 58), also possible, is less likely; insinuating and lubricious are the flatterer's words. (For the same *ip/eep* error, see III.ii.18.)

97 these] There are six instances in the text where the quartos disagree on 'these' and 'those'. Q2 reads 'these' and Q1 reads 'those' at I.i.239, III.i.150, IV.i.224; Q2 reads 'those' and Q1 reads 'these' at I.i.248, IV.iii.111, V.ii.211. From this array, it is evident that there was considerable difficulty in the various levels of scribal transmission in distinguishing between medial *e* and *o*, an easy scribal or compositorial misreading. (Comparable *e/o* differences occur in these readings (Q2/Q1): 'those'/'their' (I.i.137), 'then'/'thou' (I.i.164), 'know'/'knew' (V.i.100).) There are, to be sure, many instances where the quartos agree in reading 'these' or 'those'; they do so in the present instance. This edition predicates a scribal error in the preparation of the prompt-book, based on this same misreading, which produced in both derived texts the common error 'those', here emended to 'these'.

177 be slave] This emendation replaces a dash in the Q2: 'Or worthy to be——of
your delight', represented in Q1 as 'Or worthy to be secretary of your pleasure'.
Weber and Dyce followed Q1, presumably pronouncing the noun agent here in
two syllables ('sec'-t'ry'). But 'secretary' – metrics aside – can scarcely be right, as
it is used later to describe the Mathematicians. Latorch uses it in naming Russee,
and Russee uses it in describing the three other operators, 'the Secretaries of the
Starres' (IV.ii.83, 86 – both instances, presumably, of pronunciation of four
syllables). Latorch would not describe himself with the term he uses to venerate the
astrologers. Furthermore, as there is no justification for abandoning Q2 'delight' in
favour of Q1 'pleasure', an attempt must be made to find a term to replace the dash
of Q2.

   That dash represents, very likely, the compositor's inability to read the word; as
Weber conjectured, 'in the MS . . . the line was probably illegible' (– more probably
this single word than the line). Seward, with an ear and a finger always fixed on
metrics, observed that 'all words but Monosyllables are excluded by the Measure'. I
believe he was correct. Suggesting 'bawd', 'pimp', 'groom', he chose 'Groom',
followed by Weber. Of these suggestions, neither of the others can be accepted
(Jump chose 'bawd'), as we cannot imagine that Latorch would so debase himself –
'too coarse Names for a Man to call himself' (Seward) – or define his procuring
with a term so derogatory to the Duke. Latorch does refer to himself, however, as a
'watchman' (IV.i.46) and as 'servant' (IV.i.175), and in dealing with Edith he refers
to himself as 'servant' (III.i.410) and promises to 'serve' (III.i.419). Monosyllables
'watch' or 'spy' seem to smack in this context of voyeurism, and the present edition
proposes for 'servant' the monosyllable 'slave', a word not inappropriate, viewed
romantically, though perhaps 'slave for' might have been a preferable locution.
Aubrey calls Latorch 'knave', 'spy', 'slave' in other contexts (IV.i.45, 73; V.i.54).
('Drudge' might serve, but the word is not used elsewhere in the text; cf. *Romeo and
Juliet*, II.v.77, where the Nurse, also employed as an intermediary, uses that term.)

   How the Q1 reading developed is not easy to conjecture; perhaps the compositor
read the word in the MS perfectly well, but thinking it not fit to print, invented this
euphemism. What such an obscenity might be is undiscoverable (by this editor).
The Q2 compositor perhaps reacted similarly, with a dash. Presumably, Rollo's
intentions are not honorable; Aubrey calls Latorch 'Baude of the State' a term that
might indicate that he knew of other of his 'maisters lusts' (IV.i.47–8), though
there has been no indication that any of Rollo's many crimes are sexual in character,
or indeed, until lines 164–5, that his interest in Edith has been so.

199–200 *De Bube* | Another Gentleman] Dyce's observation that the name of one of
these topical figures has been omitted is surely correct, but the likeliest place to
insert it is not so easy to identify. The place where the new name will do least
damage to the Q2 text is at the end of line 199, blank in Q2:

   Russee an admirable man
   Another Gentleman, and then *La fiske*.

The Q1 version is also defective, though in another way:

258

> *Rusee*, an admirable man, another
> A gentleman, and then *Lafiske*,

There can be no question of social rank here, as Latorch calls them all 'Gentlemen' (IV.ii.237). The Q1 'A' seems a sophistication.

213 stooles] The passage here (lines 210–23) describes the various automata of classical and mythological times. So Aristotle (*Politics*, I.ii.5) refers to a story of objects invented by Daedalus that moved of their own volition, and Vulcan (Hephaestus) fashioned bellows that worked at his verbal command (Smith, *Dictionary*), tripods that moved 'of themselves' (*Iliad*, XVIII.370–80), and handmaidens wrought of gold who attended him (*ibid.*, 419–25). Though these objects might seem to support the Q1 reading 'Tooles', the tripods mentioned in the *Iliad* (XVIII.373) were thought by some to be stools, and are so glossed by Jonson in his note to the Viscount Haddington's *Masque* (1608): '*Vulcan* had made twenty *Tripodes* or stooles with golden wheeles, to moove of themselves, miraculously' (C. H. Herford, Percy and Evelyn Simpson, *Ben Jonson* (Oxford, 1941 (1963)), VII, 259).

The other machines (221–3) seem to derive from Cornelius Agrippa, *Of the Vanitie … of Artes and Sciences* (1569), fol. 56 (quoted in Jump, p. 95). Hiarbas presumably refers to Hiarchas, noted in the same work, but neither name can be connected significantly with any figure of classical times or of classical literature. Jump suggests (p. 95) how 'Hiarbas' might have been erroneously associated with the gymnosophists, but as that group practised extreme abstinence and poverty, under no circumstances could one of them have had a banquet of the trimalchian grandeur suggested here. The author of these lines was bluffing (probably, therefore, not Jonson). (I am obliged to my colleague Professor William Willis for his searches on my behalf.)

IV.ii

15 puddings] It has been suggested that, since the context is explicitly sexual, the plural should be emended to the singular. There is, however, no textual warrant for making that change, and as neither Eric H. Partridge, *Shakespeare's Bawdy* (1947), nor Frankie Rubenstein, *A Dictionary of … Sexual Puns …* (1989), treats 'puddings' or 'eggs' as bawdy terms, the suggestion is not adopted.

51 bay or streights] For the quartos' 'bog' Weber read, after Mason's conjecture, 'bay' and for 'sleights' Seward read 'Streights'. The former variant is an easy error; the latter not so easy, but the nautical imagery almost requires both these emendations.

56 crispe] Q2 'crispt', a likely *t/e* misreading (Q1: 'crispe') (as in line 168 below where the reverse occurs), but Dr Turner suggests that the past participial form could mean a wine 'made clear or sparkling (by the vintner)'.

110 you may] That the money is given to the Boy – so as (superficially) to preserve inviolate the integrity of the Jugglers – is suggested by the comparable situation at

line 143 where Russee specifically directs Latorch to give the money to the Boy.
142 *De Bube*] Q; *Russee?*

155 scheme] This scene of the astrologers (lines 155–236), or 'Juglers' as they are called (V.ii.179.1), has been the despair of editors since Seward: 'It is difficult to us at present to relish the Jargon of a Science so long exploded, but … [this scene] is certainly a very just Banter upon the ridiculous Credulity of our Authors age.' The 'scarcely penetrable' technical jargon has, we may suppose, at last been thoroughly penetrated and explicated by Dr J. C. Eade in 'Astrological analysis as an editorial tool: the case of Fletcher's *The Bloody Brother*', *Studies in Bibliography*, XXXIV (1981), 198–204 (henceforth in this Note, *SB*), and in *The Forgotten Sky* (Oxford: Clarendon Press, 1984), pp. 189–97 and *passim*. Dr Eade, to whose work and friendly correspondence I am entirely indebted, has demonstrated beyond any doubt that 'in its overall contour the passage is astrologically sound, following in their due order exactly those procedures that an astrologer would adopt in reading a horoscope. And it is internally consistent in a manner which it would have been impossible for the author to achieve without a very secure knowledge of his subject' (*SB*, p. 199). For examples: the 'scheme' of Rollo's horoscope is so exact that it can be illustrated visually (see *Forgotten Sky*, p. 191), and the latitude and longitude so precisely given at lines 161–2 are not gibberish but the co-ordinates of Caen, the birthplace of the historical Rollo, 'being reckoned from the meridian of Hierro, one of the Canary Islands, as it usually was in [the earlier seventeenth century]' (R. Garnett, 'Ben Jonson's probable authorship of Scene 2, Act IV, of Fletcher's *Bloody Brother*', *Modern Philology*, II (1904–5), 495.) The complexities can be somewhat simplified by noting that the astrologers discuss first the locations of the seven planets (lines 164–71) – Sun and Mercury and Mars (in the Third house), Jupiter (twelfth), Venus (second), Saturne (fifth), Luna (seventh) – and then of the signs of the Zodiac (lines 171–6) – Scorpio (first), Libra (second), [Capricorn] (fourth), Aries (seventh), though, of course, the assignments are not precise, each extending over into one or the other of the adjacent houses or signs. That Mars is everywhere 'ruling' and dominant will explain why Rollo is so bellicose and 'bloody'.

Notes for emendations credited to 'Eade' are from personal correspondence. Entries below, repeating items in the Historical Collation or the Emendation of Accidentals, explain or supplement the apparatus.

160 nocturnall:] (*confirmed by* Eade); ~ ∧ Q2. As in lines 184–5.

164 *Capricorne*——] ~ ∧ Q2. 'La Fiske is obviously being interrupted from saying what *degree* of Capricorn defines the next cardin. … [T]here is a lot in the text that points up the bickering, particularly Norbret's' – Eade.

166 in] Q1 (*confirmed by* Eade); omit Q2.

167 *fortunæ*] F2; *fortuna* Q2. '*fortuna* is an illiteracy and so is *Cacadæmon* [line 168]. … These errors are more likely to be scribal/printer's errors than attempts by the author to show the ignorance of his characters' – Eade.

171 *Scorpio* ∧] (*confirmed by* Eade); ~ , Q2.

172 (Thats … *gaudium*)] ∧ ~ … ~ ∧ Q2. (Eade proposes dashes here to set off the phrase; parentheses are the norm in this text.)

172 Thats] Eade. Neither Q2 'That' nor Q1 'Then' seems to be correct, but Eade's emendation 'That's' ('Thats') is easy enough. The contraction appears a second time in Norbret's speech at line 224 (spelled 'Thats', though emended in this edition to 'That is') and in Russee's at line 145.

172 *Mars* his] i.e., Mars's. Scorpio is the *gaudium* of Mars.

173 That joint] Though 'the text is very tricky, hereabouts', the Q2 reading is correct. In this section, 171–6, Norbret in his domineering way, 'is going round the horoscope, *still* looking at the cardins, which are houses 1, 4, 7, 10. So we have: (a) Scorpio (one of Mars' two mansions) is in the ascendant = 1; (b) Mars' exaltation is in 4 = *imum coeli*; (c) Aries, Mars' other mansion is in 7 and *also* Mars itself is there. Mars "owns" three of the four cardins and is also sitting in one of them – he *must* be owning the show! ... Norbret's finger is going anticlockwise around the "scheme" from 9 o'clock position to 3 o'clock position ... Libra, Venus' mansion, therefore has to be fitted in subordinately to this main outline; the point being (1) the fact that Libra, and not Scorpio, really defines the ascendant ... has to be skirted around, so that the part of Scorpio that is *also* there gets attention; (2) the fact that Libra is a mansion of Venus gets a look in, in order that Norbret can show off more useless pedantic knowledge; but the whole of line 173 is just as parenthetical as [is line 172]. [And because of that parenthetical subordination,] I continue to see "joint" as really meaning "joined". ... What the text then says at this point, in an incredibly compressed form, is *"that* [sign] Scorpio [being] *joint with Libra* [as we already know from line 163] *too* [which is, significantly,] *the house* [i.e., one of the two mansions] *of Venus"*.'

174 *In imo*] Eade. Q2 reads '*Imum*'; Q1 reads '*Juniu*'. Since the *imum Coeli* is the fourth house, it cannot refer also to the seventh house, and the Q2 reading must be wrong. The Q1 reading, a (presumed) non-word, is also wrong, but its error contains perhaps a representation of the original MS. The letters '*Juniu*' can be conceived as a misreading of MS '*In imo*'. With this emendation, the locations where 'Mars exerts his influence' (*SB*, p. 202) are entirely consistent: since Mars' '*gaudium* ... [is] in the first house [lines 171–2], and ... Aries, his other mansion, in the seventh house [lines 174–5], the intermediate second observation should relate to ... the fourth house (or 'imum coeli')' (*ibid.*). The Latin ending demonstrates the location, just as in line 167 'in the *Imo caeli*'.

174 exaltation] Q1 (*confirmed by* Eade); exultation Q2.

177 geniture] Q1; genitures Q2. 'The plural is certainly wrong' – Eade. I.e., Mars is absolutely in control of Rollo's birth chart.

179 *Zaell*] (Garnett after an anonymous *conj.*); *Laell* Q2, Q1. 'All editions read *Laell*, but this name occurs nowhere else, while *Zael* or *Sael* was a distinguished Arabian astrologer whose works were translated into Latin. The correction was made a few years ago by a correspondent of the *Athenaeum*' – Garnett (p. 495). Jump read '*Saell*', but as a L/Z misreading is likelier than an L/S one, it has seemed preferable to use the other spelling and follow Garnett. The name is transliterated also as Zahel and as Sahl ibn Bishr.

183 being *Libra*] Dyce and Jump emend, inserting 'in' between the words; but 'the subject of "being" is properly *Horoscope*' (*Forgotten Sky*, p. 192).

198 hilage ∧ with a quartile,]   Eade; ∼ , . . . ∼ ∧ Q2. 'The rest of the scene does support the combination that Mars looks at the *hilege* with a quartile aspect and that he rules the third house' (*SB*, p. 204). The 'quartile aspect' is mentioned again in line 201.

202 in]   Q1 (*confirmed by* Eade); *omit* Q2. '*In* is essential. . . . The sequence is as follows: lines 199–200 basically [suggest] . . . more in-fighting / more stage business. Then we get "the Lady of Life, / Here *in* the seaventh". This is a reference back to the moon and line 171' – Eade. The omission of 'in' here and in line 166 may reflect the compositor's despair.

221 Person]   Though the Q2 'Persons brings' offers a quite acceptable reading, all editors (except Jump) have followed the (modern) grammatical reading of Q1 'Persons bring', in the assumption that the Q2 'brings' is corrupt, an echoic carrying over of the '-s' from 'Persons' to 'bring'. Another interpretation, perhaps more in keeping with compositorial practice, suggests that 'Persons' is corrupt, that the Q2 corruption has proceeded in the opposite direction and that we have an anticipatory carrying over of the '-s' to 'Person' from 'brings'. Some small amount of support may come in the fact that in the conversation that follows the supposed threat is singular. See a comparable situation at I.i.302; III.i.254, 373.

The next line provides an intriguing comment on this reading – 'the starres tells'. Here, clearly, the subject is plural, and though the Q2 reading offers a quite acceptable reading, all editors have followed the (modern) grammatical reading of Q1 'Stars tell'. One is tempted to argue that the corruption (?) here is the opposite of that advanced to explain the preceding line, but the variant in Q1 of 'us not' suggests literary smoothing in this passage and confirms the notion that the modern subject–verb agreement in Q1 is also editorial. And if editorial in line 223, very likely editorial with the same correction in line 222.

IV.iii

52 have . . . they are]   The singular forms in Q1 – 'has . . . it is' – offer a good example of Q1's sophisticating tendency. The scribe of the MS behind Q1 assumed that Edith's 'poore beauty' had already shown itself sufficient to provoke Rollo (all editors agreed with him); but the Q2 plural is, I think, a little more understanding and sensitive: even the defects of Edith's beauty have been able to overpower Rollo.

80 worthy]   Q2 'worthlesse' is clearly a fusion of compositorial echoing of 'endlesse' and anticipation of 'blisse' and 'highnesse' in the next line.

V.ii

12 roring]   Dyce's conjecture, 'roaring' (in the old-spelling form here adopted), seems most plausible, the *r/v* misreading being not uncommon. 'Roring' strengthens the alliterative pattern of the line, providing another 'r'. Though 'roving' suits well enough with 'wildnesse' and storm – i.e., uncontrolled nature – what is wanted here is furious compulsion, not aimless wandering. For another *r/ v/n/* error, see V.ii.178.

13 Poure]   As all the verbs in this execration are in the present tense, this verb
should probably be emended from Q2 'Pour'd', in the assumption that we have a
simple e/d error (supplemented by a gratuitous apostrophe). Perhaps the original
MS spelled the word 'Powre' (as at III.i.223 (see Textual Note to III.i.147))
(retained here in Q1 'Powr'd').

21–32 *Take o take ... by thee.*]   The most vexatious problem in the editorial
tradition of *Rollo* is that of this song, the first stanza of which appears also in
Shakespeare's *Measure for Measure*, IV.i.1–6. The problem turns on authorship.
The quickest response – not therefore the best – is that Shakespeare wrote the first
stanza for his play (1604) and Fletcher wrote the second for his (1619). Jump
surveys the history of the arguments and concludes, on the basis of parallel phrases,
that 'Shakespeare must be recognized as the author of the [first] stanza. There is no
reason why the second, inferior, stanza should not be attributed to Fletcher' (pp.
105–6). The same attitude, from the musician's point of view, is expressed by
Cutts: 'la première strophe est, je crois, de Shakespeare ...; la deuxième strophe,
calquée sur la première ... fut écrite par Fletcher'.[1] Those appraisals sum up the
attitude of scholarship before the publication of the Oxford Shakespeare (1986,
1987) and the theory of composition for *Measure for Measure* enunciated in the
Textual Companion (1987(88)) and explained at length in Gary Taylor and John
Jowett, *Shakespeare Reshaped 1606–1623*. In the third chapter 'With new
additions', Jowett and Taylor argue that the presence of the song in *Measure* is the
work of a revising dramatist who has borrowed it from *Rollo* and interpolated it in
the prompt-book of Shakespeare's play for a late production some fifteen years after
its original production.[2]

Many are the warnings that argue against either of these opposing hypotheses. It
may be that neither playwright is responsible for either stanza: 'A hundred
examples can be found of playwrights having borrowed lyrics that were known to
the theatrical audience as the work of someone else.'[3]

Jowett and Taylor find a significance in the fact that the song is sung in both
plays by a male (a Boy) to a female: they consider this gender linking appropriate to
Rollo, inappropriate to *Measure*. But what is significant, surely, is not the gender of
the singer – all songs in this period are sung by male actors – but rather that the
song is sung in both plays at the request of a female of or to a male, that recipient
male being present only in *Rollo*.

If we consider the two-stanza form of the song as in *Rollo* as the original, it is
difficult to see in the dramatic context of *Measure* how the second stanza could ever
have been fitted to the first; so it is not easy to see in the dramatic context of *Rollo*
how the first stanza could have been fitted to the second. Cutts makes that attempt:

> La deuxième [strophe], tout à l'oppposé [de la première], dit le puissant pouvoir
> qu'un amant reconnaît à la beauté de sa maîtresse, et elle se prête ainsi
> admirablement bien au dessein d'Edith. Celle-ci cherche à faire croire à Rollo,
> par la première strophe, qu'elle a été abandonnée par son amant, et par la
> deuxième qu'elle agréerait très voluntiers les marques de son amour auquel elle
> serait heureuse de se soumettre. Cette suggestion est nécessaire au plan par
> lequel Edith veut causer la chute de Rollo.[4]

Other critics have difficulty in seeing the two-stanza form of the song as a unit; Professor Donald W. Foster concedes that 'the apparent disunity of the two stanzas ... may yet be explained as intentional, to indicate something of the betrayed lover's indecisiveness, but it points more probably, in this case, to composite authorship'.[5]

Foster has shown by his analysis of word-links that the words of the first stanza of the song are closely linked to the words of the full text of *Measure*. There is a high correlation between the words of the first stanza and the text of *Measure*, 156 word-links, and a low correlation between the words of the second stanza and the text of *Measure*, 99 word-links, i.e., 58 per cent more links with *Measure* for the first stanza than for the second. Such statistics imply that the writer of the first stanza was steeped in the vocabulary of *Measure*; the writer of the second was not.[6]

And Foster presents 'other evidence [for the composition of the second stanza], previously overlooked: for example, the phrase "hills of snow" suggests a later date of composition than 1604, when *Measure for Measure* was performed and, presumably written. "Hills of snow" is a poetic cliché of the 1620s, and is found nowhere in the Shakespeare canon and rarely elsewhere during his lifetime. Nor do we find poets urging women to hide their "hills" (breasts) and "pinks" (nipples) until after 1610, when ... the bare-breasted look became fashionable ... or at least became fashionable as a topic of English poetry.'[7]

Further, the major ideas of the first stanza bear a direct relationship to those of *Measure*: lips ... forsworn = 'That Angelo's forsworn, is it not strange?' (V.i.38); mislead the morn = Angelo's early morning messages that violate his pledge; sealed in vain = '[Angelo's] worth and credit ... seal'd in approbation' (V.i.244).

On the basis of this analysis, we may reasonably conclude that stanza 2 was not written for or available to the original performance of *Measure* in 1604. We may also conclude – on the basis of dates – that the author of stanza 2 was not Shakespeare; stanza 2 is the work of a later poet than Shakespeare. It is, on the other hand, probable, though not undeniably demonstrable, that the later poet was not the author also of stanza 1, though most early (and modern) criticism would seem to support the thesis that he was not, divided authorship being the most economical explanation of the crux.

Professor Thomas A. Pendleton observes a major improbability that in 1622 a single writer 'of the two stanzas [could have] produced a second stanza that repeats so much of the rhetoric and syntax of stanza 1 (Take, o take / Hide, o hide; That so– / That thy–; But my– / But first–), but so incoherently varies the implicit situation of [persona] and beloved. In stanza 1, there is a relationship that has attained some kind of consummation with oaths and kisses, and then has been "forsworn"; ... but stanza 2 gives us something like the stock Petrarchan sonneteer, enslaved by the various physical excellences of the lady, but simply lamenting his lack of access to the lady. Stanza 2 is undeniably addressed to a female [sung by a male lover]; stanza 1 may be ... but stanza 1 is not so heavily genderized that it cannot be responded to as [sung by a female lover,] the lyricizing of Mariana's experience; stanza 2 clearly can't be. ... All of this looks to me like a second stanza composed by another (and not too skillful) hand in imitation of a pre-existing first stanza.'

It is most unlikely, he continues, that someone in 1622 'designed the "Take o take" stanza to introduce [Edith] and at that distance produced (to introduce also [Marianna]) a lyric so exquisitely well calculated to satisfy the needs that Shakespeare created (but couldn't satisfy) [18] years before. [There can be no question] about the quality of the lyric, its suitability to Mariana's narrative and emotional situation, and to its effectiveness in establishing so significant a character so firmly and so late in the play. I would have thought Shakespeare's record with sweetly sad songs (vide *Twelfth Night* especially) would suggest this is very much in his line of work.'[8]

Part of the difficulty in dealing with this composite form is that, as Pendleton points out, while the gender of the persona of stanza 2 is clearly male, that of stanza 1 is not exclusively of either sex. It is probably female, but the first stanza cannot profitably be related to Edith's experience (*pace* Cutts). To suppose that Shakespeare wrote both stanzas for *Measure* is to make a supposition for which there can be no evidence beyond Mariana's 'break off' (at line 7 of the scene).[9] To suppose that a later poet wrote both stanzas for *Rollo* is to suppose that he adapted the first stanza particularly to the language and the themes of *Measure*. Neither of these suppositions is attractive. The stanza in *Measure* is Shakespeare's, written by him for that play (not the work of another poet); the new stanza in *Rollo* is a later poet's (probably Fletcher's) written for this play.

In an attempt to make sense of these assumptions and arguments and to assemble them into a whole, we may consider the textual and theatrical history of *Measure for Measure*, written originally in 1603–4.

Modern scholars agree that the copy for the printing of *Measure* in the Folio (1623) was prepared by Ralph Crane, transcribing the prompt-book in 1622. That printing gives evidence of several stages of revision in the prompt-book: (1) post-1606 deletions of profanity, (2) post-1609 additions of act divisions (possibly for a revival in 1610 or 1611), and, (3) Jowett and Taylor argue, among several topical references, one to the 'King of Hungary's peace' (I.ii.1–4) relevant to events only *c.* 1621 (an addition possibly for a revival about that time). The need for a 1610 revision is dependent on the move to the Blackfriars Theatre in 1609, with the consequent necessity of providing intervals and, hence, a readjustment of the lines to be spoken immediately before and after the interval. (Though there is, in fact, no external evidence that such adaptation or revision in 1610 took place, the changes in production techniques required by the move to the Blackfriars Theatre sufficiently justify, in the mind of the present editor, the need for such adaptation and explain the traces of it still visible in the F(1623) text.) Foster argues for a 'substantive revision' in 1611. Jowett and Taylor find the work of the 1621 revisions particularly apparent in I.ii and in the joint between Acts III and IV.[10]

Then we must posit a situation in which at the time of the move in 1609, Shakespeare was asked to suggest places for act breaks in *Measure* (as he was, demonstrably, I would argue, for *Hamlet* and *Lear*), and, as he did so, he provided the text of a song to be sung at Mariana's request to describe her situation before the Duke comes to make his proposition and before her meeting with Isabella. (It does not seem likely that the song could have belonged to the 1603–4 text of the play, as that text can now be reconstructed, to be sung in another scene.) At that time (or at a later date), the dialogue to introduce Isabella was provided by another hand. Jowett and Taylor confirm Alice Walker's opinion that the dialogue at the beginning of IV.i is 'clearly the work of an inexpert hand' almost certainly after Shakespeare's retirement.[11] They argue persuasively that the reviser was John Webster or, less likely, Massinger. They claim both stanzas of the song for Fletcher, and though they are convincing that the second stanza is Fletcher's they do not demonstrate that the first stanza is not Shakespeare's.[12]

If we accept the need for an act break here, added subsequent to the conception of the play originally, we enter an entirely new tradition – nothing from the past can explain the situation. A song at this point in a play is for Shakespeare a new thing. If Shakespeare wrote verse 1 in 1603–4, he placed it in a context now lost; if he wrote verse 1 in 1610–11, he would be remembering with wonderful detail the sense of the original play – a thesis surely not difficult to accept. Strange as it may seem, the evidence would seem to suggest that though he provided the act break and the song, Shakespeare did not provide the necessary dialogue or, at least, the dialogue now extant, and that whoever did provided unShakespearian text while retaining the song (= verse 1).[13] It is entirely possible that in 1609 the song was set, jewel-like, in a Shakespearian context entirely destroyed by a revision in 1616 or in 1622.

Such stages of revision can arguably be deduced from the 1623 Folio text, but as Pendleton points out, there is little evidence that *Measure* 'was still theatrically viable in ... [1621], ... disguised-duke plays were pretty well out of fashion by about 1611'.[14] Jowett and Taylor, however, 'find it impossible to avoid the conclusion that *Measure for Measure* suffered major theatrical adaptation in 1621', and they assert that 'a late revival ... did almost certainly take place'.[15] Their arguments turn primarily on the topical references already noted and on the music for the song. The extant music for the two-stanza song is acknowledged to be the work of John Wilson. Wilson, closely associated with the King's Men after 1617, prepared a number of songs for the company. Cutts points out that the musical interest of the song is always connected with the two-stanza form made for the production of *Rollo* (surviving in many manuscripts). That music, he argues, was a reworking by Wilson of an earlier tune (composer unknown), marked (perhaps) by musical repeats of the last three syllables of the last two lines (as represented in the F(1623) text only).[16] His argument derives from the fact that Wilson's Preface to his *Cheerful Ayres* (1659) acknowledges that many of the ayres in that collection – of which 'Take o take' is one – were new arrangements of songs by other musicians, 'new set by the Author [i.e., Composer]'.[17] Wilson's more sophisti-cated(?) setting, he would argue, required repeats of the entire last two lines. No settings of the song by other composers of the period survive.

When the author(s) of *Rollo* needed a song for Edith, they turned naturally to Wilson. Fletcher knew Wilson, and, we may suppose, he admired the *Measure* song. Perhaps he and Wilson agreed that the *Measure* song with a reworked tune would serve well in *Rollo*, and he added to Shakespeare's song a second stanza, adapted (as he must have supposed) to the situation in his own play; at the same time Wilson reconceived the old tune. That the first stanza did not easily conform to the narrative situation in *Rollo* was a detail that did not greatly disturb Fletcher, and that the second stanza did not exactly conform to the metrical pattern of the first was a detail that did not greatly disturb Wilson. Some music manuscripts have 'extra' notes to accommodate the extra syllables.

The song appears in print in the (Shakespeare) Folio of 1623 (first stanza only), in John Benson's collection of *Poems written by Wil. Shakespeare* (1640), in John Wilson's *Select Musical Airs and Dialogues* (Playford, 1652), in reprints and reissues of these items and in John P. Cutts, *La Musique de scène de la troupe de Shakespeare* (Paris, 1959), pp. 1, 85, 115, 171–2. It appears also in twelve manuscripts of the period, in most of which it is set to Wilson's music. The collation against the present text includes Q2 (1640), Q1 (1639), F1 (1623), F2 (1679), PW (John Wilson, *Select Ayres* [1652]), Bodl^1 (Bodleian, Mus.b.1), Bodl^2 (Bodleian, MS Eng. Poet. f. 27), BL^1 (British Library, Add. MSS. 11608), BL^2 (British Library, Harleian 6057), BL^3 (British Library, Harleian 3991, first verse only), XC (Christ Church, Oxford), DFo (Folger Library V.a.162 (formerly 424.4), NY^1 (New York Public Library, Drexel 4041), NY^2 (New York Public Library, Drexel 4257). The collation is based on observations by J. D. Jump, Donald Foster, the present editor, and on material published in Cutts, *Musique de scène*, Wells and Taylor, *Textual Companion*, Taylor and Jowett, *Shakespeare Reshaped*. (Manuscripts not included in this collation: Bodleian, Ashm. 47; Rawl., Poet. 65; Rosenbach Mus., MS 239/27.)

(NB: It is to be noted that 'F1' in these listings refers to the Shakespeare First Folio (1623), not the Beaumont and Fletcher First Folio (1647), which did not include this play.)

22 *were*]   are DFo
23 *like*]   the F1, Bodl^{1,2}, BL^{1,2,3}, XC, DFo, NY^{1,2}; that PW, XC
23 *of*]   the XC
23 *day*]   days PW
24 *Lights*]   light Bodl^2, PW
24 *doe*]   doth Bodl^2
24 *mislead*]   misled Bod^2
25 *bring againe*]   bis F1
25 *bring*]   being Q1(u)
26 *though*]   but F1, BL^3
26 *seal'd*]   seals PW; cal'd XC
26 *seal'd in vaine*]   bis F1
28 *That*]   which Q1, F2, NY^{1,2}
28 *bosome*]   blossome Q1(u) F2, PW
28 *beares*]   weares Bodl^2
29 *grow*]   growes DFo
30 *Are yet of those that*]   Sweeter are then Bodl^2
30 *yet*]   omit Q1, F2, BL^{1,2}, DFo, NY^{1,2}
30 *of*]   omit DFo
30 *wears*]   beares Bodl^2

32 *those*] omit Bodl², BL[1,2], DFo, NY[1]
32 *Icy*]   Ioy Q1(u); gay Q1(c); Ivy F2; Ice, DFo; Ivory BL²

None of these variants seems of compelling merit to supplant the text of Q2. It is tempting for musical regularity to delete the syllables in stanza 2 that are 'extra' to the pattern of verse 1 ('yet', 'those', lines 30, 32), but as the Playford–Wilson text provides a musical note for 'those' such action is unjustifiable.

It is perhaps worth observing that though F1 (1623) does not differ substantively from Q2 and corrected Q1, it does so in accidentals; F1 agrees with Q1 nine times against Q2, and agrees with Q2 three times against Q1.

77 Pree thee]   Though it is tempting to follow the pleasing metrical regularity of 'I prethee' in Q1, the careful separation of two syllables in Q2 suggests that something like 'prethee' was not intended and that, therefore, no 'I' was present in the MS. In the Crane transcript of *Barnavelt*, IV.iii.49, appears 'pre'thee' copied from Fletcher's MS. 'Preethee' is Compositor *Q*'s preferred form, appearing also in *Rule a Wife* (see in this series, vol. VI, p. 489).

80 minde]   Since the 'maide'/'minde' variant is easily understood palaeographically, the choice between the two readings depends on critical preference. The Q1 'made' (not possibly a verbal) is set off by commas as if an appositive, but the spelling is most unusual to identify a maiden. That spelling encourages the suggestion that there was something in the MS form that the Q1 compositor did not understand; that something – the present edition argues – is found in the Q2 'minde', a more sensitive and thoughtful reading than that of Q1. See also III.i.405: 'your sorrowes cloudes'.

80 thou,]   Jump follows Q2 'thou learne', but it is reasonably clear that Q2 reflects a state of the MS when the author was still thinking to continue the sentence with the predicate immediately. (Corrected in Q1.) The parenthetical flattery of lines 81–2 intruded on the sentence as the author shaped it in his mind, and he left 'learne' hanging at the end of the line. Another possible reading 'doe not learne' is presumably disallowed by the text of line 84. A contracted form 'don't thou learne' is inadmissible.

85 thine]   Though the preferred practice of the compositors in setting 'thy/thine' pronouns is not always clear, it seems that in this scene, at least, Q1 has changed the 'mine' found in Q2 to 'my' in 'mine eyes', 'mine owne' (lines 164, 225). Thus it is arguable that the line of text missing from Q2 probably included 'thine eyes' here not the 'thy eyes' of Q1.

150.1 *Enter ... Guards*].]   The earlier marginal direction in Q2 at lines 147–8a, here deleted, may mark the change in authorship: the first direction supplied by Massinger at the end of his share; the second supplied by Fletcher at the beginning of his. The latter's 'yee' forms begin at this spot. Q1 clears up the confusion by adding '*within*' in the margin.

164 quarri'd]   In Colman's edition (1778), Reed explained this verbal, a term from falconry, by reference to Robert Latham ('who wrote in the time of James I') as being formed from the noun *quarrie*, 'the fowle which is flown at ... especially when young hawks are flown thereunto'. Dyce, followed by Jump, defined the

participle as 'provided with prey' or 'supplied with quarry', but the *O.E.D.*
scarcely supports this interpretation, suggesting that the form should mean
'properly trained to fly at quarry' (adj. 1). Another use of the word by Fletcher in
'The Triumph of Death' (*Four Plays in One*, vi.96) describes the delight of a
predator in having secured his prey. The present instance seems a strange parallel:
'my eyes', says Matilda, a good woman about to marry the hero, 'are provided with
their prey', 'their joys' – the death of her brother.

195 stile] The clumsy repetition of 'place'/'place' (both quartos) suggests a
compositorial error of either anticipation or recollection. Editors have been well
content with Seward's suggestion 'Stile' to replace the second occurrence of 'place'
(though 'name' might serve and, as it preserves the vowel, might be preferable); but
one might consider the possibility that the error is in the first 'place' (not the
second) for a word like 'state', 'stage', 'name', etc. A comparable awkwardness
occurs in both quartos at II.ii.40: 'when the Tables drawne / To draw in the wine';
but no persuasive emendation comes to mind. Dr Turner may be correct in noting
the possibility of a pun on two meanings of 'draw': *O.E.D.*, *v*.12 and *v*.40.

NOTES

1 John P. Cutts, *La Musique de scène de la troupe de Shakespeare* (Paris, 1959), p.
172. In his Variorum edition of *Measure for Measure* (1980), Mark Eccles provides
an extensive record of critical opinions on the text of the song and of its music.
2 Stanley Wells and Gary Taylor, *William Shakespeare: A Textual Companion*
(Oxford, 1987 (1988)), pp. 468–9. Dr Taylor most generously made available in
advance of publication the typescript of his and John Jowett's *Shakespeare
Reshaped 1606–1623* (Oxford, 1993). This study includes a detailed and most
impressive analysis of the relationship between the printed and the MS texts of the
song and a careful record of the MS versions of the music (Appendix IV, 'The text
of "Take oh take those lips away"', pp. 272–95). The authorship of the song is
discussed in chapter 3, '"With new additions": theatrical interpolation in *Measure
for Measure*', pp. 107–236.
3 Donald W. Foster, correspondence, 21 November 1990.
4 Cutts, *La Musique de scène*, p. 172.
5 Donald W. Foster, '"Shall I die" post mortem: defining Shakespeare',
Shakespeare Quarterly, XXXVIII (1987), 58–77, esp. p. 59.
6 Foster, correspondence. At my request, Professor Foster has tested the stanzas of
the song against the lexicon that he is completing (and from which he has
published some of his findings (*Shakespeare Newsletter*, nos. 209, 210, 211). Since
the sample is so small, he writes (25 February 1992), the results cannot be
conclusive, but his objective conclusions: from an analysis of *Measure*, the song
(first stanza) was 'written by Shakespeare ca. 1604' (the lexicon offers no

conclusions about the dialogue, lines 7–27); from an analysis of *Rollo*, the first stanza 'has nearly twice what one should expect for a random distribution of words appearing also in the prior Shakespeare roles' and that the second stanza 'has (at best) a random distribution of words' in such roles.

7 Foster, '"Shall I die"', p. 59; correspondence, 25 February 1992.

8 Thomas A. Pendleton, correspondence, 11 August 1991.

9 *Textual Companion*, p. 468; *Shakespeare Reshaped*, chapter 3.

10 If Jowett and Taylor are correct in hypothesizing a popular *Rollo* in 1621 and a revision and revival of *Measure* in the same year, a speculation can be advanced that the reviser of *Measure*, adding his new dialogue to IV.i, saved Shakespeare's stanza 1, and knowing well that there was another verse to this song in another play, satisfied the curiosity of the audience by supplying 'Break off.'

   Since this section of these Notes was written, Professor Foster has shared with me his most recent findings (personal correspondence, 5 May 1994): 'From a strictly statistical standpoint, [among] the portions of [*Measure*] that look least convincingly Shakespearean are 1.2.1–81 ... and 4.1.16–25 ...; 3.2.261–82 is a tossup.'

11 Alice Walker, 'The text of *Measure for Measure*', *Review of English Studies*, XXXIV (1983), 1–20, esp. p. 3; Foster supports this view also (correspondence).

12 Jowett and Taylor, *Shakespeare Reshaped*, pp. 229–31. The most telling argument advanced by Jowett and Taylor against Shakespeare's authorship of stanza 1 is that there 'are no examples of the idiom "bring againe"' [line 25] in Shakespeare's works, though it occurs 'in Fletcher's acknowledged work at least six times' (p. 129). Though 'bring again my kisses' does indeed not occur elsewhere in the canon, there are two instances of this immediate collocation and at least seven instances of the verb and adverb in comparable constructions in the plays, generally throughout Shakespeare's career. Two instances for *All's Well*, a play close in date to *Measure*, seem comparable: 'Go speedily, and bring again the Count', 'bring this instrument of honour again into his native quarter' (V.iii.152, III.vi.65); as does a third from *As You Like It*: 'let not search ... quail / To bring again these foolish runaways' (II.ii.21). See also *Merchant*, I.i.151; *3 Henry VI*, III.iii.263; *Hamlet*, III.i.40; *Othello*, III.i.49; *Antony and Cleopatra*, III.xiii.103; and others.

13 Jowett and Taylor also believe that the author of the song was not the author of the dialogue accompanying it (*Shakespeare Reshaped*, p. 189).

14 Pendleton, correspondence. Professor Pendleton refers to his 'Shakespeare's disguised duke play ...', in *Fanned and Winnowed Opinions*, ed. J. W. Mahon and T. A. Pendleton (London, 1987), 79–98, and to Rosalind Miles, *The Problem of 'Measure for Measure'* (Baltimore, 1969): 'As I have argued and as Rosalind Miles earlier and more authoritatively, there is no reason to think that *Measure* was a popular play. It has no stage history after 1604, was not printed in quarto, and there are no references, allusions, or imitations of it, *and* disguised-duke plays were pretty well out of fashion by about 1611. I think it would be remarkable for any play to remain in repertory for [seventeen] years – those that did were in fact remarkable plays – and that such a thing happened without leaving some evidence

even more remarkable.' Foster notes (in correspondence, 25 February 1992) that on the basis of his theory that Shakespeare's plays were revived on a six-year cycle, *Measure* would have been produced in 1604, 1610 and 1616. He has lexical evidence for the first two dates of this series; none for the last; but if the play did indeed have continuing currency, a revival in 1622 would be consistent with his theory.

15 Taylor and Jowett, *Shakespeare Reshaped*, pp. 186, 126.
16 The argument that the repetition of only the last three words of each of these lines would be 'cacophonous and nonsensical' (Jump, p. 105) is not to be entertained.
17 Cutts, *La Musique de scène*, pp. 115, 172.

PRESS VARIANTS IN Q2 (1640)

[Copies collated by J. D. Jump: Bodl[1] (Bodleian, Mal. 913 (7)), Bodl[2] (Bodleian, Mal. 177 (2)), Bodl[3] (Bodleian, Mal. 217 (6)), Bodl[4] (Bodleian, 4⁰ T.36 Art. (3)), BL (British Library, 644.e.2), Dyce (Victoria and Albert Museum, Dyce 873), For (Victoria and Albert Museum, Forster 3084). Copies collated by G. W. Williams: ARB (private copy of Professor Albert R. Braunmuller), NcD (Perkins Library, Duke University).

SHEET A (*inner forme*)
First stage corrected:
Uncorrected: Bodl[2], BL, Dyce

Sig. A2
    I.i.4 *Baldwin*:] *Baldwin*,
    I.i.5 believ'd] believed
    I.i.12 up;] up,
Sig. A3v
    I.i.97 offer:] offer,

Second stage corrected:
Uncorrected: Bodl[2,4], BL, Dyce, For

Sig. A4
    I.i.104 *Gisbert*] *Gilbert*

SHEET A (*outer forme*)
Uncorrected: Bodl[2,4], BL, Dyce

Sig. A3
    I.i.55 lans-prizadoes] lans prizadoes
    I.i.56 back-fword;] back-fword,
    I.i.68 heard,] heard ∧
    I.i.77 it;] it,
Sig. A4v
    I.i.143 receiv'd;] receiv'd ∧

SHEET B (*inner forme*)
Uncorrected: Bodl, NcD

Sig. B1v
    I.i.198 you] you:

I.i.208 thee,] thee ∧
I.i.215 happy.] happy;
I.i.215 miſery ∧] miſery,
I.i.218 ons?] ons,
I.i.220 aſunder] aſſunder
Sig. B2
I.i.234 goodneſſe ∧] goodneſſe,
Sig. B3v
I.i.337 blaſpheme] blaſpheame
Sig. B4
I.i.376 honour,] honour ∧
I.i.381 good ∧] good:
I.i.382 I,] I ∧
I.i.383 eyes.] eyes ∧
I.i.384 accus'd,] accus',d
I.i.386 orecome] overcome

SHEET B (*outer forme*)
First stage corrected:
Uncorrected: BL, Dyce, For

Sig. B1
I.i.178 defences] defenees

Second stage corrected:
Uncorrected: Bodl², BL, Dyce, For, ARB

Sig. B1
I.i.189 and] aud

SHEET D (*outer forme*)
Uncorrected: For

Sig. D1
II.ii.173 o' my] o my
II.iii.1 table:] table,
II.iii.6 *Ho boyes and banquet.*] Ho boyes and banquet.
Sig. D2v
II.iii.82 uprightneſſe] upwrithtneſſe
II.iii.90 Dukedome.———] Dukedome.
II.iii.99 underſtand ∧] underſtand,
II.iii.101 difference ∧] difference,
II.iii.102 danger,] danger ∧
Sig. D3
II.iii.126 like it———] like it.
II.iii.127 ever.] ever;

273

II.iii.129 mifchiefe.] mifchiefe
III.i.2 love,] love.
III.i.4 suspicious;] suspicious ‸
Sig. D4v
   III.i.83 goe.] goe,

SHEET H (*inner forme*)
Uncorrected: Bodl[4], BL

Sig. H2
   IV.ii.191 *Fisk*.] *Fisk* ‸

SHEET H (*outer forme*)
Uncorrected: Bodl[4], BL

Sig. H2v
   IV.ii.237 it] i1

SHEET I (*outer forme*)
Uncorrected: Bodl[1-3], BL, Dyce, For, NcD, ARB

Sig. I1
   V.i.71 next——] next;——

SHEET K (*inner forme*)
Uncorrected: Bodl[1,3,4], BL, ARB

Sig K1v
   V.ii.214 *Fisk*.] *Fisk*,

SUPPLEMENT TO PRESS VARIANTS
SUBSTANTIVE PRESS VARIANTS IN Q1 (1639)

[Though it is not the practice in this series to include a record of press variants in editions other than that of the copy-text, it seems appropriate here to list the substantive press variants from the collation of Quarto 1 (1639) prepared by J. D. Jump. (See Textual Introduction.) Substantive variants appear also in the Historical Collation (two variant stage directions appear in the Emendations of Accidentals), and in the Textual Footnotes where the adopted reading diverges from the corrected reading in the Q1 text. Corrected states to the left of the brackets appear with the accidentals of Q1.

Copies collated: Bodleian (4⁰ T. 36 Art. (5); Mal. 243 (6); Mal. 205 (5)), British Library (161.i.47; 644.e.1), Victoria and Albert Museum (Dyce 872; Forster 538).]
   I.i.16 it] is
   I.i.69 due] dew

I.i.147 See't] Set
II.ii.117 *Latorch ... paper.*] *omit* Q1 (u)
II.ii.1118 Imagine] I imagine
II.ii.129 you, by you into] by you Into
II.ii.136 *All.* All:] All: All:
II.ii.150 bound ſtill to] Q1(c²); bound to ſtill Q1(c¹); found to Q1(u)
II.iii.7 *Hoboys* a] *Holboys*
II.iii.24 furniſht] furniſh
II.iii.32 And ... ceremony] *omit* Q1(u)
III.i.197 with:] which
III.i.201 flatter] flatters
IV.i.2 leg] legs
IV.i.164 felt] ſet
IV.ii.78 viſard] viſorod
IV.ii.79 the] hee
V.i.21 runs] was
V.i.36 *Rone*] *Rome*
V.i.55 nor] not
V.ii.25 *bring*] *being*
V.ii.28 *boſſome*] *bloſſome*
V.ii.32 *gay*] *Ioy*

EMENDATIONS OF ACCIDENTALS

[Because Q1 represents an independent witness, its readings are usually included in this listing, an exception to the normal custom of this series, since the copy-text is Q2; but its variant lining of verse (and the lining of its derivative texts) is usually not recorded. The siglum 'Qq' represents the concurrence of Q2 and Q1; the siglum 'Q1–3' represents concurrence of Q1, F2, Q3; the siglum Qq–3 represents concurrence of Q2, Q1, F2, Q3, i.e., the seventeenth-century editions.]

The Names of the Actors.

7 Baldwin] Q1; Balwin Q2
14 Trevile] Q1; Trevite Q2
16 Duprete] Q1; Du Prette Q2

18 De Bube] Q1; De Bubie Q2
19 La Fiske] Q1; La-Fiske Q2
21 Pipeau] Q1; Pipeane Q2

I.i

I.i] ACTUS I. SCENA I. Q2
1–2 Tis ... reconcil'd.] *one line in* Qq
2–4 Tis ... *Baldwin*.] *lined as in* Q2; *prose in* Q1
19–20 He ... him.] *lined as in* Q1; Q2 *lines:* He ... man, | And ... him.
25 proclaimed] Q1; ∼ ∧ Q2
41 themselves.] Q1; themselves. | SCENA 2. *Gisbert, Baldwin, Granpree, Verdon.* Q2
43 Romans;] Q1; ∼ ∧ Q2
54 law,] Q1; ∼ . Q2
57–58 The ... melted] *lined as in* Q1; *one line in* Q2
65 souse] Q2; Saulz Q1
69 there is] Q1; there's Q2
74 doe you] Q2; d'ye Q1
79–80 To hang ... Ruffion] *one line in* Qq
80–81 For ... see] *lined as in* Q1; *prose in* Q2
85 raskall!] Q1; raskall! | SCENA 3. Q2
85.1 *Enter*] *Enter to them* Qq–3
86 What, ... you ∧] ∼ ∧ ... ∼ ∧ Q2; ∼ ∧ ... ∼ ? Q1–3

96–97 I kisse ... another] *one line in* Q2; *prose in* Q1
98–99 be | Proud to be] Q2 *lines:* be proud | To be; *prose in* Q1
100.1 *omnes præter*] Q2; *manent* Q1–3
101 That ... men!] *lined as in* Q1; Q2 *lines:* That ... such | Should ... men!
103–104 Yet ... ones.] *one line in* Qq
104.1 *Enter* Aubrey.] *Enter to them Aubrey.* Q1; SCENA. 4. *Aubrey, Gilbert, Baldwin.* Q2
147 in.] Q1; in. SCENA 5. Q2
147 *Enter*] Q1; *omit* Q2
147 Verdon] *Trevile* Qq–3
147 Trevile] *Verdon* Qq–3
147 Duprete.] Q1; *Duprete, Gisbert, Baldwin, Aubrey.* Q2
152 Sir——] ∼ . Qq–3
152 Lord——] ∼ . Qq–3
164 (Wert ... sonne)] ∧ ∼ ... ∼ ∧ Qq–3
170–171 Nor ... infring'd.] *one line* Qq
173 place:] ∼ ∧ Q2; ∼ , Q1
176 *to* Baldwin] *in right margin* Qq

276

176 Baldwin∧] ~ . Q1; ~ , Q2
180 *To* Gisbert] *in right margin* Qq
182 I ... them?] *one line in* Q1; Q2 *lines*:
     I ... (*Gisbert*) | Would ... them.
193–194 The ... crime.] *one line in* Qq
198 you:] Q2(u); ~ ∧ Q2(c); ~, Q1
208 thee,] Q1; ~ ∧ Q2
215 *Offers*] Q2; *Hee offers* Q1
215 Otto:] ~ . Q1; ~ , Q2, F2, Q3
215 *joyneing*,] Q1; ~ ∧ Q2
215 , *between*,] ∧ ~ , Q2; ∧ ~ ∧
     Q1–3
215 misery∧] Q1; ~ , Q2
220 assunder] Q2(u), asunder Q2(c),
     Q1
234 goodnesse∧] Q1; ~ , Q2
237 againe?] Q1; ~ , Q2
238.1 *Enter* Sophia.] Q1; SCÆNA. 6.
     Sophia, Rollo, Otto and the rest. Q2
269–270 I ... how.] *one line in* Qq
275 enemies;] Q1; ~ , Q2
285 enemies;] Q1; ~ , Q2
286–287 The ... happy?] *one line in* Qq
290 of:] Q1; ~ . Q2
315 overcome:] Q1; ~ . Q2
316 strive: Q1; ~ , Q2
318 whatsoever] Q1; whatsoere Q2
337 blaspheame] Q2(u); blaspheme
     Q2(c), Q1

340–341 proves | My first, my first of]
     Q2 *lines*: proves my first | My first
     of; Q1 *lines*: proves | My first of
358–360 And ... pitty.] Qq *line*: And
     ... possessed | Good ... pitty.
360–361 End ... begun.] *one line in* Q1;
     Q2 *lines*: End ... Madam | But ...
     begun.
372 bloud,] ~ ; Q2; ~ ∧ Q1–3
376 honour,] ~ ∧ Q2; ~ ; Q1–3
381 good:] Q2(u); ~ ∧ Q2(c); ~, Q1
381.1 *The ... embrace.*] *in right margin
     beside lines* 382–383 *in* Qq
382 I,] Q1; ~ ∧ Q2
384 accus'd,] Q1; accus',d ∧ Q2
386 overcome] Q2(u); orecome Q2(c),
     Q1
393–394 With ... comforts.] *lined as in*
     Q1; Q2 *lines*: With ... feares | And
     ... comforts.
394 ones.] Q2; ones. *Exeunt.* Q1
396.1 *Exeunt ... præter*] Q2; *Manent*
     Q1
403–404 Those ... *Ottoes*] *lined as in*
     Q1; Q2 *lines*: Those ... thoughts: |
     All ... *Ottoes*
403 of.] off. Q1; ~ ∧ Q2
408 freely;] ~ , Q2; ~ . Q1–3
410 oth'] o'th' Q1; 'oth Q2

II.i

II.i] Act II. Scene 1. Q1; *omit* Q2
  4–5 Which ... to you,] *lined as in* Q1;
     Q2 *lines*: Which ... you. | Blest ...
     to you,
 11 hazards.] Q1; ~ , Q2
 12 What, ist∧] ~ ∧ ~ Q2; ~ ∧ ~
     , Q1–3
 14 prayer:] ~ ∧ Qq–3
 15–16 miserable, ... miserable;] Q1;
     ~ ∧ ... ~ , Q2
 26 ratified,] Q1; ~ ∧ Q2

29 fall:...understanding,] Q1; ~ ,...
     ~ ∧ Q2
45 shadow,] Q1; ~ ∧ Q2
52–53 Ushring ... subject?] *lined as in*
     Q1; Q2 *lines*: Ushring ... and |
     Bequeath'd ... subject?
53–54 What ... peace] *one line in* Qq
72 happinesse,] F2; ~ ∧ Qq
79 it:] Q1; ~ ∧ Q2
80 me:] me; / me: Q1; me, / me, Q2
102 craft;] Q1; ~ , Q2

277

II.ii

II.ii] Scœna 2.] Q2
  0.1 *Master*] Q1; *M^r* Q2
  0.1 *Seller*] *Cellar* Qq
  5 meats?... eating.] Q1; ~ , ... ~ ?
    Q2
  32 *Officers*] Q2 (*Omn.*); *All.* Q1
  34–36 Tis...-head] *lined as in* Q1; Q2
    lines: Tis ... Arch │ And ...-head
  34 *Yeoman.*] Q1 (*Yeo.*); *Yeo. Sel.* Q2
    (*throughout this scene*)
  41 Thou ... Butler.] *lined as in* Q1; Q2
    lines: Thou ... right │ And ...
    butler.
  41 *Butler*] Q1; *butler* Q2
  43 power,] Q1; ~ ∧ Q2
  44 it:——] ~ , ∧ Q2; ~ ; ∧ Q1–3
  58 *October.*] F2; *October.* │ *Finis.* Qq
  59 *Cook.*] *omit* Qq–3
  62 Masse, true] ~ ∧ ~ , Q2; ~ ∧
    ~ ∧ Q1–3
  62 wenches:] Q1; ~ ∧ Q2
  63 chaine] choine Q2; chine Q1–3
  67 Godamercy ... bottles,] *lined as in*
    Q1; Q2 *lines:* Godamercy dad, │
    Send ... bottles.
  69.1 *Enter* Latorch.] *location as in* Q1;
    on right margin of line 70a *in* Q2

  70 with him?——] ~ ~ ? ∧ Q1;
    within? ∧ Q2
  73 brothers?] ~ : Q2, Q1–3
  78 credit;] Q1; ~ , Q2
  78 stowage?] Q1; ~ . Q2
  86 Should] Q1; Sould Q2
  89 I,] Q1; ~ ∧ Q2
  98 doubled,] Q1; ~ ∧ Q2
  99 favour,] Q1; ~ ∧ Q2
  123 ye;] ~ , Q2; ~ : Q1–3
  134–136 Tis   done——which   ...
    mind?] Qq *line:* Yis ... undone. │
    About ... mind?
  134 done——] ~ ∧ Qq–3
  140 forward?] ~ . Qq–3
  141 drawd] Q2; drawn Q1
  142–143 What ... too,] *one line in* Q2;
    prose in Q1
  146–147 Say...right?] Q2 *lines:* Say...
    done │ Who...right?; Q1 *lines:* Say
    ... *Rollo?* │ And ... Right?
  160 seasning,] Q1; ~ ∧ Q2
  161 gentlemen,] Q1; ~ . Q2
  165–166 Blessing ... past.] Q2 *lines:*
    Blessing...first, │ Tis past.; *one line
    in* Q1
  173.1 *Exit*] *Exeunt* Qq–3

II.iii

II.iii] Scena 3. Q2
  7.2 *attendants*;] ~ ∧ Q2; ~ , Q1–3
  2 *Banquet*] *transferred from direction
    at line* 7 *in* Qq–3
  7 Hoboyes] Ho boyes and banquet. Q2;
    Hoboys a banquet. Q1(c), F2, Q3;
    Hoboys banquet. Q1(u)
  7.3 Hamond] Q1; *Hamon* Q2
  43 me,] Q1; ~ ∧ Q2–3
  48 abstinence——] F2; ~ . Q2; ~ ∧
    Q1

  96 You'l ... more.] *lined as in* Q1; Q2
    lines: You'l...else, │ Not...more.
  105 yee:——] ~ , ∧ Qq–3
  105–106 I ... Latorch.] *one line in* Qq
  106 Latorch] Q1; *La Torch* Q2
  116 Ilion] Q2; *Illium* Q1
  121 rise,] ~ ∧ Qq–3
  124.1 *Exeunt*] *Exit* Qq–3
  128–129 That ... mischiefe.] *one line in*
    Qq

278

III.i

III.i] Actus 3. Scena 1. Q2

12–14 The . . . ever.] *lined as in* Q1; Q2
  lines: The . . . binde, | The . . . sever,
  | Being . . . ever.

16 nature;] Q1; ~ , Q2

21 passion;] Q1; ~ , Q2

41 poyson'd;] ~ , Qq–3

58–59 breath ∧ . . . exhales?] ~ , . . .
  ~ , Qq–3

60–61 What . . . consult] *lined as in* Q1;
  Q2 *lines:* What . . . cause | To . . .
  consult

73 Empire:] ~ , Q1–3; ~ ∧ Q2

77 power;] ~ , Qq–3

92 her,] ~ ∧ Qq

93 thorough] through Qq–3

99 No,] F2; ~ ∧ Qq

105 more ∧ . . . fury,] Q1; , . . . ∧ Q2

118 i'th] in the Q1–3; 'ith Q2

170 with] Q1; wirh Q2

181.1 Aubrey] *He* Qq–3

242 entry,] F2; ~ ∧ Qq

243 death?] Q1; ~ , Q2

246–247 Tyrant. . . . then?] Q1; ~ ? . . .
  ~ . Q2

252 *Enter* Latorch.] *centred as in* Q1; *in*
  right margin of line 252a in Q2

297 Speak,] Q1; ~ ∧ Q2

298 life,] ~ ∧ Qq–3

306.1 *Exit . . . Guard.*] Q2 (*in right*
  margin of line 304c; Exit Guard,
  Count Bald. Q1 (*on line below line*
  305)

319 thee ∧ ——] ~ .——Q2; ~ .
  Q1–3

321 *Exit*] Q1; *Eʒit* Q2

325.1 Latorch *and*] Q1; *Latorch* Q2

327 there;] Q1; ~ ∧ Q2

328 funerall,] Q1; ~ ∧ Q2

331 rewarded:] Q1; ~ ∧ Q2

332 patience,] Q1; ~ ∧ Q2

337 Citizens,] Q1; ~ ∧ Q2

348 wives,] Q1; ~ ∧ Q2

352 sister,] Q1; ~ ∧ Q2

369 nerves,] Q1; ~ ∧ Q2

376 Citizens.] *Cit.* Qq–3

377 people:] Q1; ~ , Q2

385.1 *Exeunt . . .*] *located below line* 387
  in Q1; *in right margin of lines* 386–
  389 *in* Q2

385.1 *præter*] Q2; *Præter,* Q1 (*as a*
  character)

III.ii

III.ii] Act III. Scene. II. Q1; *omit* Q2

2 Make . . . prisoners.] *lined as in* Q1;
  Q2 *lines:* Make . . . there, | Roome
  . . . prisoners.

6 Ther'le] The'rle Q2; There will Q1

10 fellow,] Q1; ~ ∧ Q2

12 Yeoman.] Q1 (*Yeo.*); *Yeo. sel.* Q2
  (*throughout this scene*)

12–13 Pox . . . recreations?] *lined as in*
  Q1; Q2 *lines:* Pox . . . sport? | Are
  . . . recreations?

18 you chip] you sheep Q2; you, chip,
  Q1; you, Chip, F2, Q2

25 first,] Q1; ~ ∧ Q2

30–31 ——I beseech . . . people——]
  ∧ ~ . . . ~ . Q2; ∧ ~ . . . ~ ;
  Q1–3

46–51 *Come . . . halter.*] *lined and*
  indented as in Q2; *all lines flush left*
  in Q1

52–55 Three . . . tree.] *lined as in* Q2
  (*set in roman*); *printed as two lines in*
  Q1; Three . . . we, | As . . . tree.

56–82 *But . . . O Man*] *verses are*
  numbered 2, 3, 4 *in* Q1; *not numbered*
  in Q2

56–67 *But . . . spilled.*] *no indention in*
  Q1; *lines* 60–69 *indented in* Q2

279

56–59 *But ... pottles,*] *lined as in* Q1;
Q2 *lines:* But ... bottles, | That ...
pottles,
69–80 *O yet ... masters.*] *no indention*
in Q1; *lines* 73, 74 *indented one space,*
lines 75, 76 *indented two spaces in* Q2
69–72 *O yet ... stitch in*] *lined as in* Q1;
Q2 *lines:* O yet ... kitchin, | In ...
in
72 *in,*] Q1; ~ ∧ Q2
82–89 *O man ... Reason.*] *located,*
lined, and indented as in Q2; *lined but*

not indented in Q1 (*located after line*
94)
82 O Man] Q2; Pant. *O man* Q1
91–93 There's ... head.] Q2 *lines:*
There's ... now, | Farewell ... not
| Be ... head.; Q1 *lines:* There's ...
friends: | And ... printed | With ...
head.
91 ye; now] Q1; ~ ∧ ~ , Q2
92 Master] M^r Qq–3
94 March ... Pantler.] *one line in* Q1;
Q2 *lines:* March ... faire, | Afore ...
Pantler.

IV.i

IV.i] ACTUS 4. SCENA 1. Q2
11 is.] ~ , Q2, F2, Q3; ~ : Q1
41 state ward] Q2; stateward Q1–3
80 end:] ~ ∧ Q2; ~ ; Q1–3
95 *Allan.*] Q2 (*throughout the scene*);
All. Q1–3
101 by,] F2; ~ ∧ Q2; ~ . Q1
113–114 Till ... *Nero*] Q2 *lines:* Till ...
master, | To ... *Nero* Q1–Q3 *line:*
Till | his | Master ... *Nero*
114 master] Q1; amster Q2
117 Asse:——] ~ , ∧ Qq; ~ : ∧
F2–Q3
124 place:] F2; ~ ∧ Qq
134 Peace,] Q1; ~ ∧ Q2
141 obedience:——] ~ , ∧ Qq–3
142 then:] ~ ∧ Q2; ~ ; Q1–3

144 truth.] ~ , Q2; ~ ; Q1–3
146 honest?] Q1; ~ , Q2
148 *præter*] Q2; *all but* Q1–3
155 license——] ~ . Q2, Q1–3
181 Yes,] F2; ~ ∧ Q2, Q1–3
183 erected;] Q1; ~ , Q2
194 Highnesse] Highnes Q2 (*justifica-*
tion)
199 man,] Q1; ~ ∧ Q2
200 *La Fiske*] La-*fiske* Q2; *Lafiske*
Q1–3
203 looking-] Q1; lookin- Q2
212 *Automaton*] *Automicon* Q2; automaton Q1–3
213–214 Sir, ... sence,] *one line in* Qq
217 things:] ~ , Q2; ~ ; Q1–3

IV.ii

IV.ii] SCENA 2. Q2
0.1 Russee] Q1 (*Rusee*); Russe Q2
2 rumpe?] Q1; ~ . Q2
20 are: ~ ; Q1; ~ , Q2
29 spoone;] Q1; ~ : Q2
30 wanting:] ~ , Q2; ~ ; Q1–3
35 shar'd] Q1; shard Q2
59 *De Bube*] Debube Q2; *de Bube* Q1–3
61–62 So ... selfe.] *lined as in* Q1; *prose*

in Q2
68 there?] F2; ~ ∧ Q1; ~ . Q2
68 *Bells ... within.*] Q2; *the Bell rings.*
Q1–3
70–71 They ... Bedchamber] Qq *line:*
They ... is | Of ... Bedchamber
71 *Latorch!*——] ~ ∧ ∧ Q2; ~ , ∧
Q1–3
72 (*To* Norbret)] Q1; *omit* Q2

72 arriv'd:] ~ ∧ Q2; ~ , Q1–3
74 Crownes,] Q1; ~ ∧ Q2
75 againe,] Q1; ~ : Q2
75 Fidlers:] Q1; ~ ∧ Q2
81 *Exit.*] Q1; *omit* Q2
85 *De Bube*] Q1 (*de Bube*); *La Bube*
    Q2
85 they?] Q1; ~ . Q2
93 it:] Q1; ~ , Q2
96 fit t'] fitt' Q2; fit, to' Q1–3
101 know;] ~ , Q2, Q1–3
106 vertues?] Q1; ~ . Q2
112–113 We . . . successe.] *one line in* Qq
119 with] Q1; With Q2
125 doe?] Q1; ~ . Q2
128–129 Not . . . of?] Q2 *lines:* Not |
    Him . . . of?; *one line in* Q1
136–137 Sir . . . thing)] *one line in* Qq
154 yet——] F2; ~ , Q2; ~ ∧ Q1
156 now?] ~ , Qq–3
157 chamber,] ~ ∧ Qq–3
160 nocturnall:] ~ ∧ Q2; ~ , Q1–3
161 degrees,] ~ ∧ Q2; *omit* Q1–3
162 minutes;] ~ , Q2; ~ ? Q1–3

164 *Capricorne*——] ~ . Qq–3
164 see't,] Q1; ~ ∧ Q2
168 *Cacodaemon*] Q1; *Cacademon* Q2
171 seaventh. And] ~ , and Qq–3
171 *Scorpio*∧] ~ , Qq–3
172 (Thats . . . *gaudium*)] ∧ ~ . . . ~ ∧
    Qq–3
173 *Venus*;] ~ , Qq–3
174 exaltation;] ~ ∧ Q2; ~ , Q1–3
175 *Aries*,] ~ ∧ Qq–3
177 *Almuten*] F2; *Almuter* Q2, Q1
179 *Masaheles*] *Nasahales* Q2; *Mes-
    sethales* Q1–3
188, 208 *Alchocoden*] Q2; *Alchoroden*
    Q1–F2; Alchorodon Q3
190 and] Q1; fand Q2
198 hilage∧ . . . quartile,] ~ , . . . ~ ∧
    Q2, Q1–3
204 *Algoll*] F2; *Algell* Qq
207 *Hyleg*] *Hyley* Qq–3
218 *gaudium*,] Q1; ~ ; Q2
224 That is] Q1; Thats Q2
232 then,——] ~ , ∧ Q2; ~ ; ∧
    Q1–3

IV.iii

IV.iii] ACT. IIII. SCÆ. III. Q1; *omit*
    Q2
9 it, . . . grieving.] Q1; ~ ; . . . ~ , Q2
16 borne∧] Q1; ~ . Q2

23 partakings,] F2; ~ ; Q1; ~ ∧ Q2
27 consent∧ to which,] Q1; ~ , . . . ∧
    Q2
53 desire;] ~ , Q2; ~ ? Q1–3

V.i

V.i] ACTus. 5. SCENA. 1. Q2
2 me;] Q1; ~ ∧ Q2
3 object?] Q1; ~ . Q2
27 not;] Q1; ~ , Q2
36 you?] Q1; ~ . Q2
55 it;] Q1; ~ , Q2

58 it.——] ~ . ∧ Q2, Q1–3
69 will,] ~ ∧ Qq–3
86–87 but if | I] Q1; but | If I Q2
89 dye∧ so:] Q1; ~, ~ Q2
97–98 us, . . . hazards?] Q1; ~ ? . . . ~
    , Q2

V.ii

V.ii] ACT. V. SCÆ. II. Q1; *omit* Q2

0.1–0.2 Edith ... A] *Edith and a boy.*
A Q2; *Edith, a Boy, and a* Q1

1 ruine∧] ~ , Qq–3

2 raigne;] Q1; ~ , Q2

19.1 *Enter ... ./located as in* Q1; *in*
right margin of lines 18, 17 in Q2

44 lamps∧] Q1; ~ , Q2

44 with,] ~ ? Q1–3; ~ ∧ Q2

45 bow,] ~ ? Q1–3; ~ ; Q2

46 soules?] Q1; ~ , Q2

54 Sir?] Q1; ~ . Q2

57 sir?] Q1; ~ . Q2

59 direction?] Q1; ~ , Q2

62 Has] Q2; H'as Q1–3

62 ——why ... sir?——] ∧ ~ ...
~ ? Q1–3; ∧ ~ ... ~ , Q2

68 ——strengthen ... Justice,——]
∧ ~ ... ~ , Qq; ∧ ~ ... ~ . F2,
Q3

78 Alas] Q1; Ahlas Q2

82 nature——] ~ . Qq–3

85 done,] F2; ~ ∧ Qq

86 mallice;] ~ , Qq–3

88 (As ... Lady)] Q1; ∧ ~ ... ~ ∧
Q2

88 love,] Q1; ~ ∧ Q2

89 ever,] Q1; ~ . Q2

92 not:] Q1; ~ , Q2

99 me:] Q1; ~ , Q2

107 *Exeunt.*] Q1; *omit* Q2

114 justice:——] ~ : ∧ Q2; ~ ; ∧
Q1–3

117 me:——] ~ : ∧ Q2; ~ ; ∧ Q1–3

121 head——] ~ . Qq–3

145 thee,——] ~ , ∧ Q2; ~ . ∧
Q1–3

147–148 (*within*)] Q1–Q3 (*in right*
margin of line 148a); *Sophia, Matil-*
da, Aubrey, and Lords at the doore.
Q2 (*in right margin of lines* 147,
148a)

150 word——] ~ . Qq–3

152–153 Had ... Dutches] Q2 *lines:*
Had ... beene | Prevented ...
Dutches,; Q1 *lines:* Had ... sooner
| This ... prevented; | Take ...
Dutchesse.

160 round:] Q1; ~ , Q2

163 righteous:] Q1; ~ , Q2

170 grappell'd——] ~ ? Q2; ~ .
Q1–3

174–175 Of ... her,] *lined as in* Q1; Q2
lines: Of ... presently; | Goe ...
her,

200 houre; Q1; ~ ∧ Q2

205 Doctrine;] Q1; ~ , Q2

210 him.] Q1; ~ , Q2

210.1 *Exit* Latorch] Q2 (*in right margin*
of line 209); *He is led out* Q1 (*in right*
margin of line 210)

216 yee?] Q1; ~ . Q2

225 *Exeunt Juglers*] Q2; *They are lead*
out Q1

244.1 *Exeunt. Florish.*] Q2; *omit* Q1

244.2 FINIS.] Qq; *omit* F2, Q3

HISTORICAL COLLATION

[NOTE: This collation against the present text includes the two substantive quartos (Q1, 1639, Q2, 1640) of which the second is the copy-text, the Second Folio (F2, 1679), the third quarto (Q3, 1686), and the editions of Langbaine (L, 1711), Theobald, Seward and Sympson (S, 1750 [edited by Seward]), Colman (C, 1778), Weber (W, 1812), Dyce (D, 1846), Jump (J, 1948). In this record the collation of the songs at II.ii.47–58 and at V.ii.21–32 includes only those texts listed above; collation of the manuscripts appears in the Textual Notes. Omission of a siglum indicates that the text concerned agrees with the reading of the lemma.

SPECIAL NOTE: In this collation, the siglum 'Qq' represents the concurrence of the early quartos, Q2 and Q1 only. The siglum 'Qq-...' represents the concurrence of Q2, Q1, F2, Q3, etc.; the siglum 'Q1-...' represents the concurrence of the series Q1, F2, Q3, etc.]

Title: The Tragœdy of Rollo Duke of Normandy] Q2, C; The Bloody Brother. A Tragedy. Q1; The Bloody Brother; or, Rollo. A Tragedy. F2–S;   The Bloody Brother, or Rollo, Duke of Normandy W, D; Rollo Duke of Normandy or the Bloody Brother. A Tragedy. Q3, J

I.i

1 *Baldwin*. The] The Q1
1 are.] are, sir. Q1–L, W
3 does] doth Q1–J; doe Q2
4 *Baldwin*] (*printed as prefix*) F2–L
9 or] and W
10 Princes] Prince's L, S; princes' C, W, D
12 To ... practis'd] *omit* Q1–L
14 to good men proves] and good, prove Q1–L
15 *Baldwin*] *omit* Q1–L
16 it] is Q1(u)
21 And] But Q1–L, C–J
23 brothers] Brother Q1
42 eldest] Elder Q1–S, D
43 us ∧ lads,] us, lads, Q1–W, J; us, lad, D; us Q2
45 the so] your so Q1–L
48 hemp] hemps Q1–L
49 plead] shall plead Q2

50 Where ... twelve] *omit* Q1–L
68 that] *omit* Q1–W
69 due] dew Q1(u)
71 *Gisbert.*] *omit* Q1
73 which] that Q1–S, W
83 killing] kissing L
97 another] another too Q1–S
98 which] *omit* Q1–L
103 roots] weeds Q1–D
106 That] As Q1–D
109 arme] armes Q1–L, W
116 a] to be a Q2
117 of] to Q1–J
122 time] a time Q1–L
128 me] one Q1–L
137 those] their Q1–S, W
141 act] Arte Q1–L
147 See't] *Gis.* See't Q2; *Rol.* See't S; *Trev.* See't C
147 See't] Set Q1(u)

283

148 Now] *Gis.* Now S, C
148 *Gisbert.* We] We Q2, S
149 who] whom Q1
159 I ... would] It needs not, and I
    would Q1–L
162 threatning] threatned Q1–L, J
164 Wert] Wer't Qq–S
164 thou] then Q2
167 oath ... is] oaths ... are Q1–D
180 Imposture. For] Imposture for Q2
180 lawes,] lawe. Q2
181 as] when Q1–L
182 them:] them (*Gisbert*) Qq+
183 then] *omit* Q1–S, W
185 and] *omit* Q1–L
189 at] as D
192 To ... innocence] T'assure the
    Innocent Q1–J
197 Such] They Q1–L, C, W, D
199 to it] it to Qq–C
202 my] mine Q1–S
202 injustice] unjustice F2, L, S
203 enimies] enemy's C, W
207 his] this F2–L
208 merit] merits Q1–S
215 *factions*] *faction* Qq+
215 misery] miseries Q1–S, W, D
217 respect] respects Q1–W
218 ons?] on's? S; on? Q1–L, C–D; ons,
    Q2(u)
219 mad fencers] manfencers Q2
238 better] bettes Q1
239 these] those Q1–L
242 finde] finds W
247 her?] hers? Q2
248 those] these Q1–S

253 wracke] wracks Q2
255 And] I Q1–L ·
259 Are] Bee Q1–D
261 are] be Q1–L
266 *Aubrey.* No] No Q1–L
277 are] is S–D
280 Takes] Takes from mee Q1–S, W;
    Takes from D
280 Mothers power] Mother S
298 then] that Q1–L; than S–D
302 turne] turnes Q2, J
310 the] each S, C; *omit* Qq–L, J
310 not] and not Q1–L, W
310 my] mine Q1–W
319 'tis] This Q1–L
335 so] thus Q1–S, W, D
338 which] that Q1–S, W, D
338 prayers] prayer Q1–S
341 My first, my first] My first Q1–L
341 if] if that Q1–L, W
342 That] Which Q1–S, W, D
359 ev'n] *omit* Q1–L
365 latter] later Q1–F2
369 presidents] precedents F2–D
370 act] end Q1–L
370 tyrannies] Tyrants S, C
372 Scene] staine Q1–L, W
376 starres] starre Q2
377 a] an Q1–S
395–396 *Sophia. . . . it.*] *omit* Q1–L
397 hop'd for] hopefull Q1–L, W, D
403–404 of. | Fraile] of fraile Q2, C
406 apter] after Q1–L, W, D
408 walk] talk D
409 and] *omit* W

II.i

5 it] her Q1–D
10 sayling] soyling Q2
14 prayer] paper Q1–L; prayer and
    tears C, W
14 through] *omit* C, W
22 imployment] Interest S (*withdrawn
    later*)

27 of] to Q1–S
32 hath] has Q1–D
34 killes] kisses Q2
38 leave] leaves Q1–L
40 Are] Is Q1–S
41 breach] breath Q2
44 circling ... pull down] circling in

distrusts, distrusts pull down Q2;
circling distrusts, distrusts breed
Q1–L, J; Distrusts encircle; Distrusts Dangers S; circle in distrusts;
distrusts breed C; circling distrust,
distrusts breed W; circling in distrusts, distrusts breed D

45 shadow] follows S
46 Shoars] Showers Q2, J; shoare
Q1–D
48 peece patcht] peec'd patch Q1;
piec'd patcht F2–L; piece-patcht
S–D
50 he] it Q1–D
54 his peace] him Q2
56 you by] *omit* Q1–L
57 And] And's S
58 couch'd] toucht Q1–L
61 when] *omit* Q2
64 feare] teare Q2
65 Pauling] Palling F2–L, W, D;

Tasting Q2; Tainting S; Taking C
65 spirits] spirit Q1–L
69 such a curbe] *omit* Q2
70 Toth] The Q2, S, C, J; To the Q1–
L, W, D
70 puddle] puddles Q1–L
73 shaking] shading C
80 A crowne ... me.] *omit* Qq+
84 a] in Q1–D
91–92 bloud. | Nor] bloud. | A
crowne, a crowne, o sacred rule now
fire me, | Nor Qq–D
98–99 me, | No] me, | A crowne, a
crowne, o sacred rule now fire me, |
No Qq–S, J
99 much] muck S
100 high ... swallowing] high-threatn-
ing in your Execution, | *Ever*
remember, Sir, that swallowing S
104 friendship] friendships Q1–S

II.ii

1 boyes] day boyes Q1–S, W, D
3 a] of Q1–S
9 Peuh] Pish Q1–S, D; Pho! C, W
10 yee] your Q3
10 at table] *omit* S
11 sailing] sculing Q2, S, C
22 *Arion* on] Arion like Q1–3; Arion-
like on W
37 heere] Beere Q1–L, W
40 in] on, Q1–S, D
43 pastie] paste Q2, C
45 it] We Q1–W
47–58 *Drinke ... October.*] *omit* Q1
(*printed on* A3v *before the text*) (*For*
collation of MSS see Textual Notes.)
58 *leafe*] Leaf, Boys, S, W
66 and] if Q1–S; an C–D
66 shooe] shoote Qq+
66 into] in Q1–S
67 *Pantler.*] *But.* S–J
67, 82 Godamercy] Gra-mercy S
67 dad] Lad Q1–L, C, W

70 with him?] within? Q2, S
70–71 Save ye. *Latorch.* Save ye maister,] *Lat.* Save ye, Save ye maister,
Q2, S, J
71 maister] good maister S
77 daies] nights Q1–D
93 to] unto Q1–J
102 Hee'd] Hee'l Q2, C, W
102 doe] do't Q1–S, W–J
104 Pray] Pray you Q1–L
107 neither] nor Q1–S, W, D
115 good god] gods Q1–L; Good Gods
S, W, D
117 Latorch ... *paper.*] *omit* Q1(u)
118 Imagine] I imagine Q1(u)
124 up] *omit* Q2
129 you, by you into] by you Into
Q1(u)
132 you] I S, C, W
136 *Butler, Pantler, Yeoman.*] All:
Q1(u) (*as dialogue*); *All.* Q1(c),
F2–8, W; *Omn.* Q2, C, J

140 *Butler.*] *Pan.* Q1–S
140 we] you Q1–L
141 drawd] drawn Q1–J
142 What] Oh, what S, C, W
142 swinge] swing Q1–D
142 shall I] I shall Q1–L, W
144 we] yet we Q1–L, W; we too S
150 *Yeoman.*] *omit* Q1–L
150 bound still to] Q1(c²) bound to still

Q1(c¹); found to Q1(u)
157 stands] stand Q1–D
159 *podrida*] *podrilla* Q2
164 Or ... it.] *omit* Q1–L
167 *Yeoman.*] *omit* Q1–L
169 I] O, Q1–L, W
170 and now] now S, C
173 o'my] ô my Q2(u); on my Q1–D; ô
my J

II.iii

5 gapers] papers Q2
7.3 Matilda.] *Matilda, Edith.* Q1–S,
D
9 yours] you Q2
24 furnish] furnish Q1(u)
27 bower] bowes Q1; boughs F2–L
32 And ... Ceremony] *omit* Q1(u)
35 sweet] *omit* Q1–L
49–51 *Rollo.* And ... mee, sir.] *omit*
Q2
52 feaver] favour Q1–L
54 my] you] Q1–D
55 Heare,] Here, Q1–3
56 such] his Q1–S, D
58 full] dull Q1–L
59 with] for Q1–W

65 Indeed ... brother] *omit* Q1–L
71 hee's] tis Q1–D
75 and] or Q1, F2, L, S, W
80 him selfe of] of him selfe Qq+
82 to himselfe] in itself S, C
83 Being] Be Qq–L
83 use] base S
90 this] his L
101 future] further Q1, F2, L–D
105 upon] on Q1–D
107 *Sophia ... sweetnesse?*] *omit* Q1–L
107 now] not now S
116 His ... study)] *omit* Q2
119 move] runne Q1–Q3, L, S, D
131 your selfe] you Q1–D

III.i

10 affections] affection Q2, J
13 bonds] bands Q1–3, C–D
14 to cover falshood ever] to falshood
ever Q2; to cover falshood over
Q1–S
18 provoke] provok'd Qq–L
21 Bred ... of] Breed ... in Q1–L, C,
W, D
29 herself too deere] *omit* Qq–L
42 His] This Q1–L
43 Which he] *omit* Q2
58 of] And Q1–W
61 readiest] *omit* Q2
65 with] for Q2
70–71 prevented | With ends] per-
verted | To th'ends S

71 impiety? all] Impiety? thus Dark-
ness Lulls all things in Security,
all S
74 Be] By Q2, W, J
74 colour] Colours S
76 sit] since Q1–L
92 put] put'st Q1–D
93 spoile] spouse Q1–L
102 you] your F2
112 colour] bloudy Q2
115 and] or Q2, J
119 affaires] Fears S, C
123 teach] owne Q1–L
124 Counsellour] Counsellours Q1–S
126 affect] affects C
132 ground] bound Q1–D

139 mischiefe] mischiefes Q1–S
141 Wish] Which Q1–L
143 too] both Q2
147 Powr] Poure Q1–F2–D; Power
    Q2, J; Your Q3
149 None ... halfe] 'Till none that looks
    at Heav'n 's left half S
149 heaven's halfe] heaven is halfe Q1–
    L, W, D; heaven 'sleft halfe Q2;
    Heav'n's left half S, C
150 these] those Q1–S
153 Proclaiming] Complaining Q2, J
154 shall] haste Q1–S, D
156 Arise] Rise Q2
164 in] on Q1–L, C, D
169 presume] perfume Q1
170 nor] for Q1–S, W, D, J
175 it∧ so,] it, so∧ Q1–J
192 survive] survives Q1
197 with] which Q1(u); with: Q1(c)
201 flatter] flatters Q1(u), Q3
202 Matilda.] Sophia. S; Gisbert and
    Baldwin. C; Gisbert. D; Rollo. Qq–
    L, W, J
202 Rollo.] omit Qq–L, W, J
209 rais'd you] raise you Q1; rais'd me
    Q2
213 that] omit Q2
229 doe your] doe thy Q1
230 thine] thy Q1–L
232 Hamond. ... hence.] omit Q2
254 perswasion] perswasions Qq
255 here's] omit Q2
256 my Lord] sir Q1–S
258 Mine] My Q1–D
259 hence] here Qq+
263 there] them S
265 heare] here Q1
268 must] most Q1
280 teares] few teares Q1–L
284 sir] omit Q1–L

287 seize] seeke Q1–S
295 The ... him?] omit Q1–L
298 foster] softer L
303 thou] that thou Q1–L, W
309 up then] thus then Q1–L; up thus
    then Q2, S–J
310 Tyrant,] Tyrant, I defie thee S
323 howlings] howling Q1–L
326 came] am Q1–S
326 too] two Q1
327 His] And his Q1–S
329 highest] high Q2
340 that] whom Q1–D
341 belov'd] lov'd Q2
345 made mee] makes me Q1–S
346 preserv'd] preserves Q1–S
348 children,] childrens Q2
349 prey] preys Q1–S
352 fill'd] felt Qq–L, J
353 Curtian] curtain Q1; certain F2–L
358 beare] breathe Q1–S
363 mine] my Q1–C, D
365 mine] my Q1, D
370 rest] rests F2–S, W
372 In] By S
373 oblivion] oblivions Q2, J
375 yours] you Q2
378 kinsman] kinsmen Q1–L
380 Empery] Empire F2–L
385.2 præter] Præter Q1 (as a character)
386 heavens] Heav'n's S–D
386 seat] set Q1–D
399 Cast off] Taste of Q1–L
410–411 to ... blesse] make the Cour-
    tiers all | Your Servants, studious to
    amend with Joys | Your sad Estate,
    till you are blest; S
413 stay] Fall S
418 imbrac't] embrace'd Q1–L, C–D;
    embrace it S

III.ii

1 these] in these Q1–L
2, 3 afore] before Q1–S

2 there] omit Q1–S
3 get] have Q1–S

3 place] places Q1–S, W
6 nothing] nought S
8 ift ... you] if you please Q1–S, W, D
12 e'en] *omit* Q1–S
12 enough] enow S
14 Sir] *omit* F2–L
18 chip] sheep Q2
19 peaching] peaking F2–L
20 you ... rogue you.] you poor costive Rogue, you. S
22 Good] *omit* Q1–L
28 peaking] peaching S–W
32 Die] Dye F2
32 as] as if] Q1–S
33 too] to Q1; *omit* F2–L
35 Ballad] Ballads Q1–S, W, D
36 tune] time Q3
39 hang men ever] ever hang men Q1–D

42 mirth, and] mirth, W
43 and] *omit* Q1–L
45 chose] chosen Q1–L
50 *this*] *thus* Q1–D
50 *still*] *omit* Q2, J
54 three ... string] in a hempen string Q1–L, W, D
55 All ... tree.] under the gallow-tree. Q1–L, D; Under the gallows tree! W
72 *had a stitch in*] *ere had stitching* Q1–W; e're had stitch in D
73 *make*] *makes* Q1–S, W, D
79 *come ... for*] *now my selfe come* Q1–D
83 *wears*] *weare* Q1–S, D, J
86 *am thus*] *thus am* Q1–D
86 *clipt ... chipt*] *chipt ... clipt* Q2
90 Three ... etc.] *omit* Q1–L

IV.i

1 to you] with you Q1–D
2 leggs] Q2, Q1(u); leg Q1(c), F2–D
9 For] And S
14 that] it Q2, S. J
17 state] estate Q1–L
18 faire] far Q1–L
19 gin] begin Q1–L, W, D
23 out] on't Q2
26 guard] Guards S
27 thou] you Q2
30 to] *omit* Q1–L
30 so] *omit* Q2, S
31 They'r] They are Q1–D; Their Q2, J
39 whosoever] whomsoever S–W
49 dar'st] doest Q1–L
51 scale] state Q1–L, W
53 thine] thy Q1–Q3
55 darst] durst Q2
55 thought] thought's Q1–L, W, D
59 bringst] sing'st S, C; ring'st W
63 neither he can] hee can neither Q1–D

64 I] Ay L
65 whil'st] while Q1–D
68 unto] into Q1–L, W, D
76 slip'st] sleep'st Q2, Q1–S, D, J; creep'st C, W
80 spetious] spatious Qq, J
87 a] *omit* Q1–L, D
87 flatterers] flatterers' D; flatterer's C, W
92 I] I do S
97 these] those Qq +
100 the] your Q1–S, W
104 sometimes] some time C, W
108 so] such F2–S
108 causes] clauses Q2
113 in] in some Q1–L, W
113 killd] kills Q2
114 then] and then S, C
122 And] Oh Q1–W
125 You] You'le Q1–D
137 they are no] are never Q1–L, C–D
138 And] *omit* S
138 'gin] begin Q1–S, W

288

142 no word] no Q1–S, D, J
144 the] *omit* Q1–L, W
145 doe] *omit* Q1–L, S, W
147 will] will so Q2, J
147 I assure] assure F2–L
154 would, he is] would be, tis Q1–L, C–D, would be, he is S
156 and] *omit* Q1–L
159 beside] besides Q2
161 so] to Q1–S
164 at] *omit* Q1
164 felt] set Q1(u)
165 shafts] shaft Q1
175 wish] *omit* Q2, S, C, J
177 slave]———Q2; Groom S, C; bawd J; secretary Q1–L, W, D
177 delight] pleasure Q1–L, W, D
195 blanck figures] blanks figurd Q1–L, C–J
197 else Sir offer] else offer, Sir, Q1–L
199–200 man, *De Bube* | Another Gentleman,] man; another, | De Bube, a gentleman, D, J; man | Another Gentleman, Q2; man, another | A gentleman, Q1–W
210 compact] compacted Q2, J
213 stooles] tooles Q1–L, W
218 we] I Q1–S, W, D
218 of] that Q2
220 wait at the] waiting at Q1–D
222 Dove] door F2–L
224 these were] those new Q1–L
224 Sir] *omit* Q1–S
226 own] *omit* Q1–L
227 you] it Q1–D
230 know't] know Q1–S
234–235 as ... them.] as they come forth from 'em, | More and more accurate. S
234 and] *omit* Q2
234 still] *omit* Q2
235 And ... them] *omit* Q1–L
235 your] your own S

IV.ii

2 Mine] My Q1–D
3 'slid] slide Q1–L; slid Q2, J
5 look] tooke Q1
6 'Slight] S'light Q2; Slight Q1
13 I ... knack.] *omit* Q1–L
15 puddings] Pudding S–D
17 That] Whom Q1–D
19 on's] of us Q1–D
26 send in] sent to Q1–L,; sent in S–D
28 one] *omit* Q1–L
31 I not] not I Q1–S
34 then] again S, C
42 call] cal'd Q2
43 Element] Elements Q1–D
51 bay or streights] Gulf or Streights S, C; bog or sleights Qq–L
51 wh'ere] where Q2; where ere Q1–J
53 lesse] 'less F2–D
54 I'th] O'th Q1–D
56 crispe] crispt Q2
63 doe] *omit* W
66 on] of Q1–D
66 wrist-] wrists Q1
71 downe] down, Doctor, S
78 visour] visard Q1(c)–D; visorod Q1(u)
79 the] hee Q1(u)
92 minute] minutes Q1
95 heere] heere, heere Q2, J
96 illumine] illuminate Q2, J
97 *Latorch.* The ... 'em.] *omit* Q2
99 Four] For Q2
102 clothes] cloths Q1, Q3; cloathes F2
111 these] those Q2
112 late] late of Q1–L
132 these], their Q1–L
133 initiated] imitated Q2
135 him] him to Q1–L, W
136 *Latorch.* How then?] *omit* Q2
136 *La Fiske.*] *omit* Q2
137 him] *omit* Q2
141 and] *omit* S

142 Or else] *omit* S
144 He] For he S
149 good] a good Q1–S
154 a] *omit* Q1
155 here] there Q2
155 your] our Q1–L
156 see't] see Q1–S, W, D
161 At ... latitude] *omit* Q1–S
165 they are] are they Q1–S
166 in] *omit* Q2
167 *fortunæ*] *fortuna* Q2; Fortune Q1; *Fortunæ* F2–D
168 twelft] twelve Q1; twelfe Q2, J
172 Thats] That Q2; Then Q1–J
173 That joint] And joyn'd Q1–D
174 *In imo*] *Imum* Q2, S–]; *Juniu* Q1–L
174 exaltation] exultation Q2
177 geniture] genitures Q2

179 Zaell] *Laell* Qq–D; *Saell* J
181 *Cuspes*] Cusps F2–L
183 being] being in D, J
195 partile] partly Qq; Quartile S–W
202 in] *omit* Q2
222 Person] Persons Qq+
222 brings] bring Q1–D
223 tells not us] tell us not Q1–S, W, D; tell not us C
226 ift were] ift twere Q2; if 'twere Q1–D
229 on't] of't Q1–D
230 bloud] kin Q1–L, C–D
231 *Norbret.*] *Lat.* Q1
242 you shall] shall you, Q1–S, W
247 not waite] wait Q1–L, wait not W
247 your] you F2
248 on't] of't Q1–D

IV.iii

12–13 right ... force] Force ... S
15 is] has's S
16 be borne] born F2
17 flame] fame Q2
22 for] *omit* Q1–L
28 impartiall] partiall Q1
37 thine] thy Q1–D
47 Will] Shall Q1–D
52 have ... they are] hath ... it is Q1–J

57 were] be Q1 S, W, D
70 mine] my Q1–J
70 a contracted] an attracted Q2
74 Mine] My Q1–J
74 prayers] prayer C, W
75 affaires] affaire Qq–W
76 mine] my Q1–D
80 worthy] worthlesse Q2

V.i

21 taske] talke Qq–S, W; balk C
21 runnes] runs Q1(c); was Q1(u)–L
22 his owne] *omit* S
36 *Rhoane*] Rone Q1(c); *Rome* Q1(u)–L; *Roan* S–W; Rouen D
36–37 *Hamond.* True sir. | *Rollo.*] *omit* Q2
48 *Hamond.* I ... pleasure. | *Aubrey.*] *omit* Q2
55 nor] not Q1(u)–S

58 do] to Q2, D
72 *Hamond.* What ... Lordship? | *Aubrey.*] *omit* Q2
82 for] of Q1–S, W, D
92 a] *omit* Q2
100 know] knew Q1–W
101 doe] do's Q1–L
101 not] *omit* F2–L
103 where] when Q1–L, D, J
106 my] mine Q1–F, L–D

V.ii

1　a] Thy W
1　the] thy Q1–L
5　that] the Q1–L, W
5　cloud] clouds F2–L, W
7　these] those Q3
12　roring] roving Qq+
13　Poure] Pour'd Q2–J; Powr'd Q1
19　cloud] could Q1
21–32　(*For collation of MSS, see Textual Notes.*)
25　*bring*] *being* Q1(u)
28　*That*] *which* Q1–W
28　*bosome*] *bossome* Q1(c), *blossome* Q1(u)–L
30　*yet*] *omit* Q1–S, W
32　*Icy*] *Ioy* Q1(u); *gay* Q1(c); *Ivy* F2–L
49　got] bred Q1–D
50　hath] have Q1–D
58　and] *omit* Q1–L, W, D
59　direction] directions Q1–S
60　whilst] while Q1–C
62　Has] H'as Q1–S, D; H'has C; He has W
69　Thou'lt] Thou't Q1, F2; Thou'd Q3; Thou wilt W
70　and] *omit* Q1–S, W, D
77　Pree thee] I Prethee Q1–D
78　mischiefe] mischiefs Q1–S
79　mens] mans Q1–S, D
80　minde] made Q1; maid F2–J
80　thou,] thou learne, Q2
85　As ... eyes,] *omit* Q2
85　thine] thy Q1–J; *omit* Q2
94　me] one Q1
95　thou not] not thou Q1–S
99　blesse] close Q1–L
105　doore] doores Q1–D
108　I ... wish. *Rollo.* How] *Rollo.* I ... wish. | How Q2

122　ha] ha's Q1; has F2–L, D; Have S–W
132　I am] am I Q1–D
136　comes] come Q1–D
138　wilt thou] will you Q1–S
141　soules] soul F2, L–W
149　my] *omit* Q1–D
151　there] here Q1–L
156　May] My Q1–L
158　even] *omit* Q3
164　mine] my Q1–D
173　for though] though Q1–S, D
175　carry] presently carry Q2
178　faire] faint Q2
186　Should] To Q1–S, D
186　to] *omit* Q1–S, D
189　on] of Q1–D
192　bent] bend Q1–W
193　sutes] sute's Q2
193　saint] Saints Q3
195　stile] place Qq–L
198　Ha] *omit* Q1–S
199　O ... fortune,] *omit* Q1–S
202　mischiefes] mischief Q1–S
208　twenty] ten Q1–D
209　*Aubrey.*] *omit* Q2
210　Such] *Aub.* Such Q2
211　peeping] gaping Q1–S, W, D
211　those] these Q1–S, D
213　And it like] if it please Q1–S, W, D
214　We] And we Q3
225　mine] my Q1–S
229　mischiefe] mischiefes Q1–W
231　that bloud] the blood Q1–W
235　service] services Q1–S, W
237　is] *omit* Q2
238　that] the Q1–W
238　you.] you, Sir. Q1–S, W
243　Goe] So Q1–D

THE SPANISH CURATE

edited by

ROBERT KEAN TURNER

TEXTUAL INTRODUCTION

Both the main plot and the subplot of *The Spanish Curate* (Greg, *Bibliography*, no. 638) come from *Gerardo the Vnfortunate Spaniard*, Leonard Digges' translation of Gonzalo de Céspedes y Meneses' *Poema tràgico del Español Gerardo*.[1] As Dyce first pointed out, the wording of Tiveria's letter (II.i.122–33) shows that the translation rather than the original was the source;[2] except for three insignificant verbal differences and the alteration of one short phrase, the play's version of the letter and the translation's are identical. The writing of the play thus postdates the entry of the translation in the Stationers' Register on 11 March 1621/2[3] and antedates the issuance on 24 October 1622 of Sir Henry Herbert's licence for performance at Blackfriars.[4] This span is consistent with an implication of the actors' list provided by the Beaumont and Fletcher Folio of 1679 – Joseph Taylor, John Lowin, Nicholas Tooley, William Eccleston, Thomas Pollard and Robert Benfield. Eccleston was performing in 1622, but afterwards disappears from such records as survive except for listing in the Shakespeare Folio of 1623 as a principal actor in those much earlier plays.[5]

R. C. Bald noticed that the F1 text includes a number of stage-directions of the type found in manuscripts prepared for use as prompt-books.[6] Some specify hand properties – '*Enter* Leandro (*with a letter writ out*)' at II.i.0.1 and '*Enter* Amaranta (*with a note*)' at IV.iii.0.1 – and once an unusual action – 'Leandro *peeping*' at II.iv.65.[7] Numerous others warn of larger properties required:

III.ii.12 '*Two chairs set out*' anticipates 'We are set' (III.ii.108) as Lopez and Diego observe the singing and dancing.

III.ii.132 '*The Bar & Book ready on a Table*' anticipates '*A Bar. Table-booke, 2 chairs, & paper standish set out*', properties needed for III.iii, fifty lines below.

III.iii.145 '*Chess-boord and men set ready*' prepares for Egla to bring them on at III.iv.27, 107 lines below.

IV.v.6 '*Diego ready in Bed, wine, cup*' anticipates Diego's entrance at IV.v.41, near which '*Bed thrust out*' is added. His cup of wine is required at line 63.

IV.v.20 '*Table out, Standish paper, stools*' names the properties Lopez will need to write the will at IV. v. 67 approximately.

IV.vi.4 '*Pewter ready for noyse*' prepares for '*A great noyse within*' at IV.vii.23, 39 lines below.

V.i.1 '*Chaire and stooles out*' anticipates Violante's sitting at V.i.10 and Jamy's at V.i.20.

V.i.26 '*A Table ready covered with Cloath Napkins Salt Trenchers and Bread*' is 133 lines ahead of V.ii.0.1 where the direction is '*The Table set out and stooles*'.

V.i.123 '*Dishes covered with papers in each ready*' anticipates the entrance of the algazeirs at V.ii.55, 91 lines below.

These prompter's notations were added to a manuscript in the hand of Ralph Crane.[8] The text is carefully and correctly divided into acts and scenes. Round brackets punctuating subordinate expressions as well as vocatives occur frequently, occasionally the closing bracket serving as terminal punctuation (at I.i.86, 121, 168, II.i.40, 185, etc.) Hyphens are numerous, and may be superfluous, as in 'Mort-gages' (I.i.202) and 'weigh-down' (269). Colons, too, occur often as does '*em* for *them* (*em* at III.ii.46, perhaps erroneously). Crane's spelling preferences (so indicated below) seem sometimes to have collided with those of the compositors but they break through nevertheless; the compositors spell -*ie*- (but Crane's -*ei*- appears 3 times), -*nk* (-*nck* 3), -*l* (-*ll* often), -*ss* (-*sse* often), *g* undoubled after short vowels (*waggs* 1), *houre* (*howre* 1) and so on. As in Crane's transcripts of *The Witch* and *Demetrius and Enanthe*, entrance-directions (silently moved down in this edition) regularly precede the first speech of the entering character by several lines; many exit-directions seem to have been connected to the text by a horizontal line (removed here and represented in the Emendations of Accidentals as a long dash).[9] The prompter's warnings somewhat resemble those found in Crane's transcript of *Sir John Van Olden Barnavelt* except there the prompter was more concerned with casting than with properties (though he calls for a bar and table at line 2159).[10]

The title was among those entered in the Stationers' Register to Robinson and Moseley in 1646 (see vol. 1, pp. xxvii–xxviii in this series); the text appears in the Folio of 1647 as the second in Thomas Warren's Section 1 (sigs. 1E1–1H1v). It seems to have been set by three compositors, sometimes two working in tandem and sometimes one working alone, according to the following plan:

Compositor	A	A	A C	A C	C	C A	C A
Forme	E2:3v	E2v:3	E1:4v	E1v:4	F2v:3	F2:3v	F1v:4

Compositor	C	A A|C	C	D C	D C	D C	A —	A —
Forme	F1:4va4vb	G2v:3	G2:3v	G1v:4	G1:4v	H1v:4	H1:4v

In column F4vb Compositor *A* evidently set to line 41, the end of IV.i; *C* then finished the column before beginning work on his share of Quire G. The composition of H1v and H1 was preceded by work on H2v:3 and H2:3v, the beginning of *The Little French Lawyer* (for which see vol. IX, pp. 325–6 in this series).[11] In the lineation of this edition, the compositors' shares were

Compositor *A*: I.i.179–291, II.i.62–165, I.i.292–II.i.61, I.i.1–179, III.iii.199–IV.i.126.1, V.iii.144–55.1, V.iii.41–144

Compositor *C*: II.ii.27–132, II.i.166–II.ii.26, III.ii.168–III.iii.198, III.ii.42–167, II.iv.68–III.ii.41, II.ii.133–II.iv.67, IV.ii.1–14, IV.vii.3–V.iii.41

Compositor *D*: IV.v.119–IV.vii.2, IV.v.22–119, IV.ii.15–IV.v.21.

The compositors involved here not only set *The Little French Lawyer* but *A* and *B* also worked on *The Mad Lover*. As in those plays, some formes of *The Spanish Curate* were heavily press-corrected (see p. 404–7), and in invariant formes anomalies occur that could have been caused by mistaken proof correction. For example, at III.iii.166 (F3) the bracket following 'me' in F1 may have been intended to close the parenthesis in line 164, and in line 169 the punctuation may originally have been 'pretends ∧ ... conscience)' and when the bracket was correctly added to the first word the misplaced bracket was left after the second. At IV.i.21–2 (F4) F1's error in speech assignment could have resulted from the insertion of an omitted prefix on the wrong line. At IV.vii.121–2 (G3), where F1 reads 'from ye. ... to ye ∧' the full stop appears to have been placed after the wrong *ye*. Similar instances occur elsewhere in the text. Despite the care and pains that assiduous, if sometimes erroneous, proof-correction may imply, the quality of the printing is not very good. *The Mad Lover*, apparently set from foul papers, has three or four wrong substantives per Folio page (see in this series vol. V, pp. 4–5) and *The Little French Lawyer* about the same number (vol. IX, p. 326), although it seems to derive from presumably better copy, a scribal prompt-book (pp. 331–2). In *The Spanish Curate* the rate of substantive error is lower, perhaps because Crane's hand was quite legible, but accidental defects abound. Terminal punctuation is frequently omitted (and silently supplied here according to the practice of this edition) or wrong, and, as in the rest of Section 1, some commas barely print or perhaps do not print at all.

Cyrus Hoy found that *The Spanish Curate* 'affords one of the clearest examples of a Fletcher–Massinger collaboration in the canon. Linguistically, the play divides into two distinct parts', nearly all the 275 occurrences of *ye* being found in sections assigned to Fletcher and nearly all the 17 instances of *hath* in sections assigned to Massinger, these authorial traits having been preserved by Crane as well as by the F1 compositors.[12] To Fletcher are assigned II; III.i–ii, iv; IV.iii, v–vii; and V.ii and to Massinger I; III.iii; IV.i–ii, iv; and V.i, iii. Fletcher handled primarily the Bartolus–Amaranta–Leandro triangle together with the gulling of Bartolus and his counter-gulling of the gullers, Massinger primarily the fraternal conflict between Don Henrique and Don Jamy together with the fortunes of the flaccid Arsenio. Since the plots intermingle to some extent, the territory of each author is occasionally invaded by the other; Fletcher, for example, wrote the interview between Don Henrique and Bartolus (III.i) and Massinger, Bartolus with Don Henrique and the others in court (III.iii). Massinger also wrote the last scene, in which all the characters appear. There are no significant discrepancies in plot or character between the authors' shares.[13] At III.iii.105–6 Don Henrique and Violante are said to have been openly married whereas at V.iii.127–8 Don Henrique denies having married her at all, and at V.iii.78 Violante accuses him of having kept Jacinta, his cast-strumpet, under her roof, which he never did. As these small contradictions are entirely in Massinger's share, however, they must be attributed to rhetorical zeal or a leaky memory.

As the record of allusions and performances assembled by Professor Bentley (III, 418–20) indicates, *The Spanish Curate* was popular before the closing of the theatres. Returning to the stage after the Restoration, it was regularly performed during the remainder of the seventeenth century; Langbaine characterizes it as 'a Comedy frequently reviv'd with general Applause' (pp. 214–15). Diego's comic will became a droll included in *The Wits or Sport upon Sport* (1662), and in *The Kiss* (1811) Stephen Clarke employed both the seduction plot (less the seduction) and the comic plot, the latter in places being reproduced verbatim. The Fletcher–Massinger play was separately published in 1718 and included in J. St Loe Strachey's

Mermaid edition (1887). Although the former varies little from the collected edition of 1711, it is included in the Historical Collation, but the latter, which reprints Dyce, is not. The versions of the Prologue and Epilogue carelessly reprinted in Beaumont's *Poems* (1653) are also excluded, but variants in two songs –'Dearest do not you delay me' (II.iv.52–63) and 'Let the Bells ring' (III.ii.109–28) – found in several manuscript and printed sources are given on p. 423–4 below.

I am very grateful to Virginia Haas and to Cyrus Hoy for their help generally with this text and to L. A. Beaurline for supplying alternative versions of the songs. From the beginning of my work on this edition of Beaumont and Fletcher, Professor Beaurline has generously provided versions of all the songs found in sources other than the regular printed editions. Mistakes I made with them occurred when I failed to follow his expert advice.

NOTES

1 Gerard Langbaine, *An Account of the English Dramatick Poets* (Oxford, 1691), pp. 214–15.
2 See also R. B. McKerrow's introduction to *The Spanish Curate, The Works of Francis Beaumont and John Fletcher*, Variorum Edition (London, 1905), II, 104. The letter is in *Gerardo* (1622), pp. 248–9.
3 Edward Arber, *A Transcript of the Registers of the Company of Stationers of London 1554–1640 A. D.* (London, 1877), IV, 27.
4 See Joseph Quincy Adams (ed.), *The Dramatic Records of Sir Henry Herbert, Master of the Revels, 1625–1673* (New Haven, 1917), p. 24, and Gerald Eades Bentley, *The Jacobean and Caroline Stage* (Oxford), III (1956, rpt 1967), 420.
5 Bentley, *Jacobean and Caroline Stage*, II (1941, rpt 1966), 430. Professor Bentley does mention that Eccleston 'conceivably' was the W. E. who wrote verses for the 1652 edition of *The Wild-Goose Chase*.
6 *Bibliographical Studies in the Beaumont and Fletcher Folio of 1647* (Oxford, 1938), pp. 104–5.
7 Cf. '*Peepe*' and '*Peepe above*' in *The Little French Lawyer*, V.i.14–15, another text derived from a prompt-book. Yet since Fletcher wrote these lines as well as *The Spanish Curate* II.iv, the stage-directions could be his.
8 R. C. Bald (*Bibliographical Studies*, p. 113) found 'Crane's distinctive bracket punctuation' in *The Spanish Curate*, as well as in *The False One* (see in this series vol. VIII, pp. 117–18), *The Maid in the Mill* (vol. IX, p. 571) and, 'not quite so markedly', *The Prophetess* (vol. IX, p. 223). For other dramatic and non-dramatic transcripts attributed to Crane and printed texts thought to derive from MSS in his

hand, see Virgina J. Haas, 'Ralph Crane: a status report', *Analytical and Enumerative Bibliography*, n.s. III (1989), 3–10. This article also summarizes the orthographical characteristics associated with Crane, many first observed by T. H. Howard-Hill, *Ralph Crane and Some Shakespeare First Folio Comedies* (Charlottesville, 1972), pp. 64–8.

9 For Crane's handling of entrances, see Margaret McLaren Cook and F. P. Wilson (eds.), *Demetrius and Enanthe by John Fletcher*, Malone Society Reprints, 1950 (1951), p. viii.

10 T. H. Howard-Hill (ed.), *Sir John Van Olden Barnavelt by John Fletcher and Philip Massinger*, Malone Society Reprints, 1979 (1980).

11 For the printing, see Turner, *The Printers and the Beaumont and Fletcher Folio of 1647: Section 1 (Thomas Warren's)* (University Microfilms, 1973), summarized in *Studies in Bibliography* XXVII (1974), 137–56. The proof-reading has been investigated by James P. Hammersmith, 'The proof reading of the Beaumont and Fletcher Folio of 1647: Section 1 and b,' *Publications of the Bibliographical Society of America* LXXXII (1988), 201–27.

12 'The shares of Fletcher and his collaborators in the Beaumont and Fletcher canon (II)', *Studies in Bibliography*, IX (1957), 153–4.

13 To Massinger, Arsenio's mother is *Jacinta* and the Spanish city *Corduba* (I.i.15, 260), to Fletcher *Jacintha* and *Cordova* (II.i.122). The variation between *Milanes* and *Millanes* is not as clear-cut; it is perhaps compositorial. The single -*l* is used twice by Compositor *A* (I.i.o.1, II.i.o.1) and once by Compositor *C* (IV.vii.14.1). The -*ll* is used six times by Compositor *C* (II.iii.o.1, II.iii.1, III.ii.128.1, IV.ii.o.1, V.ii.12.1, V. iii.38); Compositor *D* uses it once (IV.v.41).

Prologue.

To tell ye (Gentlemen,) we have a Play,
A new one too, and that 'tis launch'd to day,
The Name ye know, that's nothing to my Story;
To tell ye, 'tis familiar, void of Glory,
Of State, of Bitternesse: of wit you'll say,
For that is now held wit, that tends that way,
Which we avoid: To tell ye to 'tis merry,
And meant to make ye pleasant, and not weary,
The Streame that guides ye, easie to attend:
To tell ye that 'tis good, is to no end,   10
If you believe not. Nay, to goe thus far,
To sweare it, if you sweare against, is war:
To assure you any thing, unlesse you see,
And so conceive, is vanity in me;
Therefore I leave it to it selfe, and pray
Like a good Barke, it may worke out to day,
And stem all doubts; 'twas built for such a proofe,
And we hope highly: if she lye aloofe
For her owne vantage, to give wind at will,
Why let her worke, onely be you but still,   20
And sweet opinion'd, and we are bound to say,
You are worthy Judges, and you crowne the Play.

[PERSONS REPRESENTED IN THE PLAY.

Don Henrique, *an uxorious Lord, cruel to his Brother.*
Don Jamie, *younger Brother to* Don Henrique.
Bartolus, *a covetous Lawyer, Husband to* Amaranta.
Leandro, *a Gentleman who wantonly loves the Lawyers Wife.*
Angelo Milanes, ⎫
Arsenio,   ⎬ *Two Gentlemen, Friends to* Leandro.
Ascanio, *Son to* Don Henrique.
Octavio, *supposed Husband to* Jacinta.
Lopez, *the* Spanish Curate.
Diego, *his Sexton.*
Assistant, *which we call a Judge.*
Algazeirs (*i.e.* Alguazils), *whom we call Serjeants.*
Andrea, *servant to* Don Henrique.
Four Parishioners; Paritor, *an officer of a court*; Singers; Officers;
Witnesses; Servants.

WOMEN.

Violante, *supposed Wife to* Don Henrique.
Jacinta, *formerly contracted to* Don Henrique.
Amaranta, *Wife to* Bartolus.
Egla, *a Woman-Moore, Servant to* Amaranta.

The Scene Spain.]

THE SPANISH CURAT.

Arsenio.   *Leandro* paid all.

Milanes.   'Tis his usuall custome,
And requisite he should: he has now put off
The Funerall black, (your rich heire weares with joy,
When he pretends to weep for his dead Father,)
Your gathering Sires, so long heape muck together,
That their kind Sonnes, to rid them of their care
Wish them in heaven; Or if they take a taste
Of Purgatory by the way, it matters not,
Provided they remove hence; What is befalne
To his Father, in the other world, I ask not,   10
I am sure his prayre is heard: would I could use one
For mine, in the same method.

Arsenio.   Fy upon thee,
This is prophane.

Milanes.   Good Doctor, doe not schoole me,
For a fault you are not free from: On my life
Were all Heires in *Corduba*, put too their oathes
They would confesse with me, 'tis a sound Tenet:
I am sure *Leandro* do's.

Arsenio.   He is th'owner
Of a faire Estate.

Milanes.   And fairly he deserves it,
He's a royall Fellow: yet observes a meane
In all his courses, carefull to on whom   20
He showres his bounties: he that's liberall
To all alike, may doe a Good by chance,
But never out of Judgement: This invites
The prime men of the Citie, to frequent

All places he resorts to, and are happy
In his sweet Converse.
Arsenio.   *Don Jamie* the Brother
To the Grandee *Don Henrique*, appeares much taken
With his behaviour.
Milanes.   There is something more in't:
Hee needs his Purse, and knowes how to make use on't,
'Tis now in fashion for your *Don*, that's poore,   30
To vow all Leagues of friendship with a Merchant
That can supply his wants, and howsoe're
Don Jamie's noble borne, his elder Brother
Don Henrique rich, and his Revenues long since
Encreas'd by marrying with a wealthy Heire
Call'd Madam *Violante*, he yet holds
A hard hand o're *Jamie*, allowing him
A bare annuity onely.
Arsenio.   Yet 'tis said
He hath no child, and by the Lawes of *Spaine*
If he die without issue, *Don Jamie*   40
Inherits his Estate.
Milanes.   Why that's the reason
Of their so many jarres: Though the young Lord
Be sick of the elder Brother, and in reason
Should flatter, and observe him, he's of a nature
Too bold, and fierce, to stoop so, but beares up,
Presuming on his hopes.
Arsenio.   What's the young Lad
That all of 'em make so much of?
Milanes.   'Tis a sweet-One,
And the best condition'd youth, I ever saw yet,
So humble and so affable, that he wins
The love of all that know him, and so modest,   50
That (in despight of povertie) he would starve
Rather then aske a courtesie; He's the Sonne
Of a poore cast-Captaine, one *Octavio*,
And She, that once was calld th' faire *Jacinta*,

Is happy in being his Mother: for his sake,
(Though in their Fortunes falne) they are esteem'd of,
And cherish'd by the best.

Enter Jamie, Leandro, *and* Ascanio.

　　　　　　　　　　O here they come,
I now may spare his Character, but observe him,
Hee'l justifie my report.

Jamie.　　　　　　My good *Ascanio*
Repaire more often to me: above Women　　　　　　60
Thou ever shalt be welcome.

Ascanio.　　　　　　　　My Lord your favours
May quickly teach a raw untutour'd Youth
To be both rude and sawcie.

Leandro.　　　　　　You cannot be
Too frequent, where you are so much desir'd:——
And give me leave (deare friend) to be your Rivall
In part of his Affection; I will buy it
At any rate.

Jamie.　　　Stood I but now possess'd
Of what my future hope presages to me,
I then would make it cleare thou hadst a Patron
That would not say but do: yet as I am,　　　　　　70
Be mine, I'le not receive thee as a servant,
But as my Son (and though I want my self)
No Page attending in the Court of *Spain*
Shall find a kinder master.

Ascanio.　　　　　　I beseech you
That my refusall of so great an offer
May make no ill construction, 'tis not pride
(That common vice is farre from my condition)
That makes you a denyall to receive
A favour I should sue for: nor the fashion
Which the country followes, in which to be a servant　　80
In those that groan beneath the heavy weight
Of povertie is held an argument

74, 111 *Ascanio.*] F2; *Ars.* F1

Of a base and abject mind: I wish my yeares
Were fit to do you service in a nature
That might become a Gentleman (give me leave
To think my self one.) My father serv'd the King
As a Captain in the field; and though his fortune
Return'd him home a poore man, he was rich
In reputation, and wounds fairly taken.
Nor am I by his ill successe deterr'd,   90
I rather feel a strong desire that swayes me
To follow his Profession, and if heaven
Hath marked me out to be a man, how proud,
In the service of my Country, should I be,
To traile a pike under your brave command.
There, I would follow you as a guid to honour,
Though all the horrours of the Warre made up
To stop my passage.

Jamie.   Thou art a hopefull Boye,
And it was bravely spoken: For this answer,
I love thee more then ever.

Milanes.   Pitty such seeds   100
Of promising courage should not grow and prosper.

Arsenio.   What ever his reputed Parents bee,
He hath a mind that speakes him right and noble.

Leandro.   You make him blush:——it needs not sweet *Ascanio*,
We may heare praises when they are deserv'd,
Our modestie unwounded. By my life
I would adde something to the building up
So fair a mind, and if till you are fit
To beare Armes in the field, you'l spend some yeares
In *Salamanca*, I'le supply your studies   110
With all conveniences.

Ascanio.   Your goodnesse (Signiors)
And charitable favours overwhelm me.
If I were of your blood, you could not be
More tender of me: what then can I pay
(A poore boy and a stranger) but a heart

Bound to your service? with what willingnes
I would receive (good Sir) your noble offer,
Heaven can beare witnes for me: but alas
Should I embrace the meanes to raise my fortunes,
I must destroy the lives of my poore Parents   120
(To whom I ow my being) they in me
Place all their comforts, and (as if I were
The light of their dim eyes) are so indulgent
They cannot brook one short dayes absence from me;
And (what will hardly win belief) though young,
I am their steward and their nurse: the bounties
Which others bestow on me serves to sustain 'em,
And to forsake them in their age, in me
Were more then murther.

                         Enter Henrique.

Arsenio.   This is a kind of begging
    Would make a Broker charitable.   [*They give* Ascanio *money.*]
Milanes.   Here (sweet heart)   130
    I wish that it were more.
Leandro.   When this is spent,
    Seek for supply from me.
Jamie.   Thy pietie
    For ever be remembred: nay take all,
    Though 't were my exhibition to a Royall
    For one whole yeare.
Ascanio.   High heavens reward your goodnes.
Henrique.   So Sir, is this a slip of your own grafting,
    You are so prodigall?
Jamie.   A slip Sir?
Henrique.   Yes,
    A slip; or call it by the proper name
    Your Bastard.
Jamie.   You are foul-mouth'd; do not provoke me,
    I shall forget your Birth, if you proceed,   140
    And use you, (as your manners do deserve)
    Uncivilly.

             *134 my ... Royall] *stet* F1–2

                         307

Henrique. So brave? pray you give me hearing,
  Who am I Sir?
Jamie.   My elder Brother: One
  That might have been born a fool and so reputed,
  But that you had the luck to creep into
  The world a yeare before me.
Leandro.   Be more temperate.
Jamie. I neither can nor will, unlesse I learn it
  By his example: let him use his harsh
  Unsavoury reprehensions upon those
  That are his hinds, and not on me. The Land   150
  Our father left to him alone rewards him,
  For being twelve moneths elder, let that be
  Forgotten, and let his Parasites remember
  One quality of worth or vertue in him
  That may authorise him, to be a censurer
  Of me, or of my manners, and I will
  Acknowledge him for a tutor, til then, never.
Henrique. From whom have you your meanes Sir?
Jamie.   From the will
  Of my dead father; I am sure I spend not
  Nor give't upon your purse.
Henrique.   But will it hold out   160
  Without my help?
Jamie.   I am sure it shall, I'le sink else,
  For sooner I will seek aid from a whore,
  Then a courtesie from you.
Henrique.   'Tis well; you are proud of
  Your new Exchequer, when you have cheated him
  And worn him to the quick, I may be found
  In the List of your acquaintance'.
Leandro [*to* Jamie].   Pray you hold——
  And give me leave (my Lord) to say thus much
  (And in mine own defence.) I am no Gull
  To be wrought on by perswasion: nor no Coward
  To be beaten out of my meanes, but know to whom   170

148 his example] F2; this example F1   *166 acquaintance'.] ~ ' ∧ F1; ~ ∧ . F2

And why I give or lend, and will do nothing
But what my reason warrants; you may be
As sparing as you please, I must be bold
To make use of mine own, without your licence.
Jamie. 'Pray thee let him alone, he is not worth thy anger,
    All that he do's (*Leandro*) is for my good,
    I think there's not a Gentleman of *Spain*,
    That ha's a better steward, then I have of him.
Henrique.   Your steward Sir?
Jamie.   Yes, and a provident one:——
    Why, he knowes I am given to large Expence,   180
    And therefore layes up for me: could you believe els
    That he, that sixteen years hath worne the yoke
    Of barren wedlock, without hope of issue,
    (His Coffer's full, his Lands, and Vineyards fruitfull)
    Could be so sold to base, and sordid thrift,
    As almost to deny himselfe, the meanes
    And necessaries of life? Alas, he knowes
    The Lawes of *Spaine* appoint me for his heire,
    That all must come to me, if I out-live him,
    (Which sure I must doe, by the course of Nature,   190
    And the assistance of good Mirth, and Seck,——
    How ever you prove Melancholy.)
Henrique.   If I live,
    Thou dearly shalt repent this.
Jamie.   When thou art dead,
    I am sure I shall not.
Milanes.   Now they begin to burn
    Like oppos'd Meteors.
Arsenio.   Give them line, and way,
    My life for *Don Jamie.*
Jamie.   Continue still
    The excellent Husband, and joyne Farme to Farme,
    Suffer no Lordship, that in a cleare day
    Falls in the prospect of your coveteous eye
    To be an others; Forget you are a Grandee,   200
    Take use upon use, and cut the throats of heires
    With cozening Mort-gages: rack your poore Tenants,

Till they looke like so many Skeletons
For want of Food; And when that Widowes curses,
The ruines of ancient Families, teares of Orphans
Have hurried you to the divell, ever remember
All was rak'd up, for me, (your thankfull Brother)
That will dance merrily upon your Grave,
And perhaps give a double Pistolet
To some poore needy Frier, to say a Masse   210
To keep your Ghost from walking.
Henrique.   That the Law
  Should force me to endure this!
Jamie.   Verely,
  When this shall come to passe (as sure it will)
  If you can find a loope-hole, though in hell,
  To looke on my behaviour, you shall see me
  Ransack your Iron Chests, and once againe
  Pluto's flame-colour'd Daughter shall be free
  To dominier in Taverns, Maskes, and Revells
  As she was us'd, before she was your Captive.
  Me thinkes the meere conceipt of it, should make you   220
  Goe home sick and distemper'd, if it do's,
  I'le send you a Doctor of mine owne, and after
  Take order for your Funerall.
Henrique.   You have said, sir,
  I will not fight with words, but deeds to tame you,
  Rest confident I will, and thou shalt wish
  This day thou hadst been dumb.   *Exit.*
Milanes. You have given him a heat,
  But with your owne distemper.
Jamie.   Not a whit,
  Now he is from mine eye, I can be merry,
  Forget the cause, and him: all plagues goe with him,   230
  Let's talke of something els: what newes is stirring?
  Nothing to passe the time?
Milanes.   'Faith, it is said
  That the next Summer will determine much
  Of that we long have talk'd of, touching the Wars.
Leandro. What have we to doe with them? Let us discourse

Of what concernes our selves. 'Tis now in fashion
To have your Gallants set downe, in a Taverne,
What the Arch-Dukes purpose is the next spring; and what
Defence my Lords (the States) prepare: what course
The Emperour takes against the encroching Turke,   240
And whither his Moony-Standards are design'd
For *Persia*, or *Polonia*: and all this
The wiser sort of State-Wormes seeme to know
Better then their owne Affaires: this is discourse
Fit for the Counsell it concernes; we are young,
And if that I might give the Theame, 'twere better
To talke of handsome women.

Milanes.   And that's one,
Almost as generall.

Arsenio.   Yet none agree
Who are the fairest.

Leandro.   Some prefer the French,
For their conceited Dressings: some the plump   250
Italian *Bona-Robas*, some the State
That ours observe; and I have heard one sweare,
(A merry friend of mine) that once in *London*,
He did enjoy the company of a Gamester,
(A common Gamester too) that in one night
Met him th'Italian, French, and Spanish waies,
And ended in the Dutch; for, to coole her selfe,
She kiss'd him drunke in the morning.

Jamie.   Wee may spare
The travell of our tongues in forraigne Nations,
When in *Corduba*, if you dare give credit   260
To my report (for I have seene her, Gallants)
There lives a woman (of a meane birth too,
And meanly match'd) whose all-excelling Forme
Disdaines comparison with any She
That puts in for a faire one, and though you borrow
From every Country of the Earth, the best
Of those perfections, which the Clymat yields

237 your] F2; you F1   241 whither] *i.e.* whether

To help to make her up, if put in Ballance,
This will weigh-downe the Scale.
Leandro.   You talke of wonders.
Jamie.   She is indeed, a wonder, and so kept,   270
    And, as the world deserv'd not to behold
    What curious Nature made without a patterne,
    Whose Copy she hath lost too, she's shut up,
    Sequestred from the world.
Leandro.   Who is the owner
    Of such a Jem? I am fir'd.
Jamie.   One *Bartolus,*
    A wrangling Advocate.
Arsenio.   A knave on Record.
Milanes.   I am sure he cheated me of the best part
    Of my Estate.
Jamie.   Some Businesse calls me hence,
    (And of importance) which denies me leisure
    To give you his full character: In few words   280
    (Though rich) he's covetous beyond expression,
    And to encrease his heape, will dare the Divell,
    And all the plagues of darknesse: and to these
    So jealous, as if you would paralell
    Old *Argus* to him, you must multiply
    His Eies an hundred times: of these, none sleepe.
    He that would charme the heaviest lid, must hire
    A better *Mercurie,* then *Jove* made use of:
    Blesse your selves from the thought of him and her
    For 'twill be labour lost: So farewell Signiors.   *Exit.* 290
Arsenio.   *Leandro?* in a dreame? wake man, for shame.
Milanes.   Trayned into a fooles paradise with a tale
    Of an imagin'd Forme?
Leandro.   *Jamie* is noble,
    And with a forg'd Tale would not wrong his Friend,
    Nor am I so much fired with lust as Envie,
    That such a churl as *Bartolus* should reap
    So sweet a harvest, half my State to any
    To help me to a share.

Arsenio.   Tush do not hope for
   Impossibilities.
Leandro.   I must enjoy her,
   And my prophetique love tells me I shall,   300
   Lend me but your assistance.
Arsenio.   Give it 'ore.
Milanes.   I would not have thee fool'd.
Leandro.   I have strange Engines,
   Fashioning here and *Bartolus* on the Anville:
   Diswade me not, but help me.
Milanes.   Take your fortune,
   If you come off, we'll praise your wit; if not,
   Expect to be the subject of our Laughter.

                                        Exeunt.

             Enter Octavio, *and* Jacinta.   [I.]ii

Jacinta.   You met *Don Henrique?*
Octavio.   Yes.
Jacinta.   What comfort bring you?
   Speake cheerefully: how did my Letter worke
   On his hard temper? I am sure I wrot it,
   So feelingly, and with the pen of sorrow,
   That it must force Compunction.
Octavio.   You are cozen'd;
   Can you with one hand prop a falling Tower?
   Or with the other stop the raging maine,
   When it breakes in on the usurped Shore?
   Or any thing that is impossible?
   And then conclude that there is some way left,   10
   To move him to compassion.
Jacinta.   Is there a Justice
   Or thunder (my *Octavio*) and he
   Not sunk unto the center?
Octavio.   Good *Jacinta,*
   With your long practised patience beare afflictions,

---

*305 off, we'll ... wit;] McKerrow; off well; ... wit, F1(c); off; well ... wit, F1(u)–F2
1 bring] F2; brings F1

                                        313

And by provoking it call not on Heavens anger,
He did not onely scorne to read your Letter,
But (most inhumane as he is) he cursed you,
Cursed you most bitterly.
Jacinta.   The bad mans charity,
  Oh that I could forget there were a Tye,
  In me, upon him! or the releife I seeke,   20
  (If given) were bounty in him, and not debt,
  Debt of a deere accompt!
Octavio.   Touch not that string,
  Twill but encrease your Sorrow, and tame silence,
  (The Balme of the oppressed) which hitherto
  Hath eas'd your grieved soule, and preserv'd your fame,
  Must be your Surgeon still.
Jacinta.   If the contagion,
  Of my misfortunes had not spread it self,
  Upon my Son Ascanio, though my wants
  Were centupli'd upon my self, I could be patient:
  But he is so good, I so miserable,   30
  His pious care, his dutie, and obedience,
  And all that can be wish'd for from a Son,
  Discharg'd to me, and I, bard of all meanes,
  To returne any scruple of the debt,
  I owe him as a Mother, is a Torment,
  Too painefull to be borne.
Octavio.   I suffer with you,
  In that; yet find in this assurance comfort,
  High heaven ordaines (whose purposes cannot alter)
  Children that pay obedience to their Parents,
  Shall never beg their Bread.

                    Enter Ascanio.

Jacinta.   Here comes our joy,   40
  Where has my dearest been?
Ascanio.   I have made (Mother)
  A fortunate voyage and brought home rich prize,
  In a few houres: the owners too contented,
  From whom I tooke it. See heres Gold, good store too,

                    314

Nay, pray you take it.

Jacinta.   Mens Charities are so cold,
That if I knew not, thou wert made of Goodnes,
'Twould breed a jealousie in me by what meanes,
Thou cam'st by such a sum.

Ascanio.   Were it ill got,
I am sure it could not be employed so well,
As to relieve your wants. Some noble Friends,   50
(Rais'd by heavens mercy to me, not my merits)
Bestow'd it on me.

Octavio.   It were a sacriledge
To rob thee of their bounty, since they gave it,
To thy use onely.

Jacinta.   Buy thee brave Cloathes with it
And fit thee for a fortune, and leave us,
To our necessities; why do'st thou weep?

Ascanio.   Out of my feare, I have offended you;
For had I not, I am sure you are too kind,
Not to accept the offer of my service,
In which I am a gainer; I have heard   60
My tutor say of all aiereall foule
The Storke's the Embleme of true pietie,
Because when age hath seiz'd upon his dam,
And made unfit for flight, the gratefull young one
Takes her upon his back, provides her foode,
Repaying so, her tender care of him,
'Ere he was fit to fly, by bearing her:
Shall I then, that have reason, and discourse
That tell me all I can doe is too litle,
Be more unnaturall then a silly Bird?   70
Or feed or cloth my selfe superfluously,
And know, nay see you want? holy Saints keepe me.

Jacinta.   Can I be wretched,
And know my selfe the Mother to such Goodnes?

Octavio.   Come, let us drie our eyes, wee'll have a Feast,
Thanks to our little Steward.

Jacinta. And in him,
Beleeve that we are rich.
Ascanio. I am sure I am,
While I have power to comfort you, and serve you.

Exeunt.

Enter Henrique *and* Violante. [I.]

Violante. Is it my fault, (*Don Henrique*) or my fate?
What's my offence? I came young to your Bed,
I had a fruitfull Mother, and you met me,
With equall ardour in your May of blood;
And why then am I barren?
Henrique. 'Tis not in Man
To yield a reason for the will of Heaven,
Which is inscrutable.
Violante. To what use serve
Full fortunes, and the meaner sort of Blessings,
When that, which is the Crowne of all our wishes,
The period of humane happines, 10
One only Child that may possesse what's ours,
Is cruelly denide us?
Henrique. 'Tis the curse,
Of great Estates to want those Pledges, which
The poore are happy in: They in a Cottage,
With joy, behold the Modells of their youth,
And as their Roote decaies, those budding Branches
Sprout forth and flourish, to renew their age;
But this is the beginning, not the end
To me, of misery, that against my will,
(Since Heaven denies us Issue of our owne) 20
Must leave the fruit of all my care and travell
To an unthankfull Brother that insults,
On my Calamity.
Violante. I will rather choose,
A Bastard from the Hospitall and adopt him,
And nourish him, as mine owne.

11 possesse] F1(c)–2; possesses F1(u)
19 To ... against] To me, of, that misery against F1; Of misery to me, that 'gainst F2

316

Henrique.   Such an evasion
  (My *Violante*) is forbid to us;
  Happy the Romane State, where it was lawfull,
  (If our owne Sonnes were vicious) to choose one
  Out of a vertuous Stock, though of poore Parents,
  And make him noble. But the Lawes of *Spaine*,   30
  (Intending to preserve all ancient Houses)
  Prevent such free elections; with this my Brothers
  Too well acquainted, and this makes him bold to
  Reigne 'ore me, as a Master.
Violante.   I will fire
  The Portion I brought with me, 'ere he spend,
  A Royall of it: No Quirck left? no Quiddit
  That may defeate him?
Henrique.   Were I but confirmed,
  That you would take the meanes I use, with patience,
  As I must practise it with my dishonour,
  I could lay levell with the earth his hopes   40
  That soare above the clouds with expectation
  To see me in my grave.
Violante.   Effect but this
  And our revenge shall be to us a Son
  That shall inherit for us.
Henrique.   Do not repent
  When 'tis too late.
Violante.   I feare not what may fall,
  He dispossess'd that doe's usurpe on all.

                                                          Exeunt.

        Enter Leandro (*with a letter writ out*) Milanes *and* Arsenio.   II.i

Milanes.   Can any thing, but wonder?
Leandro.   Wonder on,
  I am as ye see, and what will follow Gentlemen——
Arsenio.   Why dost thou put on this form? what can this do?
  Thou lookest most sillily.
Milanes.   Like a young Clerk,

36 Royall] See I.i.134 n.   *0.1 Leandro (*with a letter writ out*)] stet F1–2
0.1 Arsenio] F2; *Asermo* F1

A half pin'd-puppy that would write for a Royall.
Is this a commanding shape to win a Beautie?
To what use, what occasion?
Leandro.   Peace, ye are fooles,
More silly then my out-side seems, ye are ignorant,
They that pretend to wonders must weave cunningly.
Arsenio.   What manner of accesse can this get? or if gotten,   10
What credit in her eyes?
Ledandro.   Will ye but leave me?
Milanes.   Me thinks a young man, and a handsome Gentleman,
(But sure thou art lunatick) me thinks a brave man
That would catch cunningly the beames of Beautie,
And so distribute 'em, unto his comfort,
Should like himself appeare, young, high, and buxom,
And in the brightest form.
Leandro.   Ye are cozen'd (Gentlemen)
Neither doe I believe this, nor will follow it,
Thus as I am, I will begin my voyage;
When you love, lanch it out in silks and velvets,   20
I'le love in Serge, and will outgo your Sattins.
To get upon my great horse and appeare
The signe of such a man, and trot my measures,
Or fiddle out whole frosty nights (my friends)
Under the window, while my teeth keep time,
I hold no handsomnesse. Let me get in;
There trot and fiddle where I may have faire play.
Arsenio.   But how get in?
Leandro.   Leave that to me, your patience,
I have some toyes here that I dare well trust to:
I have smelt a Vicar out, they call him *Lopez.*   30
You are ne're the nearer now?
Milanes.   We do confesse it.
Leandro.   Weak simple men, this Vicar to this Lawyer
Is the most inward *Damon.*
Arsenio.   What can this do?
Milanes.   We know the fellow, and he dwells there.

5 Royall] See I.i.134 n.   19 as] F2; *omit* F1
20 lanch it out] *i.e.* launch it out, make a display   *25 time] Theobald; tune F1–2

318

Leandro.   So.

Arsenio.   A poore, thin theef: he help? he? hang the Vicar,
      Can reading of an Homily preferre thee?
      Thou art dead-sick in love, and hee'l pray for thee.

Leandro.   Have patience (Gentlemen) I say this Vicar,
      This thing I say, is all one with the Close *Bartolus*
      (For so they call the Lawyer.) On his nature   40
      (Which I have studied by relation,
      And make no doubt I shall hit hansomly)
      Will I work cunningly and home. Understand me:
      Next I pray leave me, Leave me to my fortune,
      Difficilia pulchra, thats my Motto (Gentlemen)
      I'le win this Diamond from the rock and weare her
      Or——

                    Enter Lopez *and* Diego.

Milanes.   Peace, the Vicar: send ye a full sail, Sir.

Arsenio.   There's your Confessor, but what shall be your pennance?

Leandro.   A fools head if I fail, and so forsake me.
      You shall heare from me daily.

Milanes.   We will be ready.   *Exit [with* Arsenio].   50

Lopez.   Thin world indeed!

Leandro [*aside*].   I'le let him breathe and mark him:
      No man would think a stranger as I am
      Should reap any great commodity from his pigbelly.

Lopez.   Poore stirring for poore Vicars.

Diego.   And poore Sextons.

Lopez.   We pray and pray, but to no purpose,
      Those that enjoy our Lands, choak our Devotions,
      Our poore thin stipends make us arrant dunces.

Diego.   If you live miserably, how shall we do (Master?)
      That are fed onely with the sound of prayers?
      We rise and ring the Bells to get good stomacks,   60

---

*36 an Homily] Theobald;—— ——F1–2
37–38 Thou ... thee. *Leandro.* Have] F2; *Lean.* Thou ... thee ʌ (|) Have F1
40 On] Theobald; or F1–2
*49–50 *Leandro.* A ... me. | You ... ready. *Exit.*] F2 (*Exeunt* Mil. Ars.); A ... me. *exit lea.* |
      You ... ready, F1   *53 pigbelly] *stet* F1–2

And must be fain to eat the ropes with reverence.

Lopeᶎ.   When was there a Christning (*Diego?*)

Diego.   Not this ten weekes:
Alas, they have forgot to get children (Master)
The Warres, the Seas, and usurie undoe us,
Takes off our minds, our edges, blunts our plough-shares,
They eat nothing here, but herbs, and get nothing but green sauce:
There are some poore Labourers, that perhaps
Once in seven yeare, with helping one another,
Produce some few pind-Butter-prints, that scarce hold
The christning neither.

Lopeᶎ.   Your Gallants, they get Honour,   70
A strange fantasticall Birth, to defraud the Vicar,
And the Camp Christens their Issues, or the Curtizans,
'Tis a lewd time.

Diego.   That they are so hard-hearted here too,
They will not dye, there's nothing got by Burialls.

Lopeᶎ.   *Diego,* the Ayre's too pure, they cannot perish:
To have a thin Stipend, and an everlasting Parish,
Lord what a torment 'tis!

Diego.   Good sensible Master,
You are allow'd to pray against all weathers,
(Both foule, and faire, as you shall find occasion)
Why not against all ayres?

Lopeᶎ.   That's not i'th' Canons,   80
I would it had, 'tis out of our way forty pence.

Diego.   'Tis strange, they are starv'd too, yet they wil not die here,
They will not Earth: a good stout plague amongst 'um,
Or halfe a dozen new fantasticall Fevers
That would turne up their heeles by whole-sale (Master)
And take the Doctors too, in their grave Counsells,
That there might be no naturall help for money;
How merrily would my Bells goe then?

Lopeᶎ.   Peace *Diego,*
The Doctors are our friends, let's please them well,
For though they kill but slow, they are certaine (*Diego*)   90
We must remove into a muddy Ayre,

A more contagious Clymat.
Diego.   We must certaine,
An ayre that is the nursery of Agues,
Such Agues (Master) that will shake mens soules out,
Ne're stay for Possets, nor good old wives plaisters.
Lopez.   Gowts and dead Palsies.
Diego.   The dead doe's well at all times,
Yet Gowts will hang an arsse, a long time (Master)
The Pox, or English Surfets if we had 'em;
Those are rich Marle, they make a Church-yard fat,
And make the Sexton sing, they never misse, Sir.   100
Lopez.   Then Wills and Funerall Sermons come in season,
And Feasts that makes us frolicke.
Diego.   Would I could see 'em.
Lopez.   And though I weepe i'th' Pulpit for my Brother,
Yet (*Diego*) here I laugh.
Diego.   The cause requires it.
Lopez.   Since people left to die, I am a dunce (*Diego*.)
Diego.   'Tis a strange thing, I have forgot to dig too.
Leandro [*aside*].   A pretious pair of youths; I must make toward 'em.
Lopez.   Who's that? look out, it seemes he would speak to us.
I hope a Marriage, or some Wil to make (*Diego*.)
Diego.   My friend, your businesse?
Leandro.   'Tis to that grave Gentleman;——   110
Blesse your good learning (Sir.)
Lopez.   And blesse you also,——
He beares a promising face, there's some hope toward.
Leandro.   I have a Letter to your worship.
Lopez.   Well Sir,
From whence I pray you?
Leandro.   From *Nova Hispania*, Sir,
And from an ancient friend of yours.
Lopez.   'Tis well (Sir)
'Tis very well:——the divell a-one I know there.   [*Aside.*]
Diego.   Take heed of a Snap (Sir) has a cozening countenance,

I doe not like his way.

Lopez.   Let him goe forward.
    Cantabit Vacuus, They that have nothing, feare nothing,
    All I have to loose (*Diego*) is my learning,   120
    And when he has gotten that, he may put it in a Nut shell.

Letter Read [by *Lopez*].

Signior Lopez, *Since my arrivall from* Cordova *to these parts, I have
    written divers Letters unto you but as yet received no Answer of any*
    (Good, and very good) *And although so great a forgetfulnesse might
    cause a want in my due correspondence yet the desire I have still to
    serve you, must more prevaile with me* (Better and better: the divell a
    man know I yet) *and therefore with the present occasion offered I am
    willing to crave a continuance of the favours, which I have heretofore
    received from you and doe recommend my Son* Leandro *the Bearer to
    you with request that he may be admitted in that Universitie till such*   130
    *time as I shall arive at home; his studies he will make you acquainted
    withall: This kindnesse shall supply the want of your slacknesse: And
    so heaven keep you. Yours* Alonzo Tiveria.

    Alonzo Tiveria, very well,
    A very ancient friend of mine, I take it,
    For till this houre I never heard his Name, yet.
Leandro.   You looke (Sir) as if ye had forgot my Father.
Lopez.   No, no, I look, as I would remember him,
    For that I never remembred, I cannot forget (Sir)
    Alonzo Tiveria?
Leandro.   The same (Sir.)   140
Lopez.   And now i'th' *Indies?*
Leandro.   Yes.
Lopez.   He may be any where,
    For ought that I consider.
Leandro.   Thinke againe (Sir)
    You were Students both at one time in *Salamanca*,
    And, as I take it, Chamber-fellowes.
Lopez.   Ha?

Leandro.   Nay, sure you must remember.
Lopez.   Would I could.
Leandro.   I have heard him say, you were Gossips too.
Lopez.   Very likely,
  You did not heare him say, to whom? for we Students
  May often-times over-reach our memories,——
  Do'st thou remember (*Diego*) this same Signiour?
    Thou hast been mine these twenty yeares.
Diego.   Remember?   150
  Why, this Fellow would make ye mad: *Nova Hispania?*
  And Signiour *Tiveria?* what are these?
  He may as well name ye Friends out of *Cataya*;
  Take heed, I beseech you your worship:——doe you heare, (my
    friend?)
  You have no Letters for me?
Leandro.   Not any Letter,
  But I was charged to doe my Fathers love
  To the old honest Sexton *Diego*; are you he (Sir?)
Diego.   Ha? have I friends, and know 'em not? my name is *Diego*,
  But if either I remember you, or your Father,
  Or *Nova Hispania* (I was never there Sir)   160
  Or any kindred that you have——for heaven-sake, Master,
  Let's cast about a little, and consider,
  We may dreame out our time.
Leandro.   It seemes I am deceiv'd (Sir)
  Yet, that you are *Don Lopez*, all men tell me,
  The Curat here, and have bin some time (sir)
  And you the Sexton *Diego*, such I am sent too,
  The Letter tells as much: may be they are dead,
  And you of the like names succeed: I thank ye gentlemen,
  Ye have done honestly, in telling truth,
  I might have bin forward els. For to that *Lopez*   170
  That was my Fathers friend, I had a charge,
  (A charge of Money) to deliver (Gentlemen)
  Five hundred Duckets, a poore small gratuity,
  But since you are not he,——

Lopez.   Good sir, let me thinke,
  I pray ye be patient. Pray ye stay a little,
  Nay, let me remember, I beseech ye stay, Sir.
Diego.   An honest noble friend, that sends so lovingly;
  An old friend too; I shall remember sure, Sir.
Lopez.   Thou sayst true *Diego.*
  Diego.   'Pray ye consider quickly,
  Doe, doe, by any meanes, me thinkes already   180
  A grave staid gentleman comes to my memory.
Leandro.   He's old indeed, sir.
Diego.   With a goodly white Beard,
  (For now he must be so: I know he must be)
  Signior *Alonzo,* (Master.)
Lopez.   I begin to have him.
Diego.   'Has bin from hence, about some twenty yeares (sir.)
Leandro.   Som five and twenty (sir.)
Diego.   You say most true (sir)
  Just to an houre; 'tis now just five and twenty,
  A fine straite timber'd man, and a brave souldier,
  He married: let me see,——
Leandro.   *De Castro's* Daughter.
Diego.   The very same.
Leandro [*aside*].   Thou art a very Rascall,   190
  De Castro is the Turke to thee, or any thing:
  The Money rubbs 'em into strange remembrances,
  For as many Duckets more they would remember *Adam.*
Lopez.   Give me your hand, you are welcome to your countrey,
  Now I remember plainly, manifestly,
  As freshly, as if yesterday I had seene him,
  Most heartily welcome, sinfull that I am,
  Most sinfull man, why should I loose this Gentleman?
  This loving old Companion? we had all one soule, sir,
  He dwelt here hard by, at a handsome——
Leandro.   Farme sir,   200
  You say most true.

---

*174–175 he,——| *Lopez.* Good … Pray] F2 (patient, | Pray); he, good … patient. | *Lop.*
    Pray F1

Lopez.   *Alonzo Tiveria*;
　　Lord, Lord, that time should play the treacherous knave thus?
　　Why, he was the onely friend, I had in *Spaine* (sir)
　　I knew your Mother too, a handsome Gentlewoman,
　　She was married very young: I married 'em:
　　I doe remember now the Maskes and Sports then,
　　The Fire-workes, and the fine delights; good faith, sir,
　　Now I looke in your face,——whose eies are those *Diego*?
　　Nay, if he be not just *Alonzo*'s picture——
Leandro [*aside*].　Lord how I blush for these two impudents?   210
Diego.　Well Gentleman, I thinke your name's *Leandro*.
Leandro.　It is indeed (sir)——
　　Gra'-mercy Letter, thou hadst never knowne els.   [*Aside.*]
Diego.　I have dandled ye, and kist ye, and plaid with ye
　　A hundred, and a hundred times, and danc'd ye,
　　And swong ye in my Bell-ropes, ye lov'd swinging.
Lopez.　A sweet Boy.
Leandro [*aside*].　Sweet lying knaves, what would these doe
　　　for thousands?
Lopez.　A wondrous sweet Boy then it was, see now
　　Time that consumes us, shoots him up, still sweeter.   220
　　How do's the noble Gentleman? how fares he?
　　When shall we see him? when will he blesse his Country?
Leandro.　O, very shortly, sir, till his returne,
　　He has sent me over to your charge.
Lopez.   And welcome,
　　Nay, you shall know you are welcome to your friend, sir.
Leandro.　And to my Study (sir) which must be the Law,
　　To further which, he would entreat your care
　　To plant me in the favour of some man
　　That's expert in that knowledge: for his paines
　　I have three hundred Duckets more: For my Diet,   230
　　Enough (sir) to defray me: which I am charged
　　To take still, as I use it, from your custodie,
　　I have the money ready, and I am weary.
Lopez.　Sit down, sit down, and once more ye are most welcome,
　　The Law you have hit upon most happily,
　　Here is a Master in that Art, *Bartolus*,

A neighbour by, to him I will preferre ye,
A learned man, and my most loving Neighbour,
I'll doe ye faithfull service (sir.)
Diego [*aside to* Lopez].   He's an Asse,
And so wee'll use him; he shall be a Lawyer.   240
Lopez. But if ever he recover this money again:——before *Diego*,
And get some pretty pittance: my Pupill's hungry.
                                              [*Exit* Diego.]
Leandro. Pray ye Sir, unlade me.   [*Gives money.*]
Lopez.   I'le refresh ye Sir;
When ye want, you know your Exchequer.
Leandro [*aside*]. If all this get me but accesse, I am happy.
Lopez. Come, I am tender of ye.
Leandro.   I'll goe with ye,——
To have this Fort betray'd, these fooles must fliece me. [*Aside.*]
                                              Exeunt.

                Enter Bartolus, *and* Amaranta.   [II

Bartolus. My *Amaranta*, a retir'd sweet life,
Private and close, and still, and houswifely,
Becomes a Wife, sets off the grace of woman:
At home to be beleev'd both young, and handsome,
As Lillies that are casde in christall Glasses,
Makes up the wonder: shew it abroad, 'tis stale,
And still, and the more eyes cheapen it, 'tis more slubberd,
And what need windowes open to inviting?
Or evening Tarrasses, to take opinions?
When the most wholsome Ayre (my wife) blowes inward,   10
When good thoughts are the noblest Companions,
And old chast stories (wife) the best discourses;
But why doe I talke thus, that know thy nature?
Amaranta. You know your own disease: distrust, and jealousies,
And those two, give these Lessons, not good meaning;
What triall is there of my honestie,
When I am mew'd at home? to what end, Husband,
Serves all the vertuous thoughts, and chast behaviours
Without their uses? Then they are known most excellent
When, by their contraries they are set off, and burnish'd;   20

If ye both hold me faire, and chast, and vertuous,
Let me goe fearelesse out, and win that greatnesse;
These Seeds grow not in Shades, and conceal'd places:
Set 'em i'th' heat of all, then they rise glorious.

Bartolus.   Peace, ye are too loude.

Amaranta.   You are too covetous,
If that be rank'd a vertue, you have a rich one,
Set me (like other Lawyers wives) off handsomely,
Attended as I ought, and as they have it,
My Coach, my people, and my handsome women,
My will, in honest things.

Bartolus.   Peace *Amaranta*.   30

Amaranta.   They have content, rich clothes, and that secures 'em,
Bindes, to their carefull Husbands, their observance,
They are merry, ride abroad, meet, laugh,——

Bartolus.   Thou shalt too.

Amaranta.   And freely may converse with proper Gentlemen,
Suffer temptations daily to their honour.

Bartolus [*aside*].   You are now too far again:——thou shalt have
    any thing,
Let me but lay up for a handsome Office,
And then my *Amaranta*——

                Enter Woman-Moore.

Amaranta.   Here's a thing now,
Ye place as pleasure to me: all my retinue,
My Chamber-maid, my Kitchin-maid, my friend,   40
And what she failes in, I must doe my selfe.
A foyle to set my Beauty off, I thanke ye,
You will place the Devill next for a Companion.

Bartolus.   No more such words (good wife)——What would you
    have (Maid?)

Moore.   Master Curate, and the Sexton, and a stranger (sir)
Attend to speake with your worship.

Bartolus.   A stranger?

Amaranta.   You had best to be jealous of the man you know not.

27 Set] F1 (*text*); See F1 (*catchword*)

327

Bartolus. 'Pree'thee no more of that.

Amaranta.   'Pray ye goe out to 'em,
That will be safest for ye, I am well here,
I onely love your peace, and serve like a slave for it.   50

Bartolus.   No, no, thou shalt not; 'tis some honest Client,
Rich, and litigious, the Curate has brought to me,
Pre'thee goe in (my Duck) I'll but speak to 'em,
And returne instantly.

Amaranta.   I am commanded,
One day you will know my sufferance.

Bartolus.   And reward it.

              Exit [Amaranta *with* Moore. Bartolus *locks doore*].
So, so, fast bind, fast find;——Come in my Neighbours,
My loving Neighbours pray ye come in, ye are welcome.

              Enter Lopez, Leandro, *and* Diego.

Lopez.   Bless your good reverence.

Bartolus.   Good-day, good Master Curate,
And neighbour *Diego*, welcome: what's your businesse?
And 'pray ye be short (good friends) the time is pretious,   60
Welcome, good sir.

Lopez.   To be short then with your Mastership,
(For I know your severall houres, are full of businesse)
We have brought ye this young-man, of honest parents,
And of an honest face.

Bartolus.   It seemes so (Neighbours)
But to what end?

Lopez.   To be your Pupill (Sir)
Your Servant, if you please.

Leandro.   I have travell'd far, sir,
To seek a worthy man.

Bartolus.   Alas, good Gentleman,
I am a poore man, and a private too,
Unfit to keep a Servant of your Reckoning;
My house a little Cottage, and scarce able   70
To hold my selfe, and those poore few live under it;
Besides, you must not blame me Gentleman,
If I were able to receive a Servant,

328

    To be a little scrupulous of his dealing
    For in these times——

Lopez.   'Pray let me answer that (sir)
    Here is five hundred Duckets, to secure him,
    He cannot want (sir) to make good his credit,
    Good gold, and coyne.

Bartolus.   And thats an honest pledge;
    Yet sure, that needs not, for his face, and carriage,
    Seeme to declare an in-bred honesty.   80

Leandro. And for I have a ripe mind to the Law (sir)
    (In which I understand you live a Master)
    The least poore corner in your house, poore Bed (sir)
    (Let me not seeme intruding to your Worship)
    With some Books to instruct me, and your Counsell,
    Shall I rest most content with: other Acquaintance
    Then your grave presence, and the grounds of Law
    I dare not covet, nor I will not seeke (sir)
    For surely mine owne nature desires privacie.
    Next, for your monthly paines (to shew my thanks,)   90
    I doe proportion out some twenty Duckets;
    As I grow riper, more: three hundred now (sir)
    To shew my love to learning, and my Master,
    My diet, I'll defray too, without trouble.

Lopez. Note but his mind to learning.

Bartolus.   I do strangely,
    Yes, and I like it too,——thankes to his money.   [*Aside.*]

Diego. Would he would live with me, and learn to dig too.

Lopez. A wondrous modest man (sir.)

Bartolus.   So it seemes,
    His deare love to his Studie must be nourish'd
    Neighbour, he's like to prove.

Lopez.   With your good counsell,   100
    And with your diligence, as you will ply him;
    His Parents, when they know your care——

Bartolus.   Come hither.

Diego. An honester young man, your worship ne're kept,

           *76 five] *stet* F1–2   *100 prove] *stet* F1–2

But he is so bashfull——
Bartolus.   O I like him better,——
 Say I should undertake yee, which indeed (sir)
 Will be no little straightnesse to my living,
 Considering my Affaires, and my small house (sir)
 For I see some promises that pull me to ye;
 Could you content your selfe, at first thus meanly,
 To lye hard, in an out-part of my house (sir?)   110
 For I have not many Lodgings to allow ye;
 And studie should be still remote from company;
 A little fire sometimes too, to refresh ye;
 A Student must be frugall: sometimes Lights too,
 According to your labour.
Leandro.   Any thing (sir)
 That's dry, and wholsome: I am no bred-wanton.
Bartolus.   Then I receive you: but I must desire ye
 To keep within your confines.
Leandro.   Ever sir,
 There's the Gold, and ever be your servant,
 Take it and give me Bookes: may I but prove (sir)   120
 According to my wish, and these shall multiply.
Lopez.   Do, study hard,——pray ye take him in, and settle him,
 He's onely fit for you; Shew him his Cell (sir.)
Diego.   Take a good heart; and when ye are a cunning Lawyer,
 I'le sell my Bells, and you shall prove it lawfull.
Bartolus.   Come, sir, with me:——neighbours I thank your
    diligence.
Lopez.   I'll come sometimes, and crack a case with ye.
Bartolus.   Welcome.   *Exit* [*with* Leandro].
Lopez.   Here's money got with ease: here, spend that jovially,
 And pray for the Foole, the Founder.
Diego.   Many more Fooles   130
 I heartily pray may follow his example,
 Lawyers, or Lubbers, or of what condition,
 And many such sweet friends in *Nova Hispania.*
Lopez.   It will do well; Let 'em but send their moneys,
 Come from what quarter of the world, I care not,

I'll know 'em instantly; nay I'll be a kin to 'em;
I cannot misse a man, that sends me money:
Let him Law there, 'long as his Duckets last, Boy,
I'll grace him, and prefer him.

Diego.   I'll turn Trade (Master)
And now live by the living, let the dead stinke,   140
'Tis a poore stinking Trade.

Lopez.   If the young Foole now
Should chance to chop upon his faire Wife (*Diego?*)

Diego.   And handle her Case (Master) that's a law point,
A point would make him start, and put on his Spectacles,
A hidden point, were worth the canvassing.

Lopez.   Now surely, surely, I should love him (*Diego*)
And love him heartily: nay, I should love my selfe,
Or any thing that had but that good fortune,
For to say truth, the Lawyer is a dog-bolt,
An arrant worme: and though I call him worshipfull,   150
I wish him a canoniz'd Cuckold (*Diego.*)
Now, if my youth doe dub him——

Diego.   He is too demure (sir.)

Lopez.   If he do sting her home——

Diego.   There's no such matter,
The woman was not borne to so much blessednesse,
He has no heate: study consumes his oyle (Master.)

Lopez.   Let's leave it to the will of Fate, and presently
Over a cup of lustie Sack, let's prophecie.
I am like a man that dreampt he was an Emperour:
Come *Diego*, hope, and whilst he lasts, we'll lay it on.

                                        Exeunt.

                    Enter Jamy, Millanes, Arsenio.   [II.]iii

Jamy.   *Angelo Millanes*, did you see this wonder?
Millanes.   Yes, yes.
Jamy.   And you *Arsenio?*
Arsenio.   Yes, he's gon (Sir)

        136 a kin] *i.e.* akin   1 *Angelo* ∧] McKerrow; ~ , F1–2

                    331

Strangely disguis'd, he's set upon his voyage.
Jamy.   Love guide his thoughts: he's a brave honest fellow,
Sit close Don Lawyer, ô that arrant knave now,
How he will stinke, will smoake againe, will burst:
He's the most arrant Beast.
Millanes.   He may be more beast.
Jamy.   Let him beare six, and six, that all may blaze him:
The villany he has sowed into my Brother,
And from his State, the Revenue he has reach'd at,   10
Pay him, my good *Leandro*, take my praiers.
Arsenio.   And all our wishes, plough with his fine white heifer.
Jamy.   Marke him (my deare Friend) for a famous Cuckold,
Let it out-live his Bookes, his paines, and heare me,
The more he seeks to smother it with Justice,
Let it blaze out the more:

        Enter [Andrea,] *a Servant.*

        what news *Andrea?*
Andrea.   Newes I am loth to tell ye: but I am charg'd (Sir)
Your Brother layes a strict command upon ye,
No more to know his house, upon your danger,
I am sorry (Sir.)
Jamy.   'Faith never be: I am glad on't,   20
He keepes the house of pride, and foolery:
I meane to shun it, so returne my Answer:
'Twill shortly spew him out;   [*Exit* Andrea.]
        Come, let's be merry,
And lay our heads together carefully,
How we may helpe our friend; and let's lodge neare him,
Be still at hand: I would not for my patrimony,
But he should crown his Lawyer, a learned Monster;
Come, let's away, I am stark mad till I see him.

                Exeunt.

      Enter Bartolus, *and* Amaranta.   [II.

Amaranta.   Why will ye bring men in, and yet be jealous?

*4 *Jamy.*] Theobald (Seward); *omit* F1–2
17 loth] F1(c)–2; both F1(u)   1 Why∧] F2; ∼ , F1

Why will ye lodge a young man, a man able,
And yet repine?
Bartolus.   He shall not trouble thee (Sweet)
A modest poore slight thing, did I not tell thee
He was onely given to the Booke, and for that
How royally he paies? finds his owne meat too.
Amaranta.   I will not have him here: I know your courses,
And what fits you will fall into of madnesse.
Bartolus.   Y'faith, I will not Wife.
Amaranta.   I will not try ye.
Bartolus.   He comes not neare thee, shall not dare to tread   10
Within thy Lodgings: in an old out-Roome
Where Logs, and Coles were layd——
Amaranta.   Now ye lay fire;
Fire to consume your quiet.
Bartolus.   Didst thou know him,
Thou wouldst thinke as I doe: he disquiet thee?
Thou mayst weare him next thy heart, and yet not warme him,
His mind (poore man) 's o'th' Law, how to live after,
And not on lewdnesse: on my conscience
He knowes not how to looke upon a woman,
More then by reading what Sex she is.
Amaranta.   I doe not like it (Sir.)
Bartolus.   Do'st thou not see (Foole)   20
What presents he sends hourely in his gratefulnesse?
What delicate meates?
Amaranta.   You had best trust him at your Table,
Doe, and repent it, doe.
Bartolus.   If thou be'st willing,
By my troth, I thinke he might come, he's so modest,
He never speakes: there's part of that he gave me,
He'll eat but halfe a dozen bits, and rise immediately,
Even as he eats, he studies: he'll not disquiet thee,
Doe as thou pleasest (Wife.)
Amaranta [*aside*].   What means this Wood-cocke?
                                        Knock within.

24 he] F1(c)–2; ye F1(u)

333

Bartolus.   Retire (Sweet) there's one knocks: [*Exit* Amaranta.]
                                       come in,

                         Enter Servant.

                                                your businesse.

Servant.   My Lord *Don Henrique* would entreat ye, Sir,   30
   To come immediatly, and speake with him,
   He has businesse of some moment.
Bartolus.   I'll attend him,——
                                       [*Exit* Servant.]

   I must be gon: I pre'thee thinke the best (wife)
   At my returne, I'll tell thee more, good morrow;——
   Sir, keep ye close, and study hard: an houre hence
   I'll read a new Case to ye.   *Exit.*
Leandro (within).   I'll be ready.

                         Enter Amaranta.

Amaranta.   So many hundred Duckets, to ly scurvily?
   And learne the pelting law? this sounds but slenderly,
   But very poorely: I would see this fellow
   Very faine see him, how he lookes: I will find   40
   To what end, and what study:——there's the place:
   I'll goe o'th' other side, and take my Fortune;
   I think there is a window.   *Exit.*

                         Enter Leandro.

Leandro.   He's gone out,
   Now, if I could but see her: she is not this way:
   How nastily he keepes his house? my Chamber,
   If I continue long, will choak me up,
   It is so damp: I shall be mortifide
   For any woman, if I stay a moneth here:
   I'll in, and strike my Lute, that sound may call her.   *Exit.*

                         Enter Amaranta.

Amaranta.   He keeps very close: Lord, how I long to see him: 50
   A Lute strooke handsomely, a voice too; I'll heare that:

36 (*within*)] *Leandro within.* as marginal direction after *Exit.* F1–2

334

Lute and Song [by Leandro *within].*

1

Dearest do not you delay me,
  Since thou knowest I must be gone;
Wind and Tide 'tis thought doth stay me,
  But 'tis wind that must be blown
    From that breath, whose native smell
    Indian Odours far excel.

2

Oh then speak thou fairest fair,
  Kill not him that vows to serve thee,
But perfume this neighboring Air;   60
  Else dull silence sure will starve me:
    'Tis a word that's quickly spoken,
    Which being restrain'd a heart is broken.

These Verses are no Law, they sound too sweetly,
  Now I am more desirous.   Leandro *peeping.*
Leandro [aside].   'Tis she certain.
Amaranta.   What's that that peeps?
Leandro [aside].   O, admirable face!
Amaranta.   Sure 'tis the man.
Leandro [aside].   I will goe out a little.
Amaranta.   Hee lookes not like a foole, his face is noble:
  How still he stands?
Leandro [aside].   I am strucken dumb, with wonder,
  Sure, all the Excellence of Earth dwells here.   70
Amaranta.   How pale he looks? yet, how his eies like torches,
  Fling their beames round: how manly his face shewes?
  He comes on: surely he will speak: he is made most handsomly:
  This is no Clerk behaviour; Now I have seen ye,
  I'l take my time: husband, ye have brought home tinder.
                                      Ex[it. Drops her glove.]

51.1 *Lute and Song.*] 1711; on line 49.1 after *Enter* Amaranta. F1; on 49 after *Exit.* F2
52–63 *Dearest ... broken.*] F2 (after line 49); *omit* F1

335

Leandro.   Sure she has transform'd me, I had forgot my tongue
    cleane,
  I never saw a face yet, but this rare one,
  But I was able boldly to encounter it,
  And speak my mind, my lips were lockt upon me,
  This is divine, and onely serv'd with reverence;   80
  O most faire cover, of a hand far fairer,   [*Takes up glove.*]
  Thou blessed Innocence, that guards that whiteness,
  Live next my heart. I am glad I have got a relick,
  A relick when I pray to it, may work wonders.   *A noise within.*
  Harke, there's some noyse: I must retire againe.
  This blessed Apparition, makes me happy;
  I'll suffer, and I'll sacrifice my substance,
  But I'll enjoy: now softly to my Kennell.

                                    Exit.

          Enter Henrique *and* Bartolus.   III.i

Henrique.   You know my cause sufficiently?
Bartolus.   I doe (Sir.)
Henrique.   And though it will impaire my honesty,
  And strike deep at my Credit, yet (my *Bartolus*)
  There being no other evasion left to free me
  From the vexation of my spightfull Brother,
  That most insultingly raignes over me,
  I must and will goe forward.
Bartolus.   Doe (my Lord)
  And looke not after credit, we shall cure that,
  Your bended honestie, we shall set right (Sir)
  We Surgeons of the Law, doe desperate cures (Sir)   10
  And you shall see how heartily I'll handle it:
  Marke how I'll knock it home: be of good cheare (Sir)
  You give good Fees, and those beget good Causes,
  The prerogative of your crownes will carry the matter,
  (Carry it sheere) The *Assistant* sits to morrow,
  And he's your friend, your monied men love naturally,
  And as your loves are cleare, so are your Causes.

           79 lockt] F2; lock F1

Henrique.   He shall not want for that.

Bartolus.   No, no, he must not,
　Line your Cause warmly (Sir) the times are Aguish,
　That holds a Plea in heart; hang the penurious,   20
　Their Causes (like their purses) have poore Issues.

Henrique.   That way, I was ever bountifull.

Bartolus.   'Tis true (Sir)
　That makes ye fear'd, forces the Snakes to kneele to ye,
　Live full of money, and supply the Lawyer,
　And take your choice of what mans lands you please (Sir)
　What pleasures, or what profits; what revenges,
　They are all your owne: I must have witnesses
　Enough, and ready.

Henrique.   You shall not want (my *Bartolus.*)

Bartolus.   Substantiall fearless soules, that will sweare suddenly,
　That will sweare any thing.

Henrique.   They shall sweare truth too.   30

Bartolus.   That's no great matter: for varietie
　They may sweare truth, els 'tis not much look'd after:
　I will serve Processe, presently, and strongly
　Upon your Brother, and *Octavio*,
　Jacinta, and the Boy; provide your proofes (Sir)
　And set 'em fairely off, be sure of Witnesses,
　Though they cost money, want no store of witnesses,
　I have seen a handsome Cause, so fowly lost (Sir,)
　So beastly cast away for want of Witnesses——

Henrique.   There shall want nothing.

Bartolus.   Then be gone, be provident,   40
　Send to the Judge, a secret way: you have me?
　And let him understand the heart.

Henrique.   I shall (Sir.)

Bartolus.   And feele the pulses strongly beat, I'll study,
　And at my houre, but mark me: goe, be happy,
　Goe, and beleeve i'th' Law.

Henrique.   I hope 'twill helpe me.

Exeunt.

*23 Snakes] *stet* F1–2

337

Enter Lopez, Diego, *and foure* Parishioners, *and Singers.*   [III.

Lopez.   Nea'r talke to me, I will not stay amongst ye,
Debaush'd and ignorant lazie knaves I found ye,
And fooles I leave ye: I have taught these twenty yeares,
Preacht spoon-meat to ye, that a child might swallow,
Yet ye are Block-heads still: what should I say to ye?
Ye have neither faith, nor money left to save ye,
Am I a fit companion for such Beggers?
1. Par.   If the Shepheard will suffer the sheep to be scab'd (sir)——
Lopez.   No, no, ye are rotten.
Diego [*aside*].   Would they were, for my sake.
Lopez.   I have nointed ye, and tar'd ye with my doctrine,   10
And yet the murren sticks to ye, yet ye are mangy,
I will avoid ye.
2. Par.   'Pray ye (Sir) be not angry,
In the pride of your new Cassock, doe not part with us,
We doe acknowledge ye a carefull Curat,
And one that seldome troubles us with Sermons,
A short slice of a Reading serves us (Sir)
We doe acknowledge ye a quiet Teacher,
Before you'll vex your Audience, you'll sleep with 'em,
And that's a loving thing.
3. Par.   We grant ye (Sir)
The onely benefactor to our Bowling,   20
To all our merry Sports, the first provoker,
And at our Feasts, we know there is no reason,
But you that edifie us most, should eat most.
Lopez.   I will not stay for all this, ye shall know me
A man borne to a more beseeming fortune
Then ringing all-in, to a rout of Dunces.
4. Par.   We will increase your Tithes, you shall have Egs too,
Though they may prove most dangerous to our Issues.
1. Par.   I am a Smith; yet thus far out of my love
You shall have the tenth horse I prick, to pray for,   30
I am sure I prick five hundred in a yeare (Sir.)

12 ye.] F2; ye. *Two chaires set out.* F1

338

2. Par.   I am a Cooke, a man of a dride conscience,
   Yet thus far I relent: you shall have tith porrage.

3. Par.   Your stipend shall be rais'd too (good neighbour *Diego*.)

Diego.   Would ye have me speak for ye? I am more angry,
   Ten times more vex'd, not to be pacified:
   No, there be other places for poore Sextons,
   Places of profit (Friends) fine stirring places,
   And people that know how to use our Offices,
   Know what they were made for: I speak for such Capons?   40
   Ye shall find the Key o'th' Church, under the doore (Neighbours,)
   You may goe in, and drive away the dawes.

Lopez.   My Surplesse, with one sleeve, you shall find there,
   For to that dearth of Linnen, you have driven me;
   And the old Cutworke Cope, that hangs by gymitrie:
   'Pray ye turne em carefully, they are very tender:
   The remnant of the Books, lie where they did (Neighbours)
   Halfe puft away with the Church-wardens pipings,
   Such smoaky zeales they have against hard places.
   The poore-mans Box is there too: if ye find any thing   50
   Beside the posie, and that halfe rub'd out too
   For feare it should awake too much charitie,
   Give it to pious uses, that is, spend it.

Diego.   The Bell-ropes, they are strong enough to hang ye,
   So we bequeath ye to your destiny.

1. Par.   'Pray ye be not so hastie.

Diego.   I'll speake a proud word to ye,
   Would ye have us stay?

2. Par.   We doe most heartily pray ye.

3. Par.   I'll draw as mighty drinke (Sir.)

Lopez.   A strong motive.

3. Par.   The stronger still, the more ye come unto me,
   And I'll send for my Daughter.

Lopez.   This may stir too: 60
   The Maiden is of age, and must be edified.

4. Par.   You shall have any thing: loose our learned Vicar?
   And our most constant friend, honest deare *Diego*?

---

*58 Sir.)] *stet* F1–2
*59–60 *3. Par.* The … me, | And] McKerrow *conj.*; The … me. | 3. And F1–2

Diego.   Yet all this will not do: I'll tell ye (Neighbours)
          And tell ye true: if ye will have us stay,
          If you will have the comforts of our companies,
          You shall be bound to doe us right in these points,
          You shall be bound, and this the obligation:
          Dy when 'tis fit, that we may have fit duties,
          And doe not seeke to draw-out our undoings,   70
          Marry tryde women, that are free, and fruitfull,
          Get children in abundance, for your Christnings,
          Or suffer to be got, 'tis equall justice.
Lopez.   Let Weddings, Christnings, Churchings, Funerals,
          And merry Gossippings goe round, go round still,
          Round as a Pig, that we may find the profit.
Diego.   And let your old men fall sick handsomely,
          And dy immediatly, their Sonnes may shoot up:
          Let women dy oth' sullens too, 'tis naturall,
          But be sure their Daughters be of age first,   80
          That they may stock us still: your queazie young wives
          That perish undeliver'd, I am vext with,
          And vext abundantly, it much concernes me,
          There's a childes buriall lost, looke that be mended.
Lopez.   Let 'em be brought abed, then dy when they please,
          These things considered (Country-men) and sworne to——
2. Par.   All these, and all our sports againe, and gambolls.
3. Par.   We must dy, and we must live, and we'll be merry,
          Every man shall be rich by one another.
2. Par.   We are here to morrow, and gone to day: for my part   90
          If getting children can be-friend my Neighbours,
          I'll labour hard, but I will fill your Font (Sir.)
1. Par.   I have a Mother now, and an old Father,
          They are as sure your own, within these two moneths.
4. Par.   My Sister must be prayd for too, she is desperate,
          Desperate in love.
Diego.   Keepe desperate men farre from her,
          Then 'twill goe hard: doe you see how melancholy?
          Doe you marke the man? do you professe ye love him?

---

*69 duties] stet F1–2   70 draw-out] Theobald; draw——out F1–2
*78 And … up] stet F1–2   *85 abed] F1(u); to bed F1(c)–2

And would doe any thing to stay his fury?
And are ye unprovided to refresh him,   100
To make him know your loves? fie Neighbours.
2. *Par.*   We'll doe any thing,
We have brought Musick to appease his spirit,
And the best Song we'll give him.
Diego.   'Pray ye sit down (Sir)
They know their duties now, and they stand ready
To tender their best mirth.
Lopez.   'Tis well,——proceed Neighbours,
I am glad I have brought ye to understand good manners,
Ye had Puritan hearts a-while, spurn'd at all pastimes,
But I see some hope now.
Diego.   We are set, proceed Neighbours.

SONG

[*by the Singers*. Parishioners *dance*].

Let the Bells ring, and let the Boys sing,
* The young Lasses skip and play,*   110
Let the Cups go round, till round goes the ground,
* Our Learned old Vicar will stay.*

Chorus.

Let the Pig turn merrily, merrily ah,
* And let the fat Goose swim,*
For verily, verily, verily ah,
* Our Vicar this day shall be trim.*

2

The stew'd Cock shall Crow, Cock a-loodle-loo,
* A loud Cock-a-loodle shall he Crow;*
The Duck and the Drake, shall swim in a lake
* Of Onions and Claret below.*   120
                    [Chorus: *Let the Pig, etc.*]

108.1–128 SONG. ... *Vicar.*] F2; *omit* F1
112.1 Chorus.] McKerrow (Fleay *conj.*); 2 F2; *omit* F1

3

Our Wives shall be neat, to bring in our meat,
  To thee our most noble adviser;
Our paines shall be great, and Bottles shall sweat,
  And we our selves will be wiser.

                    [Chorus: *Let the Pig, etc.]*

4

We'll labour and swinck, we'll kiss and we'll drink,
  And Tithes shall come thicker and thicker;
We'll fall to our Plow, and get Children enough,
  And thou shalt be learned old Vicar.

                    [Chorus: *Let the Pig, etc.]*

Enter Arsenio *and* Millanes.

Arsenio.   What ayles this Priest? how highly the thing takes it?
Millanes.   Lord how it looks? has he not bought some Prebend?   130
  Leandro's money, makes the Rascall merry,
  Merry at heart; he spies us.
Lopez.   Be gon Neighbours,
  Here are some Gentlemen: be gone good Neighbours,
  Be gon, and labour to redeeme my favour,
  No more words, but be gon: these two are Gentlemen,
  No company for crusty-handed fellowes.
Diego.   We will stay for a yeare or two, and trie ye.
Lopez.   Fill all your hearts with joy, we will stay with ye,
  Be gone, no more; I take your pastimes graciously:——
                    [*Exeunt* Parishioners & *Singers.*]
  Would ye with me (my friends?)
Arsenio.   We would looke upon ye,   140
  For me-thinks ye looke lovely.
Lopez.   Ye have no Letters?
  Nor any kind Remembrances?
Millanes.   Remembrances?

121–122 *meat, ... adviser;*] Colman; ~ ; ... ~ , F2; *omit* F1
132 Neighbours,] F2; Neighbours, *The Bar & Book ready on a Table.* F1

Lopez.   From *Nova Hispania*, or some part remote (Sir?)
   You looke like travell'd men: may be some old friends
   That happily I have forgot; some Signeours
   In *China*, or *Cataya*; some Companions——
Diego.   In the Mogulls Court, or else-where?
Arsenio.   They are mad, sure.
Lopez.   Ye came not from *Peru?*——doe they look (*Diego*)
   As if they had some mistery about 'em?
   Another *Don Alonzo* now?
Diego.   I marry,   150
   And so much money, Sir, from one you know not,
   Let it be who it will.
Lopez.   They have gracious favours.——
   Would ye be private?
Millanes.   There's no need on't (Sir)
   We come to bring ye a Remembrance from a Merchant.
Lopez. 'Tis very well, 'tis like I know him.
Arsenio.   No, sir,
   I doe not thinke ye doe.
Lopez [aside].   A new mistake (*Diego*)
   Let's carry it decently.
Arsenio.   We come to tell ye,
   You have received great summes from a young Factor
   They call *Leandro*, that has rob'd his Master,
   Rob'd him, and run away.
Diego [aside].   Let's keep close (Master)   160
   This newes comes from a cold Country.
Lopez [aside].   By my faith it freezes.
Millanes.   Is not this true? doe you shrink now (good man Curate)
   Doe I not touch ye?
Lopez.   We have a hundred Duckets
   Yet left, we doe beseech ye sir——
Millanes.   You'll hang both.
Lopez.   One may suffice.
Diego.   I will not hang alone (Master)
   I had the least part, you shall hang the highest.

Plague o' this *Tiveria*, and the Letter;
The divell sent it, post, to pepper us,
From *Nova Hispania*, we shall hang at home now.
Arsenio.   I see ye are penitent, and I have compassion: 170
 Ye are secure both, doe but what we charge ye;
 Ye shall have more gold too, and he shall give it,
 Yet ne're indanger ye.
Lopez.   Command us (Master)
 Command us presently, and see how nimbly——
Diego.   And if we doe not handsomely endeavour——
Arsenio.   Goe home and till ye heare more, keep private,
 Till we appeare againe, no words, (Vicar)
 There's something added.   [*They give money.*]
Millanes.   For you too.
Lopez.   We are ready.
Millanes.   Goe, and expect us hourely, if ye falter,
 Though ye had twenty lives——
Diego.   We are fit to loose 'em.   180
Lopez.   'Tis most expedient that we should hang both.
Diego.   If we be hang'd, we cannot blame our fortune.
Millanes.   Farewell, and be your owne friends.
Lopez.   We expect ye.
                                                                Exeunt.

                    Enter Octavio, Jacinta, Ascanio.   [II

Octavio.   We cited to the Court!
Jacinta.   It is my wonder.
Octavio.   But not our fear, (*Jacinta*) wealthy men,
 That have Estates to loose, whose conscious thoughts
 Are full of inward guilt, may shake with horrour,
 To have their Actions sifted, or appeare
 Before the Judge. But we that know our selves
 As innocent, as poore, that have no Fleece
 On which the Talons of the griping Law
 Can take sure hold, may smile with scorne on all
 That can be urg'd against us.
Jacinta.   I am confident   10

171 both, ... ye;] ~ ; ... ~ , F1–2
1 Court!] Court! *A Bar. Table-booke,* 2 *chairs, & paper standish set out.* F1–2

344

There is no man so covetous, that desires
To ravish our wants from us, and lesse hope
There can be so much Justice left on earth,
(Though sude, and call'd upon) to ease us of
The burthen of our wrongs.
Octavio.   What thinkes *Ascanio?*
  Should we be call'd in question or accus'd
  Unjustly, what would you doe to redeeme us,
  From tirannous oppression?
Ascanio.   I could pray
  To him that ever has an open eare
  To heare the innocent, and right their wrongs;   20
  Nay, by my troth, I thinke I could out plead
  An Advocate, and sweat as much as he
  Do's for a double Fee, ere you should suffer
  In an honest cause.
Octavio.   Happy simplicitie!
Jacinta.   My dearest, and my best one:——

                    Enter Jamie *and* Bartolus.
                                Don Jamie.
Octavio.   And the Advocate, that caus'd us to be summon'd.
Ascanio.   My Lord is mov'd, I see it in his lookes,
  And that man, in the Gowne, in my opinion
  Lookes like a proaguing knave.
Jacinta.   Peace, give them leave.
Jamie.   Serve me with Processe?   30
Bartolus.   My Lord, you are not lawlesse.
Jamie.   Nor thou honest;
  One, that not long since was the buckram Scribe,
  That would run on mens errands for an Asper,
  And from such basenesse, having rais'd a Stock
  To bribe the covetous Judge, call'd to the Bar,
  So poore in practise too, that you would plead
  A needy Clyents Cause, for a starv'd hen,
  Or halfe a little loyn of Veale, though fly-blowne,
  And these, the greatest Fees you could arrive at

*12 lesse hope] *stet* F1–2
  35 call'd] F1(c)–2; and F1(u)   *29 proaguing] *stet* F1–2

For just proceedings; but since you turn'd Rascall——   40
Bartolus.   Good words, my Lord.
Jamie.   And grew my Brothers Bawd
    In all his vitious courses, soothing him
    In his dishonest practises, you are growne
    The rich, and eminent knave; in the divels name,
    What am I cited for?
Bartolus.   You shall know anon,——
    And then too late repent this bitter language,   [*Aside.*]
    Or I'll misse of my ends.
Jamie.   Wer't not in Court,
    I would beat that fat of thine, rais'd by the food
    Snatch'd from poore Clyents mouthes, into a jelly:
    I would (my man of Law) but I am patient,   50
    And would obey the Judge.
Bartolus.   'Tis your best course:——
    Would every enemy I have would beat me,   [*Aside.*]
    I would wish no better Action.
Octavio.   'Save your Lordship.
Ascanio.   My humble service.
Jamie.   My good Boy, how dost thou?
    Why art thou call'd into the Court?
Ascanio.   I know not,
    But 'tis my Lord the Assistants pleasure
    I should attend here.
Jamie.   He will soone resolve us.
Officer.   Make way there for the Judge.

        Enter Assistant, Henrique, Officer, *and Witnesses.*

Jamie.   How? my kind Brother?
    Nay then 'tis ranck: there is some villany towards.
Assistant.   This Sessions purchas'd at your suit, *Don Henrique,*   60
    Hath brought us hither, to heare and determine
    Of what you can prefer.
Henrique.   I doe beseech
    The honourable Court, I may be heard

        45 You] F1(c)–2; Yon F1(u)   *45 anon,——] ~ ∧ ∧ F1–2
        *60 This] F2; 'Tis F1

                        346

In my Advocate.
Assistant.   'Tis granted.
Bartolus.   Humh, humh.
Jamie.   That preface
  If left out in a Lawyer, spoyles the Cause,
  Though ne're so good, and honest.
Bartolus.   If I stood here,
  To plead in the defence of an ill man,
  (Most equall Judge) or to accuse the innocent
  (To both which, I professe my selfe a stranger)
  It would be requisite I should deck my Language   70
  With Tropes and Figures, and all flourishes
  That grace a Rethorician; 'tis confess'd
  Adulterate Mettals, need the Gold-smiths Art,
  To set 'em off; what, in it selfe is perfect
  Contemnes a borrowed glosse: This Lord (my Client)
  Whose honest cause, when 'tis related truly,
  Will challenge Justice, finding in his conscience
  A tender scruple of a fault long since
  By him committed, thinkes it not sufficient
  To be absolv'd of't, by his Confessor,   80
  If that in open Court, he publish not
  What was so long conceal'd.
Jamie.   To what tends this?
Bartolus.   In his young yeares (it is no miracle
  That youth, and heat of Blood, should mix together)
  He look'd upon this woman, on whose face
  The ruines yet remaine, of excellent forme,
  He look'd on her, and lov'd her.
Jacinta.   You good Angels,
  What an impudence is this?
Bartolus.   And us'd all meanes
  Of Service, Courtship, Presents, that might win her
  To be at his devotion but in vaine: 90
  Her maiden Fort, impregnable held out
  Untill he promis'd Marriage; and before

*64 Humh, humh] F1(c)–2; hunch, hunch F1(u)   90 his] F1(c)–2; her F1(u)

These Witnesses a solemne Contract pass'd
To take her as his wife.

Assistant.   Give them their oath.

Jamie.   They are incompetent Witnesses, his own Creatures,
And will sweare any thing for halfe a royall.

Officer.   Silence.

Assistant.   Proceed.

Bartolus.   Upon this strong assurance
He did enjoy his wishes to the full,
Which satisfied, and then with eyes of Judgement
(Hood winck'd with lust before) considering duly   100
The inequality of the Match, he being
Nobly descended, and allyed, but she
Without a name, or Family, secretly
He purchas'd a Divorce, to disanull
His former Contract, marrying openly
The Lady *Violante.*

Jacinta.   As you sit here
The Deputy of the great King, who is
The Substitute of that impartiall Judge
With whom, or Wealth, or titles prevaile nothing,
Grant to a much wrong'd Widow, or a Wife   110
Your patience, with liberty to speake
In her owne Cause, and let me face to face
To this bad man, deliver what he is:
And if my wrongs, with his ingratitude ballanc'd,
Move not compassion, let me die unpittied;
His teares, his oathes, his perjuries, I passe o're;
To thinke of them, is a disease, but death
Should I repeat them. I dare not deny,
(For Innocence cannot justifie what's false)
But all the Advocate hath alleadged concerning   120
His falshood, and my shame, in my consent,
To be most true: But now I turne to thee,
To thee *Don Henrique,* and if impious Acts
Have left thee blood enough to make a blush,

100 Hood] F2; Had F1

348

I'll paint it on thy cheekes. Was not the wrong
Sufficient, to defeat me of mine honour,
To leave me full of sorrow, as of want,
The witnesse of thy lust, left in my womb,
To testifie thy falshood, and my shame?
But now so many yeares I had conceal'd   130
Thy most inhumane wickednesse, and won
This Gentleman, to hide it from the world
To Father what was thine (for yet by heaven,
Though in the City, he pas'd for my husband,
He never knew me as his wife,)——

Assistant.   'Tis strange:
    Give him an Oath.

Octavio.   I gladly sweare, and truly.

Jacinta.   After all this (I say) when I had borne
These wrongs, with Saint-like patience, saw another
Freely enjoy, what was (in Justice) mine,
Yet still so tender of thy rest, and quiet,   140
I never would divulge it, to disturb
Thy peace at home, yet thou, most barbarous
To be so carelesse of me, and my Fame,
(For all respect of thine, in the first step
To thy base lust, was lost) in open Court
To publish my disgrace, and on record,
To write me up an easie-yeilding wanton,
I thinke can find no president: In my extreames,
One comfort yet is left, that though the Law
Divorc'd me from thy bed, and made free way   150
To the unjust embraces of an other,
It cannot yet deny that this thy Son
(Looke up *Ascanio*, since it is come out)
Is thy legitimate heire.

Jamie.   Confederacie:
    A trick (my Lord) to cheat me; e're you give
    Your Sentence, grant me hearing.

Assistant.   New Chymera's?

    145 Court] F2; Court *Chess-boord and men set ready.* F1
    150 Divorc'd] Dyce; Divorce F1–2   *152 thy] *stet* F1–2

349

Jamie.   I am (my Lord) since he is without Issue,
    Or hope of any, his undoubted Heire,
    And this forg'd by the Advocate, to defeat me
    Of what the Lawes of *Spaine*, confer upon me,   160
    A meere Imposture, and conspiracie
    Against my future fortunes.
Assistant.   You are too bold,——
    Speak to the Cause *Don Henrique.*
Henrique.   I confesse,
    (Though the acknowledgement must wound mine honour)
    That all the court hath heard touching this Cause,
    Or with me, or against me, is most true,
    The later part my Brother urg'd, excepted:
    For what I now doe, is not out of Spleene
    (As he pretends) but from remorse of conscience
    And to repaire the wrong that I have done   170
    To this poore woman: And I beseech your Lordship
    To thinke I have not so far lost my reason,
    To bring into my Familie, to succeed me,
    The stranger-Issue of anothers Bed;
    By proofe, this is my Son, I challenge him,
    Accept him, and acknowledge him, and desire
    By a definitive Sentence of the Court,
    He may be so recorded, and full powre
    To me, to take him home.
Jacinta.   A second rape
    To the poore remnant of Content, that's left me,   180
    If this be granted: and all my former wrongs
    Were but beginnings to my miseries,
    But this the height of all: rather then part
    With my *Ascanio*, I'll deny my oath,
    Professe my selfe a Strumpet, and endure
    What punishment soe're the Court decrees
    Against a wretch that hath forsworne her selfe,
    Or plai'd the impudent whore.
Assistant.   This tastes of passion,
    And that must not divert the course of Justice;
    Don Henrique, take your Son, with this Condition,   190

350

You give him maintenance, as becomes his birth,
And 'twill stand with your honour to doe something
For this wronged woman: I will compell nothing,
But leave it to your will.——Break up the Court:——
It is in vaine to move me; my doom's pass'd,
And cannot be revok'd.   *Exit* [*with* Officer].
Henrique [*to* Bartolus].   There's your reward.
Bartolus [*aside*].   More Causes: and such Fees. Now to my Wife,
    I have too long bin absent:——Health to your Lordship.
                              Exit. [*Exeunt Witnesses.*]
Ascanio.   You all look strangely, and I feare beleeve
    This unexpected fortune makes me proud,   200
    Indeed it do's not:——I shall ever pay you
    The duty of a son,——and honour you
    Next to my Father:——good my Lord, for yet
    I dare not call you uncle, be not sad,
    I never shall forget those noble favours
    You did me being a stranger, and if ever
    I live to be the master of a fortune,
    You shall command it.
Jamie.   Since it was determin'd
    I should be cozen'd, I am glad the profit
    Shall fall on thee; I am too tough to melt,   210
    But something I will do.
Henrique.   'Pray you take leave
    Of your steward (gentle Brother) the good husband
    That rakes up all for you.
Jamie.   Very well, mock on,
    It is your turn: I may have mine.   *Exit.*
Octavio.   But do not
    Forget us deare *Ascanio.*
Ascanio.   Do not feare it,
    I every day will see you: every houre
    Remember you in my prayers.
Jacinta.   My grief's too great
    To be expressed in words.   *Exit.*

198 *Exit.*] F2; *omit* F1   *213 rakes] F1(u); takes F1(c)–2
217 *Jacinta*] Colman; *Jam.* F1; *Oct.* F2

Henrique.   Take that and leave us,
                              Gives money to Jacinta.
Leave us without reply,
              [*Exeunt* Jacinta *and* Octavio.] Ascanio *offers to follow.*
                    nay come back sirrah
And study to forget such things as these   220
As are not worth the knowledge.
Ascanio.   O good Sir,
These are bad principles——
Henrique.   Such as you must learn
Now you are mine, for wealth and poverty
Can hold no friendship: and what is my will
You must observe and do, though good or ill.

                                   Exeunt.

                    Enter Bartolus.   [III

Bartolus.   Where is my wife?——'fore heaven, I have done
      wonders,
Done mighty things to day,——my *Amaranta,*——
My heart rejoyces at my wealthy Gleanings,
A rich litigious Lord I love to follow,
A Lord that builds his happinesse on brawlings,
O 'tis a blessed thing to have rich Clyents,——
Why, wife I say,——how fares my studious Pupill?
Hard at it still? ye are too violent,
All things must have their rests, they will not last els,
Come out and breathe.
Leandro (*within*).   I do beseech you pardon me,   10
I am deeply in a sweet point Sir.
Bartolus.   I'le instruct ye:
I say take breath, seek health first, then your study.

                    Enter Amaranta.

O my sweet soul, I have brought thee golden birds home,
Birds in abundance: I have done strange wonders:
There's more a hatching too.

218.1 *Gives ... Jacinta.*] F2; *omit* F1   219 *Ascanio ... follow.*] F2; *omit* F1
10 Come ... breathe. | *Leandro.* I] F1(c)–2; *Lean.* Come ... breathe. | I F1(u)

Amaranta.   Have ye done good, husband?
    Then 'tis a good day spent.
Bartolus.   Good enough chicken,
    I have spred the nets o'th' law, to catch rich booties,
    And they come fluttering in: how do's my Pupil,
    My modest thing? hast thou yet spoken to him?
Amaranta.   As I past by his chamber I might see him,   20
    But he is so bookish——
Bartolus.   And so bashfull too,
    I faith he is, before he will speak, he will starve there.
Amaranta.   I pitie him a little.
Bartolus.   So do I too.
Amaranta.   And if he please to take the aire o'th' gardens
    Or walk i'th' inward roomes, so he molest not——
Bartolus.   He shall not trouble thee, he dare not speak to thee——
    Bring out the Chesse-board,——

            Enter Moore *with Chesse-board* [*and exit*].

                            come let's have a game wife,
    I'le try your masterie, you say you are cunning.
Amaranta.   As learned as ye are (Sir) I shall beat ye.

                Enter Leandro.

Bartolus.   Here he steales out, put him not out of countenance,   30
    'Prethee look another way, he will be gone else——
    Walk and refresh your self, I'l be with you presently.
Leandro.   I'le take the aire a little.
Bartolus.   'Twill be healthfull.
                            Play at chesse.
Amaranta.   Will ye be there? then here? Ile spare ye that man.
Leandro [*aside*].   'Would I were so neare too, and a mate fitting.
Amaranta.   What think ye (Sir,) to this? have at your Knight now.
Bartolus.   'Twas subtilly playd: your Queen lies at my service——
    Pre thee look off, he is ready to pop in again,   [*Aside to her.*]
    Look off I say, do'st thou not see how he blushes?

15 done ∧ good,] ∼ , ∼ ∧ F1–2
        18 fluttering] F2; flttering F1   18–19 Pupil, ... thing?] ∼ ? ... ∼ , F1–2
        33.1 *Play at chesse.*] F2; *omit* F1

Amaranta.   I do not blast him.

Leandro [*aside.*].   But ye do, and burn too.   40
  What killing looks she steals?

Bartolus.   I have you now close,
  Now for a Mate.

Leandro [*aside*].   You are a blessed man
  That may so have her. Oh that I might play with her——
                              Knock within.

Bartolus.   Who's there? I come,——you cannot scape me now
  wife——   *Knock.*
  I come, I come.

Leandro [*aside*].   Most blessed hand that calls him.

Bartolus.   Play quickly wife.

Amaranta.   'Pray ye give leave to think, Sir.

               Enter Moore.

Moore.   An honest neighbour that dwells hard by (Sir)
  Would fain speak with your worship about business.   [*Exit.*]

Leandro [*aside*].   The devil blow him off.

Bartolus.   Play.

Amaranta.   I will study:
  For if you beat me thus, you will still laugh at me.   *Knock.* 50

Bartolus.   He knocks again; I cannot stay.——*Leandro*
  'Pray thee come near.

Leandro.   I am well (Sir) here.

Bartolus.   Come hither:
  Be not afraid but come.

Amaranta.   Here's none will bite (Sir.)

Leandro.   God forbid Lady.

Amaranta.   'Pray come nearer.

Leandro.   Yes forsooth.

Bartolus.   'Pre thee observe these men just as they stand here,
  And see this Lady do not alter 'em,
  And be not partiall, Pupill.

Leandro.   No indeed Sir.

Bartolus.   Let her not move a pawn, I'le come back presently——
  Nay you shall know I am a Conquerour——
  Have an eye Pupill.   *Exit.*

Amaranta.   Can ye play at Chesse Sir?
Leandro.   A little Lady.
Amaranta.   But you cannot tell me
  How to avoid this Mate, and win the Game too?——
  Ha's noble eyes:——   [*Aside.*]
                    ye dare not friend me so farre.
Leandro.   I dare do any thing that's in mans power, Lady,
  To be a friend to such a noble beauty.
Amaranta [*aside*].   This is no Lawyers language:——I pray ye tell
    me,
  Whether may I remove, (Ye see I am set round)
  To avoid my husband?
Leandro.   I shall tell ye happily,
  But happily you will not be instructed.
Amaranta.   Yes, and I'le thank ye too, shall I move this man?   70
Leandro.   Those are unseemly: move one can serve ye,
  Can honour ye, can love ye.
Amaranta.   'Pray ye tell quickly,
  He will return and then——
Leandro.   I'le tell ye instantly,
  Move me, and I wil move any way to serve ye,
  Move your heart this way (Lady.)
Amaranta.   How?
Leandro.   'Pray ye heare me.
  Behold the sport of Love, when he is imperious,
  Behold the slave of Love.
Amaranta.   Move my Queen this way?——
  Sure, he's some worthy man:——   [*Aside.*]
                    then if he hedge me,
  Or here to open him——
Leandro.   Do but behold me,
  If there be pity in you, do but view me,   80
  But view the misery I have undertaken
  For you, the povertie.
Amaranta.   He will come presently.
  Now play your best Sir,——though I loose this Rook here

Yet I get Libertie.   [*Aside.*]

Leandro.   I'le seize your fair hand
  And warm it with a hundred, hundred kisses,
  The God of love warm your desires but equal:
  That shall play my game now.

Amaranta.   What do you mean Sir?
  Why do you stop me?

Leandro.   That ye may intend me.
  The time ha's blest us both: Love bids us use it.
  I am a Gentleman nobly descended: 90
  Young to invite your Love, rich to maintain it.
  I bring a whole heart to ye, thus I give it,
  And to those burning altars thus I offer,
  And thus——   [*Kisses her.*]
            divine lips, where perpetuall Spring grows!

Amaranta.   Take that, ye are too saucy.
                          [*Hits him with Chesse-board.*]

Leandro.   How proud Lady?
  Strike my deserts?

Amaranta [*aside*].   I was too blame.

Enter Bartolus.

Bartolus.   What wife, there?
  Heaven keep my house from thieves.

Leandro [*aside*].   I am wretched:
  Opened, discovered, lost to my wishes.
  I shall be whooted at.

Bartolus.   What noise was this (wife?)
  Why dost thou smile?

Leandro [*aside*].   This proud thing will betray me.   100

Bartolus.   Why these lie here? what anger (deare?)

Amaranta.   Why none, Sir,
  Onely a chance, your pupill said he plaid well,
  And so indeed he do's: he undertook for ye
  Because I would not sit so long time idle,
  I made my Liberty, avoided your mate,
  And he again as cunningly endangered me,
  Indeed he put me strangely to it. When presently

356

Hearing you come, and having broke his ambush too,
Having the second time brought off my Queen fair,
I rose o'th' sudden smilingly to shew ye,   110
My apron caught the Chesse-board, and the men,
And there the noise was.
Bartolus.   Thou art grown a Master,
For all this, I shall beat ye.
Leandro [*aside*].   Or I, Lawyer,
For now I love her more, 'twas a neat answer,
And by it hangs a mighty hope: I thank her,
She gave my pate a sound knock that it rings yet,
But you shall have a sounder if I live Lawyer,
My heart akes, yet I would not be in that fear.
Bartolus.   I am glad ye are a gamester, Sir, sometimes
For recreation we two shall fight hard at it.   120
Amaranta.   He will prove too hard for me.
Leandro [*aside*].   I hope he shall do,
But your Chesse-board is too hard for my head.
Bartolus.   I have been attoning two most wrangling neighbours,
They had no money, therefore I made even:
Come, let's go in, and eat, truly I am hungry.
Leandro.   I have eaten already, I must intreat your pardon.
Bartolus.   Do as ye please, we shall expect ye at supper.——
He ha's got a little heart now, it seems handsomly.
Amaranta [*aside*].   You'l get no little head, if I do not look to ye.
Leandro [*aside*].   If ever I do catch thee again thou vanity——   130
Amaranta [*aside*].   I was too blame to be so rash, I am sorie.

> *Exeunt.*

> *Enter* Don Henrique, Violante, Ascanio.   IV.i

Henrique.   Heare but my reasons.
Violante.   O my patience, heare 'em?
Can cunning falshood colour an excuse?
With any seeming shape of borrowed truth

---

*113 Or I] *stet* F1–2   *118 akes, yet ∧ ... fear.] ~ ∧ ~ , ... ~——F1–2
*122 head.] head, line that good Lady, F1–2   128 heart ∧ now,] ~ , ~ ∧ F1–2
2–4 excuse? ... truth ∧ ... error?] McKerrow *conj.*; ~ ? ... ~ ? ... ~ . F1; ~ ∧ ... ~ ? ...
      ~ ? F2

Extenuate this wofull wrong, not error?
Henrique.　　You gave consent that to defeat my brother
I should take any course.
Violante.　　　　　　　But not to make
The cure more loathsome then the fowle disease:
Was't not enough you took me to your bed,
Tir'd with loose dalliance, and with emptie veines,
All those abilities spent before and wasted,　　　　　10
That could conferre the name of mother on me?
But that (to perfect my account of sorrow
For my long barrennesse) you must highten it
By shewing to my face, that you were fruitfull
Hug'd in the base embraces of another?
If Solitude that dwelt beneath my roofe
And want of children was a torment to me,
What end of my vexation to behold
A bastard to upbraid me with my wants,
And heare the name of father paid to ye　　　　　20
Yet know my self no mother?
Henrique.　　　　　　　What can I say?
Shall I confesse my fault and ask your pardon?
Will that content ye?
Violante.　　　　　　If it could make void,
What is confirm'd in Court: No, no, *Don Henrique*,
You shall know that I find my self abus'd,
And adde to that I have a womans anger,
And while I look upon this Basilisk,
Whose envious eyes hath blased all my comforts,
Rest confident I'le study my dark ends,
And not your pleasures.
Ascanio.　　　　　　Noble Lady, heare me,　　　　　30
Not as my Fathers son, but as your servant,
Vouchsafe to heare me, for such in my duty,
I ever will appeare: And far be it from
My poore ambition, ever to looke on you,
But with that reverence, which a slave stands bound

21–22 *Henrique.* What ... Shall] Weber (Mason *conj.*); What ... *Hen.* Shall F1–2
28 envious] *i.e.* malicious, spiteful (*O.E.D.*)

To pay a worthy Mistris: I have heard
That Dames of highest place, nay Queenes themselves,
Disdaine not to be serv'd by such as are
Of meanest Birth: and I shall be most happie,
To be emploi'd when you please to command me   40
Even in the coursest Office: as your Page,
I can wayte on your trencher, fill your wine,
Carry your pantofles, and be sometimes bless'd
In all humilitie to touch your feete:
Or if that you esteeme that too much grace,
I can run by your Coach, observe your lookes
And hope to gaine a fortune by my service,
With your good favour: which now, as a Son,
I dare not challenge.

Violante.   As a Son?

Ascanio.   Forgive me,
I will forget the name, let it be death   50
For me to call you Mother.

Violante.   Still upbraided?

Henrique.   No way left to appease you?

Violante.   None: now heare me,
Heare what I vow before the face of heaven,
And if I breake it, all plagues in this life,
And those that after death are fear'd, fall on me:
While that this Bastard staies under my rooffe,
Looke for no peace at home, for I renounce
All Offices of a wife.

Henrique.   What am I falne to?

Violante.   I will not eate, nor sleepe with you, and those howres
Which I should spend in prayers for your health   60
Shall be emploi'd in Curses.

Henrique.   Terrible.

Violante.   All the day long, i'le be as tedious to you
As lingring fevers, and i'le watch the nights,
To ring alou'd your shame, and breake your sleepes,
Or if you doe but slumber, i'le appeare
In the shape of all my wrongs, and like a fury
Fright you to madnes, and if all this faile

To worke out my revenge, I have friends and kinsmen,
That will not sit downe tame with the disgrace
That's offer'd to our noble familie   70
In what I suffer.
Henrique.   How am I devided
Betweene the duties I owe as a Husband,
And pietie of a Parent?
Ascanio.   I am taught Sir
By the instinct of nature that obedience
Which bids me to prefer your peace of mind,
Before those pleasures that are dearest to me:
Be wholy hers (my Lord) I quit all parts,
That I may challenge: may you grow old together
And no distast e're find you, and before
The Characters of age are printed on you   80
May you see many Images of your selves,
Though I, like some false Glasse that's never look'd in,
Am cast a side, and broken: from this hower
(Unles invited, which I dare not hope for)
I never will set my forbidden feete
Over your threshold: onely give me leave
Though cast off to the world, to mention you,
In my devotions, 'tis all I sue for
And so I take my last leave.
Henrique [*aside*].   Though I am
Devoted to a wife, nay allmost sol'd   90
A slave to serve her pleasures, yet I cannot
So part with all humanity, but I must
Shew something of a Father:——thou shalt not goe
Unfurnish'd and unfriended too: take that
To guard thee from necessities;   [*Gives money.*]
                        may thy goodnes
Meet many favours, and thine innocence
Deserve to be the heire of greater fortunes,
Then thou wer't borne to.——Scorne me not *Violante*,
This banishment is a kind of civill death,

83 Am] F1(c)–2; And F1(u)   *97 Deserve] *stet* F1–2

360

And now, as it were at his Funerall,   100
To shed a teare or two, is not unmanly——
And so farewell for ever: one word more,
Though I must never see thee (my *Ascanio*)
When this is spent (for so the Judge decreed)
Send to me for supply: [*Exit* Ascanio.]
                        are you pleas'd now?
Violante.   Yes: I have cause: to see you howle and blubber
At the parting of my torment, and your shame;
'Tis well: proceed: supply his wants: doe doe:
Let the great dowre I brought serve to maintain
Your Bastards riots: send my Clothes and Jewells,   110
To your old acquaintance, your deare dame his Mother:
Now you begin to melt, I know 'twill follow.
Henrique.   Is all I doe misconstrude?
Violante.   I will take
A course to right my selfe, a speeding one:
By the bless'd Saints, I will; if I prove cruell,
The shame to see thy foolish pitty, taught me
To loose my naturall softnes, keepe off from me,
Thy flateries are infectious, and i'le fle thee
As I would doe a Leper.
Henrique.   Let not fury
Transport you so: you know I am your Creature,   120
All love, but to your self, with him hath left me,
I'le joyne with you in any thing.
Violante.   In vaine:
I'le take mine owne waies, and will have no partners.
Henrique.   I will not crosse you.
Violante.   Doe not,——they shall find   [*Aside.*]
That to a Woman of her hopes beguil'd
A viper troad on, or an Aspick's mild.

                                        Exeunt.

        Enter Lopez, Millanes, Arsenio.   [IV.]ii

Lopez.   Sits the game there? I have you: by mine order,

107 shame;] F2 (shame.); shame ∧ *Bed ready, wine, table Standish & Paper.* F1
1 you:] Sympson; ∼ ∧ F1–2

I love *Leandro* for't.

Millanes.   But you must shew it
In lending him your help, to gain him meanes
And opportunitie.

Lopez.   He shall want nothing,
I know my Advocate to a hayre, and what
Will fetch him from his prayers, if he use any:
I am honyed with the project, I would have him horn'd
For a most pretious Beast.

Arsenio.   But you loose time.

Lopez.   I am gon, instruct you *Diego*, you will find him
A sharpe and subtle knave, give him but hints   10
And he will amplifie: See all things ready,
I'll fetch him with a vengeance.   *Exit.*

Arsenio.   If he faile now,
Wee'll give him over too.

Millanes.   Tush he is flesh'd,
And knowes what vaine to strike for his owne credit.

Arsenio.   All things are ready.

Millanes.   Then we shall have a merry Scene, ne're feare it.
                    Exeunt.

Enter Amaranta (*with a note*) *and* Moore [Egla].   [IV

Amaranta.   Is thy Master gone out?

Moore.   Even now, the Curat fetch'd him,
About a serious businesse as it seem'd,
For he snatch'd up his Cloak, and brush'd his hat strait,
Set his Band handsomely, and out he gallop'd.

Amaranta.   'Tis well, 'tis very well, he went out (*Egla*)
As luckily, as one would say, goe Husband,
He was call'd by providence: fling this short paper
Into *Leandro*'s Cell, and waken him,
He is monstrous vexed, and musty, at my Chesse-play;
But this shall supple him, when he has read it: 10
Take your owne recreation for two houres,
And hinder nothing.

12 he] F1(c)–2; ye F1(u)
*15 *Arsenio.* All] F2; *Ars.* All [*preceded by catchword* Have] F1

362

Moore.   If I doe, I'll hang for't.

                                                    Exeunt.

Enter Octavio, Jacinta.   [IV.]iv

Octavio.   If that you lov'd *Ascanio* for himselfe,
       And not your private ends, you rather should
       Blesse the faire opportunitie, that restores him
       To his Birth-right, and the Honours he was borne to,
       Then grieve at his good Fortune.
Jacinta.   Grieve *Octavio?*
       I would resigne my Essence, that he were
       As happy as my love could fashion him,
       Though every blessing that should fall on him,
       Might prove a curse to me: my sorrow springs
       Out of my feare, and doubt he is not safe.   10
       I am acquainted with *Don Henrique*'s nature,
       And I have heard too much the fiery temper
       Of Madam *Violante*: can you thinke
       That she, that almost is at war with heaven
       For being barren, will with equall eyes
       Behold a Son of mine?
Octavio.   His Fathers care,
       That for the want of Issue, tooke him home,
       (Though with the forfeiture of his owne fame)
       Will looke unto his safetie.
Jacinta.   Step-mothers
       Have many eyes, to find a way to mischiefe,   20
       Though blind to goodnesse.

Enter Jamy *and* Ascanio.

Octavio.   Here comes *Don Jamy*,
       And with him our *Ascanio.*
Jamy.   Good youth leave me,
       I know thou art forbid my company,
       And onely to be seene with me, will call on
       Thy Fathers anger.
Ascanio.   Sir, if that to serve you
       Could loose me any thing (as indeed it cannot)

                        363

I still would follow you. Alas I was borne
To doe you hurt, but not to help my selfe,
I was, for some particular end, tooke home,
But am cast off againe.

Jamy.   Is't possible?   30

Ascanio.   The Lady, whom my father calls his wife,
Abhors my sight, is sick of me, and forc'd him
To turne me out of dores.

Jacinta.   By my best hopes
I thanke her crueltie, for it comes neere
A saving charitie.

Ascanio.   I am onely happy
That yet I can relieve you, 'pray you share:
My Father's wondrous kind, and promises
That I should be supplide: but sure the Lady
Is a malitious woman, and I feare
Meanes me no good.

Jamy.   I am turn'd a stone with wonder,   40
And know not what to thinke.

Enter Servant.

Servant [*aside to* Jamy].   From my Lady,
Your private eare, and this.   [*Gives a purse.*]

Jamy.   New Miracles?

Servant.   She sayes, if you dare make your selfe a Fortune,
She will propose the meanes; My Lord *Don Henrique*
Is now from home, and she alone expects you:
If you dare trust her, so, if not despaire of
A second offer.   *Exit.*

Jamy [*aside*].   Though there were an Ambush
Layd for my life, I'll on and sound this secret,——
Retire thee (my *Ascanio*) with thy Mother:
But stir not forth, some great designe's on foot,   50
Fall what can fall, if e're the Sun be set,
I see you not, give me dead.

Ascanio.   We will expect you,

*52 give me dead] stet F1

364

And those bless'd Angels, that love goodnesse, guard you.

Exeunt.

Enter Lopez *and* Bartolus.   [IV.]v

Bartolus.   Is't possible he should be rich?

Lopez.   Most possible,
He hath bin long, though he had but little gettings,
Drawing together, Sir.

Bartolus.   Accounted a poore Sexton,
Honest poore *Diego?*

Lopez.   I assure ye, a close Fellow,
Both close, and scraping, and that fills the bags, Sir.

Bartolus.   A notable good Fellow too?

Lopez.   Sometimes, Sir,
When he hop'd to drink a man into a surfeit,
That he might gaine by his Grave.

Bartolus.   So many thousands?

Lopez.   Heaven knowes what.

Bartolus.   'Tis strange,
'Tis very strange; but we see by endeavour,   10
And honest labour——

Lopez.   *Milo,* by continuance
Grew from a silly Calfe (with your worships reverence)
To carry a Bull: from a penny, to a pound, Sir,
And from a pound, to many, 'tis the progresse.

Bartolus.   Ye say true, but he lov'd to feed well also,
And that me-thinks——

Lopez.   From another mans Trencher, Sir,
And where he found it season'd with small charge,
There he would play the Tyrant, and would devoure ye
More then the Graves he made; at home he liv'd
Like a Camelion, suckt th'Ayre of misery,   20
And grew fat by th'Brewis of an Eg-shel,
Would smell a Cooks shop, and goe home and surfeit,
And be a moneth in fasting out that Fever.

6 Sir,] F2; Sir, *Diego ready in Bed, wine, cup.* F1
17 where ... charge,] Theobald *conj.*; there ... charge: F1–2
20 misery,] misery, *Table out, Standish paper, stools.* F1–2

365

Bartolus.   These are good Symptomes: do's he lye so sick, say ye?
Lopez.   Oh, very sick.
Bartolus.   And chosen me Executor?
Lopez.   Onely your Worship.
Bartolus.   No hope of his amendment?
Lopez.   None, that we find.
Bartolus.   He hath no kinsmen neither?
Lopez.   'Truth, very few.
Bartolus.   His mind will be the quieter,
    What Doctors has he?
Lopez.   There's none sir, he believes in.
Bartolus.   They are but needlesse things, in such extremities.   30
    Who drawes the good-man's will?
Lopez.   Marry that doe I, Sir,
    And to my griefe.
Bartolus.   Griefe will doe little now, Sir,
    Draw it to your comfort, Friend, and as I counsell ye;
    An honest man, but such men live not alwayes:
    Who are about him?
Lopez.   Many, now he is passing,
    That would pretend to his love, yes, and some gentlemen
    That would faine counsell him, and be of his kindred;
    Rich men can want no heires, Sir.
Bartolus.   They doe ill,
    Indeed they doe, to trouble him: very ill, Sir,
    But we shall take a care.
Lopez.   Will ye come neare, Sir?——   40
    'Pray ye bring him out;

   Enter Diego (*in a Bed*) Millanes, Arsenio, *and Parishioners.*

                    Now ye may see in what state:——
    Give him fresh ayre.
Bartolus.   I am sorry, Neighbour *Diego*,
    To find ye in so weake a state.
Diego.   Ye are welcome,
    But I am fleeting, Sir.

---

33 ye;] Theobald (ye.); ~ , F1–2   42 ayre.] F2; ayre. *Bed thrust out.* F1

Bartolus.   Me-thinkes he looks well,
  His colour fresh, and strong, his eyes are chearfull.
Lopez.   A glimmering before death, 'tis nothing els, Sir,
  Do you see how he fumbles with the sheet? do ye note that?
Diego.   My learned Sir, 'pray ye sit: I am bold to send for ye,
  To take a care of what I leave.
Lopez.   Doe you heare that?
Arsenio [*aside to* Diego].   Play the knave finely.
Diego.   So I will, I warrant ye,   50
  And carefully.
Bartolus.   'Pray ye doe not trouble him,
  You see he's weake, and has a wandring fancie.
Diego.   My honest Neighbours, weep not, I must leave ye,
  I cannot alwayes beare ye company,
  We must drop still, there is no remedie:——
  'Pray ye Master Curat, will ye write my Testament,
  And write it largely, it may be remembred?——
  And be witnesse to my Legacies, good Gentlemen;——
  Your worship, I doe make my full Executor,
  You are a man of wit and understanding:——   60
  Give me a cup of wine to raise my Spirits,
  For I speake low: [*Drinks.*]
              I would before these Neighbours
  Have ye to sweare (Sir) that you will see it executed,
  And what I give, let equally be rendred
  For my soules health.
Bartolus.   I vow it truly, Neighbour,
  Let not that trouble ye——before all these,
  Once more I give my Oath.
Diego.   Then set me higher,
  And pray ye come neare me all.
Lopez.   We are ready for ye.
Millanes [*aside to* Diego].   Now spur the Asse, and get our friend
    time.
Diego.   First then,   [*Lopez writes.*]
  After I have given my Body to the wormes   70

      *53 not, ... ye,] *stet* F1–2   65 Neighbour] Dyce *conj.*; Neighbours F1–2

(For they must be serv'd first, they are seldome cozen'd)——
Lopez. Remember your Parish, Neighbour.
Diego.   You speak truly,
  I doe remember it, a lewd vile Parish,
  And pray it may be mended: To the Poore of it,
  (Which is to all the Parish) I give nothing,
  For nothing, unto nothing, is most naturall,
  Yet leave as much space, as will build an Hospitall,
  Their children may pray for me.
Bartolus.   What doe you give to it?
Diego.   Set downe two thousand Duckets.
Bartolus.   'Tis a good gift,
  And will be long remembred.
Diego.   To your worship,   80
  (Because you must take paines to see all finish'd)
  I give two thousand more, it may be three, Sir,
  A poore gratuitie for your paines-taking.
Bartolus.   These are large summes.
Lopez.   Nothing to him that has 'em.
Diego.   To my old Master Vicar, I give five hundred,
  (Five hundred, and five hundred, are too few Sir
  But there be more to serve.)
Bartolus [*aside*].   This fellow coynes sure.
Diego.   Give me some more drink.——Pray ye buy Books, buy
      Books,
  You have a learned head, stuffe it with Libraries,
  And understand 'em, when ye have done, 'tis Justice: 90
  Run not the Parish mad with Controversies,
  Nor preach not Abstinence to longing women,
  'Twill budge the bottoms of their consciences:
  I would give the Church new Organs, but I prophecie
  The Church-wardens would quickly pipe 'em out o'th' Parish:
  Two hundred Duckets more to mend the chancel,
  And to paint true Orthographie, as many;
  They write *Sunt* with a *C*, which is abominable,
  'Pray you set that downe; to poore Maidens marriages——

Lopez.   I that's well thought of, what's your will in that point?   100
   A meritorious thing.
Bartolus [aside].   No end of this will?
Diego.   I give *per annum* two hundred ells of Lockram,
   That there be no strait dealings in their Linnens,
   But the Sayles cut according to their Burthens;
   To all Bell-Ringers, I bequeath new Ropes,
   And let them use 'em at their owne discretions.
Arsenio.   You may remember us.
Diego.   I doe, good Gentlemen,
   And I bequeath ye both good carefull Surgeons,
   A Legacy you have need of, more then money,
   I know you want good Diets and good Lotions,   110
   And in your pleasures, good take heed.
Lopez.   He raves now,
   But 'twill be quickly off.
Diego.   I doe bequeath ye
   Commodities of pins: browne papers: pack-threds,
   Rost porke, and puddings: Ginger-bread, and Jewes-trumps,
   Of penny Pipes, and mouldy Pepper: take 'em,
   Take 'em even where you please, and be cozen'd with 'em,
   I should bequeath ye Executions also,
   But those I'll leave to th'Law.
Lopez.   Now he growes temperate.
Bartolus.   You will give no more?
Diego.   I am loth to give more from ye,
   Because I know you will have a care to execute: 120
   Onely, to pious uses, Sir, a little.
Bartolus [aside].   If he be worth all these, I am made for ever.
Diego.   I give to fatall Dames, that spin mens threds out,
   And poore distressed Damsells, that are militant
   As members of our owne Afflictions,
   A hundred Crowns to buy warm tubbs to worke in:
   I give five hundred pounds to buy a Church-yard,
   A spacious Church-yard, to lay Theeves and knaves in,
   Rich men, and honest men, take all the roome up.
Lopez.   Are ye not weary?
Diego.   Never of well-doing.   130

369

Bartolus.   These are mad Legacies.
Diego.   They were got as madly;
　My Sheep, and Oxen, and my moveables,
　My Plate, and Jewells, and five hundred Acres;
　(I have no heires)——
Bartolus [*aside*].   This cannot be, 'tis Monstrous.
Diego.   Three Ships at Sea too.
Bartolus.   You have made me full Executor?
Diego.   Full, full, and totall, would I had more to give ye
　But these may serve an honest mind.
Bartolus.   Ye say true,
　A very honest mind,——and make it rich too;   [*Aside.*]
　Rich, wondrous rich,——but where shall I raise these monys?
　About your house, I see no such great promises;   140
　Where shall I find these summes?
Diego.   Even where you please Sir,
　You are wise and provident, and know businesse,
　Ev'n raise 'em where you shall think good; I am reasonable.
Bartolus.   Thinke good? will that raise thousands? What doe you
　　make me?
Diego.   You have sworn to see it done, that's all my comfort.
Bartolus.   Where I please? this is pack'd, sure, to disgrace me.
Diego.   Ye are just, and honest, and I know you will doe it,
　Ev'n where you please, for you know where the wealth is.
Bartolus.   I am abused, betrayed, I am laugh'd at, scorn'd,
　Baffel'd, and boared, it seemes.
Arsenio.   No, no, ye are fooled.   150
Lopez.   Most finely fooled, and handsomely, and neatly,
　Such cunning Masters must be fooled sometimes, Sir,
　And have their worships noses wiped, 'tis healthfull,
　We are but quit: you foole us of our moneys
　In every Cause, in every Quiddit wipe us.
Diego.   Ha, ha, ha, ha, some more drink, for my heart, Gentle-
　　men,——
　This merry Lawyer——ha, ha, ha, ha, this Scholler——
　I thinke this fitt will cure me: this Executor——

*150 boared] *stet* F1–2

370

I shall laugh out my Lungs.

Bartolus.   This is derision above sufferance, villany   160
  Plotted, and set against me.

Diego.   Faith 'tis knavery,
  In troth I must confesse, thou art fooled indeed, Lawyer.

Millanes.   Did you thinke, had this man been rich——

Bartolus.   'Tis well, Sir.

Millanes.   He would have chosen such a Wolfe, a Cancker,
  A Maggot-pate, to be his whole Executor?

Lopez.   A Lawyer, that entangles all mens honesties,
  And lives like a Spider in a Cobweb lurking,
  And catching at all Flies, that passe his pitt-falls?
  Puts powder to all States, to make 'em caper?
  Would he trust you? Doe you deserve?

Diego.   I find, Gentlemen,   170
  This Cataplasme of a well cozen'd Lawyer
  Laid to my stomach, lenifies my Fever,
  Me-thinkes I could eat now and walke a little.

Bartolus.   I am asham'd to feele how flat I am cheated,
  How grossely, and malitiously made a May-game,
  A damned Trick; my wife, my wife, some Rascall:
  My credit, and my wife, some lustfull villaine,
  Some Bawd, some Rogue,——

Arsenio.   Some craftie Foole has found ye:
  This 'tis Sir, to teach ye to be too busie,
  To covet all the gaines, and all the rumours,   180
  To have a stirring oare, in all mens actions.

Lopez.   We did this, but to vex your fine officiousnesse.

Bartolus.   God yeild ye and God thank ye: I am fooled, gentlemen;
  The Lawyer is an Asse, I doe confesse it,
  A weak dull shallow Asse: good even to your worships:——
  Vicar, remember Vicar,——Rascall remember,
  Thou notable rich Rascall.

Diego.   I doe remember, Sir,
  'Pray ye stay a little, I have ev'n two Legacies

---

170 Would ... deserve? | *Diego.* I] F2; Would ... you? | *Die.* Doe ... I F1
*178 Rogue,——| *Arsenio.* Some craftie Foole] *stet* F1–2
*183 God ... God] Weber; Good' ... go'd F1; Good ... good F2

To make your mouth up, Sir.
Bartolus.   Remember Varletts,
  Quake and remember, Rogues; I have brine for your Buttocks.   190
                                        Ex[it].
Lopez.   Oh how he frets, and fumes now like a dunghill.
Diego.   His gall containes fine stuffe now to make poysons,
  Rare damned stuffe.
Arsenio.   Let's after him, and still vex him,
  And take my Friend off: by this time he has prosper'd,
  He cannot loose this deere time: 'tis impossible.
Millanes.   Well *Diego,* thou hast done.
Lopez.   Hast done it daintily.
Millanes.   And shalt be as well paid, Boy.
Arsenio.   Goe, let's crucifie him.
                                Exeunt.

            Enter Amaranta, Leandro.   [IV

Leandro.   I have told ye all my story, and how desperately——
Amaranta.   I doe believe: let's walke on, time is pretious,
  Not to be spent in words: here no more wooing,
  The open Ayre's an enemy to Lovers,
  Doe as I tell ye.
Leandro.   I'll doe any thing,
  I am so over-joy'd, I'll fly to serve ye.
Amaranta.   Take your joy moderately, as it is ministred,
  And as the cause invites: that man's a foole
  That at the sight o'th' Bond, dances and leapes,
  Then is the true joy, when the money comes.   10
Leandro.   You cannot now deny me.
Amaranta.   Nay, you know not,
  Women have crotchets, and strange fits.
Leandro.   You shall not.
Amaranta.   Hold ye to that and sweare it confidently,
  Then I shall make a scruple to deny ye:
  'Pray ye let's step in, and see a friend of mine,
  The weather's sharp: we'll stay but halfe an houre,

4 Lovers,] F2; Lovers, *Pewter ready for noyse.* F1

372

We may be miss'd els: a private fine house 'tis, Sir,
And we may find many good welcomes.
Leandro.   Doe Lady,
   Doe happy Lady.
Amaranta.   All your mind's of doing,
   You must be modester.
Leandro.   I will be any thing.   20

                                            Exeunt.

                 Enter Bartolus.   [IV.]vii

Bartolus.   Open the dores, and give me roome to chafe in,
                                              [*Knocks.*]
   Mine owne roome, and my liberty: why Maid there,
   Open, I say, and doe not anger me,
   I am subject to much fury: when ye dish-clout?
   When doe ye come? a sleepe, ye lazie hell-hound?
   Nothing intended, but your ease, and eating?
   No body here? why wife, why wife? why jewell?
   No tongue to answer me? 'pre'thee (good Pupill)
   Dispence a little with thy carefull study,
   And step to th' doore, and let me in; nor he neither?   10
   Ha! not at's study? nor asleepe? nor no-body?
   I'll make ye heare:——the house of Ignorance,   [*Knocks.*]
   No sound inhabits here: I have a key yet
   That commands all: I feare I am metamorphiz'd.

                                    [*Exit into the house.*]

              Enter Lopez, Arsenio, Milanes, Diego.

Lopez.   He keepes his fury still, and may doe mischiefe.
Milanes.   He shalbe hang'd first, we'll be sticklers there, boyes.
Diego.   The hundred thousand Dreams now, that posses him
   Of jealousie, and of revenge, and frailtie,
   Of drawing Bills against us, and Petitions.
Lopez.   And casting what his credit shall recover.   20
Milanes.   Let him cast till his Maw come up, we care not.
   You shall be still secured.
Diego.   We'll pay him home then;
                                    A great noyse within.

                             373

Hark what a noyse he keeps within?
Lopez.   Certaine
H'as set his Chimneys o' fire, or the divell roars there.
Diego.   The Codixes o'th' Law are broke loose, Gentlemen.
Arsenio.   He's fighting sure.
Diego.   I'll tell ye that immediatly.

                                   Exit [into house].

Milanes.   Or doing some strange out-rage on himselfe.
Arsenio.   Hang him, he dares not be so valiant.

                      Enter Diego.

Diego.   There's no body at home, and he chafes like a Lyon,
And stinkes withall.   *Noyse still.*
Lopez.   No body?
Diego.   Not a creature,   30
Nothing within, but he and his Law-tempest,
The Ladles, dishes, kettles, how they fly all?
And how the Glasses through the Roomes?
Arsenio.   My friend sure
Has got her out, and now he has made an end on't.
Lopez.   See where the Sea comes? how it foams, and brussels?
The great Leviathan o'th' Law, how it tumbles?

                      Enter Bartolus.

Bartolus.   Made every way an Asse? abus'd on all sides?
And from all quarters, people come to laugh at me?
Rise like a Comet, to be wonder'd at?
A horrid Comet, for Boyes tongues, and Ballads?   40
I will run from my wits.
Arsenio.   Doe, doe, (good Lawyer)
And from thy money too, then thou wilt be quiet.

                      Enter Amaranta, Leandro.

Milanes.   Here she comes home: now mark the salutations;
How like an Asse my friend goes?
Arsenio.   She has pull'd his eares downe.

*35 brussels] *stet* F1–2

374

Bartolus.   Now, what sweet voyage? to what Garden, Lady?
    Or to what Cosens house?
Amaranta.   Is this my welcome?
    I cannot goe to Church, but thus I am scandall'd,
    Use no devotion for my soule, but Gentlemen——
Bartolus.   To Church?
Amaranta.   Yes, and ye keep sweet youths to wait upon me,   50
    Sweet bred-up youths, to be a credit to me.
    There's your delight againe, pray take him to ye,
    He never comes neare me more, to debase me.
Bartolus.   How's this? how's this? good wife, how has he wrongd ye?
Amaranta.   I was faine to drive him like a sheep before me,
    I blush to thinke how people fleer'd, and scorn'd me,
    Others have handsome men, that know behaviour,
    Place, and observance: this silly thing knowes nothing,
    Cannot tell ten; Let every Rascall justle me,
    And still I push'd him on, as he had bin comming.   60
Bartolus.   Ha! did ye push him on? is he so stupid?
Amaranta.   When others were attentive to the Priest,
    Good devout Gentleman, then fell he fast,
    Fast, sound asleepe: then first began the Bag-pipes,
    The severall stops on's nose, made a rare musick,
    A rare and lowd, and those plaid many an Antheme:
    Put out of that, he fell strait into dreaming.
Arsenio [aside].   As cunning, as she is sweet; I like this carriage.
Bartolus.   What did he then?
Amaranta.   Why then he talked in his Sleep too,——
    Nay, I'll divulge your morall vertues (sheeps-face)——   70
    And talk'd aloude, that every eare was fixt to him:
    Did not I suffer (doe you thinke) in this time?——
    Talk'd of your bawling Law, of appellations,
    Of Declarations, and Excommunications:
    Warrants, and Executions: and such divells
    That drove all the Gentlemen out o'th' Church, by hurryes,
    With execrable oaths, they would never come there again:
    Thus am I serv'd, and man'd.

---

56 fleer'd] F2; fleere F1   *60 comming] *stet* F1–2
73 Talk'd] Weber (Mason *conj.*); Talk F1–2   *76 by hurryes] *stet* F1–2

Leandro. I pray ye forgive me,
I must confesse I am not fit to wait upon ye:
Alas, I was brought up——
Amaranta. To be an Asse, 80
A Lawyers Asse, to carry Bookes, and Buckrams.
Bartolus. But what did you at Church?
Lopez. At Church, did ye aske her?——
Doe you heare gentlemen, doe you mark that question?——
Because you are halfe an heretique your selfe, Sir,
Would ye breed her too? this shall to the Inquisition,
A pious Gentlewoman, reprov'd for praying?
I'll see this filed, and you shall heare further, Sir.
Arsenio. Ye have an ill heart.
Lopez. It shall be found out Gentlemen,
There be those youths will search it.
Diego. You are warme Signiour,
But a Faggot will warme ye better: we are witnesses. 90
Lopez. Enough to hang him, doe not doubt.
Milanes. Nay certaine,
I doe beleeve has rather no Religion.
Lopez. That must be knowne too, because shee goes to Church, sir?
O monstrum informe, ingens!
Diego. Let him goe on, sir,
His wealth will build a Nunnery, a faire one,
And this good Lady, when he is hang'd, and rotten,
May there be Abbesse.
Bartolus. You are cozend, honest Gentlemen,
I doe not forbid the use, but the forme, marke me.
Lopez. Forme? what doe ye make of Forme?
Bartolus [aside]. They will undoe me,
Sweare, as I oft have done, and so betray me;
I must make faire way, and hereafter,——Wife, 100
You are welcome home, and henceforth take your pleasure,
Goe, when ye shall thinke fit, I will not hinder ye,
My eyes are open now, and I see my errour,——
My shame, as great as that, but I must hide it. [*Aside.*]
The whole conveyance now I smell, but *Basta,*
Another time must serve:——you see us friends, now

Heartily friends, and no more chiding (gentlemen)
I have bin too foolish, I confesse,——no more words,
No more (sweet wife.)
Amaranta.   You know my easie nature.   110
Bartolus.   Goe get ye in: [*Exit* Amaranta *into the house.*]
                    you see she has bin angry:
Forbeare her sight a while and time will pacify;
And learne to be more bold.
Leandro.   I would I could,
I will doe all I am able.
Bartolus.   Doe *Leandro*,
                         Exit [Leandro *into the house*].
We will not part, but friends of all hands.
Lopez.   Well said,
Now ye are reasonable, we can looke on ye.
Bartolus.   Ye have ierckt me: but for all that I forgive ye,
Forgive ye hartily, and doe invite ye
To morrow to a Breakfast: I make but seldome
But now we will be merry.
Arsenio.   Now ye are friendly,   120
Your doggednes and nigardize flung from ye
And now we will come to ye.
Bartolus.   Give me your hands, all;
You shall be wellcome hartily.
Lopez.   We will be,
For wee'll eate hard.
Bartolus.   The harder, the more wellcome,
And till the morning farewell; I have busines.
Milanes.   Farewell good bountiful *Bartolus*,
                         Exit [Bartolus *into house*].
                              'tis a brave wench,
A sudaine witty Theif, and worth all service:
Goe, wee'll all goe and crucifie the Lawyer.
Diego.   I'll clap foure tire of teeth into my mouth more
But I will grind his substance.
Arsenio.   Well *Leandro*,   130
Thou hast had a strange voyage, but I hope
Thou rid'st now in safe harbour.

Milanes.   Lets goe drinke, Friends,
  And laugh alou'd at all our merry may-games.
Lopez.   A match, a match, 'twill whet our stomachs better.

Exeunt.

Enter Violante and Servant. V.i

Servant.   Madam hees come.
Violante.   'Tis well, how did he looke,
  When he knew from whom you were sent? was he not startled?
  Or confident? or fearefull?
Servant.   As appear'd,
  Like one that knew his fortune at the worst,
  And car'd not what could follow.
Violante.   'Tis the better,
  Reach me a Chaire: So, bring him in, be carefull
  That none disturb us: [*Exit* Servant.]
                    I will try his temper,
  And if I find him apt for my employments,
  I'll worke him to my ends, if not I shall
  Find other Engines.

Enter Jamy, Servant.

Servant.   Ther's my Ladie.
Violante.   Leave us. [*Exit* Servant.] 10
Jamy.   You sent for me?
Violante.   I did, and do's the favour,
  Your present state considered, and my power,
  Deserve no greater Ceremonie?
Jamy.   Ceremonie?
  I use to pay that, where I doe owe dutie,
  Not to my Brothers wife: I cannot fawne,
  If you expect it from me, you are cozen'd,
  And so farewell.
Violante [*aside*].   He beares up still; I like it,——
  Pray you a word.
Jamy.   Yes? I will give you hearing

1 come.] come. Chaire and stooles out. F1—2

378

On equall termes, and sit by you as a friend,
But not stand as a Sutour: Now your pleasure?   20
Violante.   You are very bold.
Jamy.   'Tis fitt since you are proud:
I was not made to feed that foolish humour,
With flattery and observance.
Violante.   Yet, with your favour,
A little forme ioyn'd with respect to her,
That can add to your wants, or free you from 'em
(Nay raise you to a fate, beyond your hopes)
Might well become your wisedome.
Jamy.   It would rather
Write me a Foole, should I but onely think
That any good to me, could flow from you,
Whom for so many yeares I have found and prov'd   30
My greatest Enemy: I am still the same:
My wants have not transform'd me: I dare tell you,
To your new ceruz'd face, what I have spoken
Freely behind your back, what I thinke of you:
You are the proudest thing, and have the least
Reason to be so, that I ever read of:
In stature you are a Giantesse, and your Tailour
Takes measure of you, with a Jacobs staffe,
Or he can never reach you, this by the way
For your large size: Now, in a word or two,   40
To treat of your Complexion were decorum:
You are so far from faire, I doubt your Mother
Was too familliar with the Moore, that serv'd her:
Your Limbes and Features, I passe breifely over,
As things not worth description, and come roundly
To your soule, if you have any: for 'tis doubtfull.
Violante.   I laugh at this, proceed.
Jamy.   This Soule, I speake of,
Or rather salt to keepe this heape of flesh
From being a walking stench, like a large Inne,
Stands open for the entertainement of   50

26 hopes)] F2; hopes) *A Table ready covered with Cloath Napkins Salt Trenchers and Bread.* F1
33 ceruz'd] F2 (cerus'd); cerviz'd F1

All impious practises: but ther's no Corner
An honest thought can take up: and as it were not
Sufficient in your self to comprehend
All wicked plots, you have taught the Foole, my Brother,
By your contagion, almost to put off
The nature of the man, and turn'd him Devill
Because he should be like you, and I hope
Will march to hell together: I have spoken,
And if the limming you, in your true Colours
Can make the Painter gracious, I stand readie   60
For my reward, or if my words distaste you
I weigh it not, for though your Groomes were ready
To cut my throat for't, be assur'd I cannot
Use other Language.

Violante.   You thinke you have said now,
Like a brave fellow: in this Womans War
You ever have bin train'd: spoke big, but suffer'd
Like a tame Asse; and when most spur'd and gall'd
Were never Master of the Spleene or Spirit,
That could raise up the anger of a man,
And force it into action.

Jamy.   Yes vile Creature,   70
Wer't thou a subject worthy of my Sword,
Or that thy death, this moment, could call home,
My banish'd hopes, thou now wer't dead, dead (woman:)
But being as thou art, it is sufficient
I scorne thee, and contemne thee.

Violante.   This shewes nobly,
I must confesse it: I am taken with it
For had you kneeld, and whind and shew'd a base
And low dejected mind, I had despis'd you:
This Bravery (in your adverse fortune) conquers
And do's command me, and upon the sudaine   80
I feele a kind of pittie, growing in me,
For your misfortunes, pittie some sayes the Parent,
Of future love, and I repent my part,

82 sayes] *i.e.* say's, say is

So far in what you have suffered, that I could,
(But you are cold) doe something to repaire
What your base Brother (such *Jami* I thinke him)
Hath brought to ruine.

Jamy.   Ha?

Violante.   Be not amaz'd,
  Our injuries are equall in his Bastard:
  You are familliar with what I grone for
  And though the name of Husband holds a tye   90
  Beyond a Brother, I, a poore weake Woman,
  Am sensible, and tender of a wrong,
  And to revenge it, would break through all letts,
  That durst oppose me.

Jamy.   Is it possible?

Violante.   By this kisse:——start not: thus much, as a stranger
  You may take from me; But, if you were pleas'd,
  I should select you, as a bosome Friend,
  I would print 'em, thus, and thus,——   [*Kissing him.*]

Jamy.   Keepe off.

Violante.   Come neare,
  Neere, into the Cabinet of my Counsailes:
  Simplicity and patience dwell with Fooles,   100
  And let them beare those burthens, which wise men
  Boldly shake off; Be mine and joyne with me,
  And when that I have rais'd you to a fortune,
  (Doe not deny your selfe the happie meanes)
  You'l looke on me, with more judicious eies
  And sweare I am most faire.

Jamy [*aside*].   What would this Woman?——
  The purpose of these words? speake not in ridles
  And when I understand, what you would counsell,
  My answer shall be suddaine.

Violante.   Thus then *Jami*,
  The objects of our fury, are the same,   110
  For young *Ascanio*, whom you snake like hug'd
  (Frozen with wants to death) in your warme bosome,

Lives to supplant you, in your certaine hopes,
And kills in me all comfort.

Jamy.   Now 'tis plaine,
I apprehend you: and were he remov'd——

Violante.   You, once againe, were the undoubted heire.

Jamy.   'Tis not to be denyed; I was ice before,
But now ye have fir'd me,——

Violante.   I'l add fuell to it,
And by a nearer cut, doe you but steere
As I direct, you bring our Bark into   120
The Port of happines.

Jamy.   How?

Violante.   By *Henriques* death:
But you'l say hee's your Brother; in great fortunes
(Which are epitomes of States and Kingdomes)
The politicke brooke no Rivalls.

Jamy.   Excellent.
For sure I thinke out of a scrupulous feare,
To feed in expectation, when I may
(Dispensing but a little with my conscience)
Come into full possession, would not argue
One that desir'd to thrive.

Violante.   Now you speake like
A man that knowes the World.

Jamy.   I needs must learne   130
That have so good a Tutresse: And what thinke you,
(*Don Henrique* and *Ascanio* cut off)
That none may live, that shall desire to trace us
In our black pathes, if that *Octavio*
His foster Father, and the sad *Jacinta*,
(Faith, pittie her, and free her from her Sorrowes)
Should fall Companions with 'em? When we are red
With murther, let us often bath in blood,
The collour will be scarlet.

Violante.   And that's glorious,
And will protect the fact.

---

123 Kingdomes)] F2; Kingdomes) *Dishes covered with papers in each ready.* F1

382

Jamy.   Suppose this don: 140
  (If undiscovered,) we may get for money,
  (As that you know buyes any thing in *Rome*)
  A dispensation.
Violante.   And be married?
Jamy.   True.
  Or if it be knowne, trusse up our Gold and Jewells,
  And fly to some free State, and there with scorne———
Violante.   Laugh at the lawes of *Spaine*. 'Twere admirable.
Jamy.   We shall beget rare Children. I am rap'd with
  The meere imagination———
Violante.   Shall it be don?
Jamy.   Shall? tis too tedious: furnish me with meanes
  To hire the instruments, and to your self,   150
  Say it is done already: I will shew you,
  'Ere the Sun set, how much you have wrought upon me,
  Your province is onely to use some meanes,
  To send my Brother, to the Grove that's neighbour,
  To the west Port of th' Citie; leave the rest,
  To my owne practise; I have talk'd too long:
  But now will doe: this kisse, with my Confession,
  To worke a fell revenge a mans a foole,
  If not instructed in a Womans Schoole.

                                        Exeunt.

Enter Bartolus [*with disguiz'd*] *Algazeirs and a Paratour.*   [V.]ii

Bartolus.   You are well enough disguiz'd, furnish the Table,
  Make no shew what ye are, till I discover,
  Not a soule knowes ye here: be quick and dilligent,
  These youthes, I have invited to a Breakefast,
  But what the Sawce will be,———I am of opinion
  I shall take off the edges of their Appetites,
  And greaze their gums, for eating hartily
  This month or two; they have plaid their prizes with me
  And with their severall flurts they have lighted dangerously,
  But sure I shall be quit: I heare'em comming: 10

147 rap'd] *i.e.* rapt   0.1 *Paratour.*] Paratour. *The Table set out and stooles.* F1–2
7–8 hartily ∧ ... two;] F2 (two,); ~ ; ... ~ ∧ F1

Goe off, and wait the bringing in your service,
And doe it handsomely: you know where to have it:

[*Exeunt Algazeirs and Paratour.*]

Enter Millanes, Arsenio, Lopez, Diego.

Wellcome i'Faith.
Arsenio.   That's well said, honest Lawyer.
Lopez. Said like a Neighbour.
Bartolus.   Wellcome all: all over:
And let's be merry.
Millanes.   To that end we came Sir,
An hower of freedome's worth an age of juglings.
Diego. I am come too Sir, to specifie my Stomach
A poore reteyner to your worships bountie.
Bartolus. And thou shalt have it fill'd, my merry *Diego*,
My liberall, and my bonney bounteous *Diego*,   20
Even filld till it groane againe.
Diego.   Let it have faire play,
And if it founder then——
Bartolus.   I'll tell ye neighbours,
Though I were angry yesterday, with ye all,
And very angry, for me thought ye bobd me——
Lopez. No, no, by no meanes.
Bartolus.   No, when I considered
It was a jest, and carried off so quaintly
It made me merry: very merry, Gentlemen,
I doe confes I could not sleepe to thinke on't,
The mirth so tickled me, I could not slumber.
Lopez. Good mirth do's worke so, honest mirth: 30
Now, should we have meant in earnest——
Bartolus.   You say true Neighbour.
Lopez. It might have bred such a distast and sowrenesse,
Such fond imaginations in your Braines, Sir,
For things thrust home in earnest——
Bartolus.   Very certaine,
But I know ye all for merry waggs, and ere long

22 *Bartolus*] F2; *omit* F1

You shall know me too, in another fashion,
Though y'are pamper'd ye shall beare part 'oth burthen.

Enter Amaranta *and* Leandro.

Come Wife; Come bid 'em wellcome; Come my Jewell:——
And Pupill, you shall come too; nere hang backward,
Come, come, the womans pleas'd, her angers over,   40
Come, be not bashfull.
Amaranta [*aside*].   What do's he prepare here?
Sure ther's no meate 'ith house, at least none drest,
Do's he meane to mock 'em? or some new bred Crotchet
Come o're his braines? I doe not like his kindnes;
But silence best becomes me: if he meane foule play
Sure they are enough to right themselves and let 'em,
I'll sit by, so they beat him not to powder.
Bartolus.   Bring in the meate there, ha?——Sit downe deare
    Neighbour,
A little meate needs little Complement,
Sit downe I say.
Amaranta [*aside*].   What doe you meane by this Sir?   50
Bartolus [*aside*].   Convay away their weapons handsomely.
Amaranta [*aside*].   You know ther's none ith' house to answer ye,
But the poore Girle; you know ther's no meat neither.
Bartolus [*aside*].   Peace and be quiet; I shall make you smoak els,
Ther's men and Meate enough,——

    Enter [*Paratour and*] *Algaʒeirs with dishes.*

                              set it downe formally.
Amaranta [*aside*].   I fear some lew'd tricke, yet I dare not speake
    on't.
                                        Removes swords.
Bartolus.   I have no dainties for ye Gentlemen,
Nor lodes of meat, to make the roome smell of 'em,
Onely a dish to every man I have dedicated,
And if I have pleas'd his appetite,——
Lopeʒ.   O, a Capon,   60

---

*51 Convay ... handsomely] *stet* F1–2   56.1 *Removes swords.*] Weber; *omit* F1–2

A Bird of grace, and be thy will, I honour it.

Diego.   For me some fortie pound of lovely Beeffe,
Plac'd in a mediterranean sea of Brewisse.

Bartolus.   Fall to, fall to that we may drinke and laugh after——
Wait diligently knaves.

Millanes [*uncovers dish*].   What rare bits this?
An execution, blesse me!

Bartolus.   Nay take it to ye,
Ther's no avoiding it, 'tis somewhat tough Sir,
But a good stomach will endue it easely,
The sum is, but a thousand duckets Sir.

Arsenio [*uncovers*].   A Capias from my Surgeon, and my Silke man.   70

Bartolus.   Your carefull makers, but they have mard your diet——
Stir not, your Swords are gon: ther's no avoiding me
And these are Algazeirs,——doe you heare that passing bell?

Lopez [*uncovers*].   A strong Citation, blesse me!

Bartolus.   Out with your
Beads, Curat,
The devills in your dish: bell, booke, and Candell.

Diego [*uncovers*].   A warrant to appeare before the Judges?
I must needs rise, and turne to'th wall.

Bartolus.   Ye need not,
Your feare I hope will make ye find your Breeches.

All.   We are betraid!

Bartolus.   Invited, doe not wrong me,
Fall to, good Guests, you have dilligent men about ye,   80
Ye shall want nothing, that may persecute ye,
These will not see ye start; Have I now found ye?
Have I requited ye? You fool'd the Lawyer,
And thought it meritorious, to abuse him,
A thick ram headed knave: you rid, you spurd him,
And glorified your witts, the more ye wrongd him;
Within this hower, ye shall have all your Creditours,
A second dish of new debts, come upon ye,
And new invitements to the whip (*Don Diego*)

*68 endue] Dyce (Mason *conj.*); endure F1–2
*76 *Diego*] Dyce (Mason *conj.*); *Lop.* F1–2   *82 These ... start] stet F1–2
*89 *Don Diego*] stet F1–2

And Excommunications for the Learned Curat: 90
A Masque of all your furies shall dance to ye.

Arsenio.   You dare not use us thus?

Bartolus.   You shall be bobd (Gentlemen)
Stir, and as I have a life, ye goe to prison,
To prison, without pittie instantly,
Before ye speake another word to prison.
I have a better Guard, without, that waytes;——
Doe you see this man, *Don* Curat? 'tis a Paratour
That comes to tell ye a delightfull story
Of an old whore ye have, and then to teach ye
What is the penaltie; Laugh at me now Sir,   100
What Legacie would ye bequeath me now,
(And pay it on the naile) to fly my fury?

Lopez.   O gentle Sir,——

Bartolus.   Do'st thou hope I will be gentle,
Thou foolish unconsiderate Curat?

Lopez.   Let me goe Sir.

Bartolus.   I'll see thee hang first.

Lopez.   And as I am a true Vicar,
Hark in your eare, hark softly——

Bartolus.   No, no bribery.
I'll have my swindge upon thee;——Sirha? Rascall?
You lenten Chaps, you that lay sick, and mockt me,
Mockt me, abhominably, abused me lewdly;
I'll make thee sick at heart, before I leave thee,   110
And groane, and dye indeed, and be worth nothing,
Not worth a blessing, nor a Bell to knell for thee,
A sheete to cover thee, but that thou stealest,
Stealest from the Merchant, and the Ring he was buried with
Stealest from his Grave, doe you smell me now?

Diego.   Have mercy on me!

Bartolus.   No Psalme of mercy shall hold me from hanging
       thee:——
How do ye like your Breakfast? 'tis but short, Gentlemen,
But sweet and healthful;——Your punishment, and yours, Sir

*107 Sirha? Rascall?] *stet* F1–2

For some neare reasons, that concernes my Credit,
I will take to my self.

Amaranta.　　　　　Doe Sir, and spare not,　　　120
I have bin too good a wife, and too obedient,
But since ye dare provoke me to be foolish——

Leandro.　She has, yes, and too worthie of your usage:
Before the world, I justifie her goodnes,　　　[*Draws.*]
And turne that man, that dares but taint her vertues,
To my Swords point; that lying man, that base man,
Turne him, but face to face, that I may know him.

Bartolus.　What have I here?

Leandro.　　　　　A Gentleman, a free man,
One that made triall of this Ladies constancie,
And found it strong as fate; Leave off your fooling,　　　130
For if you follow this course, you will be Chronicled
For a devill, whilst a Saint she is mentioned;
You know my name indeed, I am now no Lawyer.

Enter Jamy *and* Assistant.

Diego [*aside*].　Some comfort now, I hope, or else would I were
　hanged up,
And yet the Judge, he makes me swet.

Bartolus.　　　　　　　What newes now?

Jamy.　I will justifie upon my life, and Credit,
What you have heard, for truth, and will make prooffe of.

Assistant.　I will be ready at the appointed hower there,
And so I leave ye.

Bartolus.　　　　Stay I beseech your worship,
And doe but heare me.

Jamy.　　　　　Good Sir, intend this busines,　　　140
And let this bawling Foole;——No more words Lawyer,
And no more angers, for I guesse your reasons,
This Gentleman, i'l justifie in all places,
And that faire Ladies worth, let who dare crosse it;
The Plot was cast by me, to make thee jealous
But not to wrong your wife, she is faire and vertuous.

*123 of] *stet* F1–2　134–135 *Diego.* Some ... And] F2; Some ... *Die.* And F1
*141 let ... Foole] *stet* F1–2

Diego.   Take us to mercy too, we beseech your honour,
  We shall be justified the way of all flesh els.
Jamy.   No more talke, nor no more dissention Lawyer,
  I know your anger, 'tis a vaine and slight one,   150
  For if you doe, i'll lay your whole life open,
  A life that all the world shall——i'll bring witnes,
  And rip before a Judge the ulcerous villanies,
  You know I know ye, and I can bring witnes.
Bartolus.   Nay good Sir, noble Sir.
Jamy.   Be at peace then presently,
  Immediately take honest and faire truce
  With your good Wife, and shake hands with that Gentleman,
  Has honour'd ye too much; And doe it cheerefully.
Lopeʒ.   Take us along, for heaven sake too.
Bartolus.   I am Friends,——
  There is no remedie, I must put up all,   [*Aside.*] 160
  And like my neighbours rub it out by'th shoulders,——
  And perfect friends;——*Leandro* now I thanke ye,
  And ther's my hand, I have no more grudge to ye,
  But I am too meane henceforward for your Companie.
Leandro.   I shall not trouble ye.
Arsenio.   We will be friends too.
Millanes.   Nay Lawyer, you shall not fright us farther,
  For all your devills wee will bolt.
Bartolus.   I grant ye.
  The Gentlemans your Baile, and thank his comming,
  Did not he know me too well, you should smart for't;
  Goe all in peace, but when ye Foole next, Gentlemen,   170
  Come not to me to Breakefast.
Diego.   I'l be bak'd first.
Bartolus.   And pray ye remember, when ye are bold and merry,
  The Lawyers Bancket, and the Sawce he gave ye.
Jamy.   Come: goe along; I have employment for ye,——
  Employment for your lewd braynes too, to cool ye,——
  For all, for every one.
All.   We are all your Servants.

      *152–153 shall——... villanies,] F2; ~ ʌ ... ~ ʌ F1
      *160–161 There ... shoulders] *stet* F1–2

Diego.   All, all for any thing: from this day forward,
  I'l hate all Breakefasts, and depend on dinners.
Jamy [*aside to* Leandro].   I am glad you come off faire.
Leandro [*aside*].   The faire has blest me.
                                        Exeunt.

          Enter Octavio, Jacinta, Ascanio.   [V.]

Octavio.   This is the place, but why we are appointed
  By *Don Jami* to stay here, is a depth
  I cannot sound.
Ascanio.   Beleev't he is too noble,
  To purpose any thing, but for our good:
  Had I assurance of a thousand Lives,
  And with them perpetuitie of pleasure,
  And should loose all, if he prov'd only false,
  Yet I durst run the hazard.
Jacinta.   'Tis our comfort,
  We cannot be more wretched then we are,
  And death concludes all misery.
Octavio.   Undiscovered   10
  We must attend him.

              Enter Henrique, Jami.

Ascanio.   Our stay is not long:
  With him *Don Henrique?*
Jacinta.   Now I feare; be silent.   [*They retire.*]
Henrique.   Why do'st thou follow me?
Jami.   To save your life,
  A plot is laid for't, all my wrongs forgot,
  I have a Brothers Love.
Henrique.   But thy false self,
  I feare no enemy.
Jami.   You have no Friend,
  But what breathes in me: If you move a step
  Beyond this ground you tread on, you are lost.
Henrique.   'Tis by thy practise then: I am sent hither
  To meete her, that prefers my life, and safetie   20
  Before her owne.

                    390

Jami.   That you should be abus'd thus
  With weake credulitie: She for whose sake,
  You have forgot we had one noble Father,
  Or that one Mother bare us, for whose love,
  You breake a contract, to which heaven was witnes,
  To satisfie whose pride, and willfull humour,
  You have expos'd a sweet, and hopefull Son,
  To all the miseries, that want can bring him,
  And such a Son, though you are most obdurate,
  To give whom entertainement Savages   30
  Would quit their Caves themselves, to keepe him from
  Bleake cold, and hunger: This dissembling Woman,
  This Idoll, whom you worship, all your love
  And service trod under her feete, designes you
  To fill a grave, or dead, to lye a pray,
  For Wolves, and vultures.
Henrique.   'Tis false; I defie thee,
  And stand upon my Guard.   [*Draws.*]
Jami.   Alas, 'tis weake:
  Come on,

  Enter [disguised] Leandro, Millanes, Arsenio, Bartolus, Lopez,
      Diego, and Servants [and seiʒe Don Henrique].

              since you will teach me to be cruell,
  By having no faith, in me, take your fortune,——
  Bring the rest forth, and bind them fast.
                    [*They seiʒe*] Octavio, Jacinta [*and*] Ascanio.
Octavio.   My Lord.   40
Ascanio.   In what have we offended?
Jami.   I am deafe,
  And following my will, I doe not stand
  Accomptable to reason:——See her Ring
  (The first pledge of your love, and service to her)
  Deliverd as a Warrant for your death:
  These Bags of gold you gave up to her trust,
  (The use of which, you did deny your selfe)

  40 Octavio, Jacinta Ascanio] *following* Diego, *in the stage-direction at line* 38 F1–2

Bestow'd on me, and with a prodigall hand,
Whom she pick'd forth to be the Architect
Of her most bloudy building; and to Fee   50
These Instruments, to bring Materials
To raise it up, she bad me spare no cost,
And (as a surplusage) offer'd her selfe
To be at my devotion.
Henrique.   O accurss'd!
Jami.   But be incredulous still; think this my plot;
Fashion excuses to your selfe, and sweare
That she is innocent, that she doats on ye;
Believe this, as a fearefull Dreame, and that
You lie not at my mercy, which in this
I will shew onely: She her selfe shall give   60
The dreadfull Sentence, to remove all scruple
Who 'tis that sends you to the other world.

Enter Violante.

Appeares my *Violante*? speake (my dearest)
Do's not the object please you?
Violante.   More then if
All Treasure that's above the earth, with that,
That lyes conceal'd in both the Indian Mines,
Were laid downe at my feet: O bold *Jamy*
Thou onely canst deserve me.
Jami.   I am forward,
And (as you easily may perceive,) I sleepe not
On your commands.

Enter Assistant *and Officers* [*unobserved*].

Violante.   But yet they live: I look'd   70
To find them dead.
Jami.   That was defer'd, that you
Might triumph in their misery, and have the powre
To say they are not.
Violante.   'Twas well thought upon:
This kisse, and all the pleasures of my Bed
This night, shall thanke thee.

392

Henrique.   Monster!
Violante.   You Sir, that
  Would have me mother Bastards, being unable
  To honour me with one Child of mine owne,
  That underneath my Roofe, kept your cast-Strumpet,
  And out of my Revenues, would maintaine
  Her riotous issue: Now you find what 'tis   80
  To tempt a woman: with as little feeling
  As I turne off a slave, that is unfit
  To doe me service; or a horse, or dog
  That have out-liv'd their use, I shake thee off,
  To make thy peace with heaven.
Henrique.   I doe deserve this,
  And never truly felt before, what sorrow
  Attends on wilfull dotage.
Violante.   For you, Mistris,
  That had the pleasure of his youth, before me,
  And triumph'd in the fruit, that you had by him,
  But that I thinke, to have the Bastard strangled   90
  Before thy face, and thou with speed to follow
  The way he leades thee, is sufficient torture,
  I would cut off thy nose, put out thine eyes,
  And set my foot on these bewitching lips,
  That had the start of mine: but as thou art,
  Goe to the grave unpittied.
Assistant [*aside*].   Who would beleeve
  Such rage could be in woman?
Violante.   For this Fellow, [*Turns to* Octavio.]
  He is not worth my knowledge.
Jami.   Let him live then,
  Since you esteeme him innocent.
Violante.   No, *Jamy*,
  He shall make up the messe: now strike together   100
  And let them fall so.
Assistant.   Unheard of crueltie!
  I can endure no longer:——seize on her.
                              [*Officers seize* Violante.]
Violante.   Am I betrai'd?

393

Is this thy faith, *Jamy?*

Jami.   Could your desires
Challenge performance of a deed so horrid?
Or, though that you had sold your selfe to hell,
I should make up the bargaine?——Live (deare Brother)
Live long, and happy: I forgive you freely;
To have done you this service, is to me
A faire Inheritance: And how e're harsh language   110
(Call'd on, by your rough usage) pass'd my lipps,
In my heart, I ever lov'd you: All my labours,
Were but to shew, how much your love was cozen'd,
When it beheld it selfe in this false Glasse,
That did abuse you; and I am so far
From envying young *Ascanio* his good fortune,
That if your State were mine, I would adopt him.
These are the Murtherers, my noble Friends,
Which (to make triall of her bloudy purpose)
I won, to come disguis'd thus.

Henrique.   I am too full   120
Of griefe, and shame to speake: but what I'le doe,
Shall to the world proclaime my penitence;
And howsoever I have liv'd, I'le die
A much chang'd man.

Jami.   Were it but possible
You could make satisfaction to this woman,
Our joyes were perfect.

Henrique.   That's my onely comfort,
That it is in my power: I ne're was married
To this bad woman, though I doted on her,
But daily did deferre it, still expecting
When griefe would kill *Jacinta.*

Assistant.   All is come out,   130
And finds a faire successe: take her *Don Henrique,*
And once againe embrace your Son.

Henrique.   Most gladly.

Assistant.   Your Brother hath deserv'd well.

Henrique.   And shall share
The moitie of my State.

Assistant.   I have heard, Advocate,
  What an ill Instrument you have bin to him,
  From this time strengthen him, with honest counsells,
  As you'le deserve my pardon.
Bartolus.   I'le change my Copy:——
  But I am punish'd, for I feare I have had   [*Aside.*]
  A smart blow, though unseene.
Assistant.   Curat, and Sexton,
  I have heard of you too, let me heare no more,   140
  And what's past, is forgotten; For this woman,
  Though her intent were bloody, yet our Law
  Calls it not death: yet that her punishment
  May deter others from such bad attempts,
  The Dowry she brought with her, shall be emploi'd
  To build a Nunnery, where she shall spend
  The remnant of her life.
Violante.   Since I have miss'd my ends,
  I scorne what can fall on me.
Assistant.   The strict discipline
  Of the Church, will teach you better thoughts.——And Signiors,
  You that are Batchelours, if you every marry,   150
  In *Bartolus*, you may behold the issue
  Of Covetousnesse, and Jealousie; And of dotage,
  And falshood in *Don Henrique*; keep a meane then,
    For be assur'd that weake man meets all ill,
    That gives himselfe up to a womans will.

                                        Exeunt.

                    Epilogue.

The Play is done, yet our Suit never ends,
Still when you part, you would still part our friends,
Our noblest friends; if ought have falne amis,
O let it be sufficient, that it is,
And you have pardon'd it. In Buildings great
All the whole Body, cannot be so neat,
But something may be mended; Those are faire,
And worthy love, that may destroy, but spare.

TEXTUAL NOTES

I.i

0.1 Angelo ∧] At II.iii.1, where F1 reads '*Angelo, Millanes*, did you see ths wonder?', Theobald omits '*Angelo*', Seward having noted that '*Angelo* makes his Appearance in [I.i], but he speaks but four Lines there [102–3 and 129–30 'This . . . charitable]; and nothing but what *Arsenio* might full well have said: And he has nothing to do here, but to spoil the Verse'. Theobald adds, 'As *Angelo* is no where else spoke of, or to . . .; as he is no manner of a Character, nor any ways conducive to carrying on the Plot . . . I have ventured to expunge him quite out of the Drama.' (He forgot, however, to expunge the *Ang.* speech-prefixes at I.i.102 and 129.) Colman and Weber put Angelo back, but McKerrow sealed his doom by pointing out that 'the names . . . are almost all taken from *Gerardo*. In this there is an Angelo Milanes but no separate Angelo'. Dyce also was aware of this fact, but he thought Fletcher (to whom he attributed the entire play) had made two gentlemen of *Gerardo's* one. His note on II.iii.0.1, however, raises the possibility that the two names 'designate a single person'.

134 my . . . Royall] *I.e.* my allowance (*O.E.D.*, Exhibition 2) up to the last Royal (ryal, real, or piece of eight; see Sandra K. Fischer, *Econolingua* (Newark, 1985), *s.v.* Royal). Editions from 1711 through Weber choose *ryal* here and at I.iii.36 and II.i.5.

166 acquaintance'.] The apostrophe in F1, which omits the full stop, may be only another of the many instances of erroneous terminal punctuation in that edition, or it may be Crane's or Compositor *A*'s indication of a supposedly missing final -*s*.

305 off, we'll . . . wit;] Although *O.E.D.* does not exactly support 'succeed' as a meaning of *come off* unmodified, McKerrow's emendation seems superior to F2's because it is nearer F1. Milanes may mean 'get away with it', a casual use of *O.E.D.* Come, *v.* 61f, 'to retire or extricate oneself from any engagement'.

I.ii

72 me] Because 'holy Saints keepe me' seems incomplete and because line 73 is several feet short, Seward begins the line with 'From such Impiety!' He does so, he says, 'without Danger of adding what is not our Author's'. He is probably right that something was omitted. See V.ii.141 and 152–3.

II.i

0.1 Leandro (*with a letter writ out*)] Regarding the parenthesis, Theobald noted: 'This is a Stage-Direction, transcrib'd from the *Prompter*'s Book; and a Memorandum to him only, that *Leandro* should go on furnish'd with such a Letter, to deliver to *Lopez* the Curate.' He is probably wrong. Three similar notations, all in Fletcher's scenes, specify properties:

III.iv.27   *with Chesse-board*
IV.iii.0.1   *(with a note)*
IV.v.41   *(in a Bed)*

If the words here are the prompter's, the others should be too, yet the last is followed at line 42 by '*Bed thrust out.*', quite evidently a prompt annotation. Unless one believes the prompter repeated himself, it appears that '*(in a Bed)*' is Fletcher's and hence that the memorandum of Leandro's letter is too.

25 time]   Theobald's emendation was rejected by later editors as unnecessary, although chattering teeth quite obviously keep time with a frosty fiddle, not tune. Theobald reasonably attributed F1's *tune* to minim misreading.

36 an Homily]   The two 7mm dashes found in F1 may represent one long dash standing for a single word, which must have been present in the prompt-book that was the printer's copy. It was evidently left out because the printer wished to avoid giving offence or could not read it. Theobald's *homily* is a good guess; it is consistent with the surviving 'an', it fits the metre, and its meaning is appropriate.

49–50 *Leandro.* A . . . me. | You . . . ready. *Exit.*]   From line 48 F1 carries down to the end of line 49 'nance?', to which it adds '*exit lea.*', mistakenly making line 49's speech-prefix a part of the stage-direction. See note II.i.174–5.

53 pigbelly]   This word has been neither questioned nor explained. *O.E.D.* (Pig, *sb.*1 12) cites this instance to illustrate a combined form of *pig*, but provides no other examples. A pigbelly at least is not a full one; not only is the pig as a type of gluttony a recent invention but Lopez's complaint is that he is starving. Instead, *belly* may signify 'the appetite for food' (Belly, *sb.* 5b), pork in this instance.

92 more]   Although F1's *most* has never been questioned, the comparative seems more natural. *Most* may have been influenced by *must* in line 91 and later in 92.

105 a]   *Dunce* might be the proper name *Duns*, but that seems unlikely in view of the word's use in its ordinary sense in line 57. Lopez means that he has become a dullard because he cannot exercise his learning in funeral sermons; as Diego has forgot to dig, he has forgot to preach. Although metre is more regular without the *a*, the churchmen speak rather loose pentameters elsewhere in this scene.

142 I consider. | *Leandro.* Thinke]   Sympson (in Theobald) reads 'I——| *Leandro.* Consider, think', causing *consider* to anticipate 'Thinke againe' and to conform with standard usage (*O.E.D.*, *v.* 5). Lopez, however, is probably using the word loosely to mean 'think' or 'know'.

174–175 he,——| *Lopez.* Good . . . Pray]   F2 assumes a garble in F1 similar to that at II.i.49–50 where a speech-prefix was made part of a stage-direction. Here F2 takes it that a speech-prefix is misplaced by two lines and that Lopez, agitated, repeats himself ('let me think' and 'let me remember' and 'pray ye be patient' and 'pray ye stay'). Another possibility, however, is that F1 preserves two versions of the speech ('good sir . . . patient' and 'Pray . . . Sir'), one of which, probably the first, should be cancelled. Yet another is that Diego's speech-prefix is the one misplaced and that he should say 'Pray ye . . . sure, Sir'.

II.ii

76 five]   Dyce emends to 'three', the sum mentioned at II.i.230 and II.ii.92. But McKerrow notes, 'Lopez seems, however, to be referring to the money already given him by Leandro, which was apparently five hundred ducats (II.i.173). He means, I think, "You need not be suspicious, for these five hundred ducats which I have just received from Leandro show him to be a person of substance." The three hundred which was intended for Bartolus was apparently an additional sum kept by Leandro in his own possession and afterwards handed over by him to the lawyer directly (cf. line 119 below).'

100 prove]   As McKerrow recognized, this word means 'turn out well' (*O.E.D.* 10). The sentence is not incomplete.

II.iii

4 *Jamy*.]   Although in III.ii it is Arsenio who forces Lopez and Diego to become instruments in the discomfiture of Bartolus, his usual role is to supply information, to ask questions about the immediate action or comment briefly on it, or to feed lines to the major characters. If F1's assignment is correct, this speech is his longest in the play. Thus Seward was probably right to give this line and those following to Jamy, who has special reason to despise Bartolus (lines 9–11).

III.i

23 Snakes]   Theobald recognizes that the 'bold Metaphor may mean poor servile Wretches that creep like *Snakes* [*O.E.D.*, *sb.* 3]'.

III.ii

58 Sir.)]   Although editors since Colman have so punctuated it, this speech does not seem to be broken off since it is unclear how it would be completed. Evidently the Third Parishioner means that his drink will be as mighty as the Second Parishioner's prayers are hearty.

59–60 *3 Par.* The ... me, | And]   If Lopez speaks 'The ... me', *come unto* would mean 'approach me (to serve me mighty drink)'. If the Third Parishioner (who runs a tavern?) speaks the line, the motive becomes stronger: Lopez downs more and more of the mighty drink while edifying the daughter.

69 duties]   *Dues* 'is the proper and customary Word on the Occasion' (Sympson). Later editors do not agree, Dyce comparing 'use our Offices' (line 39). *Duties* actually was proper on the occasion, though it was superseded by *dues* (*O.E.D.*, Duty, 3a).

78 And ... up]   Although McKerrow was suspicious of this line, it makes satisfactory sense: 'And let your old men die immediately [so that] their sons may flourish'. The allusion is to old vegetation dying back and giving light and space to new, with the idea that the sooner the sons ripen the sooner they rot.

85 abed]　James P. Hammersmith argues that 'to bed', the reading of F1(c), is a
proof-reader's modernization, *abed* being obsolete by 1646 ('The proof-reading of
the Beaumont and Fletcher Folio of 1647: Section 1 and b', *Publications of the
Bibliographical Society of America* LXXXII (1988), p. 207). *To bring abed* (or *to bed*)
is to be delivered of a child.

III.iii

12 lesse hope]　McKerrow believes these words may mean 'without hope' or
'hopeless'. If so, the usage is exceptional, but neither an alternative meaning nor an
emendation suggests itself.

29 proaguing]　*O.E.D.* gives *proague* as a form of *Prog v.*1 or of *Proke*, the former
meaning to forage or beg and the latter, figuratively, to incite, which would be
appropriate here. F2's *proguing* is also a form of *Prog*. If emendation were
necessary, *proroguing*, protracting or delaying, might be a possibility.

45 anon,——]　Dyce and McKerrow begin the aside after 'language', the latter
remarking that he is uncertain an aside is intended. Bartolus would never openly
threaten Don Jamy, however.

60 This]　F1's ''Tis', not an impossible reading, is nevertheless suspect because it
may be an erroneous repetition of ''tis' in line 59.

64 Humh, humh]　For this representation of 'an inarticulate sound', here of throat-
clearing, *O.E.D.* cites Dekker's *Wonderfull Yeare* (1603). Misreading of *m* as *nc*
evidently caused the 'hunch, hunch' of F1(u).

152 thy]　Since much of her speech emphasizes Jacinta's suffering resulting from
Don Henrique's seduction and abandonment of her and his callous public exposure
of her as a fallen woman, 1711's *my* is attractive: *my* son will be *thy* heir, a new legal
bond compensating for the violation of his contract to marry her. On the other
hand, her final emphasis is on Ascanio's status; illegitimate though he may be, he is
thy son, hence *thy* legitimate heir.

213 rakes]　Hammersmith (p. 207) argues that 'rakes' is probably right because of the
imagery of husbandry, 'takes' being a proof-reader's sophistication. Mason (p. 68)
discovered the same reading by recalling I.i.207.

III.iv

113 Or I]　Editors from Theobald on add *you*, but the line's metre is against the
change. Evidently 'shall beat ye' is to be understood with the reference of the
pronoun changed.

118 akes, yet ∧ ... fear.]　Leandro means 'my heart aches, but that is preferable to the
husband's universal fear – the headache caused by the cuckold's horns'.

122 head.]　F1 reads

<blockquote>
(good Lady,
But your Ches-board is too hard for my head, line that
</blockquote>

All editors treat 'But ... Lady' as a single line; however, none comments but

McKerrow, who says he cannot explain the expression. He adds, 'Can it be that the words "line that" are merely a proof-reader's correction requiring *good Lady* to be put into the line below, where there would be room for it?' The answer is no: first, there is no room in the line below; second, 'good Lady' added to line 122 would make it hypermetrical; and, third, 'line that' as a proof-reader's direction is unparalleled. J. Le Gay Brereton recommends *it* for 'that' because 'the confusion of these two words is not uncommon'. Leandro would then bid 'the lady line her chess-board – i.e., cover its under surface with cloth, and so make it a somewhat less formidable weapon' (*Elizabethan Drama: Notes and Studies* (Sydney, 1909), p. 153). The idea, of course, has nothing to recommend it. Perhaps the words are some incomplete dialogue that survived Crane's transcription, or perhaps they are indeed a misplaced proof-correction, for although no variants have been found on this Folio page (F4) or its forme-mate (F1v) other formes in this gathering were corrected (see p. 405–7). Where the hypothetical proof-correction should go is not evident, however. Since as they stand the words mean nothing, it seems best to omit them.

IV.i

97 Deserve] McKerrow notes, 'If the old reading is correct, *deserve* must mean "obtain by desert."' Philip Edwards and Colin Gibson find the word used in a similar sense in Massinger's unaided plays. Their gloss is 'deserve of me (?)' (*The Plays and Poems of Philip Massinger* (Oxford, 1976), V, 293).

IV.ii

15 *Arsenio. All*] This speech begins sig. G1, but the F4v catchword is 'Have', the discrepancy possibly implying that 'some text may have been lost between the two pages' (Hammersmith, p. 210). The last speech on F4v terminates in a full stop, however, rarely used in this text for internal punctuation.

IV.iv

52 give me] 'Consider me' (*O.E.D.*, Give, *v.* 31b); the idiom, without preposition, also appears in *The Humorous Lieutenant*, II.ii.15. It seems to have been outmoded by the late seventeenth century. F2 introduces *for*, which all editors adopted until Dyce recognized that F1 is correct.

IV.v

53 not, ... ye,] A heavier stop after 'not' causes Diego to utter two clauses of about the same meaning as he does in lines 54–5; a heavier stop after 'ye' causes him to say, 'Weep not *that* I must leave ye' (Dyce, who points out the understood *that* in line 57). In the similar situation at lines 33–4, one meaning is preferable to the other. Here, however, there is nothing to choose.

93 budge]　Citing this instance only, *O.E.D.* identifies this word as a variant of *bouge*, 'to bilge', meaning 'to stave in a ship's bottom or sides, cause her to spring a leak'. 'Nor ... not' (line 92) appears to be an emphatic double negative, so that Diego says, 'Don't tell yearning women to abstain; doing so will swamp their consciences', the joke turning on *conscience* = pudendum (see Eric Partridge, *Shakespeare's Bawdy* (New York, 1969)). The salacious overtone continued in 'Organs' (line 94) becomes explicit in the misspelling of *Sunt* (line 98).

97 many;]　Dyce: '"As many" means——as many *ducats*.'

150 boared]　Made a fool of (Mason, p. 70; *O.E.D.*, Bore, *v.* 1 6). In Colman's edition the word is modernized as *boor'd*, 'degraded' or 'disgraced', presumably.

178 Rogue,——| *Arsenio*. Some craftie Foole]　Because 'it cannot be supposed that *Arsenio* would call *Leandro* a Fool', Seward changes to 'Rogue. | *Ars.* Some Craftsman, Fool, ...', a reading that at least calls attention to the crux. Weber's 'rogue—— | *Ars.* Some crafty [*i.e.* crafty rogue], fool, ...' is hardly better. Mitford suggested to Dyce 'rogue, some crafty—— | *Ars.* Fool, ...', which may be right. Yet F seems preferable, for Arsenio could mean 'someone you regarded as a fool who is actually crafty has got the better of you'.

183 God ... God]　'God yield [reward] ye' is 'a common expression of gratitude or goodwill' (*O.E.D.*, Yield, *v.* 7). Because Biblical thanks run the other way, 'God thank ye' seems odd, though the Rev. Alexander Dyce did not find it so. The expression may be an inversion, 'ye thank God [for rewarding you]', if it is not a restatement, *thank* signifying 'show favour toward' rather than 'express gratitude to'. The word *God* appears at III.iv.54 (also by Fletcher), yet it may be that here the scribe or the compositor added apostrophes to compromise between *God* and *good*.

IV.vii

35 brussels]　A form of *brustle*, a word 'used of the noise of waves' (*O.E.D.*, Brustle, *v.*1 1b).

60 comming]　Bartolus would understand 'I pushed him on because he had been coming after, lagging behind, me'; Amaranta's private meaning is 'I encouraged him as he had been engagingly amorous'. Although this scene is Fletcher's, the word in the latter sense may be found in *The Plays and Poems of Philip Massinger*, ed. Philip Edwards and Colin Gibson (Oxford, 1976), v, 287. Also applicable is the strictly sexual sense, for which see James T. Henke, *Courtesans and Cuckolds* (New York, 1979). The suggestiveness of 'push him on' is comically emphasized by Bartolus' repetition of the words.

76 by hurryes]　Although this expression has never been questioned, it is not recognized by the *O.E.D.*, which does, however, cite 'What thousand noyses passe through all the roomes, What cryes and hurries' (*The Night Walker*, II.iii.1–2) as an instance of *hurry* in the sense of 'commotion or agitation'. McKerrow glosses *By hurryes* as 'in a hurry', but it may mean 'in confused crowds' (*O.E.D.* 1b].

V.i

99 Neere] Although followed by subsequent editors, Theobald's change to 'Nearer' is unnecessary. Seated side-by-side at line 20, Violante and Jamy have risen at some point; they are surely standing when Jamy pushes the osculating Violante away at line 98. When he does not fully respond to her 'Come neare', she emphatically repeats 'Neere', adding 'into the Cabinet ....'

V.ii

51 Convay ... handsomely] At line 51 Bartolus orders that the swords be taken away, and at line 72 the 'Swords are gon'. They are evidently removed at about this point, although Amaranta's response does not indicate that Bartolus is speaking to her here. She is nevertheless available, as Weber recognizes. He places the stage-direction after 'enough', line 55.

68 endue] As Mason indicates, *endure* for *endue* (a hawking term meaning 'to digest') is also found in *Love's Pilgrimage*, II.ii.150–1, Fletcher's scene: 'Chees that would break the teeth of a new handsaw, I could endure [endue] now like an Eastrich.' McKerrow objects that *endure* makes perfect sense here in *The Spanish Curate*, but had it not made sense, it would not have been substituted for the rarer word. He adds, 'Probably there was a confusion between the words', but *O.E.D.* does not bear this assertion out.

76 *Diego.*] Mason: 'This speech ... evidently belongs to Diego. Lopez had had his dish before, in a strong citation. If this speech also belongs to Lopez [as in F1–2], Diego, the principal offender, escapes unpunished.' A citation is 'a summons; "applied particularly to process in the spiritual court" (Tomlins *Law Dict.*)' (*O.E.D.* 1) and thus appropriate to Lopez, although the *O.E.D.* gives this passage as its only instance of *citation* as 'summons' in a general sense (1c).

82 These ... start] McKerrow: 'I.e. will not let ye run away'.

89 *Don Diego*] Diego is elevated in rank because Bartolus identifies him with the well-known Spaniard who committed a nuisance in Paul's. See *Love's Cure* III.i.2 and *The Captain*, III.iii.135.

107 Sirha? Rascall?] Dyce and McKerrow punctuate to indicate that Bartolus, rejecting Lopez's offer of a bribe with 'I'll have my swindge upon thee', then turns to Diego with the compound epithet 'Sirha rascall'. Because 'You lenten Chaps' must be applied to both, however, both are probably being addressed here, as F1 has it——'Sirha' insultingly to the curate and 'Rascall' to his sexton, both being lean and lenten. 'You that lay sick' goes to Diego, of course.

123 of] Emended by Seward and later editors to *for*, *of* here may be used in connection with 'any influencing circumstance, in the sense of "as regards"' (E. A. Abbott, *A Shakespearian Grammar* (London, 1870), §173).

141 let ... Foole] The clause may be incomplete or defective, for the meaning of *let* is uncertain if it is not. Jamy tells the Assistant to attend to the business they have been discussing (his dispensing justice at the end) and, perhaps, to ignore Bartolus. The closest definition to *let* in this sense, however, is 'quit, abandon, forsake'

(*O.E.D.*, *v.*1 5). Cf. lines 152–3 for another apparently pointless suspension and I.ii.72 for an apparent omission.

152–153 shall———... villanies,]   Something seems to have been omitted from F1 because there is no reason for Don Jamy to become inarticulate. Cf. line 141 and I.ii.72.

160–161 There ... shoulders]   Bartolus probably says, 'There is no help for it. I must endure this ("put up all"), and, like my neighbours (other citizens cuckolded by gentlemen), shrug it off ("rub ... shoulders")'.

PRESS VARIANTS IN F1 (1647)

[Copies collated: Bodl (Bodleian Library B.1.8.Art.), Camb¹ (University Library, Cambridge, Acton a.Sel.19), Camb² (SSS.10.8), Hoy (private copy of Dr Cyrus Hoy), ICN (Newberry Library), IU¹ (University of Illinois 822/B38/1647), IU² (q822/B38/1647 copy 2), MB (Boston Public Library G.3960.27), MnU (University of Minnesota Z823B38/fOCa), NcD (Duke University Accession 429544), NIC (Cornell University A951587), NjP (Princeton University Ex 3623.1/1647q copy 2), PSt (Pennsylvania State University PR 2420/1647/Q), ViU¹ (University of Virginia 570973), ViU² (University of Virginia 217972), WaU (University of Washington Accession 29424), WMU¹ (University of Wisconsin–Milwaukee PR2420/1647 copy 1), WMU² (copy 2), WMU³ (copy 3), WMU⁴ (copy 4), WU (University of Wisconsin–Madison 1543420).]

SHEET 1E ii (*inner forme*)

Sig. 1E2v
Uncorrected: Camb¹, IU², MnU, NIC, NjP, ViU², WMU³
  I.i.295 Envie] envie
     305 off well;] off; well
  I.ii.1 bring] brings
     21 debt] debt,
     37 that;] that
     40 *Afcanio.*] *Afcanio-*
     48 cam'ft] camft
     56 neceffities;] neceffities
     61 aiereall] aereall
     69 litle,] litle
  I.iii.0.1 *Henrique*] Henricque
     1 *Henrique*] Henrique
Sig. 1E3
Uncorrected: NIC, ViU², WMU³
First-stage corrected: MnU, IU²
  pg. no. 29] 27
Second-stage corrected: Camb¹, NjP
  I.iii.29 Stock,] Stock
     32 Brothers] Brothers.
     42 this] (*deformed* h)
  II.i.0.1 *Afermo*] *Arfemo*
     8 out-fide feems] out-fide feems
     9 wonders] wonders (*raised* r)

404

32 *Lean.*] *Leau.*
43 I] (*deformed*)
44 Leave] (*turned* a)
49 and fo forfake] andfoforfake
Third-stage corrected: Bodl, Camb², Hoy, ICN, IU¹, MB, NcD, PSt, ViU¹, WaU,
WMU¹, WMU², WMU⁴, WU
   I.iii.8 Bleffings] Beffings
     11 poffeffe] poffeffes
     12 Il*en.*] H*er.*
     23 Calamity] (*top only of* l *prints*)
     23 *Vi ol.*] *Viol.*
[Note: The '*I*' of '*Iac.* What' (I.ii.1) is absent or does not print in all uncorrected
copies but IU².]

SHEET 1F i (outer forme)

Sig. 1F1
Uncorrected: Camb², Hoy, ICN, PSt, ViU¹, ViU², WaU, WMU¹, WMU³, WMU⁴,
WU
   II.ii.140 living] living,
     152 dub] dnb
   iii.11 him] bim
     17 loth] both
     23 fpew] fpëw
   II.iv.24 he] ye
Sig. 1F4v
Uncorrected: Bodl, ICN, WaU, WMU⁴
First-stage corrected: Camb², Hoy, PSt, ViU¹, ViU², WMU¹, WMU³, WU
   IV.i.79 and before] foud bere
     83 Am] And
     92 So] So (*space type prints*)
Second-stage corrected: Camb¹, IU¹, IU², MB, MnU, NcD, NIC, NjP, WMU²
   IV.i.52 me,] me:
     55 me,] me
     107 *ready,*] *ready*
     111 acquaintance] acquaintaince
     119 Leaper] Leper
     126 Afpick's,] Afpick's
   IV.ii.12 he] ye

SHEET 1F ii (outer forme)

Uncorrected: NIC, ViU², WMU¹, WMU³
Sig. 1F2
   III.ii.85 *Lo.* Let ... to bed] *Lop.* Let ... abed
     94 moneths——] moneths,

129 Prieſt] Prieſt,
129 it?] it.
144 be] he
146 Companions——] Companions
153 *Mil.*] *Mil.*
164 ſir——] ſir.
cw The (*raised* e)] The

Sig. 1F3v

   III.iii.211 'Pray] 'pray
      213 takes] rakes
      225 i!l. *Exeunt*] i!l——*Exeunt*

   III.iv.8 ftill?] ftill,
      10 Come ... breathe. | *Lean.* I] *Lean.* Come ... breathe. | I
      25 not——] not.
      26 ſhall not] ſhall[*space type*]not
      27 let's] let,s
      31 'Prethee] 'Pre thee
      37 'Twas ſubtilly] Twas ſubt [*turned* i] ily
      63 farre.] farre

SHEET 1F ii (inner forme)

Sig. F2v

Uncorrected: Camb², WU

First-stage corrected: IU², MnU, NIC, NjP, ViU², WMU¹, WMU², WMU³

   III.iii.0.1 *Tertia*] *tertia*
      1 Court!] Court.
      1 *ſtandish*] *ſtandeth*
      1 (*ſet*] *ſet*
      14 ſude] ſuide
      17 Unjustly] Uunjustly
      32 Scribe] Scrib
      35 call'd] and
      45 You] Yon
      49 mouthes,] mouthes
      58 *Enter*] *Enſer*

Second-stage corrected: Bodl, Camb¹, Hoy, ICN, IU¹, MB, NcD, PSt, ViU¹, WaU, WMU⁴

   III.iii.40 Raſcall——] Raſcall.
      64 humh, humh] hunch, hunch

Sig. 1F3

Uncorrected: Camb², WU

First-stage corrected: Camb¹, IU², MnU, NIC, NjP, ViU², WMU¹, WMU², WMU³

   III.iii.117 diſeaſe;] diſeaſe,
      177 of] ef

PRESS VARIANTS IN F1 (1647)

Second-stage corrected: Bodl, Hoy, ICN, IU¹, MB, NcD, PSt, ViU¹, WaU, WMU⁴
   III.iii.90 his] her

SHEET 1G ii (outer forme)

Uncorrected: Camb¹, Camb², IU², MnU, NjP, WMU³, WU
Sig. 1G3v
   V.ii.16 freedome's] freedomes

EMENDATIONS OF ACCIDENTALS

(|) *indicates that the reading occurs in a line that fills the measure.*]

Prologue

4 *Glory*,] F2; ~ ; F1
8 *weary*,] ~ : F1–2

12 *war*:] ~ ∧ F1; ~ . F2
18 *highly*] F2; *high ly* F1

I.i

I.i] *Actus Primus. Scæna Prima.* F1
8 not,] F2; ~ : F1
12–13 thee,...prophane.] ~ .... ~ , F1; ~ .... ~ . F2
24 Citie,] ~ , F1 (?); ~ ∧ F2
55 sake,] F2; ~ . F1
64 desir'd:——] ~ : ∧ F1–2
83 mind:] ~ , F1–2
104 blush:——] ~ : ∧ F1–2
141–142 And ... Uncivilly.] *one line in* F1–2
161 shall, ... else,] F2; ~ ∧ ... ~ ∧ F1
164 Exchequer,] F2; ~ ∧ F1
166 hold——] ~ ∧ F1–2
175 anger,] ~ ∧ F1(|); ~ . F2
179–191 one:—— ... Seck,——] ~ :

∧ ... ~ , ∧ F1–2
190–192 Nature, ∧ ... Melancholy.)] ~ ,) ... ~ . ∧ F1; ~ , ∧ ... ~ . ∧ F2
200 Grandee,] ~ ∧ F1; ~ ; F2
214 hell,] F2; ~ ' F1
226 dumb.∧] ~ .——F1–2
227 heat,] F2; ~ . F1
228 whit,] F2; ~ ∧ F1
238 What the] F2; Whatthe F1(|)
251 Italian∧] F2; ~ , F1
262 (of] F2;) of F1
290 Signiors.∧] ~ .——F1–2
293 Forme?] ~ , F1; ~ . F2
303 here∧ ... Anville:] ~ : ... ~ ∧ F1; ~ : ... ~ , F2

I.ii

ii] *Scæna Secunda.* F1
1 *Henrique?*] F2; ~ . F1
2 worke∧] F2; ~ ? F1
7 the raging] F2; theraging F1

13 *Jacinta*,] F2; ~ . F1 ∧
21 debt,] F1 (u)-2; ~ ∧ F1 (c)
44 too,] F2; ~ ∧ F1(|)

I.iii

iii] *Scæna Tertia.* F1
  1 fate?] F2; ~ , F1
  2 What's] F2; Wha'ts F1
  2 Bed,] F2; ~ ∧ F1

13 Pledges, which ∧] F2; ~ ∧ ~ ,
   F1
16 decaies, ... Branches ∧] F2; ~ ∧
   ... ~ , F1
45 fall,] ~ ∧ F1–2

II.i

II.i] *Actus Secundus, Scena prima* F1
  0.1 Arsenio.] F2; ~ ∧ F1(|)
  2 Gentlemen——] ~ ∧ F1; ~ ? F2
  4 Clerk,] F2; ~ ∧ F1
  7 Peace,] F2; ~ ∧ F1
  8 seems, ... ignorant,] ~ ∧ ... ~ ∧
   F1; ~ , ... ~ ; F2
  10 gotten,] ~ ∧ F1(|)–2
  12 young] F2; yong F1(|)
  12 handsome] handsom F1(|)–2
  12 Gentleman,] ~ ∧ F1(|)–2
  16 buxom,] F2; ~ . F1
  19 voyage;] ~ , F1; ~ . F2
  21 I'le] F2; I le F1
  21–22 Sattins. ... appeare ∧] F2; ~ ∧
   ... ~ . F1
  26 in;] ~ ∧ F1; ~ , F2
  31 now?] ~ , F1; ~ . F2
  33 inward ∧] F2; ~ , F1
  35 he? ... Vicar,] F2; ~ ; ... ~ ∧
   F1(|)
  39 say,] ~ ∧ F1–2
  41–42 (Which ... relation, ... han-
   somly)] ∧ ~ ... ~ ; ... ~ , F1–2
  43 home. Understand me:] ~ : ~ ~ .
   F1–2
  44 fortune,] ~ ∧ F1–2

48 shall] F2; shal F1(|)
51 indeed!] F2; ~ : F1
55 purpose,] F2; ~ ∧ F1
56–57 Devotions, ... dunces.] ~ ...
   ~ , F1–2
60–61 stomacks, ... reverence.] F2;
   ~ ... ~ , F1
102 see 'em] F2; see' em F1
108 out,] ~ ∧ F1–2
110 Gentleman;——] ~ ; ∧ F1–2
111 (Sir.)] (~ ∧) F1; ∧ ~ . ∧ F2
111 also,——] ~ , ∧ F1–2
116 well:——] ~ : ∧ F1–2
121 shell.] F2; ~ , F1
140 *Tiveria?*] F2; ~ . F1
148 memories,——] ~ , ∧ F1–2
153 *Cataya;*] ~ ∧ F1; ~ . F2
154 worship:——] ~ : ∧ F1–2
185 yeares] years F1(|)–2
208 face,——] ~ , ∧ F1–2
212 sir——] ~) ∧ F1; ~ ∧, F2
218 Sweet ... thousands?] F1–2 *line*
   knaves, | What
241 money] mony F1(|)–2
241 again:——] F2; ~ : ∧ F1
241 *Diego,*] F2; ~ . F1
246 ye,——] ~ , ∧ F1–2

II.ii

ii] *Scæna Secunda.* F1
  3 woman:] F2; ~ ∧ F1
  11 Companions] F2; Campanions F1

15 meaning;] ~ , F1–2
20 burnish'd;] ~ , F1; ~ . F2
23 places:] F2; ~ ∧ F1

33 laugh,——] ~ , ∧ F1; ~ . ∧ F2
36 again:——] ~ : ∧ F1–2
44 wife)——] ~) ∧ F1; ~ ∧ , F2
44 No ... (Maid?)] F1–2 *line:* wife) |
  What
55 sufferance. ∧] ~ .——F1–2
56 find;——] ~ ; ∧ F1–2
66–67 sir,....man.] F2; ~....~ , F1
95–96 I ... money.] *one line* F1–2
96 too,——] ~ , ∧ F1–2
104 better,——] ~ , ∧ F1; ~ . ∧ F2
105 yee] ee F1; ye F2
110 out-part] F2; out——part F1
122 hard,——] ~ , ∧ F1–2

126 me:——] ~ : ∧ F1–2
126 neighbours] F2; neighbors F1(|)
127 Welcome.] ~——F1–2
129 money] mony F1(|)–2
139–141 I'll grace ... Trade.] F1–2 *line:*
  I'll grace ... living, | Let ... Trade.
140 living,] F1(u)–2; ~ ∧ F1(c)
142 *Diego?*] F2; ~ . F1
144 Spectacles,] F2; ~ ∧ F1
153 home——] ~ . F1–2
155 Master.)] ~ ,) F1; ~ . ∧ F2
158 Emperour:] ~ , F1–2
159.1 *Exeunt.*] *Exit.* F1; *Ex.* F2

II.iii

iii] *Scæna Tertia.* F1
  0.1 Jamy,] F2; ~ ∧ F1
  8–10 him: ... at,] ~ , ... ~ : F1–2
  12 wishes,] ~ ∧ F1–2

22 it, ... Answer:] ~ : ... ~ , F1–2
24 together ∧ carefully,] ~ , ~ ∧ F1–2
27 Monster;] F2; ~ , F1

II.iv

iv] *Scæna Quarta.* F1
  7 courses] F2; coutses F1
  10–11 thee,...Lodgings:] ~ : ... ~ ,
    F1; ~ : ... ~ : F2
  12 layd——] ~ . F1–2
  12–13 Now ... quiet.] *one line* F1–2
  18 woman,] ~ ∧ F1–2
  30 Lord ∧ *Don Henrique* ∧] ~ , ~

~ , F1–2
32–34 him,—— ... morrow;——]
  ~ , ∧ ... ~ ; ∧ F1–2
36 ye. ∧] ~ :——F1–2
41 study:——] ~ : ∧ F1–2
43 out,] ~ ∧ F1–2
76 Sure ... cleane,] F1–2 *line:* me, | I
82 guards] F2; gaurds F1

III.i

III.i] *Actus Tertius, Scæna Prima.*
  29 will] F2; wil F1(|)
  29 sweare] swear F1(|)–2

39 Witnesses——] ~ . F1–2
41 me?] ~ , F1–2
44 me:] ~ , F1–2

III.ii

ii] *Scæna Secunda.* F1
  0.1 Parishioners,] ~ ∧ F1–2
  3 ye:] ~ , F1; ~ . F2
  8 1. *Par.* (etc.)] 1. (etc.) F1–2

8 sir)——] F2; ~) ∧ F1
18 you'll vex] F2; You'll vex F1
31 Sir.)] ~ . ∧ F1–2
34 shall] F2; shal F1(|)

35 angry,] F2; ~ ∧ F1(|)
37 Sextons,] F2; ~ ∧ F1
41 Ye ... Neighbours,)] F1–2 *line*: Church, | Under
48 Halfe] Half F1(|)–2
48–49 pipings, ... places.] F2; ~ .... ~ , F1
51–52 too∧ ... charitie,] ~ , ... ~ ∧ F1; ~ , ... ~ , F2
57 heartily] F2; hearilty F1
63 friend,] ~ ; F1–2
68 obligation:] ~ , F1–2
70 draw-out] draw——out F1–2
77 handsomely,] F2, ~ . F1
86 to——] ~ ∧ F1; ~ . F2
96 Keepe∧] F2; ~ , F1

105 well,——] ~ , ∧ F1–2
108 set,] F2; ~ ∧ F1
116.1 2] 3 F2 (and subsequent stanzas renumbered)
121–122 meat, ... adviser;] ~ ; ... ~ , F2; *omit* F1
129 Priest?] F2; ~ ∧ F1(c); ~ , F1(u)
139 graciously:——] ~ : ∧ F1–2
143 Sir?)] ~ ∧) F1; ~ , ∧ F2
147 else-where?] ~ . F1–2
148 *Peru?*——] ~ ? ∧ F1–2
152 favours.——] ~ . ∧ F1–2
167 Letter;] ~ , F1–2
169 *Hispania,*] F2; ~ ∧ F1 (?)
171 both, ... ye;] ~ ; ... ~ , F1–2
183 ye.∧] ~ .——F1–2

III.iii

iii] *Scæna Tertia.* F1
25 one:——] ~ : ∧ F1–2
26 summon'd] F2; summond F1(|)
40 Rascall——] F2; ~ . F1
44 knave;] ~ , F1–2
45 anon,——] ~ , ∧ F1–2
51 course:——] ~ : ∧ F1–2
72 Rethorician;] ~ , F1–2
90 devotion∧ ... vaine:] ~ : ... ~ ∧ F1; ~ : ... ~ ; F2
116–117 o're; ... disease,] ~ ∧ ... ~ , F1(u); ~ ∧ ... ~ ; F1(c); ~ ; ... ~ ; F2
126 Sufficient,] ~ ∧ F1–2
135 wife,)——] ~ ,) ∧ F1; ~ .) ∧ F2
142 thou, most barbarous∧] ~ ∧ ~ ~ , F1–2
144 thine,] ~ , F1(?); ~ ∧ F2
146–147 disgrace, ... wanton,] ~ ? ... ~ ? F1–2
156 Sentence,] F2; ~ , F1 (?)
162 bold,——] ~ , ∧ F1–2
164–166 honour∧) ... against me,] ~ , ∧ ... ~ ~) F1; ~ ,) ... ~ ~)

166 true,] ~ : F1–2
169 conscience∧] F2; ~) F1
174 stranger-Issue] ~ -- ~ F1; ~ ———— ~ F2
174 Bed;] ~ , F1–2
190 Condition,] ~ ∧ F1–2
194 will.—— ... Court:——] ~ . ∧ ... ~ : ∧ F1–2
196 revok'd.∧] ~ .——F1–2
198 absent:——] ~ : ∧ F1–2
201 not:——] ~ : ∧ F1–2
202 son,——] ~ , ∧ F1–2
203 Father:——] ~ : ∧ F1–2
204 you∧] ~ , F1–2
208 determin'd] F2; determi'nd F1
210 thee;] ~ , F1–2
214 mine.] ~ ——F1–2
216 every] F2; Every F1
218 be expressed] F2; beexpressed F1
218 words.] ~ ——F1–2
221 Sir,] F2; ~ . F1
225 ill] F2; i!l F1
225.1 *Exeunt.*] F2; ~ ∧ F1

411

III.iv

iv] *Scena Quarta.* F1
  1 wife?——] ~ ? ∧ F1–2
  1 wonders,] F2; ~ ∧ F1(|)
  2 day,——my *Amaranta,*——] ~ ,
    ∧ ~ ~ , ∧ F1–2
  6–7 Clyents,——...say,——] ~ ,
    ∧ ... ~ , ∧ F1–2
  8 violent,] F2; ~ ∧ F1
  9 els,] F2; ~ ∧ F1
  10 *Leandro (within).*] *Leandro within*
    as marginal stage-direction after
    'breathe.' followed by *Lean.* as
    speech-prefix F1(c)–2. The speech-
    prefix precedes 'Come' in F1(u).
  10 me,] F2; ~ ∧ F1
  12 study.] F2; ~ , F1
  21 bookish——] ~ , F1; ~ . F2
  26 to thee——] ~ ∧ F1(|); ~ . F2
  30 countenance,] F2; ~ ∧ F1(|)
  31 else——] ~ ∧ F1–2
  36 ∧ Sir,] F2; , ~ ∧ F1
  36 now.] F2; ~ ∧ F1(|)
  37 service——] ~ ∧ F1(|); ~ . F2
  40 do∧] F2; ~ , F1
  42–43 You ... her——] F1–2 *line:*
    You ... her.| Oh ... her——
  44 come,——...wife——] ~ , ∧
    ... ~ ∧ F1(|)–2
  50 me.] ~——F1–2
  51 stay.——] ~ . ∧ F1–2
  55 men∧] ~ : F1–2
  55 here,] F2; ~ ∧ F1(|)
  56 Lady∧] F2; ~ , F1
  58 presently——] ~ ∧ F1(|); ~ ,
    F2
  59–60 Conquerour—— ... Pupill.]
    ~ .... ~——F1–2

  62–63 too?——... eyes:——] ~ ∧
    ∧ ... ~ : ∧ F1–2
  66 language:——] ~ : ∧ F1–2
  67–68 (Ye ... round) ... husband?] ∧
    ~ ... ~ ? ... ~ . F1; ∧ ~ ...
    ~ , ... ~ ? F2
  68 happily,] F2; ~ . F1
  71–72 ye, ... quickly,] F2; ~ ∧ ...
    ~ ∧ F1
  73 then——] ~ ∧ F1; ~ . F2
  73 instantly,] F2; ~ ∧ F1
  74 ye,] F2; ~ ∧ F1
  76 imperious,] F2; ~ ∧ F1
  77–78 way?——... man:——] ~ ?
    ∧ ... ~ : ∧ F1–2
  78 me,] F2; ~ ∧ F1
  79 him——] ~ . F1–2
  79 me,] F2; ~ ∧ F1
  82 you,] F2; ~ ∧ F1
  83 Sir,——] ~ , ∧ F1–2
  85 kisses,] ~ ∧ F1; ~ . F2
  86 equal:] ~ ∧ F1; ~ , F2
  94 thus——... grows!] ~ ∧ ... ~ .
    F1; ~ , ... ~——F2
  94 Spring] F2; Sping F1
  104 idle,] F2; ~ ∧ F1
  108 too,] F2; ~ ∧ F1
  115 hope: ... her,] ~ , ... ~ ∧ F1;
    ~ , ... ~ , F2
  119 a∧] F2; a' F1 (turned comma)
  122–123 But ... Lady,] *one line* F1–2
  122 Chesse-board] Ches-board F1(|);
    Chess-board F2
  124 even:] ~ ∧ F1; ~ . F2
  127 supper.——] ~ . ∧ F1–2
  131 sorie.] ~——F1–2

IV.i

IV.i] *Actus Quartus Scæna Prima.* F1
  0.1 Violante,∧] F2; ~ , . F1

  1 patience,] F2; ~ ∧ F1
  1 'em?] ~ . F1; ~ ! F2

12–13 sorrow ∧ ... barrennesse)] F2;
    ~) ... ~ ∧ F1
16–17 roofe ∧ ... me,] ~ , ... ~ ∧
    F1; ~ , ... ~ , F2
19–21 wants, ... mother?] ~ ? ... ~ ,
    F1–2
24 Court:] F2; ~ , F1
28 comforts,] ~ ∧ F1–2
35 reverence,] F2; ~ ; F1
41 Office:] ~ , F1–2
42 trencher, ∧] F2; ~ : : F1
42 wine,] F2; ~ ∧ F1
43 pantofles] F2; pontafles F1
44 feete:] F2; ~ ∧ F1
45 grace,] F2; ~ ∧ F1
46–48 Coach, ... favour:] ~ : ... ~ ,
    F1–2
49 Son? ... me,] F2; ~ , ... ~ ∧ F1
54 it,] F2, ~ ∧ F1
55 me:] ~ ∧ F1(u); ~ , F1(c)–2
59 you,] F2; ~ ∧ F1
64 sleepes,] ~ ∧ F1; ~ . F2
76 me:] ~ ∧ F1; ~ , F2

79 you,] F2; ~ ∧ F1
82 Glasse ∧ ... in,] ~ , ... ~ ∧ F1;
    ~ , ... ~ , F2
83 broken:] ~ ∧ F1; ~ ; F2
85 feete ∧] F2; ~ , F1
88 devotions,] F2; ~ ∧ F1
90 wife,] F2; ~ ∧ F1
93 Father:——] ~ : ∧ F1–2
98 to.——] ~ . ∧ F1–2
98 Violante,] F2; ~ ∧ F1
100 Funerall,] ~ ∧ F1–2
101 unmanly ∧ ——] ~ ∧ ∧ F1; ~ ,
    ∧ F2
111 Mother:] ~ ∧ F1(|); ~ . F2
114–115 selfe, ... cruell,] F2; ~ ∧ ...
    ~ ∧ F1
117 me,] F2; ~ ∧ F1
119 Leper] F1(u)–2; Leaper F1(c)
121 him ∧ ... me,] ~ , ... ~ ∧ F1;
    ~ , ... ~ . F2
122 vaine:] ~ ∧ F1; ~ , F2
124 not,——] ~ , ∧ F1–2
126 Aspick's ∧] F1(u)–2; ~ , F1(c)

IV.ii

ii] Scena Secunda. F1
  0.1 Lopez, Millanes,] F2; ~ ∧ ~ ∧
    F1
  6–7 any: ... project,] ~ , ... ~ :

11 See] F2; Se F1
11 ready,] F2; ~ ∧ F1
12 vengeance. ∧] ~ .——F1–2 ±

IV.iii

iii] Scena Tertia. F1
  5 Egla ∧] F2; ~ . F1

IV.iv

iv] Scena quarta. F1
  9 me:] F2; ~ , F1
  31 wife,] F2; ~ ∧ F1
  42 this.] ~ ——F1–2

45 you:] ~ , F1–2
48 I'll] F2 (I'le); I,ll F1
48 secret,——] ~ , ∧ F1–2
51 Fall] F2; Fa!l F1

IV.v

v.] *Scena Quinta.* F1
 4 *Diego?*] ~ , F1; ~ . F2
 13–14 Bull: ... many,] ~ , ... ~ :
  F1–2
 19 made;] F2; ~ , F1
 31 Sir,] F2; ~ . F1
 34 alwayes:] F2; ~ ∧ F1
 40–41 Sir?——...state:——] ~ , ∧
  ... ~ : ∧ F1; ~ ? ∧ ... ~ : ∧ F2
 47 that?] F2; ~ ∧ F1(|)
 55 remedie:——] ~ : ∧ F1–2
 57 remembred?——] ~ , ∧ F1–2
 58 Gentlemen;——] ~ ; ∧ F1–2
 60 understanding:——] ~ ; ∧ F1–2
 66 ye——] ~ ∧ F1–2±
 71 cozen'd ∧)——] ~ ∧) ∧ F1;
  ~ .) ∧ F2
 86–87 Sir ∧ ... serve.)] ~) ... ~ . ∧
  F1–2
 88 drink.——] ~ . ∧ F1–2
 90 Justice:] ~ , F1; ~ . F2
 95 o'th' Parish] o'th'Parish F1(|)–F2
 95 Parish:] ~ , F1–2
 99 downe;] F2; ~ , F1
 99 marriages——] ~ . F1–2
 100 well ... will] F2; wel ... wil F1(|)
 108–109 Surgeons, ... Legacy ∧] ~ ∧

 ... ~ , F1; ~ , ... ~ , F2
 111 pleasures,] F2; ~ ∧ F1
 111–112 now, ... off.] F2; ~ .... ~ ,
  F1
 120 execute:] ~ ∧ F1; ~ . F2
 126 in:] ~ , F1–2
 134 (I ... heires)——] ∧ ~ ... ~ . ∧
  F1–2
 135 Executor?] F2; ~ . F1
 138–139 mind,——...rich,——] ~ ,
  ∧ ... ~ , ∧ F1–2
 139–140 monys? ... house,] ~ , ...
  ~ ? F1–2
 142 businesse,] F2; ~ ∧ F1
 143 raise 'em] F2; ~ raise'em F1(|)
 143 shall] F2; shal F1(|)
 143 good;] ~ , F1–2
 144 Thinke ... me?] F1–2 *line:* thou-
  sands? | What
 146 pack'd, sure,] ~ ∧ ~ ∧ F1–2
 156 Gentlemen,——] ~ , ∧ F1–2±
 165 Executor?] F2; ~ . F1
 178 Rogue,——] ~ , ∧ F1–2±
 180 rumours,] F2; ~ ∧ F1
 185–186 worships:——... Vicar,——]
  ~ : ∧ ... ~ , ∧ F1–2
 197 Boy.] ~ ——F1–2

IV.vi

vi] *Scæna Sexta.* F1
 1 desperately——] ~ . F1–2

 3 words:] ~ , F1–2
 20 thing. ∧] F2; ~ .——F1

IV.vii

vii] *Scæna Septima.* F1
 1 in,] ~ ∧ F1–2
 12 heare:——] ~ : ∧ F1–2
 18 frailtie,] F2; ~ ∧ F1
 26 immediatly.] ~ ——F1–2
 63–64 fast, ... Bag-pipes,] F2; ~ ∧
  ... ~ ∧ F1
 66 Antheme:] ~ ∧ F1; ~ . F2

 69–70 too,——...sheeps-face)——]
  ~ , ∧ ... ~) ∧ F1–2
 72 time?——] ~ ? ∧ F1–2
 73 appellations,] ~ ∧ F1–2
 76 hurryes,] F2; ~ ∧ F1
 77 again:] ~ ∧ F1(|); ~ . F2
 82–83 her?——... question?——]
  ~ ? ∧ ... ~ ? ∧ F1–2

101 hereafter,——] ~ , ∧ F1–2
104 errour,——] ~ , ∧ F1–2
107 serve:——] ~ : ∧ F1–2
109 confesse,——] ~ , ∧ F1–2
112 pacify;] F2; ~ . F1
117 ye,] F2, ~ ∧ F1
119 Breakfast:] ~ , F1–2

121–122 ye ∧ ... ye.] ~ .... ∧ F1;
   ~ ... ~ . F2
126 *Bartolus*, ... wench,] F2; ~ ∧ ...
   ~ , F1(|)
128 Goe, ... goe ∧] ~ ∧ ... ~ , F1–2
134 a match,] F2; ~ ~ ∧ F1

V.i

V.i] *Actus Quintus. Scæna Prima.* F1
 1 well,] F2; ~ ∧ F1
 3 appear'd,] ~ ∧ F1–2
 5 better,] F2; ~ ∧ F1
 6 So,] F2; ~ ∧ F1
17 it,——] ~ , ∧ F1–2±
18 Yes?] ~ : F1; ~ , F2
21 fitt ∧ ... proud:] ~ :... ~ ∧ F1;
   ~ :... ~ , F2
30–31 yeares ∧ ... same:] ~ :...
   ~ ∧ F1; ~ ∧ ... ~ , F2
34 you:] ~ , F1–2
35–37 least ∧ ... of: ... Giantesse,]
   ~ , ... ~ ∧ ... ~ : F1; ~ ∧ ...
   ~ .... ~ : F2
40 word ∧ or two,] F2; ~ , ~ ~ ∧
   F1
43–45 her: ... description,] ~ , ...
   ~ ; F1–2
47–48 of, ... flesh ∧] F2; ~ ∧ ... ~ ,
   F1

51 All] F2; A!l F1
54 Brother,] F2; ~ ∧ F1(|)
66 big,] F2; ~ : F1
70 Creature,] F2; ~ ∧ F1
73 dead, dead (woman:)] ~ : ~ (~
   ∧) F1; ~ ; ~ , ~ ; ∧ F2
75 nobly,] F2; ~ : F1
78 you:] ~ ∧ F1; ~ . F2
88 Bastard:] ~ ∧ F1; ~ , F2
95 kisse:——] ~ : ∧ F1–2
98 thus,——] ~ , ∧ F1–2±
99 Neere,] ~ ∧ F1–2
106 Woman?——] ~ ? ∧ F1–2
120 direct, you ∧] ~ ∧ ~ ∧ F1; ~ ∧
   ~ , F2
130 World] F2; Wor!d F1
136 Faith,] ~ ∧ F1–2
146 Laugh ... admirable.] F1–2 *line*:
   Spaine. | 'Twere
158 revenge ∧ a] revenge: A F1–2±

V.ii

ii] *Scæna Secunda.* F1
 2 shew ∧ ... discover,] ~ , ... ~ ∧
   F1; ~ ∧ ... ~ : F2
 5 be,——] ~ , ∧ F1–2
 9 dangerously,] F2; ~ ∧ F1
10 comming:] ~ ∧ F1; ~ . F2
12 it:] ~ ∧ F1; ~ . F2
14–15 over: ... merry.] ~ ∧ ... ~ :
   F1; ~ , ... ~ . F2
20 *Diego*,] F2; ~ ∧ F1
24 angry,] F2, ~ ∧ F1
24 me——] ~ . F1–2

28 on't,] F2; ~ ∧ F1
30 so, ... mirth:] ~ : ... ~ , F1–2
33 Sir,] F2; ~ ∧ F1
34 certaine,] F2; ~ ∧ F1
36 too,] ~ . F1; ~ ∧ F2
36 fashion,] F2; ~ ∧ F1
38 Jewell:——] ~ : ∧ F1–2
40 come,] ~ ∧ F1–2
42 house,] F2; ~ ∧ F1
44 braines? ... kindnes;] ~ ; ... ~ ?
   F1; ~ ; ... ~ : F2
48 ha?——] ~ ? ∧ F1–2

48 Neighbour,] F2; ~ ∧ F1
54 els,] F2; ~ ∧ F1
55 enough,——] ~ , ∧ F1–2
58 'em,] ~ ∧ F1; ~ . F2
60 appetite,——] ~ , ∧ F1–2±
64 after——] ~ ∧ F1; ~ , F2
66 ye,] F2; ~ ∧ F1
68 easely,] F2; ~ ∧ F1
71 diet——] ~ ∧ F1(|); ~ . F2
73 Algazeirs,——] ~ , ∧ F1–2
79 betraid!] ~ ∧ F1; ~ . F2
81 ye,] F2; ~ ∧ F1
82 ye?] F2; ~ ∧ F1
90 Curat:] ~ , F1–2
93 prison,] F2; ~ ∧ F1
94 instantly,] F2; ~ ∧ F1
96 waytes;——] ~ ; ∧ F1–2
98 story ∧] F2; ~ . F1
99 whore ∧ ye have,] F2; ~ , ~ ~ ∧ F1
102 naile ∧)] ~ ?) F1–2
103 Sir,——] ~ , ∧ F1–2±
107 thee;——] ~ ; ∧ F1–2
109 abhominably, ... lewdly;] ~ ; ... ~ ∧ F1; ~ , ... ~ , F2

111 nothing,] F2; ~ ∧ F1
116 thee:——] ~ ∧ ∧ F1; ~ . ∧ F2
117 Gentlemen,] F2; ~ ∧ F1(|)
118 healthful;——] ~ ; ∧ F1–2
120 not,] ~ ∧ F1; ~ : F2
123 usage:] ~ , F1–2
132–133 mentioned; ... indeed,] ~ , ... ~ ; F1–2
134 else ... were] F2; els ... wer F1(|)
134 up,] ~ ∧ F1(|); ~ . F2
136 Credit,] ~ ∧ F1–2
141 Foole;——] ~ ; ∧ F1–2±
144 worth, let ... it;] ~ ; Let ... ~ , F1; ~ ; let ... ~ . F2
151 doe, ... open,] F2; ~ ; ... ~ ∧ F1
153 villanies,] F2; ~ ∧ F1
157–158 Gentleman, ... much; And] ~ ; ... ~ , and F1–2
159–161 Friends,——...shoulders,——] ~ , ∧ ... ~ , ∧ F1–2
161 out] F2; ou't F1
162 friends;——] ~ ; ∧ F1–2
174–175 ye,——... ye,——] ~ , ∧ ... ~ . ∧ F1; ~ , ∧ ... ~ , ∧ F2
177 thing:] ~ , F1–2

V.iii

iii] *Scena Tertia.* F1
4 thing,] F1(?); ~ ∧ F2
4 good:] ~ ∧ F1; ~ . F2
11 long:] ~ ∧ F1; ~ . F2
12 Now ... silent.] F1–2 *line:* feare; | Be
18 on,] F2; ~ : F1
21 abus'd ∧ thus] F2; ~ ' ~ F1(?)
33 worship,] F2; ~ : F1
38 Bartolus,] *Bart.* F1–2
38–40 Leandro, ... Diego, ...

Octavio,] F2; ~ ∧ ... ~ ∧ ... ~ ∧ F1
39 fortune,——] ~ , ∧ F1–2
43 reason:——] ~ : ∧ F1–2
48 prodigall] prodigal! F1; prodigal F2
102 longer:——] ~ : ∧ F1–2
107 bargaine?——] ~ ? ∧ F1–2
137 Copy:——] ~ : ∧ F1–2
149 thoughts.——] ~ . ∧ F1–2
153 *Henrique*; ... then,] ~ , ... ~ ; F1; ~ : ... ~ ; F2

Epilogue

2 *still*] F2; *stil* F1(|)

HISTORICAL COLLATION

[NOTE: The editions cited are:
F1   *Comedies and Tragedies* (1647).
F2   *Fifty Comedies and Tragedies* (1679).
1711 *Works*. Printed for Tonson.
1718 *The Spanish Curate*.
T   *Works* (1750), ed. Theobald, Seward and Sympson. *The Spanish Curate* was
         begun by Theobald, the note on IV.i.iv being the last he wrote. Seward
         carried on, guided occasionally by Theobald's marginal emendations.
C   *Works* (1778), ed. George Colman the younger and others.
W   *Works* (1812), ed. Weber.
D   *Works* (1843–6), ed. Dyce.
V   *The Spanish Curate*, ed. McKerrow, in Bullen's Variorum Edition, vol. II
         (1905).

Only substantive variants are collated. Variations between *you* and *ye* are ignored as
are insignificant differences in the positions of stage-directions. The + sign indicates
the agreement of all editions after the one to which the variant is attributed.]

Prologue

9 *Streame that guides*] streams that guide C, W

I.i

0.1 Angelo $_\wedge$] ~ , F1–D
3 heire] heirs F1
33 *Don Jamie's*] *Jamie is Fleay conj. in*
      V
35 Encreas'd] Encreasing F1
74, 111 *Ascanio.*] *Ars.* F1
83 and] *omit* F2–T, D, V
102, 129 *Arsenio.*] *Ang.* F1–D
106 Our] Or F1
127 serves] serve T–D
131 that] *omit* F2–T

132 from] to T
148 his] this F1, 1711 (F2 press-
      variant?)
156 of] *omit* F2–T
174 mine] my F2–W
217 *Pluto's*] Plutus' *Anon. conj. in* D
237 your] you F1
305 off, we'll ... wit;] off; well ... wit,
      F1; off well, ... wit; F2–D; off,
      well, ... McKerrow *conj.*

417

I.ii

1 bring] brings F1
12 Or] *omit* 1711; And 1718
15 it] *omit* F2–C, D

63 his] her F1–1718
72 me.] me From such Impiety! T

I.iii

11 possesse] possesses F1(u)
19 To ... against] To me, of, that
   misery against F1; Of misery to me,

   that 'gainst F2 +
23 will] would Dyce *conj.*
26 forbid to] to forbid 1718

II.i

0.1 (*with a letter writ out*)] *omit* T +
0.1 Arsenio] *Asermo* F1
19 as] *omit* F1
25 time] tune F1–1718, C +
36 an Homily] an—— ——F1–1718
37–38 Thou ... thee. *Leandro.* Have]
   Lean. Thou ... thee ∧ (|) Have F1
40 On] or F1–1718; o're W (Colman
   conj.)
43 Will] While 1718
49–50 *Leandro.* A ... me. | You ...
   ready. *Exit.*] A ... me. *exit lea.* |
   You ... ready, F1
65 Takes ... blunts] Take ... blunt D
67 some] some few T
68 yeare] years C, W
84 Fevers ∧] ∼ . T

92 more] most F1 +
102 makes] make F2–D
105 a] *omit* F1–2
108 out] *omit* F2–T
121 And] *Die.* And T
144 I consider. | *Leandro.* Thinke] I—
    | *Lean.* Consider, think T (Symp-
    son *conj.*)
150 often-times] oft-times F2 +
153 ye] me 1718
167 bin] been so Fleay *conj. in* V
172 to] *omit* F1
176–177 he,——| *Lopez.* Good ...
    Pray] he, good... patient. | *Lop.*
    Pray F1
180 I shall] you will T
222 consumes] consume 1711, 1718

II.ii

9 opinions] in Minions T (Sympson
  conj.)
14 jealousies] jealousie F2 +
18 Serves] Serve C–D
18 behaviours] Behaviour 1711, 1718
22 greatnesse] Chastness T (Seward
  conj.)
27 Set] See F1 (*catchword*)
72 Gentleman] Gentlemen F2–C
76 is] are C, W

76 five] three D
96–97 too,—— ... money. | *Diego.*
   Would] too;—— | *Die.* Thanks
   ... Money. ' Wou'd T (Seward
   conj.)
100 prove.] ∼ ,——T–D
108–110 For ... (sir?)] *omit* 1718
136 a] *omit* F2–T, D
149 truth] the Truth T
152 dub] but dub T

II.iii

0.1 Arsenio.] *Arsenio, and Angelo.*
    C–D
1 *Angelo* ∧] ~ , F1–1718, C–D;

omit T
4 *Jamy*] *omit* F1–1718
17 loth] both F1(u)

II.iv

1 Why ∧] ~ , F1
9 Y'faith] 'Faith F2–C
16 after] after't McKerrow *conj.*
19 More] Nor Dyce *conj.*
19 what] of what T, C
24 he] ye F1(u)
36 (*within*)] *Leandro within.* after *Exit.*
    F1–T
36.1 *Enter* Amaranta.] *omit* F2–W

51.1 *Lute and Song.*] on line 49.1 after
    Enter Amaranta. F1; on 49.1 after
    Exit. F2
52–63 *Dearest ... broken.*] *omit* F1, C
    (*text degraded*)
57 *far*] *doth* T–W
79 lockt] lock F1
79 upon me] up here F2–W

III.i

16 your monied] you monied 1718
23 Snakes] Rakes, Jacks, *or preferably*

Knaves Seward *conj. in* T
44 houre,] ~ ,——W

III.ii

3 taught] thaught 1711
12 ye.] ye. *Two chaires set out.* F1
14 ye] ye are F2–T
52 awake] awaken Dyce *conj.*
52 too] your too T
58 Sir.)] ~ ∧ ——C +
59–60 *3. Par.* The ... me, | And] The
    ... me. | *3.* And F1–W
69 duties] Dues T
70 draw-out] draw——out F1–2,
    1711, 1718
80 be] be ye Fleay *conj. in* V
85 abed] to bed F1(c) +
108.1–128 SONG. ... *Vicar.*] *omit* F1,

C (*text degraded*)
112.1 *Chorus.*] 2 F2–D
121–122 meat, ... *adviser;*] ~ ; ... ~ ,
    F2–1718; ~ ; ... ~ ; T
132 Neighbours,] Neighbours, *The Bar*
    & Book ready on a Table. F1
144 be] he F1(u)
146 *Cataya*] *Cataga* F2
167 Plague] A Plague T
171 both, ... ye;] ~ ; ... ~ , F1–2
176 keep] keep you T, C
177 *Vicar*] good Vicar T–W
179 if ye] I fye T

III.iii

1 Court!] Court! *A Bar. Table-booke,*
2 *chairs, & paper standish set out.*
    F1–C

3 thoughts] thought D
14 Though] Tough F2
35 call'd] and F1(u)

45 You] Yon F1(u)
45–46 anon,——... language, ∧]
~ , ∧ ... ~ , ∧ F1–W; ~ ; ∧ ...
~ ∧ ——D, V
56 Assistants] Asistente's McKerrow
conj.
60 This] 'Tis F1, V
64 Humh, humh] hunch, hunch F1(u)
84 heat] head 1711
90 his] her F1(u)
100 Hood] Had F1
128 thy] my 1711, 1718
131 inhumane] inhuman 1711 +

145 Court] F2; Court Chess-boord and
men set ready. F1
147 wanton,] ~ ? F2, 1711
150 Divorc'd] Divorce F1–W
152 thy] my 1711–W
174 stranger-Issue] stranger——Issue
F2, 1711
198 Exit.] omit F1
213 rakes] takes F1(c)–W
217 Jacinta] Jam. F1; Oct. F2–T
218.1 Gives ... Jacinta.] omit F1
219 Ascanio ... follow.] omit F1

III.iv

10 Come ... breathe. | Leandro. I]
Lean. Come ... breathe. | I F1(u)
15 done ∧ good,] ~ , ~ ∧ F1–1711
18 fluttering] F2; flttering F1
18–19 Pupil, ... thing?] ~ ? ... ~ ,
F1–T
33.1 Play at chesse.] omit F1
34 here?] ~ , T +
63 farre.] ~ ? 1711 +
70 I'le thank] I thank F1; thank
F2–1718
71 one] one that T; a man Fleay conj. in

V
96 too] to F2 +
98 to] to all T–W
101 anger] angry F2–T
101 Why none] No F2–T
113 Or I] Or I you T +
118 akes, yet ∧ ... fear.] ~ ∧ ~ , ...
~ ——F1 +
122 head.] head, line that good Lady,
F1 +
128 heart ∧ now,] ~ , ~ ∧ F1–T
131 too] to F2 +

IV.i

2–4 excuse? ... truth ∧ ... error?] ~
? ... ~ ? ... ~ . F1; ~ ∧ ... ~ ?
... ~ ? F2; ~ ∧ ... ~ , ... ~ ?
1711, 1718; ~ ∧ ... ~ ∧ ... ~ ?
T–D; ~ ∧ ... ~ ? ... ~ ? V
4 Extenuate] T'extenuate T–D
4 wofull] wilfull T, C
21–22 Henrique. What can I say? |
Shall] What can I say? | Hen. Shall
F1–1718; What can you say? | Hen.
Shall T, C
28 envious] venomous T

28 hath] have F2–D
42 your] you T
52 No] Is no T
83 Am] And F1(u)
88 'tis] it is T–W
96 and] for T
97 Deserve] Deserves T; Arrive Seward conj. in T
101 two] too 1711
107 shame;] shame ∧ Bed ready, wine,
table Standish & Paper. F1

IV.ii

1 you:] ~ ∧ F1–C
9 instruct you] instruct T
12 he] ye F1(u)

15 *Arsenio.* All] *Ars.* All [*preceded by catchword* Have] F1

IV.iv

41 From] This from Fleay *conj. in* V
42 New] Now 1718

52 dead] for dead F2–W

IV.v

6 Sir,] Sir, *Diego ready in Bed, wine, cup.* F1
17 where ... charge,] there ... charge: F1+
20 misery,] misery, *Table out, Standish paper, stools.* F1+
33–34 ye; ... man,] ~ , ... ~ , F1–1718; ~ , ... ~ ; W
40 a] *omit* T
41 *Enter*] *Enter, with* 1711, 1718, T
42 ayre.] ayre. *Bed thrust out.* F1
48 ye sit] sit 1718
53 not, ... ye,] ~ ; ... ~ , C, W; ~ ∧ ... ~ ; D, V
65 Neighbour] Neighbours F1+
68 pray ye] pray T
88 some] *omit* 1711–T
92 not] *omit* F2–1718; up T–W

93 budge] burge F2–1718; purge T–D
97 many;] ~ , F1–T; ~ ∧ C, W
111 pleasures,] ~ ∧ F1
128 lay] lie W
140 promises] Premises Sympson *conj. in* T
150 boared] boor'd C
165 Maggot-pate] Maggot, Rat T, C
170 Would ... deserve? | *Diego.* I] Would ... you? | *Die.* Doe ... I F1
178 Some craftie ∧] Some Craftsman, T, C; Some crafty, W; some crafty [*as concluding words of Bartolus' speech*] D, V
183 God ... God] Good' ... go'd F1; Good ... good F2–C
196 Well ... done] *Diego*, thou'st done well T

IV.vi

4 Lovers,] Lovers, *Pewter ready for noyse.* F1

6 over-joy'd] over-joyn'd F2

IV.vii

18 of ... frailtie] and Frailty; of Revenge T, C
23 Certaine] For certain Fleay *conj. in* V
35 Sea] Seal Sympson *conj. in* T (vol. II addenda)
35 brussels] bustles T

54 how ∧] ~ , F2, 1711, T
56 fleer'd] fleere F1
60 as ... coming] as he'd been the Woman T; Was that becoming? *Anon. conj. in* T; as he had been conning W (Mason *conj.*), D, V
73 Talk'd] Talk F1–C

421

V.i

1 come.] come. *Chaire and stooles out.* F1–W

14 doe owe] owe a F2–T

26 hopes)] hopes) *A Table ready covered with Cloath Napkins Salt Trenchers and Bread.* F1

33 ceruz'd] cerviz'd F1

41 were] with T (Sympson *conj.*)

58 Will] You'll T–D

99 Neere] Nearer T+

120 direct, you] direct you, wee'l F2–1718, C–D; direct, we'll T

123 Kingdomes)] Kingdomes) *Dishes covered with papers in each ready.* F1

153 is onely] only is D *conj.*

157 Confession] Conclusion *Anon. conj. in* T

158 revenge ∧ a] revenge: A F1–1718

159 If not] Unless T

V.ii

0.1 *Paratour.*] *Paratour. The Table set out and stooles.* F1+

7–8 hartily ∧ ... two;] ∼ ; ... ∼ ∧ F1

9 lighted dangerously] lighted dangers T; slighted me *or* slighted dangers *or* lighted anger Seward *conj. in* T

10 quit] quiet W

14 all over] All's over T (Sympson *conj.*)–W

22 *Bartolus*] *omit* F1

30 do's] does always T, C

42 none] not F2–W

48 Neighbour] neighbours D

56.1 *Removes swords.*] *omit* F1–C

61 and] an't C+

68 endue] endure F1–C, V

76 *Diego*] *Lop.* F1–W

93 a] *omit* W

113–115 stealest] stealedst D (Mason *conj.*)

119 concernes] concern F2–D

123 of] for T+

124 her] your C, W

134–135 *Diego.* Some ... And] Some ... *Die.* And F1

141 let] leave T

152–153 shall——... villanies,] ∼ ∧ ... ∼ ∧ F1

V.iii

31 to] and T

40 Octavio, Jacinta Ascanio] *following Diego, in the stage-direction at line 38* F1–C

50 Fee] see 1711, 1718

90 the] thy McKerrow *conj.*

93 thine] thy C

94 these] those 1711–W

101 so] *omit* T

102 seize on her.] *a stage-direction* Fleay *conj. in* V

133 well] all F2–C

137 As] And C, W

145 she] that she T

'Dearest do not you delay me'
(II.iv.52–63)

MS[1] British Library, Loan 35, no. 123, f.59; MS[2] New York Public, Drexel 4247, no. 17; A Henry Lawes, *Ayres and Dialogues* (1653), I, 20; S Henry Lawes, *Select Ayres and Dialogues* (1669). p. 10.

52 *you*] Now MS[1], MS[2], A, S
54 *doth*] will MS[1], MS[2]
56 *that*] thy MS[1], MS[2], A, S
57 *far*] doth MS[1], A, S; doe MS[2]
58 *fairest*] deerest MS[1], MS[2], A, S
59 *that*] who A, S

60 *this*] the MS[2], A, S
61 *Else ... sure*] for dumb sylence else MS[1], A, S; Else dumb silence sure MS[2]
62 *that's*] is MS[1], A, S
63 *being*] *omit* MS[1], MS[2], A, S

'Let the Bells ring'
(III.ii.109–128)

MS[1] British Library, Harl. 3991 f.44; MS[2] British Library, Harl. 3991 f.85.

Title: The Countryman's Song in the Spanish Curate MS[1]
The Spanish Curate MS[2]
109 *Let*] *omit* MS[1], MS[2]
110 *skip*] trip MS[1], MS[2]
112 *old*] *omit* MS[1], MS[2]
112 *will*] will (*written over* we'll?) MS[1]; We'l MS[2]
113 *merrily,*] *omit* MS[1], MS[2]
113, 115 *ah*] hey MS[1], MS[2]

115 *verily,*] *omit* MS[1], MS[2]
117 *a-loodle-loo*] adoodle dow MS[1], MS[2]
118 *A ... Crow;*] *omit* MS[2]
118 *Cock-a-loodle*] Cockadoodle MS[1]
119 *a*] the MS[1]; *omit* MS[2]
122 *most*] *omit* MS[1], MS[2]
123 *Bottles*] pottles MS[1], MS[2]
127 *our*] the MS[1], MS[2]
128 *old*] Oh MS[1], MS[2]

The version in *The Musical Companion*, ed. John Playford (1673) is here given in full.

The Jolly Vicar.

Let the Bells now Ring, and let the Boys Sing,
  the young Lasses trip and play;
Let the Cup go about until it be out,
  our Learned Vi-car we'll stay.

Let the Pig turn round, Hey merrily, Hey,
  and then the Fat Goose shall swim:

For merrily, merrily, merrily hey,
   our Vicar this day shall be Trim.

The stew'd Cock shall crow, Cock a doodle doo,
   aloud Cock a doodle shall crow:
The Duck and the Drake shall swim in a lake
   of Onions and Claret below.

We'll labour and toil to fertile the Soil,
   & Tithes shall come thicker & thicker:
We'll fall to the Plow & get Children enough,
   & thou shalt be learned, O Vicar.

THE LOVERS' PROGRESS

edited by

GEORGE WALTON WILLIAMS

TEXTUAL INTRODUCTION

'The Wandring Lovers' (Greg, *Bibliography*, no. 649) was licensed on 6 December 1623 as 'Written by Mr Fletcher' and performed at Whitehall on 1 January following.[1] A new licence was granted on 7 May 1634 for 'The tragedy of *Cleander*, by Philip Massinger', and two weeks later a play entitled 'Lasander & Callista, beinge a poem', was performed. As the theme of wandering lovers figures in a play called in 1641 'The Lovers Progresse', and as the two titles of 1634 name the three characters of first importance in this last-mentioned work, Professor Bentley has concluded that the first three titles 'apply to the piece published in the ... folios of 1647 and 1679', as 'The Lovers Progresse', a title which first appeared in a list prepared by the Lord Chamberlain in 1641, was repeated in the Stationers' Register in 1646, and was published in the Folio as 'The Lovers Progres.' (running heads '*Progresse*').[2] Professor Bentley notes also that the names in the cast-list for 'The Lovers Progress' in the second Folio are players who were active in the King's Men in 1623 when 'The Wandering Lovers' was licensed. Greg, indeed, accounted 'The Wandering Lovers' a lost play, but as his argument presents no evidence stronger than that offered by the inferences of Professor Bentley,[3] the present edition adopts Professor Bentley's hypothesis.

Oddly enough, six years after publishing 'The Lovers Progresse', Moseley used the old title again in the Register in 1653: 'The Wandering Lovers, or the Painter ... by Phill: Massinger'. Of this composite title, Professor Bentley suggests that '*The Painter* ... is probably a different play which Moseley was slipping in as a sub-title'.[4]

The 'Prologue', obviously spoken before a revised piece, makes it quite clear that the original play, 'long since writ', was by Fletcher and that a reviser 'did not spare / The utmost of his strengths, and his best care / In the reviving it' (lines 15–17). In fact, the work of the reviser was so thorough that he felt justified in 'Demanding, and receiving too[,] the pay / For a new Poem' (lines 12–13).

Dr Hoy has confirmed scholarly opinion that the reviser was Philip Massinger (as was claimed in 1634; he was probably also the author of the Prologue and Epilogue); and he supports the theory 'that originally the play stood as a product of Fletcher's sole authorship' without any collaboration from Massinger in that first version and 'that Massinger's role was that of reviser only'.[5] The marks of Massinger's hand are most evident in I.i, ii.1–117; III.i, iv; IV; V; less evident in I.ii.117–241; II; III.ii, iii, v, vi. No subsequent critic has suggested any change in this evaluation or these assignments.

The markedly French tone, plot and character of the play derive from the popular romance by Vital d'Audiguier, *Histoire trage-comique de nostre temps, sous less noms de Lysandre et de Caliste*, published in Paris in 1615 and reprinted many times during the next one hundred and fifty years.[6] The popularity of this unlikely work may perhaps be explained as deriving from the supposition that it concerned 'real' people, with disguised names ('sous les noms') and was current history ('de nostre temps'). The authenticity of the events here romanticized seems to have been attested by the French and German edition of 1670, the titlepage of which reads: *Histoire des amours de Lysandre et de Caliste, Liebes-Beschreibung Lysanders und Kalisten, geschehen in Frankreich, meistentheils in und bey Paris, im Jahr 1606*. The basic episode – real or imagined – clearly caught the imagination of d'Audiguier and after him of Fletcher, and its popularity manifested on the continent and in England in the subsequent decades must have suggested to Massinger that the piece still had marketable merit.

The play is the fourth item in Section 3 of the Folio, the section printed by Susan Islip; it occupies pages 3I4–3M3v (3M2 missigned '*Mmm 3*'). It is printed with normal two-skeleton work in Quires L and M, but in Quire K there is some irregularity until the system is established. The running-title is '*The Lovers Progresse*'. There are no transfers from recto to verso.

II		K1 K2 K3		L1	L4	M1
IV			K4	L2 L3		M2 M3
I	I4v	K1v		L2v L3v		M2v M3v
III		K2v K3v				
V				L1v	L4v	
VII			K4v			M1v

The page number '92', correctly located on M2v, reappears incorrectly on page 90, M1v; this error indicates that page M2v was printed ahead of page M1v, i.e., inner sheet, inner forme preceded outer sheet, inner forme, through the press – the normal sequence for printing the sheets of this section.

The compositors for the play are two, *A* and *B*.[7] These are identified in this play by the use or non-use of spacing before medial punctuation (*A* prefers to use extra space; *B* prefers not to use such space) and by the contraction for 'I will' (*A* sets 'I'le'; *B* sets 'Ile').[8] These distinctions divide the compositors into stints of four consecutive pages in each forme (or eight in successive formes):

Compositor A	I4–4	K1–2	3–4	M1–1(2)2	3v
Compositor B		K3–4	L1–2	(2)	3	3v

Some evidence suggests that *B* was assisting also on M2.[9]

The evidence from type shortage provides some suggestive statistics. Shortage of upper-case roman 'W' seems to have been solved by the usual 'VV' and by the use of 'W' sorts from two different fonts, one slightly larger than the other. Shortage of upper-case roman 'I' at the bottom of column b both of L2v and of L2 would indicate that Compositor *B* replenished his cases mid-page in both instances; he certainly seems to have done so on L1, for column a exhibits the replacement italic '*I*' (for the proper roman form) until seven lines from the bottom of the page (one 'I' in these lines) and column b exhibits only the roman 'I'. The instance of distribution near the close of L1a is confirmed by the pattern of '*C*/C' (the replacement of the proper italic form by the roman); at the same point the supply of '*C*' is replenished (L1a uses the replacement 'C' to that point, the proper '*C*' for the remainder of the page L1a–L1b). The pattern of '*C*/C' would seem to indicate that Compositors *A* and *B* had comparable experiences in setting Quire K. They began, respectively, setting K2v and K3 with the proper '*C*' for the extreme number of prefixes beginning with that letter. At mid-point in column of of K2 and of K3v, the next pages to be set, both of them experienced shortage of that sort and replaced it with the roman 'C'. (The first replacement on K3v occurs in the name 'Cupid' (II.iii.80) and undoubtedly accounts for the anomalous setting of that name in roman.) Both of them replenished their cases at the end of those pages and proceeded to K1v, K1 and to K4, K4v using the proper '*C*'. Moving in to Quire L

Compositor *A* set L3 with both sorts used indifferently but continued his pages (L3v, L4, L4v) with the proper '*C*'; Compositor *B* set L2v properly but continued his pages (L2, L1v, L1) with what seems to be a mixture, perhaps indicating frequent distribution (as at the foot of L1a). It is perhaps worthy of mention – though a small detail – that Compositor *A* seems to have had two swash '*C*' forms in his case; Compositor *B* had one. The two sorts appear on *A*'s pages K2v, K1v, L4, L3 (and M1–1v). Single sorts appear on K4v, L2v, L1 – *B*'s pages.

There is, understandably, confusion in setting the prefixes for Clarinda and Clarange. For Clarinda Compositor *A* uses only the prefix '*Clar.*' Compositor *B* uses '*Cla.*' and also '*Clarind.*', '*Clarin.*', '*Clari.*'. For Clarange, every abbreviation possible from '*Cla.*' to '*Clarang.*' is used (and two erroneous '*Clarin.*' forms); no pattern appears to distinguish between the compositors for this name.[10]

The text is reasonably well set in the Folio, though there are many turned letters and letters printing too high or low in the line. Dr James P. Hammersmith suggests that such errors – and others – indicate 'serious difficulties with the manuscript ... [which must have been] untidy'.[11] But there are few misassignments of speeches, and the entry-directions appear, in general, to have been properly located in the blocks of dialogue (for an exception, see Textual Note at II.iv.70). A few emendations of such directions have been admitted in order to enhance (supposedly) the dramatic effect (as at V.iii.236–44; see Textual Note at V.iii.244). The apparent too-early entry at IV.iv.37.1 is deliberate, as it provides the opportunity for Lidian to hear and recognize the voice of Lisander. Mislineations, on the other hand, particularly mislinings of consecutive part-lines, seem to be unusually numerous, averaging five errors for each hundred lines in the shares of both authors and both compositors. With the exception of the '*Scæna prima.*' headings that accompany the act headings of the various acts, there are no scene divisions in either Folio. Scene divisions are supplied here in brackets in the margin of the text; no further notice is taken of their absence from the Folios. The exit and immediate re-entry of Clarinda at the act-break between acts II and III suggests, probably, an interval.

Stage-directions in the play are numerous. Directions describing action on stage occur some eleven times: '*Kissing*', '*Reads*', '*Falls in a swoon*', '*Strikes Lancelot*', '*Puts the sword in Malfort's hand*', etc.

(these would seem to be authorial); directions describing conditions or actions on entering: '*his arme in a scarffe*', '*wounded in severall places*', '*in Armour*' (no doubt for comic effect), '*like a Hermite*', '*in Friers habit*' (these are discussed below in this Introduction), '*following*', '*running, Cleander following*'; directions specifying props to be brought on for immediate need: '*with lights*' (there are several such), '*with a letter*', etc., and specifying props to be brought on which must be invisible until later in the scene (see Textual Note to I.ii.97). There are many directions which would seem to derive from the book-keeper: '*two Chaires set out*', '*Caliste sitting behind a curtaine*', '*Table, Tapers, and three stooles*', '*a bar set forth*', and several announce noises off: '*Noise within*', '*A Pistoll shot within*', '*A lute is struck*'. Because there seem to be so many authorial directions in the text, one is hesitant to conclude that this latter group is not also authorial, but the technicalities of many of these directions would seem to reflect specific playhouse needs. R. C. Bald has noted that 'the numerous specific directions about properties in the Folio text make it fairly clear that the play was set up from a prompt copy'.[12]

The Folio follows the normal practice of setting in italic type the names of persons, mythological figures, cities and countries, and words of foreign extraction ('*per annum*', '*Dor*', '*Capuchin*', '*Chymera*', '*Sans*', '*Genius*'). The series of five rivers (IV.iv.180) is also set in italic as are the '*Amazons*', '*Greeks*', and '*Pythagoreans*'. As exceptions to the norm, 'Hermite' (IV.iv.53) and 'Friers' (V.iii.257) set in italics in the Folio, are standardized in this edition. (On K3v the roman 'Mars's' (II.iii.58) is corrected in the press-run to italic.)

The name of the heroine appears in the French original as 'Caliste', as it did also, presumably, in Fletcher's holograph. The English translation of the fable in 1627 named her 'Calista', as did Sir Humphrey Mildmay when he saw the play in its revived form in 1634.[13] The 1647 Folio is clear in naming her 'Caliste' (with one exception, '*Calista*', I.i.150.1); but the 1679 Folio changes the name throughout to 'Calista', and all subsequent editors have followed that lead. It is not clear why this change from F1 to F2 should have taken place or why all editors should have adopted it. Perhaps 'Calista' sounds more Latinate or Italianate than does 'Caliste', a word which is merely French, but the appropriateness of a French name in a French setting might have seemed obvious enough. In the verse of the play, both authors think of the name as trisyllabic; perhaps editors think 'Caliste' in French has only two syllables, a deficiency the Latin feminine ending would correct. The present edition names her 'Caliste', a word of three syllables.

Similarly, the name 'Clarange', which would seem to be a French disyllable, is trisyllabic in the verse of both writers. To ensure that the word be pronounced metrically Dyce printed it as 'Clarangè'; the present edition names the character 'Clarange', a word of three syllables.

The intricate disguise plot towards the close of the play may profit from some editorial assistance. When we read '*Enter* Lidian, *like a Hermite*' (IV.iv.37.1), we are to understand that Lidian is not in disguise; he identifies himself and acknowledges: 'I purpose to ... leave the world' (lines 62–3).[14] However, when a few lines later, '*Enter ... Clarange in Friers habit*' (line 113), it will be useful to know that Clarange is in disguise and remains unidentifiable by those on stage; two scenes later, Clarange, still in disguise in the Friar's habit (V.ii.26.1), reveals himself, much to the annoyance of Lidian who is offended that 'Such reverend habits juggle' (1.43). Yet in the next scene, Clarange, presumably still in the same habit, has taken holy orders, has been tonsured, and is indeed a Friar (V.iii.240–7), not in disguise. Lidian, presumably still in his hermit's weeds, now purposes to become a husband so that the play may end: Lidian, gaining their common mistress and renouncing his hermitic promise, Clarange renouncing that lady to gain 'a better Mistris, The Church' (V.iii.249–50).

The play has two songs; they are sung at the centre of the play in contiguous scenes III.iv and III.v, the first by a soprano, the second by a bass. The second song is sung by an invisible singer off-stage. Both songs survive in manuscript copies; substantive variants are listed in the Textual Notes, though none seems sufficiently authoritative to displace a reading of F. The musical settings indicate repetition of certain words or phrases (marked '*bis*' in the Collation).

The text of this edition has been set up from a typescript of a copy of the First Folio at Duke University.[15] I am indebted to James P. Hammersmith for the collation of Press Variants, to which I have added two more exemplars.[16]

NOTES

1 Gerald Eades Bentley, *The Jacobean and Caroline Stage* (Oxford, 1956), III, 360–3. The data in this opening paragraph derive from Professor Bentley's work. Professor Bentley believes that the titles, various though they may be, designated the same play by Fletcher revised by Massinger and that a single piece is intended throughout its protean namings: 'the thorough rewriting of the piece' by Massinger was 'good reason for a change in the title' – though it should be pointed out that the 1634 revision did not produce the final title.

   The Second Folio (1679) cast-list, since it includes the name of John Underwood who made his will in October 1624 and presumably died shortly thereafter, must record the cast of a 1623/4 production.

2 The term 'Lovers' would seem to be possessive plural, not singular, though the 'Catalogue' of the First Folio uses the form 'Lover's'. Greg argues for the singular: 'The title is most naturally interpreted as referring to the wanderings of the hero, Lysander', though he acknowledges that the other title, 'The Wandering lovers', 'favours the plural form'. 'Lovers can only be said to share a progress if they travel in company', he continues, 'which those in the play do not' (*Bibliography*, II, 776). This edition supposes that 'Lovers' is plural and that those lovers who wander are Lidian and Clarange (II.i.118) and Lisander (II.iii.85; see Textual Note), i.e., those who say they do. Greg is correct, of course, in respecting 'Progress' as singular (which interpretation must have influenced his conclusion that 'Lovers' was singular); but we do not require a title like 'The Lovers' Progresses', if we allow the sense that the title refers to the 'Progress' which the several lovers make in their separate movements to fulfilment. That Lisander is designed to be the singular hero of the play is clear, yet these other two lovers are by no means minor figures. And one wonders about the progress towards satisfaction undergone by Caliste, Olinda and Clarinda. To say nothing of Leon and Malfort. It is not tenable that 'Progress' should be thought a verb.

3 *Bibliography*, II, 982–4.

4 *Jacobean and Caroline Stage*, III, 361. Moseley might have supposed that a deception would be less likely to be detected if he used a discarded title for the main title. It could have been a shrewd deception, though one would like to think that Moseley would not have descended to such a subterfuge. Greg's attempts (II, 983–4) to regard 'The Wandering Lovers' and 'The Painter' as separate plays might be thought to overlook the fact that the entry seems to regard them as alternate titles to a single play. There has been no convincing identification of 'The Painter'.

5 Cyrus Hoy, 'The shares of Fletcher and his collaborators in the Beaumont and Fletcher Canon (II)', *Studies in Bibliography*, IX (1956), 151–2. Bertha Hensman, *The Shares of Fletcher, Field and Massinger in the Beaumont and Fletcher Canon* (Salzburg, 1974), finds the distribution advanced by Maurice Chelli, *Etude sur la collaboration de Massinger avec Fletcher et son groupe* (Paris, 1927), persuasive.

433

Chelli divides the play into new (Massinger), old (Fletcher) and rewritten (Massinger revising Fletcher) (pp. 80–1); but her own distribution, formed on the basis of Massinger's use of sources – D'Audiguier, Cicero, Cervantes, Robert Burton – divides the play into four strata: Fletcher's text retained, compressed, recast; Massinger's original text (p. 293).

6 See for the publishing history: F. W. Vogler, *Vital D'Audiguier* (Chapel Hill, NC, 1964); *RSTC*; *Catalogue générale … de la Bibliothèque Nationale*; *Catalogue of … the British Library* (reprints in 1616, 1620, 1622, 1624, 1633, 1637, 1645 and 1667). It was published also in Lyons and Rouen, and in Leyden in 1650 and in Amsterdam in 1659. It was translated into English by William Duncombe as *A Tragicomicall History of our Times under the borrowed names of Lisander and Calista* and published in London in 1627, 1635 and 1652, and again by W. Barwick as *Love and Valour … One part of the unfained story of the true Lisander and Caliste* and published in 1638. (Barwick suggests on the titlepage that the original work was in part autobiographical.) It was translated also into 'Nederduyts' (Dutch) and 'Hooch-Teutsche' (German) in mid-century, and an edition in parallel columns in French and Dutch was published in Amsterdam in 1663, and one in French and German in 1670. (Dyce recorded the author's first name as 'Hery'.)

7 This analysis depends on the work of Mrs Christine Richardson-Hoy and of Mrs (now Dr) Barbara Fitzpatrick. I am indebted to Professor MacD. P. Jackson for assistance here.

8 See the analysis of these compositors in the Textual Introduction to *The Nice Valour*, in this series vol. VII, p. 430.

9 The line numbers for these stints: *A* set I.i.1–II.ii.9, IV.i.16–V.i.111 (i.112–iii.35a)–iii.35b–156), Prologue; *B* set II.ii, 10–IV.i.15, (V.i.112–iii.35a), V.iii.157–265, Epilogue.

10 Errors occur: at II.iii.50 and 69, F '*Clarin.*' represents Clarange; at IV.iii.71 '*Car.*' is misprinted for '*Clar.*'. Both compositors use '*Clar.*' and '*Cla.*' for both Clarange and Clarinda, but the confusion in these doublets is minimal. In I.ii, both characters being on-stage, an editor must decide which character is speaking on four instances of the prefix '*Clar.*'; only at line 71 is there any doubt. All editors have given the speech to Clarinda – one of her asides.

11 James P. Hammersmith, 'The proof-reading of the Beaumont and Fletcher Folio of 1647 … Section 3 …', *Papers of the Bibliographical Society of America*, LXXXVIII (1982), 287–232, esp. p. 311.

12 Quoted in Bentley, *Jacobean and Caroline Stage*, III, 363.

13 *Ibid.*, p. 360.

14 Lancelot entering '*like a Fortune-teller*' (II.ii.38) is in disguise.

15 The typescript has been prepared by a former student, Mr John Marmorstein, to whom I am indebted for careful and exact work.

16 See entry at note 11 above.

PERSONS REPRESENTED IN THE PLAY.

King of France.
Cleander, *Husband to* Caliste.
Lidian, *Brother to* Caliste.⎫
Clarange, *Rival to* Lidian.⎬*both in love with* Olinda.
Dorilaus, *Father to* Lidian *and* Caliste, *a merry old man.*
Lisander, *a noble Gentleman, in love with* Caliste.
Alcidon, *a friend, and second to* Lidian.
Beronte, *Brother to* Cleander.
Lemure, *a noble Courtier.*
Leon, *a Villain, Lover of* Clarinda.
Malfort, *a foolish Steward of* Cleander.
Lancelot, *Servant to* Lisander.
Frier.
[*An Apparition, the*] Hosts ghost.
Chamberlaine.
[*A Novice.*]
Servants.
[*Guard.*]

WOMEN

Caliste, *a vertuous Lady, Wife to* Cleander.
Olinda, *a noble Maid, and rich Heir, Mistress to* Lidian *and* Clarange.
Clarinda, *a lustful Wench,* Caliste's *waiting-woman.*

The Scene France.

436

THE LOVERS' PROGRESS.

Malfort.   And as I told you Sir——
Leon.   I understand you,
  Clarinda's still perverse.
Malfort.   Shee's worse, obdurate,
  Flinty, relentlesse, my love-passions jeer'd at,
  My presents scorn'd.
Leon.   'Tis strange a waiting-woman,
  In her condition apt to yield, should hold out,
  A man of your place, reverend beard and shape,
  Besieging her.
Malfort.   You might adde too my wealth,
  Which she contemnes, five hundred Crowns *per annum*,
  For which I have ventur'd hard, my conscience knows it,
  Not thought upon, though offer'd for a Joyinture: 10
  This Chaine which my Lords Pesants worship, flouted;
  My solemne hums and ha's, the servants quake at,
  No Rhetorick with her; every houre she hangs out
  Some new flag of defiance to torment me:
  Last Lent my Lady cal'd me her poor John,
  But now I am growne a walking Skelliton,
  You may see through and through me.
Leon.   Indeed you are
  Much falne away.
Malfort.   I am a kinde of nothing,
  As she hath made me: love's a terrible glister,
  And if some Cordiall of her favours help not,   20
  I shall like an Italian dye backward,
  And breath my last the wrong way.
Leon.   As I live
  You have my pity; but this is cold comfort,
  And in a friend lip-physick; and now I think on't,

I should doe more, and will, so you deny not
Your selfe the meanes of comfort.
Malfort.   Ile be hang'd first:
One dram of't I beseech you.
Leon.   You are not jealous
Of any mans accesse to her?
Malfort.   I would not
Receive the *Dor*, but as a bosome friend
You shall direct me, still provided that   30
I understand who is the man, and what
His purpose that pleads for me.
Leon.   By all meanes.
First, for the undertaker I am he:
The means that I will practise, thus——
Malfort.   Pray you forward,
Leon.   You know your Lady, chaste *Caliste* loves her.
Malfort.   Too well, that makes her proud.
Leon.   Nay, give me leave.
This beauteous Lady, I may stile her so,
(Being the paragon of *France* for feature)
Is not alone contented in her selfe
To seem, and be good, but desires to make   40
All such as have dependance on her like her;
For this *Clarinda's* liberty is restrain'd;
And though her kinsman the gate's shut against me;
Now if you please to make your selfe the doore,
For my conveyance to her, though you run
The hazard of a check for't, 'tis no matter.
Malfort.   It being for mine owne ends?
Leon.   Ile give it o're,
If that you make the least doubt otherwise:
Studying upon't? good morrow.
Malfort.   Pray you stay sir;
You are my friend: yet as the Proverb saies,   50
When love puts in, friendship is gone: suppose
You should your selfe affect her?
Leon.   Do you think
Ile commit Incest? for it is no lesse,

She being my cousin Germane. Fare you well sir.
Malfort.   I had forgot that; for this once forgive me.
  Onely to ease the throbbing of my heart,
  (For I doe feele strange pangs) instruct me what
  You will say for me.
Leon.   First, Ile tell her that
  She hath so far besotted you, that you have
  Almost forgot to cast accompt.
Malfort.   Meere truth sir.   60
Leon.   That of a wise and provident Steward,
  You are turn'd starke Asse.
Malfort.   Urge that point home, I am so.
Leon.   That you adore the ground she treads upon,
  And kisse her foot-steps.
Malfort.   As I doe when I finde
  Their print in the Snow.
Leon.   A loving foole I know it,
  By your bloudlesse-frosty lips: then having related
  How much you suffer for her, and how well
  You doe deserve it——
Malfort.   How? to suffer?
Leon.   No sir,
  To have your love return'd.
Malfort.   That's good, I thank you.
Leon.   I will deliver her an Inventorie   70
  Of your good parts: as this your precious nose,
  Dropping affection: your high-forehead, reaching
  Almost to the crowne of your head; your slender waste,
  And a back not like a threshers, but a bending
  And Court-like back, and so forth, for your body.
  But when I touch your minde, for that must take her,
  (Since your out-side promises little) Ile enlarge it,
  (Though ne're so narrow) as your Arts to thrive,
  Your composition with the Cook, and Butler,
  For Coney-skins and Chippings, and halfe a share   80
  With all the under-officers of the house,

In strangers bounties, that she shall have all,
And you as 'twere her Bailiffe.

Malfort.   As I will be.

Leon [*aside*].   As you shall, so Ile promise.——Then your qualities,
As playing on a Gytterne, or a Jewes Trumpe.

Malfort.   A little too on the Viall.

Leon.   Feare you nothing.
Then singing her asleep with curious catches
Of your owne making: for as I have heard,
You are Poeticall.

Malfort.   Something given that way.
Yet my works seldome thrive: and the main reason   90
The Poets urge for't, is, because I am not
As poore as they are.

Leon.   Very likely: fetch her,
While I am in the vaine.

Malfort.   'Tis an apt time,
My Lady being at her prayers.

Leon.   Let her pray on.
Nay goe, and if upon my intercession
She doe you not some favour, Ile disclaime her;
Ile ruminate on't the while.

Malfort.   A hundred Crownes
Is your reward.

Leon.   Without 'em——nay, no trifling.   *Exit* Malfort.
That this dull clod of ignorance should know
How to get money, yet want eyes to see   100
How grossely hee's abus'd, and wrought upon!
When he should make his will, the rogue's turn'd rampant,
As he had renew'd his youth: A handsome wench
Love one a spittle-whore would run away from?
Well Master Steward, I will plead for you
In such a Method, as it shall appeare
You are fit to be a propertie.

Enter Malfort *and* Clarinda.

102 rogue's] F2; rogues F1

Malfort.   Yonder he walks
  That knowes my worth and value, though you scorn it.
Clarinda.   If my Lady know not this——
Malfort.   I'll answer it:
  If you were a Nun, I hope your cousin German   110
  Might talke with you through a grate, but you are none,
  And therefore may come closer: ne're hang off,
  As I live you shall bill: you may salute as strangers,
  Custome allowes it.——Now, now, come upon her
  With all your Oratory, tickle her to the quick,
  As a young advocate should, and leave no vertue
  Of mine unmentioned, Ile stand Centinell;
  Nay keep the doore my selfe.   *Exit.*
Clarinda.   How have you work'd
  This piece of motley to your ends?
Leon.   Of that
  At leasure, Mistris.   *Kissing.*
Clarinda.   Lower, you are too loud,   120
  Though the fool be deaf, some of the house may hear you.
Leon.   Suppose they should, I am a gentleman,
  And held your kinseman, under that I hope
  I may be free.
Clarinda.   I grant it, but with caution;
  But be not seen to talke with me familiarly,
  But at fit distance, or not seen at all,
  It were the better: you know my Ladies humour,
  Shee is all honour, and compos'd of goodnesse,
  (As she pretends) and you having no businesse,
  How jealous may she grow?
Leon.   I will be rul'd.   130
  But you have promis'd, and I must enjoy you.
Clarinda.   We shall finde time for that; you are too hastie:
  Make your selfe fit, and I shall make occasion,
  Deliberation makes best in that businesse,
  And contents every way.
Leon.   But you must feed

135 you] F2; yon F1

441

This foolish Steward with some shadow of
A future favour, that we may preserve him
To be our instrument.
Clarinda.   Hang him.
Leon.   For my sake sweet,
  I undertook to speak for him; any bauble,
  Or slight employment in the way of service,   140
  Will feed him fat.
Clarinda.   Leave him to me.

                    Enter Malfort.

Malfort.   She comes.
  My Lady.
Clarinda.   I will satisfie her.
Malfort [*aside*].   How far
  Have you prevail'd?
Leon [*aside*].   Observe.
Clarinda.   Mounsieur *Malfort*.
  I must be briefe, my cousin hath spoke much
  In your behalfe, and to give you some proof,
  I entertaine you as my servant, you
  Shall have the grace——
Leon.   Upon your knee receive it.
Clarinda.   And take it as a speciall favour from me,
  To tye my shooe.
Malfort.   I am ore-joy'd.
Leon.   Good reason.
Clarinda.   You may come higher in time.
Leon.   No more, the Lady.   150

                    Enter Caliste.

Malfort.   She frownes.
Clarinda.   I thanke you for this visit cousin,
  But without leave hereafter from my Lady,
  I dare not change discourse with you.
Malfort [*to* Caliste].   Pray you take

                    148 as] F2; *omit* F1

                         442

Your mornings draught.
Leon.   I thank you: Happinesse
   Attend your honour.

                              Exeunt Leon, Malfort.

Caliste.   Who gave warrant to
   This private parle?
Clarinda.   My innocence; I hope
   My conference with a kinseman cannot call
   Your anger on me.
Caliste.   Kinsman? Let me have
   No more of this, as you desire you may
   Continue mine.
Clarinda.   Why Madam (under pardon)   160
   Suppose him otherwise: yet comming in
   A lawfull way it is excusable.
Caliste.   How's this?
Clarinda.   I grant you are made of purenesse,
   And that your tendernesse of honour holds
   The soveraigntie o're your passions. Yet you have
   A noble Husband, with allow'd embraces,
   To quench lascivious fires, should such flame in you,
   As I must ne're believe. Were I the wife
   Of one that could but zanie brave *Cleander*,
   Even in his least perfections, (excuse   170
   My ore-bold inference) I should desire
   To meet no other object.
Caliste.   You grow saucie.
   Doe I look further?
Clarinda.   No, deare Madam: and
   It is my wonder or astonishment rather,
   You could deny the service of *Lisander*;
   A man without a rivall: one the King
   And Kingdome gazes on with admiration,
   For all the excellencies a mother could
   Wish in her onely sonne.
Caliste.   Did not mine honour
   And Obligation to *Cleander*, force me   180
   To be deafe to his complaints?

                              443

Clarinda.   'Tis true; but yet
     Your rigor to command him from your presence,
     Argu'd but small compassion; the Groves
     Witnesse his grievous sufferings, your faire name
     Upon the rhinde of every gentle Poplar,
     And amorous Myrtle, (trees to *Venus* sacred)
     With adoration carv'd, and kneel'd unto,
     This you (unseen of him) both saw and heard
     Without compassion, and what receiv'd he
     For his true sorrowes? but the heavy knowledge,   190
     That 'twas your peremptory will and pleasure,
     (How e're my Lord liv'd in him) he should quit
     Your sight and house for ever.
Caliste.   I confesse
     I gave him a strong potion to worke
     Upon his hot bloud, and I hope 'twill cure him:
     Yet I could wish the cause had concern'd others,
     I might have met his sorrowes with more pittie;
     At least have lent some counsell to his miseries,
     Though now for honour sake, I must forget him,
     And never know the name more of *Lisander*:   200
     Yet in my justice I am bound to grant him,
     (Laying his love aside) most truely noble.
     But mention him no more, this instant houre
     My brother *Lidian*, new return'd from travaile,
     And his brave friend *Clarange*, long since rivalls
     For faire and rich *Olinda*, are to heare
     Her absolute determination, whom
     She pleases to elect: see all things ready
     To entertain 'em: and on my displeasure
     No more words of *Lisander*.
Clarinda [*aside*].   She endures   210
     To heare him nam'd by no tongue but her owne;
     How e're she carries it, I know she loves him.   *Exit.*
Caliste.   Hard nature: hard condition of poore women!
     That where we are most su'd too, we must flye most.
     The trees grow up, and mixe together freely,
     The Oke not envious of the sailing Cedar,

The lustie Vine not jealous of the Ivie
Because she clips the Elme; the flowers shoot up,
And wantonly kisse one another hourely,
This blossome glorying in the other beauty,   220
And yet they smell as sweet, and look as lovely:
But we are ty'd to grow alone. O honour,
Thou hard Law to our lives, chaine to our freedomes;
He that invented thee had many curses;
How is my soule divided? O *Cleander*,
My best deserving husband! O *Lisander*!
The truest lover that e're sacrific'd
To *Cupid* against *Hymen*: O mine honour;
A Tyrant, yet to be obey'd, and 'tis
But justice we should thy strict Lawes endure,   230
Since our obedience to thee keeps us pure.

                                                        Exit.

              Enter Cleander, Lidian, *and* Clarange.   [I.ii]

Cleander.   How insupportable the difference
    Of deare friends is, the sorrow that I feele
    For my *Lysanders* absence, one that stampes
    A reverend print on friendship, does assure me.
    You are rivals for a Lady, a faire Lady,
    And in the acquisition of her favours,
    Hazard the cutting of that Gordion knot
    From your first childhood to this present houre,
    By all the tyes of love and amity fastend,
    I am blest in a wife (heaven make me thankefull)   10
    Inferior to none (*sans* pride I speake it)
    Yet if I were a free-man, and could purchase
    At any rate the certainty to enjoy
    Lisanders conversation while I liv'd,
    Forgive me my *Caliste* and the Sexe,
    I never would seeke change.
Lidian.   My Lord and brother,
    I dare not blame your choice, *Lisanders* worth
    Being a Mistris to be ever courted;
    Nor shall our equall suit to faire *Olinda*

                              445

Weaken, but adde strength to our true affection,   20
With zeale so long continued.
Clarange.   When we know
Whom she prefers, as she can choose but one,
By our so long tride friendship we have vow'd
The other shall desist.
Cleander.   'Tis yet your purpose,
But how this resolution will hold
In him that is refus'd, is not alone
Doubtfull, but dangerous.

                    Enter Malfort.

Malfort.   The rich heire is come sir.
Cleander.   Madam *Olinda?*
Malfort.   Yes sir, and makes choice,
After some little conference with my Lady,
Of this room to give answer to her suitors.   30
Cleander.   Already both look pale, between your hopes
To win the prize, and your despaire to lose
What you contend for.
Lidian.   No sir, I am arm'd.
Clarange.   I confident of my interest.
Cleander.   Ile beleeve ye
When you have endur'd the test.

                    Enter Caliste, Olinda, *and* Clarinda.

Malfort [apart].   Is not your garter
Unty'd? you promis'd that I should grow higher
In doing you service.
Clarinda [apart].   Fall off or you lose mee.   *Exit* Malfort.
Cleander.   Nay take your place, no *Paris* now sits judge
On the contending goddesses. You are
The Deitie that must make curst or happy,   40
One of your languishing servants.
Olinda.   I thus look
With equal eyes on both; either deserves

33 contend] Sympson; contended F1–2

446

A fairer fortune then they can in reason
Hope for from me; from *Lidian* I expect,
When I have made him mine, all pleasures that
The sweetnesse of his manners, youth, and vertues
Can give assurance of: but turning this way
To brave *Clarange*, in his face appeares
A kinde of majesty which should command,
Not sue for favour. If the fairest Lady   50
Of *France*, set forth with natures best endowments
Nay should I adde a Princesse of the bloud,
Did now lay claime to either for a husband,
So vehement my affection is to both,
My envie at her happinesse would kill me.

Cleander.   The strangest love I ever heard.

Caliste.   You can
Enjoy but one.

Clarinda [aside].   The more I say the merrier.

Olinda.   Witnesse these teares I love both, as I know
You burne with equall flames, and so affect me;
Abundance makes me poore; such is the hard   60
Condition of my fortune; be your owne judges;
If I should favour both, 'twill taint my honour,
And that before my life I must prefer,
If one I leane to, the other is disvalewed;
You are fierie both, and love will make you warmer.

Clarinda [aside].   The warmer still the fitter. You are a foole Lady.

Olinda.   To what may love, and the devill jealousie spur you
Is too apparent: my name's cal'd in question:
Your swords flie out, your angers range at large:
Then what a murther of my modesty followes?   70

Clarinda [aside].   Take heed of that by any meanes: O innocent,
That will deny a blessing when 'tis offer'd,
Would I were murther'd so, I would thank my modesty.

Cleander.   What pause you on?

Olinda.   It is at length resolved.

Clarange.   We are on the Rack, uncertain expectation,
The greatest torture.

Lidian.   Command what you please,

447

And you shall see how willingly we will execute.

Olinda.   Then heare what for your satisfaction,
And to preserve your friendship I resolve
Against my selfe, and 'tis not to be alter'd: 80
You are both brave gentlemen, Ile still professe it,
Both noble servants, for whose gentle offers,
The undeserving, and the poore *Olinda*
Is ever bound; you love both, faire, and vertuously;
Would I could be so happy to content both:
Which since I cannot, take this resolute answer;
Goe from me both contentedly, and he
That last makes his returne, and comes to visit,
Comes to my bed. You know my will: farewell;
My heart's too big to utter more:——come friend.   90

Caliste.   Ile wait on you to your Coach.

                                        Exeunt Olinda, Caliste, Clarinda.

Cleander.   You both look blank,
I cannot blame you.

Lidian.   We have our dispatches.

Clarange.   Ile home.

Lidian.   And Ile abroad again, Farewell.

Clarange.   Farewell to yee.

                            Exeunt Clarange *and* Lidian [*severally*].

Cleander.   Their blunt departure troubles me: I feare
A suddaine and a dangerous division
Of their long love will follow:

                        Enter Caliste.

                        have you took
Your leave of faire *Olinda?*

Caliste.   She is gone sir.

Cleander.   Had you brought news *Lisander* were return'd too,
I were most happy.

Caliste.   Still upon *Lisander?*   100

Cleander.   I know he loves me, as he loves his health:
And heaven knowes I love him.

---

95 blunt] Sympson; blunted F1–2   *97 Caliste.] Colman; *Caliste with a purse.* F1–2

Caliste.   I finde it so:
  For me you have forgot, and what I am to you.
Cleander.   O think not so. If you had lost a sister,
  You lock'd all your delights in, it would grieve you:
  A little you would wander from the fondnesse,
  You ow'd your husband: I have lost a friend,
  A noble friend, all that was excellent
  In man, or man-kinde, was contain'd within him.
  That losse my wife——

                    Enter Malfort.

Malfort.   Madam, your noble Father——   110
  A fee for my good newes.
Caliste.   Why? what of him sir?
Malfort.   Is lighted at the doore, and longs to see you.
Caliste.   Attend him hither.   [*Exit* Malfort.]
Cleander.   O my deare *Lisander.*
  But Ile bee merry: lets meet him my *Caliste.*
Caliste [*aside*].   I hope *Lisanders* love will now be buried:
  My father will bring joy enough for one moneth,
  To put him out of his memorie.

          Enter [Malfort *with*] Dorilaus, *his arme in a scarffe.*

Dorilaus.   How doe you sonne?
  Blesse my faire child, I am come to visit yee,
  To see what house you keep; they say you are bountifull,
  I like the noyse well, and I come to trie it.   120
  Ne're a great belly yet? how have you trifl'd?
  If I had done so (sonne) I should have heard on't
  On both sides by Saint *Denis.*
Cleander.   You are nobly welcome sir:
  We have time enough for that.
Dorilaus.   See how she blushes:
  'Tis a good signe you'll mend your fault,——how dost thou,
  My good *Caliste?*
Caliste.   Well, now I see you sir;
  I hope you bring a fruitfulnesse along with ye.
Dorilaus.   Good luck, I never misse, I was ever good at it:

                    449

Your mother groand for't wench, so did some other,
But I durst never tell.
Caliste. How does your arme sir? 130
Cleander. Have you been let bloud of late?
Dorilaus. Against my will sir.
Caliste. A fall deare father?
Dorilaus. No, a Gun, deare daughter;
Two or three Guns; I have one here in my buttock,
'Twould trouble a Surgeons teeth to pull it out.
Caliste. O me! O me!
Dorilaus. Nay, if you fall to fainting,
'Tis time for me to trudge: art such a coward,
At the meere name of hurt to change thy colour?
I have been shot that men might see clean through me
And yet I fainted not: besides my selfe,
Here are an hospitall of hurt men for yee. 140

Enter Servants, wounded in severall places.

Cleander. What should this wonder be?
Caliste. I am amaz'd at it.
Dorilaus. What think ye of these? they are every one hurt soundly,
Hurt to the proof they are, through and through I assure ye;
And that's good game, they scorne your puling scratches.
Caliste. Who did this sir?
Dorilaus. Leave crying, and Ile tell you,
And get your plaisters, and your warme stupes ready:
Have you ne're a Shepheard that can tarre us over?
'Twill proove a businesse else, we are so many.
Comming to see you, I was set upon,
I and my men, as we were singing frolickly, 150
Not dreaming of an ambush of base rogues,
Set on ith'forrest, I have forgot the name——
Cleander. 'Twixt this, and *Fountaine-Bleiu?*
Caliste. In the wilde Forrest?
Dorilaus. The same, the same, in that accursed Forrest,
Set on by villaines, that make boot of all men;

146 stupes] *i.e.,* bandages   *153 *Caliste.*] omit F1–2

The Peeres of *France* are pillage there. They shot at us,
Hurt us, un-hors'd us, came to the sword, there plide us,
Opprest us with fresh multitudes, fresh shot still,
Rogues that would hang themselves for a fresh doublet,
And for a Skarlet Cassock kill their fathers.   160

Cleander.   Lighted you among these?
Dorilaus.   Among these murtherers,
Our poore blouds were ingag'd: yet we strook bravely,
And more then once or twice we made them shun us,
And shrink their rugged heads: be we were hurt all.

Cleander.   How came you off? for I even long to hear that.
Dorilaus.   After our prayers made to heaven to help us,
Or to be mercifull unto our soules,
So neare we were———Alas poore wench, wipe, wipe.
See heaven sends remedy.

Caliste.   I am glad 'tis come sir,
My heart was even a bleeding in my body.   170

Dorilaus.   A curl'd haire gentleman stept in, a stranger,
As he rod by, belike he heard our bickering,
Saw our distresses, drew his sword, and prov'd
He came to execute, and not to argue.
Lord what a lightning me thought flew about him,
When he once toss'd his blade; in face *Adonis*,
While peace inhabited between his eye-browes:
But when his noble anger stirr'd his mettle,
And blew his firie parts into a flame,
Like *Pallas*, when she sits between two armies,   180
Viewing with horrid browes their sad events,
Such then hee look'd: and as her shield had arm'd him.

Caliste.   This man sir were a friend to give an age for.
This gentleman I must love naturally:
Nothing can keep me off; I pray you goe on sir.

Dorilaus.   I will, for now you please me: this brave youth,
This bud of *Mars*, for yet he is no riper,
When once he had drawne bloud, and flesh'd his sword,
Fitted his manly mettle to his spirit,

*189 mettle] *stet* F1

451

How he bestirr'd him? what a lane he made?   190
And through their fierie Bullets thrust securely,
The hardned villaines wondring at his confidence:
Lame as I was I follow'd, and admir'd too,
And stirr'd, and laid about me with new spirit,
My men too with new hearts thrust into action,
And down the rogues went.

Cleander.   I am strook with wonder.

Dorilaus.   Remember but the storie of strong *Hector*,
When like to lightning he broke through his van-guard,
How the *Greeks* frighted ran away by Troops,
And trod downe Troops to save their lives: so this man,   200
Dispers'd these slaves: had they been more and mightier,
He had come off the greater, and more wonder.

Cleander.   Where is the man, good sir, that we may honor him?

Caliste.   That we may fall in superstition to him?

Dorilaus.   I know not that, from me he late departed,
But not without that pious care to see safe
Me, and my weak men lodg'd, and dress'd; I urg'd him
First hither, that I might more freely thanke him:
He told me he had businesse, crav'd my pardon,
Businesse of much import.

Cleander.   Know you his name?   210

Dorilaus.   That he deny'd me too: a vow had bard him.

Caliste.   In that he was not noble to be namelesse.

Dorilaus.   Daughter you must remember him when I am dead,
And in a noble sort requite his piety,
'Twas his desire to dedicate this service
To your faire thoughts.

Caliste.   He knowes me then?

Dorilaus.   I nam'd you,
And nam'd you mine: I think that's all his knowledge.

Cleander.   No name, no being?

Caliste.   Now I am mad to know him:
Saving mine honour, any thing I had now
But to enjoy his sight, but his bare picture: 220

---

199 Troops] *See Textual Note at* II.i.94.

Make me his Saint? I must needs honour him.

Servant.   I know his name.

Caliste.   There's thy reward for't; speak it.
                            [She rewards him] with a purse.

Servant.   His man told me, but he desir'd my silence.

Caliste.   O *Jasper* speak, 'tis thy good Masters cause too:
We all are bound in gratitude to compell thee.

Servant.   *Lisander*, Yes, I am sure it was *Lisander*.

Caliste.   *Lisander?*

Servant.   'Twas *Lisander*.

Cleander.   'Tis *Lisander*.
O my base thoughts? my wicked? to make question
This act could be another mans: 'tis *Lisander*——
A handsome timber'd man?

Servant.   Yes.

Cleander.   My *Lisander!*   230
Was this friends absence to bee mourn'd?

Caliste.   I grant it:
Ile mourne his going now, and mourne it seriously:
When you weep for him, sir, Ile beare you company.
That so much honour, so much honesty
Should be in one man, to doe things thus bravely,
Make me his Saint, to me give this brave service:
What may I doe to recompence his goodnesse?
I cannot tell.

Cleander.   Come sir, I know you are sickly,
So are your men.

Dorilaus.   I must confesse I am weake,
And fitter for a bed then long discourses.   240
You shall hear to morrow, to morrow——

Cleander.   Provide Surgeons. [*Exit* Malfort.]
   Lisander——

Caliste.   What new fire is this? *Lisander*——
                             Exeunt.

Enter Lisander, *and* Lancelot.   II.i

---

*227 *Servant.* 'Twas] Dyce; 'Twas F1–2   *241 You] Colman; *Cle.* You F1–2
241 *Cleander.* Provide] provide F1–2   242(1) *Lisander*] *Dor. Lisander* F1–2

Lisander.   Prethee good *Lancelot* remember that
   Thy Masters life is in thy trust, and therefore
   Be very careful.
Lancelot.   I will lose mine owne,
   Rather then hazard yours.
Lisander.   Take what disguise
   You in your owne discretion shall think fittest,
   To keep your selfe unknowne.
Lancelot.   I warrant yee;
   'Tis not the first time I have gone invisible:
   I am as fine a Fairie in a businesse
   Concerning night-worke——
Lisander.   Leave your vanities:
   With this purse (which deliver'd, you may spare   10
   Your Oratory) convey this Letter to   [*Gives purse and Letter.*]
   Caliste's woman.
Lancelot.   'Tis a handsome girle,
   Mistris *Clarinda*.
Lisander.   I have made her mine.
   You know your work.
Lancelot.   And if I sweat not in it,
   At my returne discarde me.   *Exit.*
Lisander.   O *Caliste*!
   The fairest! cruellest!

                    Enter Clarange.

Clarange.   So early stirring?
   A good day to you.
Lisander.   I was viewing sir,
   The site of your house, and the handsomnesse about it:
   Believe me it stands healthfully and sweetly.
Clarange.   The house and master of it really   20
   Are ever at your service.
Lisander.   I returne it:
   Now if you please goe forward in your storie
   Of your deare friend and Mistris.
Clarange.   I will tell it,
   And tell it short, because 'tis breakfast time,

                         454

(And love a tedious thing to a quick stomach)
You eate not yester-night.
Lisander.   I shall endure sir.
Clarange.   My selfe and (as I then deliver'd to you)
    A gentleman of noble hope, one *Lidian*,
    Both brought up from our infancy together,
    One company, one friendship, and one exercise,   30
    Ever affecting, one bed holding us,
    One griefe, and one joy parted still between us,
    More then companions, twins in all our actions,
    We grew up till we were men, held one heart still:
    Time call'd us on to Armes, we were one souldier,
    Alike we sought our dangers and our honours,
    Gloried alike one in anothers noblenesse:
    When Armes had made us fit, we were one lover;
    We lov'd one woman, lov'd without division,
    And woo'd a long time with one faire affection;   40
    And she, as it appeares, loves us alike too.
    At length considering what our love must grow to,
    And covet in the end, this one was parted,
    Rivalls and honours make men stand at distance.
    We then woo'd with advantage, but were friends still,
    Saluted fairely, kept the peace of love,
    We could not both enjoy the Ladies favour,
    Without some scandall to her reputation,
    We put it to her choice, this was her sentence,
    To part both from her, and the last returning   50
    Should be her Lord; we obey'd, and now you know it;
    And for my part, (so truely I am touch'd with't)
    I will goe farre enough, and be the last too,
    Or ne're returne.
Lisander.   A sentence of much cruelty;
    But milde, compar'd with whats pronounc'd on me.
    Our loving youth is borne to many miseries.
    What is that *Lidian* pray ye?
Clarange.   *Caliste's* brother,
    If ever you have heard of that faire Ladie.
Lisander.   I have seen her sir.

Clarange.   Then you have seen a wonder.
Lisander.   I doe confesse: of what yeares is this *Lidian?*   60
Clarange.   About my years: there is not much between us.
Lisander.   I long to know him.
Clarange.   'Tis a vertuous longing,
    As many hopes hang on his noble head,
    As blossoms on a bough in May, and sweet ones.
Lisander.   Ye are a faire storie of your friend.
Clarange.   Of truth sir:

Enter a Servant.

    Now what's the matter?
Servant.   There is a gentleman
    At doore, would speak with you on private businesse.
Clarange.   With me?
Servant.   He saies so, and brings haste about him.
Clarange.   Wait on him in.   *Exit* Servant.
Lisander.   I will retire the while,
    To the next room.
Clarange.   We shall not long disturbe you.   70
                              [*Exit* Lisander.]

Enter Alcidon.

Alcidon.   Save ye sir.
Clarange.   The like to you fair sir: pray you come neare.
Alcidon.   Pray you instruct me for I know you not.
    With Monsieur *Clarange* I would speak.
Clarange.   I am he sir:
    Ye are nobly welcome; I wait your businesse.
Alcidon.   This will informe you.   [*Gives a Letter.*]
Clarange.   Will you please to sit down?   *Reads.*
    He shall command me sir, Ile wait upon him
    Within this houre.
Alcidon.   Y'are a noble gentleman,
    Wil't please you bring a friend? we are two of us,
    And pitty either, sir, should be unfurnish'd.   80
Clarange.   I have none now, and the time is set so short,
    'Twill not be possible.

Alcidon.   Doe me the honour;
   I know you are so full of brave acquaintance,
   And worthy friends, you cannot want a partner:
   I would be loath to stand still sir; besides,
   You know the custome, and the vantage of it,
   If you come in alone.
Clarange.   And I must meet it.
Alcidon.   Send, wee'l defer an houre, let us be equall:
   Games won and lost on equall tearmes shew fairest.
Clarange.   'Tis to no purpose to send any whither,   90
   Unlesse men be at home by Revelation:
   So please you breath a while; when I have done with him
   You may be exercis'd too: Ile trouble no man.

Enter Lisander.

Lisander [*aside*].   They are very loud.——
                   Now what's the newes?
Clarange.   I must
   Leave you a while, two houres hence Ile returne friend.
Lisander.   Why, what's the matter?
Clarange.   A little businesse.
Lisander.   And't be but a little, you may take me with ye.
Clarange.   'Twill be a trouble to you.
Lisander.   No indeed,
   To do you service, I account a pleasure.
Clarange.   I must alone.
Lisander.   Why?
Clarange.   'Tis necessity——   100
   Before you passe the walks, and back agen,
   I will be with ye.
Lisander.   If it be not unmannerly
   To presse you, I would goe.
Clarange.   Ile tell you true sir,
   This gentleman and I upon appointment,
   Are going to visit a Lady.
Lisander.   I am no *Capuchin*,

*95 Leave you] leave you | Leave you F1–2

Why should not I goe?

Alcidon.   Take the gentleman,
Come he may see the gentlewoman too,
And be most welcome, I do beseech you take him.

Lisander.   By any means, I love to see a gentlewoman,
A prettie wench too.

Clarange.   Well sir, wee'll meet you,   110
And at the place: My service to the Lady.

Alcidon.   I kisse your hand.   *Exit.*

Clarange.   Prethee read o're her Letter.

Lisander (reads).

Monsieur,

I know you have consider'd the dark sentence Olinda *gave us, and that
(however she disguis'd it) it pointed more at our swords edges then our
bodies banishments; the last must enjoy her: if we retire, our youths are
lost in wandring; in emulation we shall grow old men, and feeble,
Which is the scorne of love, and rust of honour, and so return more fit to
wed our Sepulchers, then the Saint we aime at; let us therefore make
our journey short, and our hearts ready, and with our swords in our*   120
*hands put it to fortune, which shall be worthy to receive that blessing,
Ile stay you on the mountaine, our old hunting place, this gentleman
alone runs the hazzard with me, and so I kisse your hand.*

Your servant *Lidian.*

Is this your wench? you'll finde her a sharp Mistris.
[*Aside*] What have I thrust my selfe into?——is this that *Lidian*
You told me of?

Clarange.   The same.

Lisander [*aside*].   My Ladies brother?
No cause to heave my sword against but his?
To save the father yesterday, and this morning,
To help to kill the son? this is most courteous?   130
The onely way to make the daughter doat on me.

Clarange.   Why doe you muse? would ye goe off?

Lisander.   No, no,
I must on now;——[*aside*] this will be kindly taken,
No life to sacrifice, but part of hers?——
Doe you fight straight?

458

Clarange.   Yes, presently.

Lisander [*aside*].   To morrow then,
The balefull tidings of this day will break out,
And this nights Sun will set in bloud; I am troubl'd:
If I am kill'd, I am happy.

Clarange.   Will you goe friend?

Lisander.   I am ready sir,——[*aside*] fortune thou hast made me
monstrous.

                                        Exeunt.

                Enter Malfort *and* Clarinda.   [II.ii]

Malfort.   Your cousin, and my true friend, lusty *Leon*.
Shall know how you use me.

Clarinda.   Be more temperate,
Or I will never use, nor know you more
Ith' way of a servant: all the house takes notice
Of your ridiculous fopperie; I have no sooner
Perform'd my duties in my Ladies chamber,
And she scarce down the stairs, but you appeare
Like my evill spirit to me.

Malfort.   Can the fish live
Out of the water, or the Salamander
Out of the fire? or I live warme, but in   10
The frying-pan of your favour?

Clarinda.   Pray you forget
Your curious comparisons, borrowed from
The pond, and kitchin, and remember what
My Ladies pleasure is for th'entertainment
Of her noble father.

Malfort.   I would learn the art
Of memory in your table book.

Clarinda.   Very good sir,
No more but up and ride? I apprehend
Your meaning, soft fire makes sweet mault sir:
I'le answer you in a Proverbe.

Malfort.   But one kisse
From thy honey lippe.

Clarinda.   You sight too high, my hand is   20

                    459

A faire ascent from my foot,——his slavering kisses
Spoyle me more gloves,——enough for once, you'l surfet
With too much grace.
Malfort.   Have you no imployment for me?
Clarinda.   Yes, yes, go send for *Leon*, and convey him
  Into the private Arbour, from his mouth
  I heare your praises with more faith.
Malfort.   I am gone.
  Yet one thing ere I go, there's at the dore
  The rarest Fortune-teller, he hath told me
  The strangest things; he knows ye are my Mistris,
  And under seale deliver'd how many children   30
  I shall beget on you, pray you give him hearing,
  He'l make it good to you.
Clarinda.   A cunning man
  Of your own making, howsoe're I'le heare him
  At your intreaty.
Malfort.   Now I perceive ye love me,
  At my entreaty:——come in friend:——

            Enter Lancelot *like a Fortune-teller.*

                              [*apart*] remember
  To speake as I directed:——[*aside*] he knows his lesson,
  And the right way to please her; this it is
  To have a head-peece.   *Exit.*
Clarinda.   'Tis said you can tell
  Fortunes to come.
Lancelot.   Yes Mistris, and what's past;
  Unglove your hand: by this straight line, I see   40
  You have laine crooked.
Clarinda.   How? laine crooked?
Lancelot.   Yes;
  And in that posture plaid at the old game,
  (No body heares me, and I'le be no blab)
  And at it lost your maiden-head.
Clarinda [*aside*].   A shrewd fellow;

*35 *Fortune-teller.*] *Fortune-teller, with a Purse, and two Letters in it.* F1–2. *See Textual Note at*
  I.ii.97.

'Tis truth, but not to be confess'd;——in this
Your palmestry deceaves you, some thing else sir.

Lancelot.   Ye are a great woman with your Lady, and
Acquainted with her counsels.

Clarinda [*aside*].   Still more strange.

Lancelot.   There is a noble Knight *Lisander* loves her,
Whom she regards not, and the destinies   50
With whom I am familiar, have deliver'd
That by your meanes alone, he must enjoy her.
Your hand agen, Yes, yes; you have already
Promis'd him your assistance, and what's more,
Tasted his bounty, for which, from the skye
There are two hundred crownes dropp'd in a Purse,
Looke backe, you'l find it true;
                          [*Throws*] *a Purse* [*behind her.*]
                    nay, open it,
'Tis good Gold I assure you.   [*She opens purse;*
                          finds gold] *and two Letters in it.*

Clarinda.   How, two Letters?
The first indors'd to me? this to my Lady?
Subscrib'd *Lisander.*

Lancelot.   And the Fortune-teller,   60
His servant *Lancelot.*

Clarinda.   How had I lost my eyes,
That I could not know thee? not a word of the losse
Of my virginity.

Lancelot.   Nor who I am.

Clarinda.   I'le use all speedy meanes for your dispatch,
With a welcome answer, but till you receive it,
Continue thus disguis'd; Mounsieur *Malfort*
(You know the way to humour him) shall provide
A lodging for you, and good entertainment;
Nay, since we trade both one way, thou shalt have
Some feeling with me, take that.   [*Gives gold.*]

Lancelot.   Bountifull wench   70
May'st thou ne're want imployment.

Clarinda.   Nor such pay, boy.
                          Exeunt.

Enter Lidian, Alcidon, (*at one dore*) Clarange, Lisander, (*at*   [II.i
another).

Lidian [*to* Clarange].   You'r welcome.
Alcidon [*to* Lisander].   Let us do our office first,
    And then make choice of a new peece of ground
    To try our fortunes.
Lisander.   All's faire here.
Alcidon.   And here.
    Their swords are equall.
Lisander.   If there be any odds
    In mine, we will exchange.
Alcidon.   Wee'l talke of that
    When we are farther off: [*to* Lidian] farwell.
Lisander [*to* Clarange].   Farewell friend.
                            Exeunt Lisander *and* Alcidon.
Lidian.   Come let us not be idle?
Clarange.   I will find you
    Imployment, feare not.
Lidian.   You know sir, the cause
    That brings us hether.
Clarange.   There needs no more discoursing,
    No time, nor place for repetition now.   10
Lidian.   Let our Swords argue, and I wish *Clarange*,
    The proud *Olinda* saw us.
Clarange.   Would she did;
    What ever estimation she holds of me,
    She should behold me like a man fight for her.   *Fight within.*
Lidian.   'Tis nobly said; set on; love, and my fortune——
Clarange.   The same for me, come home brave *Lidian*:   *Fight.*
    'Twas manly thrust, this token to the Lady,
    Ye have it sir, deliver it, take breath,
    I see ye bleed apace, ye shall have faire play.

                    Enter Lisander.

Lisander [*to* Alcidon *within*].
    You must lye there a while, I cannot help you.   20

*14/16 *Fight within.* | *Fight.*] (Hammersmith *conj.*); *Fight and* | *fight with.* F1 (u); *omit* F1 (c), F2

462

Lidian.   Nay, then my fortunes gone, I know I must dye:
   Yet dearely will I sell my love, come on both,
   And use your fortunes, I expect no favour;
   Weake as I am, my confidence shall meet ye.
Clarange.   Yield up your cause and live.
Lidian.   What dost thou hold me?
   A recreant, that prefers life before credit?
   Though I bleed hard, my honour finds no Issue,
   That's constant to my heart.
Clarange.   Have at your life then.
Lisander.   Hold, or I'le turne, and bend my sword against ye;
   My cause *Clarange* too, view this brave Gentleman,   30
   That yet may live to kill you, he stands nobly,
   And has as great a promise of the day
   As you can tye unto your selfe, he's ready,
   His Sword as sharpe, view him with that remembrance,
   That you deliver'd him to me *Clarange*:
   And with those eyes, that clearnesse will become ye:
   View him, as you reported him; survey him,
   Fixe on your friendship sir, I know you are noble,
   And step but Inward to your old affection,
   Examine but that soule grew to your bosome,   40
   And try then if your Sword will bite, it cannot,
   The edge will turne againe, asham'd, and blunted;
   Lidian, you are the patterne of faire friendship,
   Exampled for your Love, and imitated,
   The Temple of true hearts, stor'd with affections,
   For sweetnesse of your spirit made a Saint,
   Can you decline this noblenesse to anger?
   To mortall anger? 'gainst the man ye love most?
   Have ye the name of vertuous, not the nature?
Lidian.   I will sit downe.
Clarange.   And I'le sit by you *Lidian*.   50
Lisander.   And I'le go on, can heaven be pleas'd with these things?
   To see two hearts that have been twin'd together,

44 Exampled] F1(c); Example F1 (u)   50, 69 *Clarange.*] Langbaine; *Clarin.* F1; *Clar.* F2
*52 twin'd] *stet* F1   53 a] Sympson; to F1–2

Married in friendship, to the world a wonder,
Of one growth, of one nourishment, one health,
Thus mortally divorc'd for one weake woman?
Can love be pleas'd? love is a gentle spirit,
The wind that blowes the Aprill flowers, not softer;
She is drawne with doves to shew her peacefulnesse,
Lions and bloudy Pards are *Mars's* servants;
Would ye serve love? do it with humblenesse,   60
Without a noise, with still prayers, and soft murmurs;
Upon her Altars offer your obedience,
And not your brawles; she's won with teares, not terrors:
That fire ye kindle to her deity,
Is only gratefull when it's blowen with sighs,
And holy Incense flung with white-hand innocence;
Ye wound her now; ye are too superstitious
No sacrifice of bloud, or death she longs for.

Lidian.   Came he from heaven?

Clarange.   He tels us truth good *Lidian.*

Lisander.   That part of Noble love which is most sweet,   70
And gives eternall being to faire beauty,
Honour, you hack a peeces with your swords,
And that ye fight to crowne, ye kill, faire credit.

Clarange.   Thus we embrace, no more fight, but all friendship,
And where love pleases to bestow his benefits,
Let us not argue.

Lidian.   Nay brave sir, come in too;
You may love also, and may hope. If ye do,
And not rewarded for't, there is no justice;——
Farwell friend, here let's part upon our pilgrimage,
It must be so, *Cupid* draws on our sorrowes.   80
And where the lot lights——

Clarange.   I shall count it happinesse,
Farewell deare friend.

Lisander.   First, let's relieve the Gentleman
That lyes hurt in your cause, and bring him off,

*53 friendship, ... world ∧ a wonder,] Dyce; friendship ∧ ... world, to wonder, F1–2
65 it's blowen] F2 (blown); it blowes F1   77 ye] F2; he F1

464

And take some cure for your hurts, then I will part too,
A third unfortunate, unwilling wanderer.

Exeunt.

Enter Olinda, *and* Caliste.   [II.iv]

Olinda.   My feares foresaw 'twould come to this.
Caliste.   I would
    Your sentence had been milder.
Olinda.   'Tis past helpe now.
Caliste.   I share in your despaire, and yet my hopes
    Have not quite left me, since all possible meanes
    Are practised to prevent the mischiefe following
    Their mortall meeting: my Lord is coasted one way,
    My father, though his hurts forbad his travell,
    Hath tooke another, my brother in Law *Beronte*,
    A third, and every minute we must looke for
    The certaine knowledge, which we must endure   10
    With that calme patience heav'n shall please to lend us.

Enter Dorilaus, *and* Cleander, *severally.*

Dorilaus.   Dead both?
Cleander.   Such is the rumour, and 'tis generall.
Olinda.   I heare my passing-bell.
Caliste.   I am in a feavour.
Cleander.   They say their seconds too; but what they are,
    Is not known yet, some worthy fellows certain.
Dorilaus.   Where had you knowledge?
Cleander.   Of the Country people.
    'Tis spoken every where.
Dorilaus.   I heard it too;
    And 'tis so common, I do halfe beleeve it,
    You have lost a brother wench, he lov'd you well,
    And might have liv'd to have done his countrie service,   20
    But he is gone, thou fell'st untimely *Lidian*,
    But by a valiant hand, that's some small comfort,

---

*85 unwilling] and willing F1–2   17 too] so too F1–2   21 fell'st] F2; feld'st F1

And tooke him with thee too, thou lov'st brave company:
Weeping will do no good:——you lost a servant,
He might have liv'd to have been your Master Lady,
But you fear'd that.
Olinda.   Good sir, be tender to me,
The newes is bad enough, you need not presse it,
I lov'd him well, I lov'd 'em both.
Dorilaus.   It seemes so.
How many more have you to love so Lady?
They were both fooles to fight for such a Fidle;   30
Certaine there was a dearth of noble anger,
When a slight woman was thought worth a quarrell.
Olinda.   Pray you thinke nobler.
Dorilaus.   I'le tell thee what I thinke: the plague, war, famine,
Nay, put in dice and drunkennesse, and those
You'l grant are pretty helpes, kill not so many
(I meane so many noble) as your loves do,
Rather your lewdnesse, I crave your mercy women.
Be not offended if I anger ye.
I am sure ye have touch'd me deep, I came to be merry,   40
And with my children, but to see one ruin'd
By this fell accident——

Enter Beronte, Alcidon, Clarinda *following.*

                         are they all dead?
If they be, speake!
Cleander.   What newes?
Beronte.   What dead? ye pose me;
I understand you not.
Cleander.   My brother *Lidian,*
Clarange, and their seconds.
Beronte.   Here is one of 'em,
And sure this Gentleman's alive.
Alcidon.   I hope so,
So is your son sir, so is brave *Clarange*:
They fought indeed, and they were hurt sufficiently;

42 *following.*] *following with a Letter.* F1–2. *See Textual Note at* I.ii.97.

We were all hurt, that bred the generall rumour,
But friends againe all, and like friends we parted.   50
Cleander.   Heard ye of *Lisander?*
Beronte.   Yes, and miss'd him narrowly:
  He was one of the combatants, fought with this Gentleman,
  Second against your brother, by his wisdome
  (For certainly good fortune followes him)
  All was made peace, I'le tell you the rest at dinner,
  For we are hungry.
Alcidon.   I before I eate
  Must pay a vow I am sworne to; my life Madam
  Was at *Lisander's* mercy, I live by it;
  And for the noble favour, he desir'd me
  To kisse your faire hand for him, offering   60
  This second service as a Sacrifice
  At the Altar of your vertues.
Dorilaus.   Come, joy on all sides;
  Heaven will not suffer honest men to perish.
Cleander.   Be proud of such a friend.
Dorilaus.   Forgive me Madam,
  It was a griefe might have concern'd you neare too.
Cleander.   No worke of excellence but still *Lisander*,
  Go thy waies worthy.
Olinda.   Wee'l be merry too,
  Were I to speake againe, I would be wiser.
Caliste.   Too much of this rare cordiall makes me sick,
  However, I obey you. *Exeunt. Manent* Clarinda, *staying* Caliste.
Clarinda [*aside*].   Now or never   70
  Is an apt time to move her:—— Madam.
Caliste.   Who's that?
Clarinda.   Your servant, I would speake with your Ladyship.
Caliste.   Why dost thou looke about?
Clarinda.   I have private businesse
  That none must heare but you. *Lisander*——
Caliste.   Where?
Clarinda.   Nay, is not here, but would entreat this favor,

*70 *Exeunt ... Caliste.*] *See Textual Note.*

Some of your Balsome from your own hand given,
For he is much hurt, and that he thinkes would cure him.
Caliste.   He shall have all, my prayers too.
Clarinda.   But conceive me,
   It must be from your selfe immediately,
   Pitty so brave a Gentleman should perish,   80
   He is superstitious, and he holds your hand
   Of infinite power: I would not urge this Madam,
   But only in a mans extreames, to helpe him.
Caliste.   Let him come (good wench) 'tis that I wish, I am happy in't,
   My husband his true friend, my noble father,
   The faire *Olinda*, all desire to see him;
   He shall have many hands.
Clarinda.   That he desires not,
   Nor eyes, but yours to looke upon his miseries,
   For then he thinkes 'twould be no perfect cure (Madam);
   He would come private.
Caliste.   How can that be here?   90
   I shall do wrong unto all those that honour him,
   Besides my credit.
Clarinda.   Dare ye not trust a hurt man?
   Not straine a curtesie to save a Gentleman?
   To save his life, that has sav'd all your family?
   A man that comes like a poore mortifi'd Pilgrim,
   Only to beg a blessing, and depart againe?
   He would but see you, that he thinkes would cure him.
   But since you find fit reasons to the contrary,
   And that it cannot stand with your cleare honour,
   Though you best know how well he has deserv'd of ye,   100
   I'l send him word backe; though I grieve to do it,
   Grieve at my soule, for certainly 'twill kill him,
   What your will is.
Caliste.   Stay, I will thinke upon't;
   Where is he wench?
Clarinda.   If you desire to see him,
   Let not that trouble you, he shall be with ye,
   And in that time, that no man shall suspect ye;
   Your honour Madam, is in your own free keeping;

468

Your care in me, in him all honesty;
If ye desire him not, let him passe by ye:
And all this businesse reckon but a dreame.   110
Caliste.   Go in, and counsell me, I would faine see him,
    And willingly comfort him.
Clarinda.   'Tis in your power.
    And if you dare trust me, you shall do it safely,
    Read that,   *[Gives]* a Letter.
        and let that tell you, how he honours you.

                                                    Exeunt.

            Enter Clarinda, *with a Key, and* Leon.   III.i

Leon.   This happy night.   *Kisses her.*
Clarinda.   Preserve this eagernesse
    Till we meet nearer, there is something done
    Will give us opportunity.
Leon.   Witty girle, the plot?
Clarinda.   You shall heare that at leasure,
    The whole house reeles with joy at the report
    Of *Lidians* safety, and that joy increas'd
    From their affection to the brave *Lisander*,
    In being made the happy instrument to compound
    The bloudy difference.
Leon.   They will heare shortly that
    Will turne their mirth to mourning, he was then   10
    The principall meanes to save two lives, but since
    There are two falne, and by his single hand,
    For which his life must answer, if the King,
    Whose arme is long, can reach him.
Clarinda.   We have now
    No spare time to heare stories, take this key,   *[Gives a key.]*
    'Twill make your passage to the banquetting house
    I'the garden free.
Leon.   You will not faile to come?
Clarinda.   For mine owne sake ne're doubt it?   *Exit* [Leon].
                            now for *Lisander*.

        Enter Dorilaus, Cleander, *Servants with lights.*

                        469

Dorilaus. To bed, to bed, 'tis very late.

Cleander. To bed all,
I have dranke a health too much,

Dorilaus. You'l sleep the better, 20
My usuall phisicke that way.

Cleander. Where's your Mistris?

Clarinda. She is above, but very ill and aguish:
The late fright of her brother, has much troubl'd her;
She would entreate to lye alone.

Cleander. Her pleasure.

Dorilaus. Commend my love to her, and my prayers for her health,
I'le see her ere I goe.

Clarinda. All good rest to ye:

Exeunt. Manet *Clarinda.*

Now to my watch for *Lisander*, when he's furnish'd,
For mine own friend, since I stand Centinell,
I love to laugh i'th'evenings too, and may,
The priviledge of my place will warrant it. 30

Exit.

Enter Lisander, *and* Lancelot. [II▶

Lisander. You have done well hetherto; where are we now?

Lancelot. Not far from the house, I heare by th'owles,
There are many of your welch falkoners about it;
Here were a night to choose to run away with
Another mans wife, and do the feate.

Lisander. Peace knave,
The house is here before us, and some may heare us;
The candles are all out.

Lancelot. But one i'the parlor,
I see it simper hether, pray come this way.

Lisander. Step to the garden doore, and feele and't be open.

Lancelot. I am going, lucke deliver me from the saw pits, 10
Or I am buried quicke: I heare a dog,
No, 'tis a cricket, ha? here's a cuckold buried,
Take heed of his horns sir, here's the doore, 'tis open.

Clarinda (*at the doore*). Whose there?

470

Lisander.   A Friend.

Clarinda.   Sir, *Lisander?*

Lisander.   I.

Clarinda.   Ye are welcome, follow me, and make no noise.

Lisander.   Go to your horse, and keep your watch with care, sirah,
     And be sure ye sleep not.   *Exit* Lisander, Clarinda.

Lancelot.   Send me out the dairy-maid
     To play at trump with me, and keep me waking;
     My fellow horse, and I now must discourse
     Like two learned Almanack-makers, of the stars,   20
     And tell what a plentifull year 'twill prove of drunkards,
     If I had but a pottle of Sacke, like a sharpe prickle,
     To knock my nose against when I am nodding,
     I should sing like a Nightingall, but I must
     Keepe watch without it, I am apt to dance,
     Good fortune guide me from the fairies circles.

                                                    Exit.

Enter Clarinda *with a Taper, and* Lisander, *two Chaires set out.*   [III.iii]

Clarinda.   Come neare, I'le leave ye now, draw but that Curtaine,
     And have your wish;——
                        now *Leon* I am for thee.
     We that are servants must make use of stoln houres,
     And be glad of snatch'd occasions.   *Exit.*
          [Lisander *discovers*] Caliste *sitting behind a Curtaine.*

Lisander.   Shee is asleepe,
     Fierce love hath clos'd his lights, I may looke on her,
     Within her eyes 'has lock'd the graces up,
     I may behold and live; how sweet she breathes?
     The orient morning breaking out in odors,
     Is not so full of perfumes, as her breath is;
     She is the abstract of all excellence,   10
     And scornes a paralell.

Caliste.   Who's there?

Lisander.   Your servant,

---

14 A] Sympson; *omit* F1–2   26 fairies] F2 (Faries); faires F1
0.1 Lisander,] *Lisander with a Pistole,* F1–2. *See Textual Note at* I.ii.97.
*6 the] F2; his F1

Your most obedient slave (adored Lady)
That comes but to behold those eyes againe,
And pay some vowes I have to sacred beauty,
And so passe by; I am blind as ignorance,
And know not where I wander, how I live,
Till I receive from their bright influence
Light to direct me; for devotions sake,   [*Kneeles.*]
(You are the Saint I tread these holy steps to,
And holy Saints are all relenting sweetnesse);   20
Be not inrag'd, nor be not angry with me;
The greatest attribute of heaven is mercy;
And 'tis the crowne of justice, and the glory
Where it may kill with right, to save with pitty.

Caliste.   Why do you kneele, I know you come to mock me,
T'upbraid me with the benefits you have giv'n me,
Which are too many, and too mighty sir,
For my returne; and I confesse 'tis justice,
That for my cruelty you should despise me,
And I expect, however you are calme now,   30
A foyle you strive to set your cause upon,
It will breake out; *Caliste* is unworthy,
Coy, proud, disdainefull, I acknowledge all,
Colder of comfort than the frozen North is,
And more a stranger to *Lisanders* worth,
His youth and faith, then it becomes her gratitude,
I blush to grant it, yet take this along,
(A soveraigne medicine to allay displeasure,
May be an argument to bring me off too)
She is married, and she is chaste; how sweet that sounds?   40
How it perfumes all ayre 'tis spoken in?
O deare *Lisander*, would you breake this union?

Lisander.   No, I adore it: let me kisse your hand,
And seale the faire faith of a Gentleman on it. [*Kissing her hand.*]

Caliste.   You are truly valiant, would it not afflict you
To have the horrid name of coward touch you?
Such is the whore to me.

Lisander.   I nobly thanke ye;
And may I be the same when I dishonour ye;

This I may do againe?

Caliste.   Ye may, and worthily;   *Kissing her hand.*
Such comforts maids may grant with modesty,   50
And neither make her poore, nor wrong her bounty;
Noble *Lisander*, how fond now am I of ye?
I heard you were hurt.

Lisander.   You dare not heale me Lady?
I am hurt here;——[*aside*] how sweetly now she blushes?
Excellent objects kill our sight, she blinds me;
The roses in the pride of May shew pale to her;
O tyrant custome! and O coward honour!
How ye compell me to put on mine owne chaines?——
May I not kisse ye now in superstition?
For you appeare a thing that I would kneele to: 60
Let me erre that way.   *Kisses her.*

Caliste.   Ye shall erre for once,
I have a kind of noble pity on you.
Among your manly sufferings, make this most,
To erre no farther in desire, for then sir,
Ye adde unto the gratitudes I owe you;
And after death, your deare friends soule shall blesse you.

Lisander.   I am wondrous honest.

Caliste.   I dare try.   *Kisses [him].*

Lisander.   I have tasted
A blessednesse too great for dull mortality:
Once more and let me dye.

Caliste.   I dare not murther,
How will maids curse me if I kill with kisses?   70
And young men flye th'embraces of faire virgins?
Come pray sit down, but let's talke temperately.

Lisander.   Is my deare friend a bed?

Caliste.   Yes, and asleep;
Secure asleep, 'tis midnight too *Lisander*,
Speake not so loud.

Lisander.   You see I am a Statue,
I could not stand else as I had eaten Ice,

<hr>

*67 Kisses.] stet F1

473

Or tooke into my bloud a drowzie poyson,
And natures noblest, brightest flame burne in me;
Midnight? and I stand quietly to behold so?
The alarme rung, and I sleep like a coward?   80
I am worne away, my faith, and dull obedience
Like crutches, carry my decayed body
Down to the grave, I have no youth within me,
Yet happily you love too?

Caliste.   Love with honour.

Lisander.   Honour? what's that? 'tis but a specious title
We should not prize too high.

Caliste.   Dearer than life.

Lisander.   The value of it, is as time has made it,
And time and custome have too far insulted,
We are no Gods, to be alwaies tyed to strictnesse,
'Tis a presumption to shew too like 'em;   90
March but an houre or two under loves ensignes,
We have examples of great memories——

Caliste.   But foule ones too, that greatnesse cannot cover;
That wife that by example sins, sins double,
And puls the curtaine open to her shame too;
Me thinkes to enjoy you thus——

Lisander.   'Tis no joy Lady,
A longing bride if she stop here, would cry,
The Bridegroome too, and with just cause curse *Hymen*;
But yeild a little, be one houre a woman,
(I do not speake this to compell you Lady)   100
And give your will but motion, let it stirre
But in the taste of that weake feares call evill,
Try it to understand it, wee'l do no thing;
You'l never come to know pure good else.

Caliste.   Fie sir.

Lisander.   I have found a way, let's slip into this errour
As Innocents, that know not what we did;
As we were dreaming both, let us embrace;
The sin is none of ours then, but our fancies;

84 happily] *i.e.,* haply

What have I said? what blasphemie to honour?
O my base thoughts!   [*Drawes*] *a Pistole.*
                        pray ye take this and shoot me.   110
My villaine thoughts?
Caliste.   I weep your miserie,
And would to heaven——   *Noise within.*
                        what noise?
Lisander.   It comes on louder.
Kill me, and save your selfe; save your faire honour,
And lay the fault on me, let my life perish,
My base lascivious life, shoote quickely Lady.
Caliste.   Not for the world, retire behind the hangings,
And there stand close——

                    Enter Cleander *with a Taper.*

                    my husband!——close *Lisander.*
                        [Lisander *goes behind the Curtaine.*]
Cleander.   Dearest, are you well?
Caliste.   O my sad heart;
My head, my head.
Cleander.   Alas poore soule! what do you
Out of your bed? you take cold my *Caliste*:   120
How do ye?
Caliste.   Not so well sir to lye by ye,
My brothers fright——
Cleander.   I had a frightfull dreame too,
A very frightfull dreame my best *Caliste*:
Me thought there came a Dragon to your Chamber,
A furious Dragon (wife) I yet shake at it:
Are all things well?
Lisander [*apart*].   Shall I shoote him?
Caliste [*apart*].   No.——All well Sir.
'Twas but your care of me, your loving care,
Which alwaies watches.
Cleander.   And me thought he came
As if he had risen thus out of his den,

                    *129 As if] *stet* F1

                        475

As I do from these hangings.

Lisander [*aside*].   Dead.

Caliste.   Hold good Sir.   130

Cleander.   And forc'd ye in his armes thus.

Caliste.   'Twas but fancie
That troubled ye, here's nothing to disturbe me,
Good sir to rest againe, and I am now drousie,
And will to bed; make no noise deare husband,
But let me sleep: before you can call any body
I am a bed.

Cleander.   This, [*Kisses her.*] and sweet rest dwell with ye.

                                              Exit.

Caliste.   Come out againe, and as you love, *Lisander*,
Make haste away, you see his mind is troubled:
Do you know the doore ye came at?

Lisander.   Well sweet Lady.

Caliste.   And can ye hit it readily?

Lisander.   I warrant ye;   14(
And must I go? must here end all my happinesse?
Here in a dreame, as if it had no substance?

Caliste.   For this time friend, or here begin our ruines;
We are both miserable.

Lisander.   This is some comfort
In my afflictions; they are so full already,
They can find no encrease.

Caliste.   Deare speake no more.

Lisander.   You must be silent then.

Caliste.   Farewell *Lisander*,
Thou joy of men, farewell.

Lisander.   Farewell bright Lady,
Honour of woman-kind, a heavenly blessing.

Caliste.   Be ever honest.

Lisander.   I will be a dog else;   15
The vertues of your mind I'le make my library,
In which I'le study the celestiall beauty:
Your constancie, my armour that I'le fight in:

148 men] man F1–2

476

And on my sword your chastity shall sit,
Terror to rebell bloud.
Caliste.   Once more farewell:
O that my modestie cou'd hold you still sir,——   *Noise within.*
He comes againe.
Lisander.   Heaven keep my hand from murther,
Murther of him I love.
Caliste.   Away deare friend,
Down to the garden staires, that way *Lisander*,
We are betrai'd else.
Lisander.   Honour guard the Innocent.   *Exit* Lisander.   160

                    Enter Cleander.

Cleander.   Stil up? I fear'd your health.
Caliste [*aside*].   'Has miss'd him happily;——
I am going now, I have done my meditations,
My heart's almost at peace.
Cleander.   To my warme bed then.
Caliste.   I will, pray ye lead.   *A Pistoll shot within.*
Cleander.   A Pistoll shot i'th house?
At these houres? sure some theefe, some murtherer:
Rise ho, rise all, I am betraide.
Caliste [*aside*].   O fortune!
O giddy thing! he has met some opposition,
And kil'd; I am confounded, lost for ever.

                    Enter Dorilaus.

Dorilaus.   Now, what's the matter?
Cleander.   Theeves, my noble father,
Villaines, and Rogues.
Dorilaus.   Indeed, I heard a Pistoll,   170
Let's search about.

            Enter Malfort, Clarinda, *and Servants.*

Malfort.   To bed againe, they are gone sir,
I will not bid you thanke my valour for't;

                *160.1 *Enter* Cleander.] stet F1

                    477

Gone at the garden doore; there were a dozen,
And bravely arm'd, I saw 'em.
Clarinda [*aside*].   I am glad,
Glad at the heart.
Servant.   One shot at me, and miss'd me.
Malfort.   No, 'twas at me, the bullet flew close by me,
Close by my eare; another had a huge Sword,
Flourish'd it thus, but at the point I met him;
But the Rogue taking me to be your Lordship,
(As sure your name is terrible, and we   180
Not much unlike in the darke) roar'd out aloud,
'Tis the kill-cow *Dorilaus*, and away
They ran as they had flowne:——[*apart to* Clarinda] now you
    must love me,
Or feare me for my courage wench.
Clarinda [*apart*].   O Rogue?
O lying Rogue:——[*apart to* Caliste] *Lisander* stumbled Madam,
At the staires head, and in the fall the shot went off;
Was gone before they rose.
Caliste [*apart*].   I thanke heaven for't.
Clarinda [*aside*].   I was frighted too, it spoyl'd my game with *Leon*.
Cleander.   You must sit up; and they had come to your Chamber
What pranks would they have plaid:——how came the doore   190
    open?
Malfort.   I heard 'em when they forc'd it; up I rose,
Took *Durindana* in my hand; and like
Orlando, issu'd forth.
Clarinda.   I know you are valiant.
Cleander.   To bed again,
And be you hence forth provident, at sun-rising
We must part for a while.
Dorilaus.   When you are a bed,
Take leave of her, there 'twill be worth the taking;
Here 'tis but a cold ceremony, ere long
Wee'l find *Lisander*, or we have ill fortune.
Cleander.   Locke all the doores fast.
Malfort.   Though they all stood open,   200

478

My name writ on the doore, they dare not enter.

Exeunt.

Enter Clarange, Frier with a Letter [and a Novice]. [III.iv]

Clarange.   Turnd Hermit?

Frier.   Yes, and a devout one too:
   I heard him preach.

Clarange.   That lessens my beliefe,
   For though I grant my *Lidian* a scholler
   As far as fits a Gentleman, he hath studied
   Humanity, and in that he is a Master;
   Civility of manners, courtship, Armes;
   But never aim'd at (as I could perceive)
   The deep points of divinity.

Frier.   That confirmes his
   Devotion to be reall, no way tainted
   With ostentation, or hypocrisie,   10
   The cankers of Religion; his sermon
   So full of gravity, and with such sweetnesse
   Deliver'd, that it drew the admiration
   Of all the hearers on him; his own letters
   To you, which witnesse he will leave the world,
   And these to faire *Olinda*, his late Mistris,
   In which he hath with all the moving language
   That ever express'd Rhetorick, sollicited
   The Lady to forget him, and make you
   Blessed in her embraces, may remove   20
   All scrupulous doubts.

Clarange.   It strikes a sadnesse in me,
   I know not what to thinke of't.

Frier.   Ere he entred
   His sollitary cell, he pen'd a ditty,
   His long and last farewell to love, and women,
   So feelingly, that I confesse, however
   It stands not with my order to be taken
   With such Poeticall raptures, I was mov'd,
   And strangely with it.

479

Clarange.   Have you the copy?
Frier.   Yes sir:
    My Novice too can sing it, if you please
    To give him hearing.
Clarange.   And it will come timely,   30
    For I am full of melancholy thoughts,
    Against which I have heard with reason Musick
    To be the speediest cure, pray you apply it.

           A Song by the Novice.

    Adieu fond love, farewell you wanton powers,
      I am free againe;
    Thou dull disease of bloud and Idle howers,
      Bewitching paine,
    Flie to the fooles that sigh away their time.
    My nobler love, to heaven clime
    And there behold beauty still young,   40
    That time can ne're corrupt, nor death destroy;
    Immortall sweetnesse by faire Angels sung,
    And honour'd by eternity and joy:
    There lives my love, thether my hopes aspire;
    Fond love declines, this heavenly love growes higher.

Frier.   How do ye approve it?
Clarange.   To its due desert,
    It is a heavenly Hymne, no ditty father,
    It passes through my eares unto my soule,
    And works divinely on it; give me leave
    A little to consider;——shall I be   50
    Out done in all things? nor good of my selfe,
    Nor by example? shall my loose hopes still,
    The viands of a fond affection, feed me
    As I were a sensuall beast? spirituall food
    Refus'd by my sicke pallat? 'tis resolved.——
    How far off father, doth this new made Hermit
    Make his abode?

        34–45 Adieu ... higher.] stet F1

Frier.   Some two dayes journey son.

Clarange.   Having reveal'd my faire intentions to ye,
   I hope your piety will not deny me
   Your aides to further 'em?

Frier.   That were against   60
   A good mans charity.

Clarange.   My first request is,
   You would some time, for reasons I will shew you,
   Defer delivery of *Lidians* Letters
   To faire *Olinda.*

Frier.   Well sir.

Clarange.   For what followes,
   You shall direct me; something I will do,
   A new borne zeale, and friendship prompts me to.

                                  Exeunt.

      Enter Dorilaus, Cleander, Chamberlaine,
       Table, Tapers, and three stooles [set out].   [III.v]

Cleander.   We have supp'd well friend; let our beds be ready,
   We must be stirring early,

Chamberlaine.   They are made sir.

Dorilaus.   I cannot sleep yet, where's the joviall host
   You told me of? 'thas been my custome ever
   To parley with mine host.

Cleander.   He's a good fellow,
   And such a one I know you love to laugh with;
   Go call your Master up.

Chamberlaine.   He cannot come sir.

Dorilaus.   Is he a bed with his wife?

Chamberlaine.   No certainly.

Dorilaus.   Or with some other ghests?

Chamberlaine.   Neither and't like ye.

Cleander.   Why then he shall come by your leave my friend,   10
   I'le fetch him up my selfe.

Chamberlaine.   Indeed you'l faile sir.

Dorilaus.   Is he i'th' house?

Chamberlaine.   No, but he is hard by sir;
   He is fast in's grave, he has been dead these three weekes.

Dorilaus.   Then o' my conscience he will come but lamely,
    And discourse worse.
Cleander.   Farewell mine honest Host then,
    Mine honest merry Host;——will you to bed yet?
Dorilaus.   No, not this houre, I prethee sit and chat by me.
Cleander.   Give us a quart of wine then, wee'l be merry.
Dorilaus.   A match my son; pray let your wine be living,
    Or lay it by your Master.
Chamberlaine.   It shall be quick sir.   *Exit.*
Dorilaus.   Has not mine Host a wife?
Cleander.   A good old woman.   21
Dorilaus.   Another coffine: that is not so hansome;
    Your Hostesses in Innes should be blith things,
    Pretty, and young to draw in passengers;
    She'l never fill her beds well, if she be not beauteous.
Cleander.   And curteous too.
Dorilaus.   I, I, and a good fellow,
    That will mistake sometimes a Gentleman
    For her good man;

                Enter Chamberlaine *with wine.*

                well done; here's to *Lisander.*
Cleander.   My full love meets it;——make fire in our lodgings,
    Wee'l trouble thee no farther;   *Exit* Chamberlaine.
                        to your Son.   30
Dorilaus.   Put in *Clarange* too; off with't, I thanke ye;
    This wine drinkes merrier still, O for mine Host now,
    Were he alive againe, and well dispos'd,
    I would so claw his pate.
Cleander.   Y'are a hard drinker.
Dorilaus.   I love to make mine Host drunke, he will lye then
    The rarest, and the roundest, of his friends,
    His quarrels, and his ghests, and they are the best bauds too
    Take 'em in that tune.
Cleander.   You know all.
Dorilaus.   I did son,
    But time, and armes have worn me out.
Cleander.   'Tis late sir,

482

I heare none stirring.   *A lute is struck.*
Dorilaus.   Hark, what's that, a Lute?   40
'Tis at the doore I thinke.
Cleander.   The doores are shut fast.
Dorilaus. 'Tis morning, sure the Fidlers are got up
   To fright mens sleepes, have we ne're a pispot ready?
Cleander. Now I remember, I have heard mine Host that's dead,
   Touch a lute rarely, and as rarely sing too,
   A brave still meane.
Dorilaus.   I would give a brace of French Crownes
   To see him rise and Fidle——
Cleander.   Harke, a Song.

A song [within].

   Tis late and cold, stirre up the fire;
   Sit close, and draw the Table nigher;
   Be merry, and drinke wine that's old,   50
   A hearty medicine 'gainst the cold.
   Your beds of wanton downe the best,
   Where you shall tumble to your rest;
   I could wish you wenches too,
   But I am dead and cannot do;
   Call for the best the house may ring,
   Sacke, White, and Claret let them bring,
   And drinke apace while breath you have,
   You'l find but cold drinke in the grave;
   Plover, Patridge for your dinner,   60
   And a Capon for the sinner,
   You shall find ready when you are up,
   And your horse shall have his sup:
      Welcome Welcome shall flye round,
      And I shall smile though under ground.

Cleander. Now as I live, it is his voice.

*47 *Cleander.*] Langbaine; *omit* F1–2   47 Harke, a Song.] F2; *at line* 66 *in* F1
*48–65 *Tis ... ground.*] stet F1   *51 *the cold*] a cold F1–2
52 wanton] F2; want on F1   64 *Welcome Welcome*] F2; *Welcome* F1
66 Now ... voice.] F2; Harke, a song, now ... voice. F1

Dorilaus.   He sings well,
  The devill has a pleasant pipe.
Cleander.   The fellow lyed sure,

Enter [Apparition, *the*] Host.

  He is not dead, he's here: how pale he lookes?
Dorilaus.   Is this he?
Cleander.   Yes.
Host.   You are welcome noble Gentlemen,
  My brave old ghest most welcome.
Cleander.   Lying knaves,   70
  To tell us you were dead, come sit downe by us,
  We thanke ye for your Song.
Host.   Would't had been better.
Dorilaus.   Speake, are ye dead?
Host.   Yes indeed am I Gentlemen,
  I have been dead these three weekes.
Dorilaus.   Then here's to ye,
  To comfort your cold body.
Cleander.   What do ye meane?
  Stand further off.
Dorilaus.   I will stand nearer to him,
  Shall he come out on's coffin to beare us company,
  And we not bid him welcome? come mine Host,
  Mine honest Host, here's to ye.
Host.   Spirits sir, drinke not.
Cleander.   Why do ye appeare?
Host.   To waite upon ye Gentlemen,   80
  'Thas been my duty living, now my farewell;
  I feare ye are not us'd accordingly.
Dorilaus.   I could wish you warmer company mine Host,
  How ever we are us'd.
Host.   Next to entreate a courtesie,
  And then I goe to peace.
Cleander.   Is't in our power?
Host.   Yes, and 'tis this, to see my body buried
  In holy ground, for now I lye unhallowed,
  By the clarkes fault; let my new grave be made

484

Amongst good fellowes, that have died before me,
And merry Hostes of my kind.

Cleander.   It shall be done.   90

Dorilaus.   And forty stoopes of wine dranke at thy funerall.

Cleander.   Do you know our travell?

Host.   Yes, to seeke your friends,
That in afflictions wander now.

Cleander.   Alas!

Host.   Seeke 'em no farther, but be confident
They shall returne in peace.

Dorilaus.   There's comfort yet.

Cleander.   Pray ye one word more, is't in your power mine Host,
Answer me softly, some houres before my death,
To give me warning?

Host.   I cannot tell ye truly,
But if I can, so much alive I lov'd ye,
I will appeare againe, adieu.   *Exit.*

Dorilaus.   Adieu sir.   100

Cleander.   I am troubl'd; these strange apparitions are
For the most part fatall.

Dorilaus.   This if told, will not
Find credit; the light breakes a pace, let's lye downe
And take some little rest, an houre or two,
Then do mine hostes desire, and so returne,
I do beleeve him.

Cleander.   So do I, to rest sir.

                                              Exeunt.

               Enter Caliste, *and* Clarinda.   [III.vi]

Caliste.   *Clarinda?*

Clarinda.   Madam.

Caliste.   Is the house well ordered?
The doores look'd to now in your Masters absence?
Your care, and diligence amongst the Servants?

Clarinda.   I am stirring Madam.

Caliste.   So thou art *Clarinda,*

*2 look'd] *stet* F1

485

More then thou ought'st I am sure, why dost thou blush?

Clarinda.   I do not blush.

Caliste.   Why dost thou hang thy head wench?

Clarinda.   Madam, ye are deceiv'd, I looke upright,
I understand ye not:———(*aside*) she has spied *Leon*,
Shame of his want of caution.

Caliste.   Looke on me;
What, blush againe?

Clarinda.   'Tis more then I know Madam;   10
I have no cause that I find yet.

Caliste.   Examine then.

Clarinda.   Your Ladyship is set I thinke to shame me.

Caliste.   Do not deserv't: who lay with you last night?
What bedfellow had ye? none of the maids came neare ye.

Clarinda.   Madam they did.

Caliste.   'Twas one in your Cosins cloathes then,
And wore a sword; and sure I keep no *Amazons*;
Wench do not lye, 'twill but proclame thee guilty;
Lyes hide our sins like nets; like perspectives,
They draw offences nearer still, and greater:
Come tell the truth.

Clarinda.   You are the strangest Lady   20
To have these doubts of me; how have I liv'd Madam?
And which of all my carefull services
Deserves these shames?

Caliste.   Leave facing? 'twill not serve ye,
This impudence becomes thee worse then lying?
I thought ye had liv'd well, and I was proud of't;
But you are pleas'd to abuse my thoughts; who was't?
Honest repentance yet will make the fault lesse.

Clarinda.   Do ye compell me? do you stand so strict too?
Nay, then have at ye; I shall rub that sore Madam,
(Since ye provoke me) will but vexe your Ladyship;   30
Let me alone.

Caliste.   I will know.

Clarinda.   For your own peace,
The peace of your owne conscience aske no farther;
Walke in, and let me alone.

486

Caliste.   No, I will know all.

Clarinda.   Why, then I'le tell ye, 'twas a man I lay with,
   Never admire, 'tis easie to be done, Madam,
   And usuall too, a proper man I lay with;
   Why should you vexe at that? young as *Lisander*,
   And able too; I grudge not at your pleasure,
   Why should you stir at mine? I steale none from ye.

Caliste.   And dost thou glory in this sin?

Clarinda.   I am glad on't,   40
   To glory in't is for a mighty Lady
   That may command.

Caliste.   Why didst thou name *Lisander*?

Clarinda.   Does it anger ye? does it a little gall ye?
   I know it does, why would ye urge me Lady?
   Why would ye be so curious to compell me?
   I nam'd *Lisander* as my president,
   The rule I err'd by: you love him, I know it,
   I grudge not at it, but am pleas'd it is so;
   And by my care and diligence you enjoy'd him.
   Shall I for keeping counsell, have no comfort?   50
   Will you have all your selfe? ingrosse all pleasure?
   Are ye so hard hearted? why do ye blush now Madam?

Caliste.   My anger blushes, not my shame base woman.

Clarinda.   I'le make your shame blush, since you put me to't:
   Who lay with you t'other night?

Caliste.   With me? ye monster.

Clarinda.   Whose sweet embraces circled ye? not your husbands;
   I wonder ye dare touch me in this point Madam?
   Stir her against ye in whose hand your life lies?
   More then your life, your honour? what smug *Amazon*
   Was that I brought you? that maid had ne're a petticoat.   60

Caliste [aside].   She'l halfe perswade me anon, I am a beast too,
   And I mistrust my selfe, though I am honest
   For giving her the Helme,——thou knowest *Clarinda*,
   (Ev'n in thy conscience) I was ever vertuous;
   As far from lust in meeting with *Lisander*

*48 grudge] grudg'd F1–2

487

As the pure wind in welcoming the morning;
In all the conversation I had with him,
As free, and innocent, as yon'd faire heaven;
Didst not thou perswade me too?
Clarinda.   Yes, I had reason for't,
And now you are perswaded I'le make use on't.   70
Caliste.   If I had sin'd thus, and my youth entic'd me,
The noblenesse and beauty of his person,
Beside the mighty benefits I am bound to,——
Is this sufficient warrant for thy weaknesse?
If I had been a whore, and crav'd thy counsell
In the conveyance of my fault, and faithfullnesse,
Thy secrecie, and truth in hiding of it,
Is it thy justice to repay me thus?
To be the Master sinner to compell me?
And build thy lusts security on mine honour?   80
Clarinda.   They that love this sin, love their security;
Prevention Madam is the naile I knock'd at,
And I have hit it home, and so I'le hold it,
And you must pardon me, and be silent too,
And suffer what ye see, and suffer patiently;
I shall do worse else.
Caliste.   Thou canst not touch my credit,
Truth will not suffer me to be abus'd thus.
Clarinda.   Do not you sticke to truth, she is seldome heard Madam,
A poore weake tongue she has, and that is hoarse too
With pleading at the bars; none understands her,   90
Or if you had her, what can she say for ye?
Must she not sweare he came at midnight to ye,
The doore left open, and your husband cozen'd
With a feign'd sicknesse?
Caliste.   But by my soule I was honest,
Thou know'st I was honest.
Clarinda.   That's all one what I know,
What I will testifie is that shall vexe ye;
Trust not a guilty rage with likelihoods,
And on apparent proofe, take heed of that Madam,
If you were innocent, as it may be ye are,

(I do not know, I leave it to your conscience)   100
It were the weakest and the poorest part of ye,
Men being so willing to beleeve the worst,
So open eyed in this age to all infamie,
To put your fame in this weake barke to the venture.
Caliste [*aside*].   What do I suffer? O my pretious honour,
   Into what boxe of evils have I lock'd thee?
   Yet rather then be thus outbrav'd, and by
   My drudg, my footstoole, one that sued to be so;
   Perish both life, and honour.——Devill, thus
   I dare thy worst, defie thee, spit at thee,   110
   And in my vertuous rage, thus trample on thee;
   Awe me thy Mistris, whore, to be thy baud?
   Out of my house, proclame all that thou knowest,
   Or malice can invent, fetch jealousie
   From hell, and like a furie breath it in
   The bosome of my Lord; and to thy utmost
   Blast my faire fame, yet thou shalt feele with horror
   To thy sear'd conscience, my truth is built
   On such a firme base, that if e're it can
   Be forc'd, or undermin'd by thy base scandals,   120
   Heaven keeps no guard on Innocence.   *Exit.*
Clarinda.   I am lost,
   In my owne hopes forsaken, and must fall
   (The greatest torment to a guilty woman)
   Without revenge: till I can fashion it
   I must submit, at least appeare as if
   I did repent, and would offend no farther.
   Monsieur *Beronte* my Lords brother is
   Oblieg'd unto me for a private favour;
   'Tis he must mediate for me; but when time
   And oportunity bids me strike, my wreake   130
   Shall powre it selfe on her nice chastitie
   Like to a torrent; deeds, not words shall speake me.

                                                     Exit.

        Enter Alcidon, *and* Beronte *severally.*   IV.i

Alcidon.   Ye are oportunely met.

                        489

Beronte.   Your countenance
  Expresses hast mixt with some feare.
Alcidon.   You'l share
  With me in both, as soone as you are made
  Acquainted with the cause, if you love vertue;
  In danger not secure, I have no time
  For circumstance: instruct me if *Lisander*
  Be in your brothers house?
Beronte.   Upon my knowledge
  He is not there.
Alcidon.   I am glad on't.
Beronte.   Why good sir?
  (Without offence I speake it) there's no place
  In which he is more honour'd, or more safe,   10
  Then with his friend *Cleander*.
Alcidon.   In your votes
  I grant it true, but as it now stands with him,
  I can give reason to make satisfaction
  For what I speake; you cannot but remember
  The ancient difference between *Lisander*
  And *Cloridon*, a man in grace at Court?
Beronte.   I do; and the foule plot of *Cloridons* kinsmen
  Upon *Lisanders* life, for a fall given
  To *Cloridon* 'fore the King, as they encountred
  At a solemne tilting.
Alcidon.   It is now reveng'd: 20
  In briefe a challenge was brought to *Lisander*
  By one *Chrysantes*; and as far as valour
  Would give him leave, declin'd by bold *Lisander*:
  But peace refus'd, and braves on braves heap'd on him,
  Alone he met the opposites, ending the quarrell
  With both their lives.
Beronte.   I am truely sorry for't.
Alcidon.   The King incensed for his favourites death,
  Hath set a price upon *Lisanders* head,
  As a reward to any man that brings it

---

*4–5 vertue; . . . secure,] vertue, . . . secure; F1–2   *7 brothers] F2; fathers F1

Alive, or dead; to gaine this, every where   30
He is pursu'd, and laid for, and the friendship
Between him and your noble brother knowne,
His house in reason cannot passe unsearcht,
And that's the principall cause that drew me hither,
To hasten his remove, if he had chosen
This Castle for his sanctuary.

Beronte.   'Twas done nobly,
And you most welcome; this night pray you take
A lodging with us; and at my intreaty
Conceale this from my brother, he is growne
Exceeding sad of late; and the hard fortune   40
Of one he values at so high a rate,
Will much encrease his melancholy.

Alcidon.   I am tutor'd:
Pray you lead the way.

Beronte.   To serve you I will shew it.

Exeunt.

Enter Cleander *with a book.*   [IV.ii]

Cleander.   Nothing more certaine then to dye, but when
Is most uncertaine: if so, every houre
We should prepare us for the journey, which
Is not to be put off. I must submit
To the divine decree, not argue it,
And chearfully I welcome it: I have
Dispos'd of my estate, confess'd my sinnes,
And have remission from my Ghostly Father,
Being at peace too here: the apparition
Proceeded not from fancy, *Dorilaus*   10
Saw it, and heard it with me, it made answer
To our demands, and promis'd, if 'twere not
Deny'd to him by fate, he would forewarne me
Of my approaching end; I feele no symptome
Of sicknesse, yet (I know not how) a dulnesse
Invades me all over.——

491

Enter [Apparition, *the*] Host.

                              Ha?

Host.   I come sir,
    To keep my promise; and as farre as spirits
    Are sensible of sorrow for the living,
    I grieve to be the messenger to tell you,
    Ere many houres passe, you must resolve   20
    To fill a grave.

Cleander.   And feast the wormes?

Host.   Even so sir.

Cleander.   I heare it like a man.

Host.   It well becomes you,
    There's no evading it.

Cleander.   Can you discover
    By whose means I must dye?

Host.   That is deny'd me:
    But my prediction is too sure; prepare
    To make your peace with heaven. So farewell sir.   *Exit.*

Cleander.   I see no enemy neare; and yet I tremble
    Like a pale Coward: my sad doom pronounc'd
    By this aëriall voice, as in a glasse
    Shewes me my death in its most dreadfull shape.   30
    What rampire can my humane frailty raise
    Against the assault of fate? I doe begin
    To feare my selfe, my inward strengths forsake me,
    I must call out for helpe.——Within there? haste,
    And breake in to my rescue.

Enter Dorilaus, Caliste, Olinda, Beronte, Alcidon, *Servants and*
                    Clarinda *at severall doores.*

Dorilaus.   Rescue? where?
    Shew me your danger.

Caliste.   I will interpose
    My loyall breast between you and all hazzard.

Beronte.   Your brothers sword secures you.

Alcidon.   A true friend
    Will dye in your defence.

Cleander.   I thank yee,

                              492

To all my thanks. Encompass'd thus with friends   40
How can I feare? and yet I doe, I am wounded,
Mortally wounded: nay it is within,
I am hurt in my minde:——One word——
Dorilaus.   A thousand.
                                        [*They speake apart.*]
Cleander.   I shall not live to speak so many to you.
Dorilaus.   Why? what forbids you?
Cleander.   But even now the spirit
Of my dead Host appear'd, and told me, that
This night I should be with him: did you not meet it?
It went out at that doore.
Dorilaus.   A vaine *Chymera*
Of your imagination: can you thinke
Mine Host would not as well have spoke to me now,   50
As he did in the Inne? these waking dreames
Not alone trouble you, but strike a strange
Distraction in your family: see the teares
Of my poore daughter, faire *Olinda's* sadnesse,
Your brothers and your friends griefe, servants sorrow.
Good sonne beare up, you have many yeares to live
A comfort to us all: let's in to supper;
Ghosts never walke till after mid-night, if
I may believe my Grannam. We will wash
These thoughts away with wine, spight of Hobgoblins.   60
Cleander.   You reprehend me justly:——gentle Madam,
And all the rest, forgive me, Ile endeavour
To be merry with you.
Dorilaus.   That's well said.
Beronte [*to* Clarinda].   I have
Procur'd your pardon.
Caliste.   Once more I receive you
Into my service: but take speciall care
You fall no further.
Clarinda.   Never Madam:——[*aside to* Beronte] sir,
When you shall finde fit time to call me to it,
I will make good what I have said.
Beronte [*aside to* Clarinda].   Till when,

Upon your life be silent.

Dorilaus.   We will have

A health unto *Lisander.*

Cleander.   His name sir   70

Somewhat revives me; but his sight would cure me.

However let's to supper.   [*Exeunt. Manent* Olinda, Caliste.]

Olinda.   Would *Clarange*

And *Lidian* were here too, as they should be,

If wishes cou'd prevaile.

Caliste.   They are fruitlesse Madam.

                                                Exeunt.

                        Enter Leon.   [IV

Leon.   If that report speak truth, *Clarinda* is

Discharg'd her Ladies service, and what burthen,

I then have drawne upon me is apparent;

The crop she reapt from her attendance was

Her best Revenue, and my principall meanes

Clarinda's bountie, though I labour'd hard for't,

A younger brothers fortune: Must I now

Have soure sawce after sweet meate? and be driv'n

To leavie halfe a Crown a week, besides

Clouts, sope, and caudles, for my heire apparent,   10

If she prove, as she sweares she is, with childe;

Such as live this way, finde like me, though wenching

Hath a faire face, there's a Dragon in the taile of't

That stings toth' quick. I must skulke here, untill

I am resolv'd: how my heart pants between

My hopes and feares?

                        Enter Clarinda.

                        shee's come;——are we in the Port?

If not, let's sink together.

Clarinda.   Things goe better

Then you deserve; you carry things so openly,

I must beare every way, I am once more

72 However] F2; How ever F1   *8 meate] meats F1–2
10 caudles] Weber; candles F1–2

In my Ladies grace.
Leon.   And I in yours.
Clarinda.   It may be;   20
    But I have sworne unto my Lady never
    To sinne againe.
Leon.   To be surpriz'd——the sinne
    Is in it selfe excusable; to be
    Taken is a crime, as the Poet writes.
Clarinda.   You know my weaknesse,
    And that makes you so confident. You have got
    A faire sword; was it not *Lisanders?*
Leon.   Yes wench,
    And I growne valiant by the wearing of it:
    It hath been the death of two. With this *Lisander*
    Slew *Cloridon*, and *Chrysanthes*. I took it up,   30
    Broken in the handle, but that is reform'd,
    And now in my possession; the late Master
    Dares never come to challenge it: this sword,
    And all the weapons that I have, are ever
    Devoted to thy service: Shall we bill?
    I am very gamesome.
Clarinda.   I must first dispose of
    The foole *Malfort*; he hath smoak'd you, and is not,
    But by some new device, to be kept from me:
    I have it here shall fit him: you know where
    You must expect me, with all possible silence   40
    Get thither.
Leon.   You will follow?
Clarinda.   Will I live?
    She that is forfeited to lust must dye,
    That humour being un-fed; begone, here comes
    My champion in Armour.   *Exit* Leon.

                Enter Malfort *in Armour.*

Malfort.   What adventure
    I am bound upon I know not, but it is
    My Mistris pleasure that I should appeare thus.
    I may perhaps be terrible to others,

                        495

But as I am, I am sure my shadow frights me,
The clashing of my Armour in my eares,
Sounds like a passing-bell; and my Buckler, puts me   50
In minde of a Beere; this my broad sword a pick-axe
To dig my grave: O love, abominable love,
What Monsters issue from thy dismall den,
Clarinda's placket, which I must encounter,
Or never hope to enter?

Clarinda [*aside*].   Here's a Knight errant,——
Monsieur *Malfort*.

Malfort.   Stand, stand, or Ile fall for yee.

Clarinda.   Know ye not my voice?

Malfort.   Yes, 'twas at that I trembl'd.
But were my false friend *Leon* here——

Clarinda.   'Tis he.

Malfort.   Where? where?

Clarinda.   He is not come yet.

Malfort.   'Tis well for him,
I am so full of wrath.

Clarinda [*aside*].   Or feare——This *Leon*,   60
How 'ere my kinsman, hath abus'd you grossely,
And this night vowes to take me hence perforce,
And marry me to another: 'twas for this,
(Presuming on your love) I did entreat you
To put your armour on, that with more safety
You might defend me.

Malfort.   And Ile doe it bravely.

Clarinda.   You must stand here to beate him off, and suffer
No humane thing to passe you, though it appeare
In my Lords shape, or Ladies: be not cozen'd
With a disguise.

Malfort.   I have been fool'd already,   70
But now I am wise.

Clarinda.   You must sweare not to stirre hence.

Malfort.   Upon these lips.

Clarinda.   Nor move untill I call you?

51 Beere] *i.e.*, Bier

Malfort.   Ile grow here rather.
Clarinda.   This nights taske well ended,
    I am yours to morrow. Keep sure guard.   *Exit* Clarinda.
Malfort;   Adiew;
    My honey-combe how sweet thou art, did not
    A nest of Hornets keep it? what impossibilities
    Love makes me undertake? I know my selfe
    A naturall coward, and should *Leon* come,
    Though this were Cannon proofe, I should deliver
    The wench before he ask'd her. I heare some footing: 80
    'Tis he; where shall I hide my selfe? that is
    My best defence.   [*Withdraws.*]

Enter Cleander.

Cleander.   I cannot sleep, strange visions
    Make this poore life, I fear'd of late to lose,
    A toy that I grow weary of.
Malfort.   'Tis *Leon.*
Cleander.   What's that?
Malfort.   If you are come sir for *Clarinda*;
    I am glad I have her for you; I resigne
    My interest; you'll finde her in her chamber,
    I did stay up to tell you so.
Cleander.   *Clarinda*,
    And *Leon*!   There is something more in this
    Then I can stay to aske.   *Exit.*
Malfort.   What a cold pickle,   90
    (And that none of the sweetest) doe I finde
    My poore selfe in?
Cleander (within).   Yield villaine.

Enter Clarinda, *and* Leon, *running.* Cleander *following.*

Clarinda.   'Tis my Lord,
    Shift for your selfe.
Leon.   His life shall first make answer
    For this intrusion.   *Kills* Cleander.

*84 Malfort.] stet F1

497

Malfort. I am going away,
I am gone already. *Falls in a swoune.*
Cleander. Heaven take mercy on
My soule; too true presaging Host. [*Dies.*]
Clarinda. Hee's dead,
And this wretch little better: doe you stare
Upon your handy-work?
Leon. I am amaz'd.
Clarinda. Get o're the garden Wall, flye for your life,
But leave your sword behinde; enquire not why: 100
Ile fashion something out of it, though I perish,
Shall make way for revenge.
Leon. These are the fruits
Of lust *Clarinda.*
Clarinda. Hence repenting Milk-sop.
Now 'tis too late. *Exit* Leon.
Lisanders sword, I, that,
That is the base Ile build on. *Puts the sword in* Malforts *hand.*
So. Ile raise
The house. Help, murther, a most horrid murther.
Monsieur *Beronte*, noble *Dorilaus*,
All buried in sleep? Aye me a murther:
A most unheard-of murther.

Enter Dorilaus, *as from bed.*

Dorilaus. More lights knaves;
Beronte, Alcidon; more lights.

Enter Beronte, Alcidon, *and Servants, with lights.*

Clarinda. By this 110
I see too much.
Dorilaus. My sonne *Cleander* bathing
In his owne gore. The devill to tell truth
Ith'shape of an Host!
Beronte. My Brother?
Malfort [*apart*]. I have been
Ith'other world, in hell I think, these devills
With fire-brands in their pawes sent to torment me,

Though I never did the deed, for my lewd purpose
To be a whore-master.

Dorilaus.   Who's that?

Alcidon.   'Tis one
In Armour. A bloudy sword in his hand.

Dorilaus.   *Sans* question
The murtherer.

Malfort.   Who I? you doe me wrong,
I never had the heart to kill a Chicken;   120
Nor doe I know this sword.

Alcidon.   I doe, too well.

Beronte.   I have seen *Lisander* weare it.

Clarinda [*aside to* Beronte].   This confirmes
What yester-night I whisper'd: let it worke,
The circumstance may make it good.

Malfort.   My Lord?
And I his murtherer?

Beronte.   Drag the villaine hence,
The Rack shall force a free confession from him.

Malfort.   I am struck dumbe; you need not stop my mouth.

Beronte.   Away with him.   *Exit* [*Servant*] *with* Malfort.

Enter Caliste *and* Olinda.

Caliste.   Where is my Lord?

Dorilaus.   All that
Remaines of him lies there: look on this object,
And then turne marble.

Caliste.   I am so already,   130
Made fit to be his monument: but wherefore
Doe you, that have both life and motion left you,
Stand sad spectators of his death, and not
Bring forth his murtherer?

Beronte.   That lies in you:
You must, and shal produce him.

Dorilaus.   She *Beronte?*

Beronte.   None else.

Dorilaus.   Thou ly'st, Ile prove it on thy head,
Or write it on thy heart.

499

Alcidon.   Forbeare, there is
  Too much bloud shed already.
Beronte.   Let not choler
  Stifle your judgement: many an honest father
  Hath got a wicked daughter. If I prove not   140
  With evident proofes, her hand was in the bloud
  Of my deare brother, (too good a husband for her)
  Give your revenge the reines, and spur it forward.
Dorilaus.   In any circumstance but shew her guilty,
  Ile strike the first stroak at her.
Beronte.   Let me aske
  A question calmly: doe you know this sword?
  Have you not seen *Lisander* often weare it.
Dorilaus.   The same with which he rescued me.
Caliste.   I do,
  What inference from this to make me guilty?
Beronte.   Was he not with you in the house to night?   150
Caliste.   No on my soule.
Beronte.   Nor ever heretofore
  In private with you, when you feign'd a sicknesse,
  To keep your husband absent?
Caliste.   Never sir,
  To a dishonest end.
Beronte.   Was not this woman
  Your instrument? her silence does confesse it:
  Here lyes *Cleander* dead, and here the sword
  Of false *Lisander*, too long cover'd with
  A masque of seeming truth.
Dorilaus.   And is this all
  The proofe you can alleage? *Lisander* guilty,
  Or my poore daughter an adulteresse?   160
  Suppose that she had chang'd discourse with one
  To whom she ow'd much more?
Caliste.   Thou hast thy ends,
  Wicked *Clarinda*.   *She falls.*
Olinda.   Helpe, the Lady sinks,
  Malice hath kill'd her.
Dorilaus.   I would have her live,

Since I dare sweare shee's innocent: 'tis no time
Or place to argue now: this cause must be
Decided by the Judge; and though a Father,
I will deliver her into the hands
Of Justice. If she prove true gold when try'd,
Shee's mine: if not, with curses Ile disclaime her: 170
Take up your part of sorrow, mine shall be
Ready to answer with her life the fact
That she is charg'd with.

Beronte.   Sir, I look upon you
As on a father.

Dorilaus.   With the eyes of sorrow
I see you as a brother: let your witnesses
Be readie.

Beronte.   'Tis my care.

Alcidon.   I am for *Lidian.*
This accident no doubt will draw him from
His Hermits life.

Clarinda [aside to Beronte]*.   Things yet goe right, persist sir.

                        Exeunt [omnes, bearing off the body].

                Enter Lisander, *and* Lancelot.   [IV.iv]

Lisander.   Are the horses dead?

Lancelot.   Out-right. If you ride at this rate,
You must resolve to kill your two a day,
And that's a large proportion.

Lisander.   Will you please
At any price, and speedily, to get fresh ones?
You know my danger, and the penalty
That followes it, should I be apprehended.
Your duty in obeying my commands,
Will in a better language speak your service,
Then your unnecessary, and untimely care
Of my expence.

Lancelot.   I am gone sir.

Lisander.   In this thicket   10
I will expect you: *Exit [Lancelot].*
            Here yet I have leisure

To call my selfe unto a strict account
For my pass'd life, how vainly spent: I would
I stood no farther guilty: but I have
A heavier reckoning to make: This hand
Of late as white as innocence, and unspotted,
Now weares a purple colour, dy'd in gore,
My soule of the same tincture; per-blinde passion,
With flattering hopes, would keep me from depaire.
Pleading I was provok'd to it; but my reason   20
Breaking such thin and weak defences, tells me
I have done a double murther; and for what?
Was it in service of the King? his Edicts
Command the contrary: or for my Countrey?
Her *Genius*, like a mourning mother, answers
In *Cloridon* and *Chrysanthes* she hath lost
Two hopefull sonnes, that might have done their parts,
To guard her from Invasion: for what cause then?
To keep th'opinion of my valour upright,
Ith' popular breath, a sandy ground to build on;   30
Bought with the Kings displeasure, as the breach
Of heavens decrees, the losse of my true comforts,
In Parents, Kinsmen, friends, as the fruition
Of all that I was borne to; and that sits
Like to a hill of Lead here, in my exile,
(Never to be repeal'd, if I escape so)
I have cut off all hopes ever to look on

Enter Lidian, *like a Hermite.*

Divine *Caliste*, from her sight, and converse,
For ever banish'd.
Lidian [*apart*].   I should know this voice,
His naming too my sister, whom *Lisander*   40
Honour'd, but in a noble way, assures me
That it can be no other: I stand bound
To comfort any man I finde distress'd:
But to ayd him that sav'd my life, Religion

12 unto] F2; to F1   37.1 *like*] *i.e.*, in the attire of his hermetic life – not disguised

And Thankfullnesse commands; and it may be
High providence for this good end hath brought him
Into my solitary walke.——*Lisander,*
Noble *Lisander.*

Lisander.   Whatsoe're thou art,
That honourable attribute thou giv'st me,
I can pretend no right to: come not neare me,   50
I am infectious, the sanctity
Of thy profession (for thou appearest
A reverend Hermite) if thou flye not from me,
As from the plague or leprosie, cannot keep thee
From being polluted.

Lidian.   With good counsell sir,
And holy prayers to boot I may cure you,
Though both wayes so infected. You look wildly,
(Peace to your conscience sir), and stare upon me,
As if you never saw me: hath my habit
Alter'd my face so much, that yet you know not   60
Your servant *Lidian?*

Lisander.   I am amaz'd!
So young, and so religious?

Lidian.   I purpose
(Heaven make me thankfull for't) to leave the world:
I have made some triall of my strengths in this
My sollitarie life; and yet I finde not
A faintnesse to goe on.

Lisander.   Above beliefe:
Doe you inhabit here?

Lidian.   Mine owne free choise sir:
I live here poorely, but contentedly,
Because I finde enough to feed my fortunes;
Indeed too much: these wilde fields are my gardens,   70
The Chrystall Rivers they afford their waters,
And grudge not their sweet streams to quench afflictions;
The hollow rocks their beds, which though they are hard,
(The Emblemes of a doting lovers fortune)
Yet they are quiet; and the wearie slumbers
The eyes catch there, softer then beds of Down, friend;

503

The Birds my Bell to call me to devotions;
My Book the story of my wandring life,
In which I finde more houres due to repentance
Then time hath told me yet.
Lisander.   Answer me truely.   80
Lidian.   I will doe that without a conjuration.
Lisander.   Ith' depth of meditation doe you not
   Sometimes think of *Olinda*?
Lidian.   I endeavour
To raze her from my memorie, as I wish
You would doe the whole Sex, for know *Lisander*,
The greatest curse brave man can labour under,
Is the strong witch-craft of a womans eyes;
Where I finde men I preach this doctrine to 'em:
As you are a Scholler, knowledge make your Mistris,
The hidden beauties of the heavens your studie;   90
There shall you finde fit wonder for your faith,
And for your eye in-imitable objects:
As you are a profess'd souldier, court your honour,
Though she be sterne, she is honest, a brave Mistris;
The greater danger you oppose to win her,
She shewes the sweeter, and rewards the nobler;
Womens best loves to hers meere shadowes be,
For after death she weds your memorie.
These are my contemplations.
Lisander.   Heavenly ones;
And in a young man more remarkable.   100
But wherefore doe I envy, and not tread in
This blessed tract? here's in the heart no falshood
To a vow'd friend, no quarrells seconded
With Challenges, which answer'd in defence
Of the word Reputation, murther followes.
A man may here repent his sinnes, and though
His hand like mine be stain'd in bloud, it may be
With penitence and true contrition wash'd off;
You have prov'd it *Lidian*.

92 in-imitable] F2; in immitable F1

Lidian.   And you'll finde it true,
    If you persevere.
Lisander.   Here then ends my flight,   110
    And here the furie of the King shall finde me
    Prepar'd for heaven, if I am mark'd to dye;
    For that I truely grieve for.

        Enter Frier: *and* Clarange [*disguised*] *in Friers habit.*

Frier [*apart*].   Keep your selfe
    Conceal'd, I am instructed.
Clarange [*apart*].   How the sight
    Of my deare friend confirmes me?
Lisander.   What are these?
Lidian.   Two reverend Friers, one I know.
Frier.   To you
    This journey is devoted.
Lidian.   Welcome Father.
Frier.   I know your resolution so well grounded,
    And your adiew unto the world so constant,
    That though I am th'unwilling messenger   120
    Of a strange accident to trie your temper,
    It cannot shake you. You had once a friend,
    A noble friend, *Clarange.*
Lidian.   And have still,
    I hope good father.
Frier.   Your false hopes deceive you,
    Hee's dead.
Lisander.   *Clarange* dead?
Frier.   I buried him.
    Some said he dy'd of melancholy, some of love,
    And of that fondnesse perish'd.
Lidian.   O *Clarange.*
Clarange [*apart*].   Hast thou so much brave nature, noble *Lidian*,
    So tenderly to love thy rivalls memorie?
    The bold *Lisander* weeps too.
Frier.   I expected   130
    That you would beare this better.
Lidian.   I am a man sir,

And my great losse weigh'd duly——
Frier. His last words were
    After Confession, live long deare *Lidian*,
    Possest of all thy wishes; and of me
    He did desire, bathing my hand with teares,
    That with my best care, I should seek and finde you,
    And from his dying mouth prevaile so with you,
    That you a while should leave your Hermites strictnesse,
    And on his monument pay a teare, or two,
    To witnesse how you lov'd him.
Lidian. O my heart! 140
    To witness how I lov'd him? would he had not
    Led me unto his grave, but sacrific'd
    His sorrowes upon mine; he was my friend,
    My noble friend, I will bewayle his ashes,
    His fortunes and poore mine were born together,
    And I will weep 'em both: I will kneele by him,
    And on his hallow'd earth doe my last duties.
    Ile gather all the pride of spring to deck him,
    Wood-bines shall grow upon his honour'd grave;
    And as they prosper claspe to shew our friendship, 150
    And when they wither Ile die too.
Clarange [apart]. Who would not
    Desire to dye, to be bewaild thus nobly?
Frier. There is a Legacy he hath bequeath'd you;
    But of what value I must not discover,
    Untill those Rites and pious Ceremonies
    Are duly tender'd.
Lidian. I am too full of sorrow
    To be inquisitive.
Lisander [aside]. To think of his
    I doe forget mine owne woes.

Enter Alcidon.

Alcidon [apart]. Graze thy fill, now
    Thou hast done thy business; ha? who have we here?

160

Lisander, *Lidian?* and two reverend Friers?
What a strange Scene of sorrow is exprest
In different postures, in their looks and station?
A common Painter eying these, to helpe
His dull invention, might draw to the life
The living sonnes of *Priam*, as they stood
On the pale walls of *Troy*, when *Hector* fell
Under *Achilles* Speare:——I come too late,
My horse, though good and strong, mov'd like a Tortoise:
Ill newes had wings, and hath got here before me.
All *Pythagoreans?* not a word?

Lidian.   O *Alcidon*——   170
Deep rivers with soft murmures glide along,
The shallow roare: *Clarange?*

Lisander.   *Cloridon?*
Chrysanthes? spare my grief, and apprehend
What I should speak.

Alcidon.   Their fates I have long since
For your sake mourn'd; *Clarange's* death, for so
Your silence doth confirme, till now I heard not:
Are these the bounds that are prescrib'd unto
The swelling seas of sorrow?

Lisander.   The bounds *Alcidon?*
Can all the windes of mischiefe from all quarters,
Euphrates, Ganges, Tigris, Volga, Po,   180
Paying at once their tribute to this Ocean,
Make it swell higher? I am a murtherer,
Banish'd, proscrib'd, is there ought else that can
Be added to it?

Lidian.   I have lost a friend,
Priz'd dearer then my being, and he dead,
My miseries at the height contemne the worst
Of fortunes malice.

Alcidon.   How our humane weaknesse,
Growne desperate from small disasters makes us
Imagine them a period to our sorrowes,

<hr>

186 miseries] F2; misery's F1

When the first syllable of greater woes   190
Is not yet written.

Lidian.   How?

Lisander.   Speak it at large,
Since griefe must break my heart, I am ambitious
It should be exquisite.

Alcidon.   It must be told,
Yet e're you heare it, with all care put on
The surest Armour anvil'd in the shop
Of passive fortitude; the good *Cleander*
Your friend is murther'd.

Lisander.   'Tis a terrible pang.
And yet it will not doe, I live yet: act not
The tortrers part; if that there be a blow
Beyond this, give it, and at once dispatch me.   200

Alcidon.   Your sword dyed in his heart-bloud was found near him
Your private conference at mid-night urg'd
With faire *Caliste*; which by her whose pure truth,
Would never learne to tell a lie, being granted,
She by inrag'd *Beronte* is accus'd
Of murther and adulterie, and you
(However I dare sweare it false) concluded
Her principall agent.

Lidian.   Wave upon wave rowles o're me.
My sister? my deare sister?

Clarange [apart].   Hold great heart.

Frier.   Teare open his Doublet.

Lisander.   Is this wound too narrow   210
For my life to get out at? Bring me to
A Cannon loaded, and some pittying friend
Give fire unto it, while I nayle my breast
Unto his thundering mouth, that in the instant,
I may be peece-meale torne, and blowne so far,
As not one joynt of my dismember'd limbes
May ever be by search of man found out.
Cleander! Yet why name I him? however
His fall deserv'd an earth-quake, if compar'd
With what true honour in *Caliste* suffers,   220
Is of no moment; my good Angel keep me

508

From blasphemy, and strike me dumb before
In th'agony of my spirit, I doe accuse
The powers above, for their unjust permission
Of vertue, innocent vertue, to be branded
With the least vitious marke.

Clarange [*apart*].   I never saw
A man so far transported.

Alcidon.   Give it way,
'Tis now no time to stop it.

Enter Lancelot.

Lancelot.   Sir, I have bought
Fresh horses; and as you respect your life
Speedily back 'em; the Archers of the Kings guard,   230
Are every where in quest of you.

Lisander.   My life?   *Strikes* Lancelot.
Perish all such with thee that wish it longer:
Let it but cleare *Caliste's* innocence,
And *Nestors* age to mine was youth, Ile flye
To meet the rage of my incensed King,
And wish his favourites ghost appear'd in flames,
To urge him to revenge, let all the tortures
That tyranny ever found out circle me,
Provided justice set *Caliste* free.   *Exeunt* Lisander, Lancelot.

Alcidon.   Ile follow him.   [*Exit*] Alcidon.

Lidian.   I am rooted here.

Frier.   Remember   240
Your dear friends last request, your sisters dangers,
With the aides that you may lend her.

Lidian.   Pray you support me,
My legs deny their office.   [*Exit with* Friar.]

Clarange.   I grow still
Farther engag'd unto his matchlesse vertues,
And I am dead indeed, untill I pay
The debt I owe him in a noble way.

                                   Exit.

                    Enter Dorilaus, *and* Servant.   V.i

Dorilaus.   Thou hast him safe?

509

Servant.   As fast as locks can make him:
 He must break through three doores, and cut the throats
 Of ten tall fellowes, if that hee scape us:
 Besides, as far as I can apprehend,
 He hath no such intention, for his looks
 Are full of penitence.
Dorilaus.   Trust not a knaves looks,
 They are like a whores oaths;——how does my poore daughter
 Brook her restraint?
Servant.   With such a resolution
 As well becomes your Lordships childe.   *Knock within.*
Dorilaus.   Who's that?
Servant.   Monsieur *Lemure.*   [*Exit.*]

     Enter Lemure.

Dorilaus.   This is a special favour,   10
 And may stand an example in the court
 For courtesie: It is the Clyants duty
 To wait upon his patron; you prevent me,
 That am your humble suter.
Lemure.   My neare place
 About the King, though it swell others, cannot
 Make me forget your worth and age, which may
 Challenge much more respect; and I am sorry
 That my endeavours for you have not met with
 The good successe I wish'd; I mov'd the King
 With my best advantage both of time and place,   20
 Ith' favour of your daughter.
Dorilaus.   How doe you finde
 His Majesty affected?
Lemure.   Not to be
 Sway'd from the rigour of the Law: yet so far
 The rarity of the cause hath won upon him,
 That he resolves to have in his owne person
 The hearing of it; her tryall will be noble,
 And to my utmost strength, where I may serve her,

My aydes shall not be wanting.

Dorilaus.   I am your servant.

Lemure.   One word more: if you love *Lisanders* life,
   Advise him as he tenders it to keep   30
   Out of the way: if he be apprehended,
   This City cannot ransome him; so good morrow.

Dorilaus.   All happinesse attend you: *Exit* [Lemure].
                           goe thy wayes,
   Thou hast a cleare and noble soule: for thy sake
   Ile hold that man mine enemy, who dares mutter,
   The court is not the sphere where vertue moves
   Humanity and noblenesse waiting on her.

Enter Servant.

Servant.   Two gentlemen (but what they are I know not,
   Their faces are so mufl'd) presse to see you,
   And will not be deny'd.

Dorilaus.   What ere they are,   40
   I am to old to feare.

Servant.   They need no usher,
   They make their own way.

Enter Lisander, Alcidon.

Dorilaus.   Take you yours.   *Exit* Servant.
                       Lisander!
   My Joy to see you, and my sorrow for
   The danger you are in, contend so here,
   Though different passions, nay oppos'd in nature,
   I know not which to entertaine.

Lisander.   Your hate
   Should win the victorie from both, with justice,
   You may look on me as a Homicide,
   A man whose life is forfeit to the Law,
   But if (how ere I stand accus'd) in thought   50
   I sinn'd against *Cleanders* life, or live
   Guilty of the dishonour of your daughter,

*49 forfeit] forfeited F1-2

May all the miseries that can fall on man
Here, or hereafter circle me.
Dorilaus.   To me
This protestation's useless, I embrace you,
As the preserver of my life, the man
To whom my sonne owes his, with life, his honour,
And howsoever your affection
To my unhappy daughter, though it were
(For I have sifted her) in a noble way,   60
Hath printed some taint on her fame, and brought
Her life in question, yet I would not purchase
The wish'd recoverie of her reputation,
With strong assurance of her innocence
Before the King her Judge, with certaine losse
Of my *Lisander*, for whose life, if found,
There's no redemption; my excesse of love,
(Though to enjoy you one short day would lengthen
My life a dozen yeares) boldly commands me,
Upon my knees, which yet were never bent,   70
But to the King and heaven, to entreat you
To flye hence with all possible speed, and leave
Caliste to her fortune.
Lisander.   O blessed Saints,
Forsake her in affliction? can you
Be so unnatural to your owne bloud,
To one so well deserving, as to value
My safety before hers? shall innocence
In her be branded, and my guilt escape
Unpunish'd? doe's she suffer so much for me,
For me unworthy, and shall I decline   80
(Eating the bitter bread of banishment)
The course of justice to draw out a life?
(A life? I stile it false, a living death)
Which being uncompell'd laid downe will cleare her,
And write her name a-new in the faire legend
Of the best women? seek not to disswade me.
I will not, like a carelesse Poet, spoyle
The last act of my Play, till now applauded,

By giving the world just cause to say I fear'd
Death more then losse of honour.
Dorilaus.　　　　　　　　　　But suppose　　　　　　90
Heaven hath design'd some other saving meanes
For her deliverance?
Lisander.　　　　　　　Other means? that is
A mischiefe above all I have groan'd under:
Shall any other pay my debt, while I
Write my selfe bankrupt? or *Caliste* owe
The least beholdingnesse for that which she
On all the bonds of gratitude I have seal'd to,
May challenge from me to be freely tender'd?
Avert it mercy! I will goe to my grave,
Without the curses of my creditors;　　　　　　100
Ile vindicate her faire name, and so cancell
My obligation to her; to the King,
To whom I stand accomptable for the losse
Of two of his lov'd subjects lives, Ile offer
Mine owne in satisfaction; to heaven
Ile pay my true repentance; to the times
Present, and future, Ile be registred
A memorable president to admonish
Others, however valiant, not to trust
To their abilities to dare, and doe;　　　　　　110
And much lesse for the aërie words of honour,
And false stamp'd reputation, to shake off
The chains of their religion, and allegeance,
The pricipall means appointed to prefer
Societies and Kingdomes.　　　　　　　　　*Exit.*
Dorilaus.　　　　　　Let's not leave him;
His mind's much troubled.
Alcidon.　　　　　　　　　Were your daughter free,
Since from her dangers his distraction rises,
His cause is not so desperate for the slaughter
Of *Cloridon* and *Chrysanthes*, but it may
Find passage to the mercy of the King,　　　　　120
The motives urg'd in his defence, that forc'd him
To act that bloudy Scæne.

513

Dorilaus.   Heaven can send ayds,
    When they are least expected: let us walke,
    The houre of tryall drawes neare.
Alcidon.   May it end well.

Exeunt.

Enter Olinda *and* Lidian.   [V.ii

Olinda.   That for my love you should turne Hermit *Lidian*,
    As much amazes me, as your report
    Clarange's dead.
Lidian.   He is so, and all comforts
    My youth can hope for, Madam, with him buried;
    Nor had I ever left my cell, but that
    He did injoine me at his death to shed
    Some teares of friendship on his Monument,
    And those last Rites perform'd, he did bequeath you,
    As the best legacie a friend could give
    Or I indeed could wish, to my embraces.   10
Olinda.   'Tis still more strange, is there no foule play in it?
    I must confesse I am not sorry sir
    For your faire fortune; yet 'tis fit I grieve
    The most untimely death of such a Gentleman,
    He was my worthy servant.
Lidian.   And for this
    Acknowledgement, if I could prize you at
    A higher rate I should, he was my friend:
    My dearest friend.
Olinda.   But how should I be assur'd sir
    (For slow beleefe is the best friend of truth)
    Of this Gentlemans death? if I should credit it,   20
    And afterward it fall out contrary,
    How am I sham'd? how is your vertue tainted?
Lidian.   There is a Frier that came along with me.
    His businesse to deliver you a Letter
    From dead *Clarange*: You shall heare his testimonie.——
    Father, my reverend Father——

Enter Clarange [*disguised in Friers habit*] (*with a Letter) and* Frier.

                           looke upon him,
  Such holy men are Authors of no Fables.
Olinda.   They should not be, their lives and their opinions,
  Like brightest purest flames should still burne upwards,
                   [Clarange] *delivers the Letter.*
  To me sir?
Clarange.   If you are the faire *Olinda*——   [*She*] *Reads.* 30
Frier [*aside*].   I doe not like these crosse points.
Clarange [*aside*].   Give me leave,
  I am nearest to my selfe. What I have plotted
  Shal be pursu'd: you must not over-rule me.
Olinda.   Doe you put the first hand to your own undoing?
  Play to betray your game?——Mark but this letter.
    Lady I am come to claime your noble promise;
   If you be Mistris of your word, ye are mine,
   I am last return'd: your riddle is dissolv'd,
   And I attend your faith. Your humble servant
                          Clarange.   40

  Is this the Frier that saw him dead?
Lidian.   'Tis he.
                 [Clarange *draws back his cowl.*]
  Clarange on my life: I am defeated:
  Such reverend habits juggle? my true sorrow
  For a false friend not worth a teare, derided?
Frier.   You have abus'd my trust.
Olinda.   It is not well,
  Nor like a gentleman.
Clarange.   All strategems
  In love, and that the sharpest war, are lawfull,
  By your example I did change my habit,
  Caught you in your owne toyle, and triumph in it,
  And what by policy's got, I will maintaine   50

   26.1 *Letter*] *Letter writ out* F1–2. *See Textual Note at* I.ii.97.

With valour; no *Lisander* shall come in
Again to fetch you off.
Lidian.   His honor'd name
   Pronounc'd by such a treacherous tongue is tainted,
   Maintaine thy treason with thy sword? With what
   Contempt I heare it; in a Wildernesse
   I durst encounter it, and would, but that
   In my retired houres, not counterfeited
   As thy religious shape was, I have learn'd
   When Justice may determine; such a cause,
   And of such weight as this faire Lady is,   60
   Must not be put to fortune, I appeale
   Unto the King, and he whose wisdome knowes
   To doe his subjects right in their estates,
   As graciously with judgement will determine
   In points of honour.
Olinda.   I'le steere the same course with you.
Clarange.   I'le stand the tryall.   [*Exeunt* Lidian *and* Olinda.]
Friar.   What have you done? or what
   Intend you?
Clarange.   Aske not; I'le come off with honour.

                                        Exeunt.

   Enter Beronte, Clarinda, Malfort [*guarded by*] *Officers,*   [V.
                     a bar set forth.

Beronte.   Be constant in your proofes: should you shrinke backe
      now,
   Your life must answer it, nor am I safe,
   My honour being engag'd to make that good
   Which you affirme.
Clarinda.   I am confident, so dearely
   I honour'd my dead Lord, that no respect,
   Or of my Ladies bounties (which were great ones
   I must confesse) nor of her former life,
   For while that she was chast, indeed I lov'd her,
   Shall hinder me from lending my assistance
   Unto your just revenge——(*aside*) mine owne I meane,   10
   If *Leon* keepe far off enough, all's secure:

Lisander dares not come in, modest blushes
Parted with me long since, and impudence
Arm'd with my hate unto her innocence, shall be
The weapon I will fight with now.

Beronte.   The racke
Being presented to you, you'l roare out
What you conceale yet.

Malfort.   Conceale? I know nothing
But that I shall be hang'd, and that I looke for,
It is my destiny, I ever had
A hanging look; and a wise woman told me,   20
Though I had not the heart to do a deed
Worthy the halter, in my youth or age,
I should take a turne with a wry mouth, and now
'Tis come about: I have penn'd mine owne ballad
Before my condemnation, in feare
Some rimer should prevent me:

Enter Dorilaus, Caliste, Olinda.

                            here's my Lady?
Would I were in heaven, or a thousand miles hence,
That I might not blush to looke on her,

Dorilaus.   You
Behold this preparation, and the enemies
Who are to fight against your life, yet if   30
You bring no witnesse here, that may convince ye
Of breach of faith to your Lords bed, and hold up
Unspotted hands before the King, this tryall
You are to undergo, will but refine,
And not consume your honour.

Caliste.   How confirm'd
I am here, whatsoever Fate falls on me,
You shall have ample testimony; till the death
Of my deare Lord, to whose sad memory
I pay a mourning widdowes teares, I liv'd
Too happy in my holy-day trim of glorie,   40
And courted with felicitie, that drew on me,
With other helpes of nature, as of fortune,

517

The envie, not the love of most that knew me,
This made me to presume too much, perhaps
Too proud; but I am humbled; and if now
I doe make it apparent I can beare
Adversity with such a constant patience
As will set off my innocence, I hope, sir,
In your declining age, when I should live
A comfort to you, you shall have no cause,   50
How e're I stand accus'd, to hold your honour
Ship-wrack'd in such a daughter.
Olinda.   O best friend,
My honour's at the stake too, for——
Dorilaus.   Be silent;
The King.

Enter King, Lemure, *and Attendants.*

Lemure.   Sir, if you please to look upon
The Prisoner, and the many services
Her Father hath done for you——
King.   We must look on
The cause, and not the persons. Yet beholding
With an impartial eye, th'excelling beauties
Of this faire Lady, which we did beleeve
Upon report, but till now never saw 'em,   60
It moves a strange kind of compassion in me;
Let us survey you nearer, shee's a book
To be with care perus'd; and tis my wonder,
If such mishapen ghests, as lust and murther,
At any price should ever finde a lodging
In such a beauteous Inne! mistake us not,
Though we admire the outward structure, if
The roomes be foule within, expect no favour.
I were no man, if I could look on beautie
Distress'd, without some pitty; but no King,   70
If any superficiall glosse of feature
Could worke me to decline the course of Justice.——
But to the cause, *Cleander's* death, what proofes
Can you produce against her?

Beronte.   Royall sir,
    Touching that point my brothers death, we build
    On suppositions.
King.   Suppositions? how?
    Is such a Lady sir to bee condemn'd
    On suppositions?
Beronte.   They are well grounded sir:
    And if we make it evident she is guilty
    Of the first crime we charge her with, Adulterie,   80
    That being the parent, it may finde beliefe,
    That murther was the issue.
King.   We allow
    It may be so; but that it may be, must not
    Inferre a necessary consequence
    To cast away a Ladies life. What witnesses
    To make this good?
Beronte.   The principall, this woman,
    For many yeares her servant; she hath taken
    Her oath in Court.——Come forward.
King.   By my Crowne
    A lying face.
Clarinda.   I swore sir for the King:
    And if you are the partie, as I doe   90
    Believe you are, for you have a good face,
    How ever mine appeares, swearing for you sir,
    I ought to have my oath passe.
King.   Impudent too?
    Well, what have you sworne?
Clarinda.   That this Lady was
    A goodly tempting Lady, as she is:
    How thinks your Majestie? and I her servant,
    Her officer as one would say, and trusted
    With her closest Chamber-service; that *Lisander*
    Was a fine timber'd gentleman, and active,
    That he cou'd doe fine gambolls   100
    To make a Lady merrie; that this paire,
    A very loving couple, mutually
    Affected one another: so much for them sir.

That I, a simple waiting-woman, having taken
My bodily oath, the first night of admittance
Into her Ladiships service, on her slippers,
(That was the book) to serve her will in all things,
And to know no Religion but her pleasure,
('Tis not yet out of fashion with some Ladies);
That I, as the premises shew, being commanded   110
To doe my function, in conveyance of
Lisander to her chamber, (my Lord absent,
On a pretended sicknesse) did the feat,
(It cannot be deny'd) and at dead mid-night
Left 'em together: what they did, some here
Can easily imagine? I have said, sir.
Dorilaus.   The devills Oratrix.
King.   Then you confesse
You were her Bawd?
Clarinda.   That's course, her agent sir.
King.   So goodie agent? and you think there is
No punishment due for your agentship?   120
Clarinda.   Let her suffer first,
Being my better, for adulterie,
And Ile endure the Mulct impos'd on Bawdes,
Call it by the worst name.
Caliste.   Live I to heare this?
King.   Take her aside.——Your answer to this, Lady?
Caliste.   Heav'n grant me patience: to be thus confronted,
(O pardon Royall sir a womans passion)
By one, and this the worst of my mis-fortunes,
That was my slave, but never to such ends sir,
Would give a statue motion into furie: 130
Let my pass'd life, my actions, nay intentions,
Be by my grand accuser justly censur'd,
(For her I scorne to answer) and if they
Yeeld any probability of truth
In that she urges, then I will confesse
A guilty cause; the peoples voyce, which is

135 then] F2; and F1

The voyce of truth, my husbands tendernesse
In his affection to me, (that no dotage
But a reward of humblenesse), the friendship
Eccho'd through *France* between him and *Lisander*,   140
All make against her; for him, in his absence,
(What ever imputation it draw on me)
I must take leave to speak: 'tis true, he lov'd me,
But not in such a wanton way, his reason
Master'd his passions: I grant I had
At mid-night conference with him; but if he
Ever receiv'd a farther favour from me,
Then what a sister might give to a brother,
May I sinke quick: and thus much, did he know
The shame I suffer for him, with the losse   150
Of his life for appearing, on my soule
He would maintaine——

Enter Lisander, *and* Alcidon.

Lisander.   And will, thou cleare example
  Of womens purenesse.
King.   Though we hold her such,
  Thou hast express'd thy selfe a desperat foole,
  To thrust thy head into the Lions jawes,
  The justice of thy King.
Lisander.   I came prepar'd for't,
  And offer up a guilty life to cleare
  Hir innocence; the oath she tooke, I sweare to;
  And for *Cleanders* death, to purge my selfe
  From any colour malice can paint on me,   160
  Or that she had a hand in't, I can prove
  That fatall night when he in his own house fell,
  And many daies before, I was distant from it
  A long daies journey.
Clarinda [*aside*].   I am caught.
Beronte.   If so,
  How came your Sword into this stewards hands?——
  Stand forth.
Malfort.   I have heard nothing that you spake;

521

I know I must dye, and what kind of death
Pray you resolve me, I shall go away else
In a qualme; I am very faint.
King.   Carry him off,
His feare will kil him.   *Exit [Officer] with* Malfort.
Dorilaus.   Sir, 'twas my ambition,   170
My Daughters reputation being wounded
I'th' generall opinion, to have it
Cur'd by a publicke triall; I had else
Forborne your Majesties trouble: I'le bring forth
Cleanders murtherer,

Enter Servants and Guard [with] Leon.

                    in a wood I heard him
A I rod sadly by, unto himselfe
With some compunction, though this devill had none,
Lament what he had done, cursing her lust,
That drew him to that bloudy fact.
Leon.   To lessen
The foulenesse of it, for which I know justly   180
I am to suffer, and with my last breath
To free these Innocents, I do confesse all;
This wicked woman only guilty with me.
Clarinda.   Is't come to this? thou puling Rogue, dye thou
With prayers in thy mouth; I'le curse the lawes
By which I suffer, all I grieve for is,
That I dye unreveng'd.
Leon.   But one word more sir,
And I have done; I was by accident where
Lisander met with *Cloridon,* and *Chrysanthes,*
Was an eare witnesse when he sought for peace,   190
Nay, begg'd it upon colder tearmes then can
Almost find credit, his past deeds considered,
But they deafe to his reasons, severally
Assaulted him, but such was his good fortune,
That both fell under it; upon my death
I take it uncompel'd, that they were guilty
Of their owne violent ends; and he against

His will, the Instrument.

Alcidon.   This I will sweare too,
    For I was not far off.

Dorilaus.   They have alleadg'd
    As much to wake your sleeping mercy sir,   200
    As all the Advocates of *France* can plead
    In his defence.

King.   The criminall judge shall sentence
    These to their merits——

                              Exeunt [*Guards*] *with* Leon, *and* Clarinda.
                              with mine owne hand Lady
    I take you from the bar, and do my selfe
    Pronounce you innocent.

All.   Long live the King.

King.   And to confirme you stand high in our favour,
    And as some recompence for what you have
    With too much rigour in your triall suffered;
    Aske what you please, becoming me to grant,
    And be possest of't.

Caliste.   Sir, I dare not doubt   210
    Your royall promise, in a King it is
    A strong assurance, that emboldens me
    Upon my humble knees to make my boone
    Lisanders pardon.

Dorilaus [*aside*].   My good Genius
    Did prompt her to it.

Lemure.   At your feet thus prostrate,
    I second her petition.

Alcidon.   Never King
    Powr'd forth his mercie on a worthyer subject.

Beronte.   To witnesse my repentance for the wrong
    In my unjust suspition I did both,
    I joyne in the same suit.

Lisander.   The life you give,   220
    Still ready to lay down for your service,
    Shall be against your enemies imploy'd,
    Not hazzarded in brawles.

All.   Mercie dread sir.

523

King.   So many pressing me, and with such reasons
  Moving compassion, I hope it will not
  Be censur'd levity in me though I borrow
  In this from justice to relieve my mercie;
  I grant his pardon at your intercession,
  But still on this condition; you *Lisander*,
  In expiation of your guilt, shall build   230
  A monument for my *Cloridon*, and *Crysanthes*:
  And never henceforth draw a Sword, but when
  By us you are commanded, in defence of
  The Flower de Luce, and after one yeares sorrow
  For your deare friend, *Cleanders* wretched fate,
  Marry *Caliste*.
Lisander.   On your sacred hand,
  I vow to do it seriously.

Enter Lidian.

Lidian.   Great sir stay,
  Leave not your seat of justice, till you have
  Given sentence in a cause as much important
  As this you have determined.
King.   *Lidian?*
Lidian.   He sir,   240
  Your humblest subject,——I accuse *Clarange*
  Of falshood in true friendship at the height;
  We both were suiters to this Lady, both
  Injoyn'd one pennance——

Enter Clarange [*in Friers habit*], *and* Frier.

Clarange.   Trouble not the King
  With an unnecessarie repetition
  Of what the Court's familiar with already.
                              [*Draws back his cowl.*]

King.   *Clarange?*
Dorilaus.   With a shaven crowne?
Olinda.   Most strange.

244 Clarange.] See Textual Note.

Clarange.   Looke on thy rivall, your late servant Madam,
    But now devoted to a better Mistris,
    The Church, whose orders I have tooke upon me: 250
    I here deliver up my interest to her;
    And what was got with cunning as you thought,
    I simply thus surrender: heretofore,
    You did outstrip me in the race of friendship,
    I am your equall now.
Dorilaus.   A suite soone ended.
Clarange.   And joyning thus your hands, I know both willing,
    I may do in the Church my Friers Office
    In marrying you.
Lidian.   The victory is yours sir.
King.   It is a glorious one, and well set's of
    Our Scæne of mercy; to the dead we tender   260
    Our sorrow, to the living ample wishes
    Of future happines: 'tis a Kings duty
    To prove himselfe a father to his Subjects:
    And I shall hold it if this well succeed,
    A meritorious, and praise worthy deed.

                                                    Exeunt.

Prologue.

A Story, and a known one, long since writ,
Truth must take place, and by an able wit,
Foule mouth'd detraction daring not deny
To give so much to Fletchers *memory;*
If so, some may object, why then do you
Present an old piece to us for a new?
Or wherefore will your profest writer be
(Not tax'd of theft before) a Plagary?
To this he answers in his just defence,
And to maintaine to all our Innocence, 10
Thus much, though he hath travel'd the same way,
Demanding, and receiving too the pay
For a new Poem, you may find it due,
He having neither cheated us, nor you;
He vowes, and deeply, that he did not spare
The utmost of his strengths, and his best care
In the reviving it, and though his powers
Could not as he desired, in three short howers
Contract the Subject, and much lesse expresse
The changes, and the various passages 20
That will be look'd for, you may heare this day
Some Scænes that will confirme it is a play,
He being ambitious that it should be known
What's good was Fletchers, *and what ill his owne.*

Epilogue.

Still doubtfull, and perplex'd too, whether he
Hath done Fletcher *right in this Historie,*
The Poet sits within, since he must know it,
He with respect, desires that you would shew it
By some accustomed signe, if from our action,
Or his indeavours you meet satisfaction,
With ours he hath his ends, we hope the best,
To make that certainty in you doth rest.

TEXTUAL NOTES

I.ii

97 Caliste.] This is the first of several instances in which the Folio direction provides a hand-carried property that is not needed at the entry of the character or, indeed, is of necessity to be concealed.

I.ii.97 *Enter Caliste with a purse.*
II.ii.35 *Enter ... Fortune-teller, with a Purse and two Letters in it.*
II.iv.42 *Enter ... Clarinda, following with a letter.*
III.iii.0.1 *Enter ... Lisander with a Pistole, ...*
V.ii.26.1 *Enter Clarange (with a Letter writ out) ...*

This edition supposes that these are book-keeper's notices, reminding the actor to take the prop on stage at his entrance; as warnings to the actor, not advice to the reader, these anticipatory prop-directions are transferred from the places where they are initially mentioned to the spot where the appearance of the prop is appropriate. This direction at line 97, 'with a purse', is transferred to line 222. (It might be worth comment that Caliste comes on stage in this scene first at line 35 and leaves at line 91. Before his second entrance, at line 97, the actor is to pick up the purse from the prop table. He does not need the purse during his first appearance, and it is therefore not mentioned then.)

This kind of preliminary warning is not present at each instance; at II.i.0.1 there is no such direction, though a purse is needed at line 11. And there are instances when the direction is given and the prop is required immediately or its visible presence is significant: III.i.0.1 *with a Key;* IV.ii.0.1 *with a book.* And there are others which seem to be of the first kind but which are sufficiently ambiguous that they are not here emended: III.iv.0.1 *with a Letter.* Directions for lights are, of course, of a different sort: *with lights* (III.i.18.1); *with a Taper* (III.iii.117), etc.

One is tempted to believe that all the directions requiring props are, in fact, uniform in their significance in the book-keeper's mind: whenever a prop is needed it should be mentioned in the direction that brings on stage the actor who will need to use it. When a prop is needed or visible immediately after the actor's entrance, this edition leaves the 'warning' notice in its Folio position.

153 *Caliste.*] Though the Folio does occasionally divide one line assigned to a single speaker and print it on two lines of type, such lineation always invites an inquiry into the irregularity. One explanation is that for the second line a second speaker was intended for whom the prefix was omitted. The present instance would seem to qualify for emendation on the basis of the personalities of the two speakers. In this scene, husband and wife jointly express their concern for Dorilaus' welfare, as, for example, at lines 202–3 and at line 141 where the two split the single line. I would

528

suggest that they do so again in this single line, Cleander requiring the specific locality of the accident and Caliste expressing her fearful concern for her father. The half lines exhibit two characteristics: the analytical or reasonable, the daughterly and emotive (the *wild* forest).

189 mettle]   F2 changed the spelling of this word to 'metal', i.e., his sword, and Mason approved (Weber and Dyce followed). Mason is clearly correct in his understanding of the passage, but as 'mettle' is a variant spelling of 'metal', this edition retains the F1 form.

227 *Servant.* 'Twas]   One could argue that this speech was on the same line in the MS (as just above in the Folio at line 216) and that, again, the prefix (for an unimportant character) was omitted (see note at line 153). The Folio setting can certainly be played dramatically; much is gained by having the wife and then the husband mention the name of the hero; but as this trick is (probably) used at the end of the scene, it is not necessary here, perhaps not even desirable. (For '*Servant*', Dyce read '*Jasper*'.)

241 You]   Colman demonstrated that the Folio arrangement of these closing lines was erroneous:

> *Dor.* ...
> And fitter for a bed than long discourses.   (w)
>   *Cle.* You shall hear to morrow, to morrow provide   (x)
> *Dor. Lisander*——   (y)   (Surgeons.   (x)
>   *Cal.* What new fire is this? *Lisander*——*Exeunt.*   (z)

Colman's rearrangement recognized that the line x–x assigned to '*Cle.*' 'should come from the old man [Dorilaus] ... which expresses his faintness'. He therefore continued that line to Dorilaus; the old man was 'preparing to speak, but is forced to desist and to call for assistance'. Then as a natural consequence, he dropped the prefix for '*Cle.*' one line so that it replaced the prefix '*Dor.*' (The presence of '*Dor.*' in this particular context (line y) is clearly irregular and erroneous.) He read:

> *Dor.* ...
> And fitter for a bed than long discourses.   (w)
> You shall hear tomorrow.——Tomorrow——Provide Surgeons.   (x)
>   *Cle. Lisander*——   (y)

Weber and Dyce followed this arrangement. Dyce reported and rejected the conjecture of Heath that Caliste should speak the last two lines (y, z):

> *Cal. Lisander*——What new fire is this? *Lisander*——   (y, z)

But Colman was surely right in recognizing the need for both husband and wife to call the name of the beloved, so pointing up the conflict already suggested in this act and to become essential as the play progresses:

> *Cle. Lisander*——   (y)
> *Cal.*   What new fire is this? *Lisander*——   (z)

(This edition supposes that Caliste's question is addressed to her own heart.)

I will suggest, however, that one further refinement should be made. As it appears that the prefix '*Cle.*' was placed a line too high in the copy——or was perceived by the compositor as being a line too high——we may imagine the MS as having had this lineation:

Dor.	(a)
And fitter for a bed than long discourses.	(b)
Cle. You shall hear to morrow, to morrow	(c)
Provide Surgeons.	(d)
Lisander——	(e)
Cal. What new fire is this? *Lisander*——	(f)

Confronted with what must have appeared to be two consecutive short lines with no speakers' names, the compositor might have thought to solve the awkwardness (1) by putting line d on the end of line c (though that would require a turn-over) and (2) by supplying for line e the prefix of the other speaker prominent in this scene. This edition adjusts this perceived error in the MS by lowering the prefix '*Cle.*' from line c to line d (and eliminating the 'extra' prefix '*Dor.*').

As a literary justification for the elimination of the prefix '*Dor.*' it can be argued that though Dorilaus has seemed quite strong enough, indeed quite jocular, from line 117 to line 217, he now suddenly fails as his loss of blood begins to tell on him. His speech collapses in line 241 as he promises an even fuller account of the attack tomorrow. He might at this point ask his son-in-law to provide surgeons, but a more dramatic effect results if the son-in-law, as master of the house, orders an attendant to summon medical assistance. Though Cleander's chief concern in this scene is with the welfare of his beloved friend, he is not so far besotted that he cannot organize the pseudo-*judicium Paridis*, express concern for the disappointed lovers, act the gracious host, serve as the prime auditor and responder to Dorilaus' story, and – most important – recognize (at last) that the stage is full of wounded men needing help (lines 238–9). (This edition, taking literally Caliste's command to Malfort at line 113 that the Steward attend Dorilaus, brings him on stage with the wounded old man at line 117 and sends him off here to fetch the help that Cleander has ordered in line d.)

II.i

95 Leave you]   The duplication of this phrase (which appears in F1 at the end of line 94 and at the beginning of line 95) suggests an erroneous compositorial anticipation. Deleting one of the instances provides a metrical regularity.

A different kind of duplication, suggesting perhaps anticipation, occurs at I.ii.199–200: 'ran away by Troops | And trod downe Troops to save their lives'. The awkwardness of this repetition suggests that the second 'Troops' may have resulted from the compositor's recollection of the first 'Troops' which has displaced a word – 'Heaps', perhaps – intended to be in the later location (line 200).

II.iii

14/16 *Fight within.* | *Fight.*]   The uncorrected Folio reads at the right margin of lines
13–14, '*Fight and* | *fight with.*'. Dr James P. Hammersmith has most ingeniously
argued that '*with.*' was supposed to be '*within*', and that the corrector, 'baffled by
what he took to be a nonsensical fragment', excised the entire stage-direction ('The
proof-reading of the Beaumont and Fletcher Folio ...', *Papers of the
Bibliographical Society of America*, LXXXVIII (1982), 314). In support of that
conjecture it might be noted that line 14 is full and that line 15 has little space for any
additional run-over of the direction. As the Second Folio reprinted a corrected
copy of this page (3K3), the uncorrected puzzling stage-direction vanished from
editorial concern and has never been discussed by any editor. In the assumption that
if the off-stage duel and the on-stage duel begin simultaneously, as the uncorrected
direction would seem to suggest they should, the separate sounds of the off-stage
swords will have no significance, this edition divides the direction, commencing the
off-stage duel at line 14, the on-stage duel (as the dialogue intimates) after line 16.
(If the off-stage duel were directed to begin after line 10, the next line might seem to
be Lidian's specific response to the swords of the seconds ('Let *our* swords argue');
but that early location of one half of the direction would seem to separate the two
sections by too many lines.)

52 twin'd]   The editions of F1, F2 and Langbaine give this spelling, understanding
(we may believe) that it signified 'twinned' (as at II.i.33), and Sympson confirmed
that meaning with the spelling 'twinn'd'. Colman reverted to the F spelling: 'twin'd
[i.e., twined] is clearly the true reading', followed by Weber and Dyce. An old-
spelling edition need not pass judgement, but the present editor observes that
twinship has been mentioned in the discussion of this friendship, vegetative
interinvolvement has not. Indeed, the growing together of this relationship is seen
as characterized not by two vines, or tendrils (as 'twining' naturally supposes), but
by an extension of a single growth: 'We grew up till we were men, held one heart
still' (II.i.34), 'that soul grew to'your bosome' (II.iii.40). Only in their present
condition can the two be seen as distinct individuals capable of being separated:
'one growth ... mortally divorc'd' (II.iii.54–5). After death, the twins are indeed
envisioned as vegetatively twining together (IV.iv.148–51).
    (See also 'sin'd' (= sinned) (III.vi.71).

53 friendship, ... a wonder,]   We may suppose that the Folio 'to wonder' has
resulted from a compositor's faulty duplication of 'to' – 'to the world, to wonder,',
which in its turn stems from his misconception of the idea – 'Married in friendship
to the world'. Colman's emendation of 'to' to 'two' might well be entertained were
it not that it requires an additional 'correction' of 'wonder' to 'wonders'. For this
last there is no authorization. Furthermore, such a duality violates the sense of unity
that the passage has been stressing. (See previous note.)

85 unwilling]   In support of the emendation ('un' for 'and') it may be argued that the
compositor, momentarily dislocated by the alliteration in 'willing wanderer',
forgot the parallelism of 'unfortunate'/'unwilling', and converted the second 'un' to

'and'. Perhaps a useful parallel may be found in what would seem to be another omission of the prefix 'un-' at IV.iv.12 (F1 'to'; F2 and edd. 'unto').

As there is no indication that the rejection by Caliste, that makes Lisander wander, makes him willing to do so (as the Folio 'unfortunate, and willing wanderer' would seem to suggest), and since Caliste tells us later that she would 'willingly comfort him' (II.iv.112), we must believe that he would willingly be comforted, wander from such comfort unwillingly. Indeed he describes himself as ignorantly blind in his wandering (III.iii.15–16), and the Apparition of the Host tells us that Lisander wanders 'in afflictions ... now' (III.v.93).

It has been suggested that the Folio reading is correct, that Lisander is a willing wanderer, willing to leave the vicinity so as not to wrong his friend Cleander; nothing in his speech suggests that particular attitude. Furthermore, though it is clear that all editors have accepted the pleasant paradox of 'unfortunate' and 'willing', retaining 'willing' requires the reading 'third ... willing wanderer'; certainly the other two wanderers wander unwillingly. Lidian remarks that in living out Olinda's 'dark sentence' Clarange's and his youth will be 'lost in wandring' (II.i.115), and he refers gloomily to his 'wandring life' (IV.iv.78) in terms that suggest that he finds in such wandering no consolation other than the religious (he gives it up quickly enough at the first opportunity).

It will be proper here to recall that the original title (1623) of the play was 'The Wandring Lovers' (see Textual Introduction). The later title (1641), 'The Lovers Progress', to which we must suppose Massinger came some six years after his revision of the old play, would seem to indicate that *wandering* was an action not sufficiently directed to satisfy Massinger's conception of what the play was about. Massinger was unwilling, we may say, to allow his revision to wander casually; directed progression was his aim.

II.iv

70 *Exeunt* ... Caliste.]   This exit-direction appears in the Folio at the foot of 3K3v, in the right margins of lines 3 and 2 from the bottom of column b (lines 67a, b; Compositor *B*, who continued on to 3K4). By a quite unusual press correction, the compositor has added an asterisk before the direction and an asterisk at the end of line 68, the last line of the page. Dr Hammersmith terms this a 'desperate measure', taken as 'a last resort ... to indicate to the reader the proper position of the stage direction', though, as he recognizes also, the direction should appear (as in the present edition) after line 70a. He believes the direction was overlooked in the casting off (*op.cit.* above at Textual Note for II.iii.14/16, pp. 311–12). If, however, the compositor continued from 3K3v to 3K4, as would seem to have been the sequence followed here, he could more profitably have set the direction on 3K4 where it applies properly to the action.

III.iii

6 the]   F1 reads 'his graces'; F2 reads 'the graces'; Langbaine and Sympson read
'his Graces'. It is not clear that any of these recognized that the imprisoned graces
were the Three Graces themselves. Colman and his successors have done so. One
can readily understand that the MS might have had a lower-case initial for the
'graces' and so did not alert the compositor to the presence of these deities. The
problem with the emendation lies, then, in the F1 'his' (another problem is the
question of the source for the F2 'the' – even without the upper-case letter), but an
argument can be made that the frequency of words beginning with *h* in these lines –
'hath', 'his', 'her', 'her', 'has' – replaced the negligible 'the' in the compositor's
mind and produced the F1 'his'. But it is understandable that Love, here depicted as
'Fierce', might have violently locked up graces in Caliste's eyes – his own graces
(even though such virtues are not usually specific to Cupid). Is it forbidden to look
on the Three Graces? Does Death to the observer result?

67 *Kisses*.]   This edition regards the F1 direction, '*Kisses*' – carefully placed on the
line of Caliste's short speech – as different in kind (not in degree) from the earlier
directions: 49 '*Kissing her hand.*', 61 '*Kisses her.*'. The absence here of the feminine
object (or of any object) suggests that at line 67 the object is different from earlier
objects, is in fact masculine; it is Caliste who initiates this kiss. Sympson and Dyce
both supply '*Kisses her*'; an interpretation that this prurient note seeks to correct.
He says he is honest; she replies that she will dare to test or prove ('try') that
assertion. She kisses him. His response is immediate and masculine: he asks her to
kiss him again. She declines. Lines 69–71 make little sense if Caliste is not the
initiator here. (One is tempted to observe in this titillating scene that her trial would
seem to have demonstrated a readiness on his part not to be 'honest'.)

129 As if]   The temptation to emend Folio 'As if he had risen' to the elliptical 'As he
had risen', which offers directness and metrical regularity, is appealing (see also 'As
I were a sensuall beast' (III.iv.54)), but since the 'As' in the next line must have a
different signification, the Folio is retained.

160.1 *Enter* Cleander.]   The Folio arrangement for the entry and exit of the rivals
has merit:

Sig. 3L1(a)	We are betrai'd else.	*Ent. Clea.*
Sig. 3L1(b)	*Lis.* Honour guard the Innocent.	*Exit. Lis.*
	Clean. Stil up? I fear'd your health.	

This arrangement, exactly followed, would bring Cleander on stage – '*with a
Taper*' presumably (as at line 117.1) – before Lisander had left it. That split-second
replacement routine has something to recommend it to be sure, but the argument
supporting it depends on a care in the compositor's placement of directions that
would not be characteristic. For example, at Cleander's other unexpected entry
(line 117), the arrangement requires Cleander to speak to his wife, whom he
supposes asleep, before he is on stage. The fact that the action is split at line 160 by
the break in the folio columns would seem to suggest that not too much weight be

put on the specific location of the direction. Each interpretation offers a valid dramatic experience.

III.iv

34–45 *Adieu ... higher.*]   This song appears in British Library Manuscript Eg. 2013. F. 47b. Substantive variants in the MS:

38 *the*] those BL
38 *sigh*] BL (*bis*)
39 *to ... clime,*] BL (*bis*)
39 *clime*] clymes BL
41 *ne're*] near BL
43 *by ... and*] with th' ... of BL
44 *There ... love*] There ... thoughts BL (*bis*)
45 *this heavenly love*] BL (*thrice*)

The variant in line 43 has merit, and the variant in line 38, 'those' for '*the*', is decidedly preferable, as the -*o*- vowel is musically superior to the -*e*- at the end of an ascending vocal run; but 'clymes' in line 39 (cf. F2 '*doth climb*') indicates that the writer did not recognize that '*My nobler love*' was parallel to '*Adieu fond love*', in direct address; 'thoughts' in line 44 indicates the same inadequacy. J. P. Cutts in *Musique de scène de la troupe de Shakespeare* (Paris, 1959) attributes the musical setting to Robert Johnson on stylistic grounds and because Johnson is the composer of the other song in the play (pp. 97–9, 183–4).

III.v

47 *Cleander.*]   The song appears a line or a half-line too soon in F1; F2 solved a part of the problem by bringing the half-line speech 'Harke, a Song' up from line 66 ('Harke a Song, now as I live it is his voice.') to line 47, adding the words to Dorilaus' speech (lines 46–7) (not inappropriately) setting them off with a dash. (There is nothing in the character of Dorilaus that would prohibit his interrupting himself in this way, but F1 does give the three words to Cleander.) Recognizing the error in F1 (without consulting F2), Langbaine brought the entire line '66' '*Cle.* Harke, ... voice.') up to line 47 (followed by Sympson). This arrangement provides an interruption to Dorilaus' speech, surely a more dramatic moment than that offered by F2; and it calls attention to the forthcoming song – perhaps after hearing the opening words. The second half-line, however, properly belongs after the song, a comment on what has been heard and a fit introduction to Dorilaus' line 67, 'He sings well'. Colman split the line – placing 'Harke, a Song' before the song and 'now ... it is his voice' after it. All editors follow. Cleander is the 'regular' at this inn who knows the old Host – though Dorilaus wants to talk with him (as he talks with all old hosts), and it is Cleander who recognizes the voice as that of his old acquaintance.

48–65 *Tis ... ground.*]   This song appears in three manuscripts in the British

Library: Addl. MSS. 11608. f. 20 [43] (BL¹), 29481. f. 25b (BL²), 29396. f. 39b [46] (BL³). Substantive variants in the MSS:

51 *hearty*] heartye good BL³
51 *the*] the BL²,³; *a* BL¹ [*a* F1–2; see next note]
53 *shall* may BL¹⁻³
53 *tumble*] BL¹⁻³ (*thrice*)
54 *wish*] well wish BL¹⁻³
55 *But … dead*] BL² (*bis*)
58 *And*] omit BL¹,³
58 *while*] whilst BL¹
59 *drinke*] drinking BL³
60 *Plover*] Plovers BL³
61 *the*] a BL²,³
64 *Welcome Welcome*] BL¹,³ [*Welcome* F1; *Welcom welcom* F2]
65 *shall*] will BL²
[65.1] finis. Robt Johnson BL¹

The textual variants of these manuscripts are not such as to necessitate any changes in the received text, though the repeated 'Welcome' of two manuscripts supports the F2 reading of the line which is therefore adopted, and the 'the cold' of two manuscripts supports the present editor's conjecture, instead of 'a cold', which is therefore adopted.

BL¹ attributes one setting of the song to Robert Johnson (an attribution accepted by Cutts); the same music is found in BL³. BL² provides a different setting, no attribution, for lines 48–57 only. BL¹ also provides a heading: 'ffor a Base alone. | Myne Osts songe. | Sung in yᵉ Mad-Lover.' (The song is not stipulated to be sung in 'The Mad Lover'; see *Musique de scène*, pp. 49a, b; 184–5.) The popularity of the song is no doubt attributable to Johnson's music.
51 *the cold*]   The ameliorating effects of drink against climatic distress are traditional and are better known than are those against bronchial ('*Tis late and cold*' line 48).

III.vi

2 look'd]   Weber's emendation, 'lock'd', is attractive.
48 grudge]   As the Folio past tense seems awkward in a context of present verbs – see line 38 – a normal compositorial error of terminal *d/e* seems likely. Dr Turner points out that the past tense may have resulted also from attraction of 'err'd', 'pleas'd' (lines 47, 48).

IV.i

4–5 vertue; … secure,]   The Folio punctuation, 'if you love vertue, In danger not secure;', has caused some debate. Sympson offered a 'violent alteration' (Dyce), best not repeated; Colman thought it 'plainly a broken sentence' and placed a dash

after 'secure'. Weber and Dyce followed Mason's interpretation: 'If you love virtue
in such a dangerous situation, that it is not, as it ought to be, its own security'. Such
a reading seems almost too elliptical. A simpler interpretation results from
interchanging two points, as in the present text. Alcidon is, presumably, not
personally in danger, but the situation, in which all of them are involved, is
certainly not a secure one, and it is one requiring haste if Lisander is to be protected.
7 brothers]   Since 'brothers' is certainly correct (as in line 32 and F2), we must
suppose that the Folio 'fathers' results from Massinger's lapse of memory; his
intentions are clear.

IV.iii

8 meate]   Though the Folio plural 'meats' is acceptable, one might have expected
the spelling 'meates' as in 'meanes' in line 4. The emendation supposes the common
terminal *e/s* confusion. The parallel singular 'sawce' supports the change.
84 *Malfort.*]   Dyce marks this speech, "'Tis *Leon.*', '*Aside*', but Cleander reacts to
the speech (line 85) and refers to 'Leon' in line 89, a name he would not have known
to mention had he not heard it.

V.i

49 forfeit]   Editors from Seward to Dyce have emended at I.ii.33 and 95
Compositor *A*'s predilection to supply an extra *-ed* to verbals. They have not done
so here, supposing that the only reason for changing Folio 'forfeited' to 'forfeit' is
metrical. The same principle applies here, however, as at the earlier instances:

> You dispaire to lose
> What you contend[ed] for.
> > No sir, I am armed.   (I.ii.32–3)

> Their blunt[ed] departure troubles me: I feare.   (I.ii.95)

V.iii

244 *Clarange.*]   The Folio provides the entrance of Clarange and his Friar at line 240,
not necessarily in error, but certainly obtrusively. Colman regarded Lidian's
speech (lines 240–4) as interrupted, and Weber and Dyce transferred Clarange's
entry-direction to the end of it as the occasion for the interruption. Such an entry
provides for high melodrama – as do the entry of Lisander at line 152 (exactly
placed in F1) and the entry of Lidian at line 237 (transferred from line 236a) – and is
probably what Massinger intended.
     As Lidian and Clarange left the stage together in the Folio at the end of V.ii, both
with the express purpose of bringing their difference to the King, there is no reason
in the fiction why they should enter the stage separately in V.iii (as they do), but
there is in the theatre. And such a separated entrance encourages the thought that
they should have left the stage separately at the end of V.ii. This edition provides,

536

therefore, at the end of V.ii an additional direction for the early exit of Lidian, an emendation that the dialogue encourages. (There is a reason in the fiction why Olinda, who leaves at V.ii.66 with Lidian, should enter V.iii before him (at line 26).)

PRESS VARIANTS IN F1 (1647)

[Copies collated: Ger (private copy of Dr J. Gerritsen), Hoy (private ... copy of Cyrus Hoy), IU¹ (University of Illinois 822/B38/1647), IU² (University of Illinois q822/B38/1647 copy 2), MB (Boston Public Library G.39600.27), MnU (University of Minnesota Z823B38/fOCa), NcD (Duke University, 429544), NcD-A (Duke University, second copy), NIC (Cornell University A951587), NjP (Princeton University Ex 3623.1/1647q copy 2.), PSt (Pennsylvania State University Library PR2420/1647/Q), ViU¹ (University of Virginia 570973), ViU² (University of Virginia 217972), WaU (University of Washington Accession 29424), Wms (private copy of G. W. Williams), WMU¹ (University of Wisconsin–Milwaukee (RARE) PR2420/1647 copy 1), WMU² (University of Wisconsin–Milwaukee (RARE) PR2420/1647 copy 2), WMU³ (University of Wisconsin–Milwaukee (RARE) PR2420/1647 copy 3), WU (University of Wisconsin–Madison 1543420).

QUIRE 3K (*outer sheet, inner forme*)
Uncorrected: IU², MB, PSt, ViU¹, WMU²

Sig. 3K1v
I.ii.180 ſhe] eſh

QUIRE 3K (*outer sheet, outer forme*)
Uncorrected: ViU²

Sig. 3K2
II.i.3 Be] e
Sig. 3K3v
II.iii.44 Exampled ... Love,] Example ... Love;
II.iii.59 *Mars's* ſervants; Mars's ſervants
II.iii.68 No] No
II.iii.74 *Clara.*] *Clar.*
II.iv.38 Rather] Ra her
II.iv.67 worthy. **Ex.*] worthy. *Ex.*
II.iv.68 wiſer.*] wiſer.

QUIRE 3K (*inner sheet, inner forme*)
Uncorrected: ViU², WaU, Wms

Sig. 3K3
II.ii.33 own] ᵒwn
II.ii.34 intreaty] ⁱntreaty

II.iii.6.1 *Lisand*] *Lisaud*
II.iii.13 me,] me, *Fight and*
II.iii.14 her.] her. *fight with.*
II.iii.18 deliver] deliuer

EMENDATIONS OF ACCIDENTALS

Persons Represented
1–23.1] F2; *omit* F1
2 Caliste] Calista F2 (*and so*

throughout)
10 Lemure] Lemeor F2
12 Malfort] Mallfort F2

I.i

I.i] *Actus primus. Scæna prima.* F1–2
1 Sir——] ~ . F1–2
2 *Clarinda*'s] F2; *Clarinda's* F1
17–18 indeed ... away.] *one line in*
  F1–2
19 glister] Clyster F2
22–23 As ... comfort,] *one line in* F1–2
26–27 Ile ... you.] *one line in* F1–2
27–28 You ... her?] *one line in* F1–2
28–29 I ... friend] *one line in* F1–2
35 Lady,] F2; ~ ∧ F1
40 seem] F2; seeem F1
47 ends?] ~ . F1–2
52–53 Do ... lesse,] *one line in* F1–2
53 Incest?] F2; ~ ; F1
64–65 As ... Snow.] *one line in* F1–2
68 suffer] F2; fuffer F1
69–70 No ... return'd.] *one line in*
  F1–2
84 promise.——] ~ . ∧ F1–2
93–94 'Tis ... prayers.] *one line in*
  F1–2
97–98 A ... reward.] *one line in* F1–2

101 upon!] F2; ~ . F1
114 it.——] ~ . ∧ F1–2
118–119 Of ... Mistris] *one line in* F1–2
139 him;] ~ , F1–2
141–142 She ... Lady.] *one line in* F1–2
142–143 How ... prevail'd?] *one line in*
  F1–2
146–147 you | Shall] | You shall F1–2
147 grace——] ~ . F1–2
150.1 Caliste] *Calista* F1–2
153–154 Pray ... draught.] *one line in*
  F1–2
154–155 Happinesse | Attend] | Happi-
  nesse attend F1–2
155 Leon,] F2; ~ . F1
155–156 Who ... parle? *one line in* F1–2
159–160 No ... mine.] *one line in* F1–2
172–173 You ... further?] *one line in*
  F1–2
193–194 I ... worke] *one line in* F1–2
210–211 She ... owne;] *one line in* F1–2
216 Cedar,] F2; Cedar t F1

I.ii

4 me.] F2; ~ ∧ F1
11 *sans*] sans F1–2
17 worth∧] F2; ~ , F1
28 *Olinda*?] F2; ~ . F1
35–36 Ile ... test.] *one line in* F1–2
41–42 I ... deserves] *one line in* F1–2
56–57 You ... one.] *one line in* F1–2

90 more:——] ~ : ∧ F1–2
91–92 You ... you.] *one line in* F1–2
94.1 *Exeunt*] F2; *Exit* F1
97 Caliste.] *Caliste with a purse.* F1–2
100 *Lisander*] F2; *Lasander* F1
119 keep;] ~ , F1–2
125 fault,——] ~ , ∧ F1–2

143 proof∧ they are,] ~ , ~ ~ ∧ F1–2
155 men;] ~ . F1–2
156 there. They] ~ , they F1–2
168 were——] ~ . F1–2
191–192 securely, ... confidence:] ~ : ... ~ , F1–2
204 him?] ~ . F1–2
209 businesse,] F2; ~ ∧ F1
220 picture:] ~ ; F1–2
221 Saint?] ~ , F1–2
222.1 with a purse.] F1–2 (transferred from line 97)
227–231 'Tis ... mourn'd?] F1–2 line: 'Tis ... wicked? | To ... mans: | 'Tis ... man. | Yes. | My ... mourn'd?
229 Lisander——] ~ ∧ F1–2
230 man?] F2; ~ . F1
238–239 Come ... men.] one line in F1–2
241 to morrow——Provide] ~ ∧ provide F1–2

II.i

II.i] Actus Secundus. Scæna prima. F1–2
3–4 I ... yours.] one line in F1–2
10–11 deliver'd, ... to] F1–2 line: deliver'd | You ... to
12–13 'Tis ... Clarinda.] one line in F1–2
13–14 I ... work.] one line in F1–2
15–16 O ... cruellest!] one line in F1–2
16–17 So ... you.] one line in F1–2
27 and (as] (and ∧ as F1–2
38 lover;] ~ , F2; ~ . F1
57–58 Caliste's ... Ladie.] one line in F1–2
64 May] May F1–2
65–66 Of ... matter?] one line in F1–2
69–70 I ... room.] one line in F1–2
80 either, sir,] F2; ~ ∧ ~ ∧ F1
94 loud.——] ~ . ∧ F1–2
98–99 No ... pleasure.] one line in F1–2
105–6 I ... goe?] one line in F1–2
116 are] F2; ars F1
126 into?——] ~ ? ∧ F1–2
132–133 No, ... taken.] one line in F1–2
133 now;——] ~ ; ∧ F1–2
134 hers?——] ~ ? ∧ F1–2
139 sir,——] ~ , ∧ F1–2

II.ii

8–9 Can ... Salamander] one line in F1–2
15–16 I ... book.] one line in F1–2
16–17 Very ... apprehend.] one line in F1–2
17 ride?] ~ , F1–2
19 Proverbe] F2; Provetbe F1
19–20 But ... lippe.] one line in F1–2
21 foot,——] ~ , ∧ F1–2
26–27 I am ... dore] one line in F1–2
35 entreaty:——] ~ , ∧ F1–2
35 friend:] ~ ∧ F1–2
35 Enter ... Fortune-teller.] Enter ... Fortune-teller, with a Purse, and two Letters in it. F1–2 (on line below 38a)
36 directed:——] ~ , ∧ F1–2
38–39 'Tis ... come.] one line in F1–2
40 hand:] ~ , F1–2
41–42 Yes ... game,] one line in F1–2
45 confess'd;——] ~ ; ∧ F1–2
56 two hundred] 200. F1–2
57 a Purse] with a Purse F1–2 (transferred from line 35)
58 and two Letters in it.] F1–2 (transferred from line 35)
58–59 How ... Lady?] one line in F1–2

60–61 And ... *Lancelot*.] *one line in* F1–2

60 Fortune-teller] F2; Fortuneteller F1

66 disguis'd;] ~ , F1–2

70–71 Bountiful ... imployment.] *one line in* F1–2

71 pay,] ~ ∧ F1–2

II.iii

0.1 Clarange, Lisander,] *Lisander, Clarange*, F1–2

3–4 And ... equall.] *one line in* F1–2

3 And ... here.] ~ ~ , F1–2

4–5 If ... exchange.] *one line in* F1–2

6 off:] ~ , F1–2

7–8 I ... not. *one line in* F1–2

8–9 You ... hether.] *one line in* F1–2

15 on; love,] ~ ∧ ~ ; F1–2

16 *Lidian*:] ~ , F1–2

16 *Fight*.] *Fight and* | *fight with*. F1 (u)(*in right margin of lines* 13, 14);

omit F1(c), F2

52 together,] F2; ~ ∧ F1 (*justification*)

59 *Mars's*] F1 (c), F2; Mars's F1 (u)

66 white-hand innocence] white hand-innocence F1–2

72 Honour, you] F2; ~ . You F1

73 kill,] F2, ~ ∧ F1

77 hope.] ~ , F1–2

78 justice;——] ~ ; ∧ F1–2

80 *Cupid*] F2; Cupid F1

II.iv

1–2 I ... milder.] *one line in* F1–2

6 meeting:] ~ , F1–2

16–17 Of ... where.] *one line in* F1–2

23 company: ~ , F1–2

24 good:——] ~ , ∧ F1–2

34 thinke:] ~ , F1–2

35 Nay,] ~ ∧ F1–2

42 *Enter ... following*.] *on line below line* 43b *in* F1–2

42 *following*.] *following with a Letter*. F1–2

43 speake!] ~ ? F1–2

44–45 My ... seconds.] *one line in* F1–2

45–46 Here ... alive.] *one line in* F1–2

46–47 I ... *Clarange*:] *one line in* F1–2

70 Manent] F2; *Manet* F1

70 *staying* Caliste] *stayes Cal*. F1 (*at line* 67b); *omit* F2

70–71 Now ... Madam.] *one line in* F1–2

71 her:——] ~ ∧ F1–2

89 Madam);] ~) ∧ F1; ~), F2

95 Pilgrim,] F2; ~ ; F1

100 ye,] ~ : F1–2

101 backe;] ~ , F1–2

103–104 Stay ... wench? *one line in* F1–2

114 *a Letter*.] *with a Letter*. F1–2 (*transferred from line* 42)

III.i

III.i] *Actus Tertius. Scæna prima*. F1–2

14–15 We ... key,] *one line in* F1–2

19–20 To ... much] *one line in* F1–2

III.ii

14 (*at the doore*)] ∧ ~ ~ ~ ∧ F1; *as marginal stage direction* F2

16 sirah,] F2; ~ ∧ F1
18 waking;] ~ , F1–2

III.iii

0.1 Lisander,] *Lisander with a Pistole,* F1–2
1 Come ... Curtaine,] F1–2 *line:* neare, | I'le
2 wish;——] ~ ; ∧ F1–2
4 Caliste ... *Curtaine.*] *in right margin of line* 1 *in* F1–2
10–11 She ... paralell.] *one line in* F1–2
11–12 Your ... Lady)] *one line in* F1–2
18 me;] ~ , F1–2
19–20 (You ... sweetnesse);] ∧ ~ ... ~ ∧ ; F1; ∧ ~ ... ~ ∧ , F2
19 to,] F2; ~ . F1
30 expect,] ~ ∧ F1–2
38–39 (A ... too)∧] ∧ ~ ... ~ ∧ ; F1–2
49 againe?] ~ . F1–2
54 here;——] ~ ; ∧ F1–2
58 chaines?——] ~ ? ∧ F1–2
61–62 Ye ... you.] *one line in* F1–2
67–68 I have ... mortality:] *one line in* F1–2
68 mortality:] ~ , F2; ~ ∧ F1
84 too?] ~ , F1–2
103 thing;] ~ , F1–2
107 both,] F2; ~ ∧ F1
110 *a Pistole.*] *with a Pistole.* F1–2 (*transferred from line* 0.1)

111–112 I ... noise?] *one line in* F1–2
117 husband!——] ~ , ∧ F1–2
118–119 O ... head.] *one line in* F1–2
119–121 Alas ... ye?] F1–2 *line:* bed | You
121–122 Not ... fright——] *one line in* F1–2
126 No.——] ~ . ∧ F1–2
135–136 But ... bed.] *one line in* F1–2
137 love,] F2; ~ ∧ F1
147–148 Farewell ... farewell.] *one line in* F1–2
148 men,] F2; ~ ∧ F1
156–157 O ... againe.] *one line in* F1–2
160.1 *Enter* Cleander.] *in right margin of line* 160a *in* F1–2
161 happily;——] ~ ; ∧ F1–2
169–170 Theeves ... Rogues.] *one line in* F1–2
170–171 Indeed ... about.] *one line in* F1–2
174–175 I ... heart.] *one line in* F1–2
178 thus, ... him;] ~ ; ... ~ , F1–2
182 kill-cow] F2; kill cow F1
183 flowne:——] ~ : ∧ F1–2
185 Rogue:——] ~ , ∧ F1–2
190 plaid;——] ~ : ∧ F1; ~ ? ∧ F2

III.iv

0.1 Clarange,] F2; *Claran.* F1
1–2 Yes ... preach.] *one line in* F1–2
25 confesse,] ~ ∧ F1–2
27 raptures,] ~ ; F1–2
33.1 *A Song by the*] roman *in* F1–2
36 howers,] ~ . F1; ~ ; F2

39 *love,̄...clime*∧] ~ ∧ ... ~ , F1–2
50 consider;——] ~ ; ∧ F1–2
54 beast?] F2; ~ ∧ F1
55 resolv'd.——] ~ . ∧ F1–2
60–61 That ... charity.] *one line in* F1–2

III.v

16 Host;——] ~ ; ∧ F1–2
22 coffine:] ~ , F1–2
28 *Enter ... wine.] after* too. *line* 26 in
F1–2
29 it;——] ~ ; ∧ F1–2
38–39 I ... out.] *one line in* F1–2
39–40 'Tis ... stirring.] *one line in*
F1–2
41 doores ∧] F2; ~ , F1
42 morning, sure ∧] ~ ∧ ~ , F1–2

47 Fidle——] F2; ~ . F1
47.1 *A Song.] roman in* F1–2
60 *Patridge*] Partridge F2
66–67 He ... pipe.] *one line in* F1–2
74–75 Then ... body.] *one line in* F1–2
75–76 What ... off.] *one line in* F1–2
79 not.] F2; ~ ? F1
84 us'd.] F2; ~ ? F1
103 credit;] ~ , F1–2

III.vi

8 not:——] ~ : ∧ F1–2
8 (*aside*)] *in right margin of line in*
F1–2
9–10 Looke ... againe?] *one line in*
F1–2
13 deserve't:] ~ , F2; ~ . F1
22–23 And ... shames?] *one line in*
F1–2
40–41 I ... Lady] *one line in* F1–2
47 by:] ~ , F1–2
54 to't:] ~ . F2; ~ ∧ F1
59 life,] F2; ~ ∧ F1
60 petticoat.] ~ ? F1–2
63 Helme,——] ~ , ∧ F1–2
73 to,——] ~ , ∧ F1–2

77 it,] ~ ; F1–2
90 bars;] ~ , F1–2
94–95 But ... honest.] *one line in* F1–2
99 innocent, as ... are,] ~ (~ ... ~)
F1–2
100 (I ... conscience)] ∧ ~ ... ~ ,
F1–2
102 willing] F2; wil'ing F1
109 life,] F2; ~ . F1
109 honour.——Devill,] ~ . ∧ ~ ∧
F2; ~ , ∧ devill ∧ F1
123 (The ... woman)] ∧ ~ ... ~ ∧
F1–2
124 revenge:] ~ , F1–2
132 torrent;] ~ , F1–2

IV.i

IV.i] *Actus Quartus. Scæna prima.* F1–2
1–2 Your ... feare.] *one line in* F1–2
2–3 You'l ... made] *one line in* F1–2
6 circumstance:] ~ , F1–2
7–8 Upon ... there.] *one line in* F1–2

18–20 Upon ... tilting.] F1–2 *line:*
Cloridon | 'Fore
40 Exceeding] F2; Exceeing F1
42–43 I ... way.] *one line in* F1–2

IV.ii

14 end;] ~ , F1–2
15 (I ... how)] ∧ ~ ... ~ ∧ F1–2
16 over.——] ~ . ∧ F1–2
22–23 It ... it.] *one line in* F1–2

23–24 Can ... dye?] *one line in* F1–2
34 helpe.——] ~ . ∧ F1–2
35–36 Rescue? ... danger.] *one line in*
F1–2

38–39 A ... defence.] *one line in* F1–2
43 minde:——] ~ : ‸ F1–2
61 justly:——] ~ : ‸ F1–2
63–64 I ... pardon.] *one line in* F1–2

66 Madam:——] ~ : ‸ F1–2
68–69 Till ... silent.] *one line in* F1–2
69–70 We ... *Lisander.*] *one line in* F1–2

IV.iii

3 apparent;] ~ , F1–2
11 is,] ~ ‸ F1–2
16 come;——] ~ ; ‸ F1–2
20–21 It ... never] *one line in* F1–2
23–24 be | Taken is] be taken | Is F1–2
38 device,] ~ ‸ F1–2
55–56 Here's ... *Malfort.*] *one line in* F1–2]
55 errant,——] ~ . ‸ F1–2
70–71 I ... wise.] *one line in* F1–2
71 *Clarinda.*] F2 (*Clar.*); *Car.* F1
88–89 *Clarinda,* ... this] F1–2 *line:* Leon! | There
92 *Cleander (within).*] *Clean. speaks within.* F1–2
93 His ... answer] F1–2 *line:* life | Shall
97–98 And ... Handy-work?] F1–2 *line:* And ... better: | Doe ... your | Handy-work?

104 I,] I ‸ F1–2
106 horrid murther. |] horrid | Murther F1–2
110–111 By ... much.] *one line in* F1–2
112–113 In ... Host! F1–2 *line:* of | An
117–118 'Tis ... hand.] *one line in* F1–2
118–119 Sans ... murtherer.] *one line in* F1–2
124–125 My ... murtherer?] *one line in* F1–2
127 I ... mouth.] F1–2 *line:* dumbe; | You
133–135 Stand ... him.] F1–2 *line:* death, | And ... murtherer? | That
148–149 I ... guilty?] *one line in* F1–2
153–154 Never ... end.] *one line in* F1–2
162–163 Thou ... *Clarinda.*] *one line in* F1–2
163–164 Helpe ... her.] *one line in* F1–2
173–174 Sir ... father.] *one line in* F1–2

IV.iv

4 ones?] ~ . F1–2
9–10 Then ... expence.] *one line in* F1–2
31 breach] F2; breac F1
34 to;] ~ , F1–2
45 commands;] ~ , F1–2
47–48 Into ... | Noble *Lisander.*] *one line in* F1–2
47 walke.——] ~ . ‸ F1–2
53 Hermite] *Hermite* F1–2
58 (Peace ... sir),] ‸ ~ ... ~ ‸ F1–2
62–63 I ... world:] *one line in* F1–2
66–67 Above ... here?] *one line in* F1–2

73 though] F2; thogh F1 (*justification*)
76 Down,] F2, ~ ‸ F1
109–110 And ... persevere.] *one line in* F1–2
113–114 Keep ... instructed] *one line in* F1–2
123–124 And ... father.] *one line in* F1–2
130–131 I ... better.] *one line in* F1–2
131 –132 I ... duly——] *one line in* F1–2
140–141 O ... not] *one line in* F1–2
143 mine;] ~ , F1–2
156–157 I ... inquisitive.] *one line in* F1–2

167 Speare:——] ~ : ∧ F1; ~ ; ∧ F2
171 along,] ~ ∧ F1–2
172 *Clarange?*] ~ ! F1–2
172–173 *Cloridon?* ... apprehend] *one line in* F1–2
185 dead,] F2; ~ ∧ F1
198 yet: , F1–2
226–227 I ... transported.] *one line in*

F1–2
227–228 Give ... it.] *one line in* F1–2
232 longer:] ~ , F2; ~ ∧ F1
239–240 *Exeunt* ... Alcidon.] *Ex. Lisander, Alcidon, & Lancelot.* F1–2
240–241 Remember ... dangers,] *one line in* F1–2
246.1 *Exit.*] *Exeunt.* F1–2

V.i

V.i] *Actus Quintus. Scæna Prima.* F1–2
7 They ... daughter] F1–2 *line:* oathes; | How
7 oaths;——] ~ : ∧ F1–2
10(2) Lemure] F2; *Lemur* F1
21–22 How ... affected?] *one line in* F1–2
40–41 What ... feare.] *one line in* F1–2
41–42 They ... way.] *one line in* F1–2
46–47 Your ... justice,] *one line in* F1–2
54–55 To ... you,] *one line in* F1–2
65 with] F2; wirh F1

73–74 O ... you] *one line in* F1–2
90–92 But ... deliverance?] F1–2 *line:* some | Other
102 her;] ~ , F1–2
105 satisfaction;] ~ , F1–2
106 repentance;] ~ , F1–2
110 doe;] ~ , F1–2
112 reputation,] ~ ∧ F1–2
115–116 Let's ... troubled.] *one line in* F1–2
117 rises,] F2; ~ ∧ F1
123 expected:] ~ , F1–2

V.ii

2–3 As ... dead.] *one line in* F1–2
8 you,] ~ ∧ F1–2
9–10 give∧ ... wish,] ~ , ... ~ ∧ F1–2
15–16 And ... at] *one line in* F1–2
25 testimonie.——] ~ . ∧ F1–2
26 Father——] ~ , F1–2
26 *Enter* ... *Frier.*] *on line below line* 27 *in* F1–2
26 *Letter*)] *Letter writ out*) F1–2
30 *Reads.*] *at line* 36 *in* F1–2
31–32 Give ... plotted] *one line in* F1–2

32 plotted] F2; ploted F1 (*justification*)
35 game?——] ~ ? ∧ F1–2
36–39 *Lady ... servant*] *in roman in* F1–2
36 *promise;*] ~ , F1–2
39–40 *And ... Clarange.*] *one line in* F1–2
44 teare,] ~ ∧ F1–2
45–46 It ... gentleman.] *one line in* F1–2
51–52 With ... off.] *one line in* F1–2
59 determine;] ~ ∧ F1–2
66–67 What ... you?] *one line in* F1–2

V.iii

0.1–0.2 Malfort ... *forth.*] *Malfort, a bar set forth, Officers.* F1–2

14 hate∧ ... innocence,] ~ , ... ~ ∧ F1–2

28–29 *You ... enemies] one line in*
    F1–2
46 apparentₐ] ~ , F1–2
52–53 O ... for——] *one line in* F1–2
53–54 Be ... King.] *one line in* F1–2
72 Justice.——] ~ . ₐ F1–2
74–78 Royall ... suppositions?] F1–2
    line: Royall ... death, | We ...
    suppositions. | Suppositions? ...
    condemn'd | On suppositions?
88 Court.——] ~ . ₐ F1–2
89–90 By ... face.] *one line in* F1–2
93–94 Impudent ... sworne?] *one line
    in* F1–2
109 ('Tis ... Ladies)] ₐ ~ ... ~ ₐ
    F1–2
117–118 Then ... Bawd?] *one line in*
    F1–2
125 aside.——] ~ . ₐ F1–2
125 this,] ~ ₐ F1–2
138–139 (that ... humblenesse),] ₐ ~
    ... ~ ₐ , F1–2
152 maintaine——] ~ ₐ F1–2
152–153 And ... purenesse.] *one line in*
    F1–2

165–166 How ... forth.] *one line in*
    F1–2
165 hands?——] ~ ? ₐ F1–2
169–170 Carry ... him.] *one line in* F1–2
175 *Enter ... Leon.] Enter Leon,*
    Servants, and Guard. F1–2 (*on line*
    below faint *in line* 169a)
198–199 This ... off.] *one line in* F1–2
214–215 My ... it.] *one line in* F1–2
215–216 At ... petition.] *one line in*
    F1–2
217 mercie] F2; meocie F1
219 both,] F2; ~ ; F1
236–237 On ... seriously.] *one line in*
    F1–2
237 *Enter* Lidian.] *in right margin of line*
    236a *in* F1; *on line below* 236a *in* F2
240–241 He ... *Clarange*] *one line in*
    F1–2
241 subject,——] ~ , ₐ F1–2
241 I accuse] Iaccuse F2
244 pennance——] ~ . F1–2
244 Enter ... Frier.] *in right margin of*
    line 240b *in* F1; *on line below* 240b *in*
    F2
257 Friers] *Friers* F1–2

Epilogue

8 *rest.] rest* | FINIS. F1–2

HISTORICAL COLLATION

[NOTE: This collation against the present text includes the two seventeenth-century Folios (F1, 1647; F2, 1679), and the editions of Langbaine (L, 1711), Theobald, Seward and Sympson (S, 1750), Colman (C, 1778), Weber (W, 1811) and Dyce (D, 1843). The Song at III.iv.34–45 appears in BL MS Eg. 2013.f.47b; the Song at III.v.48–65 appears in BL Addl. MSS 11608. f. 20[43], 29481.f.25b, 29396. f.39b [46]; for collations, see Textual Notes *in locis*.]

Title Lovers'] Lovers F1–S

I.i

35 *Caliste*] *Calista* F2–D
42 *Clarinda's*] *Clarinda's* F1
49 Studying] Study F2
80 For] For the C, W; Fory F1
102 rogue's] rogues F1
115 tickle ... quick] *omit* F2
135 you] yon F1
148 as] *omit* F1
156 parle] parly L, S, C

178 excellencies] excellences C, W
199 honour sake] honours sake F2; honour-sake D
204 new] now S
216, 217 Oke ... Vine] Oak's ... Vine's S
219 wantonly] wanton L
223 freedomes] freedom W

I.ii

33 contend] contended F1–L
75 expectation] Expectation's S
95 blunt] blunted F1–L
153 *Caliste*.] *omit* F1–D
189 mettle] metal F2, W, D

227 *Servant.* 'Twas] 'Twas F1–W
241 You] *Cle.* You F1–S
241 *Cleander.* Provide] provide F1–S
242(1) *Lisander——*] *Dor. Lisander* F1–S; *Cle.* Lisander C–D

II.i

25 love] love is F2; Love's S–D
34 one] our L

95 Leave you] leave you | Leave you F1 +

II.ii

49 a] *omit* W

548

II.iii

14/16 *Fight within.* | *Fight.*] *Fight and* |
    fight with. F1(u); *omit* F1(c), F2, L;
    They fight. S–D (*at line* 16)
33 he's] as C
44 Exampled] Example F1(u)
50, 69 *Clarange.*] *Clar.* F2; *Clarin.* F1
52 twin'd] twinn'd S
53 a] to F1–L
53 friendship, ... world ∧ a wonder,]
    friendship ∧ ... world, to wonder,

F1–L; friendship ∧ ... world, a
    wonder, S; friendship, ... world
    two wonders, C, W
65 it's blowen] it blows F1–S
66 white-hand innocence] white hand-
    innocence F1–2
72 a peeces] i' pieces F2
77 ye] he F1
85 unwilling] and willing F1 +

II.iv

17 too] so too F1–S, W
21 fell'st] feld'st F1
23 tooke] took'st S–D

74 you.] your ∧ F2
75 is] he's S, C, W
110 this] his L

III.ii

8 simper] glimmer C
14 Whose] Who's F2

14 A] *omit* F1–L
26 fairies] faires F1

III.iii

6, 161 'has] h'has C; he has W; h'as D
6 the] his F1, L, S
51 her ... her] them ... their S, C
103 no thing] nothing F2–D

139 at] in at F2, C, W
148 men] man F1 +
167 he has] 'has S
182 Kill-cow] kill-Crow F2

III.iv

4 he hath] 'hath S; h'hath C
34–45 *For collation against MS, see*
    Textual Note.

39 *clime*] *doth climb* F2
52 hopes] hope F2

III.v

21 *Cleander.*] *Dor.* F2
47 *Cleander.*] *omit* F1–2
47 *Harke, a Song.*] *omit* F1
47 Song.] Song, now as I live it is his
    voice. L, S

48–65 *For collation against MSS, see*
    Textual Note.
51 *the*] *a* F1 +
52 *beds ... downe*] *bed ... down's* F2
52 *wanton*] *want on* F1

64 *Welcome Welcome*] *Welcome* F1, L,
S
66 *Cleander.* Now ... voice.] *Clean.*

Harke, a Song, now ... voice. F1;
omit L, S (*at line* 47)
91 dranke] drunk D

III.vi

2 look'd] lock'd W
32 farther] further C, W
48 grudge] grudg'd F1 +

68 yon'd] yon F2, L–W; yond D
90 understands] understand F2, C

IV.i

4–5 vertue; ... secure,] ~ , ... ~ ;
F1 +
7 brothers] fathers F1, L, S

8 *Beronte.*] *omit* S
17 kinsmen] Kinsman F2

IV.ii

9 here] hear L
60 spight] in spight L

72 However] How ever F1

IV.iii

8 meate] meats F1 +
10 caudles] candles F1–C

54 which] what L
108 Aye] Ah C, W

IV.iv

12 unto] to F1, L
92 in-imitable] in immitable F1; inimitable L +
118 resolution] resolution's S

119 world] world's S
137 you] yon F1
142 Led] Lead F1
186 miseries] misery's F1, L

V.i

5 intention] invention F1–L
6 looks] look F2

49 forfeit] forfeited F1 +
66 whose] whole L

V.ii

32 What I] What L

47 that] that's S

V.iii

118 course] coarse S +
120 your] you F2

135 then] and F1, L
166 spake] speak L

183 woman] Woman's S
221 ready] ready, Sir S
221 to lay] to be laid D

241 I accuse] Jaccuse F2
251 to] in C

THE FAIR MAID OF THE INN

edited by

FREDSON BOWERS

TEXTUAL INTRODUCTION

Although Sir Henry Herbert's licence of 22 January 1625/6 attributes *The Fair Maid of the Inn* (Greg, *Bibliography*, no. 668) to Fletcher, Cyrus Hoy finds traces of that author, who had died in August 1625, only in a few passages of IV.i. He suggests that *The Fair Maid* was 'the last play on which Fletcher worked; that his share in it was never brought to completion; that it was finished by the trio of Webster, Massinger and Ford. Massinger may have been present from the beginning, as perhaps was Webster; Ford, to judge from the evidence of IV.i, where he is overwriting Fletcher, was not.'[1] Professor Hoy makes the following assignments:

FLETCHER AND FORD: IV.i
FORD: III
MASSINGER: I, V.iii.1–253
WEBSTER: II, IV.ii, V.i–ii.253.1 on.

His hypothesis is consistent with internal evidence of the play's date. As Professor Bentley points out, Forobosco's threat that he will send the Clown to Amboina for pepper leads the latter to reply 'To *Amboyna*? so I might be pepperd' (IV.ii.264), an allusion to the Dutch massacre of English colonists there, news of which reached England in 'May 1624 and was a common subject of allusion in the summer and autumn of 1624 and on into 1625'.[2] In addition, Professor Bentley finds allusions in *The Fair Maid* 'to the same individuals and events referred to in Jonson's *Staple of News* . . ., which was also performed by the King's company in February 1625/6'.[3]

Omitted from the 1646 Stationers' Register entry of Beaumont and Fletcher copies to Robinson and Moseley, *The Fair Maid* was a late addition to the two-play Section 7 of the 1647 Beaumont and Fletcher Folio, a part of the book apparently manufactured in the shop of Susan Islip.[4] Typesetting began after the concluding two-leaf gathering of *Valentinian* was imposed, if not after it was printed, for 'The', the catchword on the last page of *Valentinian*, links as well with 'The Prologue', which begins Section 8, as it does with the head-title on

555

7E1, 'The Faire Maide ...' Type was set by formes in the following sequence:

Compositor	B B	B B	B A	B A?	A(C?)	B	?	A B	B A
Forme	E2:3v	E1v:4	E3:2v	E1:4v	F3:	2va	2vb	F3v:2	F1v:4

Compositor	B A	? A	B	B? A	? B?	B	A	A?	? ?
Forme	F1:4v	G3:2v	G2a	2b:3v	G4:1va	1vb¹	1vb²	G1a	1b:4v

In the line numbers of this edition, these attributions are

Compositor *A*: I.i.310–I.iii.24 (hurt.), IV.i.85–IV.ii.171 (spectacle), IV.ii.395.1–405,
    V.i.94–V.iii.14, V.iii.127–243
Compositor *A?*: II.ii.113–II.iv.60, IV.ii.171–233 (you)
Compositor *A (C?)*: III.ii.219b–IV.i.84
Compositor *B*: I.i.1–309, I.iii.24–II.ii.112, II.iv.61–III.ii.161a, IV.ii.354–V.i.36
Compositor *B?*: IV.ii.296–354, V.i.37–93
Compositor *?*: III.ii.162b–219a, IV.ii.233 (fortye)–295, V.iii.15–126, V.iii.244–end
    of play and Prologue

Despite the numerous uncertainties, this analysis permits a few abnormalities of the text to be ascribed to the compositors rather than to their copy. Compositor *A*, for example, tended to indent speech-prefixes unevenly; the *Exeunt* at I.ii.42.1 and the entrance at I.iii.0.1 are printed in the same line because he was short of space on E2v, E3 having been previously set. Similar crowding may be observed on *B*'s F2, composed after F2v, and F1v, where the stage-directions at III.i.132.1–2 and 144.1–3 are set in unusually small type. Since the same typecase was used by both workmen, there could have been no simultaneous composition, and 'rather than make up two full skeletons, the printers found it convenient to employ two chases and three sets of box rules in a manner approximating two-skeleton printing'.[5] The work evidently proceeded slowly, but it was not very correct; both compositors either misread words or otherwise failed to reproduce their copy (assuming it to have been accurate) and neither was expert at lining verse, which perhaps was irregularly lined in the manuscript. Little can be said of the proof-reading, for collation of twenty copies turned up only four variants: in some copies (1) the head for IV.i is *Scœna* rather than *Scæna*, (2) at IV.ii.203 'againe' is divided between two lines as 'a-|gine' rather than 'a-|gaine', (3) at V.iii.267 the 'le' of 'fooles' are turned clockwise 90 degrees so that the 'l' appears above the 'e', and (4) at V.iii.289 a space prints between 'For' and 'blessings'.[6]

The printer's copy seems to have been authorial papers prepared for use as a prompt-book. In III.i.115 '*Stooles out*' begins the line, an anticipation of their use in line 143; the double appearance of Cæsario at the start and the end of the entrance-direction at III.i.144.1 no doubt reproduces a book-keeper's duplication; and at IV.ii.36.1 the direction '*Enter* Forobosco *as in his study.* (A paper)' refers to the challenge which Forobosco shows the Host. As in *Valentinian*, many of the stage-directions are preceded by a dash connecting them with the text.

NOTES

1 'The shares of Fletcher and his collaborators in the Beaumont and Fletcher canon (v)', *Studies in Bibliography*, XIII (1960), 102.
2 Gerald Eades Bentley, *The Jacobean and Caroline Stage* (Oxford, 1956), III, 338–9. The allusion was first recognized by F. L. Lucas, 'Did Dr Forman commit suicide?' *TLS*, 7 April 1927, p. 250. In his edition of the play, Lucas had also noticed that the Ball mentioned at V.ii.79 was a tailor who had predicted that James I would be crowned in the Pope's Chair. Lucas believes Ball would not have qualified as a false prophet until after King James' death on 27 March 1625 (*The Complete Works of John Webster* (London, 1927), IV, 147).
3 Bentley, *Jacobean and Caroline Stage*, III, 339.
4 See the Textual Introduction to *Valentinian* in this series, vol. III, pp. 263–75. Originally examined by R. C. Bald, *Bibliographical Studies in the Beaumont and Fletcher Folio of 1647* (Oxford, 1938), esp. p. 36, work on this part of the Folio was more thoroughly investigated by James P. Hammersmith, 'The printers and the Beaumont and Fletcher Folio of 1647', *Papers of the Bibliographical Society of America*, LXIX (1975), 206–25. His analysis of *The Fair Maid* is found in University Microfilms OP 71, 767.
5 James P. Hammersmith, 'The proof-reading of the Beaumont and Fletcher Folio of 1647; Sections 7 and 8A–C', *Papers of the Bibliographical Society of America*, LXXXIII (1989), 188.
6 See Hammersmith, 'Proof-Reading', pp. 196–7 for further details.

[PERSONS REPRESENTED IN THE PLAY.

Duke *of* Florence.
Cæsario, *a young Gentleman of a fiery nature, Son to Alberto.*
Alberto, *Father to* Cæsario, *Admiral of* Florence.
Baptista, *A brave Sea-Commander, antient friend to* Alberto, *and Father to* Mentivole *and* Bianca.
Mentivole, *Son to* Baptista, *Lover of* Clarissa.
Prospero, *a noble friend to* Baptista.
Two Magistrates *of* Florence.
Host, *the supposed Father of* Bianca.
Forobosco, *a cheating Mountebank.*
Clown, *the Mountebanks man, and setter.*
Three Gentlemen.
Secretary *to the Duke.*
Dancer,
Taylor,
Muleti, } *Six fools and knaves, who pretend love*
Pedant, } *to* Biancà, *the Fair Maid of the Inn.*
Coxcombe,
Clerk,
Physitian.
Chirurgion.
Sailors.

WOMEN.

Mariana, *Wife to* Alberto, *a virtuous Lady.*
Clarissa, Mariana's *Daughter, in love with* Mentivole.
Juliana, *Neece to the Duke of* Genoa, Baptista's *second wife.*
Bianca, *the Fair Maid of the Inn, beloved of* Cæsario, *and Daughter to* Baptista *and* Juliana.
Hostesse, *the supposed Mother of* Bianca.

The Scene, Florence.]

PERSONS ... PLAY.] *adapted from* F2; *omit* F1

558

The Prologue.

Playes have their fates, not as in their true sence
They're understood, but as the influence
Of idle custome madly workes upon
The drosse of many-tongu'd opinion.
A worthy story, howsoever writ
For language, modest mirth, conceite or witt,
Meetes often times with the sweet commendation
Of hang't, tis scurvy, when for approbation
A Jigg shall be clapt at, and every rime
Prais'd and applauded by a clamorous chime.   10
Let Ignorance and laughter dwell together,
They are beneath the Muses pitty. Hether
Come nobler Judgements, and to those the straine
Of our invention is not bent in vaine.
The faire Maide of the Inne to you commends
Her hopes and welcomes, and withall intends
In th'Entertaines to which she doth invite ye,
All things to please, and some things to delight yee.

THE FAIRE MAIDE OF THE INNE

Cæsario.   Interpret not *Clarissa*, my true zeale
  In giving you councell, to transcend the bounds
  That should confine a brother; tis your honour,
  And peace of mind (which honour lost will leave you)
  I labour to preserve, and though you yet are
  Pure and untainted, and resolve to be so:
  Having a Fathers eye, and Mothers care
  In all your wayes to keep you faire, and upright.
  In which respects my best advices must
  Appeare superfluous; yet since love deere sister   10
  Will sometimes tender things unnecessary,
  Misconster not my purpose.
Clarissa.   Sir, I dare not:
  But still receive it as a large addition,
  To the much that I already stand ingagd for,
  Yet pardon me, though I professe upon
  A true examination of my selfe
  Even to my private thoughts, I cannot finde
  (Having such strong supporters to uphold me)
  On what slight ground the least doubt can be raisd
  To render me suspected I can fall,   20
  Or from my fame or vertue.
Cæsario.   Far be it from me,
  To nourish such a thought; and yet excuse me,
  As you would doe a lapidary, whose whole fortunes
  Depend upon the safety of one Jewell,
  If he think no case pretious enough
  To keep it in full lustre nor no locks,
  Though lending strength to Iron doores sufficient

To gard it, and secure him; you to me are
A Gemme of more esteeme, and prizd higher
Then Usurers doe their muck, or great men title.   30
And any flaw (which heaven avert) in you,
(Whose reputation like a Diamond
Cut newly from the rock, women with envie,
And men with covetous desires look up at)
By prying eyes discovered, in a moment
Would render what the braveries of *Florence*
For want of counterpoize, forbeare to cheapen,
Of little or no value.

Clarissa.   I see brother
The mark you shoot at, and much thank your love;
But for my Virgin Jewell which is brought   40
In comparison with your Diamond, rest assurd
It shall not fall in such a workmans hands
Whose Ignorance or Malice shall have power
To cast one cloud upon it, but still keep
Her native splendor.

Cæsario.   Tis well, I commend you;
And study your advancement with that care
As I would doe a Sisters, whom I love
With more then common ardor.

Clarissa.   That from me,
I hope's returnd to you.

Cæsario.   I doe confesse it,
Yet let me tell you (but still with that love,   50
I wish to increase between us) that you are
Observd against the gravity long maintaind
In *Italy* (where to see a mayd unmaskd
Is held a blemish) to be over frequent
In giving or receiving visits.

Clarissa.   How?

Cæsario.   Whereas the custome is here to wooe by picture,
And never see the substance: you are faire,
And beauty drawes temptations on; You know it,

48 ardor] Seward; order F1–2

I would not live to see a willing grant
From you to one unworthy of your birth,   60
Feature or fortune; yet there have been Ladies
Of ranck, proportion, and of meanes beyond you,
That have prov'd this no miracle.
Clarissa.   One unworthy?
    Why pray you gentle brother, who are they
    That I vouchsafe these bounties to? I hope
    In your strict Criticisme of me, and my manners,
    That you will not deny they are your equalls.
Cæsario.   Angry?
Clarissa.   I have reason, but in cold bloud tell me,
    Had we not one Father?
Cæsario.   Yes, and Mother to.
Clarissa.   And he a Souldier.
Cæsario.   True.
Clarissa.   If I then borrow   70
    A little of the boldnesse of his temper,
    Imparting it to such as may deserve it;
    (How ere indulgent to your selves, you brothers
    Allow no part of freedome to your sisters)
    I hope 'twill not passe for a crime in me,
    To grant accesse and speech to noble suitors;
    And you escape for innocent, that descend
    To a thing so far beneath you. Are you touchd?
    Why did you think that you had *Giges* ring,
    Or the herbe that gives invisibility?   80
    Or that *Bianchas* name had ne'r bin mentiond;
    The faire mayd of the grand Osteria brother.
Cæsario.   No more.
Clarissa.   A little brother. Your night walkes,
    And offerd presents, which coy she contemnd;
    Your combats in disguises with your rivalls,
    Brave Muletiers, Scullions perfum'd with grease,
    And such as cry meat for Cats must be remembred;
    And all this pother for a common trull,

59 see] F2; say F1

A tempting signe, and curiously set forth,
To draw in riotous guests, a thing exposd   90
To every Ruffians rude assault; and subject
For a poore salary, to a rich mans lust,
Though made up of diseases.

Cæsario.   Will you end yet?

Clarissa.   And this a Mistris for *Albertus* sonne,
One that I should call sister?

Cæsario.   Part not with
Your modesty in this violent heate; the truth is,
(For you shall be my Confessor) I love her,
But vertuously; report that gives her out
Only for faire, and adds not she is chast,
Detracts much from her: for indeed she is,   100
Though of a low condition; composd
Of all those graces, dames of highest birth,
Though rich in natures bounties, should be proud of;
But leave her, and to you my neerest care,
My dearest best *Clarissa.* Doe not think
(For then you wrong me) I wish you should live
A barren Virgin life; I rather ayme at
A noble husband, that may make you mother
Of many children, one that when I know him
Worth your embraces, I may serve, and sue to: 110
And therefore scorne not to acquaint me with
That man, that happy man; you please to favour.

Clarissa.   I ever purposd it, for I will like
With your allowance.

Cæsario.   As a pawne of this;
Receive this ring, but ere you part with it
On any tearmes, be certaine of your choice;
And make it knowne to me.

Clarissa.   You have my hand for't.

Cæsario.   Which were it not my sisters, I should kisse
With too much heate.

Enter Servants with lights, Alberto, Baptista, Mariana, Mentivole.

*110 to] *stet* F1

564

Clarissa.   My Father, and his guests Sir.

Alberto.   O my old friend, my tryde friend; my *Baptista*:   120
  These dayes of rest, and feasting, sute not with
  Our tougher natures, those were golden ones,
  Which were enjoyd at Sea; thats our true Mother:
  The Land's to us a stepdame; there we sought
  Honor, and wealth through dangers; yet those dangers
  Delighted more then their rewards, though great ones,
  And worth the undertakers: here we study
  The Kitchin arts, to sharpen appetite,
  Dulde with abundance; and dispute with Heaven,
  If that the least puffe of the rough Northwinde,   130
  Blast our vines burthen, rendring to our Palats
  The charming juice lesse pleasing; whereas there
  If we had bisket, powderd flesh, fresh water,
  We thought them *Persian* delicates: and for musicke
  If a strong gale but made the maine yard cracke,
  We dancde to the lowd minstrell.

Baptista.   And feard lesse,
  (So far we were in love with noble action)
  A tempest then a calme.

Alberto.   Tis true *Baptista*;
  There, there, from mutuall aydes lent to each other,
  And vertuous emulation to exceed   140
  In manly daring, the true schoole of friendship,
  We learnt those principles, which confirmd us friends
  Never to be forgot.

Baptista.   Never I hope.

Alberto.   We were married there, for bells the roring Cannon,
  A loud proclaimd it lawfull, and a prize
  Then newly tane and equally divided,
  Servd as a dowry to you, then stild my wife;
  And did enable me to be a husband,
  Fit to encounter so much wealth though got
  With bloud and horror.

Mariana.   If so got, tis fit Sir   150

131 vines] Seward; times F1–2

Now you possesse it, that you should enjoy it
In peace, and quiet; I, your sonne, and daughter
That reape the harvest of your winters labour,
Though debtors for it yet have often trembled,
When in way of discourse, you have related
How you came by it.

Alberto.   Trembled? how the softnesse
Of your sex may excuse you, Ile not argue,
But to the world, how ere I hold thee noble
I should proclaime this boy some cowards bastard,
And not the Image of *Albertus* youth: 160
If when some wishd occasion calls him forth,
To a brave tyrall, one weake artery
Of his should show a feaver, though grim death
Put on a thousand dreadfull shapes to fright him;
The Elements, the sea and all the windes
We number on our compasse, then conspiring
To make the Scæn more ghastly. I must have thee
Sirra, I must, if once you graple with
An enemies ship, to boord her, though you see
The desperat Gunner ready to give fire,   170
And blow the deck up, or like *Cesars* Souldiour
Thy hands like his cut off, hang by the teeth,
And die undanted.

Mariana.   I even dye to heare you:
My sonne, my lov'd *Cesario* runne such hazards?
Blesd Saints forbid it: you have done enough
Already for one family, that rude way;
Ile keep him safe at home, and traine him up
A compleat Courtier: may I live to see him,
By sweet discourse, and gracious demeanor,
Winne, and bring home a faire wife, and a rich;   180
Tis all I rest ambitious of.

Alberto.   A Wife!
As if there were a course to purchase one
Prevailing more then honourable action?
Or any Intercessors move so farre,
To take a Mistris of a noble spirit,

566

As the true fame of glorious victories,
Achievd by sweat and bloud! ô the brave dames
Of warlike *Genoa*! they had eyes to see
The inward man, and only from his worth,
Courage, and conquests the blind Archer knew   190
To head his shafts, or light his quenched torch,
They were proofe against them else. No Carpet Knight
That spent his youth in groves, or pleasant bowers;
Or stretching on a Couch his lazy limbes,
Sung to his Lute such soft and melting notes,
As *Ovid*, nor *Anacreon* ever knew,
Could work on them, nor once bewitch their sense;
Though he came so perfumd as he had robd
Sabæa, or *Arabia*, of their wealth;
And stord it in one sute: I still remember,   200
And still remember it with joy *Baptista*,
When from the rescue of the *Genoa* fleete,
Almost surprizd by the *Venetian* Gallies,
Thou didst returne, and wert receivd in triumph.
How lovely in thy honord wounds and scars
Thou didst appeare? what worlds of amorous glances
The beauties of the City (where they stood,
Fix'd like so many of the fairest starrs)
Shot from their windowes at thee? how it firde
Their blouds to see the Enemies captive streamers   210
Borne through the streets? nor could chast *Juliana*
The Dukes faire Neece, though garded with her greatnesse
Resist this gallant charge, but laying by
Disparity of fortune from the object,
Yeelded her selfe thy prisoner.
Baptista.   Pray you chuse
   Some other theame.
Mariana.   Can there be one more pleasing?
Baptista.   That triumph drew on me a greater torture,
   And tis in the remembrance little lesse
   Then ever Captive sufferd.

Mariana.   How? to gaine
  The favour of so great a Lady?
Baptista.   Yes,   220
  Since it prov'd fatall, t'have bin happy Madam
  Adds to calamity, and the heavie losse
  Of her I durst not hope for once injoyd,
  Turnes what you thinke a blessing to a curse,
  Which griefe would have forgotten.
Alberto.   I am sorry
  I touchd upon it.
Mariana.   I burne rather Sir,
  With a desire to heare the story of
  Your loves, and shall receave it as a favour,
  Which you may grant.
Baptista.   You must not be denyde,
  Yet with all brevity I must report it;   230
  Tis true faire *Juliana* (*Genoas* pride)
  Enamord of my actions, likd my person;
  Nor could I but with joy meet her affection;
  Since it was lawfull, for my first wife dead;
  We were closly married, and for some few months
  Tasted the fruits of't; but malitious fate,
  Envying our too much happinesse, wrought upon
  A faithlesse servant, privie to our plot,
  And Cabinet Councellor to *Juliana*,
  Who either for hope of reward, or feare,   240
  Discoverd us to the incensed Duke:
  Whose rage made her close prisoner, and pronouncd
  On me perpetuall banishment: some three yeares
  I wanderd on the Seas, since entertaind
  By the great Duke of *Florence*; but what fate
  Attended her? or *Prospero* my friend,
  That stayd at *Genoa*, to expect the issue,
  Is yet uncertaine.

Enter a Gentleman.

240 of] Dyce; or F1–2

Alberto.   From the Duke.
Baptista.   Hee's welcome,
  To end my forc'd relation.
Alberto.   Signior *Baptista*;
  The great Dukes will commands your present eare.   250
Gentleman.   It points indeed at both of you.
Baptista.   I wait it.
Alberto.   In *Mariana*, to your rest.
Baptista.   Nay leave us,
  We must be private.
Mariana.   .   Stay not long *Cæsario.*
                              Exeunt. Manet Cæsario, Mentivole.
Mentivole.   So these old men vanishd, tis allowd
  That we may speake, and how so ere they take
  Delight in the discourse of former dangers,
  It cannot hinder us to treate a little
  Of present pleasures.
Cæsario.   Which if well injoyd,
  Will not alone continue, but increase
  In us their friendship.
Mentivole.   How shall we spend the night?   260
  To snore it out like drunken *Dutchmen*, would
  Sort ill with us *Italians*. We are made
  Of other metall, fiery, quick, and active;
  Shall we take our fortune? and while our cold fathers
  (In whom long since our youthfull heates were dead,)
  Talke much of *Mars*, serve under *Venus* Ensignes,
  And seeke a Mistris?
Cæsario.   Thats a game deere friend,
  That does admit no rival in chase of it,
  And either to be undertooke alone,
  Or not to be attempted.
Mentivole.   I'le not presse you: 270
  What other sports to entertaine the time with
  The following morning?

          *250 eare] *stet* F1   268 rival] F2; rivald F1

Cæsario.   Any that may become us.

Mentivole.   Is the *Neapolitan* horse the Viceroy sent you,
   In a fit plight to runne?

Cæsario   So my Groom tells me;
   I can boast little of my horsmanship,
   Yet upon his assurance, I dare wager
   A thousand Crowns, 'gainst any horse in *Florence*,
   For an eight myle course.

Mentivole.   I would not win of you,
   In respect you are impatient of losse:
   Else I durst match him with my Barbary
   For twice the summe.

Cæsario.   You doe well to excuse it,   280
   Being certain to be beaten.

Mentivole.   Tush. You know
   The contrary.

Cæsario.   To end the controversie,
   Put it to tryall, by my life ile meete you
   With the next rising sunne.

                    Enter Clarissa.

Mentivole.   A match. But here
   Appeares a *Cynthia*, that scornes to borrow
   A beame of light from the great eye of Heaven;
   She being her selfe all brightnesse: how I envie
   Those amorous smiles, those kisses, but sure chast ones
   Which she vouchsafes her brother?

Clarissa.   You are wanton:
   Pray you think me not *Biancha*, leave I pray you;   290
   My Mother will not sleep before she see you;
   And since you know her tendernesse, nay fondnesse,
   In every circumstance that concernes your safety,
   You are not equall to her.

Cæsario.   I must leave you,
   But will not faile to meet you.

Mentivole.   Soft sleepes to you.

285 *Cynthia*] F2; *Cynthian* F1

570

Within Mariana.   Cæsario.

Clarissa.   You are calld againe.

Cæsario.   Some sonnes
    Complaine of too much rigor in their Mothers;
    I of too much indulgence; you will follow.

Clarissa.   You are her first care, therefore leade the way.
                                            Exit [Cæsario].

Mentivole.   She staies: blest opportunity, she staies?   300
    As she invited conference, she was ever
    Noble, and free; but thus to tempt my frailty,
    Argues a yeelding in her; or contempt
    Of all that I dare offer; stand I now
    Consulting? No, ile put it home.

Clarissa.   Who waites there?
    More lights.

Mentivole.   You need them not, they are as uselesse,
    As at noone-day; can there be darknesse, where
    Nature then wisely liberall, vouchsafd
    To lend two Sunnes?

Clarissa.   Hyperboles.

Mentivole.   No, truths.
    Truths beauteous virgin, so my lovesicke heart   310
    Assures me, and my understanding tels me
    I must approach them wisely, should I rashly
    Presse neare their scortching beames, they would consume me
    And on the contrary should your disdaine
    Keepe me at too much distance, and I want
    Their comfortable heate, the frost of death
    Would seise on all my faculties.

Clarissa.   Pray you pause sir.
    This vehemency of discourse must else needs tire you.
    These gay words take not me, tis simple faith,
    Honest integrity, and lawfull flames   320
    I am delighted with.

Mentivole.   Such I bring with me,
    And therefore Lady——

Clarissa.   But that you tooke me off
    Ere I came to a period, I had added

A long experience must bee requird
Both of his faith and trust with whom a virgin
Trafficks for whats dearest in this life,
Her libertie, and honor; I confesse
I oft have viewd you with an eye of favour,
And with your generous parts the many tenders
Of doing me all faire offices, have woone   330
A good opinion from me.

Mentivole.   Oh speake ever,
I never heard such musick.

Clarissa.   A playne tune sir:
But tis a hearty one; when I perceive
By evident proofes, your aimes are truly noble,
And that you bring the Engines of faire love,
Not of foule lust, to shake and undermine
My maiden fortresse: I may then make good
What now I dare not promise.

Mentivole.   You already
In taking notice of my poore deservings,
Have beene magnificent, and 'twill appeare   340
A frontlesse Impudence to aske beyond this,
Yet qualifie, though not excuse my error,
Though now I am ambitious to desire
A confirmation of it.

Clarissa.   So it wrong not
My modesty to grant it.

Mentivole.   Tis far from me,
I only am a sutor, you would grace me
With some toy, but made rich in that you wore it,
To warrant to the world that I usurp not
When I presume to stile my selfe your servant,
A riband from your shooe——

Clarissa.   You are too humble,   350
Ile think upon't; and something of more value
Shall witnesse how I prize you; it growes late,
Ile bring you to the doore.

Mentivole.   You still more binde me.

                                        Exeunt.

Enter Duke of Florence, Alberto: Baptista: *Magistrates, and*   [I.ii]
Attendants.

Duke.   You finde by this assur'd intelligence
    The preparation of the *Turke* against us.
    We have met him oft and beate him; now to feare him
    Would argue want of courage, and I hold it
    A safer policie for us and our signories
    To charge him in his passage ore the sea,
    Then to expect him here.

Alberto.   May it please your highnesse
    Since you vouchsafe to thinke me worthy of
    This great imployment, if I may deliver
    My judgment freely, tis not flattery   10
    Though I say my opinion waits on you,
    Nor would I give my suffrage and consent
    To what you have propos'd, but that I know it
    Worth the great speaker, though that the deniall
    Cald on your heavie anger. For my selfe
    I do professe thus much, if a blunt Soldier,
    May borrow so much from the oyld tongu'd Courtier,
    (That ecchoes what so-ere the Prince allowes of)
    All that my long experience hath taught me
    That have spent three parts of my life at sea,   20
    (Let it not tast of arrogance that I say it)
    Could not have added reasons of more waite
    To fortifie your affections, then such
    As your grace out of observation meerly
    Already have propounded.

Baptista.   With the honor
    To give the daring enemy an affront,
    In being the first opposer it will teach
    Your Soldiers boldnesse: and strike feare in them
    That durst attempt you.

1. Magistrate.   Victualls and ammunition,
    And mony too, the sinewes of the war,   30

17 oyld] F2 (oyl'd); old F1

573

Are stor'd up in the Magazine.

2. *Magistrate.*   And the gallies
   New rigd and traind up, and at two dayes warning
   Fit for the service.

Duke.   We commend your care,
    Nor will we ere be wanting in Our counsailes,
    As we doubt not your action; you *Baptista*
    Shall stay with us; that Merchant is not wise
    That ventures his whole fortunes in one bottome.
    Alberto be our Admirall, spare your thankes,
    Tis merit in you that invites this honor,
    Preserve it such; ere long you shall heare more.   40
    Things rashly undertaken end as ill,
    But great acts thrive when reason guides the will.

                                        Exeunt.

                Enter three Gentlemen.   [I.iii

1. No question twas not well done in *Cæsario*
   To crosse the horse of younge *Mentivole*
   In the middest of this course.

2.   That was not all,
   The switching him duld him.

3.   Would that both the jades
   Had broke their necks, when they first started; 'slight,
   We stand here prateing, give them leave to whisper,
   And when they have cut one anothers throats
   Make in to part em.

2.   There is no such hazard,
   Their fathers freindship, and their love forbid it;

                Enter Mentivole, *and* Cæsario.

See where they come!

1.   With fury in their lookes.   10

Mentivole.   You have the wager, with what fowle play got
    Ile not dispute.

Cæsario.   Fowle play.

38 *Alberto* be] Seward; *Albert.* Be F1–2   39 Tis] F2 ('Tis); His F1
5 'slight] F2 ('Slight); light F1   11 wager] F2; wages F1

Mentivole.   I cannot speak it
In a fairer language, and if some respects
Familiar to my selfe chaind not my tongue,
I should say more. I should, but Ile sit down,
With this disgrace; how ere presse me no farther.
For if once more provokd, youl understand
I dare no more suffer an Injury
Then I dare doe one.
Cæsario.   Why sir are you injur'd
In that I take my right which I would force,   20
Should you detaine it?
Mentivole.   Put it to judgement.
Cæsario.   No,
My will in this shall carrie it.
Mentivole.   Your will?
Nay farwell softnes then.   *They sodainly drawe.*
3.   This I foresaw.
2.   Hold, hold.
Cæsario.   I am hurt.
2.   Shift for your selfe, tis death.
Mentivole.   As you respect me, beare him off with care,
If he miscarry since he did the wrong,
Ile stand the shock of t.
2.   Gently, he will faint else.
                             Exeunt Gentlemen *with* Cæsario.
Mentivole.   And speedily I beseech you; my rage over
That pourd upon my reason clouds of error,
I see my folly, and at what deare losse   30
I have exchangd a reall innocence
To gaine a meere fantasticall report,
Transported only by vaine popular wind,
To bee a daring nay foole hardie man.

                    Enter Baptista.

But could I satisfie my selfe within here,
How should I beare my fathers frowne? They meet me,

                    15 more] Langbaine; no more F1–2

                             575

My guilt conjures him hither.

Baptista.   Sirra.

Mentivole.   Sir.

Baptista.   I have met the trophies of your ruffian sword:
 Was there no other Anvile to make triall
 How far thou durst be wicked, but the bosome   40
 Of him which under the adulterate name
 Of friendship thou hast murderd?

Mentivole.   Murderd sir?
 My dreams abhor so base a fact; true valor
 Imployd to keepe my reputation faire
 From the austerest judge, can never merit
 To be branded with that title; you begot me
 A man, no coward; and but call your youth
 To memory, when injur'd you could never
 Boast of the Asses fortitude, slavelike patience:
 And you might justly doubt I were your sonne,   50
 If I should entertaine it; if *Cæsario*
 Recover, as I hope his wound's not mortall,
 A second tryall of what I dare doe
 In a just cause, shall give strong witnesse for me
 I am the true heire to *Baptistas* courage
 As to his other fortunes.

Baptista.   Boy, to neither:
 But on this strict condition, which intreaties
 From Saints, nay Angels, shall not make me alter.
 A friendship so begun, and so continu'd
 Betweene me and *Alberto* my best friend,   60
 Your brawles shall not dissolve; it is my will
 And as I am thy father, I command thee,
 That instantly on any tearms, how poore
 So ere it skils not, thou desire his pardon
 And bring assurance to me he has sign'd it,
 Or by my fathers soule ile never know thee
 But as a stranger to my blood; performe it,
 And suddainly without reply, I have said it.

  42 murderd] F2 (murder'd); murder F1   59 begun] Lucas; began F1–2
  65 he] F2; *omit* F1

576

Mentivole.   And in it given a heavier sentence on me
  Then the most cruell death; you are my father   70
  And your will to be servd, and not disputed
  By me that am your sonne: but ile obey,
  And though my heart strings crack for't, make it known,
  When you command, my faculties are your own.

                                            Exeunt.

              Enter Alberto, Physitian, *and a* Chirurgion.   II.i

Physitian.   Have patience, Noble Sir; your sonne *Cæsario*
  Will recover without question.
Chirurgion.   A slight wound.
  Though it peirc't his body, it hath miss'd the vitals.
Physitian.   My life for't, he shall take the aire againe
  Within these ten daies.
Alberto.   O but from a friend,
  To receive this blody measure from a friend!
  If that a man should meete a violent death
  In a place where he had taken sanctuary,
  Would it not grieve him? such all *Florence* held
  Their friendship, and tis that which multiplyes   10
  The injury.
Physitian.   Have patience worthy Signior.
Alberto.   I doe protest as I am man and soldier,
  If I had buried him in a wave at sea,
  (Lost in some honorable action)
  I would not to the saltnesse of his grave
  Have added the least teare; but these quarrels
  Bred out of game and wine, I had as lief
  He should have died of a surfeit.

                  Enter Mariana, *and* Clarissa.

Mariana.   Oh what comfort?
  How is it with our son Sir?
Alberto.   His Work-masters
  Beare me in hand here as my Lawyer does,   20

                  20 me in] F2; in my F1

                          577

When I have a crackt title, or bad sute in Law,
All shall goe well.

Mariana.   I pray you Gentlemen, what think you of
His wound?

Physitian.   Tis but a scratch, nothing to danger.

Clarissa.   But he receiv'd it from a friend, and the unkindnesse
Tane at that, may kill him.

Mariana.   Let me see him.

Physitian.   By no meanes, he slumbers.

Mariana.   Then I cannot beleive you,
When you tell me there's hope of him.

Alberto.   Yet many Ladyes
Doe give more faith to their Physition
Then to their Confessor.

Clarissa.   O my poore lost brother,
And friend more deere then brother,

Alberto.   More loud instruments   30
To disturbe his slumbers! goe, goe, take Caroch:
And as you love me, you and the Girle retire
To our Summer house, i'th Country; ile be with you
Within these two dayes.

Mariana.   I am yours in all things,
Though with much sorrow to leave him.

Exeunt Mariana, Clarissa.

Alberto.   I pray you Gentlemen,
With best observance tend your Patient;
The losse of my heire Male, lies now a bleeding.
And think what payment his recovery
Shall showre upon you.   *Exeunt* Physitian, Chirurgion.

Enter Mentivole.

                    Of all men breathing,
Wherefore doe you arrive here? are you mad?   40
My injury begins to bleed a fresh
At sight of you; why, this affront of yours
I receive more malitious then the other.

28 give] F2; give him F1   42 yours] F2; your F1

Your hurt was only danger to my sonne:
But your sight to mee is death; why come you hither?
Do you come to view the wounds, which you have made?
And glory in them?

Mentivole.   Rather worthy Sir,
To powre oyle into them.

Alberto.   I am a Souldier Sir,
Least part of a Courtier, and understand
By your smooth oyle your present flattery.   50

Mentivole. Sir, for my Fathers sake acknowledge me
To be borne a Gentleman, no slave; I ever
Held flatterers of that breed; do not misconstrue
In your distaste of me, the true intent
Of my comming hither, for I doe protest
I doe not come to tell you I am sorry
For your sonnes hurt.

Alberto.   Not sorry?

Mentivole.   No not sorry;
I have to the lowest ebbe, lost all my fury:
But I must not lose my honesty; twas he
Gave heate unto the injury, which returnd   60
(Like a Petar ill lighted) into th' bosome
Of him gave fire to't, yet I hope his hurt,
Is not so dangerous, but he may recover;
When if it please him, call me to account,
For the losse of so much bloud, I shall be ready
To doe him noble reason.

Alberto.   You are arm'd me thinks
With wondrous confidence.

Mentivole.   O with the best Sir;
For I bring penitence, and satisfaction.

Alberto. Satisfaction? Why I heard you say but now,
You were not sorry for his wounds.

Mentivole.   Nor am I: 70
The satisfaction which I bring Sir, is to you;
You are a Gentleman ne'r injurd me;

49 a Courtier] F2; Courtier F1

One ever lov'd my Father, the right way,
And most approv'd of noble amity.
Yet I have runne my sword quite through your heart,
And slightly hurt your sonne; for't may be feard,
A griefe tane at these yeares for your sonnes losse,
May hazard yours: And therefore I am sent
By him that has most interest in your sorrow;
Who having chid me almost to the ruin   80
Of a disinheritance, for violating
So continued and so sacred a friendship
Of fiftie winters standing: such a friendship,
That ever did continue like the spring;
Ne'r saw the fall o'th leafe; by him I am sent
To say the wrong I have done Sir, is to you:
And that I have quite lost him for a Father,
Untill I finde your pardon; nay there followes
A waightier deprivation; his estate
I could with a lesse number of sighes part with.   90
Fortune might attend my youth, and my deservings
In any Climate: but a Fathers blessing,
To settle and confirme that fortune, no where;
But only here. Your pardon, give me that;
And when you have done, kill me; for tis that
Takes from me the effect of excommunication;
A fathers heavie curse.
Alberto.   Nay, may that curse
Light on himselfe, for sending thee in this minute:
When I am grown as deafe to all compassion,
As the cruellest Sea fight, or most horrid tempest.   100
That I had drownd i'th Sea a thousand duckets,
Thou hadst not made this visit: rash young man,
Thou tak'st me in an ill Planet, and hast cause
To curse thy Father; for I doe protest,
If I had met thee in any part o'th world,
But under my owne roofe, I would have killd thee.
Within there.

Enter Physitian, Chirurgion, *and* Servants.

Looke you! Here's a triumph sent

For the death of your young Master.
Servant.   Shall we kill him?
Alberto.   No, Ile not be so unhospitable; but Sir,
By my life, I vow to take assurance from you,   110
That right hand never more shall strike my sonne.
Mentivole.   That will be easily protested.
Alberto.   Not easily,
When it must be exacted, and a bloudy seale to't.
Bind him, and cut off's right hand presently:
Faire words shall never satisfie foule deeds.
Chop's hand off.
Mentivole.   You cannot be so unrighteous,
To your own honour.
Physitian.   O sir, collect your selfe;
And recall your bloudy purpose.
Alberto.   My intents of this nature,
Do ever come to action.
Chirurgion.   Then I must fetch
Another stickler.   *Exit.*
Alberto.   Yet I doe grieve at heart;   120
And I doe curse thy Father heartily,
That's the cause of my dishonour; sending thee
In such an houre, when I am apt for mischiefe:
Apt as a *Dutch man* after a Sea-fight,
When his Enemy kneeles afore him; come dispatch.
Physitian.   Intreate him Noble Sir.
Mentivole.   You shall excuse me;
Whatsoever he dares doe, that I dare suffer.

Enter Cæsario, *and* Chirurgion.

Cæsario.   Oh sir, for honours sake stay your foule purpose,
For if you do proceed thus cruelly,
There is no question in the wound you give him,   130
I shall bleed to death for't.
Alberto.   Thou art not of my temper,
What I purpose, cannot be alterd.

[*Enter* Servant.]

Servant.   Sir; the Duke
    With all speed expects you. You must instantly
    Ship all your followers, and to sea.
Alberto.   My blessing
    Stay with thee upon this condition,
    Take away his use of fighting; as thou hop'st
    To be accounted for my son, perform't.   *Exit.*
Cæsario.   You heare what I am injoynd too.
Mentivole.   Pray thee take it,
    Only this ring, this best esteemed Jewell:
    I will not give't to'th hangman chops it off;   140
    It is to deare a relique. Ile remove it
    Nearer my heart.
Cæsario.   Ha, that ring's my sisters.
    The ring I injoynd her never part withall
    Without my knowledge; come sir, we are friends:
    Pardon my fathers heate, and melancholy;
    Two violent Feavers which he caught at Sea,
    And cannot yet shake off: only one promise
    I must injoyne you to, and seriously.
    Hereafter you shall never draw a sword
    To the prejudice of my life.
Mentivole.   By my best hopes   150
    I shall not.
Cæsario.   I pray deliver me your sword
    On that condition.
Mentivole.   I shall Sir, may it hereafter
    Ever fight on your part.
Cæsario.   Noble Sir, I thank you;
    But for performance of your vow, I intreat
    Some gage from you.
Mentivole.   Any Sir.
Cæsario.   Deliver me that ring.
Mentivole.   Ha, this ring? indeed this Jewell bindes me,
    If you knew the vertue of it, never more
    To draw my sword against you.
Cæsario.   Therefore I
    Will have it.
Mentivole.   You may not.

Cæsario.   Come: you must.
  I that by violence could take your hand,   160
  Can inforce this from you; this is a token Sir,   [*Takes ring.*]
  That we may prove friends hereafter. Fare you well.
Physitian.   Why did you ceise his sword Sir?
Cæsario.   To perform
  What my father bade me, I have for the present
  Tane away his use of fighting.
Physitian.   Better so,
  Then take that which your Father meant.

                              Exeunt. Manet Mentivole.

Mentivole.   Was ever the like usage? ô that ring!
  Dearer then life, whether is honour fled?
  Cæsario? Thou are unmanly in each part,
  To seize my sword first and then split my heart.   170

                                        Exit.

                Enter Host, *and* Clowne.   [II.ii]

Host.   Thy Master that lodges here in my Hosteria, is a rare man of
  art, they say hee's a Witch.
Clown.   A witch? Nay hee's one step of the Ladder to preferment
  higher, he is a Conjurer!
Host.   Is that his higher title?
Clown.   Yes, I assure you, for a Conjurer is the Devills Master, and
  commands him; whereas a witch is the Devills Prentice and obeys
  him.
Host.   Bound Prentice to the Devill!
Clown.   Bound and inrolld I assure you, he cannot start; and   10
  therefore I would never wish any Gentleman to turne Witch.
Host.   Why man.
Clown.   Oh he looses his gentility by it, the Devill in this case cannot
  helpe him, he must go to the Herald for new armes, beleeve it.
Host.   As I am true Inkeper, yet a Gentleman borne, Ile ne'r turne
  witch for that trick. And thou hast bin a great Traveller?
Clown.   No indeed, not I Sir.
Host.   Come you are modest.
Clown.   No I am not modest, for I told you a lye, that you might the
  better understand I have bin a traveller.   20
Host.   So sir, they say your Master is a great Physitian too.

                              583

Clown.   He was no foole told you that, I assure you.

Host.   And you have beene in *England*, but they say Ladies in *England* take a great deale of Physick.

Clown.   Both wayes on my reputation.

Host.   So tis to be understood: But they say Ladyes there take Physick for fashion.

Clown.   Yes sir, and many times dye to keep fashion.

Host.   How? dye to keep fashion!

Clown.   Yes, I have knowne a Lady sicke of the small Pocks, onely to keepe her face from Pitholes, take cold, strike them in againe, kick up the heeles and vanish.   30

Host.   There was kicking up the heeles with a witnesse?

Clown.   No Sir; I confesse a good face has many times bin the motive to the kicking up of the heeles with a witnesse: but this was not.

Enter Hostesse, *and* Bianca.

Host.   Here comes my wife and daughter.

Clown.   You have a pretty commodity of this night worm!

Host.   Why man?

Clown.   She is a pretty lure to draw custome to your ordinary.

Host.   Dost think I keep her to that purpose?   40

Clown.   When a Dove-house is empty, there is cuminseed used to purloine from the rest of the neighbours; In *England* you have severall Adamants, to draw in spurres and rapiers; one keeps silk-worms in a Gallery: A Milliner has choice of Monkies, and Paraketoes; another shewes bawdy East Indian Pictures, worse than ever were *Aretines*; a Goldsmith keeps his wife wedged into his shop like a Mermaide, nothing of her to bee seene (thats woman) but her upper part.

Host.   Nothing but her upper part?

Clown.   Nothing but her upper bodies, and he lives at the more hearts ease.   50

Host.   What's the reason?

Clown.   Because her neather part can give no temptation; by your leave sir, ile tend my Master, and instantly bee with you for a Cup of Cherelly this hot weather.   [*Exit.*]

30 Pocks] F2; Pockets F1   50 bodies] *i.e.* bodice as in Colman's edition, but with a pun
*55 Cherelly] *stet* F1–2

Host.   A nimble pated rascall, come hither daughter,
   When was *Cesario* here?

Bianca.   Sir not this fortnight.

Host.   I doe not like his visits, commonly
   He comes by Owle-light, both the time and manner
   Is suspitious; I doe not like it.

Bianca.   Sir, the Gentleman   60
   Is every way so noble, that you need not
   Question his intent of comming; though you did,
   Pray Sir preserve that good opinion of me,
   That though the custome of the place I was borne in
   Makes me familiar to every guest,
   I shall in all things keep my selfe a stranger
   To the vices they bring with them.

Hostesse.   Right my daughter!
   She has the right straine of her mother.

Host.   Of her mother?
   And I would speake, I know from whence she took it;
   When I was as young I was as honest.   70

Hostesse.   Leave your prating, and study to be drunk;
   And abuse your guests over, and over.

          Enter Forobosco, *and* Clowne.

Host.   Peace wife.
   My honourable guest.

Forobosco.   My indeard Landlord! And the rest o'th complements
   o'th house.

Host.   Breakfast is ready Sir; it waites only the tide of your stomack.

Clown.   And mine gapes for't like a stale Oyster. Ere you goe to bed,
   faile not of that I pray.

          Exeunt all but Forobosco, *and* Clowne.

Forobosco.   We will instantly be with you; now we are all fellowes.
   Nine a clock, and no clyents come yet, sure thou dost not set up   80
   bills enough.

Clown.   I have set up bills in abundance.

Forobosco.   What bills?

        *77–78 Ere ... pray.] *stet* F1–2

Clown. Marry, for curing of all diseases, recovery of stolne goods, and a thousand such impossibilities.

Forobosco. The place is unlucky.

Clown. No certaine, tis scarcity of mony; doe not you hear the Lawyers complain of it? men have as much malice as ever they had to wrangle, but they have no mony: whether should this money be travell'd?   90

Forobosco. To the Devill I think.

Clown. Tis with his cofferer I am certaine, that's the Usurer.

Forobosco. Our cheating does not prosper so well as it was wont to doe.

Clown. No sure, why in *England* we coo'd cozen 'em as familiarly, as if we had travaild with a Briefe, or a Lotterie.

Forobosco. I'th Low-countries we did prety well.

Clown. So so, as long as we kept the Mop-headed butterboxes sober; marry when they were drunke, then they grew buzards: You should have them reel their heads together, and deliberate; your   100 *Dutchman* indeed when he is foxt, is like a Fox; for when hee's sunke in drink, quite earth to a mans thinking, tis full Exchange time with him, then hee's subtlest; but your *Switzer*, twas nothing to cheate him.

Forobosco. Nothing?

Clown. No nor conscience to bee made of it; for since nature aforehand cozend him of his wit, twas the lesse sinne for us to cozen him of his mony.

Forobosco. But these *Italians* are more nimble-pated, wee must have some new trick for them, I protest but that our Hostisse daughter is a   110 sweet lasse, and drawes great resort to'th house, we were as good as draw teeth a horseback.

Clown. I told 'em in the Market place you could conjure, and no body would beleeve me: but ere long I will make 'em beleeve you can conjure with such a figuary.

Forobosco. What language shal's conjure in? high *Dutch* I thinke, that's full i'th mouth.

Clown. No, no, *Spanish*, that roares best; and will appeare more dreadfull.

87 hear] F2; here F1
90 travell'd] F2; tralaunct F1   103 *Switzer*, twas] F2 ('twas); Switzert, was F1

Forobosco.   Prethee tell me thy conceit thou hast to gull them.   120
Clown.   No, no, I will not stale it; but my dear Jews-trump, for thou
   art but my instrument, I am the plotter, and when we have cozen'd
   'em most titely, thou shalt steale away the Inn-keepers daughter,
   I'le provide my selfe of another moveable: and wee will most purely
   retire our selves to *Geneva.*
Forobosco.   Thou art the compasse I saile by.

                                                  [*Exeunt.*]

                Enter Baptista *and* Mentivole.   [II.iii]

Baptista.   Was ever expectation of so Noble
   A requitall answered with such contumely!
   A wild *Numidian* that had suck't a Tigresse,
   Would not have bin so barbarous; did he threat
   To cut thy hand off?
Mentivole.   Yes Sir, and his slaves
   Were ready to perform't.
Baptista.   What hindred it?
Mentivole.   Onely his sonnes intreaty.
Baptista.   Noble youth,
   I wish thou wert not of his blood; thy pitty
   Gives me a hope thou art not.
Mentivole.   You mistake Sir,
   The injury that followed from the sonne,   10
   Was worse then the fathers; he did first disarme
   And took from me a Jewell which I prize
   Above my hand or life.
Baptista.   Take thy sword from thee?
   He stole it like a thiefe rather, he could not
   I'th field deprive thee of it.
Mentivole.   He tooke it from me,
   And sent me forth so thinne, and so unmade up,
   As if I had bin a Foote-boy.
Baptista.   O my fury!
   I must now aske thee forgivenesse, that my rashnesse
   Bred out of too much friendship, did expose thee

---

121 stale] Seward; steale F1; staele F2   1 *Baptista*] F2 (*Bap.*); *Ment.* F1

587

To so eminent a danger; which I vowe   20
I will revenge on the whole Family:
All the calamities of my whole life,
My banishment from *Genoa*, my wifes losse
Compar'd to this indignity is nothing;
Their Family shall repair't; it shall be to them
Like a plague, when the Dog-star reignes most hot:
An *Italians* revenge may pause, but's ne're forgot.   *Exit.*
Mentivole.   I would I had conceal'd this from my father,
For my interest in *Clarissa*; my care now
Must be to untangle this division,   30
That our most equall flames may be united;
And from these various and perturbed streames
Rise like a sweet morne after terrible dreames.

                                                                       Exit.

Enter Clarissa *and* Cæsario.   [II.

Clarissa.   Brother, I am happy in your recovery.
Cæsario.   And I Sister, am ever best pleased in your happinesse:
But I miss a toy should be on your finger.
Clarissa.   My Ring
This morning when I wash't I put it off,
Tis in my windowe.
Cæsario.   Wher's your Looking-glasse?
Clarissa.   Here Sir.
Cæsario.   Tis a faire one.
Clarissa.   Tis pure Chrystall.
Cæsario.   Can a Diamond cut in Crystall? let me see,
I'le grave my name in't.
Clarissa.   Oh, you'l spoyl my glasse.
Cæsario.   Would you not have your brother in your eye?
I had thought he had bin Planted in your heart,   10
Looke you, the Diamond cuts quaintly, you are cozen'd,
Your Crystal is too britle.
Clarissa [*aside*].   Tis the Ring

---

1 *Clarissa.* Brother,] F2; *Cæsar.* F1   2 *Cæsario.*] F2; *omit* F1
3 miss] F2; wish F1   9 *Cæsario.*] Seward; *omit* F1–2
10 I] Seward; *Cæs.* I F1–2

588

I gave unto *Mentivole*, sure the same.——
You put me to amazement Sir, and horror;
How came you by that ring?
Cæsario.   Does the blood rise?
Clarissa.   Pray Sir resolve me, ô for pitty doe;
    And take from me a trembling at the heart,
    That else will kill me: for I too much feare
    Nothing but Death could ravish it from his hand
    That wore it.
Cæsario.   Was it given to *Mentivole*   20
    On that condition?
Clarissa.   Tell me of his health first.
    And then I'le tell you any thing.
Cæsario.   By my life he's well,
    In better health then I am.
Clarissa.   Then it was Sir.
Cæsario.   Then shall I ever hate thee, oh thou false one;
    Hast thou a Faith to give unto a friend,
    And breake it to a brother? did I not
    By all the tyes of blood importune thee
    Never to part with it without my knowledge?
    Thou might'st have given it to a Muliter,
    And made a contract with him in a stable   30
    At as cheap a price of my vengeance: never more
    Shall a Womans trust beguile me; You are all
    Like Reliques: you may well be look't upon,
    But come a man to'th handling of you once,
    You fall in peeces.
Clarissa.   Dear Sir, I have no way
    Look't either beneath reason or my selfe
    In my election; there's parity in our blood,
    And in our fortunes, ancient amity
    Betwixt our parents: to which wants nothing,
    But the fruit of blest marriage between us,   40
    To add to their posterities: nor does now
    Any impeachment rise, except the sad
    And unexpected quarrell which divided
    So noble and so excellent a friendship,

Which as I ner'e had Magick to foresee
So I could not prevent.
Cæsario.   Well you must give me leave
   To have a hand in your disposing, I shall
   In the absence of my father be your Guardian;
   His Suit must passe through my office. *Mentivole*,
   He has too much of my blood already; he has,   50
   And he gets no more of't——

                Enter Mariana *and a* Sailor.

                         Wherefore weep you mother?
Mariana.   Tis occasion'd by a sorrow, wherein you have
   A child's part, and the mainest, your Father's dead.
Cæsario.   Dead?
Mariana.   There's one can relate the rest.
Sailor.   I can Sir,
   Your Father's drown'd, most unfortunately drownd.
Cæsario.   How? in a tempest?
Sailor.   No Sir, in a calme,
   Calme as this evening; the Gunner being drunk,
   Forgot to fasten the Ordnance to their ports,
   When came a suddain gust which tumbled them
   All to the starboord side, o'returned the ship,   60
   And sunck her in a moment, some six men
   That were upon the deck were saved: the rest
   Perish't with your Father.   [*Exit* Sailor.]
Clarissa.   O my dearest Father——
Cæsario.   I pray thee leave us.
                                      [*Exit* Clarissa.]

Mariana.   I have a sorrow of another nature,
   Equall to the former.
Cæsario.   And most commonly
   They come together.
Mariana.   The Family of the *Baptisti*
   Are growne to faction, and upon distast
   Of the injury late offerd in my house,

                61 a moment] F2; moment F1

                         590

Have vowd a most severe, and fell revenge   70
'Gainst all our family, but especially
'Gainst you my deere *Cæsario*.

Cæsario.   Let them threat,
I am prepard to oppose them.

Mariana.   And is your losse then
Of so easie an estimation, what comfort
Have I but in your life, and your late danger
Presents afore me what I am to suffer,
Should you miscarry; therefore ile advise you
When the Funerall is over, you would travaile,
Both to prevent their fury, and weare out
The injury.

Cæsario.   No Mother, I will not travaile,   80
[*Aside.*] So in my absence he may marry my Sister,
I will not travaile certaine.   [*Exit.*]

Mariana.   O my *Cæsario*,
Whom I respect and love 'bove my owne life,
Indeed with a kind of dotage, he shall never
Goe forth a doores, but the contrary faction
Will indanger's life, and then am I most wretched.
I am thinking of a strange prevention,
Which I shall witnesse with a bleeding eye,
Fondnesse sometimes is worse then cruelty.

                                                    Exit.

               Enter Host, Hostesse, *and* Bianca.   III.i

Host.   Haunted, my house is hanted with goblins. I shal be frighted
    out of my wits, and set up a signe only to invite carriers and Foot-
    posts; scar-crows to keep off the Cavelrie, and Gentry of the best
    rank. I will naile up my doors, and wall up my girle (wife) like an
    Anchoresse; or she will be ravisht before our faces, by rascalls and
    cacafugo's (wife) cacafugo's.

Hostesse.   These are your In-comes, remember your own proverb,
    the savour of every gaine smelt sweet; thank nobody but your selfe
    for this trouble.

                89.1 *Exit.*] *Exeunt.* F1–2

                        591

Host.   No gaulling (deere Spouse) no gaulling, every dayes new   10
    vexation abates mee two inches in the wast, terrible pennance for an
    Host. Girle, girle, girle, which of all this gally-maufry of mans flesh
    appears tolerable to thy choice; speak shortly, and speak truly: I
    must and will know, must and will; hear ye that?
Bianca.   Sir, be not jealous of my care and duty;
    I am so far from entertaining thoughts
    Of liberty, that much more excellent objects
    Then any of such course contents as these are,
    Could not betray mine eye to force my heart;
    Conceive a wish of any deerer happinesse   20
    Then your direction warrants. I am yours sir.
Hostesse.   What thinks the man now? is not this strange at thirteen?
Host.   Very good words, ther's a tang in 'em, and a sweet one, tis
    musicke (wife) and now I come t'ee. Let us a little examine the
    severall conditions of our Paragraphisticall suitors. The first, a
    travailing Tailor, who by the mistery of his needle and thimble,
    hath surveyd the fashions of the *French*, and *English*; this Signior
    Ginger-bread stitcht up in the shreds of a gaudy outside, sowes
    lineings with his crosse legd complement, like an Ape doing tricks
    over a staff, cringes, and crouches, and kisses his fore-finger.   30
Hostesse.   Out upon him.
Host.   A second, a lavolteteere, a saltatory, a dancer with a Kit at his
    bum, one that by teaching great *Madonnas* to foot it, has
    miraculously purchast a ribanded wastcote, and foure cleane paire
    of socks; a fellow that skips as hee walkes, and instead of sensible
    discourse vents the curious conceit of some new tune stolne from a
    Maske, or a bawdie dittie elevated for the Pole Artick of a Ladies
    chamber; in that fyle stands another of your inamoratoes.
Hostesse.   Hang him and his fiddle together, hee never fidles any
    child of ours.   40
Host.   The third, a Mongrell, got by a *Switzer* on an *Italian*, this
    puppy, being left well estated, comes to *Florence*, that the world
    may take notice, how impossible it is for experience to alter the
    course of nature, a foole (wife) and indeed a Clown turnd gallant,
    seldom or never proves other then a gallant foole, this toy prates to
    little purpose other then what's a clock, shall's go drink, de'e

forsooth, and thank ye heartily; I feare no art in him to catch thee,
and yet wee must bee tormented with this buzzard amongst the rest.

Hostesse.   Tis your owne folly, forbid him the house.

Host.   The fourth, a Mule-driver, a stubborn and a harsh knave: the 50
fifth a School-Master, a very amorous Pedant, run almost mad with
study of Sonnets and Complements out of old play-ends, the last an
Advocates clerk, that speaks pure Fustion in Law termes, excellent
Courtiers all, and all as neate as a Magnifico's post new painted at
his entrance to an office; thou shalt have none of 'em. Laugh at 'em,
doe. I say thou shalt have none of 'em.

Bianca.   Still your command to me shall stand a Law.

Host.   Now they throng like so many horse-coursers at a faire, in
clusters about the man of art, for love powders, ingredients,
potions, counsailes, postures, complements, philters: the devill and 60
the——how now? tumults? batteries, noise?

Clown *cries within. Enter* Forobosco *and* Clowne, *his head bloody.*

Forobosco. Ha, get from my sight.

Clown.   Murther me, do, pound me to Mummye, doe; see what will
come on't.

Forobosco.   Dog, leave thy snarling, or i'le cut thy tongue out,
Thou unlikt beare, darst thou yet stand my fury,
My generous rage? yet! by the sulpherous damps
That feed the hungry and incessant darknesse,
Which curles around the grim *Alastors* back,
Mutter againe, and with one powerfull word,   70
Ile call an Host up from the *Stygian* lakes,
Shall waft thee to the *Acherontick* fennes;
Where choak't with mists as black as thy impostures,
Thou shalt live still a dying.

Clown.   Conjure mee to the devill and you can. I live in hell upon
earth already, and you had any mercy, you would not practise upon
a kind heart thus.

Host.   You have drawne blood from him Signior. Is his offence
unpardonable?

Forobosco.   A lump of ignorance, pray speak not for him,   80

62 *Forobosco.*] Seward; *omit* F1–2   69 around] F2; round F1
73 impostures] F2; impostors F1   76 already] F2; 'em already F1

A drowsie grossenesse; in all christian kingdomes,
The mention of my art, my name, my practise,
Merit and glory hath begot at once
Delight and wonder; ile not be entreated;
Spare intercession for him,——ô thou scorne
Of learning, shame of duty; must thy sloth
Draw my just fame in question? I discharge thee
From my service; see me no more henceforth.

Clown. Discharge me, is that my yeares wages! Ile not be so
answerd.   90

Forobosco. Not Camell, sirra I am liberall to thee;
Thou hast thy life, begon.

Clown. Vengeance, sweet vengeance.

Forobosco. De'e mumble?

Clown. Ile be revengd, monstrously, sudainly, and insatiably; my
bulke begins to swell.

Forobosco. *Homoteleuton, Pragmatophoros, Heliostycorax.*

Clown. Call up your spirits, I defie 'em; well, Ile have law for my
broken pate, twelve ounces of pure bloud; *Troy*-weight. In
despight of thee my Master, and thy Master the grand devill   100
himselfe, *vindicta, vindicta.*   *Exit.*

Host. Signior you are exceeding mov'd.

Hostesse. Mercy upon us, what terrible words thou talk'st?

Forobosco. A slave, a curre——but be not you affrighted
Young Virgin: 'twere an injury to sweetnesse,
Should any rougher sound draw from your cheekes,
The pretious tincture which makes nature proud
Of her own workmanship.

Host. Wife. Marke, mark that wife.

Bianca. Shake then your anger off Sir.

Forobosco.   You command it   110
Faire one; mine Host and Hostesse, with your leaves
I have a motion joyntly to you all.

Hostesse. An honest one I hope.

Host.   Well put in wife.

Forobosco. A very necessary one; the Messe

And halfe of suiters, that attend to usher
Their loves sir reverence to your daughter, waite
With one consent, which can best please her eye,
In offering at a dance; I have provided
Musick. And 'twill be something I dare promise
Worthy your laughter, shal they have admittance?   120

Host.   By any means, for I am perswaded the manner will be so
ridiculous, that it will confirm the assurance of their miserable
fooleries, but no longer trouble with 'em here, then they are in these
May-games.

Forobosco.   So I am resolvd.

Hostesse.   Nor any wise word of sencelesse love.

Forobosco.   Not any; I have charm'd them, did you see
How they prepared themselves, how they stroak up
Their foretops, how they justle for the Looking-glasse,
To set their Faces by it; you would look   130
For some most impossible antick. See they muster.
You would look for some most impossible antick.

Enter Tailor, Dancer, [Coxcombe,] Mule Driver, Schoole-Master,
Clarke: (all with severall papers, and present 'em to Forobosco.)

Host.   So, so, so, so, here flutter the nest of hornets, the hotch-potch
of rascallity, now, now, now, now, the dunghill of corruption hath
yawnd forth the burthen of abhomination. I am vext, vext to the
soule, will rid my house of this unchristend fry, and never open my
doores again.

Forobosco.   Some other time, ile give no answer now,
But have preferred your suits, here shew your cunning.
First every one in order do his honour   140
To the faire mark you shoot at; courtly, courtly,
Convay your severall loves in lively measure:
Come, let us take our seates, some sprightly musick.   [*Stools.*]

Host.   Dance all and part, tis a very necessary farewell.

They all make ridiculous conges, to Bianca: *ranck themselves, and*
dance in severall postures: during the dance, Enter Cæsario, *and*
stands off.

115 And] F2; *Stooles out.* And F1   144.1 *They*] Seward; *Enter Cæsario. They* F1–2

595

Host.   Well done my lusty blouds, preciously well done, one lusty
    rouse of wine, and take leave on all sides.
Cæsario.   Thanks for your revells Gentlemen; accept
    This Gold, and drink as freely as you danc'd.
Host.   My noble Lord *Cesario*, cleer the rooms sirs.
Forobosco.   Away. Attend your answers.   150
                    Exeunt Forobosco *and those that Danc'd.*
Cæsario.   With your favour *Rolando*, I would change
    A word or two with your faire daughter.
Host.   At your Lordships pleasure, come wife, no muttering, have a
    care girle, my love, service, and duty to your good Lordship.
                            Exeunt and Wife.
Cæsario.   My often visits (sweet *Bianca*) cannot
    But constantly inform thy judgment, wherein
    Thy happinesse consists, for to steale minutes
    From great imployments, to converse with beauty,
    Lodg'd in so meane a fortune, to lay by
    Consideration of the unequall distance   160
    Between my blood and thine, to shun occasions
    Of courtship with the Ladies of the time,
    Noble, and faire, only for love to thee,
    Must of necessity invite a tendernesse;
    As low as nature could have stampt a bond womans;
    To entertaine quick motions of rare gratitude
    For my uncommon favours.
Bianca.   Deed my Lord,
    As far as my simplicity can leade mee,
    I freely thank your curtesies.
Cæsario.   To thank them,
    Is to reward them pretty one.
Bianca.   Then teach me   170
    How I may give them back again; in truth
    I never yet receiv'd a paire of Gloves:
    A trifling ring from any that expected
    An equall satisfaction, but as willingly
    I parted with the gift unto the owner,
    As he bestowd it.
Cæsario.   But I pow're before thee

Such plenties, as it lyes not in the ability
Of thy whole kindred to returne proportionable
One for a thousand.

Bianca.   You my Lord conclude
For my instruction, to ingage a debt   180
Beyond a possibilitie of paiment,
I ever thought a sinne; and therefore justly
Without conceit of scorne or curious rudenesse,
I must refuse your bounty.

Cæsario.   Canst thou love?

Bianca.   Love! is there such a word in any language
That carries honest sence?

Cæsario.   Never dwelt ignorance
In so sweet-shap't a building, love *Bianca*,
Is that firme knot which tyes two hearts in one,
Shall ours be tyed so?

Bianca.   Use a plainer word,
My Lord. Insteed of tyes, say marries hearts,   190
Then I may understand.

Cæsario.   Their hearts are married
Whose enterchange of pleasures and embraces,
Soft kisses, and the privacies of sweetes,
Keeps constant league together, when temptation
Of great mens oathes and gifts shall urge contempt,
Rather then batter resolution; novelty
Of sights, or taste of new delights in wantonnesse,
Breeds surfeit more then appetite in any
Reserv'd to noble vowes; my excellent maide
Live thou but true to me, and my contents,   200
Mine only, that no partner may pertake
The treasure of those sweets thy youth yet glories in
And I will raise thy lownesse to abundance
Of all varieties, and more triumph
In such a mistris, then great Princes doating
On truth-betraying wives.

Bianca.   Thus to yeeld up then
The cottage of my vertue to be swallow'd
By some hard-neighboring landlord such as you are

Is in effect to love, a Lord so vicious!
O where shall innocence find some poore dwelling   210
Free from temptations tirrany.
Cæsario.   Nay prethee.
Bianca.   Gay clothes, high feeding, easie beds of lust,
    Change of unseemly sights; with base discourse,
    Draw curses on your Pallaces; for my part
    This I will be confirmd in, I will eate
    The bread of labour, know no other rest
    Then what is earnd from honest paines, ere once more
    Lend eare to your vild toyles; Sir, would you were
    As noble in desires, as I could be
    In knowing vertue. Pray doe not afflict   220
    A poore soule thus.
Cæsario.   I sweare——

           [*Enter a* Gentleman.] Bianca *steales off.*

                    to me?
Gentleman.   The Duke my Lord commands your speedy presence
    For answering agreivances late urg'd
    Against you by your Mother.
Cæsario.   By my Mother.
Gentleman.   The Court is neere on sitting.
Cæsario.   I waite on it Sir.
                                        Exeunt.

       Enter Duke, *Magistrate*[s], *Secretary*, Baptista, *Attendants*,   [III
           Mentivole: (*they sit*) Mentivole *stands by.*

Duke.   What wast of bloud, what tumults, what divisions,
    What outrages, what uprores in a state,
    Factions though issuing from meane springs at first
    Have (not restraind) flowed to, the sad example
    At *Rome* between the *Ursins* and *Colonnas,*
    Nay here at home in *Florence,* twixt the *Neris*
    And the *Bianchi* can too mainly witnesse.
    I sit not at the helme (my Lords) of soveraignty
    Deputed Pilot for the Common-wealth,

---

5 *Colonnas*] Seward; *Columnies* F1; *Columni's* F2   6 *Neris*] Seward; *Neers* F1–2

To sleep whiles others steere (as their wild fancies   10
Shall councell) by the compasse of disorders.
Baptista, This short Preface is directed
Chiefly to you, the petty brawles and quarrels
Late urg'd betwixt th'*Alberti* and your family
Must, yes and shall like tender unknit joynts
Fasten againe together of themselves:
Or like an angry Chyrurgion, we will use
The roughnesse of our justice, to cut off
The stubborne rancour of the limbes offending.
Baptista.   Most gracious *Florence.*
Duke.   Our command was signified,   20
That neither of the followers of each party
Should appeare here with weapons.
Baptista.   Tis obeyd Sir, on my side.
Duke.   We must leave the generall cause
Of State employments to give eare to brawles
Of some particular grudges, pollitick government
For tutord Princes, but no more henceforth.
Our frowne shall check presumption, not our clemency.

Enter Mariana, *and* Clarissa, *at one door,* Cæsario *at the other.*
[*They kneel.*]

Mariana.   All blessings due to unpartiall Princes,
Crowne *Florence* with eternity of happinesse.
Cæsario.   If double praiers can double blessings (great Sir)   30
Mine joyne for your prosperity with my mothers.
Duke.   Rise both; now briefly (Lady) without circumstance
Deliver those agrievances which lately
Your importunity possest our counsaile
Were fit for audience, wherein you petitiond,
You might be heard without an Advocate,
Which boone you find is granted.
Mariana.   Though divided
I stand between the laws of truth and modesty,
Yet let my griefes have vent: Yet the cleernesse
Of strange necessity requires obedience   40
To nature and your mercy; in my weeds
Of mourning, emblems of too deer misfortunes,

Badges of griefes, and Widdowhood, the burthen
Of my charg'd soule must be layd downe before you;
Wherein if strict opinion cancell shame,
My frailty is my plea; stand forth young man,
And heare a story that will strike all reason
Into amasement.

Cæsario.   I attend.

Mariana.   *Alberto*
(Peace dwell upon his ashes) still the husband
Of my remembrance and unchanging vowes,   50
Has by his death left to his heire possession
Of faire revenew, which this young man claymes
As his inheritance. I urgd him gently,
Friendly, and privately to grant a partage
Of this estate to her who ownes it all,
This his supposed sister.

Baptista.   How? supposed?

Cæsario.   Pray Madam recollect your selfe.

Mariana.   The relish
Of a strange truth begins to work like Physick
Already: I have bitternesse to mingle
With these preparatives, so deadly loathsome;   60
It will quite choake digestion; shortly heare it
Cesario, for I dare not rob unjustly
The poore soule of his name; this, this *Cesario*
Neither for Father had *Alberto*, me
For Mother, nor *Clarissa* for his Sister.

Clarissa.   Mother, ô Mother.

Mentivole.   I am in a Dream sure.

Duke.   No interruptions. Lady on.

Mariana.   Mistake not
Great Duke of *Tuscany* or the beginning
Or processe of this novelty; my husband
The now deceast *Alberto*, from his youth   70
In-urd to an impatiency, and roughnesse
Of disposition, when not many monthes

---

56 How?] Langbaine; How ∧ F1–2
*67 Lady on.] F2; Lady on. | *Maria.* How ever | *Bap.* A Faulkners sonne: F1

After our marriage were worne out, repin'd
At the unfruitfull barrennesse of youth,
Which as he pleasd to terme it, cut our hopes off
From blessing of some issue; to prevent it,
I grew ambitious of no fairer honor
Then to preserve his love, and as occasions
Still call'd him from me, studied in his absence
How I might frame his welcome home with comfort.   80
At last I faynd my selfe with child; the Message
Of freedome or reliefe to one halfe stervd
In prison is not utterd with such greedinesse
Of expectation and delight as this was
To my much affected Lord; his care, his goodnesse,
(Pardon me that I use the word) exceeded
All former feares: the houre of my deliverance
As I pretended drawing neer, I fashiond
My birth-rights at a Country Garden house,
Where then my Faulkners wife was brought a bed   90
Of this *Cesario*; him I ownd for mine;
Presented him unto a joyfull Father.
Duke.   Can you prove this true?
Mariana.   Proofes I have most evident;
But O the curse of my impatiency; shortly
Ere three new Moones had spent their borrowed lights,
I grew with child indeed, so just is Heaven,
The issue of which burthen was this daughter;
Judge now most gracious Prince, my Lords and you,
What combats then and since I have indur'd
Between a mothers piety and weakenesse   100
Of a Soul trembling wife; to have reveal'd
This secret to *Alberto*, had bin danger
Of ruine to my fame, besides the conflict
Of his distractions; now to have supprest it,
Were to defeat my child, my only child,
Of her most lawfull honors, and inheritance.
Cæsario, th'art a man still, Education

78 his] F2; her F1

Hath moulded thee a Gentleman, continue so;
Let not this fall from greatnesse, sinke thee lower
Then worthy thoughts may warrant, yet disclaime   110
All interest in *Albertos* blood, thou hast not
One drop of his or mine.

Duke.   Produce your witnesse.

Mariana.   The Faulconers wife his mother,
And such women as waited then upon me,
Sworne to the privacy of this great secret.

Duke.   Give them all their oathes.

Cæsario.   O let me crave forberance, gracious Sir,
Vouchsafe me hearing.

Duke.   Speake *Cæsario.*

Cæsario.   Thus long
I have stood silent, and with no unwillingnesse,
Attended the relation of my fall,   120
From a fair expectation; what I fear'd
(Since the first sillable this Lady utter'd
Of my not being hers) benevolent Fates
Have eas'd me off; for to be basely born,
If not base-born, detracts not from the bounty
Of natures freedom or an honest birth.
Nobilitie claym'd by the right of blood,
Shewes chiefly that our Ancestors deserv'd
What we inherit; but that man whose actions
Purchase a reall merit to himselfe,   130
And rancks him in the file of prayse and honour,
Creates his own advancement; let me want
The fuell which best feedes the fires of greatnesse,
Lordly possessions, yet shall still my gratitude
By some attempts of mention not unworthy
Indeavour to returne a fit acquittance
To that large debt I owe your favours (Madam)
And great *Alberto's* memory and goodnesse;
O that I could as gently shake off passion
For the losse of that great brave man as I can shake off   140

128 deserv'd] Seward; desir'd F1–2   140 that] F2; what F1

Remembrance of what once I was reputed;
I have not much to say, this Princely presence
Needs not too strictly to examine farther
The truth of this acknowledgment; a mother
Dares never disavowe her only sonne,
And any woman must come short of Piety,
That can or dis-inherit her own issue,
Or feares the voice of rumor for a stranger.
Madam, you have confest, my Father was
A servant to your Lord and you: by interest   150
Of being his sonne, I cannot but claime justly
The honour of continuing still my service
To you and yours; which granted, I beg leave
I may for this time be dismist.
Duke.   Bold spirit.
Baptista.   I love thee now with pitty.
Duke.   Goe not yet——
A suddain tempest that might shake a rock,
Yet he stands firm against it; much it moves me,
He not *Alberto's* sonne, and she a widdow,
And she a widdow,——Lords your eare.
Omnes.   Your pleasure.
                                        Whispers.

Duke.   So, Lady, what you have avouch't is truth?   160
Mariana.   Truth onely, gracious Sir.
Duke.   Heare then our Sentence.
Since from his cradle you have fed and fostered
Cæsario as your sonne, and train'd him up
To hopes of greatnesse; which now in a moment
You utterly againe have ruin'd, this way
We with our Councell are resolv'd, you being
A widdow shall accept him for a husband.
Mariana.   Husband to me Sir?
Duke.   Tis in us to raise him
To honours, and his vertues will deserve 'em.
Mariana.   But Sir, 'tis in no Prince nor his prerogative,   170

To force a womans choice against her heart.

Duke.   True, if then you appeale to higher justice,
Our doome includes this clause upon refusall,
Out of your Lords revenues shall *Cæsario*
Assure to any whom he takes for wife
The inheritance of three parts; the lesse remainer
Is dowry large enough to marry a daughter;
And we by our prerogative which you question
Will publiquely adopt him into'th name
Of your deceas'd *Alberto*, that the memory   180
Of so approv'd a Peer may live in him
That can preserve his memory; lesse you find out
Some other meanes which may as amply satisfie
His wrong, our Sentence stands irrevocable:
What think you Lords?

Omnes.   The Duke is just and honorable.

Baptista.   Let me embrace *Cæsario*, henceforth ever
I vow a constant friendship.

Mentivole.   I remit all former difference.

Cæsario.   I am too poore
In words to thanke this Justice. Madam alwayes
My studies shall be love to you, and duty.   190

Duke.   Replyes we admit none. *Cæsario* waite on us.

Exeunt. Manent Mentivole, Baptista, Mariana, Clarissa.

Baptista.   *Mentivole.*

Mentivole.   My Lord,

Baptista.   Looke on *Clarissa*,
Shee's noble, rich, young, faire.

Mentivole.   My Lord, and vertuous.

Baptista.   *Mentivole* and vertuous.——Madam.

Mariana.   Tyranny
Of justice. I shall live reports derision,
That am compeld to exchange a gracefull widdow-hood
For a continuall Martyrdome in marriage,
With one so much beneath me.

Baptista.   I'le plead for ye
Boldly and constantly, let your daughter only
Admit my sonne her servant, at next visit   200

Madam ile be a messenger of comfort.
Mentivole, be confident and earnest.   *Exit.*
Mariana.   Married again, to him too! better t'had been
   The young man should have still retain'd the honors
   Of old *Albertos* son, then I the shame
   Of making him successor of his bed;
   I was too blame.
Mentivole.   Indeed without offence,
   Madame I think you were.
Clarissa.   You urge it fairely,
   And like a worthy freind.
Mariana.   Can you say any thing
   In commendation of a Mushroome withered   210
   Assoone as started up?
Mentivole.   You scorne an Innocent
   Of noble growth, for whiles your husband liv'd
   I have heard you boast *Cesario* in all actions
   Gave matter of report, of Imitation,
   Wonder and envy; let not discontinuance
   Of some few dayes estrange a sweet opinion
   Of vertue, cheifely when in such extremity,
   Your pitty not contempt will argue goodnesse.
Mariana.   O Sir.
Clarissa.   If you would use a thriving courtship,
   You cannot utter a more powerfull language   220
   That I shall listen to with greater greedinesse
   Then th'argument you prosecute; this speakes you
   A man compleat and excellent.
Mentivole.   I speake not,
   They are his own deserts.
Mariana.   Good Sir forbeare,
   I am now fully sensible of running
   Into a violent Lethargy, whose deadlinesse
   Locks up all reason, I shall never henceforth
   Remember my past happinesse.
Mentivole.   These clouds
   May be disperst.
Mariana.   I feare continuall night

605

Will over-shroud me, yet poore youth his trespasse   230
Lies in his fortune, not the cruelty
Of the Dukes sentence.
Clarissa.   I dare thinke it does.
Mariana.   If all faile I will learne then to conquer
Adversity with sufferance.
Mentivole.   You resolve Nobly.

                                                    Exeunt.

            Enter Cæsario *and a Servant.*   IV.i

Cæsario.   Let any freind have entrance.
Servant.   Sir a'shall.
Cæsario.   Any, I except none.
Servant.   Wee know your minde Sir.   *Exit.*
Cæsario.   Pleasures admit no bounds. I am pitcht so high
To such a growth of full prosperities
That to conceale my fortunes were an injury
To gratefulnesse and those more liberall favours
By whom my glories prosper. He that flowes
In gracious and swolne tydes of best abundance,
Yet will be Ignorant of his owne fortunes,
Deserves to live contemn'd, and dye forgotten;   10
The harvest of my hopes is now already
Ripen'd and gather'd, I can fatten youth
With choice of plenty, and supplies of comforts,
My fate springs in my owne hand, and Ile use it.

            Enter two Servants *and* Bianca.

1.   Tis my place.
2.   Yours? here faire one, Ile aquaint
My Lord.
1.   He's here, go to him boldly.
2.   Please you
To let him understand how readily
I waited on your errand?
1.   Saucy fellow,

    You must excuse his breeding.

Cæsario.   Whats the matter?

    Biancha, my *Biancha*,——to your offices.   *Exeunt* Servants. 20
    This visit (Sweet) from thee (my pretty deere)
    By how much more twas unexpected, comes
    So much the more timely: witnes this free welcome,
    What ere occasion led thee?

Bianca.   You may guesse Sir,
    Yet indeed tis a rare one.

Cæsario.   Prethee speake it,
    My honest vertuous maide.

Bianca.   Sir I have heard
    Of your misfortunes, and I cannot tell you
    Whether I have more cause of joy or sadnesse,
    To know they are a truth.

Cæsario.   What truth *Bianca*!
    Misfortunes, how, wherein?

Bianca.   You are disclaym'd   30
    For being the Lord *Albertos* sonne, and publickly
    Acknowledg'd of as meane a birth as mine is,
    It cannot chuse but greive thee.

Cæsario.   Greive me, ha ha ha ha?
    Is this all?

Bianca.   This all.

Cæsario.   Thou art sorry for't
    I warrant thee, alas good soule, *Biancha*,
    That which thou call'st misfortune is my happines,
    My happines *Biancha*.

Bianca.   If you love me,
    It may prove mine too.

Cæsario.   May it? I will love thee,
    My good good maid, if that can make thee happy,
    Better and better love thee.

Bianca.   Without breach then   40
    Of modesty I come to claime the Interest
    Your protestations both by vowes and letters

Have made me owner of, from the first houre
I saw you, I confesse I wisht I had beene
Or not so much below your ranke and greatnesse,
Or not so much above those humble flames
That should have warm'd my bosome with a temperate
Equality of desires in equall fortunes.
Still as you utter'd Language of affection,
I courted time to passe more slowly on   50
That I might turne more fool to lend attention
To what I durst not credit nor yet hope for:
Yet still as more I heard, I wisht to heare more.

Cæsario.   Didst thou introth wench?

Bianca.   Willingly betraid
My selfe to hopelesse bondage.

Cæsario.   A good girle,
I thought I should not misse what eare thy answer was.

Bianca.   But as I am a maid Sir, and I'faith
You may beleeve me, for I am a maid,
So deerely I respected both your fame
And quality, that I would first have perisht   60
In my sicke thoughts then ere have given consent
To have undone your fortunes by inviting
A marriage with so meane a one as I am.
I should have dyed sure, and no creature knowne
The sicknesse that had kill'd me.

Cæsario.   Pretty heart,
Good soule, alas, alas.

Bianca.   Now since I know
There is no difference twixt your birth and mine,
Not much twixt our estates, if any bee,
The advantage is on my side, I come willingly
To tender you the first fruits of my heart,   70
And am content t'accept you for my husband,
Now when you are at lowest.

Cæsario.   For a husband?
Speake sadly, dost thou meane so?

51 fool] F2; food F1

608

Bianca.   In good deed Sir,
  Tis pure love makes this proffer.
Cæsario.   I beleeve thee,
  What counsaile urg'd thee on, tell me, thy Father
  My worshipfull smug Host? wast not he wench?
  Or mother Hostesse? ha?
Bianca.   D'ee mock my parentage?
  I doe not scorne yours. Meane folkes are as worthy
  To be well spoken of if they deserve well,
  As some whose only fame lies in their bloud.   80
  O y'are a proud poore man: all your oathes falshood,
  Your vowes deceite, your letters forg'd, and wicked.
Cæsario. Thou'dst be my wife, I dare sware.
Bianca.   Had your heart,
  Your hand and tongue been twins, you had reputed
  This courtesy a benefit.
Cæsario.   Simplicity,
  How prettily thou mov'st me? why *Biancha*
  Report has cozned thee, I am not fallen
  From my expected honors, or possessions,
  Though from the hope of birthright.
Bianca.   Are you not?
  Then I am lost againe; I have a suit too,   90
  Youle grant it if you be a good man.
Cæsario.   Any thing.
Bianca. Pray doe not talke of ought what I have said t'ee.
Cæsario. As I wish health I will not.
Bianca.   Pitty me,
  But never love me more.
Cæsario.   Nay now y'are cruell,
  Why all these teares?——Thou shalt not goe.
Bianca.   Ile pray for yee
  That you may have a vertuous wife, a faire one,
  And when I am dead——
Cæsario.   Fy, fy.
Bianca.   Thinke on me sometimes,

82 vowes] F2 (vows); vowe F1

609

With mercy for this trespasse.
Cæsario.   Let us kisse
    At parting as at comming.
Bianca.   This I have
    As a free dower to a virgins grave,   100
    All goodnesse dwell with yee.   *Exit.*
Cæsario.   Harmelesse *Biancha*!
    Unskild, what hansome toyes are maids to play with?

                Enter Mariana *and* Clarissa.

    How innocent, but I have other thoughts
    Of nobler meditation.——My felicity,   [*To* Mariana.]
    Thou commest as I could wish, lend me a lip
    As soft, as melting as when old *Alberto*
    After his first nights triall taking farewell
    Of thy youthes conquest tasted.
Mariana.   You are uncivill.
Cæsario.   I will be Lord of my owne pleasures, Madame
    Y'are mine, mine freely. Come, no whimpering, henceforth   110
    New con the lessons of loves best experience,
    That our delights may meet in equal measure
    Of resolutions and desires; this sullenes
    Is scurvy, I like it not.
Mariana.   Be modest.
    And doe not learne *Cesario* how to prostitute
    The riot of thy hopes to common folly;
    Take a sad womans word, how ere thou doatest
    Upon the present graces of thy greatnes,
    Yet I am not falne so belowe my constancy
    To vertue, nor the care which I once tendred   120
    For thy behoof that I prefer a sentence
    Of cruelty before my honor.
Cæsario.   Honor!
Mariana.   Hear me, thou seest this girle! now the comfort
    Of my last dayes. She is the onely pledge
    Of a bed truly noble, shee had a father

        106 As] Seward; *omit* F1–2   111 experience] F2; experiencd F1

                        610

    (I need not speake him more then thou remembrest)
    Whom to dishonor by a meaner choice,
    Were injury and infamy——
Clarissa.   To goodnes,
    To time and vertuous mention.
Mariana.   I have vow'd,
    Observe me now *Cesario*, that how ere   130
    I may be forc't to marry, yet no tyranny,
    Perswasions, flattery, guifts, intreats, or tortures,
    Shall draw me to a second bed.
Clarissa.   Tis Just too.
Mariana.   Yes and tis Just *Clarissa*. I allow
    The Dukes late sentence, am resolv'd young man
    To be thy wife, but when the ceremony
    Of marriage is perform'd, in life I wil bee
    Though not in name a widdow.
Cæsario.   Pray a word t'ee,
    Shall I in earnest never be your bedfellow?
Mariana.   Never, ô never; and tis for your good too.   140
Cæsario.   Prove that.
Mariana.   Alas too many yeares are numbred
    In my account to entertaine the benefit
    Which youth in thee *Cesario* and ability
    Might hope for and require, it were Injustice
    To rob a gentleman deserving memory
    Of Issue to preserve it.
Cæsario.   No more herein,
    You are an excellent patterne of true piety,
    Let me now turne your advocate. Pray looke into
    The order of the Duke Injoynd, admit
    I satisfie the sentence without mariage   150
    With you, how then?
Mariana.   *Cesario.*
Cæsario.   If I know
    How to acquit your feares, yet keepe th'injunction
    In every clause whole and entire, your charity
    Will call me still your servant.
Mariana.   Still my son.

Cæsario.   Right Madam, now you have it, still your son.
   The Genius of your blessings hath instructed
   Your tongue oraculously, wee wil forget
   How once I and *Clarissa* enterchangd
   The tyes of brother and of sister, henceforth
   New stile us man and wife.
Clarissa.   By what authority?   160
Cæsario.   Heavens great appointment, yet in all my dotage
   On thy perfections, when I thought *Clarissa*
   Wee had beene pledges of one wombe, no loose,
   No wanton heat of youth, desir'd to claime
   Priority in thy affections, other
   Then nature might commend. Chastly I tendred
   Thy welfare as a brother ought; but since
   Our bloods are strangers, let our hearts contract
   A long life-lasting unity, for this way
   The sentence is to be observd or no way.   170
Mariana.   Then no way.
Cæsario.   I expected other answer
   Madam from you.
Mariana.   No, every age shall curse me,
   The monster, and the prodigie of nature,
   Horrors beyond extremity.
Clarissa.   Pray mother confine
   The violence of greife.
Cæsario.   Yes mother, pray do.
Mariana.   Thus some catch at a matrons honor
   By flying lust to plot Incestuous witchcrafts,
   More terrible then whoredomes; cruell mercy
   When to preserve the body from a death
   The soule is strangled.
Cæsario.   This is more then passion.   180
   It comes neere to distraction.
Mariana.   I am quieted.
   Cesario, thou maiest tell the Duke securely
   Albertos titles, honors and revenues,

167 welfare] F2; farewell F1

The Duke may give away. Injoy them thou.
Clarissas birthright, *Marianas* dower
Thou shalt be Lord of; turne us to the world
Unpittyed and unfreinded, yet my bed
Thou never sleep'st in; as for her, she heares me,
If she as much as in a thought consent,
That thou may'st call her wife, a Mothers curse   190
Shall never leave her.

Clarissa.   As a brother once
I lov'd you, as a noble freind yet honor ye,
But for a husband sir, I dare not owne you,
My faith is given already.

Cæsario.   To a Villaine,
Ile cut his throat.

Mariana.   Why this is more then passion?
It comes neere a distraction.

Clarissa.   Call to minde Sir,
How much you have abated of that goodnesse
Which once raign'd in ye, they appear'd so lovely
That such as freindship led to observation
Courted the great example.

Enter Baptista *and* Mentivole.

Cæsario.   Left and flatterd   200
Into a broad derision.

Mariana.   Why d'ee thinke so?
My Lord *Baptista*, is your sonne growne cold
In hasting on the marriage, which his vowes
Have seald to my wrongd daughter?

Baptista.   Wee come Lady,
To consummate the contract.

Cæsario.   With *Mentivole*?
Is he the man?

Mentivole.   *Clarissas* troth and mine,
Cesario are recorded in a character
So plaine and certaine, that except the hand

Of heaven, which writ it first, would blot it out againe,
No human power can raze it.
Cæsario.   But say you   210
So too young Lady?
Clarissa.   I should els betray
My heart to falshood, and my tongue to perjury.
Cæsario.   Madam, you know the sentence.
Baptista.   From the Duke,
I have particular comforts which require
A private eare.
Mariana.   I shall approve it gladly,
Wee are resolvd *Cesario.*
Baptista.   Be not insolent
Upon a Princes favour.
Clarissa.   Loose no glory,
Your younger yeares have purchast.
Mentivole.   And deservd too,
Y'have many worthy freinds.
Baptista.   Preserve and use them.
                    Exeunt: Manet Cæsario.
Cæsario.   Good, very good, why here's a complement   220
Of mirth in desperation, I could curse
My fate, ô with what speed men tumble downe
From hopes that soare to high. *Biancha* now
May scorne me justly too, *Clarissa* married,
Albertos widdow resolute, *Biancha*
Refusd, and I forsaken, let me study,
I can but dye a Batchelor thats the worst on't.
                            Exit.

Enter Host, Taylor, Muliter, Dancer, Pedant, [*Clerk,*] Coxcombe. [IV.ii

Host.   Come Gentlemen, this is the day that our great artist hath
   promist to give all your severall suites satisfaction.
Dancer.   Is he stirring?
Host.   He hath beene at his booke these two houres.
Pedant.   Hee's a rare Physitian.
Host.   Why Ile tell you, were *Paracelsus* the *German* now living,
   hee'd take up his single rapier against his terrible long sword, he

makes it a matter of nothing to cure the goute, sore eyes he takes out
as familiarly, washes them, and puts them in againe, as you'd blanch
almonds.   10

Taylor.   They say he can make gold.

Host.   I, I, he learnt it of *Kelly* in *Germany*. There's not a Chimist in
christendome can goe beyond him for multiplying.

Pedant.   Take heed then, he get not up your daughters belly my
Host.

Host.   You are a merry Gentleman and the man of art will love you
the better.

Dancer.   Does he love mirth and crotchets?

Host.   O hee's the most courteous Physitian, you may drink or drab
in's company freely, the better he knowes how your disease growes,   20
the better he knowes how to cure it.

Dancer.   But I wonder my Host he has no more resort of Ladyes to
him.

Host.   Why Sir?

Dancer.   O divers of them have great beleife in conjurers: lechery is a
great helpe to the quality.

Host.   Hee's scarce knowne to be in towne yet, ere long we shall have
'em come hurrying hither in Fetherbeds.

Dancer.   How? bedridden.

Host.   No sir, in fetherbeds that move upon four wheeles, in *Spanish*   30
caroches.

Pedant.   Pray acquaint him we give attendance.

Host.   I shall gentlemen. [*Aside.*] I would faine be rid of these
rascalls, but that they raise profit to my wine-seller; when I have
made use of them sufficiently, I will intreat the conjurer to tye
crackers to their tailes, and send them packing.

Enter Forobosco *as in his Study.*

Forobosco.   Come hither mine Host, looke here.

Host.   Whats that?

Forobosco.   A challenge from my man.

Host.   For breaking's pate?   40

Forobosco.   He writes here if I meet him not ith Feild within this halfe

36.1 *Study.*] *Study.* (A paper) F1–2

houre, I shall heare more from him.

Host.   O sir, minde your profit, nere thinke of the rascall, here are the gentlemen.

Forobosco.   Morrow my worthy clients, what are you all prepard of your questions, that I may give my resolution upon them?

Omnes.   We are sir.

Pedant.   And have brought our mony.

Forobosco.   Each then in order, and differ not for precedency.

Dancer.   I am buying of an office sir, and to that purpose I would   50
faine learne to dissemble cunningly.

Forobosco.   Doe you come to me for that? you should rather have gone to a cunning woman.

Dancer.   I sir but their Instructions are but like women, pretty well but not to the depth, as I'de have it: You are a conjurer, the devils master, and I would learn it from you so exactly——

Forobosco.   That the divill himselfe might not go beyond you.

Dancer.   You are ith right sir.

Forobosco.   And so your mony for your purchase might come in againe within a twelve month.   60

Dancer.   I would be a Graduate sir, no freshman.

Forobosco.   Here's my hand sir, I will make you dissemble so methodically, as if the divell should be sent from the great Turke, in the shape of an Embassador to set all christian princes at variance.

Dancer.   I cannot with any modesty desire any more. There's your mony sir.

Forobosco.   For the art of dissembling.   [*Writes.*]

Coxcombe.   My suite sir will be newes to you when I tell it.

Forobosco.   Pray on.

Coxcombe.   I would set up a presse here in *Italy*, to write all the   70
Caranta for Christendome.

Forobosco.   Thats newes indeed, and how would you imploy me in't?

Coxcombe.   Marry sir, from you I would gaine my intelligence.

Forobosco.   I conceave you, you would have me furnish you with a spirit to informe you.

Coxcombe.   But as quiet a Divell as the woman, the first day and a halfe after she's married, I can by no meanes indure a terrible one.

Forobosco.   No, no, Ile qualifie him he shall not fright you, it shall be

the ghost of some lying Stationer, a Spirit shall looke as if butter
would not melt in his mouth. A new *Mercurius Gallobelgicus*.   80
Coxcombe.   O there was a captaine was rare at it.
Forobosco.   Nere thinke of him, though that captaine writ a full hand
   gallop, and wasted indeed more harmelesse paper then ever did
   laxative Physick, yet wil I make you to out-scribble him, and set
   downe what you please, the world shall better beleeve you.
Coxcombe.   Worthy sir I thanke you, there's mony.
Forobosco.   A new office for writing pragmaticall Curranto's.

                                                      [*Writes.*]

Pedant.   I am a schoole-master sir, and would faine conferre with
   you about erecting four new sects of religion at *Amsterdam*.
Forobosco.   What the Divell should new sects of religion doe there?   90
Pedant.   I assure you I would get a great deale of mony by it.
Forobosco.   And what are the four new sects of religion you would
   plant there?
Pedant.   Why thats it I come about sir, tis a Divel of your raising
   must invent 'em, I confesse I am too weake to compasse it.
Forobosco.   So sir, then you make it a matter of no difficulty to have
   them tolerated.
Pedant.   Trouble not your selfe for that, let but your Divel set them
   a foot once, I have Weavers and Ginger-bread makers, and mighty
   Aquavitæ-men, shall set them a going.   100
Forobosco.   This is somewhat difficult, and will aske some conference
   with the divell.
Pedant.   Take your owne leasure sir, I have another busines too,
   because I meane to leave *Italy*, and bury my selfe in those neather
   parts of the low countries.
Forobosco.   Whats that sir.
Pedant.   Marry I would faine make nine dayes to the weeke, for the
   more ample benefit of the captaine.
Forobosco.   You have a shrewd pate sir.
Pedant.   But how this might be compasd?   110
Forobosco.   Compasd easily; tis but making a new Almanacke, and
   dividing the compasse of the yeare into larger penny-worths, as a
   Chandler with his compasse makes a Geometrick proportion of the
   Holland cheese he retailes by stivers. But for getting of it licenc'd?

Pedant.   Trouble not your selfe with that sir, there's your mony.

Forobosco.   For foure new sects of religions, and nine dayes to the
weeke.   [*Writes.*]

Pedant.   To be brought in at generall pay-dayes. Write I beseech
you.

Forobosco.   At generall pay-dayes.   120

Taylor.   I am by profession a taylor, you have heard of me.

Forobosco.   Yes sir, and will not steale from you the least part of that
commendation I have heard utterd.

Taylor.   I take measure of your worth sir, and because I will not
afflict you with any large bill of circumstances, I will snip off
particulars. I would faine invent some strange and exquisite new
fashions.

Forobosco.   Are you not travel'd sir.

Taylor.   Yes sir, but have observ'd all we can see or invent are but old
ones with new names to 'em; now I would some way or other grow   130
more curious.

Forobosco.   Let me see; to devise new fashions——Were you never
in the Moone?

Taylor.   In the *Moone* taverne! yes sir: often.

Forobosco.   No, I do meane in the new world, in the world thats in the
Moone yonder.

Taylor.   How? a new world ith moone?

Forobosco.   Yes I assure you.

Taylor.   And peopled?

Forobosco.   O most fantastically peopled.   140

Taylor.   Nay certaine then ther's worke for taylors?

Forobosco.   That there is I assure you.

Taylor.   Yet I have talked with a Scotch taylor that never discover'd
so much to me, though he has travail'd far, and was a pedlar in
Poland.

Forobosco.   That was out of his way, this lies beyond *China*: you
would study new fashions you say? Take my councell, make a
voyage, and discover that new world.

Taylor.   Shall I be a moon-man?

Forobosco.   I am of opinion, the people of that world (if they be like   150
the nature of that climate they live in) do vary the fashion of their
cloathes oftner then any quick-silver'd nation in *Europe.*

618

Taylor.   Not unlikely, but what should that be we call the man in the moone then?

Forobosco.   Why tis nothing but an Englishman that stands there starke naked, with a paire of sheires in one hand, and a great bundle of broad cloath in the other (which resembles the bush of thornes) cutting out of new fashions.

Taylor.   I have heard somewhat like this, but how shall I get thither?

Forobosco.   Ile make a new compasse shall direct you.   160

Taylor.   Certaine?

Forobosco.   Count me else for no man of direction.

Taylor.   There's twenty duckats in hand, at my returne Ile give you a hundred.

Forobosco.   A new voyage to discover new fashions.   [*Writes.*]

Muletir.   I have been a travailer too sir, that have shewed strange beasts in Christendome, and got mony by them, but I finde the trade to decay. Your Camelion, or East-Indian hedg-hog gets very little mony, and your Elephant devoures so much bread, brings in so little profit, his keeper were better every morning cram fifteen   170
Taylors with white manchet: I would have some new spectacle, and one that might be more attractive.

Forobosco.   Let me see, were you ever in *Spaine?*

Muletir.   Not yet Sir.

Forobosco.   I would have you go to *Madrill*, and against some great festivall, when the court lies there, provide a great and spacious English Oxe, and roste him whole, with a pudding in's belly; that would be the eight wonder of the world in those parts I assure you.

Muletir.   A rare project without question.

Forobosco.   Goe beyond all their garlike olla Podrithoes, though you   180
sod one in *Garguentuas* cauldron, bring in more mony, then all the monsters of *Affrick.*

Host.   Good Sir do your best for him; he's of my acquaintance, and one if ye knew him——

Forobosco.   What is he?

Host.   He was once a man of infinite letters.

Forobosco.   A Scholler?

Host.   No sir, a packet carrier, which is alwaies a man of many letters, you know: then he was Mule-driver, now hee's a gentleman, and feedes monsters.   190

619

Forobosco.   A most ungratefull calling.

Muletir.   Ther's mony for your direction; the price of the Oxe Sir?

Forobosco.   A hundred *French* crownes, for it must be a *Lincolne* shire
   Oxe, and a prime one:
   For a rare and monstrous spectacle, to be seen at *Madrill*.

                                                    [*Writes.*]

              Enter Clown, Hostesse, *and* Bianca.

Hostesse.   Pray forbeare sir, we shall have a new quarrell.

Clown.   You durst not meet me ith' field, I am therefore come to
   spoyle your market.

Forobosco.   Whats the newes with you sir.

Clown.   Gentlemen, you that come hither to be most abominably 200
   cheated, listen, and be as wise as your plannet will suffer you, keep
   your mony, be not guld, be not laught at.

Pedant.   What meanes this? would I had my mony againe in my
   pocket.

Host.   The fellow is full of malice, do not mind him.

Clown.   This profest cheating rogue was my master, and I confesse
   my selfe a more preternotorious rogue then himselfe, in so long
   keeping his villainous counsell.

Forobosco.   Come, come, I will not heare you.

Clown.   No couzner, thou wouldest not heare me, I do but dare thee 210
   to suffer me to speake, and then thou and all thy divells spit fire, and
   spoute *Aqua fortis*.

Forobosco.   Speake on, I freely permit thee.

Clown.   Why then know all you simple animals, you whose purses
   are ready to cast the calfe, if they have not cast it already, if you give
   any credit to this jugling rascal, you are worse then simple widgins,
   and will be drawne into the net by this decoy ducke, this tame
   cheater.

Forobosco.   Ha, ha, ha, pray marke him.

Clown.   He does professe Physicke, and counjuring; for his 220
   Physicke, he has but two medicins for all manner of diseases; when
   he was i'th low countryes, he us'd nothing but butterd beere,
   coloured with Allegant, for all kind of maladies, and that he called
   his catholick medicine; sure the *dutch* smelt out it was butterd beere,
   else they would never have endur'd it for the names sake: then does

he minister a grated dogs turd instead of Rubarbe, many times of
Unicornes horne, which working strongly with the conceit of the
Patient, would make them bescummer to the height of a mighty
purgation.

Forobosco.   The rogue has studied this invective.   230

Clown.   Now for his conjuring, the witches of *Lapland* are the divells
chaire-women to him, for they will sell a man a winde to some
purpose; he sells winde, and tells you fortye lyes over and over.

Hostesse.   I thought what we should find of him.

Host.   Hold your prating, be not you an hereticke.

Clown.   Conjure! Ile tell you, all the divells names he calls upon, are
but fustian names, gatherd out of *welch* heraldry; in breife, he is a
rogue of six repreives, foure pardones of course, thrice pilloried,
twice sung *Lacrymæ* to the Virginalls of a carts taile, h'as five times
been in the Gallies, and will never truly run himselfe out of breath,   240
till he comes to the gallowes.

Forobosco.   You have heard worthy gentlemen, what this lying
detracting rascall has vomited.

Taylor.   Yes certaine, but we have a better trust in you, for you have
taine our mony.

Forobosco.   I have so, truth is he was my servant, and for some
chastisement I gave him, he does practise thus upon me; speake
truly sirra, are you certaine I cannot conjure?

Clown.   Conjure! ha, ha, ha.

Forobosco.   Nay, nay, but be very sure of it.   250

Clown.   Sure of it? why Ile make a bargaine with thee, before all these
gentlemen, use all thy art, all thy roguery, and make me do any
thing before al this company I have not a mind to, Ile first give thee
leave to claime me for thy bond slave, and when thou hast done
hang me.

Forobosco.   Tis a match, sirra, Ile make you caper ith' aire presently.

Clown.   I have too solid a body, and my beleife is like a Puritans on
Good-Friday, too high fed with capon.

Forobosco.   I will first send thee to *Green-land* for a haunch of
venison, just of the thicknesse of thine own tallow.   260

Clown. Ha, ha, ha, Ile not stir an inch for thee.

---

232 chaire-] *i.e.* chare *or* char-   259 *Green-land*] F2 (*rom.*); Greeke-land F1

Forobosco. Thence to *Amboyna* ith' *East-Indies*, for pepper to bake it.

Clown. To *Amboyna*? so I might be pepperd.

Forobosco. Then will I conveigh thee stark naked to *Develing* to beg a paire of brogs, to hide thy mountainous buttocks.

Clown. And no doublet to 'em?

Forobosco. No sir, I intend to send you of a sleevelesse errand; but before you vanish, in regard you say I cannot conjure, and are so stupid, and opinionated a slave, that neither I, nor my art can compell you to do any thing thats beyond your own pleasure, the gentlemen shall have some sport: you cannot endure a cat sirra?

Clown. Whats that to thee Jugler?

Forobosco. Nor you'l do nothing at my entreaty?

Clown. Ile be hang'd first.

Forobosco. Sit Gentlemen, and whatsoever you see, be not frighted.

Hostesse. Alas I can endure no conjuring.

Host. Stir not wife.

Bianca. Pray let me go sir, I am not fit for these fooleryes.

Host. Move not daughter.

Forobosco. I wil make you dance a new dance calld leap-frog.

Clown. Ha, ha, ha.

Forobosco. And as naked as a frog.

Clown. Ha, ha, ha, I defye thee.

Forobosco *lookes in a booke, strikes with his wand, Musick playes.*
Enter four Boyes shap't like Frogs, and dance.

Pedant. Spirits of the water in the likenes of frogs.

Taylor. He has fisht faire beleeve me.

Muletir. See see, he sweats and trembles.

Forobosco. Are you come to your quavers?

Clown. Oh, oh, oh.

Forobosco. Ile make you run division on that o's ere I leave you; looke you, here are the playfellowes that are so indeerd to you; come sir, first uncase, and then dance, nay Ile make him daunce stark naked.

270

280

290

265 *Develing*] *i.e.*, Dublin   *272 cat] *stet* F1–2

622

Host.   Oh let him have his shirt on, and his Mogols breeches, here are
  women ith' house.

Forobosco.   Well for their sakes he shall.

> Clown *teares off his doublet, making strange faces as*
>   *if compeld to it, falls into the Daunce.*

Taylor.   He daunces, what a lying rogue was this to say the
  gentleman could not conjure?

Forobosco.   He does prettily well, but tis voluntary, I assure you, I
  have no hand in't.   300

Clown.   As you are a Counjurer, and a rare Artist, free me from these
  couplets; of all creatures I cannot endure a Frog.

Forobosco.   But your dauncing is voluntary, I can compell you to
  nothing.

Hostesse.   O me, daughter, let's take heed of this fellow, he'le make
  us dance naked, an' we vex him.   *Exeunt* Hostesse *and* Bianca.

Forobosco.   Now cut capers sirra, Ile plague that chine of yours.

Clown.   Oh, oh, oh, my kidneys are rosted, I drop away like a pound
  of butter rosted.

Taylor.   He will daunce himselfe to death.   310

Forobosco.   No matter, Ile sell his fat to the Pothecaries, and repaire
  my injury that way.

Host.   Enough in conscience.

Forobosco.   Well, at your entreaty vanish. [*Exeunt Frogs.*] And now I
  wil only make him breake his neck in doing a sommerset, and thats
  all the revenge I meane to take of him.

Clown.   O gentlemen, what a rogue was I to belye so an approved
  Master in the noble dark science? you can witnesse, this I did only
  to spoyle his practise and deprive you of the happynesse of injoying
  his worthy labours; rogue that I was to do it, pray sir forgive me.   320

Forobosco.   With what face canst thou ask it?

Clown.   With such a face as I deserve, with a hanging looke, as all
  here can testifie.

Forobosco.   Well gentlemen, that you may perceive the goodnes of
  my temper, I will entertain this rogue again in hope of amendment,
  for should I turn him off, he would be hanged.

307 chine] F2; chin F1

Clown.   You may read that in this foule coppy.

Forobosco.   Only with this promise, you shall never cozen any of my
patients.

Clown.   Never.   330

Forobosco.   And remember hence forward, that though I cannot
counjure, I can make you daunce sirra, go get your selfe into the
cottage againe.

Clown.   I will never more daunce leape Frog: [*aside*] now I have got
you into credit, hold it up, and cozen them in abundance.

Forobosco. [*to* Clown].   O rare rascall.   *Exit* Clown.

Enter Cæsario.

Cæsario.   How now, a *Frankford* mart here, a Mountebanke, and his
worshipfull auditory.

Host.   They are my ghuests Sir.

Cæsario.   A pox upon them, shew your jugling tricks in some other   340
roome.

Host.   And why not here Sir?

Cæsario.   Hence, or sirra I shall spoile your figure flinging, and all
their radicall questions.

Omnes.   Sir we vanish.   *Exeunt. Manet* Host *and* Cæsario.

Host.   Signior *Cæsario*, you make bold with me,
And somewhat I must tell you to a degree
Of ill manners, they are my ghuests, and men I live by,
And I would know by what authority
You command thus far.

Cæsario.   By my interest in your daughter.   350

Host.   Interest do you call't? as I remember
I never put her out to Usury
On that condition.

Cæsario.   Pray thee be not angry.
I am come to make thee happy, and her happy:

Enter Bianca *and* Hostesse.

Shee's here; alas my pretty soule, I am come
To give assurance thats beyond thy hope,

Or thy beleife, I bring repentance 'bout me,
And satisfaction, I will marry thee.
Bianca.   Ha?
Cæsario.   As I live I will, but do not entertain't
With too quick an apprehension of joy,   360
For that may hurt thee, I have heard some dye of't.
Bianca.   Do not feare me.
Cæsario.   Then thou think'st I faigne
This protestation, I will instantly
Before these testifie my new alliance,
Contract my selfe unto thee, then I hope
We may be more private.
Host.   But thou shalt not sir,
For so has many a maiden-head been lost,
And many a bastard gotten.
Cæsario.   Then to give you
The best of any assurance in the world,
Entreat thy father to goe fetch a Preist,   370
Wee will instantly to bed, and there be married.
Bianca.   Pride hath not yet forsaken you I see,
Though prosperity has.
Host.   Sir you are too confident
To fashion to your selfe a dreame of purchase
When you are a begger.
Cæsario.   You are bold with me.
Hostesse.   Doe we not know your value is cried downe
Fourescore i'th hundred.
Bianca.   Oh sir I did love you
With such a fixed heart, that in that minute
Wherein you slighted, or contemn'd me rather,
I tooke a vow to obey your last decree,   380
And never more looke up at any hope
Should bring me comfort that way, and though since
Your Foster-mother, and the faire *Clarissa*
Have in the way of marriage despis'd you,
That hath not any way bred my revenge,
But compassion rather. I have found

364 these testifie ∧] F2; this testimony, F1

So much sorrow in the way to a chaste wedlock
That here I will set downe, and never wish
To come to'th journies end. Your suite to mee
Henceforth be ever silenc't.

Cæsario.   My *Bianca.*   390

Hostesse. Henceforward pray forbeare her and my house:
She's a poore vertuous wench, yet her estate
May weigh with yours in a gold balance.

Host.   Yes,
And her birth in any Heralds office in Christendome.

Hostesse. It may prove so: when you'l say, you have leapt a
Whiteing.   *Exeunt.* [*Manet* Cæsario.]

Enter Baptista *and* Mentivole.

Cæsario. How far am I growne behind hand with fortune?

Baptista. Here's *Cesario:*
My son sir is to morrow to be married
Unto the faire *Clarissa.*

Cæsario.   So.

Mentivole.   Wee hope
Youle be a gueste there?

Cæsario.   No I will not grace   400
Your triumph so much.

Baptista.   I will not tax your breeding.
But it alters not your birth sir, fare you well.

Mentivole. Oh sir doe not greive him, he has to much
Affliction already.   *Exeunt.*

Cæsario.   Every way scorn'd and lost,
Shame follow you for I am growne most miserable.

Enter a Sailor.

Sailor. Sir doe you know a Ladies son in towne here
They cal *Cesario?*

Cæsario.   Ther's none such I assure thee.

Sailor. I was told you were the man.

Cæsario.   Whats that to thee?

Sailor. A pox on't. You are melancholy, will you drink Sir?

Cæsario. With whom?

Sailor.   With mee Sir; despise not this pitcht Canvas;   410
  The time was wee have knowne them lined with *Spanish* Duckets;
  I have news for you.
Cæsario.   For me!
Sailor.   Not unlesse you'l drink;
  We are like our Sea provision, once out of pickle,
  We require abundance of drink; I have news to tell you
  That were you Prince, would make you send your mandate
  To have a thousand bonfires made 'ith City,
  And pist out agen with nothing but Greek wine.
Cæsario.   Come, I wil drink with thee howsoever.
Sailor.   And upon these terms I wil utter my mind to you.
                                           Exeunt.

        Enter Alberto, Prospero, Juliana, *and* Saylors.   V.i

Sailor.   Shall we bring your necessaries ashore my Lord?
Alberto.   Do what you please, I am land-sicke, worse by far
  Then ere I was at sea.
Prospero.   Collect your selfe.
Alberto.   O my most worthy *Prospero*, my best friend,
  The noble favor I receivd from thee
  In freeing me from the *Turks* I now accompt
  Worse than my death; for I shall never live
  To make requitall; what doe you attend for?
Sailor.   To understand your pleasure.
Alberto.   They doe mock me;
  I doe protest I have no kind of pleasure   10
  In any thing i'th world, but in thy friendship,
  I must ever except that.
Prospero.   Pray leave him, leave him.
                                    Exeunt Sailors.
Alberto.   The newes I heard related since my landing
  Of the division of my Family,
  How is it possible for any man
  To bear't with a set patience?
Prospero.   You have suffer'd
  Since your imprisonment more waighty sorrowes.
Alberto.   I, then I was a man of flesh and bloud,

                   627

Now I am made up of fire, to the full height
Of a deadly Calenture; ô these vild women   20
That are so ill preservers of mens honors,
They cannot governe their own honesties.
That I should thirty and odde winters feed
My expectation of a noble heire,
And by a womans falshood finde him now
A fiction, a meare dreame of what he was;
And yet I love him still.

Prospero.   In my opinion
The sentence (on this tryall) from the Duke
Was noble, to repaire *Cesarios* losse
With the marriage of your wife, had you been dead.   30

Alberto.   By your favor but it was not; I conceive
'Twas disparagment to my name, to have my widdow
Match with a Faulkners son, and yet beleev't
I love the youth still, and much pitty him.
I doe remember at my going to Sea,
Upon a quarrell, and a hurt receiv'd
From young *Mentivole*, my rage so farre
Oretopt my nobler temper, I gave charge
To have his hand cut off, which since I heard,
And to my comfort, brave *Cæsario*,   40
Worthyly prevented.

Prospero.   And 'twas nobly done.

Alberto.   Yet the revenge, for this intent of mine
Hath bred much slaughter in our families,
And yet my wife (which infinitly moanes me)
Intends to marry my sole heire *Clarissa*
To the head branch of the other faction.

Prospero.   Tis the meane to work reconcilement.

Alberto.   Betweene whom?

Prospero.   Your selfe, and the worthy *Baptista*.

Alberto.   Never.

Prospero.   O you have been of a noble and remarkable freindship,
And by this match tis generally in *Florence*   50
Hop'd, twill fully be reconcild; to me
'Twould be absolute content.

628

Juliana.   And to my selfe,
  I have maine interest in it.
Alberto.   Noble Sir,
  You may command my heart to breake for you
  But never to bend that way; poore *Cæsario*,
  When thou put'st on thy mournfull willow garland,
  Thy enemy shall be suted (I do vow)
  In the same livery: my *Cæsario*
  Loved as my foster child, though not my sonne,
  Which in some countryes formerly were barbarous,   60
  Was a name held most affectionate; thou art lost,
  Unfortunate young man, not only slighted
  Where thou received'st thy breeding, but since scorn'd
  Ith' way of marriage, by the poore *Bianca*
  The In-keepers daughter.
Prospero.   I have heard of that too;
  But let not that afflict you; for this Lady
  May happily deliver at more leasure
  A circumstance may draw a faire event,
  Better then you can hope for. For this present
  We must leave you, and shall visit you againe   70
  Within these two houres.
Alberto.   Ever to me most welcome,——

                   Enter Cæsario.

  O my *Cæsario.*
Cæsario.   I am none of yours Sir,
  So tis protested; and I humbly beg,
  Since tis not in your power to preserve me
  Any longer in a noble course of life,
  Give me a worthy death.
Alberto.   The youth is mad.
Cæsario.   Nay Sir, I will instruct you in a way
  To kill me honorably.
Alberto.   That were most strange.
Cæsario.   I am turning Pirate. You may be imployed
  By the Duke to fetch me in; and in a sea-fight   80
  Give me a noble grave.

Alberto.   Questionlesse he's mad; I would give any Doctor
A thousand crownes to free him from this sorrow.

Cæsario.   Here's the Physitian.   *Shewes a Poniard.*

Alberto.   Hold Sir, I did say
To free you from the sorrow, not from life.

Cæsario.   Why life and sorrow are unseparable.

Alberto.   Be comforted *Cæsario*, *Mentivole*
Shall not marry *Clarissa*.

Cæsario.   No Sir, ere he shall,
Ile kill him.

Alberto.   But you forfeit your own life then.

Cæsario.   Thats worth nothing.   90

Alberto.   *Cæsario*, be thy selfe, be mine *Cæsario*,
Make not thy selfe uncapable of that portion
I have full purpose to confer upon thee;
By falling into madnesse: beare thy wrongs
With noble patience, the afflicteds freind
Which ever in all actions crownes the end.

Cæsario.   You well awak'd me, nay recover'd me
Both to sence and full life; ô most noble sir,
Though I have lost my fortune, and lost you
For a worthy Father: yet I will not loose   100
My former vertue, my integrity
Shall not yet forsake me; but as the wilde Ivy,
Spredds and thrives better in some pittious ruin
Of tower, or defac'd Temple, then it does
Planted by a new building; so shall I
Make my adversity my instrument
To winde me up into a full content.

Alberto.   Tis worthily resolv'd; our first adventure
Is to stop the marriage; for thy other losses,
Practis'd by a womans malice, but account them   110
Like conjurers windes rais'd to a fearefull blast,
And doe some mischeife, but do never last.

                                                    Exeunt.

---

95 afflicteds] F2 (afflicted's); afflicted F1   97 awak'd] F2; awake F1

[V.ii]

Enter Forobosco *and* Clowne.

Clown.   Now sir, will you not acknowledge that I have mightily
advancte your practice?

Forobosco.   Tis confest, and I will make thee a great man for't.

Clown.   I take a course to do that my selfe, for I drinke sack in
abundance.

Forobosco.   O my rare rascall. We must remove.

Clown.   Whither?

Forobosco.   Any whither: *Europe* is to little to be cozned by us, I am
ambitious to goe to the *East-Indies*, thou and I to ride on our brace
of Elephants.   10

Clown.   And for my part I long to be in *England* agen; you wil never
get so much as in *England*, we have shifted many countryes, and
many names: but traunce the world over you shall never purse up
so much gold as when you were in *England*, and call'd your selfe
Doctor *Lambestones.*

Forobosco.   Twas an attractive name I confesse, women were then my
only admirers.

Clown.   And all their visits was either to further their lust, or reveng
injuries.

Forobosco.   You should have forty in a morning beleager my closett,   20
and strive who should be cozend first; amongst fourescore love-
sick waighting women that has come to me in a morning to learne
what fortune should betide them in their first marriage, I have
found above ninety-four to have lost their maidenheads.

Clown.   By their owne confession, but I was faine to be your male
midwife, and worke it out of them by circumstance.

Forobosco.   Thou wast, and yet for all this frequent resort of women
and thy handling of their urinalls and their cases, thou art not given
to lechery; what should be the reason of it? thou hast wholsome
flesh enough about thee; me thinkes the divell should tempt thee   30
too't.

Clown.   What need he do that, when he makes me his instrument to
tempt others.

Forobosco.   Thou canst not chuse but utter thy rare good parts; thou wast an excellent baude I acknowledge.

Clown.   Well, and what I have done that way——I will spare to speake of all you and I have done sir, and though we should——

Forobosco.   We will for *England*, thats for certaine.

Clown.   We shall never want there.

Forobosco.   Want? the Court of Wards shall want mony first, for I   40 professe my selfe Lord Paramount over fooles and madfolkes.

Clown.   Do but store your selfe with lyes enough against you come thither.

Forobosco.   Why thats all the familiarity I ever had with the Divell, my guift of lying, they say hees the Father of lyes, and though I cannot conjure, yet I professe my selfe to be one of his poore gossips. I will now reveale to thee a rare peece of service.

Clown.   What is it my most worshipful Doctor *Lambstones*.

Forobosco.   There is a Captaine come lately from Sea, they call *Prosper*, I saw him this morning through a chincke of wainscote   50 that divides my lodging and the Host of the house, withdraw my Host, and Hostesse, the faire *Biancha*, and an antient gentlewoman into their bedchamber; I could not overheare their conference, but I saw such a masse of gold and Jewels, and when he had done he loc't it up into a casket; great joy there was amongst them and forth they are gone into the city, and my Host told me at his going forth he thought he should not returne till after supper; now sir, in their absence will we fall to our picklocks, enter the chamber, seize the Jewels, and make an escape from *Florence*, and wee are made for ever.   60

Clown.   But if they should goe to a true conjurer, and fetch us back in a whirlewinde?

Forobosco.   Doe not beleeve there is any such fetch in Astrology, and this may be a meanes to make us live honest hereafter.

Clown.   Tis but an ill road too't that lyes through the high way of theeving.

Forobosco.   For indeed I am weary of this trade of fortune-telling, and meane to give all over, when I come into *England*, for it is a very ticklish quality.

Clown.   And ith end will hang by a twine thred.   70

Forobosco.   Besides the Island has too many of the profession, they
   hinder one anothers market.
Clown.   No, no, the pillory hinders their market.
Forobosco.   You know there the jugling captaine.
Clown.   I there's a sure carde.
Forobosco.   Onely the fore-man of their jury is dead, but he dyed like
   a Roman.
Clown.   Else tis thought he had made worke for the hangman.
Forobosco.   And the very *Ball* of your false prophets, hee's quasht
   too.   80
Clown.   He did measure the starres with a false yard, and may now
   travaile to *Rome* with a morter on's head to see if he can recover his
   mony that way.
Forobosco.   Come, come, lets fish for this casket, and to Sea presently.
Clown.   We shall never reach *London* I feare; my minde runs so much
   of hanging landing at *Wapping*.

                                                         Exeunt.

                         Enter Mariana.   [V.iii]

Mariana.   This well may be a day of joy long wish'd for
   To my *Clarissa*, shee is innocent.
   Nor can her youth but with an open bosome
   Meet *Himens* pleasing bounties, but to me
   That am invirond with black guilt and horror
   It does appeare a funerall: though promising much
   In the conception were hard to mannage
   But sad in the event; it was not hate
   But fond indulgence in me to preserve
   Cesarios threatned life in open court   10
   That forc'd me to disclaime him, choosing rather
   To rob him of his birth-right, and honor
   Then suffer him to run the hazard of
   Inrag'de *Baptistas* fury; while he lives,
   I know I have a sonne, and the Dukes sentence
   A while deluded, and this tempest over,

                    *6 funerall:] ~ ∧ F1–2

                              633

When he assures himselfe despaire hath seizd him,
I can relieve and raise him——

Knock within. Enter Baptista.

                              speake, who is it
That presses on my privacies? Sir your pardon.
You cannot come unwelcome, though it were   20
To reade my secret thoughts.
Baptista.   Lady to you
Mine shall be ever open; Lady said I,
That name keeps too much distance, sister rather
I should have stilde you, and I now may claime it,
Since our divided families are made one
By this blessed marriage; to whose honor comes
The Duke in person, waited on by all
The braveries of his Court, to witnesse it,
And then to be our ghests: is the bride ready
To meet and entertaine him?
Mariana.   She attends   30
The comming of your sonne.
Baptista.   Pray you bring her forth.
The Duke's at hand——Musick in her loud voyce,
Speakes his arrivall.
Mariana.   Shee's prepard to meet it.   *Exit.*

Enter Mariana, Clarissa *led by two Maides: at the other doore,*
Baptista *meetes with* Mentivole, *led by two Courtiers, the* Duke,
    Bishop; *diverse Attendants: (A Song) whilst they salute.*

Duke.   It were impertinent to wish you joy,
Since all joyes dwell about you, *Himens* torch
Was never lighted with a luckier omen,
Nor burnt with so much splendor: to defer
With fruitlesse complement, the meanes to make
Your certain pleasures lawfull to the world;
Since in the union of your hearts they are   40
Confirmd already; would but argue us

36 lighted] F2; slighted F1

634

A boaster of our favours: to the Temple
And there the sacred knot once tyde, all triumphs
Our Dukedome can affoord, shall grace your nuptialls.

Enter Alberto *and* Cæsario.

Baptista   On there.
Mentivole.   I hope it is not in the power
  Of any to crosse us now.
Alberto.   But in the breath
  Of a wrongd Father I forbid the bannes.
Cæsario.   What, doe you stand at gaze?
Baptista.   Risen from the dead!
Mariana.   Although the sea had vomitted up the figure
  In which thy better part livd long imprisond,   50
  True love despising feare, runs thus to meete it.
Clarissa.   In duty I kneele to it.
Alberto.   Hence vile wretches,
  To you I am a substance incorporeall,
  And not to be prophand, with your vile touch!
  That could so soone forget me, but such things
  Are neither worth my anger, nor reproofe.
  To you great sir, I turne my selfe and these
  Immediate Ministers of your government,
  And if in my rude language I transgresse;
  Ascribe it to the cold remembrance of   60
  My services, and not my rugged temper.
Duke.   Speake freely, be thy language ne're so bitter,
  To see thee safe *Alberto*, signes thy pardon.
Alberto.   My pardon? I can need none, if it be not
  Receivd for an offence. I tamely beare
  Wrongs, which a slave-born *Muscovite* would check at.
  Why if for treason I had beene deliverd
  Up to the hangmans Axe, and this dead trunck
  Unworthy of a Christian Sepulcher,
  Exposd a prey to feed the ravenous vulture;   70
  The memory of the much I oft did for you,

47 bannes] F2 (Banes); bands F1

Had you but any touch of gratitude,
Or thought of my deservings, would have stopd you
From these unjust proceedings.
Duke.   Heare the motives
That did induce us.
Alberto.   I have heard them all,
Your highnesse sentence, the whole Court abusd,
By the perjuries, and practise of this woman.
(Weepest thou Crocodile) my hopefull son,
Whom I dare sweare mine owne, degraded of
The honors that descend to him from me: 80
And from that in his love scornd by a creature
Whose base birth though made eminent by her beauty,
Might well have markd her out *Cesarios* servant,
All this I could have pardond and forgot;
But that my daughter with my whole estate
So hardly purchased, is assignd a dower
To one whose Father, and whole family
I so detest, that I would loose my essence
And be transformed to a Basiliske
To look them dead; to mee's an injury,   90
Admits no satisfaction.
Baptista.   Ther's none offerd.
Alberto.   Nor would not be accepted, though upon
Thy knees twere tenderd.
Mariana.   Now the storme grows high.
Baptista.   But that I thought thee dead, and in thy death
The brinie Ocean had entombd thy name;
I would have sought a wife in a Bordello
For my *Mentivole*, and gladly hugd
Her spurious Issue as my lawfull Nephewes,
Before his blood should ere have mixd with thine;
So much I scorne it.
Alberto.   I'll not bandy words,   100
But thus dissolve the contract.   [*Parts them.*]
Baptista.   There I meet thee,

And seize on whats mine owne.

Alberto.   For all my service,
Great Sir grant me the combat with this wretch,
That I may scourge his insolence.

Baptista.   I kneele for it.

Cæsario.   And to approve my selfe *Albertos* sonne,
I'le be his second upon any odds,
Gainst him that dare most of *Baptistas* race.

Mentivole.   Already upon honorable termes,
In me thou hast met thy better, for her sake
I'le adde no more.

Alberto.   Sir, let our swords decide it.   110

Mariana.   O stay Sir, and as you would hold the title
Of a just Prince, ere you grant licence to
These mad-mens fury, lend your private eare
To the most distres'd of women.

Duke.   Speake, tis granted.

                              He takes Mariana *aside.*

Clarissa.   In the meane time, let not *Clarissa* be
A patient looker on; though as yet doubtfull,
To whom to bend her knee first, yet to all
I stoop thus low in duty, and would wash
The dust of fury with my Virgin teares,
From his blessd feete, and make them beautifull   120
That would move to conditions of peace;
Though with a snaile like pace, they all are wingd
To beare you to destruction: reverend sirs,
Think on your ancient friendship cæmented
With so much bloud, but shed in noble action,
Divided now in passion for a brawle;
The makers blush to own. Much lov'd *Cæsario*,
Brother, or friend, (each title may prevaile,)
Remember with what tendernesse from our child-hood
Wee lov'd together, you preferring me   130
Before your selfe, and I so fond of you
That it begot suspition in ill mindes
That our affection was incestuous.
Thinke of that happy time, in which I know

That with your deerest blood you had prevented
This showre of teares from me; *Mentivole*,
My husband, registred in that bright star-chamber,
Though now on earth made strangers, be the example
And offer in one hande the peacefull Olive
Of concord, or if that can be denyed   140
By powerfull intercession in the other
Carry the *Hermian* rod and force atonement,
Now we will not bee all marble. Death's the worst then
And hee shall be my bridegroome.

Mentivole.   Hold *Clarissa*,
This loving violence I needs must offer
In spite of honor.

> *He snatches away her knife and sets it to his owne*
> *breast, she stayes his hand.*

Duke.   Was it to that end then
On your religion?

Mariana.   And my hope in heaven Sir.

                              [*The Duke and* Mariana *return.*]

Duke.   Wee then will leave entreaties, and make use
Of our authority, must I cry ai-me
To this unheard of insolence? in my presence   150
To draw your swords, and as all reverence
Thats due to majesty were forfeited,
Cherish this wildenesse! sheath them instantly,
And shew an alteration in your lookes,
Or by my power——

Alberto.   Cut of my head——

Baptista.   And mine,
Rather then heare of peace with this bad man.
I'le not alone give up my throat, but suffer
Your rage to reach my family.

                Enter Prospero, Juliana, Bianca.

Alberto.   And my name
To be no more remembred.

Duke.   What are these?
Cæsario. Biancha, tis *Biancha*, still *Biancha*:   160
    But strangely alter'd.
Baptista.   If that thirteene yeares
    Of absence could raze from my memory
    The figure of my freind, I might forget thee;
    But if thy Image be graven on my heart,
    Thou art my *Prospero.*
Prospero.   Thou my *Baptista!*
Duke.   A suddaine change!
Baptista.   I dare not aske deere freind
    If *Juliana* live! for thats a blessing
    I am unworthy of, but yet deny not
    To let me know the place she hath made happy
    By having there her sepulcher.   170
Prospero.   If your highnesse please to vouchsafe a patient eare
    Wee shall make a true relation of a story
    That shall call on your wonder.
Duke.   Speake, wee heare you.
Prospero.   *Baptistas* Fortune in the *Genoa* court,
    His banishment, with his faire wifes restraint
    You are acquainted with; what since hath follow'd
    I faithfully will deliver. Ere eight moones
    After *Baptistas* absence were compleate,
    Faire *Juliana* founde the pleasures that
    They had injoy'd together were not barren,   180
    And blushing at the burthen of her wombe,
    No father neere to owne it, it drew on
    A violent sicknesse, which call'd downe compassion
    From the angry Duke. Then carefull of her health,
    Physitians were enquir'd of, and their judgment
    Prescrib'd the Bathes of *Luca* as a meanes
    For her recovery; to my charge it pleas'd her
    To be committed; but as on the way
    Wee journy'd, those throwes only knowne to women
    Came thick upon her, in a private village.   190

184 Duke. Then ... health,] Seward; ~ , then ... ~ . F1–2

Baptista.   Shee died?

Prospero.   Have patience, she brought to the world
A hopefull daughter;for her bodies sicknesse
It soone decai'd, but the greife of her minde
Hourely increas'd, and life grew tedious to her;
And desperate ere to see you, she injoyn'd me
To place her in a *Greekish* Monastery,
And to my care gave up her pretty daughter.

Baptista.   What monastery? as a Pilgrim bare-foot,
Ile search it out.

Prospero.   Pray you interrupt me not,
Now to my fortunes; the girle well dispos'd of   200
With a faithful freind of mine, my cruell fate
Made me a prisoner to the *Turkish* gallies,
Where for twelve yeares, these hands tugd at the oare,
But fortune tyr'd at length with my afflictions,
Some ships of *Malta* mett the *Ottoman* fleete,
Charg'd them and boorded them, and gave me freedome.
With my deliverers I serv'd, and gott
Such reputation with the great Master
That he gave me command over a tall
And lusty ship, where my first happy service   210
Was to redeeme *Alberto* rumor'd dead,
But was like me surpris'd by *Cortugogly.*

Alberto.   I would I had dyed there.

Prospero.   And from him learning
Baptista liv'd, and their dissolved freindship,
I hois'd up sailes for *Greece,* found *Juliana*
A votary at her beades; having made knowne
Both that you liv'd, and where you were, she borrow'd
So much from her devotion as to wish me
To bring her to you; if the object please you,
With joy receave her.

Baptista.   Rage and fury leave me.   220
                                    Throwes away his sword.
I am so full of happines, there's no room left
To entertaine you, O my long lost Jewell,
Light of mine eyes, my soules strength.

Juliana.   My best Lord, having Embrac'd you thus,
  Death cannot fright me.
Baptista.   Live long to do so. Though I should fix here,
  Pardon me *Prospero* though I enquire
  My daughters fortune.
Prospero.   That your happinesse
  May be at all parts perfect, here she is!
Cæsario.   *Biancha* daughter to a princesse.
Prospero.   True;   230
  With my faithfull Host I left her, and with him
  Till now she hath resided, ignorant
  Both of her birth and greatnesse.
Baptista.   O my blest one.
  Joy upon joy over-whelmes me.
Duke.   Above wonder.
Alberto.   I doe begin to melt too, this strange story
  Workes much upon me.
Duke.   Since it hath pleas'd heaven
  To grace us with this miracle, I that am
  Heavens instrument here, determine thus; *Alberto*
  Be not unthankefull for the blessings showne you,
  Nor you *Baptista*; discord was yet never   240
  A welcome sacrifice; therefore rage layd by,
  Embrace as freinds, and let pass'd difference
  Be as a dreame forgotten.
Baptista.   Tis to me.
Alberto.   And me, and thus confirme it.
Duke.   And to tye it
  In bonds not to be broken, with the marriage
  Of young *Mentivole*, and faire *Clarissa*,
  So you consent great Lady, your *Biancha*
  Shall call *Cæsario* Husband.
Juliana.   Tis a motion
  I gladly yeeld too.
Cæsario.   One in which
  You make a sadd man happy.   *Offers to kneele.*
Bianca.   Kneele not, all forgiven.   250
Duke.   With the Duke your Uncle I will make attonement,

And will have no denyall.
Mariana.   Let this day
Be still held sacred.

Enter Host, Forobosco, Clowne *and Officers.*

Host.   Now if you can conjure, let the Divell unbind you.
Forobosco.   Wee are both undone.
Clown.   Already wee feele it.
Host.   Justice sir.
Duke.   What are they?
Prospero.   I can resolve you, slaves freed from the Gallyes
By the Viceroy of *Sicilia.*
Duke.   Whats their offence?   260
Host.   The robbing me of all my plate and Jewels,
I meane the attempting of it.
Clown.   Please your grace I will now discover this varlet in earnest;
this honest pestilent rogue, profest the art of conjuring, but all the
skill that ever he had in the black art was in making a seacole fire;
only with wearing strange shapes he begot admiration amongst
fooles and women.
Forobosco.   Wilt thou peach thou varlet?
Duke.   Why does he gogle with his eyes, and stauke so?
Clown.   This is one of his Magicall raptures.   270
Forobosco.   I doe vilifie your censure, you demand if I am guilty,
whir sayes my cloake by a tricke of legerdemaine, now I am not
guilty, I am guarded with innocence, pure silver lace I assure you.
Clown.   Thus have I read to you your vertues, which notwithstand-
ing I would not have you proud of.
Forobosco.   Out thou concealement of tallow, and counterfeit
Mummia.
Duke.   To the Gallyes with them both.
Clown.   The onely sea physick for a knave is to be basted in a gally
with the oyle of a Bulls peesell.   280
Forobosco.   And will not you make a soure face at the same sauce,
sirra? I hope to finde thee so leane, in one fortnight thou mayest be
drawne by the eares through the hoop of a firkin.

268 peach] F2; preach F1   273 guarded] *i.e.,* garded

Duke.   Divide them and away with them to'th Gallyes.
Clown.   This will take downe your pride Jugler.
Duke.   This day that hath given birth to blessings beyond hope,
　　Admits no criminal sentence: to the Temple
　　And there with humblenesse praise heavens bounties;
　　For blessings nere discend from thence, but when
　　A sacrifice in thankes ascends from men.   290

　　　　　　　　　　　　　　　　　　　Exeunt omnes.

284 them to'th] F2; them them F1

TEXTUAL NOTES

I.i

110 serve, and sue to] 'To serve and sue' is 'to do service and homage' (*O.E.D.*, Sue, *v.* 19), an expression perhaps obsolete by the early seventeenth century, although the editor of F2 apparently recognized it. F1's 'to', not required for metre, may thus be a sophistication, which F2 nevertheless retained, altering 'to' to 'too'.

250 eare] A badly inked or partially broken type in F1 led to the misprint 'care' in F2, which was followed by editors up to Weber.

II.ii

55 Cherelly] By quoting from Howell's *Vocabulary* (1659), Lucas identifies this as 'Claret wine; Vino chiaretto, o chiarello'.

77–78 Ere . . . pray.] Editors from Colman to Dyce have assigned this speech to the Host, as if he were giving a direction to his wife. Allowing for the exaggeration of the Clown's humorous request, the clearest meaning is simply that he be not forgotten when it comes to giving out breakfast.

III.i

98 well, Ile] Owing to the compositor's habit of omitting words, the simplest repair of this crux is to add the pronoun 'Ile' even though there is a chance that 'well' is a corruption of some other word. The context makes it unlikely that 'we'll' is the word.

III.ii

67 Lady on.] Immediately below, F1 prints '*Maria*. How ever' followed on a separate line by '*Bap*. A Faulkners sonne.' This interruption is a mystery since Cæsario's birth has not yet been mentioned. One may only speculate how it got in the text. A possible though unmetrical position for it would be after line 116, but the odds seem to favour its being a false start and not a legitimate part of the completed text.

233 then] Seward's conjecture for F1–2 'thee' has been generally accepted without comment except that 'learne thee' can mean 'teach thee'. The propriety of emending 'thee' to 'then' rests on the person addressed by Mariana. Clarissa has been the last speaker but the remark is not appropriate for her, nor is it especially for Cæsario, who has given no sign of further needing Mariana's help. In fact, Mariana most appropriately addresses herself, in keeping with her preoccupation in the latter part

of the scene with her own plight. The line, then, becomes a summary of her preparation to face the extreme distress she will feel in the future.

IV.i

198 they]   The lack of an antecedent for this pronoun caused editors to emend to 'which', to 'nay', and to 'yea'. Lucas suggests that 'the confusion may be to two alternative versions – *Those virtues . . . they appear'd* and *that goodnesse . . . which* should have been followed not by *they*, but *it*' (*Webster*, IV, 236). Professor Hoy, noticing the *ye*, thinks the passage is a Fletcherian original 'worked over by the revising hand of Ford' (*Studies in Bibliography*, XIII, 102).

IV.ii

272 cat]   No rational suggestion appears why 'cat' instead of 'frog' is used here. It may be a simple *non sequitur* or else an unrevised remnant from an earlier version of the scene.

V.ii

13 traunce]   This word is a version of F2's *trance*, 'to move about actively or briskly; to prance or skip' (*O.E.D.*, Trance, *v.*2; see also Trounce, *v.*2).

V.iii

6 funerall:]   Lines 6–8 are so corrupt as to defy emendation. It would seem that matter is missing here that cannot be replaced. The sense, however, is clear enough.

EMENDATIONS OF ACCIDENTALS

Prologue

7 sweet] F2; *sweett* F1

I.i

I.i] *Actus primus. Scænaprima.* F1; *Actus Primus. Scæna Prima.* F2
2 In] F2; in F1
16–17 selfe∧ ... thoughts,] ∼ , ... ∼ ∧ F1–2
24 Jewell,] F2; ∼ ∧ F1
84 presents, ... contemnd;] ∼ ; ... ∼ , F1–2
86 Muletiers,] *Muletiers.* F1–2
119 *Enter* ...] F1–2 *place below* line 117a
129 abundance; ... Heaven,] ∼ , ... ∼ ; F1; ∼ ; ... ∼ ; F2
133–134 water, ... delicates:] ∼ : ... ∼ , F1; ∼ , ... ∼ , F2
167 ghastly.] ∼ ; F1–2
168 must, if] F2; must. If F1
190 conquests∧] ∼ : F1–2
192 They ... Knight] F1–2 *line:* else. | No
200 And ... remember,] F1–2 *line:* sute: | I
202 rescue] F2; resceu F1
212 Neece] F2; *Neece* F1
215–216 Pray ... theame.] *one line in* F1–2
219–220 How? ... Lady?] *one line in* F1–2
220–221 Yes, ... Madam] *one line in* F1–2
225–226 I ... it.] *one line in* F1–2
228 Your] F2; your F1
248–249 Hee's ... relation.] *one line in* F1–2
252–253 Nay ... private.] *one line in* F1–2
254 vanishd, ... allowd∧] F2; ∼ ∧ ... ∼ , F1
261 *Dutchmen*] F2; Dutchmen F1
273 Viceroy] F2; *Vireroy* F1
274–275 me; ... horsmanship,] ∼ , ... ∼ ; F1; ∼ ... ∼ ; F2
280–281 You ... beaten.] *one line in* F1–2
281–282 Tush ... contrary.] *one line in* F1–2
282 controversie,] ∼ . F1; ∼ ∧ F2
284 *Enter* Clarissa.] F1–2 *place as line* 283.1
286–287 Heaven; ... brightenesse:] ∼ : ... ∼ ; F1; ∼ , ... ∼ ; F2
291–292 you; ... fondnesse,] ∼ , ... ∼ ; F1–2
294–295 I ... you. I *one line in* F1–2
299 *Exit.*] *in line* 298 F1–2
305–306 Who ... lights.] *one line in* F1–2
306 uselesse] uselsse F1; useless F2
309 Sunnes?] ∼ . F1–2
309 Hyperboles] *Hyperboles* F1–2
319 faith,] ∼ ∧ F1–2
321–322 Such ... Lady——] *one line in* F1–2
322 Lady——] ∼ , F1–2
323 period,] ∼ . F1; ∼ ; F2
331–332 Oh ... musick.] *one line in* F1–2
332 A playne] F2; a Playne F1
340 'twill] F2; ∧twill F1

646

344–345 So ... it.] *one line in* F1–2   352 you;] ~ , F1–2
349 shooe——] ~ , F1; ~ : F2

I.ii

0.1 *and*] F2; | *And* F1   31 Magazine] F2; *Magazine* F1
25–26 With ... affront,] *one line in*   31–33 And ... service.] F1–2 *line*: And
   F1–2   ... up, | And ... service.
26 affront,] ~ ‸ F1–2   32 up,] F2; ~ . F1
30–31 And ... Magazine.] *one line in*   39 invites] F2; jnvites F1
   F1–2   40 more.] ~ , F1–2
30 too,] F2; ~ ‸ F1

I.iii

0.1 *three*] 3. F1–2   21 No,] ~ ‸ F1; ~ ; F2
2 *Mentivole* ‸] F2; ~ . F1   22–23 Your ... then.] *one line in* F1–2
3–4 That ... him.] *one line in* F1–2   45 From] F2; from F1
6 whisper,] F2; ~ . F1   57 intreaties] F2; jntreaties F1
9.1 *Enter* ....] F1–2 *place as line* 7.1   63 instantly] F2; jnstantly F1
9.1 Cæsario] F2; *Cesario* F1   63 tearms,] F2; ~ ‸ F1
10 lookes] F2; loookes F1   66 thee ‸] ~ : F1–2
21–22 No ... it.] *one line in* F1–2

II.i

II.i] *Actus secundus. Scæna prima.* F1;   50 By ... flattery.] F1–2 *line*: oyle |
   Actus Secundus. | *Scæna Prima.* F2   Your
0.1, 38 *Physitian*] F2; *Physition* F1   57–58 No ... fury:] *one line in* F1–2
4–5 My ... daies.] *one line in* F1–2   61–62 (Like ... lighted) ... to't,] (~
5 ten] F2; 10. F1   ... ~ ‸ ... ~) F1–2 ±
9 *Florence*] F2; Florence F1   61 th'] F2 ('th') 'th F1
18 *Enter* ....] F1–2 *place as line* 16.1   66–67 You ... confidence.] *one line in*
18–19 Oh ... Sir?] *one line in* F1–2   F1–2
22–23 I ... wound?] *one line in* F1–2   70–71 Nor ... you;] *one line in* F1–2
22 Gentlemen,] F2; *Gentl.* F1   75 heart,] F2; ~ . F1
23 wound?] ~ ‸ F1; ~ . F2   83 fiftie] 50. F1–2
24–25 But ... him.] F1–2 *line*: But ...   107 Within there.] *Within there.* F1–2
   friend. | And ... him.   (*as part of s.d.*)
27 there's] F2; ther'es F1   107–108 Looke ... Master.] F1–2 *line*:
33 i'th] F2 (i'th'); 'ith F1   Looke you! | Here's ... Master.
39 *Enter* ....] F1–2 *place as line* 37.1   112–113 Not ... to't.] *one line in* F1–2
42 why,] ~ ‸ F1–2   116–117 You ... honour.] *one line in*
47–48 Rather ... them.] *one line in*   F1–2
   F1–2   118–119 My ... action.] *one line in* F1–2

647

119–120 Then ... stickler.] *one line in*
    F1–2
124 *Dutch man*] Dutch man F1–2
127.1 Cæsario] F2; *Cesario* F1
134–135 My ... condition.] *one line in*
    F1–2
141–142 It ... heart.] *one line in* F1–2
150–151 By ... not.] *one line in* F1–2

158–159 Therefore ... it.] *one line in*
    F1–2
162 Fare you well.] *ital. and flush right*
    in F1–2
163–165 To ... fighting.] F1–2 *line:* To
    ... me, │ I ... his │ Use of fighting.
168 fled?] F2; ~ ∧ F1
169 *Cæsario*] *Cesario* F1–2

II.ii

1–2 Thy ... Witch.] F1–2 *line:* Hos-
    teria, │ Is
4 Conjurer!] ~ ? F1–2
5 title?] F2; ~ . F1
14 armes,] ~ ∧ F1–2
15–16 As ... Traveller?] F1–2 *line:* As
    ... borne, │ Ile ... trick. │ And ...
    Traveller.
16 trick.] ~ , F1; ~ ; F2
16 Traveller?] F2; ~ . F1
26–27 So ... fashion.] F1–2 *line:*
    understood: │ But
33 witnesse?] ~ . F1–2
37 worm!] ~ ? F1–2
41 cuminseed] cummin-│seed F1–2
46 *Aretines*;] ~ , F1; ~ : F2
56–57 A ... here?] F2; *prose in* F1
62 comming; ... did,] ~ , ... ~ ;
    F1–2
67, 71 *Hostesse*] *Hostis* F1–2
67 daughter!] F2; ~ ? F1
71–72 Leave ... over.] F1–2 *line:*

    Leave ... prating, │ And ... over.
72–73 Peace ... guest.] *one line in* F1–2
74–75 My ... house.] F1–2 *line:* Land-
    lord! │ And
74 Landlord!] ~ ? F1–2
76 Breakfast ... stomack.] F1–2 *line:*
    Sir; │ It
77–78 And ... pray.] F1–2 *line:*
    Oyster. │ Ere
79–81 We ... enough.] F1–2 *line:* We
    ... you; │ Now ... fellowes. │ Nine
    ... come │ Yet ... enough.
84–85 Marry ... impossibilities.] F1–2
    line: Marry ... diseases, │ Recovery
    ... goods, │ And ... impossibilities.
98 butterboxes] butter-│boxes F1–2
101 *Dutchman*] F2; Dutchman F1
106–107 afore-hand] F2; afore- │ hand
    F1
109 *Italians*] F2; Italians F1
121 Jews-trump] Jews-│trump F1–2

II.iii

5–6 Yes ... perform't.] *one line in*
    F1–2

12 And] F2; and F1
13 Above] F2; above F1

II.iv

3–5 My ... windowe.] F1–2 *line:* My
    ... wash't │ I ... windowe.
5 Tis] F2 ('tis); ti's F1
6 Tis ... Tis] T'is ... T'is F1; 'Tis ...

    'Tis F2
12 Tis] T'is F1; 'Tis F2
13 same.——] ~ . ∧ F1–2
19 it] F2; ir F1

20–21 Was ... condition?] *one line in*
F1–2
20 *Mentivole*] *Mentivola* F1–2
51 *Enter* ....] F1–2 *place as line* 51b
52–53 Tis ... dead.] F1–2 *line:* Tis ...
sorrow, | Wherein ... mainest, |
Your ... dead.
52 Tis] T'is F1; 'Tis F2

54–55 I ... drownd.] F1–2 *line:* I ...
drown'd, | Most ... drownd.
57 Calme] F2; calme F1
65–66 I ... former.] *one line in* F1–2
66–67 And ... together.] *one line in*
F1–2
72–73 Let ... them.] *one line in* F1–2
79–80 Both ... injury.] *one line in* F1–2

III.i

III.i] *Actus tertius Scæna prima.* F1;
Actus Tertius. | *Scæna Prima.* F2
12 Host.] ~ , F1–2
22 thirteen?] 13. F1–2
27 *French ... English*] French ...
English F1–2
33 *Madonnas*] F2; *Madonuas* F1
38 chamber;] ~ , F1–2
41 *Switzer ... Italian*] F2; Switzer ...
Italian F1
50 fourth] F2; 4th F1
55 at 'em,] F2; at 'em ∧ F1
61.1 *Enter* ....] F1–2 *place as line* 62.1
69 *Alastors*] F2; Alastors F1
71 *Stygian*] F2; Stygian F1
72 *Acherontick*] F2; Acherontick F1
75 can.] ~ , F1–2
78 Signior.] ~ , F1–2
81 grossenesse;] ~ , F1–2
82 practise,] F2; ~ ∧ F1
89–90 Discharge ... answerd.] F1–2
line: wages! | Ile
97 *Homoteleuton*] *Homotolenton* F1–2
105 Virgin: ... sweetnesse,] ~ , ...
~ : F1–2

111, 114 one;] ~ , F1–2
117–118 eye, ... dance;] ~ ; ... ~ ,
F1–2
121–124 By ... -games.] F1–2 *line:* By
... so | Ridiculous ... their |
Miserable ... here, | Then ...
-games.
130–131 To ... muster,] F1–2 *line:* it; |
You
131 See they muster.] *ital. like s.d.* F1–2
144.2 *dance,*] F2; ~ . F1
145–146 Well ... sides.] F1–2 *line:*
done, | One
151–152 With ... daughter.] *prose in*
F1–2
162 time,] ~ : F1–2
165 womans;] ~ .F1–2
167–168 Deed ... mee,] *one line in* F1–2
169–170 To ... one.] *one line in* F1–2
175–176 I ... it.] *one line in* F1–2
196 resolution;] ~ , F1–2
204 triumph] F2; rriumph F1
219–221 As ... thus.] F1–2 *line:* As ...
vertue. | Pray ... thus.
222 sweare——] F2; ~ .——F1

III.ii

27.1 *Enter* ....] F1–2 *place as line* 26.1
27.1 *door,*] F2; ~ ∧ F1
36 Advocate,] F2; ~ ∧ F1
37 divided ∧] ~ . F1–2
41 mercy;] ~ , F1–2

46 My ... man,] F1–2 *line:* plea; |
Stand
48–49 *Alberto ... husband*] *one line in*
F1–2
55 all,] ~ ∧ F1–2

57, 189, 194, 201 Madam] *Madam*
   F1–2

75 hopes] F2; hops F1

76 issue; ... it,] F2; ~ , ... ~ ; F1

83 greedinesse ∧] F2; ~ ; F1

85 Lord; ... goodnesse,] F2; ~ , ...
   ~ ; F1

87 feares:] ~ , F1–2

88 neer] F2 (near); nee'r F1

98 Prince,] F2; ~ ∧ F1

122 Since] F2; Sinc F1

160 truth?] ~ . F1–2

168 Tis] T'is F1; 'Tis F2

170 prerogative] F2 (Prerogative);
   preogative F1

173 refusall,] F2; ~ ∧ F1

182 memory;] F2; ~ ∧ F1

192–193 Looke ... faire.] *one line in*
   F1–2

194–195 Tyranny ... derision,] *one line
   in* F1–2

195 justice.] ~ , F1–2

206–207 Of ... blame.] *one line in* F1–2

207 blame] F2; blam F1

208–209 You ... freind.] *one line in*
   F1–2

209 Can] F2; can F1

214 report,] ~ ∧ F1–2

223–224 I ... deserts.] *one line in* F1–2

228–229 These ... disperst.] *one line in*
   F1–2

IV.i

IV.i] *Actus quartus Scæna prima.* ; *Actus
   Quartus.* | *Scæna Prima.* F2

0.1 Cæsario] *Cesario* F1–2

2 know ∧] ~ , F1–2

3 Pleasures ... high] F1–2 *line:*
   bounds. | I

5 injury ∧] F2; ~ ? F1

6 gratefulnesse] F2; gratfulnesse F1

15–16 Yours? ... Lord.] *one line in*
   F1–2

15 Yours?] F2; ~ – F1

16–17 Please ... readily] *one line in*
   F1–2

18–19 Saucy ... breeding.] *one line in*
   F1–2

19 matter?] F2; ~ ∧ F1

20 Biancha,—— ~ , ∧ F1–2

20 *Exeunt* Servants.] *Exit Ser.* F1–2

24 guesse] F2 (guess); gusse F1

25–26 Prethee ... maide.] *one line in*
   F1–2

29–30 What ... wherein?] *one line in*
   F1–2

33–34 Greive ... all?] *one line in* F1–2

37 My] F2; my F1

37–38 If ... too.] *one line in* F1–2

38 it?] F2; ~ , F1

38 thee,] ~ . F1–2

39 My ... happy,] F1–2 *line:* maid, | If

54 wench?] F2; ~ ∧ F1

56 I ... was.] F1–2 *line:* misse | What

63 am.] F2; ~ , F1

65–66 Pretty ... alas.] *one line in* F1–2

66 alas,] F2; ~ . F1

78 I ... worthy] F1–2 *line:* yours. |
   Meane

82 Your] F2; your F1

86 *Biancha*] F2; Biancha F1

88 possessions,] F2; ~ . F1

90 againe; ... too,] ~ , ... ~ ; F1–2

92 t'ee] F2; tee F1

93–94 Pitty ... more.] *one line in* F1–2

98 for] F2; fo F1

101 *Biancha!*] F2; Biancha? F1

101–102 Harmelesse ... with?] F1–2
   line: unskild, | What

103 innocent,] ~ . F1–2

104 My] my F1–2

110 Y'are ... whimpering,] F1–2 *line:*
   freely. | Come

110 freely.] ~ , F1–2

110 whimpering,] ~ ∧ F1–2

115, 130, 151 *Cesario*] F2; Cesario F1
128 infamy——] ~ , F1; ~ . F2
128 To] F2; to F1
138 t'ee] F2; Tee F1
149 Duke_∧] ~ . F1–2
151 With] F2; with F1
160 authority?] F2; ~ _∧ F1
163 loose,] ~ _∧ F1–2
171–172 I . . . you.] *one line in* F1–2
174–175 Pray . . . greife.] *one line in* F1–2
184 away.] ~ , F1–2
188 her,] ~ ; F1–2
189 consent,] ~ ; F1–2
194–195 To . . . throat.] *one line in* F1–2
196 Sir,] ~ . F1–2

200 *Enter* . . . .] F1–2 *place as line* 199.1
200–201 Left . . . derision.] *one line in* F1–2
201 d'ee] F2; dee F1
204–205 Wee . . . contract.] *one line in* F1–2
205–206 With . . . man?] *one line in* F1–2
206 *Clarissas_∧*] ~ , F1–2
210–211 But . . . Lady?] *one line in* F1–2
211 too_∧ . . . Lady?] F2; ~ ? ~ , F1
216–217 Be . . . favour.] *one line in* F1–2
218–219 And . . . freinds.] *one line in* F1–2
220 here's] F2; heres F1
222 fate,] ~ . F1; ~ : F2

IV.ii

1–172 Come . . . attractive.] F1–2 *print prose as rough verse*
5 Hee's] F2; Hees F1
6 *German*] German F1–2
7 hee'd] F2; heed F1
12 *Kelly*] Kelly F1–2
12 *Germany*] Germany F1–2
19 hee's] F2 (he's); hees
25 conjurers:] F2; ~ _∧ F1
28 'em] F2; _∧em F1
28 hurrying] F2 (Hurrying); hurring F1
30, 89, 92 four] 4 F1–2
30 wheeles,] ~ _∧ F1–2
30 *Spanish*] Spanish F1–2
37 Host,] F2; ~ _∧ F1
40 breaking's] F2; breakings F1
46 questions, . . . them?] ~ ? . . . ~ , F1; ~ ; . . . ~ ? F2
55 it:] F2; ~ , F1
56 exactly——] ~ , F1; ~ . F2
60 twelve] 12 F1–2
62 Here's] F2; Heres F1
65, 115, 163 There's] F2; Theres F1
70 *Italy*] Italy F1–2
80 mouth.] F2; ~ , F1

89 *Amsterdam*] F2; Amsterdam F1
107, 116 nine] 9 F1–2
114 *Holland*] F2; Holland F1
114 licenc'd?] F2; ~ . F1
130 'em;] ~ , F1–2
132 see; . . . fashions——] F2; ~ _∧ . . . ~ . F1
134 *Moone*] Moone F1–2
146 *China*:] F2; ~ , F1
152 *Europe*] Europe F1–2
163–164 twenty . . . a hundred] 20 . . . 100 F1–2
170 fifteen] 15 F1–2
171 manchet:] F2; ~ , F1
181 *Garguentuas*] F2; Garquentuas F1
192 Sir?] F2; ~ . F1
193 *French*] French F1–2
221 his Physicke,] ~ ~ ; F1–2
226 *dutch*] ducth F1; Dutch F2
231 *Lapland*] F2; Lapland F1
237 *welch*] welch F1–2
239 twice] F2; twince F1
265 stark] F2; strark F1
269 are] F2; ar F1
272 sport:] ~ , F1–2
284.2 *four*] 4. F1–2

305 let's] F2; lets F1
311 matter,] ~ ˄ F1–2
336.1 Enter ....] F1–2 place in line 333
337 Frankford] F2; Frankford F1
346 Signior] Signior F1–2
351–353 Interest ... condition.] prose in F1–2
354.1 Enter ... Hostesse.] F1–2 place as line 353.1
367–368 For ... gotten.] one line in F1–2
368–369 Then ... world,] one line in F1–2
372 forsaken] F2; fosaken F1
393–394 Yes ... Christendome.] one line in F1–2

395 It ... Whiteing.] F1–2 line: so: | When
395 Exeunt.] Exit. F1–2
399–400 Wee ... there?] one line in F1–2
400–401 No ... much.] one line in F1–2
403–404 Oh ... already.] F1–2 line: Oh ... him, | He ... already.
405 Shame ... miserable.] F1–2 line: you | For
405.1 Enter ....] F1–2 place below line 404a
410–412 With mee ... you.] prose in F1–2
411 Spanish] Spanish F1–2
414–415 Ī ... mandate] F1–2 line: Prince, | Would

V.i

V.i] Actus Quintus. Scæna prima. F1; Actus Quintus. | Scæna Prima. F2
0.1 Alberto] F2; Alberoto F1
6 Turks] Turks F1–2
31 not;] ~ , F1–2
32 'Twas] T'was F1–2
52–53 And ... it.] one line in F1–2
53–54 Noble ... you] one line in F1–2
58 livery:] ~ , F1–2
69–71 Better ... houres.] F1–2 line: Better ... for. | For ... you, | And

... houres.
71.1 Enter ....] F1–2 place below line 71a
71 Ever ... Cæsario.] one line in F1–2
72–73 I ... beg,] F1–2 line: I ... protested; | And ... beg,
79 Pirate.] ~ , F1–2
88–89 No ... him.] one line in F1–2
94 madnesse:] F2; ~ , F1
97–98 me, ... life;] ~ ; ... ~ , F1–2
105 building;] F2; ~ – F1

V.ii

8 Europe] F2; Europe F1
9 East-Indies] F2; East-Indies F1
11, 14, 38, 69 England] F2; England F1
15 Lambestones] Lambe-|stones F1; Lambe-|stones F2
21 first;] ~ , F1–2
24 ninety-four] 94 F1–2
29 lechery;] ~ , F1–2
36 way ——] ~ ˄ F1–2
48 Lambstones] Lamb-|stones F1; Lamb-|stones F2
49–52 There ... Host, and] F1–2 line:

There ... Sea, | They ... morning | Through ... lodging | And ... and
50 Prosper,] F2; ~ ˄ F1
67 fortune-telling] fortune-|telling F1–2
75 there's] F2; theres F1
79 Ball] F2; Ball F1
82 Rome] F2; Rome F1
85–86 We ... Wapping.] F1–2 line: feare; | My
85 London] F2; London F1
86 Wapping] F2; wapping F1

V.iii

4 *Himens*] F2 (*Hymens*); Himens F1
8 event;] ～ , F1–2
14 fury; ... lives,] ～ , ... ～ ; F1–2
18 *Knock* ....] F1–2 *place as line* 17.1
28 Court] F2; Coutt F1
29 ghests:] ～ , F1–2
30–31 She ... sonne.] *one line in* F1–2
32 Duke's] F2; Dukes F1
37 splendor:] ～ , F1–2
41–2 already; ... favours:] ～ : ... ～ ;
F1–2
43 triumphs] t'riumphs F1
54 touch!] ～ ? F1–2
66 *Muscovite*] F2; Muscovite F1
69–70 Sepulcher, ... vulture;] ～ ; ...
～ , F1–2
74–75 Heare ... us.] *one line in* F1–2
86 dower‿] ～ ; F1–2
88–90 detest, ... dead;] ～ ; ... ～ ,
F1–2
92–93 Nor ... tenderd.] F1–2 *line:*
accepted, | Though
100–101 I'll ... contract.] *one line in*
F1–2
101–102 There ... owne.] *one line in*
F1–2
116 on;] ～ , F1–2
121 peace; ～ , F1–2
127 own. Much ... *Cæsario*,] ～ , much
... ～ . F1–2
136 me;] F2; ～ ‿ F1
139 Olive] *Olive* F1–2
143 Death's] F2; Deaths F1
144–146 Hold ... honor.] F1–2 *line:*
Hold ... must | Offer ... honor‿
146–147 Was ... religion?] *one line in*
F1–2
153 Cherish] F2; cherish F1
154 And] F2; and F1
154–155 And ... power——] *one line*
in F1–2
155 power——] ～ ‿ F1–2
155 head——] ～ ‿ F1; ～ . F2
155–156 And ... man.] *one line in* F1–2

158–159 And ... remembred.] *one line*
in F1–2
158 Bianca] *Biancha* F1–2
160–161 *Biancha* ... alter'd.] *one line in*
F1–2
165 *Baptista*!] ～ ? F1–2
171–172 If ... story] F1–2 *line:* patient |
Eare
177 deliver. Ere] deliver, ere F1–2
184 Duke] F2; *Duke* F1
185 Physitians] F2: *Physitians* F1
194–195 her; ... you,] ～ , ... ～ ; F1–2
196 *Greekish*] F2; Greeekish F1
200 of] F2; off F1
202 *Turkish*] F2: Turkish F1
203 twelve] 12 F1–2
205 *Ottoman*] F2; Ottaman F1
206 freedome.] F2; ～ ‿ F1
220 me.] F2; ～ – F1
221 there's] F2; theres F1
226 so. Though ... here,] ～ ‿ though
... ～ . F1–2
227–228 Pardon ... fortune.] *one line in*
F1–2
230–233 True; ... greatnesse.] F1–2
line: True; ... her, | And ...
resided, | Ignorant ... greatnesse.
230 True;] ～ ‿ F1–2
233–234 O ... me.] *one line in* F1–2
236 pleas'd] F2; ples'd F1
248–249 Tis ... too.] *one line in* F1–2
249–250 One ... happy.] *one line in*
F1–2
251–252 With ... denyall.] *one line in*
F1–2
252–253 Let ... sacred.] *one line in* F1–2
253.1 *Enter* ....] F1–2 *place below line*
252a
263 earnest;] ～ , F1–2
279 is] F2; ia F1
286–288 This ... bounties;] *prose in*
F1–2
286 blessings‿] F2; ～ ; F1
287 sentence:] F2; ～ , F1

HISTORICAL COLLATION

[NOTE: The following editions have been collated for substantives: F1 (Folio 1647), F2 (Folio 1679), L (*Works*, 1711, intro. Gerard Langbaine), S (*Works*, 1750, ed. Seward), C (*Works*, 1778, ed. George Colman the Younger), W (*Works*, 1812, ed. Henry Weber), D (*Works*, 1843, ed. Alexander Dyce), Lc (*Works of John Webster*, 1922, ed. F. L. Lucas.)]

The Prologue

6 *For*] *In* S

I.i

4 lost] last F1–2, L	215 you] *omit* S
20 me] it S	221 fatall] so fatal S
48 ardor] order F1–2, L	234 wife] wife [was] D, Lc
59 see] say F1	240 of] or F1–2, L–W
87 And] *omit* S	250 eare] care F2, L–C
87 cry] want F2, L	254 vanishd] being vanished S
110 to] too F2+	258 injoyd] employ'd L, S
131 vines] times F1–2, W	265 our] their F2, L–D
197 bewitch] bewitch'd F2, L–W	268 rival] rivald F1
210 streamers] streames F1–2, L	285 *Cynthia*] *Cynthian* F1
212 her] their F1	

I.ii

2 *Turke*] *Turks* F2, L, S	38 *Alberto* be] *Alberto.* Be F1–2, L
11 you] yours S	39 Tis] His F1
17 oyld] old F1	

I.iii

3 this] his S, Lc	36 frowne] frowns D, Lc
5 'slight] light F1	42 murderd?] murder? F1
11 wager] wages F1	59 begun] began F1–2, L–W
15 more] no more F1–2, C, W	65 he] *omit* F1

654

II.i

20 me in] in my F1
28 give] give him F1
42 yours] your F1
49 a Courtier] Courtier F1
81 Of] To S

82 continued] constant S
103 Thou] That L, S
132 Sir;] omit S
169 *Cæsario?*] *Cæsario.* (*sp. pref.*) F2

II.ii

30 Pocks] Pockets F1
36 comes] some C, W
70 When] *Hostess.* When S
71 *Hostesse.*] omit S
77 Ere] *Host.* Ere C–D
87 hear] here F1
90 travell'd] tralaunct F1
101 indeed] omit S

103 *Swit3er, twas*] Switzert, was F1
109 more] most W
121 stale] steale F1, L; staele F2
121 but] by L
122 I] and I D
122 and] omit D
124 purely] piously S

II.iii

1 *Baptista*] *Ment.* F1
2 A] omit S

18 must] omit S
20 eminent] imminent C–D

II.iv

1 *Clarissa.* Brother] *Cæsario.* F1
1 Brother] omit F1, Lc
2 *Cæsario.*] omit F1
3 miss] wish F1

9 *Cæsario.*] omit F1–2
10 I] *Cæs.* I F1–2
61 a moment] moment F1–2
76 afore] before C, W

III.i

7 proverb,] proverb, that S
12 Girle, girle, girle] Girle, girle W
14 hear] here F1
19 my] mine L–C
32 A] The D
36 from] omit L; at S
37 a bawdie] bawdy S
38 chamber] Bed-Chamber S
52 Sonnets] new Sonnets S
52 out] omit L, S
53 in] omit S

58 -coursers] -courses W
62 *Forobosco.*] omit F1–2, L, Lc
69 around] round F1, D
73 impostures] impostors F1
76 already] 'em already F1
76 upon] on S
98 Ile] omit F1, S
103 talk'st] talk't F1
106 rougher] rough F1–2, L, W, D, Lc
115 And] *Stooles out.* And F1
122 will] will will S

655

128 prepared] prepare D(*qy*)
144.1 *They*] *Enter Cæsario. They* F1–2
145 preciously] precisely F2, S

154 to] unto S
224 agreivances] Grievances L

III.ii

5 *Colonnas*] *Columnies* F1; *Columni's*
   F2
6 *Neris*] *Neers* F1–2
10 whiles] while F2, L, C
17 Chyrurgion] Surgeon L, C, W
28 to] unto S, C
56 How?] ~ ∧ F1–2, L, C
67 Lady on.] Lady on. | *Maria.* How
   ever | *Bap.* A Faulkners sonne: F1

78 his] her F1
94 impatiency] impatience S, C, W
125 If] Is L
128 deserv'd] desir'd F1–2, L
140 that] what F1
141 what] that F1–2, L
160 have] heard F1
233 then] thee F1–2, L, W, Lc

IV.i

8 best] blest S, C
24 may] must F2, L, S
33 thee] ye F2, L, S; you C, W
38 *Cæsario.*] *omit* F1
39 My] *Cæs.* My F1
51 fool] food F1
106 As] *omit* F1–2, L

111 experience] experienced F1
119 Yet] Yea F1–2
149 of] that Lc
163 loose] lose F2
167 welfare] farewell F1
189 thought] thoughts F1
198 they] which S–W; nay D; yea Lc

IV.ii

14 get] go W
14 up] *omit* S
14 belly] belly up S
30 in *Spanish*] *Spanish* S
54 women] woman F2, L
61 sir] *omit* S
65 any more] more S
72 newes] new L
76 as] with as S
82 though] *omit* S
105 of] *omit* S, C
114 of] *omit* S
125 large] larger S
189 Mule-] A Mule- S–W

210 thou] though thou W
243 has] now has S
259 *Green-land*] *Greeke-land* F1
289, 308 oh, oh] ho, ho F2, L, C, W
290 that] those C, W
290 o's] o'r F2, L; Oh o'r S; Oh D
307 chine] chin F1
332–333 the cottage] thy cottage W; the
   coatage D (*aft.* Mason)
340, 409 pox] ——F1–2, L, S
354 I] *Hostes.* I F1
364 these testifie] this testimony F1
388 set] sit S–D

V.i

47 reconcilement] a reconcilement S
51 twill] will S–W
51 fully be] be fully S
60 were] not S, C

95 afflicteds] afflicted F1
97 You] You've S, C; You have W, D
97 awak'd] awake F1
102 yet] *omit* S

V.ii

13 traunce] trace S, C; traunt Lc
18 was] were L–D
22 has] have S–D
40 the] their F2, L–D

51 Host] Host's D
72 one] on F2, L
86 landing] and of landing S

V.iii

6 funerall:] ~ ∧ F1–2; ~ , L; ——Lc
8 But] And Lc
8 the] *omit* F2, L
12 honor] his honor D(*qy*), Lc
36 lighted] slighted F1
46 crosse us now] now to cross us S
47 bannes] bands F1
78 Weepest] Wee pest F1; We pest F2, L
92 not] it C, W
143 Now we] Nay, we W (*aft.* Mason)
145 This ... I needs] his ... needs F1–2,

149 ai-me] Ah-me L; Aim S–W
172 make] make you S
184 Duke. Then ... health,] ~ , then ... ~ . F1–2, L, Lc
195 ere] ever Lc
227 *Prospero* though] tho' of *Prospero* S
244 and] I S–D
250 all] all's S
265 was] was but S
268 peach] preach F1
284 them] them them F1

THE LAWS OF CANDY

edited by

CYRUS HOY

TEXTUAL INTRODUCTION

The first known reference to *The Laws of Candy* (Greg, *Bibliography*, no. 648) is its inclusion in the list of some thirty plays entered in the Stationers' Register by Humphrey Moseley and Humphrey Robinson in September 1646 for publication in the first Beaumont and Fletcher Folio, which appeared in the following year. The cast-list printed with the play in the second (1679) Beaumont and Fletcher Folio provides the only clue to its date: sometime between March 1619 and June 1623. The cast of principal players named there does not include Richard Burbage, the King's Company's most prominent actor, who died in March 1619, but does include the name of Joseph Taylor, who had joined the company by the middle of May of that year; and the list provides a *terminus ad quem* with its inclusion of the name of Nicholas Tooley, who was buried in June 1623.[1]

The Laws of Candy was not included in the Lord Chamberlain's list (dated 7 August 1641) of plays to be protected for the King's Company against unauthorized publication, and this apparent lack of regard for it has suggested to G. E. Bentley that it 'was one of the least popular of the Fletcher plays – and deservedly so'.[2] But Fletcher had nothing to do with the authorship of *The Laws of Candy*, nor did Beaumont, nor Massinger, despite the efforts of nineteenth-century scholars to account for its inclusion in the 1647 Folio by finding some evidence in the play of the work of one or another or all of these dramatists. Its inclusion in F1 is probably best accounted for by the nature of the play's principal source. This has been identified by Eugene Waith in his discovery that *The Laws of Candy*, as well as two other plays in the Beaumont and Fletcher canon (*The Queen of Corinth* and *The Double Marriage*), derive their basic plot materials from Senecan declamations (Controversia 2, book ten, in the case of *The Laws of Candy*).[3] The elaborate dialectic and rhetorical schemes that are such a prominent feature of Seneca's *Controversiae* exerted a crucial influence on the developing pattern of Fletcherian tragicomedy, as Waith has shown. Rhetorical texts such as those that provided the plots for *The Queen of Corinth*, *The Double Marriage* and *The Laws of*

Candy must have seemed to promise distinctively Fletcherian dramatic possibilities: uniquely rich sources for the sort of startling reversals of plot that by *c.* 1620 were becoming something of a Fletcherian theatrical speciality. Fletcher collaborated in the authorship of *The Double Marriage* (with Massinger) and in *The Queen of Corinth* (with Massinger and Field). The Senecan sources used in these plays and in *The Laws of Candy* might well have been specifically intended by the King's Company for Fletcher and his *atelier*, to be worked up into dramatic form either with his assistance or under his direction. All three of these plays date from the period *c.* 1617–21. But Field's death sometime in 1619 or 1620, the demands of Fletcher's ever-flourishing career, and Massinger's emergence as an independent playwright during these years seem to have made it necessary for the King's Company to assign another dramatist to the task of working up into a play whatever dramatic possibilities were deemed to be inherent in Seneca's Controversia 2, book ten.

When scholars investigating the play's authorship came to despair of finding any evidence of Fletcher, Beaumont or Massinger in *The Laws of Candy*, they began to look to other dramatists for a possible candidate, and the name that has been most plausibly suggested is John Ford, though there is no external evidence to associate Ford with this play.[4] The beginnings of Ford's career as a dramatist are wrapped in mystery, but it was under way by 1621 when he is found writing *The Witch of Edmonton* with Dekker and William Rowley. He is not known to have had any permanent association with the King's Company at this date. If he were, indeed, hired to make a tragicomedy *à la* Fletcher out of this particular Senecan text, it may have been in the nature of a trial performance. The result (*The Laws of Candy*) was apparently not held to be encouraging, and Ford continues through most of the 1620s to write for lesser companies, though the King's Men seem to have employed his services again in 1625 to help with *The Fair Maid of the Inn* (perhaps to take on or to complete the share of Fletcher, who died in August of that year).[5] By the end of the decade, Ford had come into his own as a dramatist and the King's Men acted three of his plays (*The Lover's Melancholy*, *The Broken Heart* and the now lost *Beauty in a Trance*). I would suggest that *The Laws of Candy* found its way into the 1647 Beaumont and Fletcher Folio (and thence into the Beaumont and Fletcher canon) because it was a King's

Company play that resembled in style and substance the work of the company's principal dramatist. By 1647, the term 'Beaumont and Fletcher' had come to subsume not only large quantities of the work of such dramatists as Fletcher and Massinger, but occasional products from such other dramatists as Nathan Field, Middleton, William Rowley and, it would seem, John Ford.

The Laws of Candy was printed in Section 3 of the 1647 Folio, the section printed by Susan Islip. It occupies sigs. 3G2–3I3 (sig. 3I3v is blank). The text seems to have been set by the two compositors whose work has been noted by previous editors of plays printed in Islip's shop.[6] Their work displays sufficiently different habits of spelling and abbreviation to make it possible to differentiate their shares. Compositor *A* spells *Ile, goe, doe* (sometimes *do*). Compositor *B* spells *I'le*, and strongly prefers *do* and *go* (though *doe* and *goe* sometimes appear in his work). Speech-prefixes for Erota are abbreviated *Erot.* or *Ero.* by Compositor *A*; Compositor *B* sometimes prints *Ero.* but more often prints simply *Er.* Speech-prefixes for Philander appear as *Phil.* when set by Compositor *A*, *Phi.* when set by Compositor *B*. At the beginning of the text, Compositor *A* had difficulty with the name of the central character (*Cassilane*); he spells it *Cassilanes* seven times when it does not occur as a genitive (sigs. G2, G3, G3v: at I.i.42; I.i.83; I.ii.0.1; I.ii.130, 146, 281, 294). Compositor *B* made an identical error once (sig. H4v: at IV.ii.16.1). The shares of the two compositors seem to be as follows:

Compositor A: 3G2–H2v (I.i.1–III.ii.177); 3I2v–3I3 (V.i.247–414)
Compositor B: 3H3–3I2 (III.ii.178–V.i.246)

The Laws of Candy is a relatively short play. Oliphant speaks of the 'corruptness of the text',[7] but in fact the F1 text is remarkably free of errors. It was probably printed from an authorial fair copy. Though the F1 text calls for music and a song at III.iii.31.1, 35 and 42.1 (the words of the song are not given), there is nothing else on display in it that could conceivably suggest it to have been printed from a manuscript that had any connection with the theatre.

As a title, *The Laws of Candy* continued to appear in long lists of King's Company plays undergoing legal transferral throughout the later years of the seventeenth century,[8] but there is no record of any performance of it. Gerard Langbaine lists it in his *Momus Triumphans*

(1688, p. 59) with the laconic comment 'not Acted these many years'. In addition to being reprinted in the second Beaumont and Fletcher Folio (1679), the play has been included in all the complete editions of their *Works* (1711, 1750, 1778, 1812, 1843–6). In the present century *The Laws of Candy* has been edited by E. K. Chambers in volume III of the Bullen Variorum (London, 1908).

NOTES

1 Gerald Eades Bentley, *The Jacobean and Caroline Stage* (Oxford, 1941–56), II, 590–2, 601–2; III, 355.

2 Bentley, *ibid.* III, 356.

3 Eugene M. Waith, *The Pattern of Tragicomedy in Beaumont and Fletcher* (New Haven, 1952), 205–7. Earlier scholars (Weber, Dyce, Chambers) had found the source of *The Laws of Candy* in Cinthio's *Hecatommithi*, x, 9, but the Senecan source is clearly the basic one. Waith (p. 206) suggests that Cinthio's novella is in some degree influenced by Seneca.

4 The attribution of *The Laws of Candy* to Ford was first proposed by William Wells whose views (unpublished at the time) were conveyed to E. H. C. Oliphant who endorsed them, in the main, in his *The Plays of Beaumont and Fletcher* (New Haven, 1927), 472–86. Acknowledging that 'It may be easier to join Mr Wells in abandoning altogether the idea of the participation of Fletcher', Oliphant went on: 'but, if we do that, we are met by the stumbling-block of having to account for the inclusion of the play in the Beaumont and Fletcher collection, and, what is of equal importance, its ascription to them in the Stationers' Register entry of September 4, 1646' (p. 482). These are not really stumbling-blocks, as I suggest in what follows. The internal evidence for Ford's authorship of the entire play is impressive, though such evidence is unlikely ever to be viewed as conclusive in all quarters. I have discussed Ford's claim to the authorship of *The Laws of Candy* in 'The shares of Fletcher and his collaborators in the Beaumont and Fletcher canon (v),' *Studies in Bibliography*, XIII (1960), 97–100.

5 I have discussed the evidence for Ford's share in the authorship of *The Fair Maid of the Inn* in *Studies in Bibliography*, XIII (1960), 100–3.

6 See, for example, Fredson Bowers' Textual Introduction to his edition in this series of *The Loyal Subject* (vol. V, p. 155), and George Williams' Textual Introductions to his editions of *The Island Princess* (vol. V, pp. 543–55) and *The Nice Valor* (vol. VII, pp. 429–31).

7 *The Plays of Beaumont and Fletcher*, p. 476.

8 See Bentley, *Jacobean and Caroline Stage*, III, 354–55; William Van Lennep (ed.), *The London Stage: 1660–1800*, Part I: 1660–1700 (Carbondale, Ill., 1965), pp. 151–2.

PERSONS REPRESENTED IN THE PLAY.

Cassilane, *General of* Candy.
Antinous, *Son to* Cassilane, *and his Competitor.*
Fernando, *a Venetian Captain, Servant to* Annophil.
Philander, *Prince of* Cyprus, *passionately in love with* Erota.
Gonzalo, *an ambitious Politick Lord of* Venice.
Gaspero, *Secretary of State.*
Melitus, *a Gentleman of* Cyprus.
Arcanes, *a noble Souldier, Friend to* Cassilane.
Decius, *Friend to* Antinous.
Porphicio, ⎫
Possenne, ⎬ *Senators.*   10
Paolo Michael, *Venetian Ambassadour.*
Mochingo, *an ignorant servant to* Erota.
Gentlemen.
Souldiers.
Servants.
[*Messenger, Attendants, Senators.*]

WOMEN

Erota, *a Princess, imperious, and of an overweaning Beauty.*
Annophil, *Daughter to* Cassilane.   20
Hyparcha, *Attendant on the Princess* Erota.

The Scene Candy.
The principal Actors were,

Joseph Taylor.	John Lowin.
William Eglestone.	John Underwood.
Nicholas Toolie.	George Birch.
Richard Sharpe.	Thomas Pollard.

PERSONS REPRESENTED ... Pollard.] *adapted from* F2; *omit* F1
*7 Cyprus] Mason; Candy F2

666

THE LAWS OF CANDY.
A TRAGICOMEDY.

Enter Gaspero, *and* Melitus.

Melitus.   Sir, you'r the very friend I wish'd to meet with,
I have a large discourse invites your eare
To be an Auditor.
Gaspero.   And what concernes it?
Melitus.   The sadly thriving progresse of the loves
Betweene my Lord the Prince, and that great Lady,
Whose insolencie, and never-yet-match'd pride,
Can by no Character be well exprest,
But in her onlie name, the prow'd *Erota*.
Gaspero.   Alas *Melitus*, I should ghesse, the best
Successe your Prince could find from her, to be   10
As harsh as the event doth prove: but now
'Tis not a time to pity passionate griefes,
When a whole Kingdome in a manner lies
Upon its death-bed bleeding.
Melitus.   Who can tell
Whether or no, these many plagues at once
Hang over this unhappie Land, for her sake,
That is a monster in it.
Gaspero.   Here's the miserie
Of having a child our Prince: else I presume
The bold Venetians had not dar'd to attempt
So bloudie an Invasion.
Melitus.   Yet I wonder   20
Why, Master Secretarie, still the Senate
So almost superstitiouslie adores
Gonʒalo the Venetian Lord, considering
The outrage of his Countrymen——

Gaspero.   The Senate
   Is wise, and therein just, for this *Gonzalo*,
   Upon a Massacre performed at Sea
   By the Admirall of *Venice*, on a Merchant
   Of *Candy*, when the cause was to be heard
   Before the Senate there, in open Court
   Professed, that the crueltie the Admirall   30
   Had shewed, deserved not only fine, but death:
   For *Candy* then, and *Venice* were at peace:
   Since when upon a motion in the Senate,
   For conquest of our Land, 'tis known for certaine,
   That only this *Gonzalo* dar'd to oppose it,
   His reason was, because it too much savoured
   Of Lawlesse, and unjust ambition.
   The wars were scarce begun, but he (in feare
   Of quarrels 'gainst his life) fled from his Countrie,
   And hether came, where (to confirme his truth)   40
   I know (*Melitus*) he, out of his owne store,
   Hath monied *Cassilane* the Generall.
Melitus.   What, without other pledges then *Cassilanes*
   Bare promise of payment?
Gaspero.   No, it may be
   He has some pettie Lordship to retire to:
   But this he hath done; now 'tis fit *Melitus*,
   The Senate should be thankefull, otherwise,
   They should annihilate one of those Laws,
   For which this Kingdome is throughout the world
   Unfellowed, and admired.
Melitus.   What Lawes are these? sir,   50
   Let me so much importune you.
Gaspero.   You shall,
   And they be worth your knowledge; briefly thus:
   Who ere he be that can detect apparently
   Another of ingratitude, for any
   Received benefit, the Plaintiffe may
   Require the offenders life; unlesse he please

42, 83 *Cassilane*] Seward; *Cassilanes* F1–2
50 Unfellowed] Dyce (Theobald *conj.*); Unfollowed F1–2

Freely, and willingly to grant remission.

Melitus.   By which strict Law the Senate is in danger,
  Should they neglect *Gonzalo.*

Gaspero.   Right; the Law
  Permits a like equalitie to Aliens,   60
  As to a home-borne Patriot.

Melitus.   Pray sir the other?

Gaspero.   Know *Melitus,*
  The elder *Cretans* flourished many yeares,
  In War, in Peace, unparalel'd, and they
  (To spurre heroicke spirits on to vertue)
  Enacted that what man so ere he were,
  Did noblest in the field against his enemie,
  So by the generall voice approv'd, and knowne,
  Might at his home-returne, make his demand
  For satisfaction, and reward.

Melitus.   They are   70
  Both famous Lawes indeed.

                    Enter a Messenger.

Messenger.   Master Secretarie,
  The Senate is about to sit, and crave
  Your presence.

Gaspero.   What, so suddenly?

Messenger.   These Letters
  Will shew the causes why.

Gaspero.   Heaven thou art great,
  And worthie to be thanked.

Melitus.   Your countenance sir
  Doth promise some good tidings.

Gaspero.   O the best
  And happiest for this land, that e're was told!
  All the Venetian Forces are defeated.

Melitus.   How Sir?

Gaspero.   And what doth adde some delight more,
  There is amongst the Souldiers a contention   80
  Who shall be the triumpher, and it stands
  Doubtfull betweene a Father and his Son,

Old *Cassilane*, and young *Antinous*.

Melitus.   Why may not both demand it?

Gaspero   The Law denies it:
    But where the Souldiers do not all consent,
    The parties in contention, are refer'd
    To plead before the Senate; and from them,
    Upon an open Audience, to be judg'd
    The Chiefe, and then to make demands.

Melitus.   You ravish me
    With wonder and delight.

Gaspero.   Come: as we walke,   90
    I shall more fully informe you.

                                        Exeunt.

            Enter Cassilane, Arcanes, Antinous, *and* Decius.   [I.]

Cassilane.   Admit no Souldier neare us, till the Senate
    Have tooke their places.

Arcanes.   You are obey'd, my Lord.

Antinous.   *Decius,* fall off.

Decius.   I shall.

Cassilane.   Give leave *Arcanes*:
                    [*Exeunt* Arcanes *and* Decius.]
    Young-man come nearer to me: who am I?

Antinous.   It were a sin against the piety
    Of filiall duty, if I should forget
    The debt I owe my father: on my knee,
    Your pleasure?

Cassilane.   What, so low? canst thou finde joynts,
    Yet be an Elephant? *Antinous*, rise:
    Thou wilt belye opinion, and rebate   10
    The ambition of thy gallantry, that they
    Whose confidence thou hast bewitched, should see
    Their little God of War, kneele to his father,
    Though in my hand I did graspe Thunder.

Antinous.   Sir,
    For proofe that I acknowledge you the Author

                0.1 Cassilane] *Cassilanes* F1–2

Of giving me my birth, I have discharg'd
A part of my obedience. But if now
You should (as cruell fathers do) proclame
Your right, and Tyrant-like usurp the glory
Of my peculiar honours, not deriv'd   20
From successary, but purchas'd with my bloud,
Then I must stand first Champion for my selfe,
Against all interposers.
Cassilane.   Boldly urg'd,
And proudly, I could love thee, did not anger
Consult with just disdaine, in open language
To call thee most ungratefull. Say freely,
Wilt thou resigne the flatteries, whereon
The reeling pillars of a popular breath,
Have rais'd thy Giant-like conceit, to adde
A suffrage to thy fathers merit, speake?   30
Antinous.   Sir, heare me: were there not a Chronicle
Well pend by all their tongues, who can report
What they have seene you do; or had you not
Best in your owne performance writ your selfe,
And been your own Text, I would undertake
Alone, without the helpe of Art, or Character,
But only to recount your deeds in Armes,
And you should ever then be fam'd a president
Of living victory: But as you are
Great, and well worthy to be stiled great,   40
It would betray a povertie of spirit
In me to obstruct my fortunes, or discent,
If I should coward-like surrender up
The interest, which the inheritance of your vertue,
And mine owne thriftie fate can claime in honour:
My Lord, of all the masse of fame, which any
That weares a sword, and hath but seen me fight,
Gives me, I will not share, nor yeild one jot,
One tittle.
Cassilane.   Not to me?

*21 From successary] *stet* F1–2   37 your] F2; you F1
38 president] *i.e.,* precedent

Antinous.   You are my father,
Yet not to you.

Cassilane.   Ambitious boy, how darst thou   50
To tell me, that thou wilt contend?

Antinous.   Had I
Been sloathfull, and not followed you in all
The streights of death, you might have justly then
Reputed me a bastard; 'tis a cruelty,
More then to murther Innocents, to take
The life of my yet Infant-honour from me.

Cassilane.   *Antinous*, looke upon this badge of age,
Thy fathers gray-hair'd beard: full fifty yeares,
(And more then halfe of this, ere thou wert borne)
I have been knowne a Souldier, in which time   60
I found no difference 'twixt War and Peace,
For War was peace to me, and Peace was war;
Antinous, marke me well; there hath not liv'd
These fifty yeares, a man whom *Creet* prefer'd
Before thy father; let me boldly boast,
Thy father, both for Discipline, and Action,
Hath so long been the first of all his Nation;
Now canst thou thinke it honest, charitable,
Nay humane, being so young, my son, my child,
Begot, bred, taught by me, by me thy father,   70
For one dayes service, and that one thy first,
To rob me of a glory which I fought for
A halfe of hundred yeares.

Antinous.   My case observes
Both equity, and presidents; for sir,
That very day whereon you got your fame,
You tooke it from some other, who was then
Chiefe in repute, as you are now; and had been
Perhaps as many yeares deserving that,
Which you gain'd in a day, as I have mine.

Cassilane.   But he was not my father then *Antinous*.   80
Thou leav'st out that.

---

71 that one] Seward; that on F1–2

Antinous.   Sir had he been your father,
    He had been then immortall: for a father
    Heightens his reputation, where his son
    Inherits it, as when you give us life,
    Your life is not diminish'd, but renew'd
    In us, when you are dead, and we are still
    Your living Images.
Cassilane.   So be thou curs'd
    In thy posterity, as I in thee,
    Dishonorable boy: O shall that Sun,
    Which not a yeare yet since, beheld me mounted   90
    Upon a fierie steed, waving my sword,
    And teaching this young-man to manage Armes,
    That was a raw, fresh novice in the feates
    Of Chivalrie, shall that same sun be witnesse
    Against this brat, of his ingratitude?
    Who to ecclipse the light of my renowne,
    Can no way hope to get a Noble name,
    But by the treading on his fathers greatnesse;
    Thou wilt not yeald?
Antinous.   My life, but not the prize
    My Sword hath purchas'd.   100

                    Enter Arcanes [*and* Decius].

Arcanes.   The Senate
    My Lord are here at hand; and all the souldiers
    Begin to throng about them.
Cassilane.   Now *Arcanes*
    The——
Arcanes.   What sir?
Cassilane.   Trifles will affront us: that
    Fine fighting Stripling!
Arcanes.   Let him have the shame on't:
    Please you withdraw on this side.
Cassilane.   My great heart
    Was never quaild before.
Decius [*to* Antinous].   My Lord be confident,

                    673

Let not your father dant you.

Antinous.   *Decius*, whether
  Must I withdraw?

Decius.   On this side.——See the Souldiers
  Attend your pleasure——courage sir; the Senate.   110

Cassilane.   Way for the Senate.

Enter Porphicio, Possenne ([*and*] *three* [*other*] *Senators*), Gonzalo,
Gaspero, *Souldiers.*

Gonzalo.   My good Lords I know not
  What taxe of arrogance I may incurre,
  Should I presume, though courted by your favours,
  To take a place amongst you: I had rather
  Give proofe of my unfeign'd humility
  By some, though meane, yet more becomming place,
  Then run the hazard of a doubtfull censure.

Possenne.   My Lord, your wisedome is both known and try'd;
  We cannot ranke ye in a nobler friendship,
  Then your great service to the state deserves.   120

Porphicio.   Wil't please you sit?

Gonzalo.   What here my Lord *Porphicio*?
  It must not be.

Porphicio.   My Lord you are too modest.

Gonzalo.   It is no season to be troublesome,
  Else——But I have done: Your Lordships are observ'd.

Enter Fernando [*led captive*] *with* Soldiers.

Gaspero.   Is the demandant ready?

Arcanes.   He is ready.

Gaspero.   Produce him then.

Arcanes.   Before this sacred presence,
  I, by a generall consent, am made
  The Souldiers voice, and to your gratious wisedomes,
  Present as chiefe in Armes, his Countries Champion,
  Cassilane.   130

---

*108 dant] *stet* F1   111 Possenne] F2; *Possenme* F1
111 speech-prefix *Gonzalo.*] Colman; *omit* F1–2
116 some] Weber (Mason *conj.*); force F1–2   130 *Cassilane*] Colman; *Cassilanes* F1–2

Decius.   Most reverend Lords, you heare the lesser number
  Of those who have been Guardians to this Countrey,
  Approve this Champion; I in all their names
  Who fought for *Candy,* here present before you
  The mightiest man in Armes, *Antinous.*
  Speak fellow souldiers.
Soldiers.   *Antinous, Antinous.*
Gaspero.   Stand by all, save the two competitors.
Possenne.   My Lords, how much your Countrey owes you both,
  The due reward of your desertfull glories
  Must to posterity remain: But yet   140
  Since, by our Law, one onely can make claime
  To the proposed honours which you both
  (It seems) have truely merited, take leave
  Freely to plead your rights: we shall attend you.
Porphicio.   Wherein priority of voyce is granted
  Lord *Cassilane* to you: for that your rare
  And long experience in the course of war,
  As well doth challenge it, as the best priviledge
  Of Order and civility, for that
  You are your brave opponents worthy father.   150
  Say Countrey-men, are you content?
Soldiers.   I, I.
Cassilane.   Right grave, right gratious fathers; how unfit
  It is for me, that all my life time have
  Been practis'd in the schoole of bloud, and slaughter,
  To bandy words now in my lifes last farewell,
  Your wisedomes will consider; were there pitcht
  Another, and another field, like that
  Which not yet three days since, this arme hath scatter'd,
  Defeated, and made nothing, then the man
  That had a heart to thinke he could but follow,   160
  (For equall me he should not) through the lanes
  Of danger and amazement, might in that,
  That onely of but following me, be happy,
  Reputed worthy to be made my rivall:

146, 294 *Cassilane*] Seward; *Cassilanes* F1–2

675

For 'tis not Lords, unknowne to those about me,
(My fellow souldiers) first with what a confidence
I led them on to fight, went on still, and
As if I could have beene a second Nature,
As well in heartning them by my example,
As by my exhortation, I gave life   170
To quicken courage, to inflame revenge,
To heighten resolution; in a word,
To out-doe action: It boots not to discover,
How that yong-man, who was not fledg'd nor skil'd
In Martiall play, was even as ignorant
As childish: But I list not to disparage
His non-ability: The signall given
Of Battaile, when our enemies came on,
(Directed more by fuerie, then by warrant
Of Policy and Stratagem) I met them,   180
I in the fore-front of the Armies met them;
And as if this old weather-beaten body
Had been compos'd of Cannon-proof, I stood
The volleys of their shot. I, I my selfe
Was he that first dis-rankt their woods of Pikes:
But when we came to handy-stroaks, as often
As I lent blowes, so often I gave wounds,
And every wound a death. I may be bold
To justifie a truth, this very sword
Of mine slew more then any twaine besides: 190
And, which is not the least of all my glorie,
When he, this young man, hand to hand in fight,
Was by the Generall of the Venetians,
And such as were his retinue, unhors'd,
I stept between, and rescu'd him my selfe,
Or horses hoofs had trampled him to dirt;
And whilst he was re-mounting, I maintain'd
The combate with the gallant Generall,
Till having taken breath, he throng'd before me,
Renew'd the fight, and with a fatall blow,   200

167–168 and | As] F2; and | And as F1   179 then by warrant] F2; then warrant F1

Stole both that honour from me, and his life
From him, whom I before my selfe alone,
Had more then full three quarters kill'd: A man
Well worthy onely by this hand to have dy'd,
Not by a Boyes weak push: I talke to much,
But 'tis a fault of Age: If to bring home
Long peace, long victorie, even to your Capitoll;
If to secure your Kingdome, Wives, and Children,
Your lives and liberties; if to renowne
Your honours through the world, to fix your names,   210
Like Blazing starres, admir'd, and fear'd by all,
That have but heard of *Candy*, or a Cretane,
Be to deserve the approvement of my man-hood,
Then thus much have I done: what more, examine
The Annalls of my life; and then consider
What I have been, and am. Lords I have said.

Gonʒalo.   With reverence to the Senate, is it lawfull,
Without your Customes breach, to say a word?

Possenne.   Say on my Lord *Gonʒalo.*

Gonʒalo.   I have heard,
And with no little wonder, such high deeds   220
Of Chivalrie discours'd, that I confesse,
I doe not think the Worthies while they liv'd
All nine, deserv'd as much applause, or memorie,
As this one: But who can doe ought to gaine
The Crowne of honour from him, must be somewhat
More then a man; you tread a dangerous path,
Yet I shall heare you gladly: for believe me,
Thus much let me professe, in honours cause,
I would not to my father, nor my King,
(My Countries father) yield: if you transcend   230
What we have heard, I can but onely say,
That miracles are yet in use. I feare
I have offended.

Porphicio.   You have spoken nobly.
Antinous use your priviledge.

Antinous.   Princely fathers,
E're I begin, one suit I have to make,

'Tis just, and honourable.

Porphicio.   *Possenne.*   Speak, and have it.

Antinous.   That you would please the souldiers might all stand
Together by their Generall.

Possenne.   'Tis granted.
All fall to yonder side: Goe on, *Antinous*.

Antinous.   I shall be briefe and plaine: All what my father   240
(This Countries Patron) hath discours'd, is true.
Fellowes in Armes: speak you is't true?

Soldiers.   True, true.

Antinous.   It followes, that the blaze of my performance
Took light from what I saw him doe; and thus
A City (though the flame be much more dreadfull)
May from a little sparke be set on fire;
Of all what I have done, I shall give instance
Onely in three maine proofs of my desert.
First I sought out (but through how many dangers
My Lords judge ye) the chiefe, the great Commander,   250
The head of that huge body, whose prowd weight
Our Land shrunke under, him I found and fought with,
Fought with, and slew. Fellowes in Armes, speak you,
Is't true or not?

Soldiers.   True, true.

Antinous.   When he was falne,
The hearts of all our adversaries
Began to quaile, till young *Fernando*, sonne
To the last Duke of *Venice* gather'd head,
And soone renew'd the field, by whose example
The bold Venetians doubling strength and courage
Had got the better of the day; our men   260
Supposing that their adversaries grew
Like *Hydra's* head, recoyle, and 'gan to flye:
I follow'd them; and what I said, they know;
The summe on't is; I call'd them back, new rankt them;
Lead on, they follow'd, shrunk not till the end:
Fellowes in Armes is't true, or no?

Soldiers.   True, true.

Antinous.   Lastly, to finish all, there was but one,

The onely great exploit; which was to take
Fernando prisoner, and that hand to hand
In single fight I did: my selfe without   270
The helpe of any arme, save the arme of heaven.
Speak souldiers, is it true, or no?

Soldiers.   *Antinous, Antinous.*

Antinous.   Behold my prisoner, Fathers.

Fernando.   This one man
Ruin'd our Army, and hath glorifi'd
Creete in her robes of mightinesse and conquest.

Possenne.   We need not use long circumstance of words,
Antinous thou art conquerer: the Senate,
The souldiers, and thy valour have pronounc'd it.

All.   *Antinous, Antinous.*

Porphicio.   Make thy demand.

Cassilane.   Please ye (my Lords) give leave   280
That I may part.

Possenne.   No *Cassilane*, the Court
Should therein be dishonour'd, doe not imagine
We prize your presence at so slight a rate.——
Demand *Antinous.*

Antinous.   Thus (my Lords) to witnesse
How far I am from arrogance, or thinking
I am more valiant, though more favour'd
Then my most matchlesse father, my demand is,
That for a lasting memorie of his name,
His deeds, his reall, nay his royall worth,
You set up in your Capitoll in Brasse   290
My fathers Statue, there to stand for ever
A Monument and Trophy of his victories,
With this Inscription to succeeding ages,
Great Cassilane, Patron of Candy's Peace,
Perpetuall Triumpher.

Porphicio.   *Possenne.*   It is granted.
What more?

Antinous.   No more.

Cassilane.   How boy?

Gonzalo.   Thou art immortall,
   Both for thy Son-like pietie, and beauties
   Of an unconquer'd minde.

Antinous.   My Prisoner (Lords)
   To your more sacred wisedomes I surrender:
   Fit you his ransome; halfe whereof I give   300
   For largesse to the Souldiers: the other halfe
   To the erection of this monument.

Cassilane.   Ambitious villaine.

Gonzalo.   Thou art all un-immitable.
   My Lords to work a certaine peace for *Candy*
   With *Venice*, use *Fernando* like a Prince;
   His ransome Ile disburse what e're it be:
   Yet you may stay him with you, till conditions
   Of amitie shall be concluded on:
   Are yee content?

Porphicio.   We are, and ever rest
   Both friends and debters to your noblenesse.   310

Gonzalo.   Souldiers attend me in the Market-place,
   Ile thither send your largesse.

Soldiers.   *Antinous, Antinous.*

                                        Exeunt.

Cassilane.   I have a sute too, Lords.

Porphicio.   *Possenne.*   Propose it, 'tis yours,
   If fit and just.

Cassilane.   Let not my services,
   My being forty yeares a drudge, a pack-horse
   To you, and to the State, be branded now
   With Ignominy ne're to be forgotten:
   Reare me no Monument, unlesse you meane
   To have me fam'd a Coward, and be stamp'd so.

Possenne.   We understand you not.

Cassilane.   Proud boy, thou dost,   320
   And Tyrant-like insult'st upon my shame.

Antinous.   Sir, heaven can tell, and my integrity,

310 and] F2 (aud); add F1

680

What I did, was but onely to inforce
The Senates gratitude. I now acknowledge it.
Cassilane.   Observe it Fathers, how this haughty boy
Growes cunning in his envy of mine honours:
He knowes no mention can of me be made,
But that it ever likewise must be told,
How I by him was master'd; and for surety
That all succeeding times may so report it,   330
He would have my dishonour, and his Triumphs
Ingrav'd in Brasse: hence, hence proceeds the falshood
Of his insinuating piety.
Thou art no childe of mine: thee and thy bloud,
Here in the Capitoll, before the Senate,
I utterly renounce: So thrift and fate
Confirme me; henceforth never see my face,
Be, as thou art, a villaine to thy father.
Lords, I must crave your leaves: come, come *Arcanes.*
                                        [*Exeunt* Cassilane *and* Arcanes.]
Gonʒalo.   Here's a strange high-borne spirit.
Possenne.   'Tis but heat   340
Of suddaine present rage; I dare assure
Antinous of his favour.
Antinous.   I not doubt it,
He is both a good man, and a good father.
I shall attend your Lordships.
Possenne.   Doe *Antinous.*
Gonʒalo.   Yes: feast thy Triumphs, with applause and pleasures.
Porphicio.   *Possenne.* Lead on.
            Flourish [*of*] *Cornets. Exeunt* [*all but* Antinous *and* Decius].
Antinous.   I utterly renounce——Twas so?
Was't not, my *Decius*?
Decius.   Pish, you know my Lord,
Old men are chollerick.
Antinous.   And lastly parted
With, never henceforth see my face: O me,
How have I lost a Father? Such a father?   350
Such a one *Decius*! I am miserable,
Beyond expression.

Decius.   Fie, how unbecomming
  This shewes upon your day of fame?
Antinous.   O mischiefe:
  I must no more come neare him; that I know,
  And am assur'd on't.
Decius.   Say you doe not?
Antinous.   True:
  Put case I doe not: what is *Candy* then
  To lost *Antinous*? *Malta*, I resolve
  To end my dayes in thee.
Decius.   How's that?
Antinous.   Ile trie
  All humble meanes of being reconcil'd,
  Which if deny'd, then I may justly say,   360
  This day has prov'd my worst: *Decius* my worst.

                                        Exeunt.

                Enter Gonzalo, *and* Gaspero.   II.i

Gaspero.   Now to what you have heard; as no man can
  Better then I, give you her Character;
  For I have been both nurs'd, and traind up to
  Her petulant humours, and been glad to beare them,
  Her brother, my late Master, did no lesse:
  Strong apprehensions of her beauty hath
  Made her believe that she is more then woman:
  And as there did not want those flatterers
  'Bout the worlds Conquerour, to make him think,
  And did perswade him that he was a god;   10
  So there be those base flies, that will not stick
  To buzze into her eares she is an Angel,
  And that the food she feeds on is Ambrosia.
Gonzalo.   She should not touch it then, 'tis Poets fare.
Gaspero.   I may take leave to say, she may as well
  Determine of her selfe to be a goddesse,
  With lesser flatterie then he a god:
  For she does conquer more, although not farther.
  Every one looks on her dyes in despaire,
  And would be glad to doe it actually,   20

                        682

To have the next age tell how worthily,
And what good cause he had to perish so:
Her beauty is superlative, she knowes it,
And knowing it, thinks no man can deserve,
But ought to perish, and to dye for her:
Many great Princes for her love have languish'd,
And given themselves a willing sacrifice,
Proud to have ended so: And now there is
A Prince so maddened in his owne passions,
That he forgets the Royaltie he was borne to,   30
And deems it happinesse to be her slave.

Gonzalo.   You talke as if you meant to winde me in,
And make me of the number.

Gaspero.   Sir,
Mistake me not, the service that I owe ye
Shall plead for me: I tell you what she is,
What she expects, and what she will effect,
Unlesse you be the miracle of men,
That come but with a purpose to behold,
And goe away your selfe.

Gonzalo.   I thanke you, I will doe it: But pray resolve me,   40
How is she stor'd with wit?

Gaspero.   As with beauty,
Infinite, and more to be admired at,
Then medled with.

Gonzalo.   And walks her tongue the same gate with her wit?

Gaspero.   Much beyond: what ere her heart thinks, she utters:
And so bold, so readily, as you would judge
It penn'd and studied.

Gonzalo.   She comes.

Gaspero.   I must leave you then,
But my best wishes shall remain with you.

Gonzalo.   Still I must thanke you.   [*Exit* Gaspero.]

Enter Erota, Philander, Annophill, Hyparcha, Mochingo,
Attendants.

29 maddened] Weber; manded F1; madded F2   38 but] Dyce (*conj.*); *omit* F1–2
44 wit] Weber (Mason *conj.*) feet F1–2

[*Aside*] This is the most passionate, most pitifull Prince,　　　50
　　Who in the Caldron of affections,
　　Looks as he had been par-boyl'd.
Philander.　If I offend with too much loving you,
　　It is a fault that I must still commit,
　　To make your mercy shine the more on me.
Erota.　You are the selfe-same creature you condemne,
　　Or else you durst not follow me with hope
　　That I can pittie you, who am so farre
　　From granting any comfort in this kinde,
　　That you and all men else shall perish first:　　　60
　　I will live free and single, till I finde
　　Something above a man to equall me;
　　Put all your brave Heroes into one,
　　Your Kings and Emperours, and let him come
　　In person of a man, and I should scorne him:
　　Must, and will scorne him.
　　The god of Love himselfe hath lost his eyes,
　　His Bow and Torch extinguish'd, and the Poets
　　That made him first a god, have lost their fire
　　Since I appear'd, and from my eyes must steale it.　　　70
　　This I dare speak; and let me see the man,
　　Now I have spoke it, that doth, dare deny;
　　Nay, not believe it.
Mochingo.　　　　　He is mad that does not.
Erota.　Have not all the nations of the earth heard of me?
　　Most come to see me, and seeing me, return'd
　　Full of my praises? teaching there Chroniclers
　　To make their Stories perfect? for where the name,
　　Meerely the word of faire *Erota* stands,
　　It is a lasting History to time,
　　Begetting admiration in the men,　　　80
　　And in my owne Sex envie; which glorie's lost,
　　When I shall stick my beautie in a cloud,
　　And dimly shine through it.
Gonẓalo.　　　　　This Woman's in the altitudes,

*83　dimly] Dyce; clearly F1–2

684

And he must be a good Astrologer
Shall know her Zodiack.
Philander.   For any man to thinke
  Himselfe an able purchaser of you,
  But in the bargaine there must be declar'd
  Infinite bounty: otherwise I vow,
  By all that's excellent and gracious in you,
  I would untenant every hope lodg'd in me,   90
  And yield my selfe up Loves, or your owne Martyr.
Erota.   So you shall please us.
Philander.   O you cannot be
  So heavenly, and so absolute in all things,
  And yet retaine such cruell tyranny.
Erota.   I can, I doe, I will.
Gonzalo [*aside*].   She is in her Moods, and her Tences: Ile
      Gramer with you,
  And make a triall how I can decline you:——
  By your leave (great Lady).
Erota.   What are you? A man, *Gonzalo.*
  A good man, that's a wealthy, a Proper man,
  And a proud man too; one that understands   100
  Himselfe, and knowes, unlesse it be your self,
  No woman on the Universe deserves him.
  Nay, Lady, I must tell you too withall,
  I may make doubt of that, unlesse you paint
  With better judgement next day then on this;
  For (plaine I must be with you) 'tis a dull Fucus.
Erota.   Knowes any one here what this fellow is?
1. Attendant.   He is of *Venice* (Madam) a great Magnifico,
  And gracious with the Senate.
Erota.   Let him keep then among them; what makes he here?   110
  Heres state enough where I am: here's a doe——
  You, tell him, if he have ought with us, let him
  Look lower, and give it in Petition.
Mochingo.   Mighty Magnifico, my Mistris bid me tell you,
  If you have ought with her, you must look lower,

---

*85–88 For any ... bounty:] *stet* F1–2   108 *1. Attendant.*] Dyce; *Attend.* F1–2

And yeeld it in Petition.

Gonʒalo.   Here is for thee a Ducket.

Mochingo.   You say well sir, take your owne course.

Gonʒalo.   I will not grace you
(Lady) so much as take you by the hand;
But when I shall vouchsafe to touch your lip,   120
It shall be through your Court a holy-day
Proclamed for so high favour.

Erota.   This is some great mans Jester:——Sirrah, begone,
Here is no place to foole in.

Gonʒalo.   Where are the fooles you talke of? I doe keep two.

Erota.   No question of it:
For in your selfe you doe maintaine an hundred.

Gonʒalo.   And besides them I keep a noble traine,
Statists, and men of action: my purse is large and deep,
Beyond the reach of riot to draw drie: 130
Fortune did vie with Nature, to bestow
(When I was borne) her bountie equally:
Tis not amisse you turne your eyes from me;
For should you stand and gaze me in the face,
You perish would, like *Semele* by *Jove*:
In *Venice* at this instant there do lye
No lesse then threescore Ladies in their graves,
And in their Beds five hundred for my love.

Mochingo [*aside*].   You lie more then they; yet it becomes him
bravely;
Would I could walke and talke so! Ile endeavour it.   140

Erota.   Sir, doe you know me?

Gonʒalo.   Yes, you were sister to the late Prince of *Candy*,
Aunt to this young one: And I in *Venice*,
I am borne a Lord; equall to you in fortunes,
In shape; Ile say no more, but view.

Mochingo [*aside*].   There needs no more be said, were I a
woman——
O he does rarely: 'in shape, Ile say no more,
But view': Who could say more, who better?

135 *Jove*] F2; *Iolus* F1

Man is no man, nor woman woman is,
Unlesse they have a pride like one of these.   150
How poore the Prince of *Cyprus* shewes to him?
How poore another Lady unto her:
Carriage and State makes us seem demi-gods,
Humility, like beasts, wormes of the earth.

Enter Antinous *and* Decius.

Antinous.   Royall Lady, I kisse your hand.
Erota.   Sir, I know you not.
Annophil.   O my noble Brother, welcome from the wars.
Antinous.   Deare sister.
Annophil.   Where is my father, that you come without him?
    We have news of your successe: he has his health I hope?   160
Antinous.   Yes sister, he has his health, but is not well.
Annophil.   How not well? what Riddles do you utter?
Antinous.   Ile tell you more in private.
Gonʒalo.   Noble sir,
    I cannot be unmindfull of your merit,
    Since I last heard it: you are a hopefull youth,
    And (indeed) the soule of *Candy.* I must speak my thoughts.
Annophil.   The Prince of *Cyprus* Brother.——Good *Decius.*
Antinous.   I am his servant.
Philander.   You are the Patron of your Countrie, sir,
    So your unimitable deeds proclame you,   170
    It is no language of my owne, but all mens.
Gonʒalo.   Your Enemies must needs acknowledge it:
    Then doe not thinke it flatterie in your friends,
    For if they had a heart, they could not want a tongue.
Erota.   Is this your brother *Annophill?*
Annophil.   Yes Madam.
Erota.   Your name's *Antinous?*
Antinous.   I am (Lady) that most unfortunate man.
Erota.   How unfortunate? are you not the souldier,
    The Captaine of those Captaines, that did bring
    Conquest and victory home along with you?   180
Antinous.   I had some share in't; but was the least
    Of the least worthy.

Gonzalo.   O sir, in your modesty youl'd make
  A double Conquest: I was an eare-witnesse
  When this young man spoke lesser then he acted,
  And had the souldiers voice to helpe him out:
  But that the Law compell'd him for his honour,
  To inforce him make a claime for his reward,
  I well perceive he would have stood the man
  That he does now, buried his worth in silence.
Erota.   Sir, I hearken not to him, but looke on you,   190
  And finde more in you then he can relate!
  You shall attend on me.
Antinous.   Madam, your pardon.
Erota.   Deny it not sir, for it is more honour
  Then you have gotten ith' field: for know you shall,
  Upon *Erota's* asking, serve *Erota.*
Antinous.   I may want answers, Lady,
  But never want a will to doe you service.
  I came here to my sister, to take leave,
  Having enjoyn'd my selfe to banishment,
  For some cause that hereafter you may heare,   200
  And wish with me I had not the occasion.
Annophil.   There shall be no occasion to divide us:
  Deare Madam for my sake use your power,
  Even for the service that he ought to owe,
  Must, and does owe to you, his friends, and countrey.
Erota.   Upon your Loyalty to the state and me,
  I doe command you Sir, not depart *Candy:*
  Am I not your Princesse?
Antinous.   You are great Lady.
Erota.   Then shew your selfe a Servant and a Subject.
Antinous.   I am your vassaile.   210
Mochingo [aside].   You are a Coward; I that dare not fight,
  Scorne to be vassaile to any Prince in *Europe:*
  Great is my heart with pride, which Ile encrease
  When they are gone, with practise on my Vassailes.

[*Enter an* Attendant.]

208 are great] Langbaine; are a great F1–2

Attendant.　The noble *Cassilane* is come to see you Madam.
Decius.　There's comfort in those words, *Antinous*:
　For heres the place, and persons that have power,
　To reconcile you to his love againe.
Antinous.　That were a fortunate meeting.

Enter Cassilane *and* Arcanes.

Cassilane.　Greatnesse still wait you Lady.　　　　　　　　220
Erota.　Good *Cassilane*, we doe maintain our greatnesse,
　Through your valour.
Cassilane.　My prayers pull dayly blessings on thy head,
　My un-offending childe, my *Annophill.*
　Good Prince, worthy *Gonzalo*! ha? art thou here
　Before me? in every action art thou ambitious?
　My duty (Lady) first offered here,
　And love to thee (my childe) though he out-strip me;
　Thus in the wars he got the start on me,
　By being forward, but performing lesse;　　　　　　　230
　All the endeavours of my life are lost,
　And throwne upon that evill of mine owne
　Cursed begetting, whom I shame to father.
　O that the heat thou robd'st me off, had burnt
　Within my Entrailes, and begot a feaver,
　Or some worse sicknesse, for thou art a disease
　Sharper then any physick gives a name to.
Annophil.　Why doe you say so?
Cassilane.　O *Annophill*; there is good cause my girle:
　He has plaid the thiefe with me, and filch'd away　　　240
　The richest jewell of my life, my honour,
　Wearing it publikely with that applause,
　As if he justly did inherit it.
Antinous.　Would I had in my Infancy been laid
　Within my grave, covered with your blessings,
　Then growne up to a man, to meet your curses.
Cassilane.　O that thou hadst.
　Then I had been the father of a childe,

234 off] *i.e.*, of (*as also below, at* IV.ii.42)　　　245 your] F2; you F1

Dearer then thou wert even unto me,
When hope perswaded me I had begot   250
Another selfe in thee: Out of mine eyes,
As farre as I have throwne thee from my heart,
That I may live and dye forgetting thee.

Erota.   How has he deserv'd this untam'd anger,
That when he might have ask't for his reward
Some honour for himselfe, or masse of pelfe,
He onely did request to have erected
Your Statue in the Capitoll, with Titles
Ingrav'd upon't, The Patron of his Countrey?

Cassilane.   That, that's the poison in the gilded cup,   260
The Serpent in the flowers, that stings my honour,
And leaves me dead in fame: Gods doe a justice,
And rip his bosome up, that men may see,
Seeing, believe the subtle practises
Written within his heart: But I am heated,
And doe forget this presence, and my selfe.
Your pardon, Lady.

Erota.   You should not aske, 'lesse you knew how to give.
For my sake *Cassilane*, cast out of your thoughts
All ill conceptions of your worthy son,   27
That (questionlesse) has ignorantly offended,
Declared in his penitence.

Cassilane.   Bid me dye (Lady) for your sake Ile doe it;
But that you'll say is nothing, for a man
That has out-liv'd his honour: But command me
In any thing save that, and *Cassilane*
Shall ever be your servant. Come *Annophill*,
(My joy in this world) thou shalt live with me,
Retired in some sollitarie nook,
The comfort of my age; my dayes are short,   280
And ought to be well spent: and I desire
No other witnesse of them but thy selfe,
And good *Arcanes*.

Annophil.   I shall obey you sir.

Gonçalo.   Noble sir:
If you taste any want of worldly meanes,

Let not that discontent you: know me your friend,
That hath, and can supply you.
Cassilane.   Sir, I am too much bound to you already,
And 'tis not of my cares the least, to give you
Faire satisfaction.   290
Gonʒalo.   You may imagine I doe speak to that end,
But trust me, 'tis to make you bolder with me.
Cassilane.   Sir, I thanke you, and may make triall of you,
Meane time my service.
Annophil.   Brother be comforted; so long as I continue
Within my fathers love, you cannot long
Stand out an Exile: I must goe live with him,
And I will prove so good an Orator
In your behalfe, that you againe shall gaine him,
Or I will stirre in him another anger,   300
And be lost with you.
Antinous.   Better I were neglected: for he is hasty,
And through the Choller that abounds in him,
(Which for the time divides from him his judgement)
He may cast you off, and with you his life;
For griefe will strait surprize him, and that way
Must be his death: the sword has try'd too often,
And all the deadly Instruments of warre
Have aim'd at his great heart, but ne're could touch it:
Yet not a limbe about him wants a scarre.   310
Cassilane.   Madam my duty——
Erota.   Will you be gone?
Cassilane.   I must (Lady) but I shall be ready,
When you are pleas'd command me, for your service.
[*To* Philander] Excellent Prince——To all my heartie love,
And a good farewell.
Mochingo.   Thanks honest *Cassilane.*
Cassilane.   Come *Annophill.*
Gonʒalo.   Shall I not wait upon you sir?
Cassilane.   From hence you shall not stirre a foot:
Loving *Gonʒalo*, it must be all my study

311 be] F2; he F1

691

To requite you.   320
Gonzalo.   If I may be so fortunate to deserve
    The name of friend from you, I have enough.
Cassilane.   You are so, and you have made your selfe so.
Gonzalo.   I will then preserve it.

        [*Exeunt* Cassilane, Annophil, *and* Arcanes.]

Erota.   *Antinous* you are my servant, are you not?
Antinous.   It hath pleased you so to grace me.
Erota.   Why are you then dejected? you will say,
    You have lost a father; but you have found a Mistris
    Doubles that losse: be master of your spirit;
    You have a cause for it, which is my favour.   330
Gonzalo.   And mine.
Erota.   Will no man ease me of this foole?
Gonzalo.   Your fellow.
Erota.   *Antinous* wait upon us.
Antinous.   I shall Madam.
Gonzalo.   Nay, but Ladie, Ladie.
Erota.   Sir, you are rude:
    And if you be the Master of such meanes
    As you doe talk of, you should learne good manners.
Gonzalo.   O Lady, you can finde a fault in me,
    But not perceive it in your selfe; you must, shall heare me:
    I love you for your pride, 'tis the best vertue
    In you.
Erota [*aside*].   I could hang this fellow now:——by whom   340
    Are you supported, that you dare doe this?
    Have you not example here in a Prince
    Transcending you in all things, yet beares himselfe
    As doth become a man had seen my beautie?
    Back to your Countrey, and your Curtizans,
    Where you may be admired for your wealth,
    Which being consum'd, may be a meanes to gaine you
    The opinion of some wit. Here's nothing to be got
    But scorne, and losse of time.
Gonzalo.   Which are things I delight in.

321 If] F2; *omit* F1

692

Erota.   *Antinous* follow me.

Exeunt [all but Gonzalo *and* Mochingo].

Gonzalo.   She is vext to the soule.   350

Mochingo.   Let her be vext, 'tis fit she should be so:
  Give me thy hand *Gonzalo*, thou art in our favour,
  For we doe love to cherish lofty spirits,
  Such as percusse ever the earth, and bound
  With an erected countenance to the clouds.

Gonzalo.   'S-foot, what thing is this?

Mochingo.   I doe love fire-works, because they mount:
  An Exhalation I professe to adore,
  Beyond a fixed starre, 'tis more illustrious,
  As every thing rais'd out of smoak is so: 360
  Their vertue is in action: what doe you think of me?

Gonzalo.   Troth sir,
  You are beyond my ghesse, I know you not.

Mochingo.   Doe you know your selfe?

Gonzalo.   Yes sir.

Mochingo.   Why you and I
  Are one: I am proud, and very proud too,
  That I must tell you; I saw it did become you,
  Cousin *Gonzalo*, prethee let it be so.

Gonzalo.   Let it be so good cousin.

Mochingo.   I am no great ones foole.

Gonzalo.   I hope so, for alliance sake.

Mochingo.   Yet I do serve
  The Mighty, Monstrous, and Magnanimous   370
  Invincible *Erota.*

Gonzalo.   O good cousin,
  Now I have you: Ile meet you in your Coat.

Mochingo.   Coat? I have my horse-mans coat I must confesse
  Lin'd through with Velvet, and a Scarlet out-side;
  If you'll meet me in't, Ile send fort;
  And cousin you shall see me with much comfort,
  For it is both a new one, and a right one,
  It did not come collaterall.

---

*354 percusse ever the earth] Dyce; percusseere the earrh F1; percusse the Earth F2

Gonzalo.   Adieu
  Good cousin; at this present I have some businesse.
Mochingo.   Farewell (excellent cousin).   380

[Exeunt severally.]

Enter Gonzalo and Fernando.   III.i

Gonzalo.   *Candy*, I say, is lost already.
Fernando.   Yes,
  If to be conqueror be to be lost.
Gonzalo.   You have it; one dayes conquest hath undone them,
  And sold them to their vassalage; for what
  Have I else toyl'd my braines, profusely emptied
  My moneyes, but to make them slaves to *Venice*,
  That so in case the sword did lose his edge,
  Then Art might sharpen hers?
Fernando.   *Gonzalo* how?
Gonzalo.   *Fernando* thus: you see how through this Land,
  Both of the best and basest I am honour'd;   10
  I onely gave the State of *Venice* notice,
  When, where, and how to land, or you had found
  A better entertainment: I was he
  Encourag'd young *Antinous* to affront
  The devill his father: for the devill I think
  Dares not doe more in battaile.
Fernando.   But why did ye?
  I finde no such great policie in that.
Gonzalo.   Indeed *Fernando*, thou canst fight, not plot:
  Had they continu'd one, they two alone
  Were of sufficient courage and performance   20
  To beat an Armie.
Fernando.   Now by all my hopes,
  I rather shall admire, then envy vertue.
Gonzalo.   Why then by all your hopes you'll rather have
  Your Braines knockt out, then learne how to be wise;
  You States-man? Well sir, I did more then this,
  When *Cassilane* crav'd from the common treasure
  Pay for his Souldiers, I strook home, and lent him
  An hundred thousand Duckets.

694

Fernando.   Marry sir,
The policy was little, the love lesse,
And honesty least of all.
Gonzalo.   How say ye by that?   30
Go fight, I say goe fight, Ile talke no more with you,
You are insensible.
Fernando.   Well, I shall observe ye.
Gonzalo.   Why look you sir, by this meanes have I got
The greatest part of *Cassilanes* estate
Into my hands, which he can ne're redeem,
But must of force sinke: do you conceive me now?
Fernando.   So:
But why have you importuned the Senate,
For me to sojourne with him?
Gonzalo.   There's the quintessence,
The soule, and grand elixer of my wit: 40
For he (according to his noble nature)
Will not be knowne to want, though he do want,
And will be bankrupted so much the sooner,
And made the subject of our scorne and laughter.
Fernando.   Here's a perfect plotted stratagem.
Gonzalo.   Why? could you
Imagine, that I did not hate in heart
My Countreyes enemies? yes, yes, *Fernando*,
And I will be the man that shall undoe them.
Fernando.   Ye are in a ready way.
Gonzalo.   I was never out on't.
Peace, here comes a wise Coxcombe, a tame Coward.   50

                    Enter Gaspero.

Now worthy *Gaspero*, what, you come (I know)
To be my Lord *Fernando's* Conductor
To old *Cassilane*?
Gaspero.   To wait upon him.
Gonzalo.   And my Lords the Senators sent you?
Gaspero.   My noble Lord they did.

39 him] Seward; them F1-2

695

Gonʒalo.   My Lord *Fernando*,
This gentleman, (as humble as you see him)
Is even this Kingdomes treasure; In a word,
'Tis his chiefe glory that he is not wiser
Then honest, nor more honest then approv'd
In truth and faith.

Gaspero.   My Lord——

Gonʒalo.   You may be bold   60
To trust him with your bosome, he'll not deceive,
If you relie upon him once.

Fernando.   Your name is *Gaspero?*

Gaspero.   Your servant.

Gonʒalo.   Goe commend me
(Right honest *Gaspero*) commend me heartily
To noble *Cassilane*, tell him my love
Is vow'd to him

Gaspero.   I shall.

Gonʒalo.   I know you will.——
My Lord I cannot long be absent from you.

Fernando.   Sir, you are now my guide.

                                   Exit [*with* Gaspero].

Gonʒalo.   Thus my designes
Run uncontroul'd; yet *Venice* though I be
Intelligencer to thee, in my braine   70
Are other large Projects: for if proud *Erota*
Bend to my lure, I will be *Candy's* King,
And Duke of *Venice* too. Ha? *Venice* too?
O 'twas prettily shov'd in: why not? *Erota*
May in her love seale all sure: if she swallow
The bait, I am Lord of both; if not, yet *Candy*
Despight of all her power shall be ruin'd.

                                        [*Exit.*]

          Enter Cassilane, Arcanes, *and* Annophill.   [II]

Cassilane [*to* Arcanes].   Urge me no farther.——*Annophill.*

Annophil.   My Lord.

Cassilane.   Thy fathers poverty has made thee happie;

          696

For though 'tis true, this solitary life
Sutes not with youth and beautie, O my childe,
Yet 'tis the sweetest Guardian to protect
Chaste names from Court-aspersions; there a Lady
Tender and delicate in yeares and graces,
That doats upon the charmes of ease and pleasure,
Is ship-wrackt on the shore; for 'tis much safer
To trust the Ocean in a leaking ship,　　　　　　　　　　10
Then follow greatnesse in the wanton rites
Of luxurie and sloth.

Annophil.　　　　　　My wishes sir,
Have never soar'd a higher flight, then truely
To finde occasion wherein I might witnesse
My duty and obedience.

Cassilane.　　　　　'Tis well said.——
Canst thou forbeare to laugh *Arcanes?*

Arcanes.　　　　　　　　Why sir?

Cassilane.　　To look upon my beggerie, to look
Upon my patience in my beggerie: Tell me,
Does it shew handsome? bravely? thou wilt flatter me,
And sweare that I'm not miserable.

Arcanes.　　　　　　　　Nothing　　　　　20
More glorifies the noble, and the valiant,
Then to despise contempt: if you continue
But to enjoy your selfe, you in your selfe
Enjoy all store besides.

Cassilane.　　　　　An excellent change:
I that some seven Apprentice-ships commanded
A hundred Ministers, that waited on
My nod, and sometimes twenty thousand souldiers,
Am now retir'd, attended in my age
By one poore maid, followed by one old man.

Arcanes.　　Sir, you are lower in your owne repute　　30
Then you have reason for.

Cassilane.　　　　　　The Romane Captaines,
I meane the best, such as with their blouds

19 handsome? bravely? thou] Variorum; handsome? bravely? | Handsome? thou F1–2
*20 I'm not miserable] Colman (Sympson *conj.*); I am miserable F1–2

Purchas'd their Countreyes peace, the Empires glorie,
Were glad at last to get them to some Farmes,
Off-from the clamours of the ingratefull great ones,
And the unsteddy multitude, to live
As I doe now, and 'twas their blessing too,
Let it be ours *Arcanes*.

Arcanes.   I cannot but
Applaud your scorne of injuries.

Cassilane.   Of injuries?
Arcanes, *Annophill*, lend both your hands.   40
So, what say yee now?

Arcanes.   Why now my Lord——

Cassilane.   I sweare
By all my past prosperities; thus standing
Between you two, I thinke my selfe as great,
As mighty, as if in the Capitoll
I stood amidst the Senators, with all
The Cretane subjects prostrate at my feet.

Annophil.   Sir, you are here more safe.

Cassilane.   And more beloved:
Why look yee sirs, I can forget the weakenesse
Of the traduced souldiers, the neglect
Of the faire-spoken Senate, the impietie   50
Of him, the villaine, whom (to my dishonour)
The World miscalls my son. But by the——

Arcanes.   Sir,
Remember that you promis'd no occasion
Should move your patience.

Cassilane.   Thou do'st chide me friendly.
He shall not have the honour to be thought upon
Amongst us.

Enter a Servant.

Now? the newes?

Servant.   The Secretarie,
With the Venetian prisoner, desire
Admittance to your Lordship.

Cassilane.   How? to me?

What mysterie is this? *Arcanes* can they
Thinkst thou, meane any good?
Arcanes.   My Lord, they dare not   60
Intend ought else but good.
Cassilane.   Tis true, they dare not;
    Arcanes welcome them:

                              [*Exeunt* Arcanes *and* Servant.]
                         Come hither *Annophill*,
Stand close to me, wee'll change our affability
Into a forme of State: and they shall know
Our heart is still our owne.

              Enter Arcanes, Fernando, *and* Gaspero.

Arcanes.   My Lord——
Cassilane.   *Arcanes,*
    I know them both: *Fernando*, as you are
    A man of greatnesse, I should under-value
    The right my sword hath fought for, to observe
    Low-fawning complements, but as you are
    A Captive and a stranger, I can love you,   70
    And must be kinde. You are welcome.
Fernando.   'Tis the all
    Of my ambition.
Gaspero.   And for proof how much
    He truely honours your heroick vertues,
    The Senate on his importunity,
    Commend him to your Lordships guard.
Cassilane.   For what?
Gaspero.   During the time of his abode in *Candy*,
    To be your houshold guest.
Fernando.   Wherein my Lord.
    You shall more make me debtor to your noblenesse,
    Then if you had return'd me without ransome.
Cassilane.   Are you in earnest Sir?
Fernando.   My sute to the Senate   80
    Shall best resolve you that.
Cassilane.   Come hither Secretarie,
    Look that this be no trick now put upon me:

                         699

For if it be——Sirrah——
Gaspero.   As I have troth
  (My Lord) it onely is a favour granted
  Upon *Fernando's* motion, from himselfe:
  Your Lordship must conceive, I'de not partake
  Ought, but what should concerne your honour; who
  Has been the prop, our Countries shield, and safety,
  But the renowned *Cassilane*?
Cassilane.   Applause
  Is *Gaspero*——puffe——nothing.——Why, young Lord,   90
  Would you so much be sequester'd from those
  That are the blazing Comets of the time,
  To live a solitarie life with me?
  A man forsaken? all my hospitality
  Is now contracted to a few; these two,
  This tempest-wearied souldier, and this Virgin;
  We cannot feast your eyes with Masques and Revells,
  Or Courtly Anticks: the sad sports we riot in,
  Are Tales of foughten fields, of Martiall scarres,
  And things done long agoe, when men of courage   100
  Were held the best, not those well-spoken youths,
  Who onely carry conquest in their tongues;
  Now stories of this nature are unseasonable
  To entertaine a great Dukes son with.
Fernando.   Herein
  Shall my Captivity be made my happinesse,
  Since what I lose in freedome, I regaine
  (With int'rest) by conversing with a Souldier
  So matchlesse for experience, as great *Cassilane*.
  Pray sir admit me.
Cassilane.   If you come to mock me,
  I shall be angrie.
Fernando.   By the love I beare   110
  To goodnesse, my intents are honourable.
Cassilane.   Then in a word, my Lord, your visitations
  Shall find all due respect: But I am now
  Growne old, and have forgot to be an host;
  Come when you please you are welcome.

Fernando.   Sir, I thank you.
Annophil.   Good sir be not too urgent; for my father
   Will soon be mov'd: yet in a noble way
   Of courtesie he is as easily conquer'd.
Fernando.   Lady, your words are like your beauty, powerfull;
   I shall not strive more how to doe him service,   120
   Then how to be your servant.
Cassilane.   Shee's my daughter,
   And does command this house.
Fernando.   I so conceive her.
Cassilane.   Doe you heare?
Gaspero.   My honour'd Lord.
Cassilane.   Commend me to them.
   Tell 'em I thank them.
Gaspero.   Whom my Lord?
Cassilane.   The Senate:
   Why how come you so dull? O they are gratious,
   And infinitely gratefull——Thou art eloquent,
   Speak modestly in mentioning my services:
   And if ought fall out in the By, that must
   Of meere necessity touch any act
   Of my deserving praises, blush when you talke on't,   130
   'Twill make them blush to heare on't.
Gaspero.   Why my Lord——
Cassilane.   Nay, nay, you are too wise now; good, observe me,
   I doe not raile against the hopefull Springall,
   That builds up monuments in Brasse; reares Trophies
   With Mottoes and Inscriptions, quaint devices
   Of Poetrie and fiction; let's be quiet.
Arcanes.   You must not crosse him.
Gaspero.   Not for *Candys* wealth.
Fernando.   You shall for ever make me yours.
Annophil.   'Twere pitty
   To double your captivity.

              Enter Decius.

Arcanes.   Who's here.
   Decius?

Cassilane.   Ha! *Decius?* who nam'd *Decius?*   140
Decius.   My duty to your Lordship: I am bold,
    Presuming on your noble and knowne goodnesse
    To——
Cassilane.   What?
Decius.   Present you with this——
Cassilane.   Letter?
Decius.   Yes my honour'd Lord.
Cassilane.   From whom?
Decius.   Please you peruse
    The in-side, you shall finde a name subscrib'd,
    In such humility, in such obedience,
    That you your selfe will judge it tyranny
    Not to receive it favourably.
Cassilane.   Hey-day.
    Good words my Masters; this is Court-infection,
    And none but Cowards ply them: Tell me, *Decius,*   150
    Without more circumstance, who is the sender?
Decius.   Your much griev'd sonne *Antinous.*
Cassilane.   On my life
    A challenge; speak, as thou art worthy speak:
    Ile answer't.
Decius.   Honour'd Sir——
Cassilane.   No honour'd Sirs——
    Foole your yong Idoll with such pompous Attributes.
    Say briefely, what containes it?
Decius.   'Tis a lowly
    Petition for your favour.
Cassilane.   Rash young man,
    But that thou art under my owne roofe, and know'st
    I dare not any way infringe the Lawes
    Of hospitality, thou should'st repent   160
    Thy bold and rude intrusion. But presume not
    Againe to shew thy Letter, for thy life;
    Decius, not for thy life.
Arcanes.   Nay then (my Lord)
    I can with-hold no longer: you are too rough,
    And wrestle against nature, with a violence

More then becomes a father: wherein would yee
Come nearer to the likenesse of a God,
Then in your being entreated? Let not thirst
Of honour, make you quite forget you are
A man, and what makes perfect man-hoods comforts,   170
A father.

Annophil.   If a memory remaine
Of my departed mother; if the purity
Of her unblemish'd faith deserve to live
In your remembrance, let me yet by these
Awake your love to my uncomforted Brother.

Fernando.   I am a stranger: but so much I tender
Your sons desertfull vertues, that I vow
His Sword nere conquer'd me so absolutely,
As shall your curtesie, if you vouchsafe
At all our instances, to new receive him,   180
Into your wonted favour.

Gaspero.   Sir, you cannot
Require more low submission.

Annophil.   Am I not
Growne vile yet in your eyes? then by the name
Of father, let me once more sue for him,
Who is the only now remaining branch
With me, of that most ancient roote, whose body
You are, deare sir.

Cassilane.   'Tis well: an host of furies
Could not have baited me, more torturingly,
More rudely, or more most unnaturally!
Decius, I say, let me no more heare from him;   190
For this time goe thou hence, and know from me
Thou art beholding to me that I have not
Killed thee already, looke to't next, looke to't.
Arcanes fie, fie *Annophil.*

                                        Exit.

Arcanes.   He's gone.
Chaf'd beyond sufferance: we must follow him.

167 a] Seward; *omit* F1–2

Decius.   Lady, this letter is to you.
Annophil.   Come with me,
  For we must speake in private:——please you sir,
  To see what entertainement our sad house
  Can yeild?
Fernando.   I shall attend you Lady.
                       Exeunt [Annophil, Arcanes, *and* Decius].
Gaspero.   How do ye like
  To sojourne here, my Lord?
Fernando.   More then to feast   200
  With all the Princes of the earth besides:
  Gonzalo told me that thou wert honest.
Gaspero.   Yes sir,
  And you shall find it.
Fernando.   Shall I?
Gaspero.   All my follies
  Be else recorded to my shame.
Fernando.   Enough,
  My heart is here for ever lodg'd.
Gaspero.   The Lady——
Fernando.   The place admits no time to utter all,
  But *Gaspero* if thou wilt prove my friend,
  I'le say thou art——
Gaspero.   Your servant: I conceive ye,
  Wee'll choose some fitter leisure.
Fernando.   Never man
  Was (in a moment) or more bless'd, or wretched.   210
                              Exeunt.

     Enter Hyparcha (*placing two chaires*), Antinous, *and* Erota.   [III.

Erota.   Leave us.
Hyparcha.   I shall.   *Exit.*
Erota.   *Antinous* sit downe.
Antinous.   Madam——
Erota.   I say sit downe: I do command you sit;
  For, looke what honour thou dost gaine by me,

3 dost] F2; didst F1

704

I cannot lose by it: happy *Antinous*,
The graces, and the higher Deities
Smil'd at thy birth, and still continue it:
Then thinke that I (who scorne lesser examples)
Must doe the like: such as do taste my power,
And talke of it, with feare and reverence,
Shall do the same unto the man I favour.   10
I tell thee youth, thou hast a conquest won,
Since thou cam'st home, greater then that last,
Which dignified thy fame; greater then if
Thou sholdst goe out againe, and conquer farther;
For I am not asham'd to acknowledge
My selfe subdued by thee.
Antinous.   Great Lady——
Erota.   Sit still, I will not heare thee else: now speake,
And speake like my *Antinous*, like my Souldier,
Whom Cupid, and not Mars, hath sent to Battle.
Antinous.   I must (I see) be silent.
Erota.   So thou maist: 20
There's greater Action in it than in clamour,
A looke, (if it be gratious) will begin the War,
A word conclude it: then prove no Coward,
Since thou hast such a friendly enemie,
That teaches thee to conquer.
Antinous.   You do amaze me Madam,
I have no skill, no practice in this War,
And whether you be serious, or please
To make your sport on a dejected man,
I cannot rightly ghesse: but be it as it will,
It is a like unhappinesse to me: 30
My discontents beare those conditions in them.
                                        Musick [within].
And lay me out so wretched, no designes
(How ever truly promising a good)
Can make me rellish ought, but a sweet-bitter,
Voluntarie Exile.   *Musick againe [within].*
Erota.   Why an Exile?
What comfort can there be in those companions

Which sad thoughts bring along with them?——*Hyparcha*!

Enter Hyparcha.

Hyparcha.   Madam.
Erota.   Whence comes this well-tun'd sound?
Hyparcha.   I know not Madam.
Erota.   Listen wench: 40
What ever friendly hands they are that send it
Let 'em play on; they are Masters of their facultie.

Song [*within*].

Doth it please you sir?
Antinous.   According to the time.
Erota.   Go to 'em wench,
And tell 'em, we shall thanke 'em; for they have kept
As good time to our disposition, as to their instruments;

[*Exit* Hyparcha.]

Unlesse *Antinous* shall say he loves,

Enter Philander.

There never can be sweeter accents uttered.
Philander.   Let then the heart, that did imploy those hands,
Receive some small share of your thankes with them,   50
'Tis happinesse enough that you did like it;
A fortune unto me, that I should send it
In such a lucky minute; but to obtaine
So gratious welcome, did exceed my hopes.
Erota.   Good Prince, I thanke you for it.
Philander.   O Madam, poure not (to fast) joyes on me,
But sprinkle 'em so gently, I may stand 'em:
It is enough at first, you have laid aside
Those cruell angry lookes out of your eyes,
With which (as with your lovely) you did strike   60
All your beholders in an Extasie.
Erota.   *Philander*, you have long profess'd to love me——
Philander.   Have I but profest it Madam?
Erota.   Nay, but heare me!

37 with them?——*Hyparcha*!] Dyce; with? F1–2   56 to] *i.e.*, too

706

Philander.   More attentively, then to an Oracle.

Erota.   And I will speake more truly, if more can be:
   Nor shall my language be wrapt up in Riddles,
   But plaine as truth it selfe: I love this Gentleman,
   Whose griefes has made him so uncapable
   Of Love, he will not heare, at least not understand it.
   I that have lookt with scornefull eyes on thee,   70
   And other Princes mighty in their states,
   And in their friends as fortunate, have now prai'd,
   In a petitionary kind almost,
   This man, this wel-deserving man, (that I must say)
   To looke upon this beauty, yet you see
   He casts his eyes rather upon the ground,
   Then he will turne 'em this way: *Philander*
   You looke pale; I'le talke no more.

Philander.   Pray go forward: I would be your Martyr,
   To dye thus, were immortally to live.   80

Erota.   Will you goe to him then, and speake for me?
   You have loved longer, but not fervener,
   Know how to speake, for you have done it like
   An Orator, even for your selfe: then how will you for me
   Whom you professe to love above your selfe.

Philander.   The curses of dissemblers follow me
   Unto my grave, and if I do not so.

Erota.   You may (as all men do) speake boldlier, better
   In their friends cause still, then in your owne;
   But speake your utmost, yet you cannot feigne,   90
   I will stand by, and blush to witnesse it.
   Tell him since I beheld him, I have lost
   The happinesse of this life, food, and rest;
   A quiet bosome, and the state I went with.
   Tell him how he has humbled the proud,
   And made the living, but a dead *Erota*.
   Tell him withall, that she is better pleas'd
   With thinking on him, then enjoying these.
   Tell him——*Philander*, Prince; I talke in vaine
   To you, you do not marke me.   100

Philander.   Indeed, I do.

Erota.   But thou dost looke so pale,
  As thou wilt spoyle the story in relating.
Philander.   Not, if I can but live to tell it.
Erota.   It may be you have not the heart.
Philander.   I have a will I am sure, how e're my heart
  May play the coward, but if you please, I'le trie.
Erota.   If a kisse will strengthen thee, I give you leave
  To challenge it, nay, I will give it you.   [*Kisses him.*]
Philander.   O that a man should taste such heavenly blisse!
  And be enjoyn'd to beg it for another.   110
Erota.   Alas, it is a miserie I grieve
  To put you to, and I will suffer rather
  In his tyranny, than thou in mine.
Philander.   Nay Madam, since I cannot have your love,
  I will endeavour to deserve your pitty:
  For I had rather have within the grave
  Your love, then you should want it upon earth.
  But how can I hope, with a feeble tongue
  To instruct him in the rudiments of love,
  When your most powerfull beauty cannot worke it?   120
Erota.   Do what thou wilt (*Philander*); the request
  Is so unreasonable, that I quit thee of it.
  I desire now no more, but the true patience,
  And fortitude of Lovers, with those helpes
  Of sighes and teares, which I think is all the Phisick——
Philander.   O if he did but heare you, 'twere enough;
  And I will wake him from his Appoplexie.——
  Antinous!
Antinous.   My Lord?
Philander.   Nay pray,
  No curtesie to me, you are my Lord,
  (Indeed you are) for you command her heart,   130
  That commands mine: nor can you want to know it.
  For looke you, she that told it you in words,
  Explaines it now more passionately in teares;
  Either thou hast no heart, or a marble one,
  If those drops cannot melt it; prethee looke up,
  And see how sorrow sits within her eyes,
  And love the griefe she goes with (if not her)

Of which thou art the parent: and never yet
Was there (by nature) that thing made so stony,
But it would love what ever it begot.　　　　　　　　　　140
Antinous.　He that begot me, did beget these cares
Which are good issues, though happily by him
Esteemed monsters: nay, the ill-judging world
Is likely enough to give them those Characters.
Philander.　What's this to love, and to the Lady? he's old,
Wrathfull, perverse, selfe-will'd, and full of anger,
Which are his faults; but let them not be thine;
He thrusts you from his love, she puls thee on,
He doubts your vertues, she doth double them:
O either use thy owne eyes, or take mine,　　　　　　　150
And with them, my heart, then thou wilt love her,
Nay, doate upon her, more then on thy duty,
And men will praise thee equally for it;
Neglecting her, condemne thee, as a man
Unworthy such a fortune: O *Antinous*,
'Tis not the friendship that I beare to thee,
But her command, that makes me utter this:
And when I have prevail'd, let her but say,
Philander, you must dye or this is nothing,
It shall be done together with a breath,　　　　　　　160
With the same willingnesse, I live to serve her.
Erota.　No more *Philander.*
Philander.　All I have done, is little yet to purpose,
But ere I leave him, I will perceive him blush;
And make him feele the passions that I do,
And every true lover will assist me in't,
And lend me their sad sighs to blow it home,
For *Cupid* wants a dart to wound this bosome.
Erota.　No more, no more *Philander*, I can endure no more,
Pray let him goe; go good *Antinous*, make peace　　　170
With your owne mind, no matter though I perish.

　　　　　　　　　　　　　　　　　　　Exeunt.

　　　　　　Enter Hyparcha, *and* Mochingo.　　　　IV.i

Hyparcha.　I cannot help it.
Mochingo.　　　　　　　Nor do I require it,

709

The malady needs no Phisitian,
Helpe hospitall people.
Hyparcha.   I am glad to heare
You are so valliant.
Mochingo.   Valiant?
Can any man be proud that is not valiant;
Foolish woman, what wouldst thou say? thou——
I know not what to call thee.
Hyparcha.   I can you,
For I can call you Coxcome, Asse, and Puppy——
Mochingo.   You do do it, I thanke you.
Hyparcha.   That you'l lose a fortune,
Which a Cobler better deserves, then thou dost.   10
Mochingo.   Do not provoke my magnanimity,
For when I am insens'd, I am insensible;
Go tell thy Lady, that hath sent me word
She will discard me, that I discard her,
And throw a scorne upon her, which I would not,
But that she does me wrong.   [*Exit.*]

Enter Erota, *and* Antinous.

Erota.   Do you not glory in your conquest more,
To take some great man prisoner, then to kill him?
And shall a Lady find lesse mercie from you,
That yeilds her selfe your Captive, and for her Ransome,   20
Will give the jewell of her life, her heart,
Which she hath lockt from all men but thy selfe:
For shame (*Antinous*) throw this dulnesse off,
Art thou a man no where but in the field?
Hyparcha [*aside*].   He must here Drums, and Trumpets or he sleeps,
And at this instant dreames he's in his Armour:
These Iron-hearted Souldiers are so cold,
Till they be beaten to a womans armes,
And then they love 'em better then their owne;
No Fort can hold them out.   [*Exit.*] 30
Antinous.   What pitty is it (Madam) that your selfe,

17 *Erota.*] F2; *Ant.* F1   25 or] Seward; ere F1–2

710

Who are all excellence, should become so wretched,
To thinke on such a wretch as griefe hath made me?
Seldom despairing men looke up to heaven,
Although it still speake to 'em in its glories;
For when sad thoughts perplexe the mind of man,
There is a plumit in the heart, that waighs,
And puls us (living) to the dust we came from;
Did you but see the miseries you pursue,
(As I the happinesse that I avoid   40
That doubles my afflictions) you would flye
Unto some wildernesse, or to your grave,
And there find better comforts then in me,
For love, and cares can never dwell together.

Erota.   They should,
If thou hadst but my love, and I thy cares.

Antinous.   What wild beast in the Desart, but would be
Taught by this Tongue to leave his crueltie,
Though all the beauties of the face were vail'd!
But I am savager than any beast,   50
And shall be so till *Decius* do arive,
Whom with so much submission I have sent
Under my hand, that if he do not bring
His Benediction backe, he must to me
Be much more crueller, then I to you.

Erota.   Is't but your fathers pardon you desire?

Antinous.   With his love, and then nothing next that, like yours.

Enter Decius.

Erota.   *Decius* is come.

Antinous.   O welcome friend; If I apprehend not
Too much of joy, there's comfort in thy lookes.   60

Erota.   There is indeed: I prethee *Decius* speake it.

Decius [*aside*].   How? prethee *Decius*? this woman's strangly alter'd.

Antinous.   Why dost not speake (good friend) and tell me how
The reverent blessing of my life, received
My humble lines; wept he for joy?

Decius.   No, ther's a letter will informe you more:

[*Gives letter.*]

711

Yet I can tell you, what I think will grieve you,
The old man is in want, and angry still,
And povertie is the bellowes to the Coale,
More then distast from you as I imagine.   70

Antinous. What's here? how's this? It cannot be: now sure
My griefes delude my senses.

Erota.   In his lookes,
I read a world of changes: *Decius* marke
With what a sad amazement he surveies
The newes: canst thou ghesse what 'tis?

Decius.   None good I feare.

Erota. I feare so too: and then——

Antinous.   It is her hand.

Erota. Are you not well?

Antinous.   Too well: if I were ought
But Rock, this Letter would conclude my miseries,
Peruse it (Lady) and resolve me then,
In what a case I stand.

Decius.   Sir, the worst is,   80
Your fathers lownesse, and distaste.

Antinous.   No *Decius*,
My sister writes, *Fernando* has made suite
For love to her: and to expresse sincerely
His constant truth, hath like a noble Gentleman,
Discovered plots of treachery; contriv'd
By false *Gonzalo*, not intending more
The utter ruine of our house, then generally
Candies confusion.

Decius.   'Tis a generous part
Of young *Fernando*.

Antinous.   'Tis, and I could wish
All thrift to his affections *Decius*.——   90
You find the summe on't Madam.

Erota.   Yes, I do.

Antinous. And can you now yet think a heart opprest
With such a throng of cares, can entertaine
An amorous thought? love frees all toyles but one,
Calamitie and it can ill agree.

Erota. Wil't please ye speake my doome?
Antinous.　　　　　　　　　　Alas great Lady,
　Why will you flatter thus a desperate man,
　That is quite cast away? O had you not
　Procured the Senates warrant to enforce
　My stay, I had not heard of these sad newes.　　　　100
　What would you have me do?
Erota. 　　　　　　　Love me, or kill me,
　One word shall sentence either: for as truth
　Is just, if you refuse me, I am resolute
　Not to out-live my thraldome.
Antinous. 　　　　　　　Gentle Lady——
Erota. Say, must I live, or dye?
Decius. 　　　　　　My Lord, how can you
　Be so inexorable: here's occasion
　Of succouring your father in his wants,
　Securely profer'd: pray sir, entertaine it.
Erota. What is my sentence?
Antinous. 　　　　What you please to have it!
Erota. As thou art Gentle, speake those words againe.　　110
Antinous. Madam, you have prevail'd, yet give me leave
　Without offence, ere I resigne the interest
　Your heart hath in my heart, to prove your secresie.
Erota. *Antinous*, 'tis the greatest Argument
　Of thy affections to me.
Antinous. 　　　　Madam, thus then,
　My father stands for certaine summes engag'd
　To treacherous *Gonzalo*; and 'has morgag'd
　The greatest part of his estate to him:
　If you receive this morgage, and procure
　Acquitance from *Gonzalo* to my father,　　　　120
　I am what you would have me be.
Erota. 　　　　　　You'l love me then?
Antinous. Provided (Madam) that my father know not
　I am an Agent for him.
Erota. 　　　　If I faile

<hr>

117 morgag'd] F2; more 'gag'd F1

713

In this, I am unworthy to be lov'd.
Antinous.   Then (with your favour) thus I seale my truth,
    To day, and *Decius* witnesse how unchangingly
    I shall still love *Erota.*
Erota.   Thou hast quickned
    A dying heart *Antinous.*
Decius.   This is well:
    Much happinesse to both.   [*Exit* Decius.]

Enter Hyparcha.

Hyparcha.   The Lord *Gonʒalo*
    Attends you Madam.
Erota.   Comes as we could wish,   130
    Withdraw *Antinous*, here's a Closset, where
    You may partake his errand;——let him enter.
                                [*Exit* Hyparcha.]
Antinous.   Madam you must be wary.
Erota.   Feare it not,
    I will be ready for him; to entertaine him
    With smiling welcome: *Exit* [Antinous].

Enter Gonzalo.

                    Noble sir, you take
    Advantage of the time; it had been fit
    Some notice of your presence, might have fashion'd
    A more prepared state.
Gonʒalo.   Do ye mocke me Madam?
Erota.   Trust me, you wrong your judgement, to repute
    My gratitude a fault: I have examin'd   140
    Your portly carriage, and will now confesse
    It hath not slightly won me.
Gonʒalo [*aside*].   The wind's turn'd;
    I thought 'twould come to this:——it pleas'd us Madam,
    At our last interview, to mention love,
    Have you consider'd on't?
Erota.   With more then common
    Content: but sir, if what you spake, you meant,
    (As I have cause to doubt) then——

714

Gonzalo.　　　　　　　　　　　　　What, (sweet Lady)?

Erota.　　Methinks we should lay by this forme of statelinesse.
　　Loves courtship is familiar, and for instance,
　　See what a change it hath begot in me,　　　　　　　　　　150
　　I could talke humbly now, as Lovers use.

Gonzalo.　　And I: and I: we meet in one selfe-center,
　　Of blest consent.

Erota.　　　　　　　I hope my weakenesse sir,
　　Shall not deserve neglect: but if it prove so,
　　I am not the first Lady has been ruin'd
　　By being too credulous: you will smart for't one day.

Gonzalo.　　Angell-like-Lady, let me be held a villaine,
　　If I love not sincerely.

Erota.　　　　　　　Would I knew it?

Gonzalo.　　Make proofe by any fit command.

Erota.　　　　　　　　　　　　What, do ye meane
　　To marry me?

Gonzalo.　　　　How? meane? nay more, I meane　　　　160
　　To make you Empresse of my earthly fortunes,
　　Regent of my desires, for did ye covet
　　To be a reall Queene, I could advance you.

Erota.　　Now I perceive you slight me, and would make me
　　More simple then my sexes frailety warrants.

Gonzalo.　　But say your mind, and you shall be a Queene.

Erota.　　On those conditions, call me yours.

Gonzalo.　　　　　　　　　　　　Enough,
　　But are we safe?

Erota.　　　　　　Assuredly.

Gonzalo.　　　　　　　　In short,
　　Yet Lady first be plaine: would you not choose
　　Much rather to prefer your own Sun-rising,　　　　　　170
　　Then any's else though ne're so neere entituled
　　By bloud, or right of birth?

Erota.　　　　　　　　'Tis a question
　　Needs not a resolution.

Gonzalo.　　　　　　　Good: what if

148 we] F2; me F1

715

I set the Crowne of *Candy* on your head?

Erota.   I were a Queene indeed then.

Gonzalo.   Madam, know
There's but a boy 'twixt you, and it: suppose him
Transhap'd into an Angell.

Erota.   Wise *Gonzalo*,
I cannot but admire thee.

Gonzalo.   'Tis worth thinking on:
Besides your husband shall be Duke of *Venice*.

Erota.   *Gonzalo*, Duke of *Venice*?

Gonzalo.   Ye are mine ye say.   180

Erota.   Pish: you but dally with me; and would lull me
In a rich golden dreame.

Gonzalo.   You are too much distrustfull of my truth.

Erota.   Then you must give me leave to apprehend
The meanes, and manner how.

Gonzalo.   Why thus——

Erota.   You shall not,
We may be over-heard; Affaires and counsels
Of such high nature, are not to be trusted
Not to the Aire it selfe, you shall in writing,
Draw out the full designe; which if effected,
I am as I professe.

Gonzalo.   O I applaud   190
Your ready care, and secresie.

Erota.   *Gonzalo*,
There is a bar yet, twixt our hopes and us,
And that must be remov'd.

Gonzalo.   What is't?

Erota.   Old *Cassilane*.

Gonzalo.   He? feare not him: I build upon his ruines
Already.

Erota.   I would find a smoother course
To shift him off.

Gonzalo.   As how?

Erota.   Wee'l talke in private,
I have a ready plot.

Gonzalo.   I shall adore you.

                                        Exeunt.

716

Enter Fernando, *and* Annophil.

Fernando.   Madam, although I hate unnoble practices,
    And therefore have perform'd no more then what
    I ought, for honours safety: yet *Annophil,*
    Thy love hath been the spur, to urge me forward
    For speedier diligence.
Annophil.   Sir your owne fame
    And memory will best reward themselves.
Fernando.   All gaine is losse (sweet beauty) if I misse
    My comforts here: The brother and the sister
    Have double conquer'd me, but thou maist triumph.
Annophil.   Good sir, I have a father.
Fernando.   Yes, a brave one;   10
    Could'st thou obscure thy Beauty, yet the happinesse
    Of being but his daughter, were a dowre
    Fit for a Prince: what say ye?
Annophil.   You have deserv'd
    As much as I should grant.
Fernando.   By this faire hand
    I take possession.
Annophil.   What in words I dare not,
    Imagine in my silence.
Fernando.   Thou art all vertue.

Enter Cassilane, *and* Arcanes.

Cassilane.   I'le tell thee how: *Baldwin* the Emperour,
    Pretending title, more through tyranny,
    Then right of conquest, or descent, usurp'd
    The stile of Lord o're all the Grecian Islands,   20
    And under colour of an amity
    With *Creet,* preferd the Marquesse *Mountferato*
    To be our Governor; the Cretians vex'd
    By the ambitious Turkes, in hope of aide
    From the Emperour, received for Generall,
    This *Mountferato*; he (the wars appeased)
    Plots with the state of *Venice,* and takes money

16.1 Cassilane] *Cassilanes* F1–2

Of them for *Candy*: they paid well, he steales
Away in secret; since which time, that right
The state of *Venice* claimes o're *Candy*, is   30
By purchase, not inheritance, or Conquest:
And hence growes all our quarrell.

Arcanes.   So a usurer
Or Lumbard-Jew, might with some bags of trash,
Buy halfe the Westerne world.

Cassilane.   Money *Arcanes*
Is now a God on earth: it cracks virginities,
And turns a Christian, Turke;
Bribes justice, cut-throats honour, does what not?

Arcanes.   Not captives *Candy*.

Cassilane.   Nor makes thee dishonest,
Nor me a Coward——Now sir, here is homely,
But friendly entertainment.

Fernando.   Sir, I find it.   40

Arcanes.   And like it, do ye not?

Fernando.   My repaire speakes for me.

Cassilane.   *Fernando* we were speaking off——how this?

Enter Gonzalo, *and* Gaspero, *with a Casket.*

Gonzalo.   Your friend, and servant.

Cassilane.   Creditors, my Lord,
Are Masters and no Servants: as the world goes,
Debters are very slaves to those to whom
They have been beholding to; in which respect,
I should feare you *Gonzalo*.

Gonzalo.   Me my Lord?
You owe me nothing.

Cassilane.   What, nor love, nor money?

Gonzalo.   Yes, love, I hope not money.

Cassilane.   All this braverie,
Will scarcely make that good.

Gonzalo.   'Tis done already: 50
See sir, your Morgage which I only took,
In case you and your son had in the wars
Miscarried: I yeild it up againe: 'tis yours.

Cassilane.   Are ye so conscionable?

Gonzalo.   'Tis your owne.

Cassilane.   Pish, pish, I'le not receive what is not mine,
That were a dangerous businesse.

Gonzalo.   Sir, I am paid for't,
The summes you borrowed, are return'd; The bonds
Cancell'd, and your acquittance formally seal'd:
Looke here sir, *Gaspero* is witnesse to it.

Gaspero.   My honoured Lord, I am.

Gonzalo.   My Lord *Fernando*,   60
Arcanes and the rest, you all shall testifie,
That I acquit Lord *Cassilane* for ever,
Of any debts to me.

Gaspero.   'Tis plaine and ample.

Arcanes.   Fortune will once againe smile on us fairely.

Cassilane.   But hearke ye, hearke ye, if you be in earnest,
Whence comes this bounty? or whose is't?

Gonzalo.   In short,
The great *Erota*, by this Secretary,
Returned me my full due.

Cassilane.   *Erota*? why
Should she do this?

Gonzalo.   You must aske her the cause,
She knowes it best.

Cassilane.   So ho; *Arcanes*, none   70
But women pitty us? soft-hearted women,
I am become a brave fellow now, *Arcanes*,
Am I not?

Arcanes.   Why sir, if the gracious Princesse
Have tooke more speciall notice of your services,
And meanes to be more thankfull than some others,
It were an injury to gratitude,
To disesteeme her favours.

Annophil.   Sir she ever
For your sake most respectively lov'd me.

Cassilane.   The Senate, and the body of this Kingdom,

---

58 formally] Langbaine; formerly F1–2   64 *Arcanes*.] Dyce; *omit* F1–2

Are herein (let me speake it without arrogance)   80
Beholding to her: I will thanke her for it;
And if she have reserv'd a meanes whereby
I may repay this bounty with some service,
She shall be then my Patronesse: come sirs,
Wee'l taste a cup of wine together now.

Gonzalo.   *Fernando,* I must speake with you in secret.

Fernando.   You shall——Now *Gaspero,* all's well?

Gaspero.   There's newes
You must be acquainted with. Come,
There is no master-peece in Art, like Policie.

                                             Exeunt.

              Enter Fernando, *and* Michael.   V.i

Fernando.   The Senate is inform'd at full.

Michael.   *Gonzalo*
Dreames not of my arivall yet?

Fernando.   Nor thinkes
'Tis possible his plots can be discover'd:
He fats himselfe with hopes of Crownes, and Kingdoms,
And laughes securely, to imagine how
He meanes to gull all but himselfe: when truly,
None is so grosely gull'd as he.

Michael.   There was never
A more arch villain.

Fernando.   Peace, the Senate comes.

        Enter Porphicio, Possenne, *Senators, and* Gaspero, [*with*]
                          Attendants.

Porphicio.   How closely, Treason cloakes it selfe in formes
Of Civill honesty?

Possenne.   And yet how palpably   10
Does heaven reveale it?

Gaspero.   Gratious Lords, the Embassadour,
Lord *Paulo Michael,* Advocate
To the great Duke of *Venice.*

8.1 Porphicio] F2; *Porphino* F1   8.1 Possenne] *Pos.* F1–2
*11 *Gaspero.* Gratious Lords] Variorum (Mason *conj.*); *Fer.* Gratious Lords. F1–2

Porphicio.   You are most welcome,
   Your Master is a just and noble Prince.
Michael.   My Lords, he bad me say; that you may know
   How much he scornes, and (as good Princes ought)
   Defies base indirect, and godlesse treacheries;
   To your more Sacred wisdomes he refers
   The punishment due to the false *Gonzalo*,
   Or else to send him home to *Venice*.
Possenne.   Herein   20
   The Duke is royall: *Gaspero* the Prince
   Of *Cyprus* answer'd he would come?
Gaspero.   My Lords,
   He will not long be absent.
Porphicio.   You *Fernando*,
   Have made the State your debter:

                    Enter Philander, *and* Melitus.

                              worthy Prince,
   We shall be sutors to you for your presence,
   In hearing, and determining of matters
   Greatly concerning *Candy*.
Philander.   Fathers, I am
   A stranger.
Possenne.   Why, the cause (my Lord) concernes
   A stranger: please you seat your selfe.
Philander.   How e're
   Unfit, since you will have it so (my Lords)   30
   You shall command me.
Porphicio.   You my Lord *Fernando*,
   With the Ambassador, withdraw a while.
Fernando.   My Lords, we shall.

                                        Exit [*with* Michael].
Possenne.   *Melitus*, and the Secretary,
   Give notice to *Gonzalo*, that the Senate
   Requires his presence.

                              Exeunt Gaspero *and* Melitus.
Philander.   What concernes the businesse?
Porphicio.   Thus noble Prince——

                              721

Enter Cassilane *and* Arcanes.

Cassilane.   Let me alone, thou troublest me,
I will be heard.
Arcanes.   You know not what you doe.
Possenne.   Forbeare:
Who's he that is so rude? whats he that dares
To interrupt our counsels?
Cassilane.   One that has guarded   40
Those Purple roabes from Cankers worse then Moaths,
One that hath kept your fleeces on your backs,
That would have been snatch'd from you: but I see
'Tis better now to be a dog, a Spanniell
In times of Peace, then boast the brused scars,
Purchas'd with losse of bloud in noble wars:
My Lords, I speake to you.
Porphicio.   Lord *Cassilane,*
We know not what you meane.
Cassilane.   Yes, you are set
Upon a bench of justice; and a day
Will come (heare this, and quake ye potent great ones)   50
When you your selves shall stand before a judge,
Who in a paire of scales will weigh your actions,
Without abatement of one graine: as then
You would be found full weight, I charge ye fathers
Let me have justice now.
Possenne.   Lord *Cassilane,*
What strange distemperature provokes distrust
Of our impartiality? be sure
Wee'l flatter no mans injuries.
Cassilane.   'Tis well;
You have a Law (Lords) that without remorse
Dooms such as are beleapred with the curse   60
Of foule ingratitude unto death.
Porphicio.   We have.
Cassilane.   Then do me justice.

*60 beleapred] *stet* F1; belepred F2

722

Enter Antinous, Decius, Erota, Hyparcha.

Decius.   Mad-man, whether run'st thou?
Antinous.   Peace *Decius*, I am deafe.
Hyparcha.   Will you forget
  Your greatnesse, and your modesty?
Erota.   *Hyparcha* leave,
  I will not heare.
Antinous.   Lady; great, gentle, Lady.
Erota.   Prethee young-man forbeare to interrupt me,
  Triumph not in thy fortunes; I will speake.
Possenne.   More uproares yet; who are they that disturb us?
Cassilane.   The viper's come; his feares have drawn him hether,
  And now (My Lords) be Chronicled for ever,   70
  And give me justice against this vile Monster,
  This bastard of my bloud.
Erota.   'Tis justice fathers,
  I sue for too: and though I might command it,
  (If you remember Lords, whose child I was)
  Yet I will humbly beg it; this old wretch
  'Has forfeited his life to me.
Cassilane.   Tricks, tricks;
  Complots, devices, 'twixt these paire of young-ones,
  To blunt the edge of your well temper'd Swords,
  Wherewith you strike offendors, (Lords) but I
  Am not a baby to be fear'd with bug-beares,   80
  'Tis justice I require.
Erota.   And I.
Antinous.   You speak
  Too tenderly; and too much like your self,
  To meane a cruelty; which would make monstrous
  Your Sexe: yet for the loves sake, which you once
  Pleas'd to pretend, give my griev'd father leave
  To urge his owne revenge; you have no cause
  For yours: keep peace about ye.
Cassilane.   Will you heare me?
Philander.   Here's some strange novelty.
Possenne.   Sure we are mock'd.

723

Speake one at once: say wherein hath your Son
Transgress'd the Law?

Cassilane.   O the grosse mists of dulnesse;   90
Are you this Kingdomes Oracles, yet can be
So ignorant? first heare, and then consider.
That I begot him, gave him birth and life,
And education, were I must confesse,
But duties of a father: I did more;
I taught him how to manage Armes, to dare
An Enemy; to court both death and dangers;
Yet these were but additions to compleate
A well accomplish'd Souldier: I did more yet.
I made him chiefe Commander in the field   100
Next to my selfe, and gave him the full prospect
Of honour, and preferment; train'd him up
In all perfections of a martiallist:
But he unmindfull of his gratitude,
You know with what contempt of my deserts,
First kick'd against mine honour, scorn'd all
My services; then got the palme of glory
Unto himselfe: yet not content with this,
He (lastly) hath conspir'd my death, and sought
Means to engage me to this Lady's debt,   110
Whose bounty, all my whole estate could never
Give satisfaction too: now honoured fathers,
For this cause only, if your Law be law,
And you the Ministers of justice; then
Thinke of this strange ingratitude in him.

Philander.   Can this be so Antinous?

Antinous.   'Tis all true,
Nor hath my much wrong'd father limn'd my faults
In colours halfe so black, as in themselves,
My guilt hath dyed them: were there mercy left,
Yet mine owne shame would be my Executioner: 120
Lords, I am guilty.

Erota.   Thou beliest Antinous,
Thine innocence: alas (my lords) hee's desperate,
And talkes he knowes not what: you must not credit
His lunacy; I can my selfe disprove

724

This accusation: *Cassilane*, be yet
More mercifull; I beg it.
Cassilane.   Time, nor fate,
The world, or what is in it, shall not alter
My resolution; he shall dye.
Erota.   The Senats
Prayers; or weeping Lovers, shall not alter
My resolution: thou shalt dye.
Antinous.   Why Madam,   130
Are ye all Marble?
Possenne.   Leave your shifts *Antinous*,
What plead you to your fathers accusation?
Antinous.   Most fully guilty.
Possenne.   You have doom'd your selfe,
We cannot quit you now.
Cassilane.   A burthen'd conscience
Will never need a hang-man: hadst thou dar'd
To have denide it, then this Sword of mine
Should on thy head have prov'd thy tongue a lyar.
Erota.   Thy sword? wretched old man, thou hast liv'd too long
To carry peace or comfort to thy grave;
Thou art a man condemn'd: my Lords this tyrant   140
Had perish'd but for me, I still suppli'd
His miserable wants; I sent his daughter
Mony to buy him food; the bread he eate,
Was from my purse: when he (vaingloriously)
To dive into the peoples hearts, had pawn'd
His birth-right, I redeemed it, sent it to him,
And for requitall, only made my suite,
That he would please to new receive his son
Into his favour, for whose love I told him
I had been still so friendly: But then he   150
As void of gratitude, as all good nature,
Distracted like a mad man, poasted hether
To pull this vengeance on himselfe, and us;
For why, (my Lords) since by the Law, all meane
Is blotted out of your commission,

---

    *154 For why] *stet* F1–2   *154 meane] Seward; meanes F1–2

As this hard hearted father hath accus'd
Noble *Antinous*, his unblemished Son,
So I accuse this father, and crave judgement.

Cassilane.   All this is but deceit, meere trifles forg'd
By combination to defeat the processe   160
Of Justice. I will have *Antinous* life.

Arcanes.   Sir, what do ye meane?

Erota.   I will have *Cassilane's.*

Antinous.   Cunning and cruell Lady, runs the streame
Of your affections this way? have you not
Conquest enough by treading on my grave?
Unlesse you send me thether in a shrowd
Steept in my fathers bloud? as you are woman,
As the protests of love you vow'd were honest;
Be gentler to my father.

Erota.   *Cassilane,*
Thou hast a heart of flint: let my intreates,   170
My teares, the Sacrifice of griefes unfained,
Melt it: yet be a father to thy son,
Unmaske thy long besotted judgement, see
A low obedience kneeling at the feet
Of nature: I beseech you.

Cassilane.   Pish, you cosen
Your hopes: your plots are idle: I am resolute.

Erota.   *Antinous,* urge no further.

Antinous.   Hence thou Sorcery
Of a beguiling softnesse, I will stand,
Like the earths Center, unmoved; Lords your breath
Must finish these divisions: I confesse   180
Civility doth teach I should not speake
Against a Lady of her birth, so high
As great *Erota,* but her injuries
And thankelesse wrongs to me, urge me to cry
Alowd for justice, Fathers.

Decius.   Whether run you?

Antinous.   For (honoured fathers) that you all may know
That I alone am not unmatchable
In crimes of this condition, lest perhaps

726

You might conceive, as yet the case appeares,
That this foule staine, and guilt runs in a bloud;   190
Before this presence, I accuse this Lady
Of as much vile ingratitude to me.
Cassilane.   Impudent Traitor!
Philander.   Her? O spare *Antinous*;
The world reputes thee valiant, do not soyle
All thy past noblenesse with such a cowardize,
As murthering innocent Ladies will stamp on thee!
Antinous.   Brave Prince, with what unwillingnesse I force
Her follies, and in those her sin, be witnesse,
All these about me: she is bloudy minded,
And turnes the justice of the Law to rigor: 200
It is her cruelties, not I accuse her:
Shall I have Audience?
Erota.   Let him speake my Lords.
Decius.   Your memory will rot.
Antinous.   Cast all your eyes
On this, what shall I call her? truthlesse woman,
When often in my discontents, the sway
Of her unruly bloud, her untam'd passion,
(Or name it as you list) had houre by houre
Sollicited my love, she vow'd at last
She could not, would not live unlesse I granted
What she long sued for: I in tender pitty,   210
To save a Lady of her birth, from ruine,
Gave her her life, and promis'd to be hers:
Nor urg'd I ought from her, but secresie,
And then enjoyn'd her to supply such wants
As I perceiv'd my fathers late engagements
Had made him subject to; what, shall I heape up
Long repetitions? she to quit my pitty,
Not only hath discover'd to my father
What she had promis'd to conceale, but also
Hath drawne my life into this fatall forfeit;   220
For which, since I must dye, I crave a like
Equality of justice against her;
Not that I covet bloud, but that she may not

Practice this art of falsehood on some other,
Perhaps more worthy of her love hereafter.

Porphicio.   If this be true——

Erota.   My Lords, be as the Law is,
Indifferent, upright, I do plead guilty:
Now sir, what glory have you got by this?
'Las man, I meant not to outlive thy doome;
Shall we be friends in death?

Cassilane.   Heare me, the villaine   230
Scandals her, honour'd Lords.

Erota.   Leave off to doate,
And dye a wise man.

Antinous.   I am over-reach'd,
And master'd in my owne resolution.

Philander.   Will ye be wilfull Madam? here's the curse
Of loves disdaine.

Cassilane.   Why sit you like dumb Statues?
Demur no longer.

Possenne.   *Cassilane, Erota,*
Antinous, death ye aske; and 'tis your doomes,
You in your follies liv'd, dye in your follies.

Cassilane.   I am reveng'd, and thanke you for it.

Erota.   Yes,
And I: *Antinous* hath been gratious.

Antinous.   Sir,   240
May I presume to crave a blessing from you
Before we part?

Cassilane.   Yes, such a one as Parents
Bestow on cursed sons.——Now, now, I laugh
To see how those poore younglings are both cheated
Of life and comfort: looke ye, looke ye, Lords,
I go but some ten minutes (more or lesse)
Before my time, but they have finely coz'nd
Themselves of many, many hopefull yeares
Amidst their prime of youth and glory; now
My vengeance is made ful.

Enter Annophil.

Welcome my joy,   250

Thou com'st to take a seasonable blessing
From thy halfe buried fathers hand; I am dead
Already girle, and so is she and he,
We all are wormes-meat now.

Annophil.   I have heard all;
Nor shall you dye alone: Lords on my knees
I beg for justice too.

Porphicio.   'Gainst whom, for what?

Annophil.   First let me be resolv'd; does the Law favour
None, be they ne're so mighty?

Porphicio.   Not the greatest.

Annophil.   Then justly I accuse of foule ingratitude
(My Lords) you of the Senate all, not one   260
Excepted.

Possenne. *Porphicio.* Us?

Philander.   *Annophill*——

Annophil.   You are the Authors
Of this unthrifty bloud-shed; when your enemies
Came marching to your gates, your children suck'd not
Safe at their mothers breasts, your very Cloysters
Were not secure, your starting-holes of refuge
Not free from danger, nor your lives your owne:
In this most desperate Extasie, my father,
This aged man, not onely undertook
To guard your lives, but did so; and beat off
The daring foe; for you he pawn'd his lands,   270
To pay your souldiers, who without their pay
Refus'd to strike a blow: but (Lords) when peace
Was purchas'd for you, and victorie brought home,
Where was your gratitude, who in your Coffers
Hoarded the rustie treasure which was due
To my unminded father? he was glad
To live retir'd in want, in penurie,
Whilst you made feasts of surfeit, and forgot
Your debts to him: The sum of all is this,
You have been unthankfull to him; and I crave   280
The rigor of the Law against you all.

729

Cassilane.   My Royall spirited daughter!
Erota.   *Annophill*
   Thou art a worthy wench; let me embrace thee.
Annophil.   Lords, why doe ye keep your seats? they are no places
   For such as are offenders.
Possenne.   Though our ignorance
   Of *Cassilanes* engagements might asswage
   Severity of justice, yet to shew
   How no excuse should smooth a breach of Law,
   I yeeld me to the triall of it.
Porphicio.   So must I:
   Great Prince of *Cyprus*, you are left   290
   The onely Moderator in this difference;
   And as you are a Prince be a Protector
   To wofull *Candy.*
Philander.   What a Scene of miserie
   Hath thine obdurate frowardnesse (old man)
   Drawne on thy Countries bosome? and for that
   Thy proud ambition could not mount so high
   As to be stil'd thy Countries onely Patron,
   Thy malice hath descended to the depth
   Of hell, to be renowned in the Title
   Of the destroyer? dost thou yet perceive   300
   What curses all posterity will brand
   Thy grave with? that at once hast rob'd this kingdome
   Of honour and of safety.
Erota.   Children yet unborne
   Will stop their eares when thou art nam'd.
Arcanes.   The world will be too little to containe
   The memorie of this detested deed;
   The Furies will abhorre it.
Decius.   What the sword
   Could not enforce, your peevish thirst of honour
   (A brave, cold, weak, imaginarie fame)
   Hath brought on *Candy*: *Candy* groans, not these   310
   That are to die.

*309 brave] *stet* F1–2

730

Philander.   'Tis happinesse enough
  For them, that they shall not survive to see
  The wounds wherewith thou stab'st the land that gave
  Thee life and name.
Decius.   'Tis *Candy's* wrack shall feele——
Porphicio. Possenne. The mischief of your folly.
Cassilane.   *Annophill*——
Annophil.   I will not be entreated.
Cassilane.   Prethee *Annophill.*
Annophil.   Why would ye urge me to a mercy which
  You in your selfe allow not?
Cassilane.   'Tis the Law,
  That if the party who complaines, remit
  The offender, he is freed: is't not so Lords?   320
Porphicio. Possenne. 'Tis so.
Cassilane.   *Antinous*, by my shame observe
  What a close witch-craft popular applause is:
  I am awak'd, and with cleare eyes behold
  The Lethargie wherein my reason long
  Hath been be-charm'd: Live, live, my matchlesse sonne,
  Blest in thy fathers blessing; much more blest
  In thine owne vertues: let me dew thy cheeks
  With my unmanly teares: Rise, I forgive thee:
  And good *Antinous*, if I shall be thy father
  Forgive me: I can speak no more.
Antinous.   Deare Sir,   330
  You new beget me now——Madam your pardon,
  I hartily remit you.
Erota.   I as freely
  Discharge thee *Cassilane.*
Annophil.   My gracious Lords,
  Repute me not a blemish to my Sex,
  In that I strove to cure a desperate evill
  With a more violent remedy: your lives,
  Your honours are your owne.
Philander.   Then with consent

---

315 *Porphicio. Possenne.*] Dyce; *Cas.* F1–2   315 *Cassilane.*] Colman; *Porp. Pos.* F1–2

Be reconcil'd on all sides: Please you fathers
To take your places.

Possenne.   Let us againe ascend,
With joy and thankfulnesse to heaven: And now   340
To other businesse Lords.

        Enter Gaspero, *and* Melitus, *with* Gonzalo.

Melitus.   Two howres and more Sir,
The Senate hath been set.

Gonzalo.   And I not know it?
Who sits with them?

Melitus.   My Lord, the Prince of *Cyprus.*

Gonzalo.   Gaspero,
Why how comes that to passe?

Gaspero.   Some waighty cause
I warrant you.

Gonzalo.   Now Lords the businesse? ha?
Who's here, *Erota?*

Porphicio.   Secretarie doe your charge
Upon that Traitor.

Gonzalo.   Traytor?

Gaspero.   Yes, *Gonzalo,* Traitor,
Of treason to the peace and state of *Candy,*
I doe arrest thee.

Gonzalo.   Me? thou dog?

        Enter Fernando *and* Michael.

Michael.   With License   350
From this grave Senate, I arrest thee likewise
Of Treason to the State of *Venice.*

Gonzalo.   Ha?
Is *Michael* here? nay then I see
I am undone.

Erota.   I shall not be your Queen,
Your Dutchesse, or your Empresse.

Gonzalo.   Dull, dull braine.
O I am fool'd!

                    732

Gaspero.   Look Sir, do you know this hand?
                              [*Shows a paper.*]
Michael.   Do you know this Seale?——First (Lords) he writes to
     Venice,
   To make a perfect league, during which time
   He would in private keep some Troops in pay,
   Bribe all the Centinells throughout this kingdom,   360
   Corrupt the Captaines; at a Banquet poyson
   The Prince, and greatest Peeres, and in conclusion
   Yield *Candy* slave to *Venice*.
Gaspero.   Next, he contracted
   With the Illustrious Princesse, the Lady *Erota*,
   In hope of marriage with her, to deliver
   All the Venetian gallantry, and strength,
   Upon their first arrivall, to the mercy
   Of her and *Candy*.
Erota.   This is true *Gonʒalo*.
Gonʒalo.   Let it be true: what then?
Possenne.   My Lord Ambassadour,
   What's your demand?
Michael.   As likes the State of *Candy*,   370
   Either to sentence him as he deserves
   Here, or to send him like a slave to *Venice*.
Porphicio.   We shall advise upon it.
Gonʒalo.   O the devills,
   That had not thrust this trick into my pate——
   A Politician foole? destruction, plague
   Candy and *Venice* both.
Possenne. Porphicio.   Away with him.
Melitus.   Come sir, Ile see you safe.
                              Exeunt Gonzalo, Melitus.
Erota.   Lords, e're you part
   Be witnesse to another change of wonder;
   Antinous, now be bold, before this presence,
   Freely to speak, whether or no I us'd   380
   The humblest meanes affection could contrive,
   To gaine thy love.

                         733

Antinous.   Madam, I must confesse it,
And ever am your servant.
Erota.   Yes *Antinous*,
My servant, for my Lord thou shalt be never:
I here disclaim the interest thou hadst once
In my too passionate thoughts.——[*To* Philander.]
                                        Most noble Prince,
If yet a relique of thy wonted flames
Live warme within thy bosome, then I blush not
To offer up the assurance of my faith,
To thee that hast deserv'd it best.
Philander.   O Madam,   390
You play with my calamity.
Erota.   Let heaven
Record my truth for ever.
Philander.   With more joy
Then I have words to utter, I accept it.
I also pawne you mine.
Erota.   The man that in requitall
Of noble and un-sought affection
Growes cruell, never lov'd, nor did *Antinous*.
Yet herein (Prince) ye are beholding to him;
For his neglect of me humbled a pride,
Which to a vertuous wife had been a Monster.
Philander.   For which Ile ranke him my deserving friend.   400
Antinous.   Much comfort dwell with you, as I could wish
To him I honour most.
Cassilane.   O my *Antinous*,
My owne, my owne good son.
Fernando.   One suit I have to make.
Philander.   To whom *Fernando*?
Fernando.   Lord *Cassilane* to you.
Cassilane.   To me?
Fernando.   This Lady
Hath promised to be mine.
Annophil.   Your blessing sir;
Brother your love.
Antinous.   You cannot sir bestow her

On a more noble gentleman.
Cassilane.   Saist thou so?
    Antinous I confirm it. Here *Fernando*,
    Live both as one; she is thine.
Antinous.   And herein sister,   410
    I honour you for your wise setled love.
    This is a day of Triumph, all Contentions
    Are happily accorded: *Candy's* peace
    Secur'd, and *Venice* vow'd a worthy friend.

                                                    Exeunt.

                    FINIS

TEXTUAL NOTES

Persons Represented in the Play.

7 Melitus, *a Gentleman of* Cyprus] F2, the only source for this *Dramatis Personae*, reads '*Gentleman of* Candy', but as J. Monck Mason pointed out (*Comments on the Plays of Beaumont and Fletcher* (London, 1798), p. 129), 'Melitus was of Cyprus, not of Candy.' This is indicated by the references to Melitus's 'Prince' (i.e., Philander, Prince of Cyprus) at I.i.5, 10; V.i.343.

I.ii

21 From successary] Regarding the meaning of this phrase, Theobald offered two conjectures: (1) 'From successors' and (2) 'From ancestry'. Seward retained 'successary' but emended 'From' to 'Nor'. But editors since Colman have recognized that 'not deriv'd | From successary' means simply 'not derived from succession', and that the passage is in no need of emendation. 'Antinous means to say, that his honours were peculiar to himself, not derived from the *blood* of his ancestors, but purchased by his own' (Mason, p. 131).

108 dant] This seventeenth-century form of 'daunt' appears in Ford's *Love's Sacrifice*, Act V (1633, sig. K2v): 'to the point | Of thy sharpe sword . . . I'le runne . . ., | This dants not me'.

II.i

83 dimly] Editors agree that the reading of F1–2 ('clearly') is unsatisfactory, but there is no general agreement on the word that ought to replace it. Seward considered 'dimly' but rejected it because it was 'rather too far from the Trace of the Letters', whereupon 'barely' seemed to him best. However, Sympson's conjecture 'merely' disarmed him, and confessing himself 'too doubtful to insert either of them in the text', allowed 'clearly' to stand in the 1750 edition. Colman printed 'scarcely' ('as it is not very different from the old books in the trace of the letters'). Weber, following Sympson's suggestion, printed 'merely'. Dyce, followed by Chambers in the Variorum, printed 'dimly', the reading that Seward had once considered but had rejected in favour of 'barely'. By way of accounting for his choice of 'dimly' as an emendation of 'clearly', Dyce stated that 'the letters *cl* are a frequent misprint for *d*'.

85–88 For any . . . bounty:] Editors since Seward have considered the passage to be defective in some degree. Seward, though he did not emend it, suggested that some words had been lost at the beginning, and proposed that line 85 might read: "Twere

736

Arrogance for any Man to think' (or – for 'Arrogance' – a stronger word such as 'Heresy' or 'Blasphemy'). Colman noted that 'some words appear to have been lost here' and quoted Seward's conjecture. It was Weber who first suggested that the passage was missing not simply some words at its beginning but one or more lines after line 86, and later editors (Dyce, and Chambers in the Variorum) have endorsed this view typographically with a row of asterisks between lines 86 and 87. This seems extravagant, and if anything has indeed been lost from the passage, I doubt that it is anything that a few words of the sort that Seward proposed would not remedy.

I think it unlikely, however, that anything is missing from the passage. It is a piece of ecstatic hyperbole wherein a lover, assessing the vast distance between his own small merit and the immeasurable worth of his beloved, can only break off in mid-sentence at the incongruity. For any man to think it possible that he might win such a woman unless, out of her 'Infinite bounty', she is generous enough to ignore the great distance that separates them; for any man to think it possible to win such a woman without this necessary condition: here, in the presence of such an improbable assumption, the speaker breaks off. He goes on: if it were otherwise (i.e. if he thought he might win Erota on his own merits) he would sacrifice all he possesses for her ('untenant every hope lodg'd in me', etc.).

354 percusse ever the earth]   The F1 compositor mangled the line. F2 restored it to something like sense. Dyce, having added the word 'ever', announced: 'This is all I can make of the corruption of the first folio.' Given the clownish character of Mochingo and the pseudo-Marlovian rant he is affecting here, it is unlikely that much else is to be made of it. 'Percusse' means 'to strike so as to shake' (*O.E.D.*).

III.ii

20 I'm not miserable]   Sympson, supposing 'a Negative dropt' in this line, suggested the insertion of 'not', but Seward found the proposed emendation unsatisfactory, and preferred instead to follow the reading of F1–2 ('and sweare that I am miserable') in his text for the 1750 edition. He gave to the unemended passage the following interpretation: '"You, Arcanes, will flatter me by talking of my former greatness and glory, and swear that this retirement is misery to a man of my abilities for the command of whole armies."' Colman adopted Sympson's emendation, but no editor since has done so. Weber, Dyce and Chambers (in the Variorum) all retain the F1–2 reading, and explain it by quoting Seward's interpretation.

Seward's account of the passage misses the ironic self-awareness that informs the exchange between Cassilane and Arcanes. It has no support from the lines of Cassilane's speech that precede it, or from its dramatic context in III.ii, where Cassilane is seeking to reconcile himself and his daughter to their present reduced circumstances. The gentle Annophil accepts calmly enough his claims (lines 2–12) for the superiority of a solitary life, exempt from the perils of courtly intrigue. But Cassilane himself is not persuaded of these, and he is grimly aware of the presence of Arcanes, who knows him too well to be taken in by his show of stoicism. Thus

737

line 16 ('Canst thou forbeare to laugh *Arcanes?*'). Cassilane knows that his present display of patience, viewed against his past pride, is bound to strike Arcanes as grotesque ('Does it shew handsome? bravely?'). Cassilane's 'thou wilt flatter me' amounts to an accusation that Arcanes will play along with the game of self-delusion that Cassilane is himself knowingly engaged in, and the flattery will consist in the assurance that he is *not* miserable. As Colman noted, 'the very answer of Arcanes [lines 20–4] confirms' the need for the emended reading. According to Seward (and all the editors who have followed his explanation), when Cassilane charges Arcanes with intending to flatter him and to swear that he is miserable, the flattery will consist in reminding him of his past military glory, and the misery will consist in the recognition of his present situation, now that his former glory is no more. But throughout the scene Cassilane is himself aware of this glaring difference in his past and present fortunes, and his words at lines 19–20 ('thou wilt flatter me, | And sweare that I'm not miserable') are his grim anticipation that Arcanes will join in the wretched game of helping him to gloze over the difference.

V.i

11 *Gaspero*. Gratious Lords]   The words are assigned to Fernando in all editions from F1–2 to Dyce, who thought they 'may be an exclamation drawn from Fernando in consequence of the two preceding speeches'. But Dyce 'felt strongly inclined to give them to Gaspero', as Mason (*Comments on the Plays of Beaumont and Fletcher*, p. 135) had suggested: 'As there can be no reason why Fernando should address the senate, when he was not about to speak to them, I suppose that those words make part of Gaspero's speech.' Chambers, in his Variorum edition, was the first editor to print them as such. The passage printed in his text reads 'Gracious lords! The ambassador . . .'.

60 beleapred]   afflicted with leprosy. Cf. Ford, *Love's Sacrifice*, Act II (1633, sig. D4): 'For were I not beleapred in my soule, | Here were enough to quench the flames of hell.'

154 For why]   'for which reason' (Mason).

154 meane]   'middle course' (Dyce).

309 brave]   vainglorious (Mason, p. 136).

PRESS VARIANTS IN F1 (1647)

[Copies collated: Hoy (personal copy of Cyrus Hoy, Rochester, N.Y.), IU (University of Illinois), MB (Boston Public Library), MnU (University of Minnesota), NcD (Duke University), NIC (Cornell University), NjP (Princeton University), ViU¹ (University of Virginia, copy 1), ViU² (copy 2), WaU (University of Washington), WMU¹ (University of Wisconsin–Milwaukee, copy 1), WMU² (copy 2), WMU³ (copy 3), WU (University of Wisconsin–Madison).]

SHEET 3G i (*inner forme*)

Uncorrected: WU
First-stage corrected: Hoy, MnU, ViU¹⁻², WMU²
Sig. 3G4
II.i.30 Royaltie] Royall tye
[Note: Second-stage corrections to sig. 3G1v in this Sheete do not relate to this play.]

SHEET 3H ii (*inner forme*)

First state (?): ViU², WMU¹
Sig. 3H2v
Catchword following III.ii.178] His
Second state (?): Hoy, IU, MB, MnU, NIc, NjP, ViU¹, WMU²⁻³, WU
Catchword following III.ii.178] *omit*
Third state (?): NcD
Catchword following III.ii.178] 'Tis
[Note: The order proposed here assumes that the correct catchword, 'His', was set, pulled and incorrectly replaced, but the sequence is uncertain. Either of the two other possible orders could be correct.]

SHEET 3I i (*outer forme*)

Uncorrected: ViU¹
Sig. 3I1
IV.ii.49 braverie,] ~ ∧
IV.ii.73 Princesse] Princes
IV.ii.74 services] seruices

739

EMENDATIONS OF ACCIDENTALS

I.i

I.i] *Actus primus. Scæna prima.* F1–2
  19 Venetians] *Venecians* F1; *Venetians*
    F2

22 adores ‸] F2; ∼ , F1
23, 78 Venetian] *Venetian* F1–2
49 Kingdome] F2; Kiagdome F1

I.ii

I.ii] Scæn. 2. F1; SCENE II. F2
  6 if] F2; If F1
  7 father: ... knee,] ∼ ‸ ... ∼ ; F1;
    ∼ ‸ ... ∼ : F2
  19 Tyrant-like] F2; Tyrant‸ like F1
  65 father] F2; farher F1
  100.1 *Enter* Arcanes] *after* yeald? (*line*
    99) *in* F1–2
  103–104 Now ... The——] *one line in*
    F1–2
  105 Stripling!] ∼ , F1; ∼ . F2
  111 *Senators*),] ∼) ‸ F1–2
  124.1 *Enter* ... Soldiers.] *Enter* ...
    Sold.] *after* 'sit?' (*line* 121) *in* F1–2
    (*where the latter reads* 'Sir?' *for*

'sit?')
177 non-ability] non ‸ ability F1–2
212 Cretane] *Cretane* F1–2
217 reverence] F2; reveremce F1
260 day;] F2; ∼ , F1
266 no?] ∼ . F1; not? F2
283 rate.——] ∼ . ‸ F1–2
295–296 It is ... more?] *one line in* F1–2
313–314 Propose ... just.] *one line in*
  F1–2
339.1 *Exeunt*] *Ex.* F1–2
345 Yes: ... pleasures.] F1–2 *line:* Yes:
  ... Triumphs, | With ... pleasures.
346 Flourish ... *Exeunt*] *Exeunt. Flor.*
  Cornets. F1–2

II.i

II.i] *Actus Secundus. Scæna prima.* F1–2
  13 Ambrosia] *Ambrosia* F1–2
  33–34 Sir, ... ye] *one line in* F1–2
  49.1–2 *Enter* ... *Attendants.*] *printed in*
    right-hand margin of lines 47–50 *in*
    F1; *following* 'studied.' (*line* 47) *in*
    F2
  50 This ... Prince,] F1–2 *line:* This ...
    passionate, | Most ... Prince,
  59 kinde] F2; klnde F1
  63 Heroes] *Heroes* F1–2
  83–85 This ... Zodiack.] F1–2 *line:*
    This ... must be | A good ...
    Zodiack.

89 that's] F2; that s F1
96 She ... you,] F1–2 *line:* She ... her |
  Moods, ... you,
97 you:——] ∼ : ‸ F1–2
98 Lady).] ∼ .) F1–2
98–102 A man ... him.] F1–2 *line:* A
  man ... wealthy; | A Proper ... one
  | That ... unlesse | It ... him.
99 wealthy,] ∼ ; F1–2
103 withall,] F2; ∼ . F1
123 Jester:——] ∼ : ‸ F1–2
123–124 This ... in.] F1–2 *line:* This ...
  some | Great ... here is | No ... in.
125 Where ... two.] F1–2 *line:* Where

... of? | I ... two.

126–127 No ... hundred.] F1–2 *line*:
No ... for | In ... hundred.

140 so!] ~ ? F1–2

166 And ... thoughts.] F1–2 *line*: And
... *Candy.* | I ... thoughts.

167 Brother.——] ~ , ∧ F1–2

191 relate!] ~ ? F1; ~ : F2

279 nook,∧] ~ ,) F1–2

330 it,] F2; ~ . : F1 [*sic*]

334–336 Sir ... manners.] F1–2 *line*: Sir
... *Master* | *Of* ... should | *Learne*
... manners.

340 now:——] ~ : ∧ F1–2

348–349 The opinion ... time.] F1–2

line: The opinion ... nothing | To
be ... time.

350 *Exeunt*] *Exit* F1–2

364–367 Why ... be so.] F1–2 *line*:
Why ... proud, and | Very ... saw
| It did ... prethee | Let ... be so.

369–370 Yet ... Magnanimous] *one line
in* F1–2

371–372 O good ... Coat.] *one line in*
F1–2

378–379 Adieu ... businesse.] *one line in*
F1–2

380 cousin).] ~ .) F1; ~ . ∧ F2 (*cf.
below*, IV.i.147)

III.i

III.i] *Actus Tertius. Scæna prima.* F1–2

50–53 Peace, ... *Cassilane*?] F1–2 *line*:
Peace, | Here ... Coward. | Now
... what, | You ... *Fernando's* |
Conductor ... *Cassilane*?

50.1 *Enter* Gaspero.] *after line* 49 *in*
F1–2

60 Lord——] ~ . F1–2

66 will.——] ~ . ∧ F1–2

III.ii

1 farther.——] ~ ∧ ∧ F1–2

15 said.——] ~ , ∧ F1–2

17–19 To look ... flatter me,] F1–2
line: To look ... to look upon | My
... Tell me, | Does ... bravely? |
Handsome? ... flatter me,

31 Romane] *Romane* F1–2

46 Cretane] *Cretane* F1–2

52 The World ... by the——] F1–2
line: The World ... son. | But by
the——

52–53 Sir, ... occasion] *one line in*
F1–2

54 friendly.] ~ . , F1 [*sic*]; ~ , ∧ F2

57 Venetian] *Venetian* F1–2

76 *Candy*,] F2; ~ . F1

89 Applause∧] ~ ? F1–2

90 nothing.——Why] ~   ∧ ——
why F1–2

138–139 'Twere ... captivity.] *one line
in* F1–2

139–140 Who's here. | *Decius*?] Who's
here, *Decius*? F1–2

154 Sir——] ~ . F1–2

170 man-hoods∧ comforts,] ~ , ~ ∧
F1–2

189 unnaturally!] ~ ? F1; ~ . F2

197 private:——] ~ : ∧ F1; ~ ; ∧ F2

199 *Exeunt*] *Ex.* F1 (*after* 'yeild?'');
Exit. (*after* 'yield?') F2

205 Lady——] ~ , F1–2

III.iii

0.1 Hyparcha ∧ (*placing ... chaires*),]
~ , (~ ... ~) ∧ F1–2

1 Madam——] ~ : F1; ~ . F2

30 is] F2; ir F1

741

42.1 Song] *on line* 41 *in* F1–2
62 love me——] ~ ~ , F1; ~ ~ .
    F2
63 heare me!] heare me? F1–2

121 (*Philander*);] (~) ∧ F1–2
127 Appoplexie.——] ~ . ∧ F1–2
128 *Antinous*!] ~ . F1–2
171.1 *Exeunt.*] *Ex.* F1–2

IV.i

IV.i] *Actus Quartus. Scæna prima.* F1
  8 Puppy——] ~ . F1–2
 90 *Decius.*——] ~ . ∧ F1–2
104 Lady——] ~ . F1–2
109 it!] ~ ? F1; ~ . F2
132 errand;——] ~ ; ∧ F1–2
135 *Exit*] F2; *Ex.* F1 (*both* F1–2 *print the s.d. after* 'wary' *on line* 133)

135 *Enter* Gonzalo.] F1 (*in margin beside lines* 132–133); F2 (*following line* 132)
143 this:——] ~ : ∧ F1; ~ ; ∧ F2
147 Lady)?] ~ ?) F1–2 (*cf. above,* II.i.380)
159–160 What … me.] *one line in* F1–2

IV.ii

20 Grecian] *Grecian* F1–2
23 Cretians] *Cretians* F1–2
24 Turkes] *Turkes* F1–2
63 ample.] ~ : F1–2

87 well?] ~ . F1–2
88–89 You … Policie.] F1–2 *line:* You … with. | Come, … Policie.
89.1 *Exeunt.*] F2; *Ex.* F1

V.i

V.i] *Actus Quintus. Scæna prima.* F1–2
  1 The] F2; TThe F1
  1 *Gonʒalo* ∧] F2; ~ . F1
  2 yet?] ~ . F1–2
  8.1 Possenne] *Pos.* F1–2
 11 Lords,] ~ . F1–2
 11 the] The F1–2
 22 come?] ~ . F1–2
 24 *Enter* … Melitus.] *following* 'absent' (*line* 23) *in* F1–2
·33 *Exit*] *Ex.* F1–2
 35 *Exeunt*] *Ex.* F1–2
38–39 Forbeare … dares] *one line in* F1–2
 40 guarded ∧] ~ , F1–2
64–65 *Hyparcha* … heare.] *one line in* F1–2
81–82 You … self,] *one line in* F1–2
 82 much ∧] F2; ~ , F1

 82 self,] ~ ∧ F1–2
 88 mock'd.] ~ , F1–2
 92 consider.] F2; ~ , F1
161 Justice.] ~ , F1–2
196 thee!] ~ ? F1; ~ . F2
239–240 Yes … gratious.] *one line in* F1–2
240–241 Sir, … you] *one line in* F1–2
242 Part?] F2; ~ . F1
243 sons.——Now] ~ , ∧ now F1–2
273 home,] F2; ~ ; F1
321 by] By F1–2
356 fool'd!] ~ ? F1–2
357 Seale?——] ~ ? ∧ F1–2
360 kingdom] F2; kindom F1
366 Venetian] *Venetian* F1
377 *Exeunt* ∧] F2; ~ . F1
386 thoughts.——] ~ . ∧ F1–2

HISTORICAL COLLATION

[NOTE: The F1 (Folio 1647) copy-text has been collated with the following editions: F2 (Folio 1679), L (*Works*, 1711, intro. Gerard Langbaine), S (*Works*, 1750, ed. Theobald, Seward and Sympson), C (*Works*, 1778, ed. George Colman the Younger), W (*Works*, 1812, ed. Henry Weber), D (*Works*, 1843–6, ed. Alexander Dyce), V (Bullen Variorum, 1908, ed. E. K. Chambers). Omission of a siglum indicates that the text concerned agrees with the reading of the lemma.]

I.i

6 insolencie] insolence F2–D

15 many] *omit* F2, L

42, 83 *Cassilane*] *Cassilanes* F1–2, L

43 pledges] pledge S, C

44 payment] repayment S, C, W

45 pettie] pretty F2, L

46 this] thus F2–W

50 Unfellowed] Unfollowed F1–W

50 these] those F2–C, D

61 home-borne] home-bred F2, L, S

I.ii

0.1 *Cassilane*] *Cassilanes* F1–2, L

9 rise] arise C

21 From] Nor S

26 Say] But say S

36 or] to S

37 your] you F1

69 humane] human L, S, D, V

71 one thy] on thy F1–2, L

77 had] has F2, L

108 dant] daunt F2 +

108 whether] whither F2–V

111 *Cassilane.*] *Gonzalo* S (*in Errata List (but 'Cassilane' in the main text) of edn 1750, vol. IV, p. 10*)

111 Possenne] *Possenme* F1

111 speech-prefix *Gonzalo.*] *omit* F1–2, L, S, W (*where the speech is printed as a continuation of Cassilane's words*

at line 111)

116 some] force F1–2, L; this S, C

119 ye] you F2–D

121 sit] Sir F2, L

121 What] What's F2, L

130 *Cassilane*] *Cassilanes* F1–2, L, S

144 you] ye F2–W

146, 294 *Cassilane*] *Cassilanes* F1–2, L

151 I, I.] Ay, Ay. L–V

167–168 and | As] and | And as F1

179 then by warrant] then warrant F1

224 But who] But he who S

255 adversaries] adversaries then D (*conj.*)

265 Lead] Led F2–V

280 Lords] Lord F1

281 *Cassilane*] *Cassilanes* F1

310 and] add F1; aud F2

II.i

6 hath] have C, D

18 farther] further C, W

23 Her] Here F2, L, D

29 maddened] manded F1; madded F2,

743

L, S, C
29 owne] *omit* S
38 but] Dyce (*conj.*); *omit* F1–2, L, S, C, W, D; here V
44 wit] feet F1–2, L, S, C
45 what ere] what S; whatever C, W
46 And so bold] And so boldly F2, L, C; So boldly S
63 brave] bravest S, C, W
76 there] their F2+
83 dimly] D; clearely F1–2, L, S; scarcely C; merely W
85 For any] 'Twere Arrogance for any S; W, D, V *assume one or more lines to be lost following line 86*
96 Ile Gramer] I'll then Grammar S; I will grammar C, W, D
102 on] in L, S, C, W
127 your selfe] your own self S
135 *Jove] Iolus* F1
139 bravely] bravel F2
143–144 I in *Venice,* | I am] I in *Venice,* | Am F2, L, S, C, W; in Venice I | Am D, V
144 I am borne] Am borne F2
147–148 'in ... view':] ∧ ~ ... ~ : ∧ F1–2, L, S
156 Sir, I know you not] I know you not, Sir S
162 well?] well then? S
166 And] *omit* S
167 Good] O good S
170 unimitable] inimitable W
178 are] Why, are S
182 youl'd] you'll L, S; you would W

186 for] and S, C
187 To inforce] Inforc'd S, C
194 gotten] *omit* L; got S, C
204 Even] Ever L
208 are great] are a great F1–2, C, W
227 first] I first S
228 out-strip] out-stript W
234 off] of F2+
245 your] you F1; *omit* S
245 blessings] blessings rather F2+
248 I had] had I W
249 even] ever F2, L
254 he deserv'd] he, Sir, deserv'd S
293 Sir, I thanke you] I thank you, Sir S, W
300 in] with L
311 be] he F1
315 a] *omit* S
321 If] *omit* F1
336 doe] *omit* S
342 example here] here example S
354 percusse ever the earth] percusseere the earrh F1; percusse the Earth F2, L, S, C, W
372 Now I have you] I have you now S
375 fort] for't F2, L; for it S, C, W, D, V

III.i

18 not] nor C
27 strook] struck L, S, C, W, D
29 lesse] loss F2
39 him] them F1–2, L
51 Now] *omit* S
63 speech-prefix *Gaspero.] Erot.* F2

III.ii

1 farther] further C, W
19 Does it shew handsome? bravely? thou] Does it shew handsome? bravely? | Handsome? thou F1–2, L, S; does it show handsome? bravely handsome? Thou C, W, D
20 I'm not miserable] I am miserable

F1–2, L, S, W, D, V
32 best] bravest S
35 ingratefull] ungrateful W
49 traduced] seduc'd (Mason *conj.*)
104 with] *omit* S
122 I so] So I F2, L, S
159 way] ways L, S

167 a] *omit* F1–2, L
189 most] *omit* C

192 beholding] beholden S, C, W
199 ye] you F2–D

III.iii

3 dost] didst F1
4 by] *omit* F2–W
12 greater] far greater S
14 farther] further C, W
35 Voluntarie] And voluntary S
37 bring along with them?——
  Hyparcha!] bring along with? F1–2,
  L; bring along? Hyparcha? S, C;
  bring along with? Hyparcha! W
54 hopes] Hope L, S
68 griefes] grief F2–D

79 Pray go] Pray ye go C
87 and if] an if C, W, D
95–98 Tell him how he … enjoying
  these.] *lines* 97–98 *placed before lines*
  95–96 *in* S
113 In his] Under his S
150 thy] thine F2–W
164 leave him,] leave, S
166 And every] Every S, C
168 this] his S

IV.i

6 Foolish] You foolish S
9 You do do it] You do't S
17 *Erota.*] *Ant.* F1
18 then] than F2+
25 here] hear F2+
25 or] ere F1–2, L
51 do] does F2, L, S
55 crueller] cruel F2, L, C
55 I to] I am to C
59 I apprehend not] I not apprehend S,

C
64 reverent] reverend F2–W, V
69 to] of L, S
96, 159, 162, 180 ye] you F2–D
117 morgag'd] more 'gag'd F1
126 To day] *omit* S
138 ye] you F2+
146 spake] spoke F2, L, S
148 we] me F1
194 He] Ha F2–D

IV.ii

3 safety] sake S, C
16.1 Cassilane] *Cassilanes* F1–2
32 a] an F2–D
42 off] of S, C, W, D, V
42 how] how's C
46 beholding] beholden S, C
58 formally] formerly F1–2
63–66 *Gaspero.* 'Tis … ample. |
  Arcanes. Fortune … fairely. | *Cas-*

silane. But … is't?] *Gas.* 'Tis …
ample: | Fortune … fairely. | *Cas.*
But … is't? F1–2, L; *Cas.* 'Tis …
is't? S; *Gasp.* 'Tis … ample. | *Anno.*
Fortune … fairly! | *Cass.* But …
is't? C, W
81 Beholding] Beholden S, C, W
87 *Gaspero.*] *Gonȝ.* S, C

V.i

8.1 Porphicio] *Porphino* F1
8.1 Possenne] *Pos.* F1–2

11 *Gaspero.* Gratious Lords,] *Fer.* Gratious Lords F1–2–D

745

37   I will] I'll S
37–39 doe. | *Possenne. Forbeare:* |
     Who's] do: Forbear—— | *Pos.*
     Who's S
58   flatter] father S
61   unto] to S
77   devices] Device L
112 too] to F2+
154 meane] meanes F1–2, L
170 intreates] intreaties F2+
190 runs] run C, W

197 force] enforce C
204 truthlesse] ruthless S, C
294 frowardnesse] forwardness L
309 brave] bare S, C
315 *Porphicio. Possenne.*] *Cas.* F1–2, L;
     Arc. S; *assigned to Decius as conti-*
     nuation of his speech at line 314 in C,
     W
315 *Cassilane.*] *Porp. Pos.* F1–2, L, S
397 beholding] beholden S, C, W

INDEX

TITLES OF THE DRAMATIC WORKS
IN THE BEAUMONT AND FLETCHER
CANON

Title	*Volume*
Sir John Van Olden Barnavelt	VIII
Beggars' Bush	III
The Bloody Brother. *See* Rollo.	
Bonduca	IV
The Captain	I
The Chances	IV
Cleander. *See* The Lovers' Progress.	
The Coxcomb	I
Cupid's Revenge	II
The Custom of the Country	VIII
Demetrius and Enanthe. *See* The Humorous Lieutenant.	
The Double Marriage	IX
The Elder Brother	IX
The Fair Maid of the Inn	X
The Faithful Shepherdess	III
The False One	VIII
Father's Own Son. *See* Monsieur Thomas.	
Four Plays, or Moral Representations, in One	VIII
Generous Enemies. *See* The Humorous Lieutenant.	
Henry VIII	VII
The Honest Man's Fortune	X
The Humorous Lieutenant	V
The Island Princess	V
A King and No King	II
The Knight of Malta	VIII
The Knight of the Burning Pestle	I
The Laws of Candy	X
The Little French Lawyer	IX
The Little Thief. *See* The Night Walker.	
Love Lies a Bleeding. *See* Philaster.	
The Lovers' Progress	X
Love's Cure	III
Love's Pilgrimage	II
The Loyal Subject	V

749

The Mad Lover   V
The Maid in the Mill   IX
The Maid's Tragedy   II
The Martial Maid. *See* Love's Cure.
The Masque of the Inner Temple and Gray's Inn   I
Monsieur Thomas   IV
The Nice Valour   VII
The Night Walker   VII
The Noble Enemy. *See* The Humorous Lieutenant.
The Noble Gentleman   III
The Passionate Mad-man. *See* The Nice Valour.
Philaster   I
The Pilgrim   VI
The Prince of Tarent. *See* A Very Woman.
The Prophetess   IX
The Queen of Corinth   VIII
Rollo, Duke of Normandy   X
Rule a Wife and Have a Wife   VI
The Scornful Lady   II
The Sea Voyage   IX
The Spanish Curate   X
The Tamer Tamed. *See* The Woman's Prize.
Thierry and Theodoret   III
The Two Noble Kinsmen   VII
Valentinian   IV
A Very Woman   VII
The Wandering Lovers. *See* The Lovers' Progress.
A Wife for a Month   VI
The Wild-Goose Chase   VI
Wit at Several Weapons   VII
Wit Without Money   VI
The Woman Hater   I
The Woman's Prize   IV
Women Pleased   V

(*The Coronation*, published in 1640 as 'written by J. Fletcher' and included in the Second Folio (1679) as his, is recognized now to be the work of James Shirley.)

AUTHORS OF THE DRAMATIC WORKS
IN THE BEAUMONT AND FLETCHER
CANON

[We cannot emphasize too much the tentative nature of many of these ascriptions; readers should consult the Textual Introductions to the several plays for specific information. Plays of presumed single authorship are set in capitals.]

FRANCIS BEAUMONT

I   The Captain(?), The Coxcomb, THE KNIGHT OF THE BURNING PESTLE, THE MASQUE OF THE INNER TEMPLE AND GRAY'S INN, Philaster, The Woman Hater;

II   Cupid's Revenge, A King and No King, Love's Pilgrimage, The Maid's Tragedy, The Scornful Lady;

III   Beggars' Bush, Love's Cure, The Noble Gentleman(?), Thierry and Theodoret.

GEORGE CHAPMAN

X   Rollo, Duke of Normandy(?).

NATHAN FIELD

VIII   Four Plays, or Moral Representations, in One, The Knight of Malta, The Queen of Corinth;

X   The Honest Man's Fortune, Rollo, Duke of Normandy(?).

JOHN FLETCHER

I   The Captain, The Coxcomb, Philaster, The Woman Hater;

II   Cupid's Revenge, A King and No King, Love's Pilgrimage, The Maid's Tragedy, The Scornful Lady;

III   Beggars' Bush, THE FAITHFUL SHEPHERDESS, Love's Cure, The Noble Gentleman, Thierry and Theodoret;

IV   BONDUCA, THE CHANCES, MONSIEUR THOMAS, VALENTINIAN, THE WOMAN'S PRIZE;

V   THE HUMOROUS LIEUTENANT, THE ISLAND PRINCESS, THE LOYAL SUBJECT, THE MAD LOVER, WOMEN PLEASED;

VI   THE PILGRIM, RULE A WIFE AND HAVE A WIFE, A WIFE FOR A MONTH, THE WILD-GOOSE CHASE, Wit Without Money;

AUTHORS

VII   Henry VIII, The Nice Valour(?), The Night Walker, The Two Noble Kinsmen, A Very Woman, Wit at Several Weapons;

VIII   Sir John Van Olden Barnavelt, The Custom of the Country, The False One, Four Plays, or Moral Representations, in One, The Knight of Malta, The Queen of Corinth;

IX   The Double Marriage, The Elder Brother, The Little French Lawyer, The Maid in the Mill, The Prophetess, The Sea Voyage;

X   The Fair Maid of the Inn, The Honest Man's Fortune, The Lovers' Progress, Rollo, Duke of Normandy, The Spanish Curate.

JOHN FORD

X   The Fair Maid of the Inn, THE LAWS OF CANDY(?).

BEN JONSON

X   Rollo, Duke of Normandy(?).

PHILIP MASSINGER

III   Beggars' Bush, Love's Cure, Thierry and Theodoret;

VII   A Very Woman;

VIII   Sir John Van Olden Barnavelt, The Custom of the Country, The False One, The Knight of Malta, The Queen of Corinth;

IX   The Double Marriage, The Elder Brother, The Little French Lawyer, The Prophetess, The Sea Voyage;

X   The Fair Maid of the Inn, The Honest Man's Fortune, The Lovers' Progress, Rollo, Duke of Normandy, The Spanish Curate.

THOMAS MIDDLETON

VII   The Nice Valour, Wit at Several Weapons.

WILLIAM ROWLEY

VII   Wit at Several Weapons;

IX   The Maid in the Mill.

WILLIAM SHAKESPEARE

VII   Henry VIII, The Two Noble Kinsmen.

JAMES SHIRLEY

VI   Wit Without Money(?);

VII   The Night Walker.

JOHN WEBSTER

X   The Fair Maid of the Inn(?).

WITHDRAWN